Children's Literature Review

Guide to Gale Literary Criticism Series

When you need to review criticism of literary works, these are the Gale series to use:

If the author's death date is:	You should turn to:
After Dec. 31, 1959 (or author is still living)	***CONTEMPORARY LITERARY CRITICISM*** for example: Jorge Luis Borges, Anthony Burgess, William Faulkner, Mary Gordon, Ernest Hemingway, Iris Murdoch
1900 through 1959	***TWENTIETH-CENTURY LITERARY CRITICISM*** for example: Willa Cather, F. Scott Fitzgerald, Henry James, Mark Twain, Virginia Woolf
1800 through 1899	***NINETEENTH-CENTURY LITERATURE CRITICISM*** for example: Fedor Dostoevski, Nathaniel Hawthorne, George Sand, William Wordsworth
1400 through 1799	***LITERATURE CRITICISM FROM 1400 TO 1800 (excluding Shakespeare)*** for example: Anne Bradstreet, Daniel Defoe, Alexander Pope, François Rabelais, Jonathan Swift, Phillis Wheatley
	SHAKESPEAREAN CRITICISM Shakespeare's plays and poetry
Antiquity through 1399	***CLASSICAL AND MEDIEVAL LITERATURE CRITICISM*** for example: Dante, Homer, Plato, Sophocles, Vergil, the Beowulf poet *(Volume 1 forthcoming)*

Gale also publishes related criticism series:

CHILDREN'S LITERATURE REVIEW

This ongoing series covers authors of all eras. Presents criticism on authors and author/illustrators who write for the preschool through high school audience.

CONTEMPORARY ISSUES CRITICISM

This two volume set presents criticism on contemporary authors writing on current issues. Topics covered include the social sciences, philosophy, economics, natural science, law, and related areas.

ISSN 0362-4145

volume 13

Children's Literature Review

Excerpts from Reviews,
Criticism, and Commentary
on Books for Children
and Young People

Guest Essay, "Biography and the
Writer's Voice," by Milton Meltzer

Gerard J. Senick
Editor

Melissa Reiff Hug
Associate Editor

Gale Research Company
Book Tower
Detroit, Michigan 48226

STAFF

Library of Congress Catalog Card Number 75-34953
ISBN 0-8103-0348-5
ISSN 0362-4145

Computerized photocomposition by
Typographics, Incorporated
Kansas City, Missouri

Printed in the United States

CONTENTS

PREFACE

As children's literature has evolved into both a respected branch of creative writing and a successful industry, literary criticism has documented and influenced each stage of its growth. Critics have recorded the literary development of individual authors as well as the trends and controversies that resulted from changes in values and attitudes, especially as they concerned children. While defining a philosophy of children's literature, critics developed a scholarship that balances an appreciation of children and an awareness of their needs with standards for literary quality much like those required by critics of adult literature. *Children's Literature Review* (*CLR*) is designed to provide a permanent, accessible record of this ongoing scholarship. Those responsible for bringing children and books together can now make informed choices when selecting reading materials for the young.

Scope of the Series

Each volume of *CLR* contains excerpts from published criticism on the works of authors and author/illustrators who create books for children from preschool through high school. The author list for each volume is international in scope and represents the variety of genres covered by children's literature—picture books, fiction, folklore, nonfiction, poetry, and drama. The works of approximately fifteen authors of all eras are represented in each volume. Although earlier volumes of *CLR* emphasized critical material published after 1960, successive volumes have expanded their coverage to encompass criticism written before 1960. Since many of the authors included in *CLR* are living and continue to write, it is necessary to update their entries periodically. Thus, future volumes will supplement the entries of selected authors covered in earlier volumes as well as present criticism on the works of authors new to the series.

Organization of the Book

An author section consists of the following elements: author heading, author portrait, author introduction, excerpts of criticism (each followed by a bibliographical citation), and illustrations, when available.

- The **author heading** consists of the author's full name followed by birth and death dates. The portion of the name outside the parentheses denotes the form under which the author is most frequently published. If the majority of the author's works for children were written under a pseudonym, the pseudonym will be listed in the author heading and the real name given on the first line of the author introduction. Also located at the beginning of the introduction are any other pseudonyms used by the author in writing for children and any name variations, including transliterated forms for authors whose languages use nonroman alphabets. Uncertainty as to a birth or death date is indicated by question marks.

- An **author portrait** is included when available.

- The **author introduction** contains information designed to introduce an author to *CLR* users by presenting an overview of the author's themes and styles, occasional biographical facts that relate to the author's literary career, a summary of critical response to the author's works, and information about major awards and prizes the author has received. Where applicable, introductions conclude with references to additional entries in biographical and critical reference series published by Gale Research Company. These sources include past volumes of *CLR* as well as *Contemporary Authors, Something about the Author, Something about the Author Autobiography Series, Yesterday's Authors of Books for Children, Contemporary Literary Criticism, Twentieth-Century Literary Criticism, Nineteenth-Century Literature Criticism, Dictionary of Literary Biography,* and *Authors in the News.*

- **Criticism** is located in three sections: **author's commentary** and **general commentary** (when available) and within individual **title entries,** which are preceded by **title entry headings.** Criticism is arranged chronologically within each section. Titles by authors being profiled are highlighted in boldface type within the text for easier access by readers.

The **author's commentary** presents background material written by the author or by an interviewer. This commentary may cover a specific work or several works. Author's commentary on more than one work appears after the author introduction, while commentary on an individual book follows the title entry heading.

The **general commentary** consists of critical excerpts that consider more than one work by the author being profiled. General commentary is preceded by the critic's name in boldface type or, in the case of unsigned criticism, by the title of the journal.

Title entry headings precede the criticism on a title and cite publication information on the work being reviewed. Title headings list the title of the work as it appeared in its country of origin; titles in languages using nonroman alphabets are transliterated. If the original title is in a language other than English, the title of the first English-language translation follows in brackets. The first publication date of each work is listed in parentheses following the title. Differing U.S. and British titles of works originally published in English follow the publication date within the parentheses.

Title entries consist of critical excerpts on the author's individual works, arranged chronologically by publication date. The entries generally contain two to six reviews per title, depending on the stature of the book and the amount of criticism it has generated. The editors select titles that reflect the entire scope of the author's literary contribution, covering each genre and subject. An effort is made to reprint criticism that represents the full range of each title's reception—from the year of its initial publication to current assessments. Thus, the reader is provided with a record of the author's critical history.

Entries on author/illustrators will occasionally feature commentary on selected works illustrated but not written by the author being profiled. These works are strongly associated with the illustrator and have received critical acclaim for their art. By including critical comment on works of this type, the editors wish to provide a more complete representation of the author/illustrator's total career. Criticism on these works has been chosen to stress artistic, rather than literary, contributions. Title entry headings for works illustrated by the author being profiled are arranged chronologically within the entry by date of publication and include notes identifying the author of the illustrated work. In order to provide easier access for users, all titles illustrated by the author/illustrator will be boldfaced.

• Selected excerpts are preceded by **explanatory notes,** which provide information on the critic or work of criticism to enhance the reader's understanding of the excerpt.

• A complete **bibliographical citation** designed to facilitate the location of the original book or article follows each piece of criticism.

• Numerous **illustrations** are featured in *CLR.* For entries on author/illustrators, an effort has been made to include illustrations that reflect the author's styles as discussed in the criticism. Entries on major authors who do not illustrate their own works may also include photographs and other illustrative material pertinent to the authors' careers.

Other Features

• A list of **authors to appear in future volumes** follows the preface.

• A **guest essay** appears before the first author entry. These essays are written specifically for *CLR* by prominent critics on subjects of their choice. Past volumes have included essays by John Rowe Townsend, Zena Sutherland, Sheila A. Egoff, Rudine Sims, Marcus Crouch, and Anne Pellowski. Volume 13 contains Milton Meltzer's "Biography and the Writer's Voice." The editors are honored to feature Mr. Meltzer in this volume.

• An **appendix** lists the sources from which material has been reprinted in the volume. It does not, however, list every book or periodical consulted for the volume.

• *CLR* volumes contain **cumulative indexes** to authors, nationalities, and titles.

The **cumulative index to authors** lists authors who have appeared in *CLR* and includes cross-references to *Contemporary Authors, Something about the Author, Something about the Author Autobiography Series, Yesterday's Authors of Books for Children, Contemporary Literary Criticism, Twentieth-Century Literary Criticism, Nineteenth-Century Literature Criticism, Dictionary of Literary Biography,* and *Authors in the News.*

The **cumulative nationality index** lists authors alphabetically under their respective nationalities. Author names are followed by the volume number(s) in which they appear. Authors who have changed citizenship or whose current citizenship is not reflected in biographical sources appear under both their original nationality and that of their current residence.

The **cumulative title index** lists titles covered in *CLR* followed by the volume and page number where criticism begins.

Acknowledgments

No work of this scope can be accomplished without the cooperation of many people. The editors especially wish to thank the copyright holders of the criticism included in this volume, the permissions managers of many book and magazine publishing companies for assisting us in securing reprint rights, and the staffs of the Kresge Library at Wayne State University, the University of Michigan Library, the Detroit Public Library, and the Wayne Oakland Library Federation (WOLF) for making their resources available to us. We are also grateful to Sylvia Makowski, Coordinator of Children's and Young Adults' Services for WOLF, and to Anthony J. Bogucki for his assistance with copyright research.

Suggestions Are Welcome

In response to various suggestions, several features have been added to *CLR* since the series began:

- Since Volume 3—**Author's commentary,** when available, which presents the viewpoint of the author being profiled.

  —An **appendix** listing the sources of criticism in each volume.

- Since Volume 4—**Author portraits** as well as **illustrations** from works by author/illustrators, when available.

  —**Title entries** arranged chronologically according to the work's first publication; previous volumes listed titles alphabetically.

- Since Volume 5—A **guest essay,** when available, written specifically for *CLR* by a prominent critic on a subject of his or her choice.

- Since Volume 6—**Explanatory notes** that provide information on the critic or work of criticism to enhance the usefulness of the excerpt.

  —A **cumulative nationality index** for easy access to authors by nationality.

- Since Volume 8—Author entries on retellers of traditional literature as well as those who have been the first to record oral tales and other folklore.

  —More extensive illustrative material, such as holographs of manuscript pages and photographs of people and places pertinent to the authors' careers.

- Since Volume 10—Occasional entries devoted to criticism on a single work by a major author.

- Since Volume 12—Entries on author/illustrators featuring commentary on selected works illustrated but not written by the author being profiled.

Readers are cordially invited to write the editor with comments and suggestions for further enhancing the usefulness of the *CLR* series.

AUTHORS TO APPEAR IN FUTURE VOLUMES

Aardema, Verna (Norberg) 1911-
Adams, Harriet S(tratemeyer) 1893?-1982
Adams, Richard 1920-
Adler, Irving 1913-
Aesop 620?BC-564?BC
Ahlberg, Janet 1944- and Allan 1938-
Anderson, C(larence) W(illiam) 1891-1971
Arnosky, Jim 1946-
Arundel, Honor (Morfydd) 1919-1973
Asbjörnsen, Peter Christen 1812-1885 and Jörgen Moe 1813?-1882
Asch, Frank 1946-
Avery, Gillian 1926-
Avi 1937-
Aymé, Marcel 1902-1967
Bailey, Carolyn Sherwin 1875-1961
Ballantyne, R(obert) M(ichael) 1825-1894
Banner, Angela 1923-
Bannerman, Helen 1863-1946
Barrett, Judi(th) 1941-
Barrie, J(ames) M(atthew) 1860-1937
Baum, L(yman) Frank 1856-1919
Baumann, Hans 1914-1985
Beatty, Patricia Robbins 1922- and John 1922-1975
Behn, Harry 1898-1973
Belloc, Hilaire 1870-1953
Berenstain, Stan(ley) 1923- and Jan(ice) 1923-
Berger, Melvin H. 1927-
Berna, Paul 1910-
Beskow, Elsa 1874-1953
Bianco, Margery Williams 1881-1944
Bishop, Claire Huchet
Blades, Ann 1947-
Blake, Quentin 1932-
Blos, Joan W(insor) 1928-
Blumberg, Rhoda 1917-
Blyton, Enid 1897-1968
Bodecker, N(iels) M(ogens) 1922-
Bødker, Cecil 1927-
Bonham, Frank 1914-
Brancato, Robin F(idler) 1936-
Branscum, Robbie 1937-
Breinburg, Petronella 1927-
Bridgers, Sue Ellen 1942-
Bright, Robert 1902-
Brink, Carol Ryrie 1895-1981
Brinsmead, H(esba) F(ay) 1922-
Brooke, L(eonard) Leslie 1862-1940
Brown, Marc Tolon 1946-
Browne, Anthony (Edward Tudor) 1946-
Bryan, Ashley F. 1923-
Buff, Mary 1890-1970 and Conrad 1886-1975
Bulla, Clyde Robert 1914-
Burch, Robert (Joseph) 1925-
Burgess, Gelett 1866-1951
Burgess, Thornton W(aldo) 1874-1965
Burkert, Nancy Ekholm 1933-
Burnett, Frances Hodgson 1849-1924
Butterworth, Oliver 1915-
Caines, Jeannette (Franklin)
Caldecott, Randolph 1846-1886
Carlson, Natalie Savage 1906-
Carrick, Carol 1935-
Chambers, Aidan 1934-
Childress, Alice 1920-
Chönz, Selina
Christopher, Matt(hew F.) 1917-
Ciardi, John (Anthony) 1916-1986
Clapp, Patricia 1912-
Clark, Ann Nolan 1896-
Clarke, Pauline 1921-
Cohen, Barbara 1932-
Colby, C(arroll) B(urleigh) 1904-1977
Colman, Hila
Colum Padraic 1881-1972
Cone, Molly 1918-
Coolidge, Olivia E(nsor) 1908-
Coolidge, Susan 1835-1905
Cooney, Barbara 1917-
Courlander, Harold 1908-
Cox, Palmer 1840-1924
Crane, Walter 1845-1915
Cresswell, Helen 1934-
Crompton, Richmal 1890-1969
Cunningham, Julia (Woolfolk) 1916-
Curry, Jane L(ouise) 1932-
Dalgliesh, Alice 1893-1979
Daly, Maureen 1921-
Danziger, Paula 1944-
Daugherty, James 1889-1974
D'Aulaire, Ingri 1904-1980 and Edgar Parin 1898-1986
De la Mare, Walter 1873-1956
Denslow, W(illiam) W(allace) 1856-1915
De Regniers, Beatrice Schenk 1914-
Dickinson, Peter 1927-
Dillon, Eilís 1920-
Dillon, Leo 1933- and Diane 1933-
Dodge, Mary Mapes 1831-1905
Domanska, Janina
Drescher, Henrik
Duncan, Lois S(teinmetz) 1934-
Duvoisin, Roger 1904-1980
Eager, Edward 1911-1964
Edgeworth, Maria 1767-1849
Edmonds, Walter D(umaux) 1903-
Ende, Michael 1930(?)-
Epstein, Sam(uel) 1909- and Beryl 1910-
Ets, Marie Hall 1893-
Ewing, Juliana Horatia 1841-1885
Farber, Norma 1909-1984
Farjeon, Eleanor 1881-1965
Field, Eugene 1850-1895
Field, Rachel 1894-1942
Fisher, Dorothy Canfield 1879-1958
Fisher, Leonard Everett 1924-
Flack, Marjorie 1897-1958
Forbes, Esther 1891-1967
Forman, James D(ouglas) 1932-
Freeman, Don 1908-1978
Fujikawa, Gyo 1908-
Fyleman, Rose 1877-1957
Galdone, Paul 1914-1986
Gantos, Jack 1951-
Garfield, Leon 1921-
Garis, Howard R(oger) 1873-1962
Garner, Alan 1935-
Gates, Doris 1901-
Gerrard, Roy 1935-
Giblin, James Cross 1933-
Giff, Patricia Reilly 1935-
Ginsburg, Mirra 1919-
Goble, Paul 1933-
Godden, Rumer 1907-
Goodall, John S(trickland) 1908-
Goodrich, Samuel G(riswold) 1793-1860
Gorey, Edward (St. John) 1925-
Gramatky, Hardie 1907-1979
Greene, Constance C(larke) 1924-
Grimm, Jacob 1785-1863 and Wilhelm 1786-1859
Gruelle, Johnny 1880-1938
Guillot, René 1900-1969
Hader, Elmer 1889-1973 and Berta 1891?-1976
Hague, Michael 1948-
Hale, Lucretia Peabody 1820-1900
Haley, Gail E(inhart) 1939-
Hall, Lynn 1937-
Harnett, Cynthia 1893-1981
Harris, Christie (Lucy Irwin) 1907-
Harris, Joel Chandler 1848-1908
Harris, Rosemary (Jeanne) 1923-
Haywood, Carolyn 1898-
Heide, Florence Parry 1919-
Heine, Helme
Heinlein, Robert A(nson) 1907-
Highwater, Jamake (Mamake) 1942-
Hoberman, Mary Ann 1930-
Hoff, Syd(ney) 1912-
Hoffman, Heinrich 1809-1894
Holland, Isabelle 1920-
Holling, Holling C(lancy) 1900-1973

Howker, Janni 1957-
Hughes, Langston 1902-1967
Hughes, Shirley 1929-
Hunter, Mollie 1922-
Hurd, Edith Thacher 1910- and Clement 1908-
Hyman, Trina Schart 1939-
Ipcar, Dahlov (Zorach) 1917-
Iwasaki, Chihiro 1918-1974
Jackson, Jesse 1908-1983
Janosch 1931-
Johnson, Crockett 1906-1975
Johnson, James Weldon 1871-1938
Jones, Diana Wynne 1934-
Judson, Clara Ingram 1879-1960
Juster, Norton 1929-
Kelly, Eric P(hilbrook) 1884-1960
Kennedy, (Jerome) Richard 1932-
Kent, Jack 1920-1985
Kerr, (Anne-)Judith 1923-
Kerr, M. E. 1927-
Kettelkamp, Larry (Dale) 1933-
King, (David) Clive 1924-
Kipling, Rudyard 1865-1936
Kjelgaard, Jim 1910-1959
Kraus, Robert 1925-
Krauss, Ruth (Ida) 1911-
Krumgold, Joseph 1908-1980
La Fontaine, Jean de 1621-1695
Lang, Andrew 1844-1912
Langton, Jane (Gillson) 1922-
Latham, Jean Lee 1902-
Lauber, Patricia (Grace) 1924-
Lavine, Sigmund A(rnold) 1908-
Leaf, Munro 1905-1976
Lenski, Lois 1893-1974
Levy, Elizabeth 1942-
Lightner, A(lice) M. 1904-
Locker, Thomas 1937-
Lofting, Hugh (John) 1866-1947
Lunn, Janet 1928-
MacDonald, George 1824-1905
MacGregor, Ellen 1906-1954
MacLachlan, Patricia
Mann, Peggy
Marshall, James 1942-
Masefield, John 1878-1967
Mayer, Marianna 1945-
Mayne, William (James Carter) 1928-
Mazer, Harry 1925-
Mazer, Norma Fox 1931-
McCaffrey, Anne (Inez) 1926-
McGovern, Ann
McKee, David (John)
McKillip, Patricia A(nne) 1948-
McNeer, May 1902-
Meader, Stephen W(arren) 1892-1977
Means, Florence Crannell 1891-1980
Meigs, Cornelia 1884-1973
Merriam, Eve 1916-
Merrill, Jean (Fairbanks) 1923-
Miles, Betty 1928-
Milne, Lorus 1912- and Margery 1915-
Minarik, Else Holmelund 1920-
Mizumura, Kazue
Mohr, Nicholasa 1935-
Molesworth, Mary Louisa 1842-1921
Moore, Lilian
Morey, Walt(er Nelson) 1907-
Mowat, Farley (McGill) 1921-
Naylor, Phyllis Reynolds 1933-
Neufeld, John (Arthur) 1938-
Neville, Emily Cheney 1919-
Nic Leodhas, Sorche 1898-1969
Nielsen, Kay 1886-1957
North, Sterling 1906-1974
Norton, Andre 1912-
Ofek, Uriel 1926-
Ormondroyd, Edward 1925-
Ottley, Reginald (Leslie)
Oxenbury, Helen 1938-
Parish, Peggy 1927-
Peck, Richard (Wayne) 1934-
Peck, Robert Newton 1928-
Perl, Lila
Perrault, Charles 1628-1703
Petersen, P(eter) J(ames) 1941-
Petersham, Maud 1890-1971 and Miska 1888-1960
Picard, Barbara Leonie 1917-
Platt, Kin 1911-
Politi, Leo 1908-
Price, Christine 1928-1980
Pyle, Howard 1853-1911
Rackham, Arthur 1867-1939
Rawls, Wilson 1919-
Reeves, James 1909-1978
Richards, Laura E(lizabeth) 1850-1943
Richler, Mordecai 1931-
Robertson, Keith (Carlton) 1914-
Rockwell, Anne 1934- and Harlow
Rodgers, Mary 1931-
Rollins, Charlemae Hill 1897-1979
Ross, Tony 1938-
Rounds, Glen H(arold) 1906-
Rylant, Cynthia 1954-
Sandburg, Carl 1878-1967
Sandoz, Mari 1896-1966
Sawyer, Ruth 1880-1970
Scarry, Huck 1953-
Scott, Jack Denton 1915-
Sebestyen, Ouida 1924-
Seton, Ernest Thompson 1860-1946
Sharmat, Marjorie Weinman 1928-
Sharp, Margery 1905-
Shepard, Ernest H(oward) 1879-1976
Shotwell, Louisa R(ossiter) 1902-
Sidney, Margaret 1844-1924
Silverstein, Alvin 1933- and Virginia B(arbara Opshelor) 1937-
Sinclair, Catherine 1800-1864
Skurzynski, Gloria (Joan) 1930-
Sleator, William (Warner) 1945-
Slobodkin, Louis 1903-1975
Smith, Doris Buchanan 1934-
Smith, Jessie Willcox 1863-1935
Snyder, Zilpha Keatley 1927-
Spence, Eleanor (Rachel) 1928-
Sperry, Armstrong W. 1897-1976
Spykman, E(lizabeth) C. 1896-1965
Steele, William O(wen) 1917-1979
Stevenson, James 1929-
Stolz, Mary (Slattery) 1920-
Stratemeyer, Edward L. 1862-1930
Streatfeild, (Mary) Noel 1897-1986
Taylor, Sydney 1904?-1978
Taylor, Theodore 1924-
Tenniel, Sir John 1820-1914
Ter Haar, Jaap 1922-
Thiele, Colin 1920-
Thompson, Julian F(rancis) 1927-
Titus, Eve 1922-
Tolkien, J(ohn) R(onald) R(euel) 1892-1973
Trease, (Robert) Geoffrey 1909-
Tresselt, Alvin 1916-
Treviño, Elizabeth Borton de 1904-
Turkle, Brinton 1915-
Twain, Mark 1835-1910
Udry, Janice May 1928-
Unnerstad, Edith (Totterman) 1900-
Uttley, Alison 1884-1976
Ventura, Piero (Luigi) 1937-
Vining, Elizabeth Gray 1902-
Waber, Bernard 1924-
Wahl, Jan 1933-
Walter, Mildred Pitts
Ward, Lynd 1905-1985
Wells, Rosemary 1943-
White, T(erence) H(anbury) 1906-1964
Wiese, Kurt 1887-1974
Wilkinson, Brenda 1946-
Wyeth, N(ewell) C(onvers) 1882-1945
Yates, Elizabeth 1905-
Yonge, Charlotte M(ary) 1823-1901
Yorinks, Arthur 1953-
Zemach, Harve 1933-1974 and Margot 1931-
Zion, Gene 1913-1975

Readers are cordially invited to suggest additional authors to the editors.

GUEST ESSAY

Biography and the Writer's Voice

by Milton Meltzer

Some years ago, when I was doing research for my adult biography *Dorothea Lange: A Photographer's Life* (1978), I ran across a curious coincidence in remarks about her made by a few of the people I was interviewing. These few—distinguished photographers in their own right—had known Lange well in various periods of her life, and I was trying to gather from them all the facts I could about Lange, as well as their opinions of her personality. They had many useful things to tell me about Lange, who had died some ten years before, but during the interview each of them uttered one lie—or misstatement, if you will. At some point, when they got around to assessing some of Lange's personal traits, and they were recalling something negative, they would say, as if by way of explanation, "She was Jewish, you know."

I had learned long before these interviews that she was not Jewish. But each time, when I interrupted politely to say "Are you sure? The documents show she was of German Lutheran stock," my remark was ignored. The interviewee went right on seeking to establish and confirm a painful aspect of Lange's personality by giving it a cause—Jewishness.

From their testimonies, corroborated by many others, I concluded that Lange did upset or anger people by a certain kind of abrasive behavior. But in studying her relationships with friends and colleagues, it was clear that some, perhaps envious of Lange's achievements and reputation, harbored intensely negative feelings which they justified to themselves on prejudicial grounds.

It is odds and ends like this that make biography "the unpredictable spectacle of life" that Edmund Wilson once called it. One learns to approach this study of humanity with humility and the capacity to be astonished by what one finds. It can tell the biographer as much about himself as about his subject. Why do I single out the above references to Jewishness to make a point? Because in my growing years I had considerable trouble facing my own Jewish origins. And that was reflected in maturity when I began to write history and biography; I spent fifteen years producing many books about other ethnic figures and groups before I got down to writing about my own people. Well, that is a side of the biographer and historian worth exploring, too. Why does he choose to write what he does? How does who he is and where he comes from affect what he writes? What values does he bring to his work and how are they reflected in it? Does his work in turn change him in any way? (Of course he hopes it changes his readers).

About those readers: here we are talking about the younger ones, readers up through the high school years. Do they read biography? Teachers and librarians know better than I. Judging by the sales of biography for the young, not enough of them do. Certainly not enough to make it possible for most writers to earn even a modest living from their work. But if a writer finds biography to his taste, he will go on telling lives he cares about. Even if he has to hold another job to support himself, or to lean heavily upon a salaried spouse.

You, as teachers and librarians working with young people, may want to know how a biographer-historian sees his work in the light of the readers he hopes will come to it. What experiences will it open up to them? Can it be a pleasure for them to read? Can it entertain them as well as extend them and fulfill them?

I will try to pursue these questions as both historian and biographer, but perhaps with more attention to biography. Of course, you cannot really separate the two. The French historian, Marc Bloch, wrote that the true subject of history is essentially man. Wars, politics, revolutions, institutions, technology, science, culture, economies, religion—all these are of great concern to history. But it is men and women that the historian tries to get hold of. As one writer said, "The good historian is like the giant in the fairy tale—anywhere he smells human flesh is where his quarry lies."

When you write history, it is people you try to place in the real world, people who love and hate, work and play, invent fantasies and tell lies. When you write biography, you present history through the prism of a single life, a life that is, of course, connected to other lives. Is that life worth writing about? *Every* life is worth recording, worth getting down truthfully. And isn't the truth about human character desirable, no matter what the character is? The biographer investigates that life, eager to find and tell the truth about it, no matter what the outcome of his search. What could be more fascinating, and more useful, than to explain a human life in all its strength and frailty, even when we are reading about a life long gone, a life lived a hundred, five hundred, a thousand years ago? For the life we live today is enlarged and enriched by what we learn about past lives.

Writing biography, like writing history, is taking part in the creation of the collective memory. All too often, the historian Peter Gay points out, the writer gives in to the demands of his culture by remembering events that did not happen, and in forgetting events that did.[1] The culture—or its dominant powers—want a past that they can use. But there are times when society calls not for reassuring tales but for the harsh facts about the past. We should not forget that for many decades following the defeat of Reconstruction, historians created a damning indictment of that brief time when blacks and whites tried to build freedom, equality, and democracy in the postwar South, just as other historians before them created a myth about the beneficence of slavery. Memory, Peter Gay warns us, can be "the supple minister of self-interest."[2]

Such historians were "creative," but in the harmful sense of building false legends about the past. In the practice of history and biography the word "creative" does not mean to invent. It means to give the past, to give those many lives or the single life, an artistic form. Teachers of English in search of literary values they can illuminate for young readers can surely seek—and find—evidence of literary art in biographical history.

There may be some teachers who still think of biography as some sort of poor relation to literature. But if a novel may illuminate human character, does biography try to do less? In the case of the best biographies of artists—whether they be poets, painters, musicians—the point should be especially clear. Take Leon Edel's *Henry James,* or R.W.B. Lewis's *Edith Wharton,* or Quentin Bell's *Virginia Woolf.* The biographical knowledge of these novelists that they give us provide revelations that enhance our approach to the writer's art. Such biographies can tell us how the artist produces his or her work, what their motive and meaning was in doing it. Such biographies illuminate and extend our knowledge of the creative process. And they teach us that you cannot isolate the creation from the creator.

How does the biographer go about his work? Perhaps some details taken from my own experience will offer clues. If you know what went into the making of a biography, it might be of help in assisting young readers to draw the most out of it. I will use my *Langston Hughes: A Biography* (1968) as an example. Early in the 1950s Hughes and I collaborated on a book about black history, *A Pictorial History of the Negro in America* (1956). Strangers at the beginning, we became friends during the course of the work. Years later, we collaborated on a second book about blacks in the performing arts, *Black Magic: A Pictorial History of the Negro in American Entertainment* (1967). As this was entering proofs, a publisher asked me to write some short sketches of various people for a project designed to appeal to young readers in black communities. One of the sketches I did was of Langston Hughes's life. When he saw it he called to say how much he liked it. Then it occurred to me—why not try to do a biography of Langston for young adults? "What would you think of if," I asked him hesitantly, because, of course, he could easily do it himself. (He had already published two volumes of his autobiography for adults.) "Go right ahead," he said, "and I'll try to help you however I can." So, with a contract from a publisher, I set to work.

Since this was to be a book about a writer, the most important source of information was his own work. I was not trying to do the kind of biography I would come to years later, when I wrote Dorothea Lange's story for adults. I knew that here my audience was young people, that they were primarily interested in Hughes for his poems, stories, and plays, and that the role of his blackness in his work was of paramount interest.

So I began research with a very detailed analysis of the Hughes autobiography—*The Big Sea* (1940) and *I Wonder as I Wander: An Autobiographical Journey* (1956). These volumes carried his life story only up to the age of forty, by the way, and now he was sixty-five. In a book for young readers I was constrained to keep the text down to some forty thousand words. This limit—not necessarily a handicap—meant a careful choice of material to be included. One had to leave out a lot in writing about so richly varied a life. That necessity can be a blessing. Some biographies are enormous compendia of facts, full of the clutter of daily life, with the subject's every ticket stub and laundry bill thrown in.

You have probably found yourself swamped by such biographies. "Too many card indexes are flung into the face of the public instead of being molded into the semblance of a life," Leon Edel once said.[3] Virginia Woolf put it more positively: "Almost any biographer, if he respects facts, can give us much more than another fact to add to our collection. He can give us the creative fact, the fertile fact, the fact that suggests and engenders."[4] Another biographer, Robert Gittings, sees it this way: "The sheer weight of evidence available to a biographer does not in itself make a successful biography."[5] He continues, "It is not mass and variety of evidence that counts but its quality, reliability and relevance to the subject."[6]

It is important to remember that the biographer does not imagine the facts. He selects them. His imaginative powers come into play when he shapes the form into which the facts will go.

As I made notes on Hughes's writing I built a list of things to do to clarify, corroborate, or extend what his work suggested to me. Hughes also gave me certain materials from his own files, and he answered the many questions I asked him. In addition, I got help from more than fifty people who had known him, some from as far back as his early schooldays, some from college years, and some way on up through the decades of his long professional career as the first black American to seek to make a living entirely from his writing. Other writers, editors, publishers, agents, actors, directors, singers, dancers, and composers who had played some part in his multifaceted work gave me interviews or answered my queries by letter and phone. Some lent me letters, papers, photographs, clippings.

Much material on Hughes is held at Yale, the Schomburg Center for Research in Black Culture in Harlem, and Lincoln University in Pennsylvania. Among the liveliest sources were newspapers and periodicals. They carried news stories about him and articles by him, as well as editorial comment on him. And then there were the fat files of his own newspaper columns which appeared weekly for over twenty years, first in the *Chicago Defender* and then also in the *New York Post.*

Beyond his autobiography were Hughes's other writings, of course. It is an incredibly long bibliography. I read every one of these publications, for they voiced what he thought and felt and dreamed and feared and hoped. The biographer must be constantly sensitive to what he finds that characterizes his subject. Not any fact, but this *particular* fact or phrase or word is what is wanted to represent a facet of the life for the reader to see. Anything that is vivid and human will help bring the portrait to life.

A kind of compulsion seizes you as you work to build a life on paper. You scan the index of every book, hoping for a mention of your man. And miraculously, it seems, the name of your subject keeps popping up in the most unexpected places. Of course it is because you are sensitized to it. It becomes a fevered pursuit, full of delights when you uncover unknown documents about your subject or find long-lost friends of his. What special joy when you succeed in tracking down a vital detail!

Then one day you get the feeling that this is enough. You have gone everywhere you have time or money to go, you have read everything there is to read, you have talked to everyone who will see you. On your desk are piled files of documents and stacks of 3 x 5 notes. You are nagged by a sneaking feeling that if you wait a month or two more before starting to write, still another essential fact will come to light. But I'd learned to put down such impulses. The truth is, nobody writes the definitive biography, the book that will never need revision.

Each generation feels itself compelled to reexamine the past or to reconsider the value of an individual's life. It brings to that task the questions its own generation is concerned with. So the biographer stops research at some reasonable point. He must do his own job, and there will be others after him to do it again, and differently.

So you begin writing, shuttling from one document to another, trying to form in your mind an image of your subject. When you are writing about someone you have known, an image is already there, though it may be modified by what your research has unearthed. Your personal relationship with your subject is only one of many such relationships in his life. You see him from your narrow perspective. Now that perspective is altered, perhaps, by what you have learned from the views of many others. To the testimony of your own eyes you add the testimony of others.

That testimony is not always corroborative. It can often be contradictory. That was not the case with my life of Langston Hughes, but it was often the case with my life of Dorothea Lange. Just the awareness of such possible contradictions can give the biographer an advantage in his quest for the truest picture he can paint.

You can only conclude, after a considerable amount of work in this field, that any interpretation you provide, no matter how carefully done, will be oversimplified. There is always something you can't account for. The British critic, A. O. J. Cockshut, puts it this way: "When we say a man acts out of character do we mean that the character we impute to him is thus shown to be a slightly inaccurate version? Or do we mean that on certain rare occasions a man can act contrary to his own character as it really is."[7]

This point came into sharp focus when I was working on the Lange books, first for adults, and much later the one for young readers, *Dorothea Lange: Life through the Camera* (1985). There was, for example, the contrast between her marvelous photographs of the dispossessed farmers wandering the West during the Great Depression and her treatment of her own children. The photographs of those migratory farm workers are warm, sympathetic, respectful of their innate dignity and worth. How could such a humanistic artist be as cruel to her own children as the evidence shows she sometimes was? Well, people are not all of a piece.

That is why the biographer needs to maintain sympathy with his subject. You should be "neither forbearing nor adulatory," as Leon Edel warns, retaining "your capacity to be aware at every moment that the subject is human and therefore fallible."[8]

One of the biographer's biggest problems is identification with his subject. It can lead to triumphs or disasters. The biographer seeks to understand a life by coming as close as he can to that person. Yet, he must be careful not to reshape his subject in his own image. When writing about Hughes, of course, the inward and spiritual life was reflected in his work—his poems, his songs, his plays, his stories, his novels, his autobiography, his columns about that most delicious of creations Jesse B. Semple. It is easier, when your subject is a writer, to take part in his inner life.

But to convey that inner life, while always difficult, is only part of your task. The biographer is interested in every aspect of his subject's history. The physical as well as the psychic, the public as well as the private. The economic and social circumstances that helped shape him are part of the story. The world of his lifespan, as he experienced it, must be considered. In the case of Hughes, you started out with the fact that he was an American, and black. And for the Afro-American, life in the land where "white is right" has always been difficult. It is this that Hughes's poetry and his life illuminate. Before he was twenty-five, he had made himself the poet laureate of his people. Their life was his life. So it was that life, too, which the biographer had to try to make clear.

It sounds like a daunting task, the writing of biography, and believe me, it is. Its difficulties are such that it takes great enthusiasm to start and go through with it. Confronting that blank sheet of paper, you wonder how you will ever revive that life scattered in bits and pieces all over your desk. You know what you know, but you know too what you *don't* know and may *never* know. Still, you are convinced that this is a worthwhile thing to do. And, inadequate as you feel, you make a beginning.

You work with two elements: facts and words. With them you try to create character. Not character as in a still life, but character in a life as it is being lived, which means its development through time. And that brings up narrative. Biography is really character told through a story. And not your central character alone, but his or her story through the developing relationships with others. The biographer chooses the facts about the subject that are relevant to the portrait he wants to paint, and then he uses words to paint that portrait. There are no doubt many ways or styles in which that portrait could be painted. Because he is what he is, the creative biographer does it in his own particular and unique way.

There are biographers who borrow the methods of the novelist, while being careful not to create fiction. It is not necessary to tell the life story by a strict and straight chronology. The biographer may move back and forth in time, using his documentary evidence in imaginative ways without ever departing from their truth. He will do whatever his creative powers permit in the hope that, in some magic way, what he reveals about this singular life will connect, will resonate, with the reader.

I have said nothing about style, a question sure to arise whenever teachers discuss literature with students. *This* writer has style, someone will say, while *that* writer has none. But the truth is, every writer has style. The word is really a neutral one—it simply means a way of expressing thought in language, oral or written. One writer's style may be ugly and another's beautiful. You may be indifferent to a writer's style, scarcely noticing it, or you may be angered by it if you find it offensive.

No one is born with a style; it is a mode of expression shaped by your personal history and by the culture you live in—its ways of feeling, thinking, acting. For me the most useful way of thinking about style is as a tone of voice. That tone develops through the exercise of will and intelligence and it is refined by the struggle with your material. The historian Edward Gibbon said it is the mark of style to express the writer's mind and the task of style to hold the writer's audience.[9] Every writer is influenced by what he reads and tends to imitate in his early career. He works hard to break free of his models and find his own voice.

In reading history and biography, then, one listens to a writer's voice. In that voice he tells his story of an epoch or his story of a man or woman. Through his research he thinks he has discovered what they are like and he is trying to tell you about it. He must meet the task of any writer: being read. As that extremely talented historian Peter Gay tells us, there is no law holding that the historian or biographer must be unreadable.[10] Do your job well, and you will give pleasure without compromising the telling of truth.

Notes

1. Peter Gay, *Style in History* (New York: McGraw-Hill, 1974), 206.
2. Ibid.
3. Leon Edel, *Literary Biography* (Garden City, N.J.: Doubleday, 1959), xiii.
4. Ibid., 154.
5. Robert Gittings, *The Nature of Biography* (Seattle: University of Washington Press, 1978), 66.
6. Ibid., 71.
7. A. O. J. Cockshut, *Truth to Life: The Art of Biography in the Nineteenth Century* (New York: Harcourt, 1974), 15.
8. Edel, 133.
9. Gay, 44.
10. Ibid., 217.

Bibliography

Bell, Quentin. *Virginia Woolf.* New York: Harcourt, 1972.

Edel, Leon. *Henry James: A Life.* New York: Harper, 1985.

Hughes, Langston. *The Big Sea.* New York: Knopf, 1940.

Hughes, Langston. *I Wonder as I Wander: An Autobiographical Journey.* New York: Rinehart, 1956.

Hughes, Langston and Milton Meltzer. *Black Magic: A Pictorial History of the Negro in American Entertainment.* Englewood Cliffs, N.J.: Prentice-Hall, 1967.

Hughes, Langston and Milton Meltzer. *A Pictorial History of the Negro in America.* New York: Crown, 1956.

Lewis, R. W. B. *Edith Wharton.* New York: Harper, 1975.

Meltzer, Milton. *Dorothea Lange: A Photographer's Life.* New York: Farrar, 1978.

Meltzer, Milton. *Dorothea Lange: Life through the Camera.* New York: Viking, 1985.

Meltzer, Milton. *Langston Hughes: A Biography.* New York: Crowell, 1968.

Milton Meltzer is an American author, editor, critic, teacher, and lecturer. The creator of approximately sixty books for children, young people, and adults, he is well known as a writer of social histories which center on the struggle of the oppressed and biographies which highlight figures in the human rights movement and the arts. Among his many acclaimed works are *A Pictorial History of the Negro in America* (with Langston Hughes, 1956); the three-volume series *In Their Own Words: A History of the American Negro* (1964-67; revised edition as *The Black Americans: A History In Their Own Words, 1619-1983,* 1984): *Thaddeus Stevens and the Fight for Negro Rights* (1967); *Langston Hughes: A Biography* (1968); *Underground Man,* a novel (1972); *Never to Forget: The Jews of the Holocaust* (1976): *Dorothea Lange: A Photographer's Life* (for adults, 1978); *The Chinese Americans* (1980); *The Jewish Americans: A History in Their Own Words, 1650-1950* (1982); *Ain't Gonna Study War No More: The Story of America's Peace Seekers* (1985); *Dorothea Lange: Life through the Camera* (for children, 1985); and *Winnie Mandela: The Soul of South Africa* (1986). Since 1962, Meltzer has served as the editor of the "Women of America" series for Crowell. He also edited the series of "Zenith Books" for Doubleday from 1963 to 1973 and served as a consulting editor of the "Firebird Books" series from 1968 to 1972. After the publication of his young adult biography *Tongue of Flame: The Life of Lydia Maria Child* (1965), Meltzer received a four-year grant from the National Publications and Records Commission to head a team of scholars formed to edit the letters of Mrs. Child. As part of the grant, Meltzer received an adjunct professorship in the W. E. B. DuBois Department of Afro-American Studies at the University of Massachusetts, Amherst, a position he held from 1977 to 1980. The letters were published as *The Collected Correspondence of Lydia Maria Child, 1817-1880: Guide and Index to the Microfiche Edition* (with Patricia Holland and Francine Krasno, 1980). Meltzer is also the editor of *Lydia Maria Child: Selected Letters, 1817-1880* (with

Patricia Holland, 1982). In 1960, Meltzer founded the *Pediatric Herald* and served as its editor for eight years. He has also worked as a journalist, a public relations writer, and a scriptwriter for radio, television, and documentary films. Since 1972, he has served on the national council of the Authors Guild and has been a member of the editorial board of *Children's Literature in Education* since 1973.

For further information on Meltzer's books for children and young adults, see pages 114-52 of this volume.

Children's Literature Review

Franklyn M(ansfield) Branley

1915-

American author of nonfiction and fiction and editor.

Branley is the well-regarded author of over one hundred science books that center mainly on astronomy, space science, and meteorology. Writing for a preschool through high school audience, he is noted for the authority, clarity, and simplicity of his prose and for the ease with which he explains complex concepts. Branley's respect for a child's innate intelligence is evident in his use of accurate terminology and his careful discrimination between fact and theory. Usually adopting an informal approach, he enhances his well-organized accounts with interesting examples and easy experiments, and employs sufficient repetition to highlight salient points. Formerly a chairman of the American Museum-Hayden Planetarium, Branley first saw the need for child-oriented science books as an elementary school teacher. He began writing for children by collaborating with scientist Nelson F. Beeler on *Experiments in Science* (1947); together, they successfully produced several other volumes of experiments designed to educate and entertain middle grade and junior high school students. Branley's first solo publication was his only venture into science fiction, *Lodestar, Rocket Ship to Mars* (1951). With Eleanor K. Vaughan, he then coauthored three stories that introduce preschoolers to magnets, electric currents, and sound waves. His later titles include contributions to many series, such as "Exploring Our Universe" which is directed towards ten- to fourteen-year-olds. A major achievement of Branley's career is his conception, coeditorship, and frequent authorship of volumes in the popular "Let's-Read-and-Find-Out" series for listeners and beginning independent readers. In addition, he is recognized as being one of the first writers for juveniles to spotlight the topics in *Exploring by Satellite* (1957), *The Mystery of Stonehenge* (1969), and *Think Metric!* (1972).

Critics commend Branley for his clear, concise, readable style and for his ability to clarify sophisticated concepts and convey the excitement of scientific discovery. While reviewers object to occasional minor errors and misleading statements that often result from oversimplification, most agree that his books serve as sound introductions to diverse subjects and ably demonstrate the potentialities as well as the limitations of science. Branley is generally acknowledged as an author of wide scholarship and enthusiasm, whose prolific works over a period of four decades underscore his commitment to science education.

Branley has received many adult-selected awards for his nonfiction contributions to children's literature.

(See also *Contemporary Literary Criticism*, Vol. 21; *Something about the Author*, Vol. 4; *Contemporary Authors New Revision Series*, Vol. 14; and *Contemporary Authors*, Vols. 33-36, rev. ed.)

Photograph by Margaret Branley. Courtesy of Franklyn Branley.

AUTHOR'S COMMENTARY

[*The following excerpt is from an interview by S. V. Keenan.*]

[Children's] ability to understand, study, and persevere is terribly underrated by adults. . . .

We throw away a tremendous potential when we delay the exposure of young people to the excitement of science until they have become cynical sophisticates—say twelve years old . . . ; young children have the open mindedness, the willingness to make errors, the spirit of enquiry, the courage to take a challenge—attitudes that are requisites to solid scientific investigation.

S. V. Keenan, "Franklyn M. Branley," in Wilson Library Bulletin, *Vol. 36, No. 1, September, 1961, p. 66.*

GENERAL COMMENTARY

H. H. HOLMES

[***Experiments in the Principles of Space Travel*** and ***Mars***] contain a certain amount of useful material, along with a great many "do-it-yourself" experiments (which seem to entail far more trouble than they're worth) and far too many misleading or flatly inaccurate statements, the oddest of which is that Sir Isaac Newton advanced his theories "several decades ago."

H. H. Holmes, in a review of "Experiments in the Principles of Space Travel" and "Mars," in New York Herald Tribune Book Review, *November 13, 1955, p. 14.*

MAY HILL ARBUTHNOT

Franklyn M. Branley is almost as prolific a writer as Herbert Zim. . . . [Branley's] simplest book is ***Mickey's Magnet. . .,*** which explains the characteristics of the magnet, a perennially fascinating object for young children. ***A Book of Planets for You, A Book of the Milky Way Galaxy for You,*** and ***The Big Dipper*** are also for children six to seven or eight. All of his books are . . . remarkably informative. ***A Book of the Milky Way Galaxy for You*** gives a fascinating and understandable explanation of how vast distances are measured. ***The Sun: Star Number One*** and ***The Earth: Planet Number Three*** are fuller and more advanced than books on similar subjects by Zim, but the style and striking pictures by Helmut K. Wimmer make them comprehensible and fascinating. ***Experiments in Sky Watching,*** which won the Edison Foundation Award for the best science book for children in 1959, is also for advanced readers. Clear directions are given for locating and observing the stars and planets and even for performing simple experiments. The Branley books are well written and have made a brilliant contribution to children's science interests, especially in the field of astronomy. (p. 292)

May Hill Arbuthnot, "Informational Books: Science Books," in her Children's Reading in the Home, *Scott, Foresman and Company, 1969, pp. 290-97.*

DONALD MACRAE AND ELIZABETH MACRAE

The "Let's-read-and-find-out" series is titled optimistically insofar as [the] books on astronomy are concerned. The choice of subject is good but they are disappointingly written. . . . There is a point beyond which simplification leads to smugness if not to absurdity.

Consider ***The Moon Seems to Change. . . .*** (F. M. Branley is the author of the very good book ***Mars*** written for young adults). This simple book seems to end in complete confusion, having attempted to explain the size, distance, and particularly the phases of the moon. The time required to reach the moon in a car is estimated and is off by a factor of ten, unless the car were to travel at the rate of a tricycle. . . .

These overly simple books, ***What Makes Day and Night, The Moon Seems to Change, The Sun Our Nearest Star,*** are neither fish nor fowl. They do not lend themselves to being read aloud by a parent to a very young child. They are foolishly garrulous. They have no information or excitement to offer the alert six-year-old who is beginning to read for himself. At best, then, they are practice reading books, but dull. (p. 100)

Donald Macrae and Elizabeth Macrae, "Astronomy Books for Children" in Reading about Adolescent Literature, *edited by Dennis Thomison, The Scarecrow Press, Inc., 1970, pp. 99-109.*

THE HORN BOOK MAGAZINE

Comets, Meteoroids, and Asteroids contains little new information but does present a good, up-to-date description of the "mavericks" of the solar system. . . .

[***A Book of Flying Saucers for You***] aimed at the very young, demonstrates rather well that just about everything which can be said about UFO's can be said to first graders. The presentation seems perfectly fair to me; it repeats a few reports which are still unexplained, describes some of the accepted explanations, and lists a number of the proven hoaxes. The likelihood of life on other planets is discussed. In short, it is better balanced than most UFO books.

A review of "Comets, Meteoroids, and Asteroids: Mavericks of the Solar System" and "A Book of Flying Saucers for You," in The Horn Book Magazine, *Vol. LI, No. 1, February, 1975, p. 74.*

BARBARA BADER

For their particular audience, ["the very youngest reader," ***A Book of Moon Rockets*** and ***A Book of Satellites***], without a wisp of a story or the least lyricizing, were the first entries of the space age.

From recognition of "the child's serious quest for science information" came the Let's-Read-and-Find-Out series, by any standard—commercial, educational, creative—the most successful enterprise of its sort. Dr. Branley, whose idea it was, enlisted as co-editor his erstwhile mentor at Teachers College, Dr. Roma Gans, and himself wrote two of the first five. (p. 400)

Branley continued to be the leading author, responsible for astronomy and space science and meteorology and physics, and it can only be said that as a group the nineteen titles he produced between 1960 and 1973 dominate the field or fields, especially in astronomy and space science. (p. 402)

Barbara Bader, "More Information: Crowell and Science, Inc., 'Let's-Read-and-Find-Out'," in her American Picture Books from Noah's Ark to the Beast Within, *Macmillan Publishing Company, 1976, pp. 399-409.*

HARRY C. STUBBS

The contrast in style of [***Comets*** and ***Mysteries of the Universe***] is interesting and, of course, indicative of the different ages for which they were intended. ***Comets*** barely mentions the uncertainties in our slowly-built picture of the "dirty snowball"; the book mainly contains descriptions of how comets move and what they look like; only the most solidly established of the "why's" are mentioned (elliptical orbits, eventual disappearance). Several pages are devoted to the return of Halley's Comet, and for once a correct pronunciation of the name is indicated. Even with this comet there is some uncertainty. Its apparent path through the sky can hardly be very wrong, but any prediction about its brightness is extremely risky. Dr. Branley is following the pessimistic school—probably with justification. The 1910 apparition was a disappointment, and this comet may be nearing the end of its career. I am rather dubious about the role suggested for Jupiter on page twenty-seven. . . .

Mysteries of the Universe is far more open-ended and potentially more interesting. The structures of galaxy and universe, the natures of neutron stars and black holes, and the life history of a star are discussed with the clear understanding that space and time have prevented direct observation of most of the items mentioned. . . . The bibliography is very good.

Harry C. Stubbs, "Astronomy," in The Horn Book Magazine, *Vol. LXI, No. 2, March-April, 1985, p. 214.*

ZENA SUTHERLAND AND MAY HILL ARBUTHNOT

Both [Franklyn Branley's] professional knowledge and his familiarity with presenting facts to the lay person are reflected in his many books on astronomy and other scientific subjects. He collaborated with Eleanor K. Vaughan on two interesting books for the very young, ***Mickey's Magnet*** (1956) and ***Timmy and the Tin-Can Telephone*** (1959), which present scientific facts in attractive format.

The Milky Way (1969) is one of his books for older readers, using scientific terminology and a scholarly approach. It begins with a history of astronomy, describing early telescopes, the beliefs of early scientists and the ordinary people, and the conflict between Ptolemaic and Copernican theories. The book includes an appendix for finding stellar magnitudes and distances, intended for those who understand logarithms, and a bibliography. ***Mysteries of the Universe*** (1984) probes the many questions that scientists have, some answered and some still unsolved.

Branley has also written many books for younger children. ***The Sun: Our Nearest Star*** (1961) is a simple explanation in picture-book format, and ***A Book of Mars for You*** (1968) speculates about an unmanned landing. . . . [An] intriguing title is ***Is There Life in Outer Space?*** (1984). Branley is particularly skilled at selecting salient facts and omitting minor ones, so that his books for readers in lower and middle grades are succinct as well as accurate. In ***Eclipse*** (1973) he defines terminology in order to explain clearly the phenomenon of total solar eclipse, and in ***Pieces of Another World*** (1972) he discusses the collection and analysis of moon rocks, carefully distinguishing between fact and theory, and making clear the interdisciplinary effort of scientists, and in ***Color: From Rainbows to Lasers*** (1978) he discusses color in relation to light.

In ***Water for the World*** (1982) a discussion of the water cycle is followed by separate chapters on sources of water supply. Branley's versatility is demonstrated in the authority with which he writes on such diverse subjects as ***Dinosaurs, Asteroids, and Superstars: Why the Dinosaurs Disappeared*** (1982) and ***Shivers and Goose Bumps: How We Keep Warm*** (1984).

None of Franklyn Branley's books has been more popular than ***The Christmas Sky*** (1966), which is based on the Christmas lecture at the Hayden Planetarium. It discusses the Biblical, historical, and astronomical clues to the true date of the birth of Jesus, and deftly combines scientific facts and a reverent approach.

Zena Sutherland and May Hill Arbuthnot, "Informational Books: Franklyn M. Branley," in their Children and Books, *seventh edition, Scott, Foresman and Company, 1986, p. 490.*

EXPERIMENTS IN SCIENCE (with Nelson F. Beeler, 1947)

The mothers of America better get what rest and peace of mind they can right now, because after the boys of America get a good look at ***Experiments in Science,*** home isn't going to be the same any more. . . . [Here] are fifty simple experiments, which should be absolutely fascinating to any child, all in one book, and the urge to go right out to the kitchen and start messing around is irresistible.

The Messrs. Beeler and Branley are true scientists, and all on the children's side. They never flinch or turn away, although when making coke from coal they suggest, "you better hold your nose when you do this because the smell is awful." However, most experiments are innocent enough, and all are entertaining. ***Experiments in Science*** should prove a godsend to any teacher or parent faced with the problem of holding a pack at bay during a rainy afternoon.

Creighton Peet, in a review of "Experiments in Science," in The New York Times Book Review, *August 3, 1947, p. 18.*

EXPERIMENTS WITH ELECTRICITY (with Nelson F. Beeler, 1949)

These experiments will satisfy the boys and girls of ages ten to twelve. They go beyond the elementary stage, and yet they can all be performed with very simple equipment. Explanations of dry cells, fuses, electromagnets, and armatures are all clear and direct enough to be understood. There are some chapters on tricks to do for fun. Highly recommended.

Elsie T. Dobbins, in a review of "Experiments with Electricity," in Library Journal, *Vol. 74, No. 7, April 1, 1949, p. 555.*

Teen-agers, summer counselors and just plain parents, who have to face long, irritating, wet days indoors, will welcome this book. For with a little patience and with material that is lying around the house or that can be easily and inexpensively bought, a host of ingenious contraptions can be rigged up and made to work: a household buzzer, a magic bulb that lights, apparently without wires, a nail file sparkler or an elaborate Halloween mask complete with interior illumination. Since these "experiments" use only dry cells or flashlight batteries, they are safe; besides furnishing a frolicsome time they will also take the "magic" out of electrical phenomena. A good deal of information is nicely blended in with the instructions. The language is simple enough for youngsters from 9 to 12. . . . A scientific-minded youngster will find this volume a cornucopia of knowledge and enjoyment.

Thomas Lask, "Contraptions," in The New York Times Book Review, *July 10, 1949, p. 18.*

MORE EXPERIMENTS IN SCIENCE (with Nelson F. Beeler, 1950)

[This book] should be a hit with readers of junior high school age. In the wide variety of simple, interesting problems in the physical and biological sciences the materials needed for the experimentation are simple and easily obtained. Best of all, each activity is related to familiar mechanical and natural phenomena—compasses and magnets, helicopters, roots and soil, the wind, and color are some of the subjects discussed—so that the experiments take on significance rather than being merely stunts in science. A very worthwhile supplementary book for schools and libraries.

A review of "More Experiments in Science," in Virginia Kirkus' Bookshop Service, *Vol. XVIII, No. 4, February 15, 1950, p. 103.*

In this second volume of experiments in many areas of science, modern developments appear in experiments on supersonic barrier, gardening without soil, heating by refrigeration, a grapefruit map, a foam fire extinguisher, and others. Magic tricks, dancing mothballs, the straightline curve are intriguing experiments. For each experiment a list of common, inexpensive materials and equipment precedes concise, simply worded, very readable directions. Easy enough for a beginner of 10 working at home but interesting enough for general science demonstrations at school.

Frances L. Morrison, in a review of "More Experiments in Science," in Library Journal, *Vol. 75, No. 7, April 1, 1950, p. 566.*

LODESTAR, ROCKET SHIP TO MARS: THE RECORD OF THE FIRST OPERATION SPONSORED BY THE FEDERAL COMMISSION FOR INTERPLANETARY EXPLORATION, JUNE 1, 1971 **(1951)**

Neither a novel nor exactly a pretend record, it is a good science-fiction item, on the junior high level, the first fiction written by a high school science teacher well known for several titles on science experiments.

First we learn in detail, which adds much to former imaginings in this field, of the 1971 rocket ship, its construction, the testing of its crew and its departure. The crew includes an older boy. They sail the skies safely, make the first landing on the red dust of Mars and find its strange inmates, a slowly dying race of peculiar build, living underground. They are imprisoned, finally escape and leave for home with valuable specimens, information and photographs.

It is a relief to this adult to escape for awhile from the emotions of the girls' books to the cold stellar spaces; yet, actually, this kind of imagining seems fruitless, however exciting. Probably boys who pursue a period of this reading become such specialists in its details that they apply their true knowledge rather keenly to each new title. They may read such books as they would play chess, and who is to criticize such mental exercise? It is a far step above the doings of Superman.

Louise S. Bechtel, in a review of "Lodestar: Rocket Ship to Mars," in New York Herald Tribune Book Review, *March 11, 1951, p. 10.*

Although the dramatic and literary possibilities of the story have not been fully realized and the characters are stiff, the scientific aspects are quite engrossing and there is plenty of fantastic adventure.

F. C. Smith, "The Red Planet," in The New York Times Book Review, *March 11, 1951, p. 26.*

Scientific technique and paraphernalia are here described in just sufficient detail to make the tale convincing without making it exceptional. Though the author is always reasonable in his conjectures and although most of his lines of thought have been expounded of recent years at a high level . . . , the text is at times a little bare, and the 204 pages of the book seem inadequate for a really live treatment of the theme. The Martians and their installations are skilfully composed but there is no mention of the social aspect of life on Mars, a fact which detracts from its reality.

Some slightness apart, this is a good yarn and most boys, scientifically minded or not, will enjoy it though it may date with unexpected rapidity. (pp. 170-71)

A review of "Lodestar: Rocket Ship to Mars," in The Junior Bookshelf, *Vol. 16, No. 3, October, 1952, pp. 170-71.*

EXPERIMENTS IN OPTICAL ILLUSION **(with Nelson F. Beeler, 1951)**

A fascinating little book with lots of tantalizing "now you see it; now you don't" home experiments. Beginning with a discussion of the physiology of the eye, the authors, with the aid of experiment suggestions and "optical illusion" diagrams by Fred Lyon, investigate the phenomena of image reversal, focus, light and dark, space and line arising from the peculiar construction of the eye. Such famous diverting illusions such as the deceiving size of the rising moon, mirages, after-images, color tricks, and light "ghosts" are also explained in lucid, informal style. Pleasant supplementary material for science courses, for intrepid "experimenters" and fun for the whole family.

A review of "Experiments in Optical Illusion," in Virginia Kirkus' Bookshop Service, *Vol. XIX, No. 12, June 15, 1951, p. 298.*

EXPERIMENTS IN CHEMISTRY **(with Nelson F. Beeler, 1952)**

The authors of books of experiments in general science, electricity and optical illusion, with a substantial one on chemistry that should be fun to read and to work with. Here are the kinds of experiments to do in the kitchen or a home-devised basement lab—simple yet interestingly presented—and often with a practical end in view—on the major fields such as salt and its properties, soaps, emulsions, crystals, nutrients and their products. A drawback is the lack of explanations of techniques needed for experiments like wiring a salt bath for electrolysis, but the inquisitive, if he doesn't know how already, can easily get help. Fine for junior high school supplementary reading.

A review of "Experiments in Chemistry," in Virginia Kirkus' Bookshop Service, *Vol. XX, No. 19, October 1, 1952, p. 660.*

EXPERIMENTS WITH AIRPLANE INSTRUMENTS **(with Nelson F. Beeler, 1953)**

It is a pleasure to see in this book the method adopted for describing the various instruments on the instrument panel of an aircraft.

After outlining some principles common to most of the instruments, the authors proceed from the simplest gauges to the complicated gyros, ending, as it should be, with the automatic pilot. Several experiments, easy to carry out, are described, and model instruments can be built, according to the directions given in the book, without making a dent in the weekly allowance. The clear text is well supported by excellent diagrams [by Leopold London]. This book should be a must for anyone interested in flying—including adults.

Vladimir Specktor, in a review of "Experiments with Airplane Instruments," in The Saturday Review, *New York, Vol. XXXVI, No. 20, May 16, 1953, p. 58.*

Boys over twelve will find this a wonderfully interesting book. . . . Even a boy (or girl) too lazy to do the experiments would learn much from reading this. It is not intended to teach you how to fly, but it is a fine introduction to a plane for any future pilot.

Both authors have extensive science-teaching experience, and both use their own children and home laboratories as bases for their books.

A review of "Experiments with Airplane Instruments," in New York Herald Tribune Book Review, *May 17, 1953, p. 25.*

Easy-to-follow directions for constructing working models of many kinds of airplane instruments. Most of the materials required for the models will be found around any home. . . . The book contains more information than the title might indicate since it includes accurate, detailed information about the basic principles on which airplane instruments operate. Excellent.

A review of "Experiments with Airplane Instruments," in Bulletin of the Children's Book Center, *Vol. VI, No. 11, July, 1953, p. 73.*

EXPERIMENTS WITH ATOMICS **(with Nelson F. Beeler, 1954)**

Beeler and Branley have had a stable record of good information and safe experiments in their past books . . . , though they have been occasionally weak in organization and explanation. This one as far as we can tell upholds that standard, though we'd advise checking with a science teacher or some other authority—as would doubtless be necessary due to the advanced nature of the material. Definitely it will need grounding and pre-established interest or a combination of both. Topics discussed—with simpler experiments and projects outlined to illustrate theory—include basics of atomic structure and electrical charges, the atomic family, discovery of radioactivity, natural and artificial radioactivity, particle acceleration for bombardment, separation of isotopes, fission, atomic reactors, plutonium and weapons—a pretty wide coverage of a big topic. The projects which are as simple as rubbing a fountain pen and as advanced as making a geiger counter, leave something to be desired *as per* instructions, and they'll also take time, space and money. But for the right person in the right setting, this is inspiration.

A review of "Experiments with Atomics," in Virginia Kirkus' Bookshop Service, *Vol. XXII, No. 5, March 1, 1954, p. 156.*

Messrs. Beeler and Branley present the facts needed to understand the basic elements of nuclear physics. . . . Beeler and Branley are experts at imparting considerable information without calling on technical terms and mathematical equations.

John Pfeiffer, "Atoms for Everyone," in The Saturday Review, *New York, Vol. XXXVII, No. 34, August 21, 1954, p. 20.*

MARS **(1955; revised edition as *Mars: Planet Number Four*)**

The author has attempted to bring together all the known facts concerning the planet Mars and to present, also, the various theories regarding life there. His style is suitable for the high-school reader, . . . but much of his material is highly technical and the subject too specialized for this age. Furthermore, the discussion of conflicting or contradictory theories is likely to be confusing. Definitely not for science fiction enthusiasts but would interest amateur astronomers.

Dorothy Schumacher, in a review of "Mars," in Junior Libraries, *an appendix to* Library Journal, *Vol. 2, No. 2, October, 1955, p. 139.*

[Dr. Branley] has given us a fully revised, interesting, clearly written book about the red planet, explaining all the difficulties we may encounter with regard to probes or manned vehicles. There . . . [is an index] and suggestions for further reading.

Alice Dalgliesh, in a review of "Mars: Planet Number Four," in Saturday Review, *Vol. XLV, No. 38, September 22, 1962, p. 44.*

EXPERIMENTS IN THE PRINCIPLES OF SPACE TRAVEL **(1955)**

Well-written, graphic presentation of the scientific laws basic to the development of space travel. Consideration is given to rocket design, temperature control, power, and pressure in space. The purpose of the book, to make a clear distinction between scientific and fictional possibilities in space travel, is successfully fulfilled through the illustrations and tables [by Jeanyee Wong] and the experiments, which can be performed with very simple equipment. The material should be of interest to the science fiction reader as well as to those wanting scientific information. The book could also be used for checking the scientific accuracy of science fiction.

A review of "Experiments in the Principles of Space Travel," in Bulletin of the Children's Book Center, *Vol. X, No. 3, November, 1956, p. 35.*

Scientists' understanding and proper application of basic principles of science can, according to Branley, determine the success or failure of space exploration. The author's succinct presentation of some of these principles is given in tandem with a highly technical yet comprehensible series of experiments. The experiments discuss the principles behind space measurement, rocket design and streamlining, rocket engines, power and pressure in space, temperature control in space, and gravitational force. Clear explanations, illustrations, and charts expose the reader to the scientific tools and framework needed to develop problem-solving abilities while orienting the reader toward research as well. Completely updated from the 1955 edition. . . .

A review of "Experiments in the Principles of Space Travel," in The Booklist, *Vol. 70, No. 8, December 15, 1973, p. 444.*

MICKEY'S MAGNET **(with Eleanor K. Vaughan, 1956)**

No scientific explanations here, but nevertheless a completely vivid and humorous object lesson about magnets and how handy they are, especially for picking up pins around the house. Mickey, who couldn't be much younger, spills a box of them one day, but Father produces a magnet. Wonderful as this is, Mickey is still more thrilled when he sees he can make his own magnet—by rubbing a needle with the magnet and picking up the pins with the needle. A pleasant "Aha!"

A review of "Mickey's Magnet," in Virginia Kirkus' Service, *Vol. XXIV, No. 16, August 15, 1956, p. 569.*

Two books that give a primary child with very limited knowledge of reading fascinating bits of scientific information are ***Mickey's Magnet*** . . .and *I Know A Magic House* by Julius Schwartz. . . . We like ***Mickey's Magnet*** especially, because it gives precise knowledge on a specific topic in a form to appeal to a very young child.

Margaret Sherwood Libby, "Simple Science," in New York Herald Tribune Book Review, *November 4, 1956, p. 9.*

Where in an ostensible science book a child is usually a puppet put through the requisite motions, or alternatively fancy takes over from fact, ***Mickey's Magnet*** is one and indivisible; it is a demonstration, a success story, and—thanks to Crockett Johnson's pictures—spontaneously funny: a complete pleasure.

Barbara Bader, "More Information: 'Mickey's Magnet'," in her American Picture Books from Noah's Ark to the Beast Within, *Macmillan Publishing Company, 1976, p. 399.*

EXPERIMENTS WITH A MICROSCOPE **(with Nelson F. Beeler, 1957)**

This experienced writing team has produced a useful and much needed book on the microscope and its uses. A readable and well-organized text . . . [describes] the microscope, how to use it, mount specimens, and prepare many experiments. While the introductory material is sufficiently simple to aid the young reader in fourth or fifth grade, enough development is included to attract the more experienced and older boy and girl. Culturing protozoa, observing bacteria, photomicrography are treated in separate chapters. An index increases the usefulness of this welcome addition to books on science for boys and girls.

Ruth Hewitt Hamilton, in a review of "Experiments with a Microscope," in The Saturday Review, *New York, Vol. XL, No. 19, May 11, 1957, p. 60.*

Another "experiment" book by Nelson Beeler and Frank Branley is welcome, especially one dealing with the use of the microscope. This one is useful for those fortunate young people who have a microscope and all who are beginning laboratory science. There are excellent chapters on the instrument itself, its construction and how it works. . . . Wise advice is given on careful observation and the keeping of records as well as on ways of mounting specimens, staining colorless ones, and even on photo-micrography with a Brownie Hawkeye camera. With its index, detailed sketches and occasional photographs [by Anne Marie Jauss], this is a fine new science book.

A review of "Experiments with a Microscope," in New York Herald Tribune Book Review, *May 12, 1957, p. 12.*

This is as excellent as the authors' other books for 5th-8th-graders, with similar well-spaced print, photographs, diagrams, simple explanations and directions complete with index. There is no comparable book on the subject for this age group.

Miriam S. Mathes, in a review of "Experiments with a Microscope," in Junior Libraries, *an appendix to* Library Journal, *Vol. 4, No. 1, September 15, 1957, p. 36.*

SOLAR ENERGY **(1957)**

Mr. Branley gives the science-minded reader a highly articulate account of the frontiers of solar energy and the surprising advances already made in this field. Americans with homes to heat, and autos, washing machines and TV sets to operate, consume 2000 times as much energy per person as their ancestors of 1776, with the result that new energy sources are needed. Results of sun-energy experiments include a telephone relay operated by Bell Laboratories with solar energy, emergency life rafts equipped with stills capable of converting seawater into fresh water, thousands of homes in the South which get their hot water from the sun's rays, and solar furnaces which have attained temperatures of 8500 degrees. Directions for practical experiments are included. Thoroughly . . . indexed.

A review of "Solar Energy," in Virginia Kirkus' Service, *Vol. XXV, No. 14, July 15, 1957, p. 489.*

For a child . . . solar energy is eminently practicable. . . .

My only complaint about this book is that sometimes it confuses light and heat; but in context it makes little difference. A readable and fascinating book. (p. 496)

J. D. Bloom, in a review of "Solar Energy," in The School Librarian and School Library Review, *Vol. 9, No. 6, December, 1959, pp. 495-96.*

RUSTY RINGS A BELL **(with Eleanor K. Vaughan, 1957)**

Rusty had a bad cold; he had to stay in bed. When he could not find the bell to call his parents, his father showed Rusty how to attach wires to a dry cell to make his own bell ring. Rusty had fun. He even lit a light bulb using the same principles. The mechanics of electricity seem advanced for this early reading level and large type but this approach to science in story form might be just the thing in a community of children whose background has upped their interests somewhat. A challenge for highly scientific children, it might also be considered solely on its informational content for average third grade youngsters.

A review of "Rusty Rings a Bell," in Virginia Kirkus' Service, *Vol. XXV, No. 20, October 15, 1957, p. 770.*

A rather contrived story that is too difficult for beginning readers to handle alone and does not have enough specific information to interest readers who could handle the text.

Zena Sutherland, in a review of "Rusty Rings a Bell," in Bulletin of the Children's Book Center, *Vol. XI, No. 8, April, 1958, p. 78.*

EXPLORING BY SATELLITE: THE STORY OF PROJECT VANGUARD **(1957)**

With the Sputnik-sputter, this brief pictorial approach to satellites ought to answer the fundamental questions of the uninitiated. The author . . . predigests some of the technical terminology, leaving plenty of gristle for the teen-aged reader to tackle. The tone of the book is admirable. The author does not project with assertions of certainty the time intervals or the exact procedures through which man will vault to the planets. His predictions seem guardedly cautious enough to be reliable. This is capsule photo-journalistic treatment, quite brief, for a quick run-down on the satellite situation.

A review of "Exploring by Satellite," in Virginia Kirkus' Service, *Vol. XXV, No. 21, November 1, 1957, p. 816.*

EXPERIMENTS WITH LIGHT **(with Nelson F. Beeler, 1957)**

Like the other fine experiment books by these authors, [this one] is planned for young people who want to make things for themselves, a lens, a light meter or a kaleidoscope. Through demonstrations the students learn the nature of light and lenses, something of polarized light and photosynthesis. A valuable book.

A review of "Experiments with Light," in New York Herald Tribune Book Review, *May 11, 1958, p. 25.*

[***Experiments with Light***] is, in the main, a do-it-yourself book, suggesting experiments with simple apparatus. The writers also attempt to clarify some rather sophisticated notions about light—

diffraction, interference and polarization. Although these efforts are by no means uniformly successful, some of them come off well—for example, the lucid discussion of the stroboscope.

Robert E. K. Rourke, in a review of "Experiments with Light," in The New York Times Book Review, *August 31, 1958, p. 16.*

THE NINE PLANETS **(1958)**

Franklyn M. Branley has lectured to crowds of people, young and old. For those who have his book in hand, the strain of trying to take notes in the darkness of a planetarium dome will be eliminated. Here is a solidly packed reference book on the nine planets which yields an exceptionally rich harvest of information per page.

Mr. Branley writes sincerely, accurately and with no attempt at glamorizing the facts. Any references he makes to things that are speculative are clearly identified with qualifying words. . . . Impressive also are the tables of statistics which have been included in the body of the text rather than in an appendix.

Near the end of the book the author has suggested nine titles for further reading. I wish he had listed twice as many because I believe he will stir in his readers a wider range of interest than is encompassed by these few titles.

Alfred D. Beck, "Orbs and Orbits," in The New York Times Book Review, *November 23, 1958, p. 48.*

[The Nine Planets *was revised in 1971 and 1978.*]

This is a very basic description of the major planets in our solar system. . . . Its strong advantages are its easy readability, coherent story design, and relative absence of ambiguity or equivocation. Its faults probably are not too important, but a few are worth mentioning. The explanation of mean value . . . is wrong. An alternate symbol . . . for Uranus is still used by some astronomers. The term "minor planets" . . . is not correct as a substitute for "terrestrial planets." Once again, Isaac Newton's illustration of orbital and suborbital speed is reproduced . . . without credit. The geometric utility of Venus transits . . . is no longer relevant, because the same information is available to much higher accuracy by modern means. The mass of Pluto is now known to be much smaller than previously believed. Also, the myth that Pluto is sometimes nearer the sun than is Neptune is perpetuated. There is a list of sources of further information, and a useful index is appended.

A review of "The Nine Planets," in Science Books: A Quarterly Review, *Vol. 7, No. 3, December, 1971, p. 216.*

The author has obviously made an effort to incorporate the latest information on the planets, and has been successful to a limited extent. Still, information obtained in the last five years does not seem to have made its way into this revision to the extent that it might have. In the case that would have been of most interest—Mars—there is a striking failure to bring us up to date on the most recent information and theories. The text also suffers from the author's obsession to tell us a little bit about everything remotely connected with the planets. This concern means that many essentially irrelevant topics—thermocouples, ellipses, and Bode's Law for example—are treated so inadequately that they are not readily understandable. Most important of all, perhaps, is the deadliness of the text. It is, for the most part, a recital of unconnected and uninteresting facts. We are at the point now that someone could write a really fascinating story of the planets, making the tale an object lesson in the way scientists work. Here is a chance to show students what scientists do with conflicting and inadequate data. The last chapter of the text makes a beginning in this direction. Finally, the sexist use of "man" whenever "humans" is meant is especially striking in a field in which women have had so much to contribute! What we really should have had here is a totally new book on the planets, not another revision of a twenty-year old text.

David E. Newton, in a review of "The Nine Planets," in Appraisal: Children's Science Books, *Vol. 12, No. 2, Spring, 1979, p. 10.*

A BOOK OF SATELLITES FOR YOU **(1958)**

[This book] initiates the pre-reader into the realms of outer space. Various aspects of the satellites, natural and manmade, are simply explained with the emphasis on today's attempts at launching man-made moons. The author . . . indicates, in language simple enough for children to grasp, the mechanical devices which are employed, the problems presented in launching a satellite, the importance of such a move, and the ramifications a successful launching may have in our future. In an age where children become as quickly aware of Sputnik as they do of the moon, it is helpful to use their enthusiasm constructively by imparting to them facts, which in this case are infinitely more stimulating than much of the fiction revolving about the subject. The author's hypothesis that facts, simply stated, no matter how technical, can be absorbed by the young uncluttered mind . . . do much to make this a profitable project for the pre-reader and his parents.

A review of "A Book of Satellites for You," in Virginia Kirkus' Service, *Vol. XXVI, No. 23, December 1, 1958, p. 871.*

A Book of Satellites for You is a lucid and accurate explanation of the subject for the very youngest reader. The author vividly reviews what science has accomplished and hopes to accomplish in the exploration of space. . . . Although he writes of thermistors, cosmic rays, meteors and magnetism, Mr. Branley has been careful not to overwhelm his audience. Particularly helpful are his comparisons of the unfamiliar sizes, shapes, weights and speeds of rockets and satellites with familiar objects.

Michael McWhinney, "Endless Frontiers," in The New York Times Book Review, *March 29, 1959, p. 32.*

[A Book of Satellites for You *was revised in 1971.*]

The youngster is introduced to the concept of satellites in a very satisfying and elementary fashion. The blend of illustrations [by Leonard Kessler] and text is excellent and provides the color to make the book hold the elementary reader's attention. There are a limited number of minor inaccuracies and impressions that are somewhat annoying and could be confusing to the child. It is stated that Laika died after a few days, which might leave the impression that beings cannot live in space for a longer period. A statement to the effect that people have since lived in space for extended periods would have helped. . . . The impression left that a thermistor measures temperature only in outer space is inaccurate. Intellectually, it would have been more satisfying to see the statements: "A thermometer measures temperature. A thermistor measures temperature. Thermistors are small," etc. . . . On the last page it would have been helpful to introduce the concept of the length of time required to travel to the planets and stars since the only other time mentioned was the orbital time of 2 hours or less. Again, by lack of statement, the child could be left with the impression that travel time to the planets and stars would be the same 2 hours. The book is short and easy for the youngster to follow and should prove popular with the pre-school and lower grade elementary school child. It should also help parents and teachers answer questions posed by the children.

A review of "A Book of Satellites for You," in Science Books: A Quarterly Review, *Vol. 7, No. 4, March, 1972, p. 327.*

TIMMY AND THE TIN-CAN TELEPHONE **(with Eleanor K. Vaughan, 1959)**

Timmy and Kit are next door neighbors, but unlike some of their neighbors, they are early risers. In an attempt to subdue their early morning communiques, Timmy's father helps them construct a tin-can telephone, over which they can speak without rousing the entire community. A step-by-step description of the machine . . . not only makes up an easy-reading book of considerable suspense, but suggests an interesting experiment in do-it-youself engineering.

A review of "Timmy and the Tin-Can Telephone," in Virginia Kirkus' Service, *Vol. XXVII, No. 3, February 1, 1959, p. 88.*

A story book, for the first-graders and pre-schoolers, that also shows a child how to build a tin-can telephone. The instructions (carefully built into a story) are clear and, given the materials, youngsters ought to be able to build their own and get their first introduction into gadgeteering. A pleasant way, this book, of combining entertainment and education.

Isaac Asimov, in a review of "Timmy and the Tin-Can Telephone," in The Horn Book Magazine, *Vol. XXXV, No. 4, August, 1959, p. 305.*

A book about the transmission of sound for beginning readers with scientific curiosity, written so simply and clearly that it can be read aloud to a non-reader and usable, also, for older children who are slow readers. . . . [Materials] easily available, instructions clear.

Zena Sutherland, in a review of "Timmy and the Tin-Can Telephone," in Bulletin of the Center for Children's Books, *Vol. XIII, No. 1, September, 1959, p. 3.*

EXPERIMENTS IN SKY WATCHING **(1959)**

This book covers an area for junior high students that their textbooks rarely do. It clearly demonstrates where, how, and what to look at in the sky. Construction directions for instruments are explicit. . . . Vocabulary is geared to junior high age, and crispness of the style makes for readability. Index and list of books for further reading. Although written for young readers, many adults will find this useful, particularly teachers who wish to encourage student projects.

Barbara Sheehan, in a review of "Experiments in Sky Watching," in Junior Libraries, *an appendix to* Library Journal, *Vol. 6, No. 3, November, 1959, p. 44.*

Experiments in Sky Watching is a real do-it-yourself book that will provide many opportunities for the thrill of discovery. . . . [Franklyn M. Branley] describes, clearly and simply, interesting experiments tht can be performed with homemade apparatus. The reader is not only told how to make observations of the sun, moon, planets and stars (even on man-made satellites), but he is told exactly what to look for. Valuable supplementary information is provided, including star charts and planet positions to 1969.

Robert E. K. Rourke, "Wild Blue Yonder," in The New York Times Book Review, *November 1, 1959, p. 12.*

A BOOK OF MOON ROCKETS FOR YOU **(1959)**

Although other juvenile books deal with space travel, none answers as clearly and accurately as this the timely questions of young children. The fascination with space travel of the primary child is recognized and heightened by the excellent, accurate information. . . . Difficult reading for those below third grade but good for listening and quick reference above the age of four. Though recent scientific discoveries have provided answers to some questions Branley poses, they tend to enhance rather than detract from the desirability of this book.

Alvin Hertzberg, in a review of "A Book of Moon Rockets for You," in Junior Libraries, *an appendix to* Library Journal, *Vol. 6, No. 4, December, 1959, p. 40.*

[A Book of Moon Rockets for You *was revised in 1970.*]

Several instances of error, omission, or poor wording make this small book less than it could have been. . . . Lunar orbiters functioned for weeks or months, not just days. . . . [The] Saturn rocket is credited with lifting 6 million pounds into space. That is its weight on the launch pad; only about 100,000 pounds reaches orbit. . . . [It] is correctly stated that there are advantages to moon-based astronomy, but the author missed the opportunity to tell why! (It is simply because one does not have to look through all the air that surrounds the earth.) The most annoying error, to one who has fought many public misconceptions about space, is the statement . . . that the lunar orbiters were "pulled into the moon by lunar gravity." Gravity does not "pull an orbiting satellite down" unless some external force such as atmospheric friction slows its orbital velocity. In addition to perpetuating a common misconception, this statement is incorrect under the most liberal interpretation. The orbiters were deliberately crashed into the moon to avoid accidental collisions with later orbiters or Apollo vehicles. In spite of the objections listed above, the book is simple, clear, usually accurate, and liberally illustrated [by Leonard Kessler]. It may rank among the better children's "space" books, but it could have been improved.

A review of "A Book of Moon Rockets for You," in Science Books: A Quarterly Review, *Vol. 6, No. 4, March, 1971, p. 337.*

Admittedly, writing effective science books for a very young audience is difficult; but, at the very least, authors not technically trained themselves should enlist help. Most of the dozen or so glaring errors in this volume could be found in ten minutes of review by most any engineer or scientist. This problem aside, the content is an unbalanced mixture, with unimportant detail taking up space which would be better used for some of the missing simple fundamentals. . . . In the only table in the book, the listing of launch dates and rockets used for lunar missions curiously leaves off all the Apollo missions even though they are discussed in the text and constitute the natural climax of the theme.

David G. Hoag, in a review of "A Book of Moon Rockets for You," in Appraisal: Children's Science Books, *Vol. 5, No. 1, Winter, 1972, p. 9.*

THE MOON: EARTH'S NATURAL SATELLITE (1960)

[This is] an excellent introduction to a subject that is becoming more and more newsworthy. The moon's story is told here in a style that is simple, clear and direct. The lunar motion, orbit, atmosphere, temperature, mass and density are covered with a minimum of technicalities. . . .

The author deals also with the moon's role in tides and in eclipses, its place in mythology, and with man's efforts across the centuries to reach it. The book contains convenient tables, index and a list of references for those who wish to probe more deeply. Mr. Branley has given us a fine and timely science study.

Robert E. K. Rourke, "Lunar Probe," in The New York Times Book Review, *May 8, 1960, p. 14.*

This is a minimal revision of the author's 1960 edition. Covered are the appearance of the moon, its movements, effects on the earth, physical characteristics, and treatment in folklore and fiction. A few paragraphs have been added sporadically to include information gained from the Apollo missions. In the chapter on the atmosphere of the moon, two sentences near the end refer to direct observations; the rest of the chapter describes indirect observations which led to the conclusion that the moon had little, if any, atmosphere. The discussion of color vision by moonlight is inconclusive and does not mention current theories about how the human eye works at low light levels. The existence of a facility for generating electricity from ocean tides is denied though there now is such a power station in operation on the north coast of France. This new book would not replace the previous edition.

Ovide V. Fortier, in a review of "The Moon: Earth's Natural Satellite," in School Library Journal, *an appendix to* Library Journal, *Vol. 19, No. 2, October, 1972, p. 116.*

The original copyright date for this book about the moon predates the adventures and discoveries of the manned lunar landings of Apollo. This [1972] edition has been updated with only a cursory and superficial acknowledgment of Apollo. This is not bad, however, since it leaves room for much of the fundamental coverage of lunar science and the earth moon system which would otherwise be displaced by material covered elsewhere in many new books about Apollo. However, although the organization is logical. . . , the text has many serious flaws. . . . [The] author identifies the intersection of the ecliptic with the horizon as being in the constellation Aries. It hasn't been there since ancient times. . . . [He] equates the ecliptic with the moon's orbit. They are 5 degrees different. . . . He confuses the convention for the east and west sides of the moon's face, both as seen directly and by inverting telescope. This, of course, disagrees with the correct convention shown later in a NASA lunar chart reproduction. These and other errors are too serious to ignore. Without them the book would be very good. As it is, I rank it only fair.

David G. Hoag, in a review of "The Moon: Earth's Natural Satellite," in Appraisal: Children's Science Books, *Vol. 7, No. 1, Winter, 1974, p. 9.*

BIG TRACKS, LITTLE TRACKS (1960)

A clear and simple introduction to the subject. . . . The text gives, in sentences that are short and repetitive, only the necessary amount of information. . . . Mr. Branley describes the tracks of human beings (with and without shoes), dogs (big and little), cats, and rabbits; he then gives a few other examples to show variation in tracks. A fine first nature study book for the beginning independent reader, and a good book to read aloud to stimulate interest on the part of the pre-school child.

Zena Sutherland, in a review of "Big Tracks, Little Tracks," in Bulletin of the Center for Children's Books, *Vol. XIV, No. 5, January, 1961, p. 75.*

WHAT MAKES DAY AND NIGHT (1961)

Simply written, with no confusing extraneous material, an explanation of the revolution of the earth and the consequent changes from light to dark. . . . The short sentences, logical sequence of statements, and the recapitulation combine to make this an excellent science book for beginning independent readers.

Zena Sutherland, in a review of "What Makes Day and Night," in Bulletin of the Center for Children's Books, *Vol. XIV, No. 9, May, 1961, p. 138.*

[What Makes Day and Night *was revised in 1986.*]

What Makes Day and Night is an enormous improvement over the 1961 edition: less repetitive, much clearer in presentation and more specific about physical phenomena. However, brevity causes some of the explanations to be oversimplified, and some further explanations may be necessary. . . . The simple science experiment remains from the old edition, and Branley has included a new discussion of day and night on the moon. . . .

John Peters, in a review of "What Makes Day and Night," in School Library Journal, *Vol. 33, No. 1, September, 1986, p. 117.*

A BOOK OF PLANETS FOR YOU (1961)

Elementary graders enthralled but thoroughly confused by the labyrinth of facts about planets will emerge triumphant from this basic description of the nine planets that revolve around the sun, their temperatures, relative sizes, atmospheres and satellites. Where they are located in relation to the sun, the earth and each other, what characteristics distinguish each one, and some of the unknown avenues open to discovery are the major topics explored via the doubly effective technique of clear language involving the child's experiences, and colorful eye-catching illustrations supplied by Leonard Kessler. Basic, and lucidly presented, this is recommended for use both inside and outside the second through fourth grade classrooms.

A review of "A Book of Planets for You," in Virginia Kirkus' Service, *Vol. XXIX, No. 12, June 15, 1961, p. 500.*

A very good science book for the primary level: straight information, no talking down or popularization. . . . Dr. Branley combines his professional competence with a deft ability to present material in a style that is crisp without being dry. (pp. 3-4)

Zena Sutherland, in a review of "A Book of Planets for You," in Bulletin of the Center for Children's Books, *Vol. XV, No. 1, September, 1961, pp. 3-4.*

Here is a delightful little book to carry young readers (age 6-10) away to the planets. The basic facts of our solar system are set forth simply and interestingly. They should entertain the space cadets in your family and help answer their questions.

Robert C. Cowen, in a review of "A Book of Planets for You," in The Christian Science Monitor, *November 16, 1961, p. 11B.*

EXPLORING BY ASTRONAUT: THE STORY OF PROJECT MERCURY **(1961)**

Exploring by Astronaut is an authoritative, unemotional survey of Project Mercury. It is highly detailed but readily comprehensible. . . . Mr. Branley's book is well worth reading by all serious students of space science, including adults.

Henry W. Hubbard, in a review of "Exploring by Astronaut: The Story of Project Mercury," in The New York Times Book Review, *June 18, 1961, p. 22.*

New addition to the growing body of books about Project Mercury, this covers the usual material, i.e. the capsule, booster, astronauts, testing men and equipment, the orbit, etc., and has an interesting chapter on previously launched satellites. However, author's style is pedantic, and the suggested further readings include too few of the best books on the subject and a number of government publications not readily available in many libraries. Index.

Albert Monheit, in a review of "Exploring by Astronaut: The Story of Project Mercury," in Library Journal, *Vol. 86, No. 13, July, 1961, p. 2540.*

A lucid, readable account of Project Mercury. . . . Although some of the material is already outdated, the detailed information is accurate and the book will be a welcome addition to collections of materials on space flight. As in most of his books, the author leaves the reader with a sense of the challenge of the future.

A review of "Exploring by Astronaut: The Story of Project Mercury," in The Booklist and Subscription Books Bulletin, *Vol. 58, No. 1, September 1, 1961, p. 30.*

THE SUN: OUR NEAREST STAR **(1961)**

A good science book for beginning independent readers, in which the author successfully establishes a few basic facts with lucidity and with no digression. At the end of the book, the facts that have been learned are recapitulated. . . . In the simplicity of presentation and in the limitation of concepts, this is one of the best books in the [Let's-Read-and-Find-Out] series.

Zena Sutherland, in a review of "The Sun: Our Nearest Star," in Bulletin of the Center for Children's Books, *Vol. XV, No. 9, May, 1962, p. 138.*

ROCKETS AND SATELLITES **(1961)**

In very simple language, the difference between rockets and satellites is explained. . . . As in other books by Dr. Branley, the limitation of the text to the topic at hand is nicely appropriate for the beginning independent reader.

Zena Sutherland, in a review of "Rockets and Satellites," in Bulletin of the Center for Children's Books, *Vol. XVI, No. 4, December, 1962, p. 54.*

[Rockets and Satellites *was revised in 1970.*]

[***Rockets and Satellites***] is the Dick and Jane of the space age. It should talk, but it lisps instead. Designed as a primer for the just-learning-to-read, it is too late with too little. Eagle has landed. But this book with its oversimplified drawings [by Al Nagy] and its There-are-little-Rockets They-don't-go-very-high They-don't-go-very-far text never gets off the ground.

John C. Waugh, "Orbiting in Space," in The Christian Science Monitor, *May 7, 1970, p. B7.*

A book aimed for this level obviously takes some license with explanation which could be annoying to a more sophisticated reader. An example would be the fact that upper stages of rockets actually orbit as does a satellite although the book explains that the difference between a satellite and a rocket is the fact that a rocket does not orbit. The book is quite short and easy for the youngster to follow.

A review of "Rockets and Satellites," in Science Books: A Quarterly Review, *Vol. 6, No. 2, September, 1970, p. 165.*

AIR IS ALL AROUND YOU **(1962)**

This very elementary presentation of the importance of air might be suitable for classroom use if it said a little more. There's very scanty information given and over one-third of the book is devoted to the empty-glass-upside-down-in-water experiment which simply proves the presence of air.

A review of "Air Is All around You," in The New York Times Book Review, *May 13, 1962, p. 32.*

[Air Is All around You *was revised in 1986.*]

The text replaces the earlier, singsong repetitive style with a direct but simple approach. As in the 1962 edition, Branley gives directions . . . for two easy experiments that show how air is in everything, including water. The new edition also explains how spaceships need rocket power to go beyond the earth's atmosphere, that astronauts must carry air with them, and that undersea divers need to take air tanks along. Replacement of old editions with this attractive new one is recommended because of the updated, well-presented information. . . .

Mary Lathrope, in a review of "Air Is All around You," in Booklist, *Vol. 82, No. 16, April 15, 1986, p. 1216.*

WHAT THE MOON IS LIKE (1963)

A simplified description of the surface and atmosphere of the moon, with a prediction of man's exploration there. Dr. Branley explains lunar seas and craters, mountains and valleys. . . . A lucid and unified first science text. . . .

Zena Sutherland, in a review of "What the Moon Is Like," in Bulletin of the Center for Children's Books, *Vol. XVI, No. 8, April, 1963, p. 123.*

[What the Moon Is Like *was revised in 1986.*]

The text, drawings [by True Kelley], and photographs of this interesting book are designed to stimulate questions and discussion about the moon and the Apollo lunar landings. They accomplish this and more, creating excitement and interest at the prospect of further lunar exploration and discovery. The book is primarily intended for third to fifth graders, but even kindergarteners will enjoy having it read to them. The children with whom I shared the book were stimulated by the text and illustrations and asked questions that went beyond the material presented. . . . This book is a good choice for school or home libraries.

Robert Bissell, in a review of "What the Moon Is Like," in Science Books & Films, *Vol. 22, No. 3, January-February, 1987, p. 183.*

SNOW IS FALLING (1963)

[A] good science book for beginning independent readers. The text describes briefly what makes snow, what snowflakes are like, and some of the ways in which snow may benefit or may harm living things. A simple and useful introduction to the topics of weather or seasons. (pp. 74-5)

Zena Sutherland, in a review of "Snow Is Falling," in Bulletin of the Center for Children's Books, *Vol. XVII, No. 5, January, 1964, pp. 74-5.*

A BOOK OF ASTRONAUTS FOR YOU (1963)

A succinct and simple description of the astronaut: his selection, training, testing, performance, and problems. The author explains clearly the reasons for all of the educational, physical, and psychological training and screening. Although the text is simple, it is not over-simplified; neither does it diverge to ancillary subjects.

Zena Sutherland, in a review of "A Book of Astronauts for You," in Bulletin of the Center for Children's Books, *Vol. XVII, No. 11, July-August, 1964, p. 166.*

EXPLORATION OF THE MOON (1963)

[*The following excerpt is from a review of the 1965 British edition.*]

Many books have been written about man's attempt to land on the moon, but, for once, this new book is an agreeable surprise, for Dr. Branley . . . has a refreshingly easy style and a gift for clear explanation. The standard of the work is quite elementary and begins with an account of the nature of the moon, including a very fair description of the controversy over its origin. Methods of exploring the moon by unmanned and manned probes are then discussed (with results up to the end of 1964), and the third part describes some of the plans for the future establishment of permanent bases on the moon. This is popular science writing at its best.

A review of "Exploration of the Moon," in The Times Literary Supplement, *No. 3312, August 19, 1965, p. 721.*

RAIN AND HAIL (1963)

[This is Branley's 1983] revision of his clear, simple explanation of where rain and hail come from, tracing the cycle from water vapor to raindrops and hail. The text is similar to that of the original edition—careful and logical, giving examples from everyday life of the processes described. . . . As in the original edition, Branley succinctly summarizes at the end, without becoming boringly repetitive, which provides a good chance for readers to check their understanding. Very useful for primary science concepts. (p. 79)

Nancy Palmer, in a review of "Rain and Hail," in School Library Journal, *Vol. 30, No. 4, December, 1983, pp. 78-9.*

[This book has one error] and it's not too bad a one at that: . . . "All clouds . . . are made of . . . drops of water." That's a little too sweeping—some clouds, Cirrus in particular, are made of ice crystals. The error is compounded . . . where the author neglects the formation of rain by, in effect, large ice crystals, forming, falling and melting before they reach the ground. Happens all the time.

A few qualifiers: "Most clouds. . ."; "One way rain falls. . ." would have saved the day. Oh well, just short of outstanding. (pp. 14-15)

John D. Stackpole, in a review of "Rain and Hail," in Appraisal: Science Books for Young People, *Vol. 17, No. 1, Winter, 1984, pp. 14-15.*

There are no errors of fact, and the material is suitable primarily for the lower elementary grades, although some of the vocabulary is too high-level. The book uses everyday examples of rain clouds, hail storms, and evaporation to help students feel familiar with what they are learning about the effects of heat and cold on water vapor. However, the writing is poor, the sentences dreary. . . . The writing style is Dick-and-Jane, inexcusable in a book that uses words such as evaporation and condensation. . . . This book could be used to lead a discussion on weather in a class of very young children, and second- or third-grade students could use it to prepare science reports about rain and hail; however, I'm not sure I would welcome these uses. For the young developing taste, accuracy should be complemented by literary excellence, and this book doesn't have it.

Joanne D. Denko, in a review of "Rain and Hail," in Science Books & Films, *Vol. 20, No. 2, November-December, 1984, p. 93.*

THE SUN: STAR NUMBER ONE (1964)

A detailed, technical, and up-to-date study of the sun as a star. . . . The instruments used and the type of information they provide: sun spots and associated phenomena, solar energy and its effect on earth, solar motion and eclipses, the evolution of the sun are discussed. Not an introductory book, this requires some math and physics background. The explanations are clear, but the style is plodding.

Elizabeth MacRae, in a review of "The Sun: Star Number One," in School Library Journal, *an appendix to* Library Journal, *Vol. 11, No. 1, September, 1964, p. 135.*

FLASH, CRASH, RUMBLE, AND ROLL (1964)

[Flash, Crash, Rumble, and Roll *was revised in 1985.*]

The information presented is basically the same [as in the original edition], covering the formation of clouds, the causes of lightning and thunder and safety precautions to follow during a storm. The revised wording, although close to the original, explains the scientific concepts more clearly. . . . There are few books available for this age group that deal solely with thunder and lightning. *Storms* (Childrens, 1982) by Ray Broekel mentions lightning and thunder but doesn't have the detail found here.

Phyllis Sue Alpert, in a review of "Flash, Crash, Rumble, and Roll," in School Library Journal, *Vol. 32, No. 1, September, 1985, p. 113.*

Good, concise explanations are given for the causes of thunder and lightning, helping to demystify these scary phenomena for young children. The explanations are enhanced by excellent examples . . . , such as a balloon bursting to simulate thunder. . . . The "game" of counting the seconds between lightning and thunder to determine the distance is explained. . . . Several pages are devoted to precautions children can take to prevent being hit by lightning. In sum, . . . the limit of a few sentences per page [makes this] a good read-along book—an excellent choice for both classroom and home use.

Mark McDermott, in a review of "Flash, Crash, Rumble, and Roll," in Science Books & Films, *Vol. 21, No. 2, November-December, 1985, p. 71.*

In almost every way the second edition is significantly better. The text is more focused and less verbose. The reasons for safety rules during thunderstorms are explained where they were not before. (pp. 18-19)

Gone are the discussions about ions and sonic booms. Gone are a few gratuitous condescending remarks.

Studying [the original and revised editions] and seeing the development and growth that they reveal gladdens me: what a fine body of work we have from Franklyn M. Branley. . . . (p. 19)

Diane Holzheimer, in a review of "Flash, Crash, Rumble, and Roll," in Appraisal: Science Books for Young People, *Vol. 19, No. 2, Spring, 1986, pp. 18-19.*

A BOOK OF THE MILKY WAY GALAXY FOR YOU (1965)

The size, location, and components of the Milky Way are described here for the young reader. The attempt at simplification results in statements which need considerable clarification for the elementary school child. A teacher would need to demonstrate how "as the earth spins, it revolves around the sun." Also, "satellites are followers of the planets" does not indicate that they revolve around the planets. "You can never see Venus late at night. That's because Venus and the sun are always on the same side of the earth." What does this mean to a third-grader? "We think new stars are being created while old stars fade away." What does "fade" mean in this context?

Ethel C. Kutteroff, in a review of "A Book of the Milky Way Galaxy for You," in School Library Journal, *an appendix to* Library Journal, *Vol. 12, No. 4, December, 1965, p. 70.*

In a brief, simplified account using scientifically accurate terminology, the author describes the solar system, explains how astronomers acquire information about the stars, and what they have discovered about the shape and composition of the Milky Way and other galaxies. He ends his discussion with provocative questions about the stars, planets, and galaxies for which scientists are still seeking answers. An excellent introduction to the complexities of the universe for young children. . . .

A review of "A Book of the Milky Way Galaxy for You," in The Booklist and Subscription Books Bulletin, *Vol. 62, No. 7, December 1, 1965, p. 360.*

THE EARTH: PLANET NUMBER THREE (1966)

This is book number five in this popular science writer's *Exploring Our Universe* series. . . . This may be the most useful one in the series, for summarized in it is detailed, up-to-date material in various fields of earth study. The subdivisions deal with the physical components of the earth, its geologic history, "motions of the earth and their effects," and "gravity and the shape of the earth." The text is concise without being superficial and brings together separate but related topics for the alert student interested in the physical sciences. There is a very helpful table of "some facts about the earth." Suggestions for Further Reading.

A review of "The Earth: Planet Number Three," in Virginia Kirkus' Service, *Vol. XXXIV, No. 7, April 1, 1966, p. 379.*

A stimulating account of man's present knowledge of planet Earth. . . . At times the text is difficult, but the careful presentation of the subject matter, within historical perspective, brings to the reader a sense of excitement and wonder at man's endeavor to learn more about the universe. Useful table of facts about the earth and an excellent bibliography. (pp. 160-61)

Elizabeth F. Grave, in a review of "The Earth: Planet Number Three," in School Library Journal, *an appendix to* Library Journal, *Vol. 12, No. 9, May, 1966, pp. 160-61.*

NORTH, SOUTH, EAST, AND WEST (1966)

An attractive picture book which the primary-grade child might read with interest, since it gives useful information in terms he can understand. It does, however, assume two facts; first, that the small reader already knows right from left, and, second, that he is situated somewhere in the general latitude of the United States. The latter is quite likely to be true, but there is no recognition of the fact that several statements made about shadows would not be true in South Africa or Argentina. One statement, intended to clarify "up" and "down" in relation to the earth, implies a misleading concept of gravity, the ever present danger in over-simplification. However, the book meets in general the purpose for which it was intended, and should be useful, especially in school libraries.

Della Thomas, in a review of "North, South, East, and West," in School Library Journal, *an appendix to* Library Journal, *Vol. 13, No. 2, October, 1966, p. 214.*

In trying to get down to a pre-school level all scientific value is lost. A thinking, observant child will question validity, and a less perceptive youngster may get ideas which must later be discarded.

Priscilla L. Moulton, in a review of "North, South, East, and West," in Appraisal: Children's Science Books, *Vol. 1, No. 1, Winter, 1967, p. 2.*

[A] good first book on the points of the compass. The author explains fixed position by reference to the more familiar left and right, and up and down. He establishes east by the sun's position, and gives step-by-step directions for a simple demonstration of shadows that indicate directions at different times of day. The text has just enough repetition to give emphasis to important points without making the writing dull. (pp. 85-6)

Zena Sutherland, in a review of "North, South, East, and West," in Bulletin of the Center for Children's Books, *Vol. 20, No. 6, February, 1967, pp. 85-6.*

THE CHRISTMAS SKY (1966)

The Star of Bethlehem is here sought by reason. Page by page in this clear and gentle book the possibilities are explored. It was not a meteor, because it endured; it was not a comet, because it was welcome; it was not a nova. The birth of Jesus is carefully and convincingly dated from the circumstances of history. It is assigned to the spring (the flocks are not in the fields at the winter solstice), probably of the year 6 B.C. In that very season there was a rare close triple conjunction of Mars, Jupiter and Saturn in the constellation Pisces, where a similar event had traditionally heralded the birth of Moses.

Philip Morrison and Phylis Morrison, in a review of "The Christmas Sky," in Scientific American, *Vol. 215, No. 6, December, 1966, p. 141.*

Written simply and clearly . . . , the book considers the question of what star it was the Wise Men followed. Incipient astronomers will acquire a wealth of basic astral information, and the author makes a strong case as well for several earth-bound hypotheses: that Jesus was not born in 1 A.D., as we might imagine; that, in all likelihood, he was not even born in December, the date merely providing a convenient occasion for persecuted Christians to celebrate their Saviour's birth. Dr. Branley's ultimate conclusion seems entirely plausible, but his text would benefit from a more substantial depiction of the conjunction of planets he feels accounted for the great star. (p. 22)

Selma G. Lanes, "Stocking Tales," in Book Week—New York Herald Tribune, *December 4, 1966, pp. 22, 28.*

[This is] a rather dry and conservative look at possible astronomical explanations for the "Star of Bethlehem". Personally, I find the astronomy too conservative in places, and the author makes argumentative statements without showing his evidence for them. In all, the book is a good example of what happens when you try to dissect a fairy tale.

Benjamin W. Bova, in a review of "The Christmas Sky," in Appraisal: Children's Science Books, *Vol. 1, No. 2, Spring, 1968, p. 3.*

A BOOK OF STARS FOR YOU (1967)

Dr. Branley's better books for young people usually fall in his area, astronomy; this one may be the exception. From time to time in his writing for youngsters the author shows lack of perception of the fact that children's understanding of certain science concepts is not tied merely to reading ability. Often, no amount of clear exposition can make a relationship real to a child because of cognitive immaturity which cannot be overcome by interesting writing. The detail in this book of stars is accurate and interesting and, for the most part, valuable. But, for the younger reader, one or two incomprehensible ideas make the whole book very frustrating thereby devaluing even the good parts (e.g., the concept of relativity of position in space and the resulting inconstancy of arrangement of stars in the constellations). If an older youngster could stand the childish styling there would be much he could gain.

A review of "A Book of Stars for You," in Kirkus Service, *Vol. XXXV, No. 19, October 1, 1967, p. 1211.*

Branley has written an elementary and lucid summary of stellar astronomy for very young readers. He clearly explains the place and importance of the solar system in the galaxy; the numbers, distances, motions, and properties of stars; and even describes something of the way stars are formed and evolve—all in so few words that an adult can read the entire booklet in about 10 minutes. One arithmetic error occurs (at the rate of one per second, it would take about 3,000 years to count 10^{11} stars, not 30,000 years as stated). Also the use of the term "billions" to describe almost any large number—even be it many trillions—is a little objectionable. The figures are given for dimensions and temperatures of stars that are not entirely up to date. These criticisms, however, are nit-picking. There are no serious errors that give a generally wrong impression. The book is excellent and goes a long way to introducing children to a descriptive account of the astronomical universe as it is understood today. Some younger children may require explanation of some of the technical terms, hence it is a good book for children to share with their parents.

A review of "A Book of Stars for You," in Science Books: A Quarterly Review, *Vol. 3, No. 3, December, 1967, p. 204.*

Written as a continuous narrative, . . . this presentation of elementary information about the stars is authoritative and interesting. Crowded into its few pages . . . are diverse and difficult subjects. . . . [However], this is not a beginning book, and readers will need some prior information to understand many of the concepts. For the child who is equipped with some facts about the solar system and the galaxy of which it is a part, this should make interesting reading, but the young reader who is attracted by the picture book format but is less well equipped with background information might find difficulty in handling some of the ideas.

Beryl Robinson, in a review of "A Book of Stars for You," in Appraisal: Children's Science Books, *Vol. 1, No. 3, Fall, 1968, p. 7.*

HIGH SOUNDS, LOW SOUNDS **(1967)**

Interest is immediately captured in this exploration of the causes of high and low pitched sounds and sustained through several entertaining and highly informative activities. (Have you ever tried to make a tablespoon resonate like a church bell, or a soda straw like a multipitched whistle?) From these experiences Dr. Branley moves to a brief and simple explanation of the physiology of hearing.

A review of "High Sounds, Low Sounds," in Kirkus Service, *Vol. XXXV, No. 19, October 1, 1967, p. 1211.*

The physics of sound is clearly explained through an accurate and interesting text. . . . Several activities are suggested for children, although the expected findings will be found in the text. Occasionally a child will be led to an unanticipated observation with profit. The simplicity of the approach is admirable, yet the vocabulary makes reading a little difficult for the youngest elementary group. Older children who can handle the content may easily be encouraged to explore sound in other books at a more sophisticated level.

A review of "High Sounds, Low Sounds," in Science Books: A Quarterly Review, *Vol. 3, No. 3, December, 1967, p. 210.*

FLOATING AND SINKING **(1967)**

The basic principles of the statics of fluids are taught by this colorful little book in which the child is invited to experiment as part of his learning process. One wishes that the author had introduced the terms "buoyancy" and "density" which he explains very well, thus providing the reader with unit scientific ideas he will need the rest of his life. (pp. 209-10)

A review of "Floating and Sinking," in Science Books: A Quarterly Review, *Vol. 3, No. 3, December, 1967, pp. 209-10.*

A smattering of information on buoyancy is contained in this book. The terms "floating" and "sinking" are not defined and the reader is not led to formulate his own definition. Evidently the terms are related only to water. One page carefully proves that a thing floats or does not because of its weight—a fact which a preceding page has said "can't be right." In the end we are told we won't know whether something floats or sinks but we can find out because we know why! Water play is encouraged but no scientific concept is clearly developed.

Priscilla L. Moulton, in a review of "Floating and Sinking," in Appraisal: Children's Science Books, *Vol. 1, No. 3, Fall, 1968, p. 7.*

[***Floating and Sinking***] must be judged unsatisfactory, raising more questions than it solves. "When you weigh more than the water you push aside, you sink." How does this help a child to understand why he can sometimes float for a few seconds and then sinks under the water? His weight has not changed. "A ship sinks until the weight of the water it pushes aside equals the weight of the ship and its load." This indicates that there is always a point of balance. The next sentence states "If a ship with its cargo weighs more than the water it pushes aside, the ship will sink". It will be an unusual child of four to eight years, the age group for which these books cater, who will be able to equate these two sentences.

A review of "Floating and Sinking," in The Times Literary Supplement, *No. 3484, December 5, 1968, p. 1384.*

A BOOK OF MARS FOR YOU **(1968)**

This is a collection of interesting, relevant bits of information about Mars which compares favorably to the recent, more mature looking Bergaust *Mars, Planet for Conquest* . . . in that, unlike the latter, it remains free of speculation. Dr. Branley uses the technique of relating one by one the facts of Mars—its gravity, atmosphere, surface features—to their counterparts in earth science; it works well. He concludes with a selection of major unanswered questions which scientists are investigating via space probes.

A review of "A Book of Mars for You," in Kirkus Service, *Vol. XXXVI, No. 4, February 15, 1968, p. 186.*

An easily understood history of man's advancing knowledge about the planet Mars is followed by a discussion, as thorough as the simplified treatment allows, of the findings that resulted from the Mariner IV probe in 1965. . . . [Scientifically] accurate, this is an excellent introduction to Mars.

A review of "A Book of Mars for You," in The Booklist and Subscription Books Bulletin, *Vol. 64, No. 17, May 1, 1968, p. 1040.*

An informative . . . presentation of the latest scientific findings about Mars. The information about Mariner IV and the exciting predictions of Martian exploration constitute a high-interest framework for other astronomical concepts, including comparisons between early and modern telescopes and discussions of air pressure, the Van Allen belts, and magnetism. Difficult terms are explained as they come up. . . . [The book has] concise writing.

Rose Henninge, in a review of "A Book of Mars for You," in School Library Journal, *an appendix to* Library Journal, *Vol. 15, No. 2, October, 1968, p. 151.*

THE MILKY WAY: GALAXY NUMBER ONE **(1969)**

Taking much-explored topics, Mr. Branley manages the usual range with ease: the known "facts" of our universe and galaxy; the historical dilemmas which have plagued sky watchers; the chronological history of great astronomers and their achievements relevant to galactic understanding. But he goes further: with the ease of a teacher, one very good at his trade, he leads the reader into the fascinating area of how we estimate some of our facts and in so doing presents more science than all of the "facts" taken together. The reader is introduced to the assumptions upon which total concepts are placed, often rather cautiously. He comes to realize that the great debates of science may arise from disputes about the validity of axioms rather than about the reliability of the data. Thus he will be able to appreciate such problems as the computation of stellar magnitudes, galactic distance, and the probable age of the milky way (including its likely future). (pp. 58-9)

A review of "The Milky Way: Galaxy No. 1," in Kirkus Reviews, *Vol. XXXVII, No. 2, January 15, 1969, pp. 58-9.*

Branley at his desk. Photograph by Margaret Branley. Courtesy of Franklyn Branley.

In this book Dr. Branley presents another gem among his "Exploring our Universe" books. The text is well researched and clearly presented. . . . The author presents early optical observations of Ptolemy, 127 AD, up to present day exploring by radio astronomy. The progess of man's study of our Galaxy is explained by measuring distances, what is known about nebulas, how the age of our Galaxy is determined and the discovery of other galaxies. Charts at the back of the book show how to compute stellar magnitudes and how to find stellar distances from the magnitudes. There is also a bibliography, tables and index. The mathematical computations are geared to high school level but the book is an excellent reference tool for ages twelve and up.

Dorothy Comfort, in a review of "The Milky Way: Galaxy No. 1," in Appraisal: Children's Science Books, *Vol. 3, No. 3, Fall, 1970, p. 6.*

This could have been an excellent book. It is up-to-date, well-organized, . . . and for the most part, is well written. Most of the technical explanation is clear and particularly good. However, the several places in the text having mathematical or geometrical descriptions are needlessly complex, confusing, not always relevant, and often wrong. The volume would be ever so much better over-all if these parts were removed. It would be excellent if a competent scientist helped the author make the needed repairs. In spite of these serious flaws, this is a worth-while science book about optical and radio astronomy explaining what we know and how we know about our galaxy: the Milky Way.

David G. Hoag, in a review of "The Milky Way: Galaxy No. 1," in Appraisal: Children's Science Books, *Vol. 3, No. 3, Fall, 1970, p. 6.*

THE MYSTERY OF STONEHENGE (1969)

The elusives of the stone circle near Salisbury are suggested in this sharp, self-contained approach. Possibilities of transport . . . are elaborated with a diagram [by Victor Ambrus]. . . . Carbon 14 dating suggests 1800 B.C. as the start of construction that must have lasted 300 years. Finally, theories of its general purposes—Hawkins' sun calendar, religious worship—are suggested but not examined for significance. . . . None of the other circles in the British Isles are mentioned but there is more than enough here to engage a youngster's imagination. The first full juvenile on the subject, and a very strong draw.

A review of "The Mystery of Stonehenge," in Kirkus Reviews, *Vol. XXXVII, No. 10, May 15, 1969, p. 561.*

This is a very readable account of this marvellous workmanship of mysterious origin. The author notes the efforts of many specialists including anthropologists, astronomers, engineers and others, using their knowledge and modern "know-how" even to the extent of computerizing this information, to try to bring forth some evidence as to the probable origin and methods of constructing this wonder and perhaps some reasons for its purpose of erection in the now lush area of Salisbury Plain in southwest England. Whether or not any authentic conclusions were found this slim book about Stonehenge is an intriguing piece of writing complemented by some powerful drawings to make it a fascinating book for all ages.

Celeste H. Vincent, in a review of "The Mystery of Stonehenge," in Appraisal: Children's Science Books, *Vol. 3, No. 2, Spring, 1970, p. 4.*

The megalithic trilithons of Stonehenge rising in a majestic circle on Salisbury Plain indeed evoke an air of mystery, but this book does little to convey this mystery and is only moderately successful in throwing light on it. It is hard to escape the feeling that the author doesn't have quite the necessary grasp of his subject. For instance, in his introductory remarks he says, "Modern investigators wonder why the Stonehenge people did not survive—or if they did survive, why they moved away." Who says they did either? Cultures change and there is ample evidence of continuity in the cultures of southern Britain from the Late Neolithic of Stonehenge into the historic period. New elements were added, it is true, for example, Iron Age Celts, Romans and Anglo-Saxons, but they didn't replace those who came before them but rather blended with them.

While Branley gives a clear enough explanation of how radiocarbon dating works, he errs in stating the half-life of Carbon-14 to be 5,760 years when in fact it is 5,730 years. He is also at fault in attributing high accuracy to radiocarbon dates, in using uncalibrated radiocarbon dates as if they referred to real calendar dates, and in claiming only a "small pinch" of charcoal is needed (although techniques developed since the book was written have corrected this last error for him).

Throughout the text Branley persists in referring to linear earthen embankments as mounds, although it must be admitted that this abuse of archaeological terminology is common in popular American usage. He also claims that Stonehenge was "most likely built by men who knew nothing about metals and metalworking," despite the firm dating of the later megalithic phases to the Early Bronze Age, after 2200 B.C. His discussion of the effort needed to move the stones assumes scores of men were needed because there were no horses, disregarding the fact that there certainly were oxen. His discussion of the astronomical implications is similarly marred by a misunderstanding of the apparent motion of the moon and by the almost certainly erroneous assumption that the ancient inhabitants of Britain used our modern calendrical seasons, which go back only a few centuries.

One of the book's main flaws, repeated references to a possible Mycenaean connection for the megaliths at Stonehenge, is not really the author's fault since the book was published before new radiocarbon dates made it clear that Stonehenge predates the likely period for such eastern Mediterranean contact by four centuries or so. . . .

While ***The Mystery of Stonehenge*** does do a moderately competent job of discussing the monument and successfully avoids the excesses of the lunatic fringe, its numerous minor errors and rather uncoordinated discussions leave one feeling mildly annoyed; a child would find it merely boring. (pp. 72-3)

Ronald Hicks, in a review of "The Mystery of Stonehenge," in Archaeology, *Vol. 34, No. 5, September/October, 1981, pp. 72-3.*

A BOOK OF VENUS FOR YOU (1969)

This book is a model of science writing for children. The elementary level of writing provides an adequate explanation of the relation between the orbits of the Earth and Venus and how this makes Venus both the Morning and Evening star and accounts for the phases of the planet. . . . The book is accurate and authoritative in addition to being interestingly written. There is one serious omission in the book. Results of the flights of Mariner V and Venera 4 are not mentioned. Reports were published in 1967 and should have been widely available since summer of 1968. Had these data been used, the surface temperature would have been given as 800° F rather than 625° F, the surface pressure as 100 atmospheres rather than 20, and instead of speculating that the atmosphere might be 80 per cent or more nitrogen, it would have simply stated that it was more than 80 per cent carbon dioxide. It would also have given the new value of 243 days for the sidereal day on Venus. It seems a shame for such an excellent book to be already five years out of date at the time it is published.

A review of "A Book of Venus for You," in Science Books: A Quarterly Review, *Vol. 5, No. 4, March, 1970, p. 308.*

As usual, [Branley's] attempts to simplify the complex leave him open to criticism. However, he covers the important ground without being dogmatic about the imponderables and concludes with a list of unresolved questions for future scientists. . . . To activate the reader, Branley includes a list of dates for evening and morning observation of Venus from winter 1969 through the summer of 1970.

Allison Hamlin, in a review of "A Book of Venus for You," in Appraisal: Children's Science Books, *Vol. 3, No. 3, Fall, 1970, p. 5.*

This book gives an excellent, extremely up-to-date survey of what is known about Venus. Every recent discovery about the planet by United States and Russian space probes and United States radar observations is included. The explanations are very clear and concise, and the book is quite readable. There is one quibble, however. Dr. Branley says a "day" on Venus is 247 days long, while a year is 225. "Day" is an ambiguous word in astronomy but most people would assume the author meant time from sunrise to sunrise. On Venus a Solar Day is only about 120 days long, while it is the "sidereal day" which is about 247 days long. Other than this little inaccuracy the book is flawless. (pp. 5-6)

Edmund R. Meskys, in a review of "A Book of Venus for You," in Appraisal: Children's Science Books, *Vol. 3, No. 3, Fall, 1970, pp. 5-6.*

GRAVITY IS A MYSTERY (1970)

[***Gravity Is a Mystery***] . . . and so, rightly, it remains, distinguishing this from the several (Berger, Fischer, King, Pine) aimed at approximately the same age level: whereas these offer an operative definition—e.g. "a force that pulls down on everything"—as the final answer, Dr. Branley illustrates the pull with the stipulation that "no one knows exactly what gravity is." His opening illustration (which may raise some questions of its own) hypothesizes a hole through the earth and a boy's body falling back and forth through it, going slower toward each end (the surface) and a shorter distance each time until it comes to a stop at the center. Thereafter come familiar examples of gravity's holding power and its pull in terms of weight (but not mass) whereupon we spin off to the relative gravity of the moon and the other planets for several pages. But there are not the sorties into rocketry and other peripheral matters that dot the others: this is simple, centered, and instructively inconclusive.

A review of "Gravity Is a Mystery," in Kirkus Reviews, *Vol. XXXVIII, No. 13, July 1, 1970, p. 682.*

The differences in gravitational forces on the sun, on the earth, and on other planets are carefully explained. A question that recurs frequently among youngsters is answered and explained satisfactorily: If a hole is dug through the earth from one side to the other, and someone jumps in the hole, what will happen? A few simple open-ended exercises involving gravitational forces would have been a good addition. . . . (p. 212)

A review of "Gravity Is a Mystery," in Science Books: A Quarterly Review, *Vol. 6, No. 3, December, 1970, pp. 211-12.*

The book is very free-flowing. . . . The book is perfect for its intended audience and should be available to the parents in a public library and to teachers in the grade school library to answer the small child's "wonder" questions.

Edmund R. Meskys, in a review of "Gravity Is a Mystery," in Appraisal: Children's Science Books, *Vol. 4, No. 2, Spring, 1971, p. 7.*

This update of the 1970 edition remains a succinct and lively presentation of a baffling scientific phenomenon. Although Branley never defines gravity, its effect on life is clearly shown in terms easily comprehensible to its target audience. . . . The major change in the text is a comment about one's weight on Pluto, which was based on conjecture in the original edition, and which is stated as fact here. *Gravity All Around* (McGraw-Hill, 1963; o.p.) by Tillie S. Pine and Joseph Levine offers similar information, but the presentation is not as well-suited to the very young.

Renée Steinberg, in a review of "Gravity Is a Mystery," in School Library Journal, *Vol. 33, No. 6, February, 1987, p. 64.*

A BOOK OF OUTER SPACE FOR YOU (1970)

Dr. Branley is undoubtedly one of the most lucid science writers for the very young, particularly in his own discipline, astronomy. Here the text, which is continuous, is no less lucid than usual, but is not quite as well-organized. It discusses the galaxy and the universe, the extent of space, variation in the density of air in space, gravitation, and the ways in which space explorers must be protected. The format (continuous text, very large print) seems a bit juvenile for the vocabulary and the difficulty of some of the concepts.

Zena Sutherland, in a review of "A Book of Outer Space for You," in Bulletin of the Center for Children's Books, *Vol. 24, No. 3, November, 1970, p. 38.*

A flawed but generally interesting and useful beginner's book. . . . [The author] discusses in simple terms the relative sizes of the sun and planets; the properties of space both in the solar system and beyond; and the atmospheres of the planets. However, his use of the formula for volume is inconsistent with the level of his audience. And, his oversimplification of the reason why objects "stay up" leads readers to believe that "speed" and "stay up" ability are equivalent; a helium-filled balloon would pose a serious dilemma for the author here. This poor treatment of one idea decreases the quality of the book from excellent to satisfactory.

Phillip Alley, in a review of "A Book of Outer Space for You," in School Library Journal, *an appendix to* Library Journal, *Vol. 17, No. 4, December, 1970, p. 32.*

MAN IN SPACE TO THE MOON (1970)

With just enough appreciative comment and historical background to keep the book from being arid, Franklyn Branley gives a detailed and accurate report of the Apollo 11 mission. There is some discussion of the importance of the data gathered, but the book is primarily devoted to what happened: the stages of flight and the manipulation of modules; how the three astronauts ate, slept, disposed of human waste; the mechanics of landing and communication with Mission Control; investigation on the moon, and the details of the return flight, reentry, and recovery. One of the best books on the subject, it is dignified enough for slow older readers, though primarily intended for ages 9-11.

A review of "Man in Space to the Moon," in Saturday Review, *Vol. LIII, No. 51, December 19, 1970, p. 32.*

Much of the information is a straight repeat of what the fifth or sixth grader has already seen during TV coverage of the moon flights, but here and there the author makes some excellent points. For instance, he shows that the LM (lunar module) is the first true space ship designed for exclusive use in space, having no streamlining. This book will give the child a good summary of what has happened—he should find the list of all manned space craft interesting—and should inspire the imagination of the curious. I believe every public and grade school library should have this. (pp. 7-8)

Edmund R. Meskys, in a review of "Man in Space to the Moon," in Appraisal: Children's Science Books, *Vol. 4, No. 2, Spring, 1971, pp. 7-8.*

OXYGEN KEEPS YOU ALIVE (1971)

Oxygen Keeps You Alive is written for the early and intermediate elementary school grades. It is a collection of statements about the necessity of oxygen in the function of animals and plants. In addition, it suggests a simple experiment to demonstrate the presence of gases in water. Examples are given of conditions in which environmental oxygen is not available in sufficient quantities to sustain life in man; for example, at high altitudes, in space, and underwater—in these cases oxygen must be supplied in tanks. It is well-written, easy to read, and only a few simple concepts are presented to the reader. The text is accurate, except that it should have pointed out that some living things can and do survive on anaerobic metabolism. . . . The only criticism of this little book is that it is limited to statements about the importance of oxygen in life processes without any attempt to explain how oxygen is necessary in energy transformation. It is, however, a good introduction to the significance of respiration for children 7 to 9 years old.

A review of "Oxygen Keeps You Alive," in Science Books: A Quarterly Review, *Vol. 7, No. 3, December, 1971, p. 232.*

This book relates the need for oxygen throughout the animal kingdom, but not much else. The subject matter is abstract and the scope limited. . . . Teachers may derive great use from the book as a motivational device, but, as a library inclusion, without reading guidance, ***Oxygen . . .*** may keep you alive but not interested.

Robert J. Stein, in a review of "Oxygen Keeps You Alive," in Appraisal: Children's Science Books, *Vol. 5, No. 2, Spring, 1972, p. 5.*

[This] is an excellent, simple treatise on the subject of respiration in animals and plants. Branley limits his presentation to the oxidation function in living organisms, preferring not to becloud the concept with the chemistry of oxygen or its genesis as an end-product of photosynthesis. . . . This is a unique, useful addition to primary science materials.

Leone R. Hemenway, in a review of "Oxygen Keeps You Alive," in School Library Journal, *an appendix to* Library Journal, *Vol. 19, No. 1, September, 1972, p. 113.*

***WEIGHT AND WEIGHTLESSNESS* (1972)**

There are few science books for children which can effectively simplify a difficult concept with a creative approach to the topic. This is one of the few. With . . . succinct text . . . , Branley explains weightlessness—how it affects astronauts, how orbits are computed so that spaceships fall weightlessly around the earth without crashing or drifting. There is no comparable book on the subject for this grade level and few science books with such universal appeal. An excellent companion book to the author's ***Gravity Is a Mystery*** (. . . 1970).

Shirley A. Smith, in a review of "Weight and Weightlessness," in Library Journal, *Vol. 97, No. 16, September 15, 1972, p. 2931.*

[An] engagingly written book on weight and weightlessness for the younger reader. A timely topic, but one must wonder why the author does not come to grips with the concept of mass. In this respect the book seems incomplete, although the author deals primarily with kinematical problems of parabolic and circular motion later in the book. Because the concepts of force and mass are not emphasized, the reader is prone to problems of misunderstanding or misinterpretation. For example, the reader is likely to think that if an astronaut is not tied down he will float or move around. What would make him move? Although the author does touch on such problems in places . . . , erroneous notions about weightlessness from the use of terminology in the popular press should be dealt with according to some basic concepts of dynamics.

Richard H. Weller, in a review of "Weight and Weightlessness," in Appraisal: Children's Science Books, *Vol. 5, No. 3, Fall, 1972, p. 11.*

Weight and Weightlessness will certainly encourage the child to enquire into the strange phenomenon of men floating in space on the surface of the moon, gravity, rocket propulsion and the rest. But for all the gay illustrations [by Graham Booth] and careful text, the opportunity has been missed for directing the child towards his own discoveries. Simple ideas and indications of the type of experiment which the child could perform for himself would make the book a much more useful teaching tool. Not that teachers will not welcome its appearance for with such a nebulous subject books are hard to find and this one is lively, accurate and up to date (weights in kilogrammes) and easy for children to use.

J. Russell, in a review of "Weight and Weightlessness," in The Junior Bookshelf, *Vol. 37, No. 4, August, 1973, p. 249.*

***THE BEGINNING OF THE EARTH* (1972)**

In keeping with current thinking Branley describes the sun, earth and other planets forming from the same cloud of dust and gases ("maybe ten billion years ago"), the gradual cooling of the earth and formation of water, air and rocks ("about five billion years ago"), the rains and storms and volcanoes, and the formation of islands and (barely mentioned) mountains and valleys. It's no more than the hint of an introduction but as such it is sound and judiciously geared to a young child's understanding.

A review of "The Beginning of the Earth," in Kirkus Reviews, *Vol. XL, No. 21, November 1, 1972, p. 1242.*

Succinct and direct as always, Franklyn Branley demonstrates in this excellent book for young readers that he has become as skilled in writing for this audience as he is authoritative in his field. While there is no extraneous material in this description of the evolution of the earth through the long millennia of whirling dust, heat, and rain, the text has an almost lyric cadence and is imbued with an appreciation of the slow, slow passage of time during which the earth formed.

Zena Sutherland, in a review of "The Beginning of the Earth," in Bulletin of the Center for Children's Books, *Vol. 26, No. 8, April, 1973, p. 120.*

This successfully explains a complex subject to children in simple, easy-to-read terms. Much about planet formation is still unknown to scientists and the book states, "We don't know where the earth came from. We don't know how the earth was formed. But we have ideas about such things." . . . [Children] will like the question-and-answer approach of the Branley book.

Evelyn Weible, in a review of "The Beginning of the Earth," in School Library Journal, *an appendix to* Library Journal, *Vol. 19, No. 8, April, 1973, p. 52.*

***THINK METRIC!* (1972)**

A history of measures for weight, length, volume, distance, and temperature—including derivations of the systems in use today—leads into Branley's explanation of the simplicity and logic of the metric system. . . . Problem solving and examples are well integrated into the text, and English-metric equivalents are listed at the end. The clarity of the writing . . . [makes] this a good introduction to essential information on a timely subject.

A review of "Think Metric!" in The Booklist, *Vol. 69, No. 19, June 1, 1973, p. 945.*

While the writing style is clear and the explanations lucid, this is a book so filled with solid paragraphs of facts that it seems heavier than most of Branley's books, perhaps in part due to the fact that the text is continuous.

Zena Sutherland, in a review of "Think Metric!" in Bulletin of the Center for Children's Books, *Vol. 27, No. 3, November, 1973, p. 38.*

PIECES OF ANOTHER WORLD: THE STORY OF MOON ROCKS (1972)

In an orderly progression, the author tells how the rocks were collected by astronauts on the moon, how they were handled at the receiving laboratory, and what the rocks contained. Three succeeding chapters discuss what the significance of the rocks is for life on the moon, for formation of craters and mass concentrations, and for the origin and history of the moon. The descriptions are adequate for the intended audience, but the text is full of unexplained technical terms, and no glossary is included. The suggested readings and index are helpful. . . . Speculations are kept to a minimum, and those introduced are reasonable ones. Coverage is only through Apollo 14, thus important later observations are not included.

A review of "Pieces of Another World: The Story of Moon Rocks," in Science Books: A Quarterly Review, *Vol. IX, No. 2, September, 1973, p. 160.*

Jules Verne himself would revel in this fascinating account of the moon rocks. There is a sense of real discovery on every page. An absolute must for the young geologist, astronomer or space scientist, the book gives insight into the interplay of the most precise scientific work and the theories this work promotes.

Douglas B. Sands, in a review of "Pieces of Another World: The Story of Moon Rocks," in Appraisal: Children's Science Books, *Vol. 6, No. 3, Fall, 1973, p. 9.*

[This] is—as Branley books are wont to be—well written and organized, authoritative and meticulously careful in distinguishing fact from theory. . . . While general readers may be interested in the findings, it is to the budding geologist or astronomer that the book should have most appeal; it is nevertheless clear that interpretation of scientific findings will require and contribute to many disciplines.

Zena Sutherland, in a review of "Pieces of Another World: The Story of Moon Rocks," in Bulletin of the Center for Children's Books, *Vol. 27, No. 2, October, 1973, p. 22.*

A BOOK OF FLYING SAUCERS FOR YOU (1973)

Dignified in approach, informal in style, and written with authority, this text discusses some of the phenomena that have been reported as unidentified flying objects and the known or probable explanations. Some of the reports have been revealed as hoaxes, but many of those made by reputable observers (professional pilots, for example) have no explanation. Branley describes some of the natural and man-made phenomena that might explain some reports, describes the atmosphere and temperature of planets in our system, and discusses the possibilities of intelligent life on other solar systems and of interplanetary travel. (pp. 58-9)

Zena Sutherland, in a review of "A Book of Flying Saucers for You," in Bulletin of the Center for Children's Books, *Vol. 27, No. 4, December, 1973, pp. 58-9.*

Interesting, informed and sober coverage of flying saucers is needed for younger readers, and this author provides it. In his usual readable and enjoyable prose, he offers a good selection of bizarre sightings, reveals a few hoaxes, and explains what most "saucer" sightings turn out to be. Perhaps this explanation could have been stressed more strongly—but then, the reader of any age who wants to believe in little green men in magic saucers will believe in them anyhow. This absolution covers the "Who Knows" ending, although the author might have made it a bit plainer that he was admitting, not predicting, that any real extraterrestrials who might arrive might just (who knows?) arrive in "saucers" such as we have "seen." However, the discussion along the way includes much information worthwhile in itself—on mirages, on fireballs, on satellites, on when to expect to see Jupiter and Venus (with simple timetables through 1981), on how easy it is to perpetrate a photographic hoax, and much else.

A review of "A Book of Flying Saucers for You," in Science Books: A Quarterly Review, *Vol. IX, No. 3, December, 1973, p. 250.*

The whole vexed topic—hoaxes, the will to believe, Ezekiel, balloons, St. Elmo's fire and all—is spelled out in simple language without either rancor or credulousness. If there are saucers (and there is no good evidence for them), they would have to come from the stars. Who knows? So the book ends. Although the most severe skeptics might not accept even this faintly agnostic air, the experienced astronomical author has made a model of honest approach and genuine content.

Philip Morrison and Phylis Morrison, in a review of "A Book of Flying Saucers for You," in Scientific American, *Vol. 229, No. 6, December, 1973, p. 133.*

ECLIPSE: DARKNESS IN DAYTIME (1973)

Branley effectively explains the phenomenon of solar eclipses. The simple analogy of a penny held close to the eye and covering the larger image of a car answers the question of how the comparatively tiny moon can cover a large sun. Final portions of the text narrowly miss condescension. . .; however, the end result remains a lucid conceptual explanation for the youngest skywatchers.

A review of "Eclipse: Darkness in Daytime," in The Booklist, *Vol. 70, No. 8, December 15, 1973, p. 444.*

In his usual capable fashion, an eminent astronomer explains the phenomenon of the total solar eclipse. . . . There's some discussion of the effect of the eclipse on animals and on the people of ancient times, and a home demonstration project that will enable the reader to see the image of the eclipse in safety. Succinct, lucid, and authoritative. . . .

Zena Sutherland, in a review of "Eclipse: Darkness in Daytime," in Bulletin of the Center for Children's Books, *Vol. 27, No. 7, March, 1974, p. 107.*

COMETS, METEOROIDS AND ASTEROIDS: MAVERICKS OF THE SOLAR SYSTEM **(1974)**

[Franklyn Branley] has given us an interesting and informative book about the many other small bodies that move among our nine planets and their thirty-two satellites. . . . This is the book for one who is looking for concise, accurate descriptions of meteorites, asteroids, tektites, comets, the zodiacal light, the solar wind, and cosmic rays. Even included is a set of instructions for meteor-watching. This fine book would certainly encourage me to read some of the other books in Dr. Branley's series ''Exploring Our Universe.''

Rev. Francis B. Carmody, S.J., in a review of ''Comets, Meteoroids, and Asteroids,'' in Best Sellers, *Vol. 34, No. 12, September 15, 1974, p. 285.*

SUNSHINE MAKES THE SEASONS **(1974)**

This picture book for younger readers explains the cycle of seasons as an effect of the earth-sun relationship. An occasional vague statement may lead to misunderstanding: ''During winter the sun shines all day and all night at the South Pole.'' That is, winter in the northern hemisphere but *summer* at the South Pole. However, the text is generally clear in describing the progress of the tilted earth and the changes in amounts of daylight and dark or heat and cold as we revolve around the sun.

A review of ''Sunshine Makes the Seasons,'' in The Booklist, *Vol. 70, No. 6, November 15, 1974, p. 341.*

[Sunshine Makes the Seasons *was revised in 1985.*]

Colorful illustrations [by Giulio Maestro] and clear easy-to-read text give this revised edition more appeal than the 1974 edition. The completely rewritten text is better organized with less repetition. It includes less descriptive information about the four seasons and places more emphasis on the causes of seasonal changes. A simply stated and carefully illustrated experiment using an orange, a pencil and a flashlight to help children actually see the differences on earth caused by the tilt of the earth as it rotates on its axis and revolves around the sun is particularly useful. A worthwhile addition. . . .

Eunice Weech, in a review of ''Sunshine Makes the Seasons,'' in School Library Journal, *Vol. 32, No. 5, January, 1986, p. 54.*

Sunshine is a nifty little description of astronomical meteorology. The clear text and dramatic illustrations make the march of the seasons quite clear and understandable. The minor carping I can offer is that the reader might be left with the impression that it is the variation of the length of the day (caused by the tilt of the earth's axis) that induces the seasons. That's not really the case; what's important is the angle that the sun climbs above the horizon during the day—the higher in the sky, the more heating per unit area of the earth's surface—and not the length of time that the sun is up. The two do go together, high sun angle and long days, but the former is the immediate cause of the seasons. (pp. 25-6)

John D. Stackpole, in a review of ''Sunshine Makes the Seasons,'' in Appraisal: Science Books for Young People, *Vol. 19, No. 4, Fall, 1986, pp. 25-6.*

SHAKES, QUAKES, AND SHIFTS: EARTH TECTONICS **(1974)**

Oddly enough, while the several recent YA books on drifting continents and plate tectonics achieved some dramatic and human interest by taking a chronological approach to the piecing together of the puzzle, Branley's explanation for much younger children presents the theory (and the fossil, magnetic, and sea floor evidence that supports it) straight—with an unfocused introduction that takes some time to hint at what it is leading up to. Nevertheless, . . . Branley does make the currently important subject comprehensible to young children, and his usual well-ordered clarity combined with the subject's fascination makes this a useful introduction.

A review of ''Shakes, Quakes and Shifts: Earth Tectonics,'' in Kirkus Reviews, *Vol. XLII, No. 23, December 1, 1974, p. 1254.*

The text presents a fine summary of the current ''plate tectonics'' concept of continental evolution; yet the book has some serious flaws, including . . . a very lengthy and somewhat irrelevant introduction which detracts from the inherent impact and excitement of the subsequent subject matter; a conflict of format and content. The general layout of the book seems designed to appeal to the reader at a very elementary level, but the concepts presented and the terminology used would be unsuitable for readers at anything less than a junior high school level.

Ronald J. Kley, in a review of ''Shakes, Quakes, and Shifts: Earth Tectonics,'' in Appraisal: Children's Science Books, *Vol. 8, No. 1, Winter, 1975, p. 8.*

While Branley always writes lucidly and authoritatively, here he discusses a topic perhaps too broad and complex to be covered adequately in a text so brief and without division. A bibliography and an index are appended.

Zena Sutherland, in a review of ''Shakes, Quakes, and Shifts: Earth Tectonics,'' in Bulletin of the Center for Children's Books, *Vol. 28, No. 7, March, 1975, p. 106.*

THE END OF THE WORLD **(1974)**

An eminent astronomer discusses the ways in which the explosion of the moon and the cooling of the sun—although billions of years in the future—will so affect the surface and atmosphere of our world that life cannot be sustained. Informative, depressing, authoritative, and fascinating. . . .

Zena Sutherland, in a review of ''The End of the World,'' in Bulletin of the Center for Children's Books, *Vol. 28, No. 6, February, 1975, p. 90.*

Though cataclysmic in its implications, the presentation is confusing. Theories run together, as they are attributed to no particular scientist, but to ''scientists'' in general. Young readers will need a good understanding of concepts, such as gravitational force, mass and solar radiation, for there is very little explanation of terms and no glossary or index. (p. 9)

Judith C. Botsford, in a review of ''The End of the World,'' in Appraisal: Children's Science Books, *Vol. 8, No. 2, Spring, 1975, pp. 9-10.*

Branley speculates on a number of possible ways in which the earth will eventually become uninhabitable. He has been only moderately successful in digesting a very complex subject for consumption by primary grade readers. He has not managed to avoid being dogmatic. He has also followed a couple of standard mistakes. It is about four million tons of mass, not of hydrogen, which the sun's fusion reaction consumes (the hydrogen loses only about a third of one percent of its mass in the reaction, so over a billion tons of hydrogen are used). The Roche limit value is that for a satellite of equal density with its primary; for a less dense body like our own moon the value would be larger. Granting that the distinction is beyond the grasp of the intended readers, why not mention only the correct figure? I am dubious about the statement that the early earth was covered by deep layers of ice, and I take strong objection to the claim that carbon dioxide would act as a "mirror" to reflect solar radiation back into space. It is generally credited with enhancing the greenhouse effect, keeping the heat in. The speculations themselves are interesting, but I would have been happier if their underlying reasons had been brought out more clearly. It seems to me that this might have provided more stimulation for readers to investigate the pertinent sciences more deeply.

Harry C. Stubbs, in a review of "The End of the World," in Appraisal: Children's Science Books, *Vol. 8, No. 2, Spring, 1975, p. 10.*

MEASURE WITH METRIC (1975)

There are not many ways to write a book about the metric system. One can describe its nature, tell its history, and discuss the pros and cons of using it.

Franklyn Branley has stressed the first approach, telling what the metric units of length, volume, and weight are called and showing how large they are. He does not, I am glad to say, translate from English units into the metric ones. He provides a small metric scale for his readers to copy, tells how to make a meter stick and a liter cube and how to measure familiar things. With distances and volumes, Mr. Branley does well; with weight, he has a little trouble. Probably wise not to have his readers weigh a cubic centimeter of water, he simply labels pictures of a few familiar things with their weights in grams. The weighing device he proposes, however—which uses a pencil and a ruler—is not very promising. The ruler which forms its beam has a center of gravity above the level of support. If the beam rests on a flat side of the pencil fulcrum, as seems to be intended, it can be balanced but will not be very sensitive; if an edge of the pencil is upward, the beam cannot be balanced at all—or it will balance only with the aid of friction, which again impairs sensitivity.

Harry C. Stubbs, in a review of "Measure with Metric," in The Horn Book Magazine, *Vol. LI, No. 3, June, 1975, p. 294.*

This Young Math book helps to explain the metric system (meters, grams, and liters) in easily understood terms and reinforces the information through the use of activities. . . . This is indeed an excellent *introduction* to the metric system.

Roberta A. Donnelly, in a review of "Measure with Metric," in Appraisal: Children's Science Books, *Vol. 9, No. 1, Winter, 1976, p. 11.*

Without launching into arguments for the advisability of America's going metric, the author does state that most of the world uses the metric system. He then involves his readers in a series of simple projects to learn and absorb metric measures. . . . It is all so clear and practical, moving in such orderly sequence, that reluctant Americans of any age could profit from this introduction to the inevitable.

Ethanne Smith, in a review of "Measure with Metric," in Appraisal: Children's Science Books, *Vol. 9, No. 1, Winter, 1976, p. 11.*

ROOTS ARE FOOD FINDERS (1975)

Branley explores a single important biological phenomenon—the mineral- and water-absorbing properties of plant roots and root hairs. The focus is consistent throughout, a summary concludes the text, and easy experiments demonstrate points in the discussion. The book's relatively difficult vocabulary level is largely due to the inclusion of some scientific terms. These are balanced by a low-level general vocabulary and a direct, clear approach, which combine to facilitate reading and comprehension.

Judith Goldberger, in a review of "Roots Are Food Finders," in The Booklist, *Vol. 72, No. 4, October 15, 1975, p. 307.*

This is one of the newest additions to Crowell's "Let's-Read-and-Find-Out Science Books," and it is, for the most part, as successful as its predecessors. It is a very thorough treatment of the food needs of plants and how the roots with the help of their root hairs get this food. . . . I found an error . . . where mention is made of the prickly pear: "It is a small plant, only a few inches high." The prickly pear can grow to many feet in height, and I have seen it taller than a person. Checking this should have been routine for the author or editor, especially as much is made of the point of its being small in the text.

Beryl B. Beatley, in a review of "Roots Are Food Finders," in Appraisal: Children's Science Books, *Vol. 9, No. 2, Spring, 1976, p. 10.*

Elementary pupils with good reading skills can use Branley's book to learn about some functions of plant roots. He includes instructions for a "lab" exercise which can be easily and effectively performed at home. Without technical terminology the author explores the external structure of roots and compares the advantages of different types. The relationship between these types and ecological principles is clearly described. Branley's method of calling on the reader to do things with familiar objects rather than only to read about them should prove to be popular with children and certainly will stimulate their interest in science.

Howard J. Stein, in a review of "Roots Are Food Finders," in Science Books & Films, *Vol. XII, No. 1, May, 1976, p. 39.*

LIGHT AND DARKNESS (1975)

A brief, simple introduction to the basics of optics and illumination. Although the phenomenon of reflection is clearly explained with a number of examples, there are serious omissions which detract from the book's usefulness—e.g., Branley does not mention that light travels at different speeds in different media; diffraction, the slight spreading of light rays which occurs when light passes the edges of an obstacle, is not discussed; nor is any information on light as a source of energy included. . . . Far from an illuminating treatment.

Michele Woggon, in a review of "Light and Darkness," in School Library Journal, *Vol. 22, No. 3, November, 1975, p. 42.*

This attempt to explain the simplest and most basic principles of light appears to work satisfactorily. . . . My feeling is that a book of this type ought to involve more and better activities for the student, but then it is a volume in the "Let's-Read-and-Find-Out" series rather than being a truly "scientific" book which encourages the student to "work-and-find-out." I do take some exception to the author's continual insistence that only "hot" things produce light, since that may cause students to wonder about, among other things, fireflies and "cold lights."

David E. Newton, in a review of "Light and Darkness," in Appraisal: Children's Science Books, *Vol. 9, No. 2, Spring, 1976, p. 9.*

[The] total information conveyed is rather limited. The author makes the same points repeatedly: It is very difficult to achieve total darkness, light comes from hot things, light travels very fast, and we see things because light falls on them. The suggestion that even a "dark" room has some light is made early, but not until it is repeated toward the end of the book are children urged to experiment by going into a dark room to see if they can discern shapes. Branley keeps close to the hard facts of science, but ignores the possible psychological significance of dark rooms (or darkness at bedtime) for small children. Unfortunately, he does not comment on the playful uses of light and dark. There is no mention of shadows, outlines, the movement of the sun's image or its shadow with time, or the many activities which make use of the phenomenon of light and shadow.

George E. Hein, in a review of "Light and Darkness," in Science Books & Films, *Vol. XII, No. 2, September, 1976, p. 102.*

ENERGY FOR THE 21ST CENTURY **(1975)**

An authoritative, well-written, and interesting discussion of the history of fuels and possibilities for the future—e.g., solar energy, photosynthesis, solar sea power, geothermal, wind, hydro-electric, and tidal power. Branley also spices his account with unusual and intriguing facts. . . . Solid, basic coverage, this is better than Rothman's *Energy and the Future* (Watts, 1975). (pp. 68, 71)

Shirley A. Smith, in a review of "Energy for the 21st Century," in School Library Journal, *Vol. 22, No. 3, November, 1975, pp. 68, 71.*

Since Branley discusses the abstract concept of energy only in the first chapter, the idea does not come across too clearly. For example, the discussion of energy as work done against a force field (such as gravity) is rather weak; the distinction between recoverable and irrecoverable energy is missed. In the rest of the book, the history of man's increasing demand for energy is especially well done; the quantitative examples are good. . . .

Some of his details are questionable. In the nuclear chapter he speaks of the heat wasted by atomic power plants and of the damage done to the environment; he fails to mention that a fossil fuel plant wastes at least as much heat in producing the same power. . . . [He] perpetuates the superstition that a nuclear power plant can explode like a nuclear bomb. (p. 183)

Harry C. Stubbs, in a review of "Energy for the 21st Century," in The Horn Book Magazine, *Vol. LII, No. 2, April, 1976, pp. 182-83.*

If one is looking for a good review of present and possible future sources of energy for human use, this book will do very well. But don't be misled by the title to expect a projection into the next century of the desirable energy policies for that period. Brief mention is made of current "optimistic" or "pessimistic" views of our energy future, and Branley tentatively promises to "discover which idea is correct." After an excellent cataloging of human energy sources, from firewood to exotic windmills, he simply extrapolates the present into the future, seemingly avoiding moral and ethical concerns by telling us all to "get to work right now." With enough effort in the next 25 years, we shall enter "a new era for mankind," with everyone having "abundant energy." No mention anywhere, in spite of early promises, of what citizens of the 21st century may well face, with every one of the 4 to 6 billion people having, wanting, or needing "abundant energy." As both an engineer and an anthropologist, I think in terms of alternatives to "energy-intensive" ways of life, and I believe many people, technologists and others, are beginning to give serious thought to moderation and even radical redirection of current energy needs and production. Unfortunately, these very necessary considerations are not adequately emphasized here.

Thomas J. Maloney, in a review of "Energy for the 21st Century," in Science Books & Films, *Vol. XII, No. 3, December, 1976, p. 132.*

A BOOK OF PLANET EARTH FOR YOU **(1975)**

In this book, I like Branley's approach of describing the earth as it would be seen from another part of the universe. He contrasts what would be obvious to a distant observer with what would be obscure when one is too close—such things as the shape, the rotation, and the other motions of our planet. In the process, he does a good job of making clear how we actually did learn some of these facts.

There are some errors, mostly arithmetical, which even a young reader should be able to spot if he has been trained to read critically. On page 71, the figures given for Earth's distance from the sun suggest that there are 16 kilometers in a mile instead of 1.6; on page 78 the implication seems to be that there are only 0.16 kilometers per mile. However, on other pages, figures implying the correct ratio are provided. The inconsistency should be obvious to the careful reader; and if he cannot decide which pages to believe, he should at least be moved to check elsewhere.

Some of the statements are a bit dogmatic; I am not at all sure that "Earth is the only one of the nine planets that is teeming with life." In any case, the book should be fun for young readers. If they find the few inconsistencies, so much the better; it will help preserve them from growing up with the conviction that the written word is infallible.

Harry C. Stubbs, in a review of "A Book of the Planet Earth for You," in The Horn Book Magazine, *Vol. LII, No. 2, April, 1976, p. 183.*

When I had finished reading ***A Book of Planet Earth For You*** I was hard put to decide for what age group it was intended. The format . . . [gives] the book a deceptive air of simplicity. The opening paragraphs introduce us to a theoretical distant planet among the vast galaxy of stars, out there in space, the planet Omega. Omega supports life and the Omegans are very advanced, for they can study the world of space through super telescopes; in this way they have studied the earth. So Franklyn Branley introduces us to humanity's study of the earth discussing the developing theories from ancient times to the present day. All this is very interesting and up to the first third of the book not too complex and would entertain and be comprehensible to a child of nine and his parent. But then the author begins to put in too much, pre-supposing some sophistication on the part of his reader, and tries to explain too many things in too few words. On some pages there are too many numbers (in both kilometers and miles) for comfort, and a young reader, unfamiliar with the subject or unable to retain so many facts, may close the book, or may go back to the beginning of the argument to be sure she understands. In truth, the book attempts too much. "Weather" cannot be explained in a few words. There is confusion . . . [in the sentence]: "Winds blow northeastward from the equator." Surely northeast trades move from the northeast? The concept of "precession" . . . is much too difficult and is not really explained, and the reader's parent would have trouble explaining it. The closing pages of this extended essay (for there are no chapter headings, no obvious organization, and no index) again, like the opening ones, are more general and much more comfortable to read. I cannot, altogether, dismiss this most attractive book; it tells much but not in a way that the reader can think about and understand without the added help of a specialist in this field.

Beryl B. Beatley, in a review of "A Book of Planet Earth for You," in Appraisal: Children's Science Books, *Vol. 9, No. 3, Fall, 1976, p. 11.*

The imaginative manner of presenting astronomy in this book is clever; but unfortunately, the execution of it is careless. A hypothetical astronomer on a fictitious planet "Omega" . . . describes his observations of earth and our solar system. The astronomer observes that our earth "turns 365 ¼ times while it goes around its star." Actually he would see it turn 366 ¼ times (adding one extra turn to the number of days in our year for the one revolution about the sun). Perhaps the author could be excused for this somewhat subtle point. But, he cannot be excused for saying . . . that the Foucault pendulum would always "be lined up with the same stars." Not so—only at the North or South Pole would this happen. An even more serious error . . . , both on a figure and in the text, has the earth one billion, five hundred million kilometers from the sun. That is ten times too far. The blue color of earth seen from space is attributed . . . to the blueness of the water. In truth, it is blue due to scattered sunlight in the atmosphere. In a bit of whimsey in the back, the author credits an imaginative consultant on Omega. He would have been better served by a real scientist or engineer on earth to proofread his work. Instead, a potentially very good book came out poorly. (pp. 11-12)

David G. Hoag, in a review of "A Book of Planet Earth for You," in Appraisal: Children's Science Books, *Vol. 9, No. 3, Fall, 1976, pp. 11-12.*

BLACK HOLES, WHITE DWARFS, AND SUPERSTARS (1976)

Though the subject is mind-boggling and still vastly unsettled, Branley comes through once again and gives us a splendidly clear, totally non-mathematical presentation of what is currently known about the life cycles of stars. Beginning with our sun, . . . he goes back to young, still unstabilized T Tauri stars, then on to the red giants, where gravity takes over in a complicated sequence of stages, and to the tremendously dense white and yellow dwarfs (beyond atoms) that come next. Whether the question is how we know T Tauri are young; why stars move as they do and some of the older ones pulsate; what makes novas explode; or how, in "neutron stars" and then black holes, atoms themselves can collapse until volume becomes zero and density reaches infinity—Branley is always on hand to explain the process of discovery, review rival theories, or, in the end, admit that neither "ordinary laws of science" nor "the special ones discovered by Einstein" seem to apply. Fuel for cosmic thoughts.

A review of "Black Holes, White Dwarfs, and Superstars," in Kirkus Reviews, *Vol. XLIV, No. 19, October 1, 1976, p. 1104.*

Branley gives a clear and concise account of current *theories* (the word is continually stressed) on the nature and significance of these intriguing stellar objects and of stellar evolution in general. . . . This book requires some background, but for those interested in the newer horizons of astronomy it presents a good deal of material not generally available outside of texts. Whether it might be a little too simplified and orderly, I will leave to the experts, but it is a clear, understandable, and most interesting introduction to a complex subject, and should be of use in either adult or comprehensive juvenile collections. Appendixes, bibliography, and index. (pp. 9-10)

Daphne Ann Hamilton, in a review of "Black Holes, White Dwarfs, and Superstars," in Appraisal: Children's Science Books, *Vol. 10, No. 3, Fall, 1977, pp. 9-10.*

The general descriptions here are very clear, and, as far as we know at the moment, quite accurate. Some of the statements given very definitely are still a bit controversial, but the picture is very acceptable. There are a few slips. The statement . . . that the distinction between "gas" and "dust" is merely one of elemental composition is wrong; dust consists of particles containing vast numbers of atoms or molecules, while gas means just what it does in earthly laboratories—the state of matter in which atoms and molecules are far enough apart to have negligible effect on each other.

Harry C. Stubbs, in a review of "Black Holes, White Dwarfs, and Superstars," in Appraisal: Children's Science Books, *Vol. 10, No. 3, Fall, 1977, p. 10.*

COLOR: FROM RAINBOWS TO LASERS (1978)

Branley begins with a businesslike background chapter on light theory from the Greeks through Newton to the present, using simple, easily understandable equations in explaining the concepts of "light waves," the speed of light, and the diffraction of white light. And though Branley's writing style is more carefully geared to a juvenile audience, his approach is less attractive superficially; he deals with physiological, psychological, and physical basics before getting into his very wide range of specific topics: laser light, color blindness, rainbows and other atmospheric phenomena, pigments and dyes, and color TV, printing, and photography. Unfortunately all of this skipping about produces its own scattering effect and sometimes gives an impression of aimlessness. However, many of the explanations are interesting in themselves, and despite a few minor slips (the text mixes up the two rings of a solar halo, and in two of the colored diagrams blue comes out purple) both text and [Henry Roth's] illustrations are clear and to the point.

A review of "Color: From Rainbows to Lasers," in Kirkus Reviews, *Vol. XLVI, No. 14, July 15, 1978, p. 755.*

The clarity of Branley's explanation of light waves and light energy and what they have to do with color is admirable. Technical aspects are present but in a basic, understandable way. . . . A fine introduction. (p. 43)

Denise M. Wilms, in a review of "Color: From Rainbows to Lasers," in Booklist, *Vol. 75, No. 1, September 1, 1978, pp. 42-3.*

There are many treasures here but unfortunately most will be accessible to only the very proficient young reader. The first chapter is packed with new concepts and terminology—frequency, wavelength, Angstrom unit, photon, electron-volt, scientific notation. Chapter two uses these ideas in a fairly involved discussion of the color spectrum. By this point, the tone of the book has been set. Each of the remaining chapter-topics are given intricate treatments. (p. 61)

Teachers should be confident, however, that their most talented students will find the material in ***Color: From Rainbows to Lasers*** stimulating and worthy of their time. Also available is an extensive index for easy reference. (p. 62)

Charles Piemonte, in a review of "Color: From Rainbows to Lasers," in Curriculum Review, *Vol. 18, No. 1, February, 1979, pp. 61-2.*

THE ELECTROMAGNETIC SPECTRUM: KEY TO THE UNIVERSE (1979)

Branley brings his trademark of good scientific writing, clear, accurate and concise, to bear on a difficult albeit interesting subject: the spectrum of invisible radiation that abounds throughout the universe from radio waves, light waves, infrared and ultraviolet radiation to x-rays and gamma rays. The early investigations of such historical figures as Max Planck, Einstein, Rutherford, and Niels Bohr are explained, as is the interest of the electromagnetic spectrum to branches of science, including medicine, biology, chemistry, astrophysics, and radio-astronomy. Hard-to-grasp concepts, such as the invisibility and speed of light, are defined in context. Equations and formulas are frequent and require effort to understand as well as some mathematical background. But Branley has succeeded in presenting a complex topic with clarity, while stimulating curiosity and encouraging experimentation and study. Little on the subject for any age group exists, and what is available is primarily found in scattered chapters of physics books.

Connie Tyrrell, in a review of "The Electromagnetic Spectrum," in School Library Journal, *Vol. 26, No. 3, November, 1979, p. 84.*

Branley is a practiced and lucid writer, as well as an authoritative voice; what may limit the readership for this book is the amount of information so tightly packed into the text, and the fact that the reader with no scientific background may find the terminology discouraging. . . . [A] brief bibliography and an index are appended. (p. 168)

Zena Sutherland, in a review of "The Electromagnetic Spectrum: Key to the Universe," in Bulletin of the Center for Children's Books, *Vol. 33, No. 9, May, 1980, pp. 167-68.*

Here we have an authoritative and interesting survey of the electromagnetic spectrum and related topics. Although the book has many of the usual difficulties associated with "explaining" the electromagnetic spectrum, it is, nevertheless, written with a highly readable, engaging style. As is usual for this subject, the text gets tangled up in the piano keyboard analogy, complete with the low notes and high notes as metaphors. In addition, the author brings in ocean waves to help clarify things. Hopefully, the young reader will be sufficiently familiar with sound waves and ocean waves to be able to employ these analogies as intended. . . . This book might be added to any high school science library, if for no other reason than the sheer number of interesting topics which are discussed. Students who become interested in a specific topic can turn elsewhere for a deeper, more rigorous treatment.

Clarence C. Truesdell, in a review of "The Electromagnetic Spectrum: Key to the Universe," in Appraisal: Science Books for Young People, *Vol. 14, No. 1, Winter, 1981, p. 15.*

COLUMBIA AND BEYOND: THE STORY OF THE SPACE SHUTTLE (1979)

In a smooth, graceful text that is remarkably free of jargon, Branley introduces the space shuttle operation by way of the orbiter Columbia, depicted here carrying the European Space Agency's Spacelab into outer space. Orbiter descriptions are nontechnical but full, and just as much attention is paid to projected Spacelab operations and to the future space utilization that orbiter vehicles promise to make possible. The topics Branley chooses to zero in on are well selected. One area of perpetual curiosity that he addresses is space vehicle bathroom facilities; his description here is the most complete in a children's book. Information on Spacelab experiments for industry and what they might mean for future manufacturing is concise and clear; the usual space colony description wrap-up is relatively restrained in its speculation. Overall, this is an excellent introduction, more attractive and accessible than either [Charles] Coombs' *Passage to Space* or [Frank] Ross' *Space Shuttle*. . . . (pp. 608-09)

Denise M. Wilms, in a review of "Columbia and Beyond: The Story of the Space Shuttle," in Booklist, *Vol. 76, No. 8, December 15, 1979, pp. 608-09.*

The latest entry into the space shuttle book race is the best so far. Branley's book will be understandable to children a grade or so younger than those who will read Ross' *Space Shuttle* (Lothrop, 1979). Each book includes different details. Where Ross explained heat shielding in depth, Branley has introduced the weightless showerstall and rescue balls to be used by escaping passengers in an emergency.

Carolyn Caywood, in a review of "Columbia and Beyond: The Story of the Space Shuttle," in School Library Journal, *Vol. 26, No. 6, February, 1980, p. 52.*

AGE OF AQUARIUS: YOU AND ASTROLOGY (1979)

Branley describes the origins of astrological belief in ancient times, and the role of the astronomers who also functioned as astrologers during the medieval era. His explanation of the origins of astrological signs and applications in horology are lucid, and he shows readers how they can cast their own horoscopes; he then discusses the facts from a scientific viewpoint, noting the effects that other bodies in our solar system do or don't have on earth and its people, and pointing out the fallacies of astrological beliefs. This should satisfy readers who are curious about astrology but it does not deviate from facts or encourage credulity. In sum, just what one would expect from Branley: directness, accuracy, and clarification in a text that is well-organized and clearly written.

Zena Sutherland, in a review of "Age of Aquarius: You and Astrology," in Bulletin of the Center for Children's Books, *Vol. 33, No. 7, March, 1980, p. 128.*

This is one of very few books on the subject for this age level, and unlike Liz Greene's attractive *Looking at Astrology* (Crane Russak, 1978) and many adult astrology books, it goes beyond the sun signs and explains the calculation of houses, ascendants, etc. Larry Kettlekamp's *Astrology: Wisdom of the Stars* also deals with these astrological elements, and in slightly more detail, but is also aimed at a slightly higher reading level. Although at the end it is clear that the author does not believe in astrology, throughout the text he maintains an admirably detached attitude which leaves the reader quite free to decide either way. This objectivity, combined with its clarity and readability, make this a good introduction to the subject for young readers. A bibliography and an index are included. (pp. 13-14)

Daphne Ann Hamilton, in a review of "Age of Aquarius: You and Astrology," in Appraisal: Children's Science Books, *Vol. 13, No. 3, Fall, 1980, pp. 13-14.*

This book deserves a place in every library for it performs a much-needed service. Astrology is in no way a science. . . . Branley completely dispels any doubts about the validity of astrology by means of a clear and lucid description of its so-called principles. In addition, he describes its origins, its spread, and the emotional basis of its appeal. Perhaps his most significant contribution is the way he weaves astronomical facts and scientific thinking into a thorough debunking of astrology as a source of guidance in everyday life. As thorough as Branley is, however, his argument suffers a bit by what seems to be an effort to be gentle with those who believe in astrology. Unfortunately, it is necessary to read the book carefully, and, above all, to finish it to get the full impact of the author's case. The child who reads the book carelessly or does not finish it could conceivably come away with a mistaken idea of what astrology is and what it offers.

A. H. Drummond, Jr., in a review of "Age of Aquarius: You and Astrology," in Appraisal: Children's Science Books, *Vol. 13, No. 3, Fall, 1980, p. 14.*

FEAST OR FAMINE? THE ENERGY FUTURE (1980)

The book promises to be a worthwhile addition to available titles on energy. Dr. Branley describes in balanced style several possible energy sources with their advantages and failings and seems to have avoided the common tendency to go overboard either for or against any one of them. He presents a particularly rational discussion about cutting down on waste, without falling into the common trap of suggesting that this is the whole answer to the energy problem—or denying that there is a problem at all. List of further reading. (pp. 668-69)

Harry C. Stubbs, in a review of "Feast or Famine? The Energy Future," in The Horn Book Magazine, *Vol. LVI, No. 6, December, 1980, pp. 668-69.*

Dr. Branley has produced a fine summary of the overall energy situation, without falling into the trap of trying to blame it on anyone. While he does not actually use the terms, he makes evident the difference between primary and secondary sources. A hasty reader may forget that shifting to a hydrogen economy does not lessen the actual demand for energy but actually increases it, but this is not the author's fault. I would question his choice of words in one or two places; . . . for example, *lessening* the amount of sulfur, ash, and other by-products of burning can hardly be said to *eliminate* one of the main objections to coal.

The book does not attempt to cover the basic thermodynamics which anyone seriously concerned with solutions to the energy problem must understand, but it does a very fine job within its planned scope.

Harry C. Stubbs, in a review of "Feast or Famine? The Energy Future," in Appraisal: Science Books for Young People, *Vol. 14, No. 2, Spring, 1981, p. 10.*

Although marred by an apocalyptic start, in which an alternative future of feast versus famine is limned, this book does a creditable job of presenting a melange of information on energy—its uses, sources and forms. The child reading this might wonder how that view fits with what is actually happening now: reduced oil consumption, vigorous energy conservation, in short, a future in which the manner of our lives is basically retained, albeit with energy thrift becoming a norm of transportation planning, housing design and industrial manufacturing. There are occasional gee whizzes ("within a few decades, people will not need to 'go shopping'") and some asides spurious to the intent of the book ("the race to produce the biggest bombs, the fastest planes, the most powerful tanks, the heaviest and fastest ships is nonsense"). These blemishes are, however, redeemed by the author's overall effect: accurate, reasonably fair, and for the most part, providing a careful description and assessment of various energy options. The part on nuclear fission power is particularly well done, one that might even satisfy both sides of that debate.

Norman Metzger, in a review of "Feast or Famine? The Energy Future," in Science Books & Films, *Vol. 16, No. 5, May-June, 1981, p. 273.*

SUN DOGS AND SHOOTING STARS: A SKYWATCHER'S CALENDAR (1980)

This "calendar"—arranged by season and month—is a compendium of myths, facts, information, and activities relating to the sky (primarily, of course, weather and astronomy). . . . Directions are given for such activities as meteor-watching, calculating a north-south line by sun shadows, keeping weather records, making a sextant or a weathervane, and finding your latitude. There are a few errors or confusing statements, such as "there is no wetness in water vapor." . . . Information on any single topic is necessarily rather superficial, but usually clear and hopefully will encourage readers to investigate further into anything that catches their interest. This book is an entertaining series of facts and diversions which should prove most useful as a browsing item and as a source for science projects. There is a bibliography but no index. (pp. 10-11)

Daphne Ann Hamilton, in a review of "Sun Dogs and Shooting Stars: A Skywatcher's Calendar," in Appraisal: Science Books for Young People, *Vol. 14, No. 2, Spring, 1981, pp. 10-11.*

The author's month by month approach to locating and observing sky phenomena is well organized. Several interesting and informative activities, e.g. the one for constructing a quadrant for measuring sky angles, are situated throughout the book. Particularly intriguing are the explanations for the origin of many familiar words, terms, and titles. . . . In addition, Branley offers many novel and exciting ways to understand information. When describing the Earth's speed of revolution around the Sun he reports this velocity as 30 times faster than a speeding bullet (29,792 meters per second)! . . .

Yet, despite several good points, ***Sun Dogs and Shooting Stars*** often leaves much to be desired. Many concepts are presented which certainly require further explanation for a young reading audience. In a discussion of the winter constellations, we are introduced to the stars of Orion and told of their distance in light years. However, there is neither an attempt to explain what indeed a light year is nor a glossary or index to lend a helping hand. . . .

Many times we are given interesting science insights, but left hopelessly without a clue to understanding the concept. For example, we are shown how to find the direction South by using a wristwatch and the afternoon sun—the activity is accurate and fun, but why and how does it work? We are also presented with a formula for calculating the Sun's height on the summer solstice but never informed as to the underlying theory.

Conversely, however, Branley does reach concept completion on many of his chosen skywatcher phenomena. For example, his description of the "green flash" at sunset and his explanation of sunburn are both quite excellent.

All in all, ***Sun Dogs and Shooting Stars*** would be a readable addition to a library collection, albeit somewhat incomplete on the explanations of some scientific wonders.

James E. Palmer, in a review of "Sun Dogs and Shooting Stars: A Sky Calendar," in Appraisal: Science Books for Young People, *Vol. 14, No. 2, Spring, 1981, p. 11.*

The subtitle is important, for Branley provides a guide for meteorological as well as astronomical observations. . . . The style is chatty and encouraging; the solid information clearly presented. Similar books do not usually cover *both* subjects. [Jamie] Jobb's *The Night Sky Book* (Little, 1977) for a slightly older age group also has a project-oriented approach, but lacks this book's emphasis on daytime and weather. An interesting and worthwhile addition, despite the lack of an index.

Elaine Fort Weischedel, in a review of "Sun Dogs and Shooting Stars: A Skywatcher's Calendar," in School Library Journal, *Vol. 28, No. 3, November, 1981, p. 88.*

THE PLANETS IN OUR SOLAR SYSTEM (1981)

Astronomer-author Branley has written another valuable book in the admirable Let's-Read-and-Find-Out Science line, a text with easily grasped and absorbing information about the nine planets, the moon, asteroids and satellites in the solar system. . . . There are facts about meteorites, comets and "shooting stars," what they consist of, etc. Branley also offers directions for making two models, one showing the planets' sizes and the other, their relative distances from the sun.

A review of "The Planets in Our Solar System," in Publishers Weekly, *Vol. 219, No. 15, April 10, 1981, p. 70.*

The Planets In Our Solar System is an authoritative introduction to the solar system. It is well-written. . . . This book, like many others, tells how to construct a scale model of the solar system. To facilitate model making, all of the scaled down diameters of the planets, and their distances from the sun, are provided. Unfortunately, the scale for planet diameters is quite different from the scale for the distances. Although this results in a solar system model of manageable proportions, it also creates a seriously distorted model. Any child who compares the solar system model in this book to one in another book, say, the one in *The Stars,* by H. A. Rey, could be very confused. At the very least, the authors should have indicated their use of two different scales.

Clarence C. Truesdell, in a review of "The Planets in Our Solar System," in Appraisal: Science Books for Young People, *Vol. 15, No. 1, Winter, 1982, p. 21.*

Branley does his usual good job on this elementary survey of our solar system. Facts and figures reflecting the latest discoveries are clearly and simply presented. . . . Other titles available on the subject, such as the [Mae and Ira] Freeman's *The Sun, the Moon, and the Stars* (Random, 1979) and Rutland's *The Planets* . . . are for a slightly older audience and are broader in scope. If you're still using Branley's ***A Book of Planets for You*** (. . . 1966), update it with this one; if you're not, buy it anyway.

Elaine Fort Weischedel, in a review of "The Planets in Our Solar System," in School Library Journal, *Vol. 28, No. 5, January, 1982, p. 60.*

JUPITER: KING OF THE GODS, GIANT OF THE PLANETS (1981)

Using the latest information available from the Voyager space missions, Branley introduces readers to the planet Jupiter and its satellites. Although not as detailed as Asimov's *Jupiter: the Largest Planet* (Lothrop, 1976), Branley's book is thorough and has the advantage of currency. In addition to the "discovery" of Jupiter and its satellites and the usual physical data, Branley includes descriptions of the two Voyager probes and looks ahead to the Galileo probe of the late '80s, which will enter the Jovian atmosphere. A good reading list is included. This would be useful paired with [Margaret] Poynter's recent *Voyager: the Story of a Space Mission. . . .*

Elaine Fort Weischedel, in a review of "Jupiter: King of the Gods, Giant of the Planets," in School Library Journal, *Vol. 28, No. 5, January, 1982, p. 84.*

An up-to-date account of fascinating facts about our largest planet, written by an excellent author of astronomy and science books for young readers. Much attention is given to the remarkable space probes to the planet and its moons. The book really stirs one's imagination. Highly recommended.

George Barr, in a review of "Jupiter: King of the Gods, Giant of the Planets," in Children's Book

Review Service, *Vol. 10, No. 8, March, 1982, p. 75.*

The book is informative, accurate, and reasonably well written. The information presented, however, is hardly more illuminating than that presented in popular journals. . . . While Branley writes clearly enough for most readers, there is little information that is unique or outstanding. Except for the first and last chapters, the book is a rather routine presentation. Although it can serve as a concise, easy-to-read reference on the subject and should be considered as an addition to a reference library, it possesses no attributes that make it a clear choice over other easily accessible references. (pp. 89-90)

Van E. Neie, in a review of "Jupiter: King of the Gods, Giant of the Planets," in Science Books & Films, *Vol. 18, No. 2, November-December, 1982, pp. 89-90.*

SPACE COLONY: FRONTIER OF THE 21ST CENTURY **(1982)**

Branley's overview of what life will be like in space colonies features solid research peppered with speculation and "letters home" from a mythical immigrant couple, Jenny and Tom. The book is at its best when discussing documented knowledge such as the effect of zero gravity on humans or the hazards of space life. More questionable are speculative details of space existence that are presented as definites, e.g., "Most people will rent their apartments, though a few will be owned by the occupants." For students doing reports or just browsing, this is an informative peek into the twenty-first century, but it should not be taken as gospel.

Ilene Cooper, in a review of "Space Colony: Frontier of the 21st Century," in Booklist, *Vol. 78, No. 16, April 15, 1982, p. 1093.*

Branley's book should find a wide audience and deservedly so: it is not only full of exciting ideas and fascinating scientific facts and plans, it forms them into a coherent, understandable, and believable scenario for our future in space. The author covers not only colonies of several types and their development from temporary close-earth-orbit stations through permanent "life" colonies far out in the solar system; he also deals with solar power satellites (to provide energy both to Earth and the space stations) and lunar and asteroid mining (for the materials to construct the colonies). In addition to technical matters like mass drivers and waste recycling, practical concerns such as gravity differentials for living and manufacturing (not to mention space hazards like radiation and meteoroids), he also takes into account such human factors as government and various types of living quarters. This latter aspect is not so well covered as in [James S.] Trefil's *Living in Space* . . . , but is adequate, and the hypothetical "letters home" are not as awkward and intrusive as such things usually are. . . . There is a list of further reading and an index.

Daphne Ann Hamilton, in a review of "Space Colony: Frontier of the 21st Century," in Appraisal: Science Books for Young People, *Vol. 15, No. 3, Fall, 1982, p. 15.*

WATER FOR THE WORLD **(1982)**

Water for the World is an excellent effort to provide both suitable and informative supplementary material for [classroom discussions on environmental and ecological issues]. . . . The book is readable, concise, and full of information about water, the water cycle, its sources, and its pollution by humankind. . . . Several recent additional readings are included. This book should be required reading for classroom students who are studying water. While the book is recommended for junior-high students, some advanced elementary school students may be able to get a lot of information from it about water.

Lowell J. Bethel, in a review of "Water for the World," in Science Books & Films, *Vol. 18, No. 2, November-December, 1982, p. 64.*

Frankly, I expected to find this rather dull. I was agreeably surprised to read an interesting text. . . . There are a few simple experiments, including one on solar evaporation of salt water. The visionary idea of towing icebergs to coastal cities is discussed. Timely material, such as the entrance of salt into groundwater as a result of the salting of winter roads, is here. . . . A good style, not condescending . . . [characterizes] the text. (pp. 13-14)

Elizabeth Gillis, in a review of "Water for the World," in Appraisal: Science Books for Young People, *Vol. 16, No. 1, Winter, 1983, pp. 13-14.*

DINOSAURS, ASTEROIDS, AND SUPERSTARS: WHY THE DINOSAURS DISAPPEARED **(1982)**

Branley, a prolific and always explicit science writer, discusses the various theories that have tried to explain the disappearance of the dinosaurs. The text begins with a discussion of the Mesozoic Era in which these creatures thrived and of the ways in which scientists can date and describe varieties from fossil remains. Clues from plankton and pollen grains of the time, from differences in the thickness of dinosaur egg shells, from knowledge of continental drift and change of climate may have contributed, but Branley also posits the possibility of volcanic disturbance, of some extraterrestrial influence such as the explosion of a supernova, or of collision of a very large asteroid with the earth. He presents the problem as a fascinating puzzle yet to be solved, and his text—lucidly written and carefully organized—is a fine example of the ways in which a scientific body of knowledge is built. A relative index is appended.

Zena Sutherland, in a review of "Dinosaurs, Asteroids, and Superstars: Why the Dinosaurs Disappeared," in Bulletin of the Center for Children's Books, *Vol. 36, No. 5, January, 1983, p. 83.*

Branley's book discusses only the theories of the causes of [the dinosaur's] sudden extinction. But the subject matter broadens to include an explanation of some of the most important concepts of science: geologic ages, drifting continents, the formation of super stars, sources of atmospheric dust, and asteroids that collide with Earth. Inducing readers to be interested in such heady information is no mean feat. Branley succeeds brilliantly by offering enough background material in the first chapter to intrigue them with the mystery of dinosaur disappearance. The reader is then left to solve the mystery by following the pros and cons of successive theories. The biological end of the discussion suffers slightly. While Branley does not repeat the discredited idea that because of their small brains dinosaurs must have been stupid, he states the reverse: Tiny mammals must have "used their wits in order to survive." Theoretically, brain volume could be devoted as much to sensory perception as to "wits." . . . By writing an intriguing text and by integrating several important scientific concepts, Branley has produced one of the outstanding books of the year. With . . . a general bibliography.

Sarah Gagné, in a review of "Dinosaurs, Asteroids, & Superstars: Why the Dinosaurs Disappeared," in The Horn Book Magazine, *Vol. LIX, No. 1, February, 1983, p. 81.*

The idea behind this brief book is a good one. Paleontological data that are related to dinosaur extinction are presented in the context of ancient and modern physical terrestrial as well as astronomical environments. . . . The exposition is clear and reasonably comprehensive; the treatment is balanced. . . . Unfortunately, the book contains misstatements or factual errors on 17 of 78 pages of text. Although few of these errors affect the author's main argument, they are fundamental to paleontology and are not likely to be detected by the intended readers. What is especially frustrating is that few of the errors would have escaped the most cursory technical review, and all could have been corrected easily. The book is acceptable for the realistic impression it gives of the scientific treatment of dinosaur extinction, but it should be rated no higher than "acceptable" because of the pervasiveness of technical errors that it contains.

Nicholas Hotton, III, in a review of "Dinosaurs, Asteroids, and Superstars: Why the Dinosaurs Disappeared," in Science Books & Films, *Vol. 18, No. 4, March-April, 1983, p. 209.*

SATURN: THE SPECTACULAR PLANET (1983)

Newly discovered information about Saturn makes this introduction to the planet an especially useful addition to any collection. This is the most up to date book about Saturn available, and Branley's writing here is as consistently good as in his many other books—clear and easy to follow and understand.

Frances E. Millhouser, in a review of "Saturn: The Spectacular Planet," in School Library Journal, *Vol. 30, No. 1, September, 1983, p. 118.*

This is a very good, though not spectacular book about the planet Saturn. . . . Author Branley covers the history of discovery and the facts known about this planet in an easy reading text. . . . There are a few problems which may not be too important. For instance, Branley describes Galileo's puzzlement in trying to understand the "ears" he first saw on Saturn which later he observed had gone away. The curious young reader is not helped in understanding that Galileo first saw the rings at an oblique aspect like ears and then later saw the planet when the plane of the rings was in his line of sight and invisible. A nice feature of this U.S. published book is the almost exclusive use of the metric system without the distracting translation of each measurement into English units.

David G. Hoag, in a review of "Saturn: The Spectacular Planet," in Appraisal: Science Books for Young People, *Vol. 17, No. 1, Winter, 1984, p. 15.*

[This] is a terse but quite acceptable book. It begins with naked-eye and telescope observations and culminates with information from the Pioneer and Voyager missions. The author is careful to avoid leading the reader to accept certain explanations of Saturnian structures—such as the rings—when alternative theories abound. The message is that science doesn't always know—a good lesson for elementary school children to learn. I have few serious criticisms of this book if it is to be considered a very elementary treatment of Saturn. . . . The short sentences make the reading somewhat choppy, but this might enhance the book's readability for a young audience.

Frank D. Stekel, in a review of "Saturn: The Spectacular Planet," in Science Books & Films, *Vol. 19, No. 3, January-February, 1984, p. 154.*

HALLEY: COMET 1986 (1983)

The impending return of Halley's comet has sparked a number of books on the subject, but this is the first intended solely for school-aged readers. It is a good, concise, and accurate account of comets in general and Halley's in particular. The book begins with a historical review of the sightings of Halley's comet and the earthly events attributed to these sightings. It then gives a brief description of the "dirty snowball" theory of how comets work, discusses their possible origins, and describes famous comets from the past. The final two chapters tell what to watch for when Halley returns in 1986 and describes the activities of the International Halley Watch. All of the chapters are short, well-written, nontechnical, and interesting. . . . A short bibliography of nontechnical information sources is also provided. The only flaw, however minor, is that the chapter on past notable comets is too long, comprising more than one-fourth of the entire book.

David Tyckoson, in a review of "Halley: Comet 1986," in Science Books & Films, *Vol. 19, No. 3, January-February, 1984, p. 154.*

The newest entry in the "Halley's Comet preparation library" by the redoubtable Dr. Franklyn Branley is up to his highest standards. It is crammed with historic and scientific information. . . . The information is comprehensive and detailed, though not so technical as to discourage the interested browser. The reader will come out of this with a sound knowledge of comets in general, the principles of which are almost invariably presented in terms of (or in relation to) Halley's Comet specifically. . . . The writing is excellent. . . .

This title is more comprehensive than [Norman D.] Anderson and [Walter R.] Brown's *Halley's Comet* (Dodd Mead, 1981 . . .), but also somewhat more difficult reading. The Anderson/Brown title is also a bit more thorough on the historical and superstitious aspects of the comet. Those who can manage it may want both; limited to one, I would choose Branley's book as having more complete information and being better written.

Daphne Ann Hamilton, in a review of "Halley: Comet 1986," in Appraisal: Science Books for Young People, *Vol. 17, No. 2, Spring-Summer, 1984, p. 13.*

One fault with the book lies in the author's failure to always lay the groundwork for new concepts before introducing them. . . . [For] example, he discusses the possibility of a comet colliding with Earth, and then examines the theory that holds such a collision responsible for the extinction of the dinosaurs, all before telling the reader what a comet is or describing the solar system. Such knowledge cannot be assumed on the part of every sixth-grade student who might read this book.

Another problem with ***Halley: Comet 1986*** is Branley's tendency to oversimplify his explanations. This often results in misleading statements. For example, in discussing the extinction of the dinosaurs, he ignores the layer of iridium (a constituent element of meteorites) found in the sediments containing dinosaur fossils. Then he states that there is "little evidence to prove the belief" that cometary impact was responsible for the dinosaur's extinction. Again, . . . the author says that "Newton concluded that planets and comets moved in elliptical orbits." Actually, Kepler had already demonstrated that the planets' orbits were elliptical. All readers, regardless of age, deserve to be told facts.

The book contains suggestions for viewing the comet, . . . and there is an account of the various countries' plans to send space probes to it. Some of this information is now dated, however, since the United States will not be sending a spacecraft to Halley's Comet as once was hoped. (p. 306)

Stephen L. Gallant, "Halley's Comet: A Bibliographic Essay," in Voice of Youth Advocates, *Vol. 8, No. 5, December, 1985, pp. 306-07, 310-11.*

***COMETS* (1984)**

Branley's knowledgeable elementary text makes astronomical principles easily accessible with fundamental explanations of how comets are probably formed and why they follow elliptical orbits. A short history of Halley's comet introduces a discussion of Edmund Halley's discoveries, which dispelled early, superstitious notions that considered comets harbingers of disaster. Best of all, precise instructions for spotting Halley's comet during the early months of 1986 by locating nearby constellations are handily detailed. . . . A timely introduction that maintains the high standards of this popular beginning science series [Let's-Read-and-Find-Out].

Karen Stang Hanley, in a review of "Comets," in Booklist, *Vol. 81, No. 3, October 1, 1984, p. 243.*

[Branley] and illustrator [Giulio Maestro] work together here to introduce sophisticated scientific concepts through simply worded explanations and illustrative diagrams and paintings. Although easy, the explanations do not sacrifice the integrity of the concept. . . . It is refreshing to see difficult concepts such as solar pressure explained in simple language for young audiences without talking down or distorting the concept.

Margaret M. Hagel, in a review of "Comets," in School Library Journal, *Vol. 31, No. 4, December, 1984, p. 68.*

This book tells the young reader about as much as she or he might want to know about comets. And it presents this information in an interesting and understandable way. . . . My primary concern is that the text relies so heavily on a discussion of Halley's Comet, which the reader is advised to watch for in 1986. The story line reads in such a way that I would expect the book to be unnecessarily dated by the middle of that year. While this approach may take advantage of excitement surrounding the return of the comet next year, it need not have done so in such a way as to make the book seem "old hat" within two years of its copyright date.

David E. Newton, in a review of "Comets," in Appraisal: Science Books for Young People, *Vol. 18, No. 2, Spring, 1985, p. 14.*

***SHIVERS AND GOOSE BUMPS: HOW WE KEEP WARM* (1984)**

Man has numerous ways to keep warm, some instinctive, others well-reasoned. Franklyn Branley brings these together in a text as intriguing as the book title. The opening story of Jean Hilliard, who blacked out in the snow for five hours, is fascinating. . . . Chapters include discussions of human survival in cold, the physics of heat loss, garments and housing among Eskimos and Lapps, clothes and hypothermia, and astronauts' needs in space. The book is perhaps slightly easier to read than Joan Rahn's *Keeping Warm, Keeping Cool* (Atheneum). For a discussion of achieving coolness as well as warmth, Rahn's book is invaluable. But Branley substitutes some specifics about keeping cool with information on how space suits are made to maintain warmth in space. The main considerations on active and passive solar heating are covered concisely in three pages. Recommended for further reading are three excellent periodical articles and two earlier books by Branley.

Sarah S. Gagné, in a review of "Shivers and Goose Bumps: How We Keep Warm," in The Horn Book Magazine, *Vol. LXI, No. 1, January-February, 1985, p. 83.*

[***Shivers and Goose Bumps***] weaves a complicated web of high interest facts around the factors associated with human thermoregulation. It initiates the reader with the miraculous survival story of Jean Hilliard who survived unharmed after being "frozen stiff." (Unfortunately the author missed the opportunity to explain the physiological mechanisms of tissue damage due to freezing and the technical details of reviving Ms. Hilliard). . . . Branley dealt with some critical issues well: arctic dwellings were not lumped into the usual all-Eskimos-live-in-igloos imagery, . . . and traditional and modern household heating techniques were compared for efficiency. My major criticisms of ***Shivers and Goose Bumps*** are that it adhered to the Fahrenheit scale (it would have provided an excellent framework for introducing Celsius in situations familiar to most students, such as standard body temperature and room temperature), and it neglected some fundamental definitions such as true hibernation. What it lacks in accuracy, though, it replaces with breadth. I would recommend this book as an effective motivator for students who have the sophistication to comprehend basal metabolism and the stability to survive notions of swelling explosively if exposed to low pressure situations like outer space.

Nancy Murphy, in a review of "Shivers and Goose Bumps: How We Keep Warm," in Appraisal: Science Books for Young People, *Vol. 18, No. 2, Spring, 1985, p. 15.*

The information is accurate, but it may be too thorough and overwhelming to a juvenile audience. The first page introduces a formula for converting Fahrenheit temperatures to Celsius, which will confuse most readers. This is followed by a gruesome story of a child who survives a night in below-freezing temperatures with a body temperature of 64 degrees. Once you get past the first chapter, there is much information, but complicated concepts are often explained superficially. . . . The bright child who is a good reader will enjoy this book and be stimulated to learn more. The average child will probably give up while trying to understand the second chapter's explanation of radiation, conduction, and convection. Much of what the book covers requires formal thinking levels beyond the age of the intended audience. Most of those who are able to understand these concepts would not read them in what is obviously a child's book.

Robert A. Bernoff, in a review of "Shivers and Goose Bumps: How We Keep Warm," in Science Books & Films, *Vol. 20, No. 5, May-June, 1985, p. 308.*

IS THERE LIFE IN OUTER SPACE? (1984)

This should be as intriguing and, when read aloud, as comprehensible to the preschool child as it is to the independent reader. It is written simply, but with no condescension, . . . and it is both succinct and lucid in describing what investigations have shown about the moon and Mars, what is known about other planets in the solar system that makes it unlikely that they sustain life, and what probably exists of life on planets in other galaxies. Good scientist that he is, Branley makes it clear that his opinions on the last topic are conjectural.

Zena Sutherland, in a review of "Is There Life in Outer Space?" in Bulletin of the Center for Children's Books, *Vol. 38, No. 6, February, 1985, p. 100.*

A children's book with this title might be expected to be either a "fun" book for recreational reading or a "science" book that offered insights on some interesting technical questions, concepts and ideas. . . . In my judgement, [Branley] and artist [Don Madden] have achieved the "fun" objective with spectacular success, but have produced only the most modest of "science" books. Largely because of the wonderful and imaginative drawings of creatures from outer space by the artist, the book will delight readers from the age of five to ninety-five. I don't think those same readers will find out very much, however, about the questions that scientists have about life in outer space, the methods they use to answer those questions, the issues involved in defining "life" for such studies, the wide varieties of life forms that could be hypothesized and searched for, and so on. In fact, the book does a surprisingly poor job of meeting the objectives of the series for which it was prepared, the "Let's-Read-and-Find-Out" series. Readers won't really "find out" much science in this book at all. I highly recommend the book for recreational reading, but a book in which readers—of any age—learn more about the truly exciting and challenging *scientific* questions of life in outer space yet remains to be written.

David E. Newton, in a review of "Is There Life in Outer Space?" in Appraisal: Science Books for Young People, *Vol. 18, No. 3, Summer, 1985, p. 15.*

MYSTERIES OF THE UNIVERSE (1984)

A distinguished astronomer who has been a prolific author of excellent science books for children and young people, Branley here again exemplifies good scientific principles. There are clear distinctions drawn between facts and theories, the information is authoritative and is logically arranged, and the text moves always from the more to the less familiar. Giving background information to help readers understand the nature of the questions he poses (What are supernovas? How and when did galaxies form? Why do pulsars pulse?) and answers. A bibliography and a carefully compiled index are appended.

Zena Sutherland, in a review of "Mysteries of the Universe," in Bulletin of the Center for Children's Books, *Vol. 38, No. 6, February, 1985, p. 100.*

Branley looks at some of the unanswered questions astronomers have about the nature and function of the universe: how did it start; why does it have certain elements in its makeup; how big is it; and what are mysterious bodies such as black holes, quasars, and pulsars. The book's strength is in Branley's explanations, which both clarify the substance of the question and trace the scientific logic that suggests certain solutions. He defines many concepts and procedures along the way so that readers get a good dose of basic background information. Where controversy exists, readers learn of that as well. There is no glossary for quick reference, but the care of the text in outlining terms and concepts should render that less a liability.

Denise M. Wilms, in a review of "Mysteries of the Universe," in Booklist, *Vol. 81, No. 11, February 1, 1985, p. 786.*

Sometimes in attempting to simplify, an author can make a subject more complicated and confusing. Essential information is omitted, and difficult concepts are passed over with a quick sentence. In this book, Branley creates some simple analogies ("the galaxy is shaped somewhat like two fried eggs back to back"), but he runs into trouble when he says that "energy seems to come from electrons spinning at high speed in a magnetic field . . . called synchrotron radiation." Some ideas just do not lend themselves to the simple language used in much of this book. . . . This book is a worthy attempt at presenting some of the fundamental mysteries of the universe to young people by using as little physics as possible; however, physics may be necessary to delve satisfactorily into questions of the origin and nature of the universe.

Deborah Allen, in a review of "Mysteries of the Universe," in Science Books & Films, *Vol. 20, No. 5, May-June, 1985, p. 307.*

MYSTERIES OF OUTER SPACE (1985)

Branley uses a question-and-answer format to provide information about outer space and man's accommodation to exploring it. Accurate and authoritative, the author has grouped his questions logically; the material is under such headings as Kinds of Space, Weightlessness and Zero Gravity, Uses of Space, and The End of Space—The End of Time. . . . A knowledgeable and interesting survey. . . . A few books are suggested for further reading; an index is appended.

Zena Sutherland, in a review of "Mysteries of Outer Space," in Bulletin of the Center for Children's Books, *Vol. 38, No. 8, April, 1985, p. 142.*

Despite the ostensible groupings, I felt the book lacked organization; certainly there is rarely any continuity between questions, and no sense of focus to the book. It seems to be merely a random collection of disconnected information about outer space.

As Dr. Branley's ability to explain things simply and clearly remains intact, this may have some use as a browsing item in large collections, but its lack of organization and/or purpose keeps it from being more. A disappointment.

Daphne Ann Hamilton, in a review of "Mysteries of Outer Space," in Appraisal: Science Books for Young People, *Vol. 19, No. 2, Spring, 1986, p. 20.*

In this book, thirty-six questions are used as springboards for discussion of a good variety of interesting topics related to the universe beyond the Earth. Unfortunately, in most of the "answers" there are minor technical inaccuracies, and there are a few more serious errors of fact. For example, the author incorrectly states that solar gravity pulls dust away from comets—the role of sublimated vapor is not even mentioned. The "explanation" of the twin paradox is incorrect. (Perhaps a technically correct explanation would be too subtle for a juvenile reader. In such cases, I would favor a straightforward admission that the "proof" is something for the reader to seek when he/she is a bit older.) There are misleading statements about weightlessness, orbital motion, the solar wind, and the interaction between charged particles and the Earth's magnetic field. There are some really good sections, such as those which address the questions "How would time be regulated in space colonies?" and "Can asteroids be mined?". But I believe that the overall technical accuracy of this book is inadequate even for a juvenile audience: it is possible to omit complex details without blurring the logical structure of a scientific description or explanation. . . . I wish that I could be more enthusiastic about this book. The overall concept is certainly reasonable, but the technical inaccuracies and a fair number of stylistic shortcomings detract from the final product.

William H. Ingham, in a review of "Mysteries of Outer Space," in Appraisal: Science Books for Young People, *Vol. 19, No. 2, Spring, 1986, p. 20.*

VOLCANOES **(1985)**

A new Let's-Read-and-Find-Out Science Book by Branley shouldn't be missed. He invariably tells children what they want to know about complicated subjects in simple but not simplistic terms. . . . The text starts with a description of [Mount Vesuvius]. . . . There are details on the recent Mt. Helena blowup and other eruptions, interspersed with explanations of how they are caused. Data on the work of geologists are included, with reference to how they can predict when an old volcano may go off again and when a new one may be created.

A review of "Volcanoes," in Publishers Weekly, *Vol. 227, No. 18, May 3, 1985, p. 73.*

A slim, straightforward volume on volcanoes explains why they occur where and when they do. . . . [The] author writes in simple, general terms about the movement of the earth's plates and the other physical phenomena involved in the development of a volcano. . . . Incorporating details sparingly, the book provides clear, easily understandable descriptions of technical points—explaining, for example, that the earth's plates move "only about as fast as your fingernails grow."

Karen Jameyson, in a review of "Volcanoes," in The Horn Book Magazine, *Vol. LXI, No. 3, May-June, 1985, p. 326.*

Simple declarative sentences are used and there is a minimum of technical terms. Plate tectonics, although not named, is described but the concept may not be clear enough for comprehension by young readers. . . . The final sentence may get a debate. It states that we should not worry too much, since geologists usually "are able to warn us long before a volcano blows its top." (p. 20)

John R. Pancella, in a review of "Volcanoes," in Appraisal: Science Books for Young People, *Vol. 19, No. 3, Summer, 1986, pp. 19-20.*

SPACE TELESCOPE **(1985)**

In 1986 the space shuttle will carry into orbit a space telescope that will be able, because of its position above the earth's atmosphere, to gather data previously unavailable to astronomers. Branley briefly discusses the history and limitations of earthbound telescopes, then explains the special structure, workings, and maintenance of the Space Telescope. Because observations by the new telescope may increase our understanding of questions about black holes, the size of the universe, and the possibility of intelligent life on other planets, Branley touches briefly on these and other enigmas. Although clearly written and well organized, the book omits some basic information that students may need for reports. Oddly, Branley does not discuss who conceived, developed, and financed Space Telescope, as he calls it, or even its official name. Other than mentioning that the European Space Agency supplied solar panels and a faint-object camera and will use 15 percent of the observation time, he ignores the question of who will have access to the telescope and who will control its use. Although photos are credited to NASA, the agency is never mentioned in the text. In spite of these omissions, the book is useful within its scope.

Carolyn Phelan, in a review of "Space Telescope," in Booklist, *Vol. 82, No. 2, September 15, 1985, p. 127.*

[Space Telescope's] longer range will enable astronomers to explore deeper into space (and consequently further into the past) and perhaps find more clues about the origin (and future) of the universe. Branley describes this exciting event fully and accurately. However, some statements, although accurate, will be confusing to children without some background in astronomy. . . . ***Space Telescope*** captures the special excitement of anticipated and yet undreamed of scientific discovery. (p. 169)

Margaret M. Hagel, in a review of "Space Telescope," in School Library Journal, *Vol. 32, No. 2, October, 1985, pp. 168-69.*

HURRICANE WATCH **(1985)**

Branley describes hurricane formation, paths and destructive power using short sentences and colorful vocabulary. The descriptions don't include the real-life stories found in books on hurricanes for grades four and up, but this is more than made up for in [Giulio Maestro's] illustrations, which clearly convey the pounding force of the hurricane winds and water. . . . Branley and Maestro are to be lauded for effectively portraying the inherent drama of a hurricane as they explain the science behind such a storm and provide common-sense safety advice.

Jonathan R. Betz-Zall, in a review of "Hurricane Watch," in School Library Journal, *Vol. 32, No. 5, January, 1986, p. 54.*

Unfortunately, the narrative opens with the statement that "the air that surrounds the earth weighs five quadrillion tons" or an amount equal to that of one quadrillion 5-ton elephants. It is doubtful that the juveniles will comprehend the enormity of the number. A simpler example, such as the weight of a bar of iron 1,000 miles long, 1,000 miles wide, and ½-mile thick might have been better. The narrative then indicates that hurricanes "are big, powerful and dangerous storms that happen in August, September and October." These three months are the hurricane season, but hurricanes have been recorded in every month of the year. . . . [An] overall examination of this book indicates that the emphasis is on destruction and damaged homes, with less emphasis on hurricane formation. This book should certainly interest juveniles, but it is not likely to be highly edifying. (pp. 226-27)

George G. Mallinson, in a review of "Hurricane Watch," in Science Books & Films, *Vol. 21, No. 4, March-April, 1986, pp. 226-27.*

Hurricane Watch is a very nice description of hurricane formation, the effects of hurricanes on coastal areas, what (little) can be done to control them or protect yourself from them . . . , and some mention of current observational methods—satellites, and airplane flights through hurricanes, for example. Nothing on forecasting other than simple extrapolation of observed motion. There were no errors of commission that I could spot.

The first page is a tad off-putting: it means very little to tell the reader that the earth's air weighs five "quadrillion" tons, and then write all 15 zeros out. (It should be "mass" and not "weight" anyway). But it helps even less to "explain" five quadrillion as equal to one quadrillion 5-ton elephants! What, in my view, is more impressive is a description of how *thin* the atmosphere is relative to the rest of the earth—just a layer of paint. Then again, we people aren't very big either.

John D. Stackpole, in a review of "Hurricane Watch," in Appraisal: Science Books for Young People, *Vol. 19, No. 4, Fall, 1986, p. 26.*

FROM SPUTNIK TO SPACE SHUTTLES: INTO THE NEW SPACE AGE (1986)

"Satellites are changing the way we live" is Branley's theme (he says it twice); for a discussion aimed at such young readers, he's pleasantly specific about the capabilities, both of current satellites and those that are planned for the near future. The text's brevity results in some oversimplification (the Strategic Defense Initiative is presented as an offensive anti-satellite system) and gives Branley's occasional editorial comments a higher profile, but children who don't understand orbits might after reading the first chapter. There is a reference to the *Challenger* disaster, and some of the projects mentioned here will come to pass within the next year or two. . . . This can be used to introduce longer books on communications, space exploration, geography or new technology (seven of which are cited in the short bibliography).

John Peters, in a review of "From Sputnik to Space Shuttles: Into the New Space Age," in School Library Journal, *Vol. 33, No. 1, September, 1986, p. 132.*

A nice up-to-date book about artificial satellites, explaining in Branley's clear and interesting prose what satellites are, and how they are put and remain in orbit. Most of the book is devoted to the marvelous usefulness of satellites in communications, whether it be radio/television, or weather forecasting information which can track hurricanes or inform farmers about harmful crop freezing. Among the wealth of information provided by land survey satellites (Landsats) is to show pollution areas and rock formations to aid in locating mineral deposits. Branley also writes about satellite use in space exploration, as in studying comets and solar winds, as well as their military surveillance of countries around the world. . . .

[The text] makes the reader aware just how much satellites are part of our everyday lives. In doing so, Branley consciously or unconsciously makes an effective case for continued space exploration, a fitting tribute to the Challenger crew to whom the book is dedicated.

Mary Johnson-Lally, in a review of "From Sputnik to Space Shuttle: Into the New Space Age," in Appraisal: Science Books for Young People, *Vol. 20, No. 1, Winter, 1987, p. 17.*

The only misleading explanation concerns geosynchronous orbit. St. Louis is used as an example of a terrestrial point above which a geostationary satellite might orbit. Since St. Louis is not on the equator, the fuel cost to keep a satellite over that point would preclude this example in the real world. The only error noted was the implication that the U.S. space station would be made out of space shuttle external fuel tanks. Since funding for the space station began, NASA has made plans only for modules manufactured on earth that would be transported into space in the shuttle cargo bay. This book was written for the general awareness and understanding of students who are familiar with space terminology. It would be good for book reports and outside class reading because it has many good illustrative examples. Overall, it is recommended for its excellent photographs and coverage of the basic concepts of satellites.

Timothy L. Stroup, in a review of "From Sputnik to Space Shuttles: Into the New Space Age," in Science Books & Films, *Vol. 22, No. 3, January-February, 1987, p. 186.*

JOURNEY INTO A BLACK HOLE (1986)

This Let's-Read-and-Find-Out Science Book helps children visualize and understand what black holes really are and how they are created. In simple but precise terms, Branley takes the reader-astronaut on the voyage of the title. . . . The author refrains from wild speculation about worlds beyond the hole, instead staying well-grounded in current scientific theory. The trip to the dark point is, as Branley explains, purely imaginary, since no one will ever get close enough to witness the process. A perfect introduction for children to an astronomical wonder.

A review of "Journey into a Black Hole," in Publishers Weekly, *Vol. 230, No. 18, October 31, 1986, p. 66.*

Branley's lucid text . . . skillfully streamlines the explanation of a complicated astronomical phenomenon so that it will be comprehensible to primary grades readers. It isn't just that Branley is an expert on the subject (he is) but that he's an expert on what to omit and to include when writing for younger children. . . .

Zena Sutherland, in a review of "Journey into a Black Hole," in Bulletin of the Center for Children's Books, *Vol. 40, No. 3, November, 1986, p. 42.*

An imaginary journey to a black hole is used to convey scientific information about black holes, but because the sophistication of the concept is not easily described in beginning-reader vocabulary, children will be left with unclear science and a bad story. The science is confused because of the difficulties in communicating clearly comparative sizes and time periods to this age group and in defining specific words used to present ideas (*mass, gravity, X-ray, atom*). The story is dull because the need to convey information severely limits the imagination. Science and story are not smoothly integrated, and as a result the focus is unclear. . . . Although this is the only book in print on the subject for this age group, children attracted to its appealing format will be disappointed or confused by its content.

Allen Meyer, in a review of "Journey into a Black Hole," in School Library Journal, *Vol. 33, No. 3, November, 1986, p. 72.*

MYSTERIES OF THE SATELLITES **(1986)**

There are still many unanswered questions about the satellites that circle the planets according to Branley's third entry in the Mysteries of the Universe series. He likens the way scientists gather and interpret information to the way detectives solve crimes and involves the reader through a question-and-answer technique that keeps the text lively. Branley is careful to differentiate between what is known and what is merely hypothesized as he discusses the origin, composition, size, shape, rotation, and orbits of each of these circling bodies. . . . [This is] an enticing, up-to-date introduction. For readers who may have a problem with the exclusive use of the metric system throughout the book, a conversion table is supplied. A short bibliography appended.

Mary Lathrope, in a review of "Mysteries of the Satellites," in Booklist, *Vol. 83, No. 5, November 1, 1986, p. 404.*

The information about the satellites is as up to date as possible, and it is presented on a level that young readers can understand. The book should be included in all libraries for young people as a scientifically current reference for information about the satellites.

Thomas Lesser, in a review of "Mysteries of the Satellites," in Science Books & Films, *Vol. 22, No. 3, January-February, 1987, p. 186.*

Elizabeth (Ann Mrazik) Cleaver

1939-1985

Canadian author/illustrator of picture books, reteller, and illustrator.

One of Canada's leading contemporary illustrators of children's books, Cleaver is internationally acclaimed for her ingenuity, boldness of design, and scholarship. She is best known for her collaborations with author/editor William Toye—*How Summer Came to Canada* (1969), *The Mountain Goats of Temlaham* (1969), *The Loon's Necklace* (1977), and *The Fire Stealer* (1979)—in which she visually interpreted Tsimshian and Micmac Indian legends. By combining thorough research of tribal customs and artifacts with a firsthand study of British Columbia's mountains and trees, Cleaver conveyed the physical and spiritual life of these natives in a rich blend of Euro-American and primitive Indian art that is considered uniquely her own. Cleaver provided the texts as well as the illustrations for several books. She retold and produced a filmstrip of *The Miraculous Hind: A Hungarian Legend* (1973), a myth based on the historical founding of Hungary, and *The Enchanted Caribou* (1985), an Inuit transformation tale, and also produced *Petrouchka* (1980), a picture book version of Igor Stravinsky's Russian ballet. Each of these works involved extensive inquiry and artistic experimentation to authenticate details of story, setting, and costume. As a child, Cleaver created paper cutouts and shadow images which she later developed into her characteristic illustrative style. Using torn and scissor-cut paper, monoprints, linocuts, and natural materials such as twigs, pine needles, birch bark, and fur, she fashioned drawn and pasted images into distinctive collages noted for sharp contrasts of color and texture. Cleaver's diminutive *ABC* (1984) features mini-collages in bright colors and utilizes objects like a button and a key. In *The Enchanted Caribou*, she demonstrated her love of puppetry by photographing original, three-dimensional shadow puppets onto paper.

Critics praise Cleaver for the beauty, innovation, and proficiency of her stylized but expressive art and for her accurate portrayal of multicultural backgrounds, folk motifs, and clothing styles. Although some observers find her texts flat and question the appeal of *The Miraculous Hind* and *Petrouchka* for the very young, the majority of reviewers agree that Cleaver's striking collages and attention to both nature and native tradition have made an enduring contribution towards a distinguished, recognizably Canadian school of children's illustration.

Cleaver was elected to membership in the Royal Canadian Academy of Arts and was highly commended for her illustrations by the Hans Christian Andersen Award committee in 1972. She also won the Amelia Frances Howard-Gibbon Medal for *The Wind Has Wings: Poems from Canada* in 1971 and *The Loon's Necklace* in 1978, and received the Canadian Library Association Award for *The Miraculous Hind* in 1974. *Petrouchka* merited the Canadian Children's Literature Award in 1981 and was placed on the International Board on Books for Young People (IBBY) Honor List in 1982. To honor Cleaver's memory, the Canadian section of IBBY created the annual Elizabeth Mrazik-Cleaver Canadian Picture Book Award in 1986.

Photograph by William Toye

(See also *Something about the Author*, Vols. 23, 43 [obituary] and *Contemporary Authors*, Vols. 97-100, 117 [obituary].)

AUTHOR'S COMMENTARY

[I begin] with a great sense of inadequacy because I realize how difficult it is to talk about pictures and because words cannot substitute for sensory experience and perceptual awareness. Accepting this limitation, I would like to share with you what I experience when I am working on a picture book.

One of the greatest pleasures in creating picture books is the way I change and grow and travel on to many new levels of existence. I love picture books. As a visual artist I find it a necessity to make art and I find the book form an ideal way to express my ideas. Through picture books and fine limited-edition books . . . , I can create a world for myself. My work is a result of my ideas as an artist, and is subject to change as my experience changes. By making books I am involved not just with pictures, but with words and ideas, as well, and find out in the process what is important to myself. Also, by making books I can create a world and live twice: once when I have an experience or idea, and then again when I re-create it. Through picture books I can talk to myself and also to others. (p. 71)

In my visual memory I can still recall the pictures from my picture books as a child. I can also remember the cut-out paper dolls that I used to cut and play with. Unconsciously, perhaps, I have retained this child-like love for cutting paper as can be seen in my collage pictures.

Picture books are a precious art form which combines word and picture. Picture books create many different worlds for a child, worlds in which art, music, literature, language and ideas can be discovered, experienced and explored. . . . But pictures also *are* a language, and it is important that we understand this visual language because what we see is a major part of what we know. All children's books will influence the way in which the child will see. But artistically valuable books will educate the child's taste and visual sense. They will stimulate imagination. They will also encourage the child to create his own image of life and thus help him find his own way. Through picture books we can help develop visual literacy.

Creating picture books demands great discipline. After having gone through the experience a number of times, I am quite aware of the different phases of my work. I will try to describe the process for you. Picture book making is an activity that demands all of my attention and so it is necessary to be alive, because it is so easy for our spirits to be dead. By "to be alive," I mean to have dreams, to have desire, to have ideas and feelings, to love, to transform the realities of the spirit. It is important to be able to visualize, which is the ability to think and form multiple images in the mind. What I find exciting, and what is probably most important, is the forming of mental pictures that I have never seen before and the being able to put them down as they move through my mind. It is not the visualizing of an idea that takes time, however, as the sculptor Brancusi has declared: to make art is easy, but the difficulty is to be in a state to make it. During this phase I am in a very vulnerable state and might even feel insecure. Every time I begin a project it is as if it's the first time I am attempting a book. There is an uncertainty. But then I also have reassurance in the fact that I have done it before. But having created books before does not guarantee that I can do it again. My mind seems to be constantly working on problems, even in my dreams. Finally there comes a time when I cannot put off getting into the work and it is necessary consciously to start selecting the materials, ideas I have taken in. This phase may take days, weeks, months, sometimes only a few minutes; every artist works in a different way. This phase requires great discipline and concentration.

The searching for images often involves playing around with a number of possibilities. I find solitude is necessary. While working on a picture I have a conversation with it constantly. Through collage it is possible to try out endless numbers of combinations and find the best possible solution. This is why I find collage such a creative medium to work in. It is not planned completely, but is in part discovered and revealed. It is necessary to play with the materials, but this is creative play. . . . With collage, collagraphs and other forms of printmaking, I create pictures to form a framework through which I can express my ideas. By making collages from monoprints (textured papers) that I paint, and by tearing and cutting, I can exploit the accidental. Collage is a way of making pictures by pasting, cutting and tearing paper. Discovering and developing the unexpected configurations is a form of visual play. Let me tell you about my early attempts at collage. In 1967 I illustrated a dragon story written by Ted Wood for which I prepared twenty pictures. This took me almost a year to complete. It was a most difficult time because I was trying to find my own way, and I knew that if I wanted to be good, I would have to be original. In examining these collage pictures I find that I have used sophisticated monoprints as backgrounds. The figures are almost silhouette images with very little detail or none at all. From here I gradually added other elements into my work.

Every book represents a new world I have to enter with a unique set of problems I will have to confront. After receiving a manuscript I read it many times for days, weeks, and even months, until my mind begins to formulate images spontaneously. This takes a lot of energy. To receive and realize new ideas, to be able to form mental pictures, requires a special kind of devotion, tranquility and self-confidence. For me to do my work it is necessary to be inspired by the piece of literature I am working with, and to believe in it, to have a great feeling and love for it.

During the first phase when I take ideas in to be digested, ideas come from everywhere. Everything I do and feel and hear and think and read is absorbed and becomes part of my memory or unconscious. Artistic structure does not evolve in a single line of thought but on several superimposed strands at once. The steps may include scribbles, sketches, drawings, failed work, thoughts, conversations, research and reading. From all these processed images, some predominate, and then I make a selection. Some ideas will crystallize, others won't. For example, ideas and inspiration for the pictures in ***The Wind Has Wings: Poems from Canada*** came from the poems themselves. Poets draw pictures too. They do it with words instead of with paint, pencils or collage. And, like the artist, the poet doesn't literally copy what he sees. He is able to describe things in an exciting way—the way his imagination sees them. This is similar to making visual pictures.

In the Indian legends, ***How Summer Came to Canada*** and ***The Mountain Goats of Temlaham,*** it was necessary to research Tsimshian and Micmac artifacts in order to understand more fully their art. I was greatly influenced by Tsimshian art and tried to recreate the ceremonies the Indians might have had. It was necessary to try to re-create their spectacular environment along the shores of the Pacific against the mountain ranges. You have to put yourself in the right frame of mind to imagine the legend being re-enacted for the glorification of chiefs, for the spiritual benefit of individuals, and for the pleasure and instruction of spectators. It was important to convey the communication they had with nature and animals, and their highly developed art forms. I received a Canada Council travel grant to visit British Columbia. I went through the mountains by air and by bus to get impressions of the spectacular environment. I did research at various museums: the Museum of Anthropology, University of British Columbia; The Royal Ontario Museum, Toronto; the McCord Museum, McGill University; and the National Museum of Man in Ottawa. At times, when visualizing a book, I find it necessary to comprehend the total structure, rather than to analyse single elements. For example, when working on ***Summer*** and ***Temlaham,*** which were both 32-page books, certain pages were worked out more easily than others, and there was no order in the way the sequence evolved.

During the final phase it is possible to reject bad ideas and search for better ones if necessary. Finally a picture will emerge with an independent life of its own. The picture acts like a living person with whom I can converse. If the picture can talk back to me, it will also be capable of talking to others.

Through collage I have found I can create feelings and moods in a contemporary way. With colour I can express feelings of ice and frost and cold in contrast to warmth and fertility. Paper edges have a character of their own. Torn paper may represent snow.

Leonardo da Vinci in his note books says he was intrigued with the images he could discover in cloud formations and walls; he exercised a form of visual imagination. I had a somewhat similar experience when I discovered Glooskap's profile in a monoprint I created [for ***How Summer Came to Canada***]. From the hundreds of monoprints I prepare, I choose and select very carefully and try to use my visual imagination. Since I was struggling with the problem of creating an image for Glooscap, I did not know what form he would take, but when I saw a profile appearing in the grey/brown monoprint, all I had to do was follow the outline. I knew instantly that this would be the Glooscap, that mythical lord and creator of the Micmacs I was looking for. According to an Indian tradition, he had a rock-like face with moss in his hair. I then added the green leaves symbolizing the moss in his hair.

A similar experience was the creation of an illustration for an Eskimo poem entitled **"Eskimo Chant"** in ***The Wind Has Wings.*** Very little had to be added to complete this picture. (pp. 71-5)

In ***How Summer Came to Canada*** I introduced pine needles, cedar twigs, green plants and potato prints into my compositions. In ***The Mountain Goats of Temlaham*** I used linoelum cuts to add impact to the developing scenes. (p. 76)

In ***The Miraculous Hind*** I have used linoleum cuts and have introduced lace into the aprons of the women's costumes. I also used cut-out words as images so that children should feel and see that there is beauty in the sound and look of words. There are words that seem to merge into the background. When the cut-out words cannot do justice any more to the ideas in them, at that moment they become pictures themselves. Words become images—the two become one. (pp. 76-7)

Elizabeth Cleaver, "The Visual Artist and the Creative Process in Picture Books," in Canadian Children's Literature: A Journal of Criticism and Review, *No. 4, 1976, pp. 71-9.*

GENERAL COMMENTARY

KIRKUS REVIEWS

[***How Summer Came to Canada***] is a Glooskap legend of the Micmac Indians of eastern Canada, [and ***The Mountain Goats of Temlaham***] a tale of the Tsimshian Indians of British Columbia; both are reduced to their plot structure—which is strong, and forms the captions to the vivid mixed-media illustrations, which are also strong. In sum, there's not much to linger over. But just as the pictures show better at a distance (the compositional elements tending to cancel each other out close up), the brief, forceful stories [by William Toye] are well suited for reading aloud.

A review of "How Summer Came to Canada," and "The Mountain Goats of Temlaham," in Kirkus Reviews, *Vol. XXXVII, No. 22, November 15, 1969, p. 1192.*

NANCY D. HERBERT

[Elizabeth Cleaver] confesses she has been influenced by Persian art, Van Gogh, Matisse, Chagall and Helen Frankenthaler. . . .

As a picture book artist, Elizabeth is involved in current trends in literature, art, music, concrete poetry and conceptual art, people and travel. Because of the artist's various interests, she has produced impressive work in the fields of filmstrip, puppet theatre and graphics as well as picture books. (p. 68)

I believe that Elizabeth Cleaver in her pictures has discovered the means of expressing universal truths. (p. 70)

Illustrations should add understanding to the text. To meet this criterion Elizabeth did extensive research for ***The Mountain Goats of Temlaham,*** visiting museums in British Columbia, Ottawa and Toronto. As a result, authentic Tsimshian artifacts were used in totem poles, wall paintings and clothing. Dr. MacDonald, ethnologist with the National Museum in Ottawa, remarked on seeing the totem poles on the cover illustration that it was truly Tsimshian. This pleases Elizabeth Cleaver very much.

In 1969/70, Prof. Gazetas of the Theatre Arts faculty at Sir George Williams University used the above book and especially pages 16-17 as an introduction to stage design. He stated that the double page spread revealed an interesting theatrical device in the revelation of an inner light both in faces and bodies even though there was no focal fire in the "stage setting".

In analysing the original art work I discussed with the artist the techniques that were used in its production. "After selecting various monoprints which I felt suited the mood of the wall paintings, I overprinted a linoblock taken from a Tsimshian wall painting. The 'people' were composed of collage papers." Leafing through the book and suddenly coming upon an open ended painting in which abstract shapes and symbols flow, I felt the desire to examine it further and in greater detail. I enjoy this painting very much. Black type on white pushes up against a red blue line which fuses with its contiguous colours. The eye then moves over graffito reminiscent of other walls we have known. Because of the knowledge that the painting has been executed by hand (hand printed linoleum) there is an affinity between the onlooker (the reader) and the work under discussion. The turbulent wall becomes part of a theatrical movement. Raven Feather and the young boy participating in the action itself are fused in background and foreground. A scintillating range of tonal blues and reds cause colour tensions on the weathered surface. Primary yellow is negated. The shapes of blues repeated rhythmically on the ground unify left and right pages. Repetitions of abstract shapes and curved lines mingle, cross, fade and reappear on the lodge wall painting. This is turn complements the repetition of the outline of two people.

The surface texture is tactile. We can trace our fingers around the corner wall post which leads into the young boy with the red markings, then around his eyes into the rattle held by Raven Feather, until we are gradually led through all the abstract maze-like Tsimshian wall painting. Certain areas are reminiscent of frescoes in which the paint has flaked away.

In analysing ***How Summer Came to Canada,*** a Micmac Indian legend, Elizabeth explained her use of found materials to add to the surface of her paintings, for example, pine needles, cedar branches and moss, which are used together with monoprinted paper, producing a three-dimensional effect on a two-dimensional surface. She researched at the McCord Museum in Montreal for Micmac artifacts and has used Micmac designs in Summer's costumes. The limited amount of research material available necessitated an inventive use of symbols. How does one invent symbols for Winter's tent? How does one invent

He went to the beautiful place where Winter lived. The giant's tent glistened white and cold in the rays of the moon. Above it the sky was filled with flashing, quivering lights and the stars shone like diamonds.
6
7

From How Summer Came to Canada, *retold by William Toye. Pictures by Elizabeth Cleaver. Oxford University Press, Canadian Branch, 1969. © Oxford University Press (Canadian Branch) 1969. Reproduced by permission of the publisher.*

symbols for a dream sequence? How does one invent symbols for Winter melting away? Here the artist must create her own world. Throughout the book symbolic colour is used to create the four seasons of Canada. (pp. 70-1)

Margaret Johnston, Head of Boys and Girls House, Toronto Public Library, mentions . . . that "Elizabeth Cleaver's books have shown new Canadian directions in illustration and are a good indication of what we can hope for in future Canadian picture books." (p. 72)

Nancy D. Herbert, "Elizabeth Cleaver," in Bookbird, *Vol. 11, No. 1 (March 15, 1973), pp. 66-73.*

SHEILA EGOFF

The appearance in the last few years of new and gifted artists and of several books illustrated, with great beauty and distinction, in colour may have signalled the beginning of a productive and distinctive Canadian tradition of book illustration. Elizabeth Cleaver, Laszlo Gal, Ann Blades, William Kurelek, and Frank Newfeld . . . have produced the kind of illustrated books that we hardly dared hope for ten years ago.

In 1968 a colourful breakthrough was made in illustration with ***The Wind Has Wings: Poems from Canada*** illustrated by Elizabeth Cleaver. All Cleaver's art work has a splendid royal magnificence—whether in this poetry anthology or in her Indian-legend picture-books, ***The Mountain Goats of Temlaham*** (1969) and ***How Summer Came to Canada*** (1969), or in ***The Miraculous Hind*** (1973), a Hungarian legend that she both illustrated and retold. Beginning with densely coloured and textured monoprints, she does paper cut-outs and linocuts and assembles them in collages, creating a rich and beautiful style of illustration. In ***The Mountain Goats of Temlaham*** the rhythmic, rippling strips of collage paper capture the mountainous folds of earth and the tactile feel of rock and cliff in British Columbia. The figures of people, animals, and birds are stylized in the totemic silhouette shapes of Indian art; they are frozen and static in a ceremonial, ritualistic sense. This aura of Indian mystery is also present in the linocuts of totem poles and longhouses, which are sombre, black, and dramatic against the white pages. ***How Summer Came to Canada*** is set in the Eastern woodlands, and forest greenery is immediately, tangibly present in the striking use of cedar leaves, ivy, moss, and grass in the collages. However, collage is not everything here: new intricacies of line and brush work are used in the details of snow, costume, loon feathers, and faces. The landscape changes—from north to south, in winter and summer—and receives a sparkling representation in scenes of icy desolation and sunny, flowering splendour. ***The Miraculous Hind,*** in keeping with its lavish theatrical style, was originally prepared as a film strip for the National Film Board, and in spite of the foreign subject matter it has many technical similarities to her previous books. Cleaver's visual imagery, though beautiful, might change with advantage in the future, for we would not like to see her work become monotonous and overfamiliar. . . . Her latest illustrations—a further treatment of Indian subject matter—are attractive linocuts for Cyrus Macmillan's ***Canadian Wonder Tales*** (1974) that show a definite advance on her earlier black-and-white work. They suggest that, given the opportunity, she will continue to grow as an illustrator. (pp. 260-63)

. . . . .

The best examples of picture-book art in Canada can be seen in the work of Elizabeth Cleaver, the young Montreal artist. For ***The Mountain Goats of Temlaham*** . . . and ***How Summer Came to Canada*** . . . William Toye provided satisfying retellings of West Coast (Tsimshian) and East Coast (Micmac) Indian legends. In ***The Miraculous Hind*** . . . Elizabeth Cleaver, herself of Hungarian descent, retold one of the most famous legends of Hungary, that of Hunor and Magyar who helped to form the Hungarian nation. Her collage technique is the same as in her illustrations for ***The Wind Has Wings,*** but in the three legend books the pictures are more illustrative. With the Indian legends Cleaver and Toye have achieved that integration of text and pictures found in all the best picture-books: the stories stand on their own, the pictures tell the stories without the text, yet when used together the two complement each other perfectly. As in her Indian books, Cleaver enriches the theme of ***The Miraculous Hind***—the Hungarian spirit—with details of landscape, customs, and dress. The attention to cultural tone as well as to meticulously researched details of costume is certainly an Elizabeth Cleaver signature: the book is a visual *tour de force*. The placement of the minimal number of lines of text on each page is primarily aesthetic and is only secondarily concerned with ease of reading. A fascination with typographical effect is chiefly seen in the change from a modest modern typeface to bold, decorative cut-out letters on a brightly coloured ground, which disrupts the flow of the story and at times makes the text difficult to read. In the Indian books there is no such dichotomy. (pp. 273-74)

Sheila Egoff, "Illustration and Design" and "Picture-Books and Picture-Storybooks," in her The Republic of Childhood: A Critical Guide to Canadian Children's Literature in English, *second edition, Oxford University Press, Canadian Branch, 1975, pp. 255-70, 271-91.*

PATRICIA MORLEY

Elizabeth Cleaver and William Toye make a great team. Toye's simple but suggestive text touches on pain, fear, humour, bravado, fantasy and joy. Cleaver's paintings remain stamped on the inner eye after one shuts the book's covers. Story and drawings are comfortable together, natural partners.

Cleaver's colours are both bold and subtle, but her textual effects are particularly remarkable. One thinks of the super-realism of contemporary Maritime painters like Pratt and Forrestall. A patch of fur draws the testing finger, irresistibly; surely a bit of fur has been pasted on, here? Birchbark is also rendered super-realistically, with fine detail.

This technique co-exists with the wet-wash effect of traditional watercolour, and with woodcut effects. In ***The Loon's Necklace,*** there is a large owl, and a man's face, close up, in woodcut technique. A night scene of a hut, beautifully stippled, resembles wood covered with moss or lichens, and contrasts dramatically with the flat bright washes on the human figures in the doorway. These visual techniques reinforce the moods created by the narrative.

Both stories have a youthful hero, but ***The Loon's Necklace*** sets both old and young in heroic roles. A young boy helps his blind father to kill a bear, but is unable to deal with the sinister malevolence of a hag who forbids him to tell his father the good news. The magical intervention of a loon (aided by the father's will to *trust* and to *try*) restores the man's sight. The loon is rewarded by a necklace whose shells become the bird's beautiful white markings. The hag, defeated, becomes an owl, to annoy the family by screeching. Her cloak, covered with totemic markings, contrasts with the family's plain robes and adds a note of awe, even terror, to a story with a happy ending.

The Fire Stealer is the story of a young Indian boy who steals fire to aid and comfort his people. Magical elements, including the boy's ability to take what shape he chooses, will delight young readers. The book has the feeling of fire throughout, starting with its frontispiece, a fiery red-orange finely veined with yellow. Autumn foliage reflects the fire's colours and reminds the youth of his triumph. (pp. 134-35)

Cleaver's rich and beautiful collages have justly earned her work many prizes. (p. 135)

Patricia Morley "The Delights of Texture: Cleaver's Colourful Mixed-Media Effects," in Canadian Children's Literature: A Journal of Criticism and Review, *Nos. 15 & 16, 1980, pp. 134-35.*

JON C. STOTT

There is no doubt about it! Elizabeth Cleaver and Ann Blades are Canada's foremost illustrators of children's books, and each has a long list of awards and prizes to prove it. . . .

Both artists have easily recognizable styles; however each uses her style differently for each book, making the artwork the appropriate vehicle for tone, theme, and characterization. Elizabeth Cleaver uses the technique of collage as well as any illustrator alive today; it has been the medium by which she has illustrated traditional European stories and Native Canadian legends. ***The Fire Stealer*** is the fourth in a series of retellings of Native legends, the earlier works having been ***The Mountain Goats of Temlaham, The Loon's Necklace,*** and ***How Summer Came to Canada. The Fire Stealer*** is a story about Nanabozho, the Central Woodlands trickster-hero. To provide warmth for his ailing grandmother, he steals fire; to give his people something to remember him by, he tinges the leaves of the maples red with his fire stick. Every autumn, when we see the leaves we can remember him.

Unfortunately, William Toye's simplified text is somewhat limping and awkward. However, Cleaver's collages are as good as any she did for the earlier retellings. Using such natural materials as birch bark, she gives a sense of the terrain and the dwellings. This is most appropriate for a story which is, in effect, a study of a people's relationship to their environment.

In retelling the story ***Petrouchka,*** Igor Stravinsky's famous ballet, Cleaver has combined lino-cuts with collage. The story of a clown-puppet who falls in love with a beautiful ballerina, but who dies a tragic death, ***Petrouchka*** presents a major challenge for any illustrator: not only must costumes and settings be accurate, but also, the many moods of the tale must be communicated. Cleaver has succeeded extremely well on both counts. As was the case in her award-winning ***The Miraculous Hind,*** she has carefully researched customs and costumes. A variety of background colors depict the passion, violence, and sadness of the story. Moreover, the stylized quality of the linocuts parallels the stylization one would expect to find in a puppet theatre or ballet.

Jon C. Stott in a review of "Petrouchka," in The World of Children's Books, *Vol. VI, 1981, p. 28.*

PERRY NODELMAN

Elizabeth Cleaver has illustrated quite different materials: her own retelling of the Hungarian legend ***The miraculous hind;*** the folk tales of French Canada adapted by Mary Alice Downie in ***The witch of the north;*** the many different poems of ***The wind has wings,*** an anthology compiled by Downie and Barbara Robertson; and most notably, four picture books of Indian legends retold by William Toye. But her pictures are always recognizably hers. They are always collages that combine drawn images and found objects, and they all use startlingly bright colours, made all the more startling because the collage technique makes separations between figures and ground so abrupt. Cleaver's backgrounds tend to be subtly textured, her figures solid patches of less textured colour that seem relatively flat and unmoving. The intense energy of her pictures comes, not from their accurate depiction of action or even of mobile faces, but from their surprising discontinuities.

While Cleaver's work is especially consistent in the four picture books containing William Toye's retellings of Indian legends, those legends come from three quite different cultures. The publishers identify ***How summer came to Canada*** as Micmac, ***The fire stealer*** as Ojibway, and ***The mountain goats of Temlaham*** and ***The loon's necklace*** as Tsimshian. But the Tsimshian of the West Coast were a tightly organized society with complex clan relationships, while the Ojibway of the north shore of Lake Superior spent much of their time apart from each other in separate hunting territories. Not surprisingly, traditional Tsimshian culture emphasized status and lineage; the more solitary Ojibway focussed on the difficulties of living in an often hostile world. Surely Cleaver's illustrations misrepresent stories from such different sources by evoking much the same mood.

But misrepresentation might be inevitable. The problem begins before illustrations, in the old controversy about how culture-bound Native American materials might be and about how successfully they might be evoked for those of us immersed in the values of contemporary Euro-American culture. According to Ruth Landes, "in the world view provided by Ojibwa religion and magic, there is neither stick nor stone that is not animate and charged with potential hostility to man, no accident that is accidental or free of personalized intent, nor one human creature to be taken for granted." In such a world, Nanabozho's theft of fire, retold in ***The fire stealer,*** is not just a more commonplace, more expectable event than it might appear to be when understood by the values I take for granted, but also, as the act of a *real* superhuman being, a more significant one. Among the Tsimshian, meanwhile, the mistreatment of animals described in ***The mountain goats of Temlaham*** is not merely a violation of the sentimental concern we like to feel nowadays for those we think of as needing our protection, but a serious crime both against beings greater than mere men and against the communal food supply.

In *Once more upon a totem,* Christie Harris offers paradoxical advice to those who want to retell such stories: they "must change the old text sufficiently to make it really come to life for people who do not know the region, the old culture or the ways behind the action. Yet they must keep the new text deeply true to the old story." She does not explain how both are possible; and she goes on to offer illustrators the same paradoxical guidelines, saying that storytellers "need illustrators as dedicated as themselves to depicting the culture authentically." The difficulty of both being authentic and being an illustrator who "depicts" a culture different from one's own becomes clear in Douglas Tait's pictures for the Northwest Coast legends in *Once more upon a totem.* While Tait uses the imagery of Northwest Coast Native art, he manipulates it according to the conventions of Euro-American art. He overlaps the traditional figures as they never overlapped in traditional art; and he provides them with backgrounds, so that they become representational figures in scenes with the depth of perspective. As these symbolic representations "come to life"—as life is understood to be represented in Euro-American representational art—they turn into rather silly-looking cartoons.

Shelia Egoff suggests that Cleaver's illustrations for ***The mountain goats of Temlaham,*** a legend from the same Northwest Coast area, *are* authentic: "The figures of people, animals and birds are stylized in the totemic silhouette shapes of Indian art; they are frozen and static in a ceremonial, ritualistic sense. This aura of Indian mystery is also present in the linocuts of totem poles and long-houses, which are sombre, black and dramatic against the white pages" [see excerpt dated 1975]. Now, while books on primitive art frequently show the images of Northwest Coast art as black figures on white grounds, no such images appear in ***Mountain goats.*** Perhaps Egoff's faith in Cleaver's authenticity let her see something that isn't there. In fact, the vibrant background colours of ***Mountain goats*** are a good part of what makes Cleaver's pictures seem so unlike Native art; Northwest Coast art used only black, yellow, a brownish red, and rarely, blue green. Furthermore, Cleaver's pictures for ***How summer came to Canada*** are similarly vibrant, whereas the Micmac originally had dyes only for red, white, black, and yellow, and words for no other colours; and while the Ojibwa favoured red, yellow, green, blue and brown, they certainly didn't favour the intense values of those colours found in ***The fire stealer.***

In any case, Cleaver's pictures are inauthentic simply because they are representational. The people who produced these legends had little representational visual art. Since the Micmacs who told ***How summer came to Canada*** have been in contact with European civilization for 450 years, it's hard to tell what their original culture may have been like; but the objects our own prejudices cause us to recognize as art among their artifacts are mainly decorative. Even the floral patterns of "authentic" beadwork sold as tourist souvenirs are European in origin. It seems that French nuns taught the Natives how to do the beadwork, and the Micmacs originally favored geometric patterns, particularly the double curve found in native artifacts from across Eastern Canada. The presence of that curve on Summer's cap in Cleaver's picture of her is the only thing in ***How summer came to Canada*** that could be safely identified as Micmac. Even then, the Carmen Miranda flowers on top of the hat rather spoil the authenticity.

While what we identify as authentic Northwest Coast art was influenced by such things as the availability of European adzes and ideas, it is clearly unlike Euro-American art. It contains black formlines in curves surrounding unpainted spaces, strong bilateral symmetry, and the use of eye-shapes at joints representing, for instance, knees and elbows. Representations always fill the space available, so there is a strong sense of pattern. Also, this art is exclusively interested in human, superhuman, and animal subjects, depicted symbolically and always shown complete; no landscape or vegetation appears, and no heads are shown separated from bodies. The meaning of these figures is implied by small details: a beaver by large incisors, a hawk by a curved beak turning inward at the bottom. Except for these distinguishing details, figures might look much like each other; and because joints contain eye-shapes, it is sometimes hard to determine which parts of the highly patterned fields are heads, and which are bodies.

In Cleaver's illustrations for ***Mountain goats*** and ***The loon's necklace,*** people and animals are represented, not by conventional details, but by what conventionally represents figures in Euro-American art: their outlines. There are no formlines, and no excess eyes. Perhaps most significantly, Cleaver's figures have a ground; they have depth and occupy space. The pictures have clearly defined tops and bottoms; we understand that incomplete trees and bodies continue past the edge that cuts them off, and that smaller things and things closer to the top are further back in the space depicted.

Nevertheless, the totem pole on the title page of ***Mountain goats*** accurately represents one originally used as a ceremonial entrance to the Tsimshian village of Kitwancool; appropriately, the hole was called "place-of-opening." The village pole on the cover and on page three seems to be modelled on one depicted in a photograph taken in 1909 and reproduced in Garfield and Wingert's *Tsimshian arts,* even though Cleaver's imaginary village contains traditional Tsimshian lodges, while the photograph, disappointingly, shows European cabins. The hunters of page four wear traditional wood hats, the one on page six a chief's ceremonial head-dress that seems out of place on a hunting expedition. But the use of authentic chilkat robes during the ceremony later in the book is accurate; and so is the background of the pictures depicting that ceremony, a rendering of a painted wooden screen of the sort used in Tsimshian dancing society performances. (pp. 69-72)

In ***Mountain goats,*** then, Cleaver uses the conventions of Euro-American representational art to depict people using the objects of Tsimshian art. Her pictures imply a detached point of view that prevents involvement. Like viewers of a travelogue about people with customs different from our own, we *observe* these people and comment on how interesting their artifacts and customs are.

While the Ojibway had little we would recognize as representational art, Cleaver acknowledges the culture of ***The fire stealer*** by including representations of some of the mysterious rock paintings found throughout Ojibway territory. The rock in the background of the first page of the story contains, on the left, a set of images found eighty miles north of Red Lake in the Lake Winnipeg watershed that may depict a shaman, a porcupine, and a canoe; and on the right, a moose found at Lac La-Croix, west and south of Quetico Park. No one knows who made any of these rock paintings, so there's no way of knowing if these images are relevant to ***The fire stealer.*** I suspect Cleaver chose these particular images merely because they are clearer than many of the other rock paintings.

Selwyn Dewdney, who found many of the rock paintings, suggests that their imagery is similar to the pictographic symbols used to set down the secret rituals of the Midiwiwin, the Ojibway secret society. The secrecy of these images makes them highly incommunicative. . . . Similar mystery surrounds the images of Tsimshian art, the patterns of which become so complicated that even different Tsimshian people interpret some of them differently.

Since totem poles and birchbark scrolls were primarily means of communicating information visually and were only secondarily meant to be aesthetically pleasing, we might assume a similarity between these objects and picture books: both tell stories by visual means, both have the practical purpose of expressing information. But the ambiguities of both Ojibway pictographs and Tsimshian symbols suggest that the primary function of visual images in these cultures was not communication. Intensely preoccupied with the legendary history of their ancestors as a means of defining social position, the Tsimshian used art "to illustrate the actors and incidents (of that history) so that they would be readily recognized by observers familiar with the tales." Unlike Cleaver's pictures, these pictures are meant to remind initiates of what they already know, not inform newcomers about what is unfamiliar to them. (p. 72)

In *The voices of silence,* André Malraux sums up a significant difference between primitive art and illustration: "like the Byzantine artists, these artists might be described as manufacturers of the numinous—but the numinous object is manufactured only for people who can put it to appropriate use."

Given its numinous purpose, North American Native art was not much interested in depicting the way things look. Franz Boas compares the conventional imagery of most Northwest Coast art with the realism of a head made to be used in a ceremony depicting decapitation. That they could make such representations but usually chose not to suggests that their art was more symbolic than illustrative—that what an image represented was meaning and not appearance; it's not surprising that they should have reduced the appearances of animals to assemblies of disconnected elements, or that their art emphasizes symmetry of pattern over verisimilitude.

But picture book illustration is a representational art, almost singlemindedly concerned with the way things look. The assumptions behind picture books are ones common in Euro-American culture: that differences in specifics like place and time influence both the characters of people and the meaning of events; that surface appearances therefore help to make people and events what they are by creating differences that matter; that such differences are noteworthy enough to be recorded; that they are noteworthy not just because surface appearances create feelings and attitudes but because they also *mirror* interior feelings and attitudes; and that therefore, the way things look is highly evocative of what they mean. In Cleaver's books as in most picture books, we see both how the characters look and where they act. The figures occupy space because we believe that people are significantly influenced and explained by the spaces they occupy. As we look at Cleaver's pictures, we stand outside and apart from her characters; and we understand how the appearances of places and people explain the events occurring to those people in that place. In other words, if these images are symbolic it is a symbolism that demands a relationship between appearance and meaning. The Tsimshian people who knew the conventional imagery representing a mountain goat could identify a symbolic mountain goat in a confusing field of disconnected symmetrical patterns; but Euro-Americans, trained to identify objects by standing back and

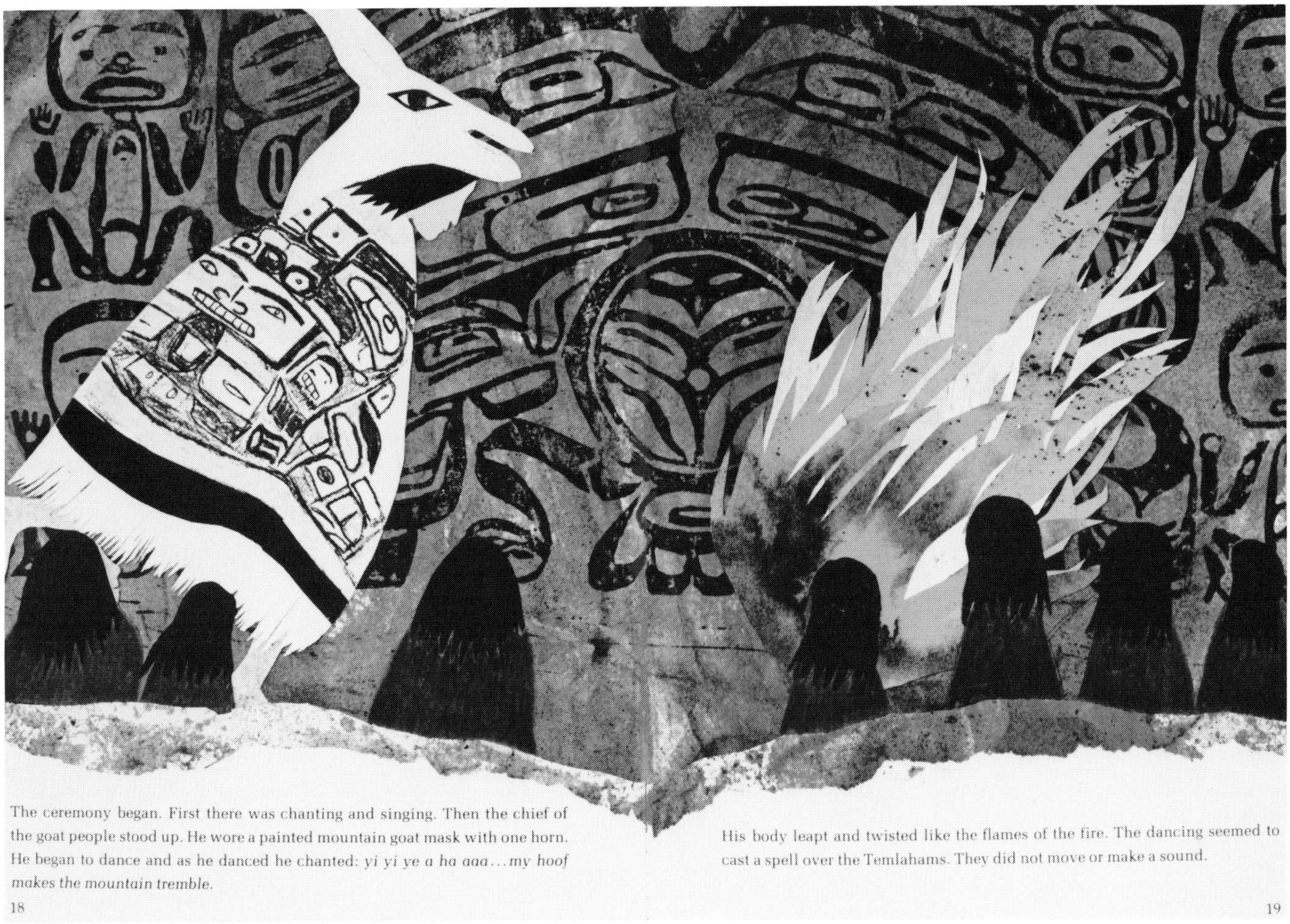
The ceremony began. First there was chanting and singing. Then the chief of the goat people stood up. He wore a painted mountain goat mask with one horn. He began to dance and as he danced he chanted: *yi yi ye a ha aaa... my hoof makes the mountain tremble.*
18
His body leapt and twisted like the flames of the fire. The dancing seemed to cast a spell over the Temlahams. They did not move or make a sound.
19

From The Mountain Goats of Temlaham, *retold by William Toye. Pictures by Elizabeth Cleaver. Oxford University Press, Canadian Branch, 1969. © Oxford University Press (Canadian Branch) 1969. Reproduced by permission of the publisher.*

perceiving their outlines, can recognize Cleaver's mountain goat because it has the outline of a mountain goat.

While Egoff's comment that Cleaver's animals and people in ***Mountain goats*** are "stylized in the totemic silhouette shapes of Indian art" is wrong, it is suggestive. For while the qualities Egoff finds in Cleaver's work are not Native, they are certainly ones we identify with the art we call primitive: it is stylized, static, and mysterious. . . . Cleaver's pictures are intensely expressive, clear in structure, and simple in technique. Her work is "primitive" in the way a Matisse is primitive, not the way Tsimshian art is primitive. In fact, her imagery is frequently reminiscent of Matisse. Her picture of the Fairies of Light and Sunshine and Flowers dancing around their queen Summer in ***How summer came to Canada*** is clearly modelled on Matisse's *The dance;* the figures form the same grouping, and Summer's face could have been drawn by Matisse. Ironically, Cleaver evokes the primitive for those of us familiar with Euro-American culture by evoking a by now traditional art of our own culture that tried to evoke primitive art.

In some ways, Cleaver's work does evoke the Native cultures of the legends it depicts. But it does so in terms meaningful within Euro-American culture. For instance, for the Ojibway, birchbark was charged with significance, not just as the material of cooking vessels and wigwam coverings, but also of the scrolls used in the sacred rites of the Midiwiwin. Cleaver's use of real birchbark in the collages of ***The fire stealer*** evokes Ojibway culture; it also evokes Nanabozho the fire stealer himself, for another legend credits him with giving the birchbark its marks in a fit of anger. But Cleaver evokes these things with a technique quite alien to Ojibway culture, or for that matter, to any culture not equipped with scissors and glue. Furthermore, the same pictures contain artifacts made of real birchbark and drawn birchbark on the drawn trees; Cleaver implies a distinction between the natural material and human uses of it that would have made little sense in traditional Ojibway culture.

Similarly, all four of Cleaver's Indian books suggest the basic cosmology of many Native North American cultures, the idea that the world consists of a series of interacting layers of what we would call physical and spiritual reality; for the Eskimo, Beaver, Sioux, Hopi, Tewa, and others, the world beyond what we ordinarily perceive "is above and below the horizontal plane of our everyday world." Cleaver suggests that by showing people moving against a background of quite untraditional coloured layers. While horizontal layering is common in Euro-American landscape painting, Cleaver's simplified layers seem symbolic; so her pictures refer to two different traditions but represent neither. In fact, the use of layered colours and layered landscapes on the title pages and on the last pages of all four books suggests how significant a part landscape plays in Cleaver's interpretation of these legends.

The focus on setting in ***How summer came to Canada*** is logical; the story is about the seasons and masterfully evokes the way different things look differently at different times of the year. Surrounded by huge symbolic snowflakes and simplified representations of snow-covered bushes against rich layers of bluish green and reddish purple, Cleaver's stiff figure of Glooskap almost disappears. He is too static to compete with his energetic setting.

More significantly, Cleaver's Winter and Summer are not actual beings whose presence is acknowledged by meteorological changes; they are personifications of the facts of meteorology, extensions of the landscape rather than the landscape being extensions of them. When Winter first appears, his blue torso does actually extend from a bluish-green background, and while he looms gigantically against the red and orange sky in Glooskap's dream, his blue-green colour still makes him part of the background. On the next page, Cleaver shows Winter's defeat as the triumph of background over figure, as his diminished form almost disappears in abstract layers of the same red and orange and blue-green. Summer is also an extension of the landscape. When she first appears her robe is the yellow of the sky above her; later, when she stands out against the blues and whites of winter, her yellow robe is echoed by a yellow sun not present in earlier winter pictures.

The subtle detail of the actual foliage Cleaver includes in these pictures draws attention because it is so different from the boldly outlined shapes of the drawn objects, and it confirms the focus on natural landscape. The winter pictures emphasize the actual bits of cedar rather than the drawn rabbits and wigwams; and when Cleaver wants us to pay attention to Glooskap, she puts him in a landscape containing no actual foliage but with actual leaves on his head.

The pictures of Glooskap's dream contain no actual foliage; actual grass appears only as Glooskap and Summer leave her home, and it acts like a barrier they must pass through before they can enter the world containing actual cedar on the next page. It seems that both Glooskap's dream and Summer's home are places of the imagination, places that affect reality but are not themselves quite real; Cleaver's use of actual foliage implies a distinction between the mundane and the imagined, a distinction that explains the relationship between the layers of the title page, of Glooskap's dream, and of the last page. The title page is an abstract layering of pretty but meaningless colours; the last page shows a landscape built on the same layers of colour in the same order, and containing actual cedar. The abstract has become representational, just as, perhaps, the myth has affected reality, and Summer and Winter have become imaginative explanations of summer and winter. The dream, which shows the same colours in a disorderly jangle and the shapes of both landscape elements and supernatural beings but no actual foliage, may represent the transition; dreams are where reality meets imagination.

The last page of ***Mountain goats*** duplicates the layers of the last page of ***How summer came to Canada.*** But this time the landscape contains people, and Cleaver's focus in this book is on people rather than backgrounds; specifically, on the relationships of natural and conventional behaviour, as represented by the differences between Cleaver's personal style and the Tsimshian artifacts she depicts, and by careful use of pictorial dynamics.

The orange sky seen through the totem pole on the title page is echoed on the next page both by the village and by the large totem that divides the picture. The orange of totem and village interrupts the natural green of the landscape; its connection with the heavens implies a preoccupation with rituals that evoke the supernatural and ignore physical reality. Not surprisingly, the totem separates the village from the naturalistically outlined goats. On the next page, the goats disappear in a collage of disorderly natural forms as they run from the hunters. While the hunters have moved into this relative chaos past the restraining rigidity of the totem on the left, they bring its influence with them in the embroidery on their garments. But the conventionalized bird of the totem is muted in comparison to the heavy black outline of the real raven beside it; and the black of that destructive raven is echoed by the hunter's dog and by their spears. The picture implies a natural bloodlust emerging from cultural conventions that condone it.

As the allowable violence of hunting gives way to the chaos of needless torment, the pictures contain no Tsimshian elements, no restraining borders, no layers; just chaotic shapes. But when the boy helps the goats, he does so in a world returned to the order of layering, and within a framework of natural trees on the left and a ritual totem on the right; both suggest order, and both represent forces beyond the merely human and merely anarchic.

The four strangers who appear on the next page combine these natural and supernatural forces. They move out of the trees, spirits of the wild come to avenge unnatural human behavior; and their ritual robes contain naturalistic goat outlines. They represent a balance lost by the villagers, who use supernatural ritual to condone unnatural violence. While the villagers wear ritual garb as they move past the protection of their totem into the strangers' territory, the totem has come to represent what is *not* supernatural about them; no longer orange, it has become the green the earth was before. The sky is no longer orange either, but the purple of the stranger's garments; the balance has shifted.

In the central sequence of the book, the action takes place against a ritual screen, in a territory divorced both from ordinary reality and the truly supernatural—just as a church is neither of earth or of heaven but connects the two. The only unritualized portions of these pictures are the goat headdresses of the chief and the asymmetrical fire his dancing is compared to; paradoxically, the supernatural breaks through convention by taking on naturally organic or anarchic forms. Cleaver uses collage to good effect as the ceremony reaches its climax; the screen is literally torn apart as supernatural forces emerge from the ritual patterns that evoke them.

In the next picture, the totem once more implies a restraining safety; it saves the boy who clings to it, while those who misused ritual to condone violence fall past it to their violent deaths. As the boy himself plunges down the mountain in his own supernaturally sanctioned defiance of the natural, backgrounds and border disappear as they did earlier in the scenes of violence; and as he returns to safety, he does so against a landscape returned to layers and borders. The village totem on the left separates the boy from the goats, and another totem on the right separates him from the village he heads toward. He occupies a space between goats and village, between the natural/supernatural and the human; a space defined by ritual objects. The village totem has itself achieved balance in this balanced picture; it is the colour of neither sky nor of earth, but a mixture of both. The last picture echoes that balancing of natural and supernatural, as the boy preaches good sense to his people in an orderly, layered landscape, his robe embroidered with the naturalistically outlined goat that has come to represent the supernatural strangers.

In ***Mountain goats,*** Cleaver uses conventions quite alien to Tsimshian art to depict Tsimshian artifacts. While her pictures for ***The loon's necklace*** have few Tsimshian elements, they do convey some of the feeling of Tsimshian art. Only one totem pole appears, and it doesn't stand out as do the totems in ***Mountain goats*** because the totem, the trees, and the people are all drawn with the same heavy black lines against solid grounds. These heavy black lines, used throughout the book, are not quite formlines, but they are enough like them to provide a consistent Tsimshian feeling. That consistency involves even the old hag and her robe; her face and her robe are both the same colour, and the face embroidered on her robe looks much like her own, something Cleaver uses to advantage when she shows the hag from behind, so that the demonic embroidered face replaces her real one.

As in Cleaver's other books, the characters in ***The loon's necklace*** are static single-coloured shapes that interrupt layered landscapes. But since the landscapes and figures are drawn similarly, and since the colours are quieter, the energy of these pictures derives less from startling contrasts than from a consistent point of view. Almost every picture shows the characters moving through similar landscapes as seen from a similar distance; even when there is a close-up of the old man, he appears against a background consistent in scale with the others in the book, so that he seems to come closer and the background remains the same distance away. As in the theatre, the action seems to unfold within settings. Only four of the openings show two scenes rather than just one, and even these are composed to form one picture; the setting continues across both pages even though we see the same characters twice. For instance, the old man dives with the loon on one opening that shows the two characters twice. The four figures form a semicircle that swoops down and up again; the loon's beak pointing the way. That sort of implied action confirms the sense of theatre; it's like watching actors move against a fixed backdrop. These pictures seem to comment on the story less than the pictures in the earlier books; but they combine the conventions of Tsimshian art and Euro-American techniques of visual storytelling, particularly those derived from stagecraft, to tell a Tsimshian story in Euro-American terms. They are less an interpretation of the story than a translation of it into the idioms of another culture—the closest Cleaver comes to the ideal Christie Harris suggested.

While the pictures in ***The fire stealer*** are similar to those in ***The loon's necklace,*** Cleaver once more makes a distinction between figures and background. Devoid of heavy black lines and carefully textured, the backgrounds seem quite representational; drawn in the same style as both people and trees in ***The loon's necklace,*** the people seem like unmoving intrusions in a mutable world. Perhaps they evoke a traditional Ojibway alienation from a hostile environment; these people do not seem to belong in these landscapes. Nor do their artifacts, the things made out of actual birchbark.

But one element of landscape is depicted similarly to the people: birch trees. That's probably inevitable in the pictures which show Nanabozho turning into a birch; but birches have heavy black lines throughout the book. Birches do have black lines, of course; but Cleaver uses that fact of nature to imply the symbolic connections between her hero and birches. She uses actual birchbark in the same way. In ***The fire stealer,*** people, birches, and the things people make from birch all stand out in a way that draws attention to their connections with each other.

The fire stealer returns to the colour dynamics of Cleaver's earlier books. The first opening shows a world without reds, the closest being the red-orange of the rock in the background. Red is the colour of fire, of course; but Cleaver makes the people who sit by fires and are warmed by them red also. Outside her father's wigwam, the girl is brown; inside she is reddish brown. Later, Nanabozho's people are the reddish orange of the forest fire he started; and on the last page, a typical layered landscape repeats the layers of the first page, except that, now that fire has entered the world, fire colours in rocks and trees interrupt the layers. This picture adds fire to the landscape, just as the last picture in ***Mountain goats*** added people and the last picture in ***How summer came to Canada*** added landscape to mere abstract layers. Not surprisingly, the last page of ***The loon's necklace,*** Cleaver's most internally consistent book, merely echoes the layers of the first page, but from a slightly different point of view; we look up at a flying loon instead of down at a floating one.

All four of these books are subtle and highly personal statements about the legends they contain. Cleaver uses the visual conventions of Euro-American art to evoke something like the feeling of the Native materials she illustrates; at least, something like that feeling for those of us familiar with the conventions of Euro-American art. These books succeed not because they are in any way authentic, but because they show a mastery of techniques quite alien to Native art. (pp. 73-8)

Perry Nodelman, "Non-Native Primitive Art: Elizabeth Cleaver's Indian Legends," in Canadian Children's Literature: A Journal of Criticism and Review, *Nos. 31 & 32, 1983, pp. 69-79.*

WILLIAM TOYE

After absorbing shock and sadness at the death . . . of Elizabeth Cleaver at the age of 45, I turned to her books, renewing my pleasure in them and appreciating her accomplishment. Elizabeth's use of the collage technique introduced something quite new into the illustration of Canadian children's books. Creating forms and backgrounds from brilliantly coloured and densely textured monoprints, and childlike figures from linocuts; sometimes using real materials (grass, birch-bark, evergreen branches, fur, pearls); and controlling all these elements with an intuitive sense of design—she brought to the texts she illustrated what is most wanted in picture-books for children: a colourful world of visual delight and imaginative suggestion.

In a profile of her published in the June 1985 issue of [*Quill & Quire*], she described our meeting in November 1967. Towards the end of that year she underwent surgery for cancer. In early January she phoned me from the hospital to ask if the book I had mentioned that she might illustrate—which developed into ***The Wind Has Wings*** (1968)—was still a possibility. I assured her it was. Much later she told me she had prayed that if she were spared she would devote her life to making beautiful books for children. This goal remained constant and paramount in the 17 years that remained to her, and resulted in 13 books, three of which she wrote.

Our collaboration on many of them enabled me to observe admiringly both her character and her creativity as she engaged in the difficult process of bringing a book to life. Her pictures were not achieved easily, but she knew that in time everything—elements, colour, design—would come together and be clearly right. Rejoicing briefly when that point was reached in one picture, she would then press on to the next, summoning amazing reserves of energy and determination that carried her over all discouragements. When the illustrations lay in sequence on her living-room floor, her joy and pride were wonderful to behold. This was her greatest moment. Her work then entered the production process, every detail of which she participated in. Later, whe she held the finished book in her hands, she was detached and quiet. It was a gift she had made for children, what she was here to do, and she knew she had done it well.

I was greatly privileged to be associated with Elizabeth—both professionally and as a friend—in this highly creative period of her life. I think now particularly of the unusually productive last year and a half, when we worked so happily on ***The New Wind Has Wings,*** her ***ABC,*** and ***The Enchanted Caribou.*** Her wish to be remembered by these and all her other books will surely be fulfilled.

William Toye, "Elizabeth Cleaver," in Quill and Quire, *Vol. 51, No. 10, October, 1985, p. 21.*

***THE WIND HAS WINGS: POEMS FROM CANADA* (1968)**

[The Wind Has Wings *was compiled by Mary Alice Downie and Barbara Robertson.*]

On dull winter days and all year round, young library patrons will enjoy reading from and looking through this latest anthology of Canadian verse.

The compilers have chosen 77 poems ranging from modern verse and nonsense rhymes to Eskimo chants and French Canadian folksongs. . . .

Selections cover a variety of topics—animals; people, real and imaginary; and nature. . . .

Illustrator Elizabeth Cleaver has done an admirable job of integrating text and drawings with the result the book is an indivisible literary and artistic unit. The illustrations which imaginatively combine a variety of techniques are bold and dramatic. Colors appear richer, more dazzling and striking when juxtaposed with the stark black and white used in the wood cuts.

Though recommended for children 8 to 12 years of age, ***The Wind Has Wings*** with its intrinsic charm and beauty, will undoubtedly appeal to a wider reading audience.

Barrie Kullman, in a review of "The Wind Has Wings: Poems from Canada," in In Review: Canadian Books for Children, *Vol. 3, No. 1, Winter, 1969, p. 23.*

[***The Wind has Wings*** is designed] to be visually enjoyed; the strongly pictured pages are always exciting and sometimes ravishing; indeed, the black-and-white woodcut effects seem no less vivid than the pages in glowing colour.

"Personal Pleasures," in The Times Literary Supplement, *No. 3501, April 3, 1969, p. 353.*

This book is an unusual event in children's publishing. It presents a lively selection of 77 Canadian poems that 8 to 12 year

From The Wind Has Wings: Poems from Canada, *compiled by Mary Alice Downie and Barbara Robertson. Illustrated by Elizabeth Cleaver. Henry Z. Walck, Inc., 1968. © Oxford University Press (Canadian Branch) 1968. Reproduced by permission of the Literary Estate of Elizabeth Cleaver.*

olds will enjoy. . . . [All are placed] in a setting of brilliant and colourful illustrations. ***The Wind Has Wings*** is in the best tradition of illustrated children's books. Children will find it irresistible and its exceptional qualities will not be lost on adults who will also want to own and to read it.

A review of "The Wind Has Wings," in Bookbird, *Vol. IX, No. 3 (September 15, 1971), p. 45.*

The unrivalled anthology of Canadian poetry selected for children is ***The Wind Has Wings***. . . . Compilers Mary Alice Downie and Barbara Robertson along with the award-winning illustrator Elizabeth Cleaver have succeeded in arranging and presenting a thoughtful collection that allows the poems to speak for themselves.

Their judicious sampling of nineteenth- and twentieth-century Canadian poetry, and Cleaver's splendid linocut and collage art, account for the book's outdistancing of more recent collections like Louis Dudek's *all kinds of everything* (Clarke, Irwin, 1973) and Fran Newman's *Round Slice of Moon* (Scholastic, 1980). . . . In contrast to [Dudek's and Newman's] often ponderous mood and didactic zeal stands the colourful and unencumbered ***The Wind Has Wings.*** With nothing fussy or pedantic about it this collection skillfully upholds the delicate aerial wisps of wonder that its title, excerpted from an Inuit chant, leads the reader to expect. The book's excellence has been recognized not only by the Canadian Association of Children's Librarians' prize of the Amelia Howard-Gibbon Award for Illustration, in 1971, but also by the critical doyenne of Canadian children's literature, Sheila Egoff, who has praised ***The Wind Has Wings*** as "a welcome and celebratory riot of colour" and called it "the first really impressive illustrated book to be published in Canada." (p. 60)

[Each] page of ***The Wind Has Wings*** presents new subjects and moods, both usually animated by unmannered and varied art work. . . .

All of the selections take their lead from A. M. Klein's wish expressed in **"Orders,"** which opens the book:

Let me sit silent
Let me wonder.

Cleaver's illustration for this eight-line poem consists of a spattering of different shades of green across a double-page layout, a sharply defined tree on each side with vivid coral blooms, and, stretched under one tree, a relaxed child figure done in ochre hues. Engaging without being overworked, its expert design prepares the reader for a collection of uniformly fine craftsmanship complementing an imaginative choice of texts. By the end of the book and the appearance of the last Klein poem, **"Psalm of the Fruitful Field,"** the compilers have not forgotten the title's claim and the first order. The psalm asserts that "field and meadowland / Can teach a lad that there are things / That set upon his shoulders wings." The collage reinforces this theme—through its waves of sea-green grass dotted with violet, pink, and golden flowers, blue wash depicting mountains, sky, and birds, and a brilliantly non-geometrical sun.

The harmonious marriage of text and picture makes ***The Wind Has Wings*** a remarkable achievement. Just as Downie and Robertson have roamed widely in choosing and placing their texts, Cleaver has responded instinctively to the poems' images. She has described her collage art as "a form of visual play," an opportunity to "exploit the accidental," which, in this project, enables the poems to be both "discovered and revealed" [see excerpt in Author's Commentary]. The elephant, for instance, that she has created as part of the collage for Bliss Carman's **"The Ships of Yule"** is an unmenacing, potato-skinned pachyderm. Fitting this catalogue of a young boy's exotic fantasies—"with elephants and ivory, . . . with figs and dates from Samarcand . . . and scented silver amulets"—the jungle animal is scaled down to manageable, almost domestic size. The lumbering grey-brown presence that occupies a whole page opposite David McFadden's **"Elephant,"** by contrast, visualizes and retains the mysteriousness of the poet's observation, "His prisonwall-thick flesh / encloses living blood." Frequently Cleaver's art performs double and triple duty. When her aquamarine tints and human shapes are spread over two pages, they serve both W. W. E. Ross' evocation of an underwater world with "the undulating / Fronds of weeds," in **"The Diver,"** and Roy Daniells' tribute to a scorned and arthritic old survivor, in **"Noah."** Textured and coloured pages illumine the poets' words with a magical clarity. Through the turquoise structures of a single collage, A. B. Demille's **"The Ice King"** and C. G. D. Roberts' **"Ice"** freeze together, "irised with memories of flowers and grass." In a similar artistic partnership, Cleaver's texturing of blue and green collages intensifies the sharply individualized character of each of the bodies of water in James Reaney's **"The Great Lakes Suite."** . . .

Sometimes [the compilers] rely on black-and-white linocuts to accompany poems. A particular favorite is the linocut of a child safely nestled in bed, vivifying Raymond Souster's central image of "the four-poster of a dream" (**"All Animals Like Me"**). Significantly, the quilt covering Cleaver's four-poster is patterned with motifs of wingspread birds—another instance of the successful intermingling of visual and verbal images in this highly recommendable anthology. (p. 61)

Patricia Demers, "The Place of Poetry: Poems from Canada," edited by Alethea Helbig, in Children's Literature Association Quarterly, *Vol. 7, No. 3, Fall, 1982, pp. 60-1.*

HOW SUMMER CAME TO CANADA **(1969)**

[How Summer Came to Canada *was retold by William Toye.*]

It is unlikely that a Micmac legend has been revived in more charming fashion than has this story of the seasons. . . . Elizabeth Cleaver's illustrations are as fine as one would expect from her related works, ***The Wind has Wings: Poems from Canada*** and ***The Mountain Goats of Temlaham.***

How Summer Came to Canada has an appeal for all age groups. The text is brief, simple and full of colour, a fine modern reflection of Anglo-Saxon style. The mythology is informative and an invitation to further study. Children will delight in the pictures' tasteful hues and their blendings and appositions. They will appreciate the individuality of the anthropomorphic figures of the god Glooskap, the giant Winter, and the queen Summer. This book will gain at once a position of primacy in libraries and on the child's (and adult's) shelves at home. (pp. 34-5)

Helen M. Pace, in a review of "How Summer Came to Canada," in In Review: Canadian Books for Children, *Vol. 4, No. 2, Spring, 1970, pp. 34-5.*

Astonishingly beautiful pictures by Cleaver persuade the reader to linger on the double spreads in an irresistible book. She uses a variety of media—fiery colored torn paper, spattered watercolors, paints in icy whites and chilly blues as well—all appropriate to continual happenings.

A review of "How Summer Came to Canada," in Publishers Weekly, *Vol. 215, No. 9, February 26, 1979, p. 184.*

Cleaver's tissuey primitivist collages, in splashy colors and a jumble of media (speckled paint, torn paper, cedar leaves), decorate this Canadian Indian tale about the origin of winter and summer. . . . As in ***The Loon's Necklace*** (1977), . . . Cleaver's breathtaking effects are shallow and showy.

A review of "How Summer Came to Canada," in Kirkus Reviews, *Vol. 47, No. 6, March 15, 1979, p. 327.*

THE MOUNTAIN GOATS OF TEMLAHAM **(1969)**

[The Mountain Goats of Temlaham *was retold by William Toye.*]

A simple and direct re-telling of a legend of the Tsimshian Indians of British Columbia with colourful and dramatic illustrations, this book so fully achieves its intention that there is, in a sense, very little to say about it beyond description.

Mr. Toye's re-telling is effective and fits well with the pictures. He has respected his story as a legend and has avoided the rationalization so often found in attempts of this kind: for instance, when the hero, Red Feather, is given a goatskin so that he may descend the steep mountain side there is no suggestion in the text that the skin acts as a parachute: rather, he simply becomes, for the time being, a mountain goat with a mountain goat's abilities. (p. 35)

Elizabeth Cleaver's pictures are, like those in her other books, full of life and of exciting colour and design. She has made full use of the two obvious motifs, mountains and totem poles, but has varied these enough to prevent the total effect from becoming static or boring.

To me this is a book about which only the children can decide. Illustrating fairy tales is surely rather a chancey thing, because it is in the nature of such a story to create in the mind of the reader or listener images so vivid and so dramatic that the effectiveness of illustrations becomes simply a matter of whether or not the two happen to fit i.e. the reader's and the illustrator's. My own personal reaction to this book is that it lacks what I can only call atmosphere: I don't seem to smell any wood smoke or see any mist on mysterious peaks, and the mountains don't overwhelm me as mountains should. While I sense the artist's excitement in her use of the splendid totem designs and the vivid colour, I don't find myself identifying with the hero.

There can be no doubt however that this is a book of distinction in the field of Canadian publishing, and one that every library will want to offer to its readers. (pp. 35-6)

Helen Armstrong, in a review of "The Mountain Goats of Temlaham," in In Review: Canadian Books for Children, *Vol. 4, No. 2, Spring, 1970, pp. 35-6.*

This beautifully illustrated, unfamiliar folk tale will delight both readers and viewers. . . . The large, brilliantly colored illustrations, utilizing torn and cut paper shapes, vividly interpret the simple story.

Clara Hulton, in a review of "The Mountain Goats of Temlaham," in School Library Journal, *an appendix to* Library Journal, *Vol. 16, No. 8, April, 1970, p. 108.*

THE MIRACULOUS HIND: A HUNGARIAN LEGEND (1973)

AUTHOR'S COMMENTARY

The preparation and conception of ***The Miraculous Hind*** was a long one. . . . [It] was originally produced for the National Film Board of Canada as a filmstrip. . . . (p. 7)

This legend is based on actual historical events that took place on the borders of Europe and Asia 1500 years ago. It was transmitted orally for centuries before it was written down. The end piece written by Dr. Veronika Gervers of the Royal Ontario Museum describes in detail the early history of the Hungarians, the history of the Miraculous Hind and the figures of the legend. I worked closely with Veronika in developing ideas for costumes and folk motifs used throughout.

Inspiration for the legend came from Arany Janos's epic poem *The Death of Buda* (in Hungarian *Buda Halala)* written in 1863. It is the sixth canto which describes the Miraculous Hind (Rege a csoda szarvasról). With Veronika and Michael Gervers I often sat up until early hours of the morning translating the poem and developing a series of picture ideas. It was our love and enthusiasm for this legend that sparked off many beautiful ideas.

The legend tells the story of Hunor and Magyar, the sons of Menrot and Eneh, who start with their 100 horsemen upon a hunting expedition. They feel mysteriously impelled to follow the Hind. They swim across the Kur River; they cross desert plains; they come to a land where great pools of oil burned; they continue day after day to pursue the chase until they come to the shores of the Sea of Azov. The Hind vanishes from view, the horsemen settle and make camp. At twilight, they are attracted by the sounds of distant music. They ride off to find the source of the music and come upon a group of fairy maidens whom they carry off and make their wives. The two noblest of these become the wives of Hunor and Magyar and their children and their children's children became the Hungarian nation.

The pictures and the retelling were re-created with great feeling and love. I tried to think back to my impressions of the few years I spent in Hungary, the customs, the landscape, the spirit that I know is Hungarian. My Hungarian cultural background certainly greatly influenced me.

It was necessary to read and study paintings, drawings, engravings, photographs and contemporary representations of original ethnographic material housed in The Royal Ontario Museum since this legend originated 1500 years ago. Because it was difficult to reconstruct the ancient Hungarian costumes, the figures of the legend are dressed in costumes now considered typical of the traditional Hungarian dress.

The main characters wear the traditional dress characteristic of the Hungarian nobility between the 16th and 18th centuries that has survived as Hungarian gala costume. The remaining figures: the horsemen, the maidens and the bard are dressed in traditional regional Hungarian folk costume.

During excavations at the Castle of Sarospatak in 1964-65 Veronika Gervers discovered Turkish tiles, which were ordered in 1640 by the Transylvanian Prince, George Rakoczi I, for decorating the walls of his audience chamber. I have incorporated the floral motifs from these tiles into the maiden's costumes and as the backgrounds in pages 6, 7 and 9.

I chose the legend of the Miraculous Hind because of its universal appeal and because I found it most beautiful to illustrate. I love fairy tales, myths and legends; they are my 'inner world,' the world I love and want to re-create. (pp. 7-8)

Elizabeth Cleaver, "An Artist's Approach to Picture Books," in In Review: Canadian Books for Children, *Vol. 8, No. 1, Winter, 1974, pp. 5-8.*

In a year which has seen several fine books for children the appearance of this book is still an important event in Canadian publishing for children. ***The Miraculous Hind***—even the words of the title are carefully chosen—is an old Hungarian legend retold. . . . The story will be familiar to readers of Kate Seredy's *White Stag*.

The legend was first written down in the 13th century. In the 19th a famous Hungarian poet turned it into verses which are memorized by every schoolchild, and it is this poetic version that Mrs. Cleaver follows. In the legend the two princes and their entourage follow the form of the strange deer. A hind is the female of the red deer, the same word in Hungarian as the name of the mother of the two princes. The significance is that the hind is both mother of the race and leader of the nomads from Persia to their new land of Hungary. The deer disappears halfway through the tale. The country is the real "hero" of the story. It is never easy to condense such a legend into captions and there will always be readers who wish for more.

There are a few lines of print on each page except for five pages of text done in cutout letters on coloured backgrounds, repeating the poetical description of the new land and of its beautiful maidens. The print on page 48 is hard to read because the cherry red letters blur on the mottled mauve background. The technique used for the illustrations is the collage familiar from Mrs. Cleaver's other books. The colours are gold, cherry red, strong green, purples and blues, and all seem to suit an ancient tale. The two princes appear in colour but their 100 horsemen and horses are in black and white. Every detail of costume and background is carefully planned and executed. . . . These details are all meticulously described in notes at the back of the book, provided by Dr. Veronika Gervers, a specialist in Hungarian costume on the staff of the Royal Ontario Museum.

After the glorious colour of the illustrations the next thing you notice is the scholarship which has gone into the work. In these days when books of folklore come out without any sources given at all, these three pages of notes are impressive and enlightening in the most scholarly way. This is a good example to the general reader who may not always realize the amount of research there is in books for children. This book is not a picture book for little children, which is not to say that they may not enjoy it, but an illustrated legend to be read and examined and reread and savoured again and again. (pp. 31-2)

Elinor Kelly, in a review of "The Miraculous Hind: A Hungarian Legend," in In Review: Canadian Books for Children, *Vol. 8, No. 2, Spring, 1974, pp. 31-2.*

Looking deceptively like a picture book for very young children, this simplified retelling of a major Hungarian legend is illustrated with vivid collage pictures in which the figures are stiff, formalized woodcuts. . . . The writing is rather stiff, the text overshadowed by the illustrations. A final section by an art historian seems directed to adults; it interprets the legend in the light of history, describes the major figures. . . , and analyzes the details of costumes in the illustrations.

Zena Sutherland, in a review of "The Miraculous Hind: A Hungarian Legend," in Bulletin of the Center for Children's Books, *Vol. 27, No. 10, June, 1974, p. 155.*

Montreal artist Elizabeth Cleaver, whose flaming colors literally engulf text and all, and whose art work has been deservedly acclaimed in ***The Wind Has Wings, How Summer Came to Canada,*** and ***The Mountain Goats of Temlaham*** (all highly successful volumes of the late sixties), has produced both narrative and drawings for ***The Miraculous Hind.*** . . . The volume is of oversized width to permit the artist the expansive scope required by her distinctive style. Often it is necessary to gaze intently into the artwork in order to discover the very letters of the text, another fulfilling variation of what might well be a hallmark of the better Canadian children's books—if not of children's books everywhere—the preeminence of the image, and its narrative-provoking potential. (p. 146)

Leonard R. Mendelsohn, "The Current State of Children's Literature in Canada," in Children's Literature: Annual of the Modern Language Association Seminar on Children's Literature and The Children's Literature Association, *Vol. 4, 1975, pp. 138-52.*

Speaking of her craft. . . , Elizabeth Cleaver said: "Artistically valuable books will educate the child's taste and visual sense. They will stimulate imagination. . . . Through picture books we can help develop visual literacy" [see excerpt in Author's Commentary]. Her own picture book ***The Miraculous Hind*** and Lucienne Fantannaz' *Les Perles de Pluie* are excellent examples to support this thesis. Both books succeed to a very large extent in presenting illustrations that are suitable and exciting for children and, at the same time, are uncompromisingly good art by any standard. (p. 53)

[***The Miraculous Hind*** is the story] of two princes and their hundred horsemen who pursue but finally lose a magic hind, gaining instead royal and fairy brides for all and the land of Hungary forever. This episodic but potentially dramatic tale of high adventure and romance is, unfortunately, retold in a somewhat pedestrian manner.

Elizabeth Cleaver is, however, a far better artist than writer. Every page is a blaze of colour, brilliant wash and collage backgrounds on which are imposed plants, animals and people in collage and linoleum block. Detail from the last three hundred years of Hungarian culture (not from the obscure historical period concerned, 400-800 AD) is visually stimulating. [One] illustration, for instance, shows not only the collage and block technique, but also the imprint of real lace in the woman's costume. The seventeenth century originals of the floral tiles were only recently excavated in Hungary.

The cut-out and linoleum block figures, mostly in stark black and white, give an effect of primitive or child-like art, of intentionally nonnaturalistic humans dominating a more realistic world. The composition of the pictures is imaginative, full of contrast of line, shape, texture and colour. But they could be better disciplined. This is the more surprising as Elizabeth Cleaver is known for her powerful illustrations for other writers (e.g., ***The Wind Has Wings, The Witch of the North***); it seems that the weakness of her own story-telling here has led to an art that is diffuse rather than dramatic.

At moments of decision in the story, the printed text is replaced by cut-out words "so that children should feel and see that there is beauty in the sound and look of words. . . . When the cut-out words cannot do justice any more to the ideas in them, at that moment they become pictures themselves. Words become images—the two become one" [see excerpt in main Author's Commentary]. Apart from the fact that the letters are very hard to read, and were consequently disliked by the children we tested the book on, this theory is only valid when meaning and symbol unite, and here they do not. Furthermore, it totally ignores the symbolic and imagistic value of type itself. Lead block can be as powerful as linoleum block. In fact, Ms Cleaver could have been better served by her book designers. The printed text is often obscured by dark backgrounds, layout is undistinguished, and the pictures should probably be within borders to avoid the effect of similar colours running unrelated scenes together.

The Miraculous Hind is nevertheless a better book than the above criticisms suggest. Though not totally successful, it is such an ambitious conception as to have much greater value than more modest successes. The motifs from folk art are beautiful and the composite "Hungarianess" is visually and intellectually satisfying. But best of all is the sense of observing an artist experimenting with the artistic process. (pp. 53-5)

David Carnegie and Pauline Neale, "Deux Illustratrices Québécoises," in Canadian Children's Literature: A Journal of Criticism and Review, *Nos. 5 & 6, 1976, pp. 53-6.*

THE LOON'S NECKLACE **(1977)**

[The Loon's Necklace *was retold by William Toye.*]

AUTHOR'S COMMENTARY

The Loon's Necklace is a famous Tsimshian Indian legend that is best known through a film dramatization released in 1950. The editor and writer William Toye initially thought of converting this film version directly into a picture book, but later decided against this because the characters in the film wore elaborately articulated ritual masks and he felt that children would find it easier to relate to more simplified stock characters already familiar to them: an old man, a wicked witch, a mother. . . . ***The Loon's Necklace*** is a story about an old man whose eyesight is restored by a loon; as a reward the man gives the loon his precious shell necklace. That, the legend tells us, is why the loon has a white collar and speckles on its back.

In northwest-coast mythology the loon is featured as a messenger from the spirit world; it is the animal part of the psyche, the guide, the instinct; it sees and knows the way. Thus, on the literal level, the old man regains his physical eyesight. Symbolically, he attains inner vision and becomes whole as he is cleansed by the deep water, symbol of purification, regeneration and birth.

I am able to document the process by which ***The Loon's Necklace*** was created because I had just started working on my Master in Fine Arts thesis at Concordia University, Montreal, and I thought then that it would be interesting to keep a diary tracing the origin and development of the pictures. My work on ***The Loon's Necklace*** provides a representative example of how I create a picture book, and what follows is an extended look at the evolution of that book. The work embodies my preoccupations as an artist and demonstrates how interest, invention, and technique coalesce. The following adaptation of my diary entries shows the development of the project from drawings, linoleum cuts, collage compositions, and reference material to the finished work.

From The Loon's Necklace, *retold by William Toye. Pictures by Elizabeth Cleaver. Oxford University Press, 1977. © Oxford University Press 1977. Reproduced by permission of the Literary Estate of Elizabeth Cleaver.*

April 13, 1977: William Toye's manuscript arrived from Oxford University Press. From this time onward I will spend time on the book virtually every day.

April 15: I start my research by going to the National Museum of Canada Library in Ottawa, where I discovered variants of the legend. Even though William Toye has done the retelling I will illustrate, I am interested in understanding how the characters are portrayed, and what incidents are important, in other versions. I collect visual material relating to Tsimshian artifacts that I may use in my pictures: totem poles, huts, articles of clothing. During my two-hour bus drive each way between Montreal and Ottawa, I work on an outline for the twenty-four page picture book.

April 19: I continue my picture research at McCord Museum and its library in Montreal. I consult anthropological journals and books by Diamond Jennesses, Franz Boaz, Marius Barbeau, and Viola Garfield. I think about my travels in 1969 through the mountains of British Columbia, by air and by bus and try to recapture the spectacular environment, especially the mountains and the trees.

April 22: I make my first linocut of the loon and try to visualize a cover design.

April 28: I meet with William Toye to show him my sketches. We go over the text and rough drawings very carefully, discussing the content of each picture.

April 29: I begin very slowly, and with many difficulties along the way, to produce final art. After the pictorial narrative and the text of a work have been developed, I begin to prepare drawings for linoleum blocks. With a block, a drawing, a pencil, and an eraser, I redraw or trace the image, working on several blocks at one time. The process of cutting a block is different from drawing in that not only is intense concentration required, but it is physically tiring to cut linoleum. But I love the line I can achieve by using different cutting knives for thicker or thinner lines. After the first stage of cutting has been done, I make a pencil rubbing (frottage) of the image and reevaluate my work. I will then decide whether to cut further or start again.

My colors are obtained from my collection of hundreds of monoprinted papers that I have produced over the years. On some of these I print my lino blocks, which provide the figures and trees in my collage compositions. It is wonderful how strips of cut and torn paper, in appropriate colors and textures, can become a landscape; and how they can give the picture a three-dimensional quality as they are built up into a background in the struggle to arrive at a harmonious color relation. The artist's intuition plays a very big part.

May 10: A bad day. I can't work, so I decide to visit the museum to see an exhibition on Russian stage design (this later proved useful in my illustrations for ***Petrouchka***).

May 11: I create my first good picture for the double spread of the underwater scene, pages 14 and 15. I experiment with various inks and paper and finally use painted acetate to get the watery effect I am looking for. The text this illustrates is as follows:

> The old man did as he was told. He grasped Loon's wings and together they dove—down, down, down. Then they floated up, up, up.

May 12 to 17: Perhaps the greatest difficulty in the reading of a text is in finding equivalent symbols and forms for those in the text. On pages 10 and 11 of ***The Loon's Necklace,*** for the picture of the old man sitting by the edge of the lake, I went through six variations. In the earliest version, the boy is seen waving good-bye to his father who is sitting by the lake to await the loon's return. In the final version his son has already left and the old man is looking out over the lake alone. In this way, I was able to emphasize, as the story does, the solitary nature of the old man's journey. The text for pages 8 and 9 merely states that the old man and child are walking through the forest. It does not specify the setting in any detail. It was necessary to invent a forest and mountains like those of British Columbia where the Tsimshian Indians lived. I tried to get the essence of the experience, the old man's feeling of grief as he goes through the forest, his patience as he waits for the loon to appear. The next problem was with pages 2 and 3, where I had difficulty working out the colors from the mountains and the boy's face (four versions), and trouble with the bear and stream. Pages 6 and 7: At first the witch was puppet-like; I had to make her more wicked. Pages 18 and 19: The design of the shell necklace required research in shells that are found on the West Coast. I finally based the necklace on dentalium shells because, when broken, they can look like the shapes that appear on the loon's back. The illustration of the necklace was made from rolled paper creating a three-dimensional effect. Pages 20 and 21: This part of the manuscript changed several times, necessitating different images for each change. The final version developed into a double spread. The hut, first a linoleum cut, was later made from textured folded paper creating the feeling of wood covered with moss.

May 28 to June 2: Mr. Toye came to Montreal and examined what I had done. We spent a full day discussing and agreeing on various changes—some had to do with the figures and their placement, some with the background colors. However, there was one big change, a serious one at this late stage, and this was in the overall color treatment. It was clear to both of us when we looked at the pictures all laid out together on the floor that the colors were too dark. I had to make fresh monoprints and reassemble every composition. This took me until June 2, and while it entailed a great deal of unexpected effort, the results were very worthwhile. . . .

[On] June 18, Mr. Toye accepted the finished art.

I parted with my pictures reluctantly. I knew I would miss having them to look at each morning. I would even miss solving the visual problems. But I took pleasure from knowing that the pictures were good enough to stand with the text of a wonderful story. (pp. 162-70)

Elizabeth Cleaver, "Idea to Image: The Journey of a Picture Book," in The Lion and the Unicorn, *Vols. 7-8, 1983-84, pp. 156-70.*

Hurray! Elizabeth Cleaver and William Toye are back together again. It's been too long since their last collabortion on a picture book and this new one is a delight.

This Indian folk-tale will be no stranger to librarians and teachers; the film has been a staple of library film programs for years. It is a simple yet strong tale of a loon who cures an old man's blindness and is given a necklace of white beads in return. This necklace becomes the beautiful white markings on the loon's neck.

Cleaver's technique of woodcut and collage is admirably suited to both the British Columbia setting and the folkoric style. Her work here is less abstract than in previous books. Blue and white mountains and gold sky provide a soft backdrop to stark evergreens, totem poles and earth-toned woodcuts of people and animals. The loon, as befits the hero, is depicted in prominent black and white and has a distinctly devilish gleam in his eye. (pp. 68-9)

Purchasers should be aware that $5.95 is buying a shiny paper-covered book whose many double-page spreads will not take kindly to binding. However it is little enough to pay for the glorious artwork and should not deter anyone from buying this commendable book. (p. 69)

Callie Israel, in a review of "The Loon's Necklace," in In Review: Canadian Books for Children, *Vol. 12, No. 1, Winter, 1978, pp. 68-9.*

Elizabeth Cleaver is one of Canada's top picture book artists. Such works as ***The Mountain Goats of Temlaham, How Summer Came to Canada, The Wind Has Wings,*** and ***The Miraculous Hind*** are justly acclaimed as major books in the tradition of Canadian Children's Literature. In her use of collage, with its sensitive but vivid use of color, she has brought to life three major aspects of our literary culture: its poetry, its native legends, and its immigrant folk tales. Last fall, she continued the tradition with the third of her interpretations of native tales: ***The Loon's Necklace.*** It's a very good book, one that should be in every school and public library in Canada; but I'm not sure it's her best book. (p. 51)

The story is . . . a pourquoi tale—explaining why the owl hoots at night and how the loon acquired his configuration (a speckled necklace)—and a presentation of the interrelationship between human and non-human life—a theme central to our native tales. Unfortunately the prose of the tale, supplied by a distinguished Canadian author-editor, William Toye, fails in two ways. While it gives the bare bones of plot, it does not help to communicate the emotions of the story; and it isn't effectively integrated with Elizabeth Cleaver's art. It doesn't help to create the marriage of murals and verbals found in all great picture books.

Elizabeth Cleaver's collages do their fair share and, indeed much more, although they don't achieve the intensity of those in ***The Mountain Goats of Temlaham*** a book which is, in my opinion, her finest. True to the British Columbia setting, the dominant colors are blue and green, conveying the feeling of wetness and chill so prevalent to West Coast winters. The human figures seem muted and diminutive set against the backgrounds. However, while this may be true of the geographical area, it doesn't completely harmonize with the text which emphasizes the triumph and joy which the family finally feels. Ultimately, the book may be Elizabeth Cleaver's most successful portrayal of environment; but, although good, it is not her best depiction of human emotions. And aren't they, after all, the essential ingredients of any story? (pp. 51-2)

Jon C. Stott, in a review of "The Loon's Necklace," in The World of Children's Books, *Vol. III, 1978, pp. 51-2.*

[***The Loon's Necklace*** has been] illustrated by a gifted Canadian artist, whose work deserves to be better known in the United States. . . . Rich and varied in color, texture, and design, the strong, dynamic pictures are unified in spirit and make a striking book.

Ethel L. Heins, in a review of "The Loon's Necklace," in The Horn Book Magazine, *Vol. LIV, No. 2, April, 1978, p. 157.*

Elizabeth Cleaver is a Canadian artist whose original technique of illustration will attract children and indeed stimulate them to experiment for themselves with pictures made from torn tissue paper and lino-cut. In ***The Loon's Necklace,*** she uses her craft to create a sense of the huge loneliness of the Canadian lakes and mountains with their pine forests and wildlife.

Elaine Moss, "The Art of Non-Conformity," in The Times Literary Supplement, *No. 3966, April 7, 1978, p. 385.*

[The] atmosphere of melancholy is sustained in the brief and effective text and in Elizabeth Cleaver's formal woodcuts. . . . Children may respond to [the story's] strange appeal, as they may to the stiff, soft-toned designs, but the book will not be to all tastes. It may find its true home in the schools of art. (pp. 195-96)

M. Crouch, in a review of "The Loon's Necklace," in The Junior Bookshelf, *Vol. 42, No. 4, August, 1978, pp. 195-96.*

THE FIRE STEALER (1979)

[The Fire Stealer *was retold by William Toye.*]

Toye and Cleaver, recognized for their outstanding achievements in Canada, where they have garnered enviable awards, teamed up for the fourth time to create this adaptation of an Indian legend. Set in a time long gone, when Earth's people lived without fire, the myth stars Nanabozho, Great Trickster. As a boy, he revels in changing himself into a rabbit or a tree, sometimes trying the patience of his kind grandmother Nokomis. As a youth, however, Nanabozho dares the magician who owns fire and escapes with a flaming torch that warms his old grandmother and becomes his most welcome gift to his tribe. Combined with the suspenseful telling, Cleaver's marvelously crafted collages—suffused with fiery reds and jumping with action—add up to a splendid book.

A review of "The Fire Stealer," in Publishers Weekly, *Vol. 217, No. 9, March 7, 1980, p. 90.*

The award-winning team of author William Toye and illustrator Elizabeth Cleaver have collaborated once again to produce another beautiful book. . . .

In her latest pictures, Elizabeth Cleaver shows that she possesses maturity as an artist. The medium she uses is the same, that is, collage, but she assembles new and interesting combinations. Besides linocuts and bits of cut and torn paper, she has added found objects such as rabbit fur and botanical elements such as corn husks and the inner and outer layers of birch bark. . . . She demonstrates a good control and blend of colour. Her scenes, painted in rich tones and carefully structured, are captivating. Her fire scene, for instance, has been printed on acetate to convey the impression of glowing flames. Her compositions reflect perspective and movement and her forms, suppleness. One of the mythological symbols that keeps recurring in her books is the tree. There are four splendid pictures at the beginning of the tale in which Nanabozho changes himself into a tree; Ms. Cleaver has used the cyclic method in which the transformation takes place in a series of four scenes. The reader senses that Ms. Cleaver immersed herself in the story which has been fully researched. ***The Fire Stealer*** will be enjoyed for the story and the pictures which complement each other in a most harmonious way.

Irene E. Aubrey, in a review of "The Fire Stealer," in In Review: Canadian Books for Young People, *Vol. 14, No. 2, April, 1980, p. 58.*

Brilliant mixed-media collages do justice to the tale with spectacular hues and an appropriately primitive feeling. One especially fine sequence of pictures shows Nanabozho changing himself into a tree. (p. 289)

Ann A. Flowers, in a review of "The Fire Stealer," in The Horn Book Magazine, *Vol. LVI, No. 3, June, 1980, pp. 288-89.*

The Fire Stealer is a Red Indian Prometheus story. Elizabeth Cleaver's pictures are backed by the authority of her undisputed scholarship, but I find them, in purely artistic terms, a little lacking in dynamism and humanity.

M. Crouch, in a review of "The Fire Stealer," in The Junior Bookshelf, *Vol. 44, No. 6, December, 1980, p. 283.*

PETROUCHKA (1980)

One of Canada's most illustrious artists, Cleaver expresses her deep feelings about the ballet commissioned by Diaghilev, the title character danced by Nijinsky at the premiere in Paris, 1911. At the Shrovetide Fair, the celebrators watch a puppet show manipulated by a master who pulls the strings of a Moor, a ballerina and the clown Petrouchka. The ballerina flirts with the Moor and with the clown, then shows her contempt for the poor clumsy buffoon and dances with his rival. Petrouchka and the Moor fight and the clown dies but his spirit appears above the curtain; he is ecstatic because he's free to be himself. The telling is staid, formalized and illustrated by Cleaver's magnificent collages with such bright blues, reds, greens and other hues that they seem filled with light. A beauty of a book.

A review of "Petrouchka," in Publishers Weekly, *Vol. 218, No. 18, October 31, 1980, p. 86.*

[Cleaver] faces the interesting challenge of presenting in book form a work that was originally conceived for non-verbal presentation: music and dance. Her solution is to keep the narrative very simple, and to rely on her illustrations to flesh out the story. Her collage paintings (using monoprints, linoprints and cut and torn paper) give a rich yet poetic carnival atmosphere; her techniques and use of colour lend a sense of theatre and mystery to these very Russian scenes. The puppet figures are, to a dancer's eye, less successful. Given the tragic intensity associated with the ballet, Cleaver's three linoprint figures lack the expected emotional clout.

Nonetheless, the book has much charm and visual appeal. I showed the book to some 12-year-old non-dancing female readers, and they enjoyed it though they were perplexed about the status of the puppets (marionnette or human). A six-year-old male wanted the book read three times through on first exposure. Depending on interests, children in this age range should respond well to this book. (pp. 44-5)

Jocelyn Allen, in a review of "Petrouchka," in Quill and Quire, *Vol. 46, No. 11, November, 1980, pp. 44-5.*

The romantic triangle of the Stravinsky ballet, inconstruable to young children, . . . is here presented as a very young picture book. The text under the framed picture on each facing page is a flat, terse, clumsily-written caption ("They watched an organ grinder begin to play; and everyone else came to listen, too. And to watch a girl with a triangle dance and pirouette to the music"); the pictures themselves, though not unattractively done (and very attractively colored), have neither verve nor emotional conviction. The puppets *are* puppets here, but then so are the people in the crowd scenes that precede the performance. On the stage all this comes alive, and the action, whether fully intelligible or not, sweeps the audience along. Here it's inert—another instance of good intentions misdirected.

A review of "Petrouchka," in Kirkus Reviews, *Vol. 48, No. 21, November 1, 1980, p. 1390.*

Integrating her "love for the magic of the puppet theater, ballet, music, costume and stage design," the Canadian artist has made a brilliantly colorful picture book; with artwork done in collage, using monoprints, linoleum cuts, and torn paper, she captures much of the spirit, the drama, and the energy of the ballet. Only the ending of the book is rather softened; the description of the final scene fails to convey the essential irony and tragedy of the original conception, stated with crystalline clarity by both the music and the pantomime in a work which has been called the *Hamlet* of ballet.

Ethel L. Heins, in a review of "Petrouchka: Adapted from Igor Stravinsky and Alexandre Benois" in The Horn Book Magazine, *Vol. LVI, No. 6, December, 1980, p. 631.*

Elizabeth Cleaver has put together exquisite, three-dimensional pictures to illustrate this appealing story and her choice of alternate bright and dark colours admirably suits its theme and setting. The different shades of blue and purple which are used to depict the evening scenes or the gloom and loneliness of Petrouchka in his cell contrast effectively, for instance, with the brilliant reds and greens of the Moor's room. Two worlds are portrayed, that is, the real world of the fair and the imaginary world of the puppet show and the link between the two materializes when Petrouchka's spirit appears in the final scene. All the characters, as well as the set pieces, are made from linoleum prints which are collaged together, and Ms. Cleaver has skilfully drawn the mechanical and the animated forms of the puppets and the people.

Since ***Petrouchka*** is a ballet, the various coloured borders framing the pictures create the proper atmosphere of a stage setting. Moreover, the space provided for the type at the bottom of each page is also framed and complements the picture as a whole. It is interesting to note the several ballet positions illustrated throughout the tale such as the pied à la main, grand écart, coupé front and passé, as well as the miming actions of Petrouchka and the character dancing of the participants at the fair. . . .

The enchantment, style of movement and inherent feelings of the Russian ballet have successfully been captured in this beautiful, carefully researched book.

Petrouchka has been chosen among the 17 books published in the United States to be featured in the biennale of illustrations in Bratislava. . . . (p. 28)

Irene E. Aubrey, in a review of "Petrouchka," in In Review: Canadian Books for Young People, *Vol. 15, No. 2, April, 1981, pp. 27-8.*

While complexities of character and plot can be realised in ballet by means of music, choreography, costume, and the dancers' physical and dramatic skills, it is much more difficult to achieve a corresponding effect through the illustrations and text of a picture book. Cleaver has been only partially successful. (p. 55)

The first six pages correspond to the ballet's Act I; the animation of a Shrovetide Fair held during the Russian winter is expressed through a multitude of forms and colours. Act II focuses on the puppet stage. Against a cool blue background (pp. 7-11), the puppets develop their love-jealousy relationship while the orange puppet master blends into the orange-red frame of his puppet theatre. . . . Pages 12 to 15 depict Petrouchka's "world"—a narrow cell (painted dark blue) enlarged by schematic stars and mountains drawn on the walls. The orange portrait of the puppet master with its hypnotic eyes presumably reminds Petrouchka that he is subject to the master's spell, while the colour link between the master and the ballerina suggests that she, too, is evil. Pages 16 to 19 show the elegant room of the Moor. . . . The set's exotic blue and green plants on a red background overpower the muted orange of the silly ballerina and the purple of the Moor; the dazzling background foliage optically moves forward while the purple and orange recede with a consequent diminishment of character and action. The Moor's coconut loses its identity, becoming a black hole in the red background. Bursting in upon the flirtation scene, Petrouchka in his white costume is powerfully silhouetted against the garish background. But the ominous mood which should be created by the Moor's attack is frustrated by the fact that his scimitar is lost in the obtrusive foliage.

The story ends with a return to the street where the fair is being held. The dominance of red and purple symbolises the violent action as the Moor kills Petrouchka. . . . Unfortunately, the impact of the Moor as an evil character is diminished because his colour fuses optically with that of the set. The final illustrations lack the strong delineation required by the dramatic climax. In the original ballet production, the soul or ghost of Petrouchka was illuminated in green (the color of hope) on top of the puppet theatre while his body was dragged away below. Cleaver's adoption of a similar colour differentiation might have enhanced a child's understanding of the conclusion.

The confusions created in the illustrations by a sometimes inappropriate choice of colours and by disproportionate formal relationships are not always clarified by the text. In some cases, the text does not correspond closely to the matching illustration. For example, an illustration of Petrouchka lying on the floor of his cell is paired with:

> The dance was over. The puppet master kicked Petrouchka into his bare, narrow room. Left alone, the poor puppet rose to his feet and tried to find a way out.

There are also inconsistencies in verbal style. Some sentences use the simple structures and restricted vocabulary that are thought appropriate for younger children. Others present unfamiliar words with meanings that might not be deduced from the verbal or visual context—"Shrovetide," "pirouette," "competition," "pointes," "rigid," "despair," "idly," "elegant," and "scimitar," for example. Grace, correct structure and euphony are often lacking:

> The ballerina danced to the music she made herself on the trumpet, and found that she liked to please the Moor.
>
> As the Moor began to flirt with her, Petrouchka became very jealous. This made the puppet master very angry because this was not a part of the dance.

In the re-tellings of Canadian myths and folktales which Cleaver has illustrated, there are clear-cut contrasts between good and evil. The characters are easily classified, their motives easily ascertained. The forms and colours of the illustrations complement the development of plot, character, and mood. In the ballet "Petrouchka," however, there are many problems. The central character is complex and contradictory. The characters are not recognisably Russian but the setting is. The puppet body is controlled by a master while the puppet soul struggles for independence. One comes to the conclusion that "Petrouchka" is too sophisticated a subject for a children's picture book. This particular work is more likely to be a collector's item than a nursery favourite. (pp. 55-8)

Muriel Whitaker and Jetske Ironside, "Puppet with a Soul," in Canadian Children's Literature: A Journal of Criticism and Review, *No. 25, 1982, pp. 55-9.*

A B C (1984)

[This small, square alphabet book offers] a group of 26 brilliant collage-miniatures, each composed of objects beginning (in trusty ABC fashion) with a single letter. To start at the zingo end, Z is represented by a zebra leaping out of a zippered page; the dominant colors are tomato red, tangerine, and for the lordly letter Z, lime green. (All the letters are similarly imposing, and part of the ensemble.) The number of objects varies, and they may or may not have a natural relationship. Almost all are easily recognizable, however—and the more arresting (like the tomato, toy soldier, teddy bear, and tree) for not belonging together. Apart from being three-dimensional collages, many of the pictures contain real objects: a needle, a paper clip, a key. But the binding element is what can now be called—in reference to Cleaver's illustrations for ***The Loon's Necklace,*** and the work of others—bold Canadian coloring design. Each little page, viewed close-up as it should be, delivers an intimate punch. (pp. J3-J4)

A review of "ABC," in Kirkus Reviews, *Juvenile Issue, Vol. 53, Nos. 1-5, March 1, 1985, pp. J3-J4.*

From The Enchanted Caribou, *written and illustrated by Elizabeth Cleaver. Atheneum, 1985. Text and pictures copyright © 1985 by Elizabeth Cleaver. Reprinted with the permission of Atheneum Publishers. In Canada by the Literary Estate of Elizabeth Cleaver.*

This small-scale *ABC* book features bright colors, bold collages, and a practical, alliterative word lineup to show how each letter sounds. Strong reds, blues, greens, and yellows grab the eye, while occasional small objects and shaded, textured color overlays add depth and visual interest. The pictures can act as a puzzle, motivating youngsters to pick out all of the words beginning with a particular letter. Listed words will also encourage sight word recognition and perhaps discussion of some of the less common items (*loon, parsnip, vulture*). An engaging presentation.

Denise M. Wilms, in a review of "ABC," in Booklist, *Vol. 81, No. 20, June 15, 1985, p. 1455.*

Another variation on the ABC, a trendy, upmarket version. It is a pocket-sized, go-anywhere book with double-page spread word lists and pictures, headed by upper- and lower-case letters: 'Cc carrot caterpillar celery cow'. Each word has its pictorial representation in brightly-coloured, collage-type illustrations on the accompanying page. These might become, for the child, an exercise in visual discrimination (of Kit Williams proportions?) and/or a game of 'I-spy'. For this latter, the word list for the letter *u* might present a problem for the discerning child: 'Uu umbrella under unicorn' ('Where is the under?'). As always, they will be learning far, far more than what we think we set out to teach them.

Christine Wilkie, in a review of "ABC," in The School Librarian, *Vol. 33, No. 3, September, 1985, p. 228.*

Not an aid for preschoolers learning their letters, ***ABC*** presents two-page spreads with lists of words facing collages constructed around each upper-case letter. Familiar words such as *apple* and *red* are used along with the obscure: *parsnip, oyster* and *vulture*. Since the words appear in a list rather than as labels, the book's use as a vocabulary builder is limited. The illustrations, while brightly colored, are in some cases so primitive that they are difficult to identify. Cleaver has attempted to create landscapes using some of the objects, with limited success. *L*, for example, is illustrated by a loon on a lake with red autumn leaves overhead and a rather incongruous lemon floating nearby. The abstract nature of the artwork makes the leaves difficult to identify, and the lake could be mistaken for the background of the page rather than an object to name. There are dozens of excellent alphabet books available, and any one would be a better choice.

Lucy Young Clem, in a review of "ABC," in School Library Journal, *Vol. 32, No. 1, September, 1985, p. 114.*

THE ENCHANTED CARIBOU **(1985)**

[Elizabeth Cleaver] created some of Canada's most exciting pictures for children's books. Her brilliant collages frequently illustrated native legends. . . . Her last book, ***The Enchanted Caribou*** . . . , is illustrated in a new and intriguing way. Each episode in Cleaver's retelling of this Inuit story is accompanied by a tableau of dramatic silhouettes, created by photographing shadow puppets.

The story itself is lovely, telling how Tyya, a young woman, is transformed into a white caribou by an evil shaman and then rescued from her enchanted form by the man who loves her. In an afterword, Cleaver explains how she feels shadow theatre is particularly well-suited "for showing dreams, visions and magical happenings, like a human turning into an animal." She also provides instructions showing readers how to create their own shadow puppets and construct a simple back-lit shadow box to tell their own stories. ***The Enchanted Caribou*** is a wonderful addition to Cleaver's legacy to Canadian children.

Mary Ainslie Smith, "Identity Crisis," in Books in Canada, *Vol. 14, No. 9, December, 1985, p. 12.*

The shadow puppets have the primitive quality of folk art and yet also have grace and movement. The illustration of the four young people dancing the caribou dance is particularly memorable for its whirling joy of movement. Cleaver has accomplished the difficult task of adapting a three-dimensional image to a flat page using this rare, fine-art medium. The story of ***The Enchanted Caribou*** contains several traditional elements: a visit from the spirit world, an evil shaman, a human being transformed into an animal form, and the white caribou symbolizing good luck.

At the back of the book, Cleaver has outlined for children directions on how to make shadow puppets so that they can re-create the story. The instructions are clear, the materials are cheap and easily obtainable, and patterns for the main characters are given. Directions are also provided for making a simple screen with lighting.

For generations, there have been many retellings of native stories but, until recently, the books have not been particularly appealing to children. [***The Enchanted Caribou*** and Anne Cameron's *How Raven Freed the Moon* and *How The Loon Lost Her Voice*] contain all the elements of a good story: drama, character, humour, and suspense and point the way to a revival of native story-telling for children.

Eva Martin, "Enchanting New Views Help Re-create Native Folk-Tales," in Quill and Quire, *Vol. 52, No. 2, February, 1986, p. 16.*

Cleaver's clear prose matches the composition and drama of the black-and-white illustrations, which combine stark simplicity with a mysterious, softly blurred effect. The pictures move from the solitary figure in the bare landscape to the rhythm and vigor of the communal dance around the fire. Tyya's transformation from woman to caribou and back again is shown in stages that reinforce the story's sense of closeness between animal and human.

Hazel Rochman, in a review of "The Enchanted Caribou," in Booklist, *Vol. 82, No. 12, February 15, 1986, p. 865.*

This Canadian tale is illustrated with black shadow puppets against a stark white background. These full-page illustrations work well with the story. Unfortunately the telling is bland and lacks energy and excitement. . . .

As a picture book this title will have limited appeal, but as an additional purchase for the story-telling collection, it's worth consideration.

Chris-tine Lisiecki, in a review of "The Enchanted Caribou," in School Library Journal, *Vol. 32, No. 7, March, 1986, p. 158.*

Elizabeth Cleaver retold this story using a storyteller's fluid language, rich with imagery. The shadow puppet pictures are a perfect visual extension of the text. Their stark black and white forms evoke images of snow and the bleak environment of the tundra, and perfectly capture the essence of the culture.

Melissa Cain, in a review of "The Enchanted Caribou," in The Advocates Newsletter, *December, 1986, p. 10.*

Rosa (Cuthbert) Guy

1928-

West Indian-born black American author of fiction, reteller, and editor.

Guy is a powerful writer who offers insight and empathy to a young adult audience, particularly black inner-city young adults. Her novels are distinguished by Guy's perceptive treatment of friendships and family relationships and by her appealing, well-developed characters. Setting many of her books in Harlem, she presents her readers with an unsweetened view of the violence, racism, and poverty of inner-city life while outlining the ways in which this lifestyle affects her characters, both teenagers and adults. Although she addresses such topics as abortion, child abuse, abandonment, starvation, betrayal, and murder, Guy most often explores the struggle for personal identity faced by adolescents as well as the variables of their personal interactions. Underscoring her works is the message that young people can learn to cope with, and ultimately survive, their circumstances and problems. Guy is best known for *The Friends* (1974), *Ruby* (1976), and *Edith Jackson* (1978), a trilogy which addresses the prejudice, social isolation, and search for love that confront three young black women and their families. With *Ruby,* Guy created a novel which is often considered the first work for young adults to include a lesbian relationship. Published as an adult work in England, the book's controversialism made it the only one of the series not to be adopted for use in English secondary schools. Guy has also written *The Disappearance* (1979) and *New Guys around the Block* (1983), two well-received mysteries which feature the resourceful Imamu Jones. In addition, she has created a humorous adventure for middle-grade children, a romance which focuses on upper-class white society, and an original folktale with a Caribbean setting. For a younger audience, Guy adapted *Mother Crocodile* (1981), an African fable with an antiwar theme originally written in French by Senegalese author Birago Diop. Guy fills her books with urban street language and West Indian dialect, characteristics noted for adding texture and richness to her texts.

Reviewers applaud Guy's gripping stories and vivid characterizations as well as her objective and sophisticated approach to her subjects. While some critics find her settings and dialogue difficult or unfamiliar, most comment favorably on the authenticity and universality of her books. They praise Guy for writing honest, compelling works which provide young readers with determination and hope.

(See also *Contemporary Literary Criticism,* Vol. 26; *Something about the Author,* Vol. 14; *Contemporary Authors New Revision Series,* Vol. 14; *Contemporary Authors,* Vols. 17-20, rev. ed.; and *Dictionary of Literary Biography,* Vol. 33: *Afro-American Fiction Writers after 1955.*)

AUTHOR'S COMMENTARY

I am a storyteller. I hope that young people of today are like I was yesterday in reading tastes. I have always liked interesting books with exciting characters, held together by invisible but well-conceived plots. And I always wanted to believe, when putting down a book, that my time had not been wasted in pure enjoyment and that I had learned something more than I knew before I picked it up. I wanted to know about people, places, and those things that had not drawn my attention before.

© *Jerry Bauer*

I am concerned for young people for all the clichéd reasons; the most obvious and truest being that they are the future. We depend on them, most selfishly, for posterity. It is through them that our civilization shall be measured. I take young readers seriously; I treat them with respect. They bear the responsibility for the future. The sooner they accept it, the better.

When I see, or hear, our elders joke about or discuss seriously the problems facing the world—nuclear rockets to destroy the world's peoples, nuclear warheads being placed in countries contrary to the wishes of their citizens—my concern for the future deepens. Even when the threat of a future holocaust is woven into fantasy—as the suggestions about rockets being recalled once fired or the building of more weapons to prevent their use—my concern grows. Even fables of mass murder and mass destruction leave an indelible impression on young minds, impressions reinforced by the acceptance of parents.

Once upon many times—the times of the crusaders, the times of the slave trade, the times of imperialism—hundreds of thousands of men, women, and children, and unborn babies were slaughtered. Villages were razed and peoples enslaved as invaders—later to be called explorers—pillaged little-known regions in the name of religion and empire. In those days the young lived in innocence, shielded from the knowledge that their conquering heroes were motivated by nothing more than pure greed. That's no longer true; the media doesn't allow it.

Today, young people are exposed to the realities of war in all its brutality on the televisions in their living rooms: the foot of an infant here, the arm of another there, babies lying on the streets of bombed-out towns as their rotting flesh nourishes flies, napalmed forests securing starvation to generations—all done in the name of religion and democracy.

The age of innocence is gone, done away with by television. Young people are forced to ask now: Who are these people? That young boy? That little girl? Are we, my people, responsible in any way in their death? Are we really supermen? Are we really wonder women? Who are these elder statesmen? Who are they to tell me that what I'm seeing guarantees my democracy? The way these questions are asked, and answered, must determine young people's future—and the future of our civilization.

I'm a storyteller. I write about people. I want my readers to know people, to laugh with them, to be glad with, to be angry with, to despair with people. And I want them to have hope with people. I want a reader of my work to work a bit more and to care.

In England, where ***The Friends*** . . . has been on the syllabus since the 1970s, and where ***Measure of Time,*** my latest book, was number one on the best-seller lists, there is a magazine that has been put out for students, detailing the neighborhood where ***The Friends*** is set. The magazine explains the conditions under which my characters Phyllisia Cathy and Edith Jackson lived, even the subway stop nearest their homes. This means, of course, that young people in England can speak with authority about a place called Harlem in America, of which Americans—some living a mile away—know nothing. A young Londoner can describe conditions in American "inner cities"—places white Americans drive miles around to avoid, even as they discuss how to bring "democracy" to El Salvador and Nicaragua.

A novel to me is an emotional history of a people in time and place. If I have proven to be popular with young people, it is because when they have finished one of my books, they not only have a satisfying experience—they have also had an education. (pp. 220-21)

Rosa Guy, "Young Adult Books: I Am a Storyteller," in The Horn Book Magazine, *Vol. LXI, No. 2, March-April, 1985, pp. 220-21.*

GENERAL COMMENTARY

LINDA BACHELDER AND OTHERS

[Like Katherine Paterson's *Bridge to Terabithia*], Rosa Guy's trilogy, ***The Friends, Ruby,*** and ***Edith Jackson,*** also explored human relationships. . . . These novels revealed life as lived by West Indian blacks in Harlem and created a world for the reader that evoked understanding of the characters. The adolescent homosexual relationship between Ruby and Daphne, in ***Ruby,*** was sensitively and tastefully handled. The author analyzed perceptively the problems of black teenagers in all three books. The use of the West Indies idiom was beautifully done and added a dimension of credibility to the novels and their characters.

Both Paterson and Guy demonstrated that the young adult novel can develop depth of characters and lucid style and still weave a plausible story to maintain young adult interest. These authors raised the young adult novel above the shallow characterizations and saccharin themes so characteristic of this genre in its early stages. (p. 88)

Linda Bachelder and others, "Looking Backward: Trying to Find the Classic Young Adult Novel," in English Journal, *Vol. 69, No. 6, September, 1980, pp. 86-9.*

R. BAINES

Rosa Guy is a black author writing with power, authority and insight about an underprivileged and inward looking world which is strange to most of us. Her themes are distressing, disturbing and unappealing ones which she deals with honestly and sympathetically.

R. Baines, in a review of "Ruby," in The Junior Bookshelf, *Vol. 46, No. 2, April, 1982, p. 76.*

BEVERLY ANDERSON

[The following excerpt is taken from an interview by Beverly Anderson.]

[***New Guys Around the Block*** is] the second in a trilogy about Imamu Jones, in [Rosa Guy's] words "a brilliant young cat from the block, who solves mysteries the police can't." As usual with this author's work an exciting story is set in an unflinchingly observed inner city, and deals with adolescent preoccupations—their relations with each other and with their parents. It reveals her respect and concern for the young trapped in urban slums, and conveys to them a robust and optimistic message.

Imamu is back from his temporary middle-class haven in Brooklyn, the setting of ***The Disappearance,*** in which he first appeared. He has returned to Harlem determined to make a decent home for his mother, now a full-time drunk. His decorating squad includes two new guys on the block—Olivette, a mysterious, assured and intelligent Creole from New Orleans and his more diffident brother, Pierre. Their attempt to clean up Imamu's apartment coincides with a series of local robberies and violent attacks which baffle the police, and with the return from jail of Iggy, an old friend of Imamu's, who has been doing time for murder.

There are a number of vivid and distinctive characters including big-mouthed Fergusson, Gladys the local man-eater who is nearly killed by the mysterious thief, Flame Larouche, self-styled aristocrat and mother of the "new guys", Detective Otis Brown, whose case Imamu solves, and on the edge of the action but very much on Imamu's mind, his girl-friend Gail. She is a member of the family which fostered him in Brooklyn and is trying to persuade Imamu to start studying again so he can join her at university.

Imamu's relationship with Olivette, whose confidence and fastidious insistence on excellence attract him, is delicately contrasted with his feeling for Gail. In ***Ruby,*** one of Rosa Guy's earlier trilogy about a group of girls in the same setting, the chief character has an intense affair with another girl, Daphne. I asked Ms Guy why she had chosen to write about what could be seen as an unsuitable subject. She said that if it was seen as daring that had to do with some people's hypocrisy.

> The majority of young girls growing up go through some sort of homosexual relationship, or at any rate feelings, sometimes only for a teacher. They sit back and drool over teachers, particularly when their mother is dead, and their father is not understanding. So they reach out and love. People should be able to love one another.

She feels that it is a natural, powerful but transient stage for most growing people and what causes the harm is calling it a sin, which makes any self-respecting young rebel regard it as a challenge, "then you have to do it if you are going to fight against society."

In the case of Olivette and Imamu, the nature of their feelings for each other is never made conscious or explicit by themselves or the author but left intangible and undefined as such feelings must often be in reality. Ms Guy remarked in passing on how difficult it was for some adult males to come to terms with their own feelings of tenderness, to see that "a sensitive person is not necessarily a homosexual". Olivette, though damaged, passes on something valuable to Imamu, which he in turn resolves to teach his mother. At the end of the book he is about to move with her back to Brooklyn, which is the setting of the final Imamu mystery.

I asked Rosa Guy why she wrote trilogies and she said that she became so fond of her characters that she hated to break away from them, so she follows them as far as she can. Certainly to read the books in order is to acquire a much richer appreciation of the various characters as well as to find out the unexpected ways in which their stories develop.

The Friends was the first of the original trilogy, which has been very popular. . . . Like the author, the main character, Phyllisia, comes to Harlem from the West Indies at the age of seven and has to make her way in an alien culture, among classmates some of whom are as snobbish as she is, and all of whom regard West Indians as "monkeys" and mock her accent. She is at first appalled to be befriended by tough and scruffy Edith, whose story continues in the second book ***Edith Jackson.*** Phyllisia's father Calvin, modelled on Ms Guy's own, is a dominant West Indian patriarch. Though he died when the writer was 15, the struggle to deal with her father, to wrestle with her love for him and the need for independence stayed with her for years, she says. She thinks that this sort of father was more common among West Indian than American blacks, and may be one reason for the former's greater confidence. . . .

Despite this powerful father in her background (her mother having died when she was nine) she sees herself as essentially an orphan, looking in and telling the stories of people as she sees them from outside, rather than someone primarily dealing with her own experience. She thinks that one of the main reasons she chose to write at all was because she was an orphan, and that this can stand as a metaphor for her people in the Western Hemisphere, brought over as slaves to help develop the American continent.

> I broaden the metaphor to show that everyone in the hemisphere is really an expatriate, even the Europeans pouring into the United States were, to a large extent, the orphans of Europe; a whole hemisphere of expatriates working on each other emotionally, socially, economically

for what she calls "the orphan reason—they felt stronger, grabbed and killed off the Indians and felt 'I did it' and tried to prevent everyone else from having it.". . .

She married and had a son very young and continued to work, as she had done since her father's death, in a garment factory stitching brassières. Through acting she met people who had been to university. She began to read voraciously and then started to write as an outlet for the anger she felt at the circumstances blacks were forced to live in. She helped found the Black Writers Guild and her first novel was for adults. . . .

She decided to write for young people as a way of challenging society to do something about the conditions in which many young blacks have to live.

> I write these novels because I am so up in arms about what is happening, that young people can be brought up in such situations and no one really does anything about it. I am saying to the world that there are many inner cities in this world, and the destruction of these people is your future; you are destroying your future. . . .
>
> You go round Harlem and see bombed-out buildings for blocks, blocks. It's as though we had actually been at war and I understand it's that way throughout the country in the inner cities. . . .

This background is unsparingly painted in her novels. There is no attempt to glamorize the characters or setting, but her message to the young is an optimistic one. Many of her main characters come to feel that they can take control of their lives and climb out of the destructive environment in which they are placed. Edith Jackson learns to let the young siblings she has struggled to rear go their individual ways, and to accept that for herself an abortion is the necessary first step to a life of her own. Ruby learns to cope when Daphne makes her new bid for freedom through a "bourgie" college. And Imamu tells Brown, the detective, that he is going to make his mother see that "there is such a thing as perfection."

Rosa Guy wants to reach the young because she sees them as the ones to change the world which our generation has brought to the brink of annihilation.

> If you understand where you are in society and learn to grow, it makes you a very valuable tool for self-preservation, not just for yourself, but for other people and eventually, probably the world. It's coming to that; each must stand up and be counted.

And her message is conveyed in powerful, vivid and exciting books.

Beverly Anderson, "The Orphan Factor," in The Times Educational Supplement, *No. 3492, June 3, 1983, p. 42.*

BOOKS FOR KEEPS

Rosa Guy is a Black American writer who has been described as 'the creator of some of the most memorable adolescent characters in modern literature'. Her stories are hard-hitting and compellingly realistic, with a powerful message for young people. She demonstrates a deep understanding and sympathy for young people and the many difficulties they face growing up or purely surviving today. Her books are mainly about Black characters but she doesn't see herself writing only for Black young people:

> I write for a world audience. I want to feel it's a universal not a specifically Black audience. I do believe that people are not that different. What helps one helps another and what destroys one destroys another.

She writes from the conviction that her books have a message.

> I'm trying to raise the consciousness of young people because I believe that the future of the world is in the hands of young people. They are going to become the leaders of another generation. They need to understand it as fully as they can—the survival of the human race may depend on it. . . .

Her first book ***The Friends*** established Rosa Guy as a sympathetic chronicler of contemporary Black life, Black pride and Black expectations and at the same time it introduced one of teenage fiction's most poignant heroes, Edith Jackson.

The Friends chronicles the unlikely and at first unwanted friendship between Phyllisia, newly arrived in Harlem from the West Indies, and scruffy, irrepressible, Edith. Things are bad at home for Phyllisia; she hates her tyrannical father and her mother is slowly dying, but things are infinitely worse for Edith who takes enormous responsibility for her younger family and lives in abject poverty. It is a harrowing story of the pressures, the violence, the poverty of urban America. Nothing is really changed at the end of the book but Phyllisia has begun to come to terms with herself and her father and the point is made very forcibly that real friendship entails responsibilities and obligations. (p. 12)

[***Edith Jackson***] takes up the story of Edith, now 17, and her three surviving sisters living in a foster home. The sisters are learning individually to find their own solutions to their problems but Edith is blind to her own potential and worth, and is passionately concerned to keep the family, the only secure element of her life, together. It is a deeply moving novel which offers a perceptive, harsh account of Edith's search for love and identity. Rosa Guy admits it contains autobiographical elements: being an orphan; the strong father (Calvin); the sister; the West Indian coming to the United States and feeling an outsider. 'Edith Jackson is another extension—a part—of me,' says Rosa.

> At first I thought of killing Edith off, then I wanted to develop her more, in line with things that were really happening to young people around her age, things that really needed to be talked about. Phyllisia, too, emerges as a strong character. She has to be strong to go through that Calvin who is very hard to go through—because they bend your will you never get over them, strong mothers and fathers. It is very hard to get past them, to assert a sense of self.

The book actually written between ***The Friends*** and ***Edith Jackson,*** but published here much later, because of its problematic theme of lesbian love, was ***Ruby,*** which concentrates on Phyllisia's elder sister, Ruby. Ruby is unsure of herself, bored and desperately lonely until she meets fellow classmate, Daphne, and forms a deep and intimate relationship with her. For Ruby, it is a blissful, painful first love affair which is started, shaped and finished by Daphne. At first desolate, Ruby finally sees that her time spent with Daphne has given her the confidence she hitherto lacked to challenge her father and seek her own freedom. The book lacks the intensity of the other two titles but the lesbian relationship is perceptively observed.

The Disappearance introduces for the first time a male central character, Imamu Jones. It is a dramatic thriller for older teenagers which gives a brutally disturbing picture of contemporary American society, contrasting the squalor of downtown Harlem with the outwardly cosy Brooklyn environment.

When Imamu leaves the detention centre where he has been held for a month for robbery with violence, he is flattered to be offered a foster home in Brooklyn by Ann Aimsley, a respectable, socially-minded Black woman with two daughters of her own. Imamu's arrival is inevitably fraught with emotion and when the eight-year-old Aimsley daughter, Perk, disappears, Imamu is an obvious first suspect. Imamu is deeply hurt but his much-despised street wisdom leads him to a horrifying denouement and the discovery of Perk.

New Guys Around the Block continues the story of Imamu in his role as detective (and a third title is promised), helping to solve a mystery which the police have failed to clear up, whilst at the same time working out a pattern for his own survival. Imamu now lives with his alcoholic mother in a run-down apartment. Most of his friends have become victims of the racist society and of life in the ghetto, forced into drug addiction, theft and violence. It is an intense and powerful novel with a strong political message about the destruction of Black family life through the pressures of the ghetto.

Why did Rosa choose a male central character?

> I wrote it particularly because boys in the States find it difficult to read. There's too much television. I questioned myself. How do I get young people to read? I believe profoundly that reading develops the mind. The mind is forced to create images. Wherever that happens, it's strengthening something there, after a while you cease to be the person you were and you become another person intellectually—it's active rather than passive learning. I am taking Imamu from the very lowest possible place—almost accused of murder and could have easily been committed for that crime. He had been a drop-out, was going around with the worst people who were mentally unbalanced because of poverty and all those things and I've put him into another setting, opening a little door for him and following him through that door to see him expand to the very end, to see what decisions he will finally make.

In several of Rosa's books there is a 'mentor' figure, Mrs Aimsley, Mrs Bate. Is this the role Rosa sees herself in, as a writer? 'Young people need the help of older people. With a bit of help, I want to show they could go a long way. So many bright kids are being wasted.'

Rosa's most recent book, ***Paris, Pee Wee and Big Dog,*** is her first novel for younger readers. It is a fast-moving, compelling story about three young Black boys. Paris and his mother have moved to a new apartment away from their previous slum home. It is Saturday morning and Paris has been told to clean the apartment while his mother is out at work, because his bedroom particularly is beginning to look like a tip. But when his friend Pee Wee calls, with compelling arguments about why they should go out to play and leave the cleaning 'till later', Paris succumbs. They are joined by Paris's cousin, Big Dog, and gradually and very convincingly one dramatic event leads to another and the day passes, until it is much too late to do the housework and his mother is distraught with worry. Rosa catches very effectively the youthful language, humour and relationships of the streets in this very readable story about three likeable and individual characters.

Does Rosa Guy see herself as a political writer?

> No, basically, I am not—more sociological, socially conscious sort of writing. My hope, my aim, is to raise awareness in people who read. Reading does that anyway but that's what I want to feel is my contribution—raising awareness of people to things around them, things that are happening because I think that's important.

Can you really be non-political when writing as Rosa does so memorably about poverty, squalor, violence, people often in despair, deprived of both love and material things?

> If you raise the level of awareness of people, it automatically goes into the political, into the need to seek change. You can have all kinds of rhetoric which really has no meaning to you. But if you have awareness, if you basically understand and feel about things, then when you do challenge prevailing concepts, you are in the mental position that you cannot be changed easily.

Passionately she describes one of the most important influences on her life:

> The lack of concern for what does destroy, particularly amongst the minority youth, particularly Black kids. Prejudice, lack of concern, translates itself into lack of money for schools, lack of money for well-trained teachers, lack of money for decent housing. Many inner cities in the States have been bombed out since the 1960's, with no programme of rehabilitation or rebuilding. It's worse now. Houses are bombed out/boarded up. Drugs have taken a terrible toll, have ruined the infrastructure of the cities. It was all of little consequence to law enforcement until it became part of the white drugs scene. Then people cared. All these facts glare at you, it really glares at you: little kids on the block at 12 o'clock at night, 1 o'clock, 2 o'clock in the morning in these bombed-out places. I put it in ***New Guys Around the Block.*** It's traumatic. It really traumatises me. I *have* to write about it. I call it genocide—it's a sure way to kill off the people.

This passionate concern with what she sees around her and the need to transmit a message to young people comes across strongly in all her work, but does it worry her that her books are not taken seriously by the people in power, because they are published as young adult books?

> I think my books *are* taken seriously. That's why there was flack about ***Ruby.*** Young people read and things of importance stick. I don't think my books are easily forgotten.

Many young people both black and white in Britain today would wholeheartedly endorse that, as they anxiously await her next book and absorb her enduring message. (pp. 12-13)

"Authorgraph No. 30: Rosa Guy," in Books for Keeps, *No. 30, January, 1985, pp. 12-13.*

AUDREY LASKI

Why do Rosa Guy's novels make those of almost all other writers for adolescents seem washed-out? Is it pure talent, or some special quality of the Black experience that gives them their hard-edged power? It's perhaps a pity that Puffin Plus have brought out ***Edith Jackson*** . . . and ***The Disappearance*** . . . at the same time, since it highlights the family resemblance between her tough mother figures, but this and a small measure of implausibility in the mystery plot of ***The Disappearance*** are all the faults I can find in these two stunning stories; ***Edith Jackson*** is an almost unbearably powerful and somehow entirely unmelodramatic account of the horrors that can assail an orphaned ghetto family in care.

Audrey Laski, in a review of "Edith Jackson" and "The Disappearance," in The Times Educational Supplement, *No. 3583, March 1, 1985, p. 29.*

THE FRIENDS **(1973)**

I feel especially blessed when reading the books of Virginia Hamilton, Toni Cade Bambara, Lucille Clifton, June Jordan, Louise Merriweather, Toni Morrison and other fine *engagé* black women writers; for I am thinking of a young black girl who spent the first 20 years of her life without seeing a single book in which the heroine was a person like herself. . . .

I do not know what damage being that girl has done me; I suspect a good deal. But now, with books like Rosa Guy's heart-slammer, ***The Friends,*** I relive those wretched, hungry-for-heroines years and am helped to verify the existence and previous condition of myself.

A young girl, Phyllisia Cathy, moves from an island in the West Indies to Harlem. She is 14; her sister, Ruby, two years older. Phyllisia's problems seem overwhelming: New York, after life on her sunlit island, is cold, cruel and filthy; Harlem is a sea of stuck-up neighbors on one side and rowdy classmates on the other. Her sister Ruby is completely ruined for intelligent thought by her beauty and her need to "get along" no matter what. Phyllisia, a bright student who takes her lessons seriously, is insulted daily by remarks on her West Indian ancestry, and is beaten up by classmates for giving correct answers in school.

Her white teacher, Mrs. Lass, long prodded by racist impulses, bursts her restraints one day to call her ninth graders the children of pigs. Phyllisia's father, Calvin, is a menacing braggart who can show concern for his daughters in only the most tried, trusted and useless ways: he beats them, locks them in and makes constant comments on the salaciousness of their characters. To him the only ambition of pride is to be wealthy. And, most devastating of all, Phyllisia's beautiful mother, Ramona, is dying of cancer.

What Phyllisia needs, God not being interested, is a friend. But when Edith Jackson approaches her, she is refused.

Edith Jackson, 15, always comes to school late (when she comes at all), "her clothes unpressed, her stockings bagging about her legs with big holes . . . on each heel, to expose a round, brown circle of dry skin the size of a quarter." Her knowledge of school studies is near zero; her grammar—especially to Phyllisia's prim and proper thinking—a threat to nerve and ear. She has no parents, she swears and she steals. But she is kind and offers her friendship *and protection* to the haughty Phyllisia, who constantly thinks up new reasons to be ashamed of her.

And so begins the struggle that is the heart of this very important book: the fight to gain perception of one's own real character; the grim struggle for self-knowledge and the almost killing internal upheaval that brings the necessary growth of compassion and humility *and courage*, so that friendship (of any kind, but especially between those of notable economic and social differences) can exist.

This book is called a "juvenile." So be a juvenile while you read it. Rosa Guy will give you back a large part of the memory of those years that you've been missing.

Alice Walker, in a review of "The Friends," in The New York Times Book Review, *November 4, 1973, p. 26.*

[***The Friends***] is a penetrating story of considerable emotional depth. . . . A strong, honest story—often tragic but ultimately hopeful—of complex, fully-realized characters and of the ambivalence and conflicts in human nature.

Ethel L. Heins, in a review of "The Friends," in The Horn Book Magazine, *Vol. L, No. 2, April, 1974, p. 152.*

There is affection . . . in Rosa Guy's short novel, ***The Friends,*** but also a hard core of toughness, which goes with its New York setting. . . .

Rosa Guy's evocation of the hot, steamy city, the subways, the coolness of air-conditioned shops after the sweltering streets, the oasis of Central Park, the narrow restaurant where Phyllisia's father works, aproned and sweating, alongside his employees, make this a vigorous and unusual book. Nor is the New York scene so alien as to be incomprehensible, perhaps because the heroine is herself an outsider and so views it all through foreign, critical eyes. And if the details of the plot smack slightly of the Dickensian—Edith's father vanished, her brother shot by the police, her little sister dead of meningitis and herself consigned to an orphanage—the feelings are very true to life.

"Lives against the Odds," in The Times Literary Supplement, *No. 3785, September 20, 1974, p. 1006.*

Neither friend is very endearing; one a rather priggish girl from a proud West Indian family, the other a sluttish, thieving but ever loyal and loving drudge struggling to keep her parentless family together. . . . The style of writing is idiomatic and rather difficult in its unfamiliarity, the setting and life style is alien—one is conscious of being an outsider to the Harlem community—and this leads to difficulty in identifying with the characters despite—perhaps even because—of the author's very real sympathy with them.

M. R. Hewitt, in a review of "The Friends," in The Junior Bookshelf, *Vol. 38, No. 6, December, 1974, p. 378.*

Rosa Guy has written a real novel about real people in a real world. The characters' problems arise naturally from their background, circumstances, personalities and relationships; they are not problems imposed by an author who wants to write about problems. The story is full of incident; the life of Harlem is ever-present, though rarely obtrusive; the writing is alive, with extra richness in the West Indian speech. Highly recommended.

M. H. Miller, in a review of "The Friends," in Children's Book Review, *Vol. IV, No. 4, Winter, 1974-75, p. 152.*

In this harsh, candid book prejudice, social and personal, sway the behaviour of the various characters and lead to serious mistakes and tragic occurrences. The close atmosphere of the city, the feeling of suppressed violence in the streets, match the tensions in the homes of the two girls—the one as needy and disorganised as the other is disciplined. It is not too fanciful, perhaps, to see the alliance between Phyllisia and Edith as an image of that unity in freedom and understanding which society tries in vain to achieve.

Margery Fisher, in a review of "The Friends," in Growing Point, *Vol. 13, No. 7, January, 1975, p. 2558.*

RUBY **(1976)**

[***Ruby*** is] an intensely committed novel talking directly to teenagers, black, white, particularly those who are uncertain and scared of what their loneliness may involve them in. This is a very sensitive novel in which adolescent homosexuality is viewed as nothing so frightening, but perhaps just a way-step towards maturity. Ruby is desperately unhappy, unfairly labeled as an "Uncle Tom" in her school. She becomes drawn to Daphne, a strong, dramatic black girl, who, we will learn, has her own secret fears and family problems. Ruby's father is a lost, lonely widower. Her younger sister is spunky, a reader finding release in books. If Rosa Guy had taken a camera and put it down in 1970 (the year of her novel) on a completely believable black middle class family situation in any big city in America, she could not have achieved a more riveting picture of basically decent people, floundering because of the generation gap. Neatest of all, she has a sense of humor and hope for the future. (pp. 80-1)

A review of "Ruby," in Publishers Weekly, *Vol. 209, No. 16, April 19, 1976, pp. 80-1.*

Ruby, Rosa Guy's newest novel, reminds us that as parents, as teachers, as friends, as lovers, this business of being responsible in any major way for the development of the delicate fibers of somebody else's psyche, spirit, personality—somebody else's life—is an awesome, frightening and dangerous challenge. Consciously or subconsciously, our own insecurities and fears, our own niches of pleasure, our own safe patterns of respectability guide the hands that slap or pat, the eyes that see, don't see or see too much, the tongue that won't move, moves right or moves wrong—slashing indelibly. All of us are largely determined by these various strokes, and maybe despite or maybe because of them we get to be eighteen and older and have kids that get to be eighteen and so forth. If we're lucky in the process, everybody connected grows.

The realization that we all need to belong somewhere, to ourselves, to each other, is not new. What Rosa Guy has done in

Ruby, however, is to place under the microscope a why and how not dealt with in any books about Black people that come to mind. (pp. 118-19)

The novel centers around Ruby's struggle toward self. . . . Ruby, moving from father-fear, cannot define herself except through Daphne who, in the end, pushes her out of her life, a step away from loneliness and a step closer to self-discovery. We expect that Ruby, the great compassionate, the profound and instinctive lover, will find her way.

The first novel about this family, ***Friends,*** gives us a beautiful opportunity to explore its beginnings in New York. ***Ruby*** is a chance to say "Amen" to the importance of love in our search for self definition and personal security. ***Ruby*** is a truly exciting life-love-people adventure. I hadn't expected to find myself crying as I read the last words. Ruby, Phyllisia, their father, Calvin, the amazing Daphne, Mrs. Duprey, Uncle Frank—all the characters are richly dimensional, joyously real. ***Ruby*** is an almost-for-everybody novel. A great story for almost everybody wrestling life to some manageable proportion. (pp. 119-20)

Ruby Dee, "'Ruby': Notes on a New Novel," in Freedomways, *Vol. 16, No. 2, second quarter, 1976, pp. 118-20.*

Rosa Guy is an extraordinary writer. In her novels ***Bird At My Window, The Friends,*** and now ***Ruby,*** Ms. Guy's characters are so vivid, her language so true, her sense of the emotional life, especially, of young adults so on target, that reading her is like listening to those rousing, nearly forgotten lyrics of one's youth which though not immediately recognized by the brain are nonetheless responded to quickly by the emotions. In her upbeat sense of economic struggle, and her awareness of and willingness to engage sexual as well as political complexity in her characters, she produces books that are crucial to an understanding of ourselves and our time. Though ostensibly written for young adult readers her stories have a richness and maturity that appeals to any age. She writes of young lives with the respect and integrity they deserve, without condescension either in language or in tone. (p. 51)

Daphne is a rare character in black American fiction. Not only is she a very young woman who takes her destiny into her own hands, she becomes, somehow, a master over her own history. She *decides,* after careful reasoning, what kind of life she intends to lead, then calmly pursues it. Her struggles over moral questions are minimal because her faith in herself, and her right to *be* herself, is absolute. Though not nearly so sympathetic a character as Ruby, she is distinctly admirable. And above all, intelligent.

What she has already given up: a softness for cripples, American racists (which the white woman teacher is) among them, she values in Ruby, whom she realizes is "civilized," uncorrupted by the pervasive American indifference to human suffering. Loving Ruby, however, (who can not stand up to her father in affirming her love for Daphne) reinforces Daphne's contempt for this very softness and generosity in Ruby's character. She realizes that because of these qualities in Ruby, there is a chance that the love they share will inhibit her, Daphne's, educational and political growth: college, a preparation for future revolutionary work. She could ruin her life—which she understands is valuable, both to herself and to black people, "on a hummer," i.e., (in this case) too deep a love for the wrong person. Who, being the wrong person, would ask the wrong sacrifices of her.

It is in the handling of the love affair between Daphne and Ruby that Ms. Guy shows herself a master in writing of the emotions, ideas and fears of post-adolescents. For it is not, this story, sensational. It is not about—really—being gay or bisexual. (At the end Daphne "decides" to go straight, "for a while," because she has promised her mother. Ruby thinks of returning the affections of a male friend.) It is a love story, and like most love stories it is about the search for someone who cares, the discovery—after immense longing and loneliness—of the ideal person in whom to trust, upon whom one may rely, to whom one may offer one's bruised and yearning heart, and from whom one may expect gentle and loving treatment of this gift.

When I finished the book I was most grateful for Ms. Guy's ability to depict her characters' intelligence. For these are characters who *think* about the world, who *talk* about politics, who are at ease with ideas of more than one interpretation. It has distressed me that some recent novels by black writers are devoid of any such complexity, and that the characters seem mere sexual *compulsions,* mindless, soulless, frightening in their limited ability to comprehend a world beyond the genitals. Though it is unfortunately true that novels about black folks endlessly fucking sell better than those in which blacks exhibit an ability to think, this hardly seems a valid reason to sell back to society the same stereotype it has so cleverly foisted upon us.

Ruby we need. Very much. (pp. 51-2)

Alice Walker, in a review of "Ruby," in The Black Scholar, *Vol. 8, No. 3, December, 1976, pp. 51-2.*

Daphne is an arrogant, domineering person who seeks to exercise absolute control over the elements of her environment, including and especially over the people to whom she is exposed. Disinclined to accommodate other people's needs and desires, she is strikingly authoritarian and power-oriented. Ruby, being unsure of herself and of her identity, is passive, submissive and dependent—a perfect foil for the superiority syndrome out of which Daphne operates.

Instead of the two young women engaging in a relationship of equality, mutual support and exchange, Daphne manipulates Ruby and enjoys their relationship wholly on her own terms. There is little evidence that Daphne cares for Ruby. Indeed, Daphne seems to lack warmth or deep affection for anyone.

Basically, Ruby's personality problems come off as being the story's central element, yet they remain unresolved. In the end, father Calvin promotes the rekindling of a relationship between Ruby and a neighborhood boy whom Calvin had previously spurned as a suitor for his daughter. In the absence of any evidence that Ruby has grown in the course of the story's events, the implication is that she will once again neurotically seek fulfillment through another person—this time a male.

Sexism is reflected both in the aggressive/passive relationship between Ruby and Daphne and in the implications of the book's conclusion. Another component of the story's sex-role stereotyping is the Daphne characterization itself, which recalls the pervasive image of lesbians as being universally "mannish" in their behavior. The story is further marred by a general unevenness in the writing. Attitudes and actions are assigned to people that would have been more characteristic of the 1940's or 1950's than the story's 1960's setting, and occasional passages of "purple prose" are cloying. In the case of Daphne, her super-intellectual manner of speech and ultra-sophisticated behavior are unrealistic.

Anti-Semitism taints the portrait of the racist teacher, who is named Miss Gottlieb. Given the extremely negative qualities that are assigned to this character (she is crippled, ugly and seems to possess no redeeming virtues), her clearly ethnic name automatically evokes negative images of the cultural group with which the name is associated. Unfortunate also is the author's choice of words in describing Daphne's mother as "fair, much fairer than Daphne (Ruby is "bronze" with light brown eyes). To describe light-skinned Black persons as "fair" in 1976 is both anachronistic and reinforces the concept that lightness—in skin, hair, eyes—is a more desirable state of being.

Due to its mixed messages and murky style, ***Ruby*** fails as a novel for young adults. (p. 15)

Regina Williams, in a review of "Ruby," in Interracial Books for Children Bulletin, *Vol. 8, No. 2, 1977, pp. 14-15.*

Ruby is unique in two respects. First, it is the first young adult book ever hailed as important for *adult* readers by a respected reviewer—Alice Walker—in the prestigious pages of *Black Scholar* magazine. Because of this highly unusual praise, five Council people (in addition to the reviewer whose comments appear above) were asked to read the book and comment. One found it "sensitive," and the four others agreed in substance with our own reviewer that the book should *not* be recommended.

Secondly, ***Ruby*** is the first young adult book to deal with a lesbian love affair. Moreover, the two young protagonists express no feelings of guilt about their affair—a welcome relief. These factors may account for the selection of ***Ruby*** as one of the year's ten best by the ALA's Young Adult Services Division. If so, we are reminded of the period when there were no children's books about Third World people; hence, when the first few appeared, people were so delighted that a vacuum was beginning to be filled that they tended to receive the new books uncritically. Later, people became more selective and began to criticize the subtle stereotypes some of the books reinforced. ***Ruby*** reinforces sexist stereotypes about heterosexual males, heterosexual females *and* lesbians by implying that *real* lesbians are "masculine" types like Daphne, while "feminine" types like Ruby are destined to "go straight."

A review of "Ruby," in Interracial Books for Children Bulletin, *Vol. 8, No. 2, 1977, p. 15.*

Sibling rivalry is, by common consent, the curse of adolescence. . . . Rosa Guy's trilogy is unusual, however, in that patriarchal authority is the source of the girls' problems, not their salvation and solace. . . .

Ruby takes up the story where ***The Friends*** left it, elaborating earlier motifs, such as the conflict between black pupils and racially prejudiced teachers who are themselves vulnerable and intimidated.

Publication in Britain may have been delayed by misgivings about Ruby's passion for her class-mate, Daphne, a voluptuous autodidact who combines grooming with genius, and quotes Shakespeare, Longfellow and chairman Mao. The girl's mental and physical communion is indeed embarrassing, but no more so than the routine insertion of Young Adult love-scenes elsewhere—"Lizzie had, so to speak, stayed kissed." An occasional qualm, blush or squirm of embarrassment is a small price to pay for the rare authenticity of Rosa Guy's Harlem and her unrivalled knowledge of the milieu she depicts.

Marion Glastonbury, "Bites of the Apple," in The Times Educational Supplement, *No. 3412, November 20, 1981, p. 35.*

EDITH JACKSON **(1978)**

The reader becomes intimately involved with the life of Edith Jackson from the first sentence in this powerfully written novel. On one level, the novel is a skillfully written account of the seventeen-year-old hero's determination to assume full responsibility for her three orphaned sisters, "her family," as soon as she reaches eighteen. But in 187 pages of tight, dramatic writing, Ms. Guy manages to address several critical social issues and to bring into sharp focus those special problems that are encountered by women of varying ages.

There is a devastating indictment of the residential care bureaucracy, referred to in the novel as "The Institution." Exposed are the gross insensitivity to the needs of children, the damaging effect of the constant shunting of children from one foster home to another, and the physical and mental retardation that can result from emotional starvation and physical neglect. The sexuality and sexual problems of women of varying ages and their male relationships are explored with great sensitivity and honesty. Running through the entire book is the theme of the special vulnerability of women and that special strength which enables so many to survive.

It is impossible not to become emotionally involved while reading this book. Ms. Guy deserves high praise for her remarkable achievement.

Beryle Banfield, in a review of "Edith Jackson," in Interracial Books for Children Bulletin, *Vol. 9, No. 6, 1978, p. 15.*

In a first-person account, occasionally colloquial and only infrequently coarse, the seventeen-year-old orphan [Edith Jackson] tells of her efforts to keep her young sisters—Bessie, Suzy, and Minnie—together as a family. . . . The novel, written in a naturalistic vein, is powerful in its depiction of character and creates scenes memorable for their psychological truth; and so well integrated are theme, character, and situation that they redeem whatever is superficially sordid in the story.

Paul Heins, in a review of "Edith Jackson," in The Horn Book Magazine, *Vol. LV, No. 5, October, 1978, p. 524.*

[Both ***Edith Jackson*** and *The Wind Is Not a River* by Arnold A. Griese] have found their drama at the same source: they are stories of children without parents, young people who are displaced from ordinary society. It is an animating source and in ***Edith Jackson*** it has been mined to include an even larger world, one in which the superficial difference between outsider and insider has been understood and transcended. . . .

[Set in the present], ***Edith Jackson*** is narrated by its namesake in a tough idiomatic vernacular which exactly mirrors the violent and exhausting events that assault its characters. . . .

With extreme care and skill, Rosa Guy makes poverty into a dynamic in her story. As Dickens does, she uses it as a character and a setting, as if it were a manipulative cruel uncle hiding just out of sight. . . .

A harrowing, rich picture, Edy's strengths and virtues are tested and stretched and seem to fail. For these events demand more, demand that she change, that she be strong and brave as she has been, but in new ways. Whether she can do so provides a climax of merit and power to a strong, good book. . . .

[Rosa Guy] firmly leaves her story in Edith's grasp. This location is important for it further humanizes those seeming outsiders and thereby further diminishes the distance between them and the reader. Works dealing with unfamiliar worlds, with outsiders, are helpful for the opportunity of those on the outside to be able publicly to express their pain and their sovereignty, (and are no doubt useful as well if only for their educational value for others). But even better, a book such as ***Edith Jackson*** which can speak to "them" as well as to "us" will not admit to any such a human division, and that is a statement of great value, spoken with passion and courage, to be heard and shared.

Victor Kantor Burg, "Novels of Children Alone against the World," in The Christian Science Monitor, *October 23, 1978, p. B13.*

Rosa Guy's reputation as a novelist of exceptional skill was established with her novel ***Ruby.*** Here it is reaffirmed in ***Edith Jackson,*** written in simple language that belies its power, depth and perceptions. Though seemingly written for an adolescent and young adult readership, the novel has appeal for all, with its love story of unrequited love and teenage characters, with its gargantuan problem of orphanage and black femininity, and how the former becomes an acid test to the latter's realization. It is a novel for all who desire a better understanding of the conditions of Afro-American female youth in a society bent on their destruction.

Edith Jackson is not a novel of fantasy or escapism; it is a gut-hitting story rooted in present day U.S. life. Today, the attack on the working-class family structure, especially that of the Afro-American community, has become an intricate part of the oppressive apparatus of U.S. society. However, few of our writers have explored with such realism, love for, and condemnation of, the plight of the Afro-American orphan within this context. Ms. Guy has done so, singling out the special problems of female orphans. (pp. 47-8)

Ms. Guy develops her female characters and situations sensitively and masterfully. Her knack for weaving an intricate story laced with subplots and scenes is superlatively demonstrated; the novel virtually steps off the page, as a poignant, painfully tragic slice of Afro-American womanhood. Death dogs this family's and Edith's footsteps—physical, spiritual, psychological and emotional death. . . . Ms. Guy also explores interracial adoption and its problems effectively. But it is the confrontation between the older and younger female Afro-American orphan-generations that emerges as the highlight of the novel; between Edith, the orphan groping for air and light, and Mrs. Bates, the orphan who seized both. The chemistry of their relation is revealed in the following:

> You want to get away, Edith. I'll never keep you if you don't want to stay. But remember, you can keep your hands on your hips, tap your feet, stare the world in the eyes, use every four-letter word invented to defy goodness, chew gum as hard as your jaw will allow, and until *you* decide that you are a person who can make choices and fight for them—you will never begin to count.

This is experience and an indomitable will speaking here; it is mother-to-daughter talk, lessons learned well in the University of Hardknocks: Life. With the fineness of this novel there does, however, remain one harsh and disconcerting, hard-to-accept tenet that runs throughout it. The image and treatment of Afro-American manhood. There are no whole, healthy and redeemable males in this novel, unless I missed him/them. This fact in no way belittles or diminishes the truth of the situations presented by Ms. Guy. That Afro-American men, men in general, have quite a lot to learn and demonstrate in the struggle for woman's equality and treatment is, in my opinion, uncontestable.

Still, it is equally uncontestable that the image rendered by Ms. Guy is hardly a reflection of a whole and accurate, majoritive, image of male Afro-America. One comes away from her novel with a narrow, one-sided picture of men, who are family deserters (Edith's father), statutory rapists (Mr. Daniels), stepfathers, "dominated" weak husbands (Mr. Bates), "cop and split, sell your buddy a bit" young adults (James), or better dead (?) at an early age (Randy). It is a trail of horrors and living/dead corpses, beyond redemption.

In light of the racist filth and stereotypes projected, in barrages, by the Banfields, Shockleys and Jensens, and finding an echo in reverse, in such works by Afro-Americans as *Black Macho and the Myth of the Superwoman* by Michele Wallace, Ms. Guy's treatment of Afro-American men is tragic and disheartening. I have to ask, where are the men like my father, and many other fathers and men I know, who are direct opposites, in her novel? Are we to believe and accept the view that our men (and one has to include white men too—the white male orphan and his derelict father) aren't worth the earth immediately under their feet? This is the only conclusion to be drawn from this novel. Seen in social-political terms, are we to conclude there is no hope for Afro-American male/female unity, a prerequisite in our fight for national equality and liberation?

True, Ms. Guy's novel cannot hope to answer all these questions definitively, and one would be remiss to demand or expect it. However, what is possible and necessary is that Ms. Guy can and does assist in answering them, albeit negatively in this case. The failure of the novel to address this problem adequately is not peculiar to Ms. Guy's work. It is a problem presently resounding through U.S. literature as a whole, and most recently in the literature of some Afro-American women. That it is a reflection of a crisis in our social-personal relations is uncontestable. What is missing are the social, political and economic roots of the problem; i.e., capitalist, racist society; and the solution of the problem; i.e., joint struggle to correct the problem.

How this reflects itself in any artistic work is not an easy answer, and is intricately tied to the author's outlook, perception and recognition of the problem and possible answers. It is not remiss, however, for a readership to demand such an approach from an author. It is this relationship that can become the basis of truly great and lasting art—art rooted in reality, seeking to define it, but above all change it. This ***Edith Jackson*** doesn't do.

Still, Ms. Guy's novel is not primarily concerned with the treatment of the male condition as such, but with that of women, and must be finally judged on this basis as to its overall merit. And on this score she does not fail you. The characters have personalities of multidimensional diversity and complexity. The subject matter is certainly topical and implicative of the overall condition of Afro-American youth. The novel has opened a new corridor of social life for our writers and readers to further explore and define. Ms. Guy has made the start seriously; she deserves your attention. (pp. 48-50)

Antar Sudan Katara Mberi, "Through a Teenager's Eyes," in Freedomways, *Vol. 19, No. 1, first quarter, 1979, pp. 47-50.*

Throughout, Edith is believable as a survivor who holds on to her own identity and integrity. She can be confused, misguided, vulnerable—but she is never defeated.

Rosa Guy is a novelist with exceptional abilities. Her work is emotionally demanding for YA readers, some of whom aren't perhaps ready for the starkness of her work.

Janet Julian, in a review of "Edith Jackson," in Kliatt Young Adult Paperback Book Guide, *Vol. XVI, No. 1, January, 1982, p. 8.*

A world away from the glossy clichés of television's 'Different Strokes', this is a gritty look at the lives and destinies of four black girls. . . . If the catalogue of horrors it portrays from child molesting, through indifferent state caring, to deaths of various and distressing kinds, leaves no comfort for the reader, it may be that there is no comfort to be given. The idiomatic first person narration is sometimes difficult to relate to and initially the book is very unapproachable, but is worth persevering with.

George English, in a review of "Edith Jackson," in Books for Your Children, *Vol. 20, No. 2, Summer, 1985, p. 17.*

THE DISAPPEARANCE (1979)

Worlds collide when streetwise, 16-year-old Imamu, acquitted of murder and robbery, is released into the custody of the middle-class Aimsley family. Harlem-bred Imamu knows life with all its raw edges. Nurtured during his short childhood by his now-alcoholic mother, Imamu has learned to be a survivor. He responds with intelligence and street-taught instinct to the sights and signals of Harlem's stark realities.

Conversely, the Aimsley home is the picture of perfection—a successful middle-class black family living on a quiet, tree-lined Brooklyn street. A capable, concerned mother, who engineered Imamu's placement with her family; hardworking, authoritarian father; intelligent older daughter, a college student; lovely but impish younger daughter; and voluptuous family friend all share this world of beauty and perfection.

But from the first Imamu discovers that the signals here are different and that the trappings of this ordered and beautiful life hide small dangers. Within 36 hours of his arrival, the Aimsley's beloved younger daughter, Perk, has disappeared and the stage is set for a series of confrontations that shatter the veneer of quiet civility in the household and place Imamu in an all-too-familiar danger. He is once again accused. The police and Ann Aimsley, his much idealized "rescuer," suspect him in the disappearance of young Perk.

The Disappearance . . . is a compelling and suspenseful story. The reader is immediately captured by the characters, who are so sharply defined, so clearly who they are. Dora Belle could only be a quirky, middle-aged West Indian and only Ann Aimsley, as Guy draws her, could be the queen of her dust-free, plastic-covered home. It is as if Guy excised whole chunks of life and brought her characters up whole. Juxtaposing characters and details of their lives, Guy outlines a picture. She paints a picture of images built up and arduously maintained to mask those common human frailties—fear, loneliness and insecurity—which touch people wherever they live. And so we see those frailties as they move an Ann Aimsley in Brooklyn or Imamu's mother in Harlem and set off events that march steadily toward tragedy.

And it is tragedy and victims that we find here, victims—intended or unintended—of false images. The victimizers are here as well. But there are no happy endings. What we are offered, and I think more realistically, is characters who are "willing to move from where they are," to use their experiences as a basis for growth. In Imamu, Guy gives us such a character, a victim who turns adversity to his benefit, one who dares to find some advantage in his disadvantaged life style.

The Disappearance will be no disappointment to readers of Guy's previous work or to young adults and adults newly discovering her. It is a suspenseful and readable novel that treats thought-provoking and complex issues.

Jerrie Norris, "Urban Strife on Suburban Streets," in The Christian Science Monitor, *October 15, 1979, p. B4.*

There are some soft points [in ***The Disappearance***]: surely the police spend more time and effort searching for lost Black girls than is indicated here, and the Aimsley family seems to accept Perk's disappearance a bit too readily. Some readers might have difficulty with the Black and West Indian speech; others may not appreciate the "down" ending. But, by story's close, each character has touched us and the fine delineation of all of them stands out as Guy's greatest strength.

Robert Unsworth, in a review of "The Disappearance," in School Library Journal, *Vol. 26, No. 3, November, 1979, p. 88.*

Her publisher once said about Rosa Guy that her "literary themes stem from the fact that she is black and a woman." I suppose this kind of labeling is inevitable, but it is misleading. For a great strength of Guy's work is her ability to peel back society's labels and reveal beneath them highly individual men and women.

The Disappearance . . . brings together Imamu, a boy from the Harlem streets, the Aimsleys, a middle-class Brooklyn family, and their West Indian friends and neighbors. All of these people are black, which in no way diminishes the distance each must travel if he is to understand the other. Nor is there a single definition of womanhood. Imamu's wino mother; the immaculate, socially aware Ann Aimsley; the man-baiting Dora Belle; and Gail, a sheltered college student, spouting undigested liberal slogans—each is a carefully drawn character whose hidden strengths and weaknesses have the power to heal or to destroy. Imamu has cause to fear each one of them, and they, him.

This is a story about fear and its tragic consequences. Not just the fear of the powerless black in an unfeeling or cruel white society, but the myriad fears which cause black persons to mistrust and hurt each other. . . .

This is a harsh book, but not a hopeless one. It is a book which cries to its readers to resist being sucked in—crushing and being crushed—but it is not a polemic. For Rosa Guy, the writer, is not primarily a black or a woman, but one of that rare and wonderful breed, a storyteller. May her tribe increase.

Katherine Paterson, "A Family of Strangers," in Book World—The Washington Post, *November 11, 1979, p. 21.*

When the blurb on the jacket says 'a powerful and disturbing novel for teenagers' it is interesting to guess how many will say 'Goody, goody,—sex and violence' and how many, 'Oh Lord. More grim and shabby reality'. Well, on this occasion we simply have a first-rate novel. . . . That [Guy] is writing of a scene she knows intimately is very obvious and she has succeeded in putting the throbbing problems of an underprivileged community into words which ricochet off the pages till the reader is awash with impressions, and the world she is writing of is made manifest. It would be impossible to read this book and not understand what it is like to be a young black boy in trouble with the police; intelligent, ambitious, tough, but alone. . . . This is the writing of an intelligent, well-balanced woman who can see all the complex reasons for situations being as they are, and who can write about them without bitterness or prejudice. I look forward eagerly to seeing her name again.

Eileen A. Archer, "The Disappearance," in Book Window, *Vol. 7, No. 3, Summer, 1980, p. 26.*

[***The Disappearance,*** *Harper's Mother* by Wendy Simons, and *Catherine Loves* by Timothy Ireland] are a depressing trio, continually reminding the reader that life is nasty and that growing up is extremely painful; the authors' creativity hamstrung by the feeling that problems and messages are more important than any other consideration. ***The Disappearance*** . . . is the best, being particularly good in its ability to evoke a sense of place—the contrasts between middle-class black New York (Brooklyn) and the crime-ridden ghetto of Harlem. . . . It is interesting to see how black liberal modes of thinking crumble; how the tensions within the family turn to ugly hysteria when the smooth easy-going surface of their lives is destroyed.

The characters are credible; they develop and grow, not always in the way the reader expects. But the book is marred by absurdly improbable twists in the plot—Perk is killed by her Aunt Dora and buried in wet cement when she discovers that Dora's beautiful hair is a wig. No one of any age is going to accept that very easily. It reflects the author's uncertain feelings about writing for adolescents—that somehow subtly changing relationships are not enough; that, to hold the reader's attention, a grisly crime story has to be tagged on to what is otherwise a persuasive portrayal of real life.

David Rees, "Approaching Adulthood," in The Times Literary Supplement, *No. 4034, July 18, 1980, p. 807.*

There is violence and tragedy in the book, developed with ruthless honesty, and a scrutiny of human motives that depends on a brilliant realisation of individuals, from spoiled, pretty little Perk to the vain, beautiful Dora Belle and the elderly lodger who is drawn into a complex situation. Above all, the story carries in its formal structure and vigorous dialogue an optimistic view of adolescence, as it follows the harsh process of growing up in Imamu and his new foster-sister Gail.

Margery Fisher, in a review of "The Disappearance," in Growing Point, *Vol. 19, No. 3, September, 1980, p. 3757.*

MIRROR OF HER OWN (1981)

Mary Abbot, 17, is shy and plain and stutters. Her efforts to find acceptance within her high-school crowd are handicapped not only by her unfortunate friendship with abrasive and prejudiced Gloria but also by the contrast between Mary and her beautiful, talented 22-year-old sister Roxanne, the object of attention from the very eligible John Drysdale. In Oak Bluff, an affluent enclave, the Drysdales represent money, power and position while the Abbots, comfortable enough, seem ordinary and meek, to the point of having allowed the Drysdales to usurp property rightfully belonging to the Abbots. The main theme is Mary's unrequited "love" for John, obviously unworthy, unrequited only until too much wine, pot and cocaine bring about the outcome for which Mary has yearned. It is, however, clearly a case of exploitation on the part of John, and Mary's flight through a swampy wood after her escapade is made to seem like a purgatorial punishment. The empty values of the white characters, as exemplified by their conspicuous consumption of clothes, homes, yachts, liquor and drugs, are contrasted with those of a few Black characters, who are proud, dignified and financially secure, and by a patronizingly superior African visitor. Though this purports, on the book jacket blurb, to be "a strong and perceptive novel of a young woman's search for an end to a life lived in the shadow of an older sister," it delivers a cliché-laden, moralistic story about cardboard figures.

Lillian L. Shapiro, in a review of "Mirror of Her Own," in School Library Journal, *Vol. 27, No. 9, May, 1981, p. 73.*

Rosa Guy should be commended on her new book, ***Mirror Of Her Own.*** This story for young adults is very good and will give many young readers food for thought.

The food for thought comes from the main story line as well as some underlying themes brought to the surface. The primary theme is one of self-identity. . . . How Mary finally comes into her own can best be told by the story itself, but important here is that perhaps some teenagers (and even some of us adults) will benefit from Mary's experience and hopefully avoid some of the traps she gets herself entangled in on her journey to herself.

As I said before, there are other themes here. One is the question of "power", who holds it, why etc. Through the character of John, Roxanne's rich boyfriend, we are given some interesting insights into that question. While other characters, Anikwi, an African prince, Fatima, the daughter of an Egyptian diplomat, Ron, a rich Jew, and Emma, the daughter of the only Black family living in Oak Bluff, present varying views on that same question.

Though the character of Anikwi comes off as a little too good to be true, he nonetheless is key as a focal point around which important questions are raised. Secondly, the perspective of the book is important as it gives us insight into the white middle and upperclass family and their relationships in a small affluent community. This is the type of community from which many of this country's future leaders in government and in particular business will come. (pp. 67, 72)

Jadi Z. Omowale, in a review of "Mirror of Her Own," in Black Books Bulletin, *Vol. 7, No. 3, 1981, pp. 67, 72.*

It is impossible to respond to such a work with pleasure or to write about it without scorn. In ***Mirror of Her Own*** no one except foreigners behaves well; no one is honest, brave, or sincere; no one has the sense to reject the slobs and cruel little misses who inhabit the Abbots' world. The novel has no center, no moral compass. When Mary turns away from the Drysdales of this world, she retreats into herself. But what kind of solution is this? Emulating her narcissistic sister will not bring this profoundly confused adolescent any improvement in virtue or strength of character. At the end of the book she is just as pathetic as she was before. Ditto her parents, her sister, and her friends.

The literary style does not help. Ms. Guy specializes in pomposity: "Drizzle, mist, gloom, permeated her spirits"; "the stench of their awful capabilities, their spoiled friendship, had already become a casualty"; "she fell, and her face dug in to the smell of rotten leaves." Young people interested in writing can only pick up bad habits from ***Mirror of Her Own.***

Where are you, Jane Austen, when we need you?

Francis Goskowski, in a review of "Mirror of Her Own," in Best Sellers, *Vol. 41, No. 6, September, 1981, p. 238.*

Except for Mary, the characters are one dimensional. However, in this form they serve as important symbols and foils for her learning experience. Roxanne is a beacon of clarity who can separate truth from illusion. John Drysdale is like the town and much of society, self-centered and stunted. Mary has both strengths and weaknesses; she denies both until the shadow of death forces her to truth. The entire style is reminiscent of Guy's earlier works such as ***The Friends*** and ***Ruby.*** This should have a wide audience and should be a nominee for the Best Books list.

Debra Loop Maier, in a review of "Mirror of Her Own," in Voice of Youth Advocates, *Vol. 4, No. 5, December, 1981, p. 30.*

Mary is described as stuttering "only when very upset," but she seems troubled by this disorder frequently. The central premise that emotional trauma combined with physical danger would provide a cure for this disorder is romantic nonsense. Stuttering in this novel appears to be a costume effect, a means to contrast the two sisters even more: Mary has the common name and dingy brown hair, is so homely that she is mistaken for a "retarded" child, is withdrawn and masochistic in her choice of a friend, and stutters; Roxanne has the glamorous name, blue eyes, and blond hair, is talented, vibrant, and articulate. The writing is awkward and overblown: "Was what she had done so horrible that she deserved such an end? John? She had been mad! Mad on moonlight and drugs." The characters in this soap opera are flimsy and completely predictable caricatures. The narrative serves mainly as a vehicle to deliver unsubtle sermons against speeding, drinking, drugs, colonialism, and racism. (p. 229)

Barbara H. Baskin and Karen H. Harris, "An Annotated Guide to Juvenile Fiction Portraying the Disabled, 1976-1981: 'Mirror of Her Own'," in their More Notes from a Different Drummer: A Guide to Juvenile Fiction Portraying the Disabled, *R. R. Bowker Company, 1984, pp. 228-29.*

MOTHER CROCODILE (1981)

Because the little crocodiles believe Golo the gossiping, vengeful monkey, who has it in for their mother Dia, and don't listen to her stories of old-time wars, don't heed her "crazy talk" (as Golo calls it) of a new war approaching, they are almost killed by bullet-fire . . . a lesson, says elderly Uncle Amadou at the close of this long, intricate, quite adult tale, "that when little crocodiles close their ears, their skins may someday cost them dear." The last refers back to the victorious soldiers' talk of taking crocodile-skin purses home to their wives—one of the many heterogeneous elements that make this a rather strong story (a convincingly updated fable, that is) but for an older than picture-book audience. . . . It's suggested on the jacket that the story can be read also "as a symbolic retelling of the history of Africa"; and certainly that interpretation, if a considerable oversimplification, might commend the book to some classroom teachers.

A review of "Mother Crocodile," in Kirkus Reviews, *Vol. XLIX, No. 15, August 1, 1981, p. 931.*

Neither the moral for adults (remember history so you won't have to repeat it) nor the moral for children (heed the wise, ignore the foolish) is too obtrusive. Although this is a translation of a translation, the prose is rhythmic and touched with folk-poetry.

Patricia Dooley, in a review of "Mother Crocodile," in School Library Journal, *Vol. 28, No. 1, September, 1981, p. 107.*

Novelist Guy has translated a tale told to her by Senegalese poet-diplomat Birago Diop, who heard the tale as a child from his grandmother's household storyteller. The story breaks from the usual folklore format found in children's tales by combining traditional characters with modern antiwar sentiments. . . . The story is told with color and verve; children will find it thought-provoking entertainment. (pp. 43-4)

Denise M. Wilms, in a review of "Mother Crocodile," in Booklist, *Vol. 78, No. 1, September 1, 1981, pp. 43-4.*

Mother Crocodile relates some wonderful stories, and translator-adaptor Rosa Guy is at her best in the lyrical passages, in leisurely descriptions of mythical landscapes. She has a good ear, and her prose has pleasing rhythms.

The book is aimed at readers 4 to 7 years old. But the text is long, and the vocabulary would be difficult even for advanced readers of this age. Read aloud, however, the story is accessible to the young age group.

Marguerite Feitlowitz, in a review of "Mother Crocodile," in The New York Times Book Review, *October 4, 1981, p. 38.*

NEW GUYS AROUND THE BLOCK (1983)

AUTHOR'S COMMENTARY

Believing as I do that world survival rests with the young, I like to think that my contribution as a writer to their understanding of the world lies in exposing a segment of society often overlooked, ignored, or treated with contempt. It's a segment that cannot be wished away, and in the final analysis, our approach to its problems can determine the kind of people we shall ultimately be. As spokesman for that segment, I give to my readers Imamu Jones—detective.

"Issue oriented" books or "required reading" can most times be a bore. But the world loves a good mystery. So do I. A good mystery can force the mind to reach just a bit further than it believes it's capable of reaching. And because I have great respect for the capabilities of the young, the possibility that I might provide stimulation, forcing minds to stretch just a bit beyond, is a great challenge. I like to imagine that in attempting to unravel a tightly woven work old prejudices and fixed ideas may be examined and rethought. And I live in hope that with rethinking comes joy.

In ***The Disappearance*** and also its sequel, ***New Guys Around the Block,*** the challenge to the reader is two-fold: solving a mind-boggling whodunit on the one hand, and on the other, attempting to unlock secret passages of minds that have been closed to us—minds developed in the so-called underbelly of our society, where wits are sharpened by the constant struggle for survival—from criminal elements and from daily confrontation with the law.

Thus Imamu Jones—poor, orphaned by the death of his father and chronic alcoholism of his mother—rises above the ugliness of his environment to shoulder the burden of *my* imposed responsibility. A shrewd observer of people, sensitive, with a natural intelligence, a boy who accepts as normal the fragility of his friends' morals, a high school dropout, Imamu with his street wisdom can solve crimes that baffle the police.

In ***New Guys Around the Block,*** the second of the Imamu series, Imamu is joined in his detective pursuits by Olivette, an exceedingly brilliant youth who because of his great intelligence and broad experiences—he has lived in every inner city in the country—is able to bring a new approach to Imamu, a new insight, as they join forces in their attempt to solve the series of crimes plaguing the city.

What a joy it is to construct a mystery! How challenging to scatter carefully thought-out clues that must fit into the novel through characters, their motives, patterns of thought, and environmental framework. Every piece must matter. Each detail must be studied. What excitement for me, the author, to imagine the alert reader attempting to unravel those events I so painstakingly knitted. Can anyone solve the crimes that took so much hard work and time to render insoluble? How nerve-splitting it is to contemplate: readers crossing ideas like swords, with the uneducated, though highly intelligent, Imamu Jones.

My characters are drawn from life. In ***The Disappearance,*** Imamu Jones, Mama, and the Aimsleys are to be found within black communities. In ***New Guys Around the Block,*** the intriguing Olivette, a rare sort, is always a phenomenon wherever he's encountered. But the Olivettes are mesmerizing, especially when found in their natural habitat of the inner cities.

What happens to individuals like Imamu Jones and Olivette when there are no outlets to channel their active minds or to absorb their energies? Here is the double challenge confronting the reader. The question must occur to many while reading the books and searching for clues. Surely the answers to that question are as important as those leading to the solution of the crimes. But the question confounds even the experts.

So, although I intend to write novels more in line with my trilogy, ***The Friends, Ruby, Edith Jackson,*** and love stories in the vein of ***Mirror of Her Own,*** I'm continuing also to work on the thought-provoking Imamu Jones series. The third book of the series, ***The Grand Decision*** (working title), is already in progress.

Rosa Guy, in a promotional piece published by Delacorte Press, 1983.

New Guys around the Block continues with the encounters and endeavours of Imamu Jones, who in ***The Disappearance*** renounced a comfortable life with well-to-do foster-parents in Brooklyn to care for his mother, victim of depression and drink, in Harlem. The 'new guys' are two brothers from New Orleans, Pierre and Olivette, whose sophisticated manners intrigue Imamu and successfully hide the destructive side to their natures until they have drawn him far into their neighbourhood depredations. In the character of Olivette, who like a succubus exists through the demands he makes on his friends to satisfy his distorted philosophy, Rosa Guy has drawn a highly complex character, a youth of eighteen at once the product of his environment and the prisoner of his own cruelties; through Olivette's plots and acts of violence the villainous Iggy and pathetic Gladys both suffer, but Imamu's emotional pain as he gradually realises what his new friends are really like is, for the purpose of the book, the true central theme. Rosa Guy keeps a firm authorial hold on the points she wants to make about certain areas of black experience in New York but her lucid view of the society she describes is slanted very clearly through the eyes of the sensitive, troubled adolescent Imamu, who is winning his place in the world, not without pain and strife.

Margery Fisher, in a review of "New Guys around the Block," in Growing Point, *Vol. 22, No. 2, July, 1983, p. 4101.*

The bleak metaphor that opens Rosa Guy's seventh novel is almost Dreiserian in its vision and power. The author records a dream of her 18-year-old hero, Imamu Jones, in which he is a desperate rat hellbent on escaping the pointless destiny of his mindlessly running pack. . . . If Mrs. Guy's earlier trilogy . . . was richer-textured and more subtle, Imamu's story—to be continued in a third installment—is nonetheless absorbing and moving. The reader cannot resist rooting for Imamu, with his intelligence and growing self-awareness, as he negotiates the booby traps of a difficult life. One hopes this novel will be read by countless other Imamus in need of encouragement.

Selma G. Lanes, in a review of "New Guys around the Block," in The New York Times Book Review, *August 28, 1983, p. 22.*

I tried while reading to keep at least part of my mind focused on the young men and women of British inner city areas, some of whom have told me that Guy's ***The friends*** is the best book they have ever read. Many of them will want to read this one, though they will find it different from the others, with the exception of ***The disappearance,*** which is an earlier episode from the life of Imamu Jones. What I admire about Guy is the way she makes a fairly predictable plot, with a surprise ending which is no surprise at all, into a texture of events and predicaments and arguments that make me think, in virtually the same way as much more sophisticated novelists like Toni Morrison make me think, about black experience and politics and sexuality. I hope that as well as recommending it, librarians may find time to read it thoughtfully. (pp. 269-70)

Alex McLeod, in a review of "New Guys around the Block," in The School Librarian, *Vol. 31, No. 3, September, 1983, pp. 269-70.*

If description and dialogue were all that was required of a novel, then Rosa Guy's ***New Guys Around the Block*** . . . could be wholeheartedly recommended to romantically inclined white, middle-class daughters of liberal parents, who are unlikely to verify ghetto conditions personally as they are to be racist. Rosa Guy's socio-aesthetic fix on contemporary Harlem is as impressive here as in her earlier books. . . . Observation of an inner-city tenement or of streets of burnt-out buildings and their inhabitants—junkies, winos, numbers' runners—is sharp and detailed. Jive talk accurately jives, and through it Imamu . . . is seen to be as resilient and lively as Claude Brown's quasi-autobiographical hero in *Manchild in the Promised land.*

The problem is that the plot (where it exists) is pitched impossibly low. Eighteen and nineteen-year olds (when not beating women over the head with bricks or attempting rape or robbery) engage in the kind of sleuthing familiar to readers of Enid Blyton's "Famous Five" books. The notion that the identification and subsequent incarceration of "the phantom burglar" (a black who preys on rich whites) would gain the support of a cynical police force and rid the neighbourhood of police harassment just about persuades: the methods of deduction employed by Imamu and his friends are at best simplistic, at worst farcically improbable.

It is infuriating that Rosa Guy should offer an unbalanced and unbelievable fiction—through the lack of a well-constructed storyline.

Holly Eley, in a review of "New Guys around the Block," in The Times Literary Supplement, *No. 4200, September 30, 1983, p. 1046.*

Guy draws characters and presents social issues that are painful but accurate. It is as if she has a double-edged knife that cuts the reader first one way, then the other. Her forte is in character development, growth of characters, and realistic dialogue and setting. This is not a dismal portrait of inner-city life but it is a seemingly hopeless, no win situation with Imamu struggling to be more than he is; the policeman who hounds him proving to be not quite so obnoxious; the numbers runner who society sees as being unredeemable, actually turning out to be quite the opposite. Guy shows, very well, that people are not always what they seem. There is some hope (just a glimmer) at the end.

Penny Parker, in a review of "New Guys around the Block," in Voice of Youth Advocates, *Vol. 6, No. 4, October, 1983, p. 202.*

I am in no position to question the accuracy and the essential truth of Rosa Guy's picture of life in the inner city. It certainly carries conviction. To what extent it is relevant or appropriate for British teenagers to read such profoundly depressing accounts of the hopeless society in which some of their American contemporaries live is a question to which each reader must provide his own answer. Certainly Rosa Guy is a powerful writer—the Harlem slang in which her story is written presents some formidable problems of comprehension—and she draws her central character, a boy who rejects the easy solution to all his troubles, with deep understanding. I found her book compulsively readable, although I often found myself wishing it were less so! At least there is a small glimmer of light at the end of this long tunnel. Imamu's mother is coming out of hospital to a newly painted apartment and to the hope of change . . . perhaps gardening. Imamu may be able to 'remake the world . . . with a little help from the sun—and rain—and a few other things'. Let us be grateful for this crumb of comfort.

M. Crouch, in a review of "New Guys around the Block," in The Junior Bookshelf, *Vol. 48, No. 1, February, 1984, p. 32.*

PARIS, PEE WEE, AND BIG DOG (1984)

[In ***Paris, Pee Wee and Big Dog,*** Rosa Guy] writes for the first time for a younger age group. The story describes an eventful day in the life of three boys who live in New York City. . . .

[The] illustrations—by Caroline Binch—are better than the text, which is stronger on plot than character. Though the three boys are carefully differentiated and their relationship is convincingly complicated, with sometimes hilarious results, the author's presence obtrudes:

> Racing up the hill to the avenue, Paris forget all about the sun and its dip to the west. He no longer worried about work that had to be done. His mind was set on new adventure. He turned the corner, dashing into the little store that sold everything from groceries to hardware.

While it is probably no mean task to convey convincingly the mind of a ten year old, the plodding prose is surprising from an author who has written so brilliantly about adolescents.

Beverly Anderson, in a review of "Paris, Pee Wee and Big Dog," in The Times Educational Supplement, *No. 3569, November 23, 1984, p. 40.*

Guy's challenge is considerable, for Paris and his friends Pee Wee and Big Dog live in a ghetto world where bullies carry weapons and hang out in burned out buildings, and mothers are often not home, even on Saturdays. . . .

There's a lot of reality floating through this gentle book, as Moms keep fighting and Paris is almost led astray. But the pain of the city streets and of life for boys without fathers is touching and engrossing without being sentimental. It's not sociology, it's a story. Though all three boys are poor and black, it is the differences among them which intrigue us. For Paris, with his strong mother, there is redemption even in near disaster, but for Pee Wee, whose brother runs a gang and whose mom is never around, things don't look so bright. The counterpoint is Big Dog, younger, fat, with a pocket full of change and a father who takes him fishing. He adds poignance and perspective to this tale of one almost tragic day as the three friends encounter adventures Tom Sawyer never dreamed of. School librarians would do well to add this story to their shelves, even though its ending is pretty sad. City kids might find it familiar, and for the suburbs it offers a glimpse into a world far from that of Fourth Grade Nothings and Great Brains. (p. 17)

Cynthia Samuels, in a review of "Growing Up Reading," in Book World—The Washington Post, *November 10, 1985, pp. 17, 20.*

Stories about Kids in the City are often not about kids *and* the city. In some, the city is only a hard presence implied in the shadows; in others, the children are merely pawns of the nasty, thrilling street-force that becomes the book's best characters.

Rosa Guy has written extensively for young adults and adults, and her first book for younger readers does justice to New York City's people and streets. . . . Miss Guy gives us no heavy social lessons about our urban horrors and keeps the boys free of "turning-point experiences." Instead, they have a play day that is both tough and fun, and so do we. . . .

Miss Guy wisely runs the boys through timeless, universal adventures—skating, fishing, snacking and rope-swinging. But the city makes its influence clear enough: the skating leads to collisions with mean drivers in heavy traffic, the fish are polluted, the snacks shockingly expensive and the rope nearly a deathtrap.

The boys' talk is a constant crackle alongside the events, a good mix of banter and insight, gamesmanship and frankness. Paris learns quite a few things simply by listening, and so do we. Another constant crackle is the threat of violence from a narrowed-eyed 14-year-old bully named Marvin who keeps popping up to push Paris around. The fear of Marvin works better in the book than Marvin himself: most of the scenes in which he appears are oddly slack. Such, of course, is the nature of bullies—they are stronger in the fright than in the flesh—and the awkwardness of the early Marvin scenes is partly redeemed by his final flicker through the twilight of Paris's day.

Caroline Binch's 20 pencil drawings, like Rosa Guy's descriptions, are sharp and amusing. Together the pictures and story lead us very naturally through a day we somehow feel will happen again: cities and boys will always attract each other. Miss Guy and Miss Binch make us believe that for now and maybe even next week no one will really be hurt and perhaps nothing—not even innocence—will really be lost. Perhaps.

Bruce Brooks, "The Concrete Canyon Rangers," in The New York Times Book Review, *November 10, 1985, p. 36.*

This is an action-packed, fast-moving and appealing adventure story. Rosa Guy has portrayed a broad range of personalities, family situations and lifestyles. Big Dog, the most affluent of the three friends, lives in a two-parent home, gets a big allowance and is envied because of the close relationship he has with his father. Pee Wee, from a poor, single-parent family, has a brother in a gang. (Although his mother is not too pleased with their friendship, Paris is able to see good qualities beneath Pee Wee's rough exterior.)

Paris' mother works hard and strives to make a better life for them in a better neighborhood. It is not clear why his father left the household as a result of this move, but it is apparent that this is a family that has taught Paris some positive moral values.

Guy manages to avoid the stereotypes of ghetto life without sugar-coating Harlem. The characters are warm and well developed. Parents can feel good about Paris' courage and sense of fairness, and every twelve-year-old can identify with Paris when he is confronted by a bully.

Adults are generally depicted as caring, responsible people, although there are not many females in the book except for Paris' mother and a girl Paris secretly likes. This book is highly recommended.

Judy Rogers, in a review of "Paris, Pee Wee, and Big Dog," in Interracial Books for Children Bulletin, *Vol. 16, No. 8, 1985, p. 16.*

The three boys have a series of usually cheerful, action-packed adventures. . . . Though it is refreshing to have an upbeat inner city story, this doesn't have the power of Guy's young adult fiction. The episodic plot drags at times, and the conflict between the excitement of the streets and the loving bond with his mother that pulls Paris home is overplayed. Setting and characterization, however, are strong (Pee Wee, particularly, is movingly drawn: sad, neglected, manipulative), and the last few episodes build to a satisfying climax.

Hazel Rochman, in a review of "Paris, Pee Wee, and Big Dog," in Booklist, *Vol. 82, No. 7, December 1, 1985, p. 572.*

Rosa Guy has taken a big risk, and succeeded. Instead of concocting a plot or a storyline to make a life in the day of three black kids in New York more 'readable', she has trusted her own skill and the book's engine—the relationships among the boys inside a fourth character, the city—to make a beautifully finished but entirely open narrative. The book can be read as a scamps-'n-scrapes story, but it's more than that; it's a revelation of the art of hanging-out and a truly contemporary tale of quest and adventure.

Nancy Chambers, "'Paris, Pee Wee and Big Dog'," in The Signal Selection of Children's Books 1984, *The Thimble Press, 1985, p. 18.*

MY LOVE, MY LOVE; OR, THE PEASANT GIRL (1985)

This slim, deceptively simple novel takes its shape from Hans Christian Andersen's "Little Mermaid." Like her briny sister, Rosa Guy's heroine, Désirée Dieu-Donné, rescues a dying prince, falls in love, is loved in return and then betrayed. Rosa Guy's mermaid, however, is not a princess of the deep but a mud-cloaked young Creole peasant, and her prince the son of a rich landowning family on a Caribbean island. But the central metaphor of Andersen's tale resonates through this modern transposition: the gulf of poverty and racism that separates Désirée from her aristocratic lover seems no less enormous than the physical distance between man and mermaid. While Rosa Guy's strange fairy tale is a moving evocation of the political realities of the Caribbean, her depiction of the Creole peasants tells us a great deal more about the complex culture that reinforces those political realities. The peasants blame the loas (the gods) as much as the landowners for their poverty. Untrustworthy and querulous, the loas withhold their favors for trivial reasons and must be appeased with offerings the peasants can hardly afford to spare. Désirée Dieu-Donné has defied the loas in order to rescue her rich landowner, but is finally unable to free herself of their influence. When a motherly woman warns Désirée that her only chance of happiness lies in leaving the Antilles, "the peasant girl" replies that she belongs to the island—the gods have willed it so. "Then the gods did curse you," the woman cries. Rosa Guy's last novel was the widely praised ***Measure of Time*** [a work for adults]. Her new fable captures the spirit of the Caribbean as unforgettably as ***A Measure of Time*** did jazz-age Harlem.

Angeline Goreau, in a review of "My Love, My Love: Or the Peasant Girl," in The New York Times Book Review, *December 1, 1985, p. 24.*

This novel's jacket bills it as a fable, but it isn't that, quite, for like the Hans Christian Andersen story "The Little Mermaid," on which it is loosely based, it has no heavy-handed moral. And it isn't quite a fairy tale, either. It has, rather, the tragic feel of a myth, in which self-consumed, petty gods play hob with human innocence. . . .

Andersen's Little Mermaid differs in significant ways from Guy's Désirée. The reader may be saddened by the fate of the mermaid, but she is a denizen of the fairy world dying for the love of a human—her story can end no other way. And her prince never knows that it is she who has saved his life, so he is innocent of responsibility. But Désirée is a flesh-and-blood girl barred from the marriage she longs for only by a rigid caste system that is the construction of other flesh-and-blood people. The man she loves is well aware of her role in saving his life, and for a time he treats her like a princess. . . . Though his nature is portrayed as gentle and good, he has used Désirée and, in the end, deserts her. He is not innocent of responsibility.

Told in another kind of voice, Désirée's story would be a simple cry of despair over the blindness of social injustice. But it is more than that because of the richness of its texture. The island, its peasants and their gods are presented in a fulsome vernacular, shot through with French words and phrases, that conjures up wonderfully the beauty and mystery of the tropics. . . . The gods are palpable presences, bickering threatening, entering the bodies of the peasants or materializing dream-like to accuse or cajole. The demon Papa Gé, with his top hat, is a vivid figure of horror: "He grinned around a cigar between brown teeth that were dripping with blood." And the picture of social injustice is balanced by the peasants' resigned acceptance of their place. A wise man of Désirée's village tells her, "To be tranquil, one must hang one's hat where one can reach it." Thus she has been warned, but she ignores the warning. So, like the mermaid, her fate is unavoidable.

Largely because of the voice Guy has chosen, ***My Love, My Love*** will be difficult reading for young people who are accustomed to something more accessible. It may miss a portion of the very audience for which it is intended. But for those who will give it the time and the careful attention it deserves, it will be a story important on many levels, and long remembered.

Natalie Babbitt, "Caribbean Gods' Spell," in The Washington Post, *December 17, 1985, p. B3.*

Rosa Guy has written a hauntingly simple story. The plot has been used by many authors before, but this time there is a poignancy that makes it a fresh experience. . . .

[***My Love, My Love***] reflects a large talent. She has told a simple story in a marvelous way. It is poetic, fanciful and yet bears universal truths. Slight though it is, the impact is great. It is a joy to read such a treasure. This is for the discriminating reader and observer of life.

Lucille G. Crane, in a review of "My Love, My Love," in Best Sellers, *Vol. 45, No. 10, January, 1986, p. 366.*

This allegory abounds in vivid, sensual images and symbols, many of which parallel Hans Christian Andersen's *Little Mermaid,* on which it is based. The last scene, however, in contrast to the fairy tale, is devastating in its ugliness. (Désirée's corpse is left with the garbage by the side of the road.) Some young adults who enjoy the fast-paced realism and memorable characterizations of the author's other books may be disappointed in the allegorical romantic mood and the story's illusive and allusive symbolism. Other readers, however, will find the message particularly relevant and will be moved by the tragic love story so eloquently captured by Guy's lilting prose.

Jackie Gropman, in a review of "My Love, My Love, or, the Peasant Girl," in School Library Journal, *Vol. 32, No. 5, January, 1986, p. 84.*

It's a fable set on a Caribbean island that captures the imagination through Guy's notable storytelling talent and another memorable character. . . . The island dialect and French language affect readability and events in voodoo worship might disturb the prudish. However, sexuality and sexual experiences are handled without vulgarity for a spellbinding story with horror, tragedy and romance. (pp. 30-1)

Virginia B. Moore, in a review of "My Love, My Love, or the Peasant Girl," in Voice of Youth Advocates, *Vol. 9, No. 1, April, 1986, pp. 30-1.*

Eric Hill

1927-

English author/illustrator and illustrator of picture books.

An internationally popular creator of toy and board books, Hill is recognized for his lovable characterizations, sense of humor, and well-designed illustrations. He gained acclaim with his first work, *Where's Spot?* (1980), a flap book which depicts the antics of an endearing, mischievous puppy. By lifting flaps in various shapes, children find such humorous surprises as a hippo and a bear while helping Spot's mother look for him. Combining a simple text with bright, smooth ink-and-watercolor pictures set against a white background, *Where's Spot?* has several sequels which detail such milestones in Spot's life as his first day of school; the series is noted for its appeal to an audience ranging from infants to beginning readers. In addition to these works, Hill has created other Spot toy books, including some made of plastic for bathtub use, and two series of board books—the "Little Spot Board Books" and the "Baby Bear Books." A cheerful stuffed animal, Baby Bear enjoys such activities as going to the park, looking up at the sky, and getting ready for bed.

Critics praise Hill as an innovative author/illustrator who catches and holds the attention of his young audience through a fresh approach, compelling concepts and stories, and vibrant, uncomplicated pictures. While some reviewers note that the colors in Hill's books have become more harsh, the details less precise, and that Spot has lost some of his puppyish charm by performing more human activities, most observers find that Hill has a keen awareness of the needs of children and produces works which have universal appeal.

***Where's Spot?* was selected as a runner-up for the Mother Goose Award in 1981.**

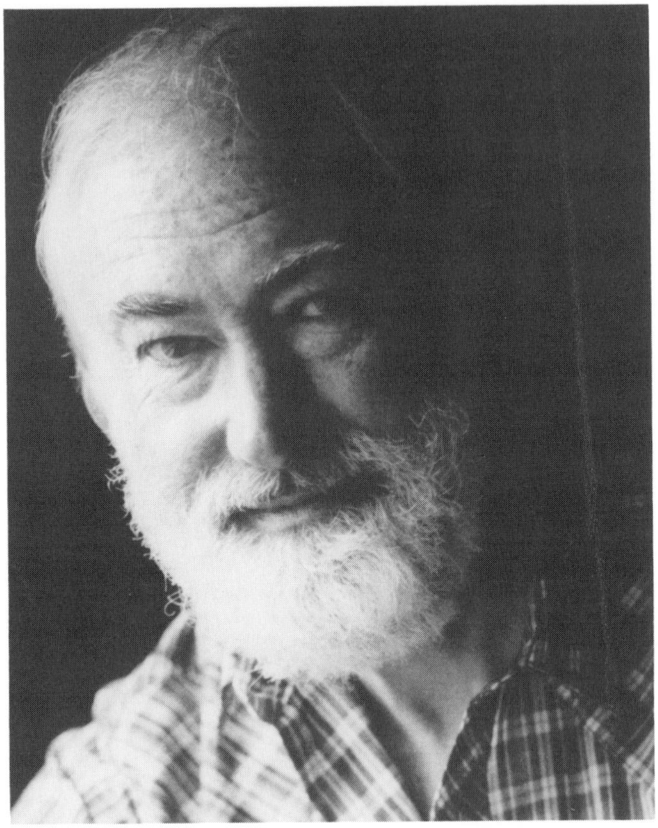

Courtesy of The Putnam Publishing Group

AUTHOR'S COMMENTARY

[*The following excerpt is from an interview by Tony Bradman.*]

When ***Where's Spot?*** appeared in 1980 it rapidly became a bestseller, and not only in Britain. More Spot books have followed—***Spot's First Walk*** and ***Spot's Birthday Party,*** and more are to come after the newest title, ***Spot's First Christmas.*** In fact, Spot has been so successful that his creator, Eric Hill, can now afford to shake the dust of the Old World from his feet and go west—to be precise, to Arizona. That's a long way for a self confessed townie, born and brought up in North London.

'I was born in 1927, and when the war came in 1939 I was evacuated to Bluntisham, in Huntingdon. I hated the countryside, so before Christmas I just took me bike and me little bag of sprouts and came home.'

Home was Holloway, and Eric experienced the blitz there. Although it wasn't all bad. 'That was what started me drawing. Like all kids, I was fascinated by aircraft, the Spitfires, Hurricanes and Messerschmitts.

'I had a minimal education and left as soon as I could, at about 15. I had no art school training at all. My first job was pretty futile—it was as a clerk in a shipping office. But I saw an ad in the paper for a messenger in an art studio, applied and got it. I've never looked back.'

Working in that studio was an Austrian refugee called Wilhelm Timyn—better known as the cartoonist Tim. 'He taught me an awful lot. I was brought up on the cartoon style—very few words.'

Children's books and Spot came along after many successful years in advertising and as a freelance graphic designer, and after a second marriage, to Gillian who is also an artist. 'I got interested in children's books because we had a little boy, Chris, who's seven now. When my first daughter, who's now in her twenties, was born I was too busy earning a living to be very involved.

'I'd noticed from Chris and from friends' children that they loved using their hands. At the time I was doing some novelty shots for some ads I was working on, with a man raising his bowler hat to reveal something underneath. Chris was fascinated by that.

'So I started making up the story of a little puppy called Spot, and the two ideas merged—puppy and flaps. It was all done for Chris.'

The rough of ***Where's Spot?*** actually sat around in a drawer for a year before Eric did anything about it. ('I was too busy earning a living then too.') But eventually he gave it to a packaging company—Ventura—and the rest is history.

'I was really pleased because it went international straightaway, and became a bestseller. I think the first four countries it was sold to were France, Germany, the States and Britain. So I took a chance and decided to give up my graphic work entirely and devote myself to children's books.

'I knew it wasn't just a novelty, that there would be a sequel at least. I couldn't leave the poor little sod in the basket, after all, could I? It's like a cartoon, you've got to find out what happens next.'

Spot is now available in more than 20 languages all over the world—including Welsh and Gaelic. And Eric Hill hasn't just restricted himself to everybody's favourite puppy, either. He's also worked on books with Allan Ahlberg—the Learning to Read series of paperbacks from Granada, featuring characters like Silly Sheep and Double Ducks—the Peek-a-Books from Piccolo, and the Baby Bear books from Heinemann. He says that in 1982 he produced 17 books—and he looks set for the same figure this year.

Eric intends Spot to have a very long future. 'What's pleased me most is that the Spot books have had a great success with children who've got difficulties, kids who are slow readers, for example. I get a terrific kick if I know that something I've done helps kids as well as entertains them.

'I was pleased with the praise I had from the academic world, too. I wasn't aware of what I was doing in using key words, for example—it seemed natural and right to write the text in that way. But then I got feedback from nursery teachers and reviewers that this was just what was needed and I started to learn from that.

'Spot's changed a little with each book. I like there to be some progress. I'll always stick to the flaps and the basic idea, but a character like Spot takes on a life of his own. It's like childhood in a way; at first it's just him and his mum, Sally, then he has some mates, and then you can do things like ***Spot's First Christmas,*** and the one that's going to come after that—***Spot Goes to School.*** All themes which are familiar to kids. I'm committed to at least one Spot book per year for the foreseeable future.' . . .

Eric Hill is a happy man who creates happy books. 'All my books are gentle. I suppose that's in my character. I could never have anything nasty happening in one of my books'. . . .

Tony Bradman, "Tony Bradman Meets Spot's Creator—Eric Hill," in Books for Keeps, *No. 23, November, 1983, p. 26.*

GENERAL COMMENTARY

ANGELA HUTH

After 17 years I have reasons once again to immerse myself in the bewilderingly vast world of books for small children. Our two-and-a-half-year-old daughter, Eugenie, demands four stories a night. Such an early appetite for literature means that her parents, in search of suitable material, are kept very busy. . . .

But of the many new authors and illustrators, few real stars have emerged to join such talent as Quentin Blake, Raymond Briggs, Maurice Sendak, John Burningham and Richard Scarry. One of them, new to me, is the simple genius of Eric Hill. His ***Spot*** books are a marvel of ingenious conception: small children eternally delight in joining the plump puppy's search for animal friends beneath simple flaps, much less likely to tear than those complicated pop-up books. (***Spot's First Christmas*** should be included in the stockings of all Spot fans this year.)

Angela Huth, "Ruined Fairy Tales," in The Listener, *Vol. 110, No. 2833, November 3, 1983, p. 27.*

DONNARAE MacCANN AND OLGA RICHARD

A shopper can hardly enter a bookstore these days without tripping over displays of Eric Hill's "Spot" books and the stuffed, furry replicas of the puppy. It may seem like overexposure to give these books any further visibility. However, since they have now been issued in a Spanish language edition, we think they deserve special commendation. . . .

It isn't necessary to say much about the content of ***¿Dónde está Spot? (Where's Spot?), La Primera Navidad de Spot (Spot's First Christmas), El Cumpleanos de Spot (Spot's Birthday Party),*** and ***El Primer Paseo de Spot (Spot's First Walk).*** A puppy makes discoveries by opening a door, peering under a basket, lifting a lid. This game is a well-tested audience pleaser, although we know of one two-and-one-half-year-old who screamed bloody murder at the sight of the suddenly visible bear in ***¿Dónde está Spot?*** This child is not always afraid of bears in books, so we presume that the picture presented a special kind of optical illusion to this viewer. Perhaps the lack of open space around the bear image makes the beast seem overlarge and scary. For a bookish three-year-old, this kind of problem is rare.

Eric Hill has a guileless mode of expression that makes his illustrations easy to read visually. On most pages he features one large object with an animal concealed behind its lift-up flap. The effect is free, uncluttered, and clever. Objects are drawn knowledgeably with a contour line and a few textual details. There are rarely any overlapping or background objects.

Two classrooms of Spanish-speaking children in the Los Angeles area responded to ***¿Dónde está Spot?*** with great enthusiasm.

Donnarae MacCann and Olga Richard, in a review of "¿Dónde está Spot?" and other titles, in Wilson Library Bulletin, *Vol. 58, No. 8, April, 1984, p. 578.*

MARGARET CARTER

Some pictures are 'aah' pictures and who could resist an 'aah' at the sight of that lovable puppy Spot. Don't all children want to stroke him? You can almost feel his fat warmth under your hand. Now, even bathtime can also be book time with the new Spot Bathbooks.

The Spot books have sent thousands of children happily to bed. . . .

Margaret Carter, in a review of "Spot's Toys" & Others, in Books for Your Children, *Vol. 21, No. 3, Autumn-Winter, 1986.*

WHERE'S SPOT? **(1980)**

Only a few children's books have the eternal quality of a classic; but considerably more possess the quality which enables them to last out a generation or so of children as good and intimate

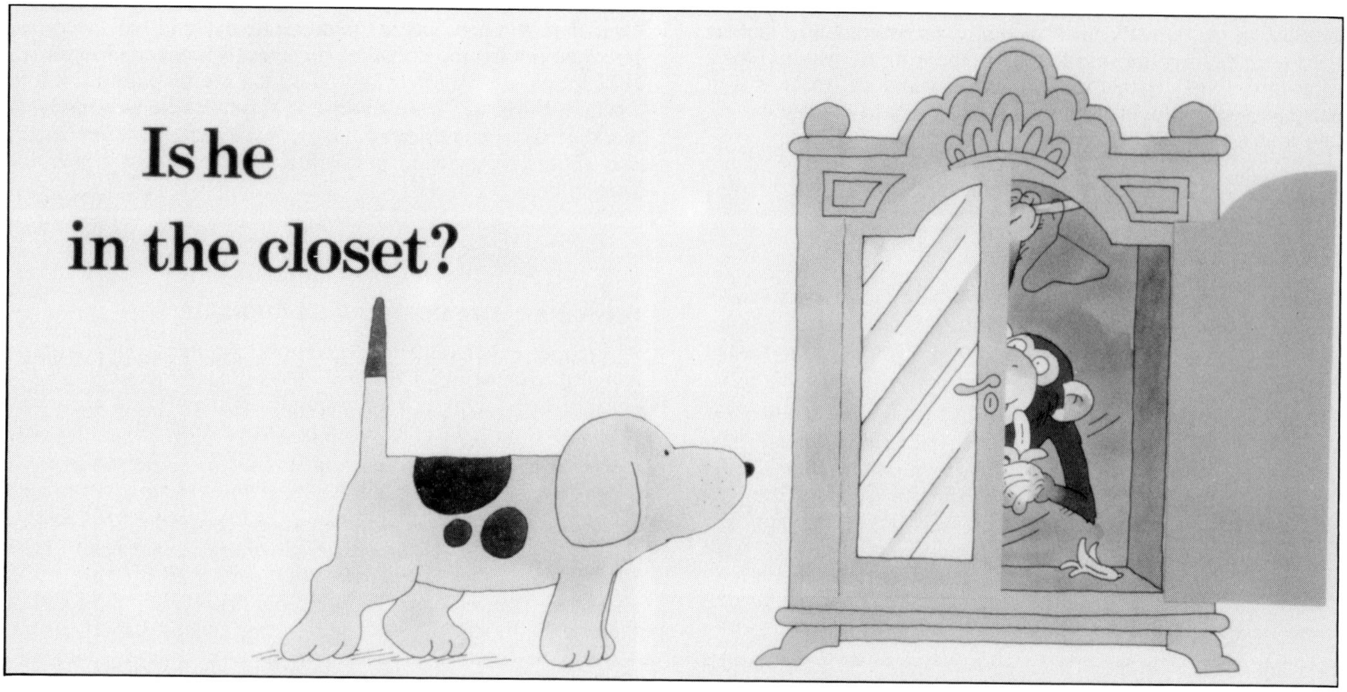

From Where's Spot? *written and illustrated by Eric Hill. G. P. Putnam's Sons, 1981. Copyright © 1980 by Eric Hill. All rights reserved. Reprinted by permission of the Putnam Publishing Group.*

family friends. Such books do not have to be completely original; ***Where's Spot?,*** by Eric Hill, for example, is an old idea: Spot is a puppy, and his mother is searching for him all round the house, that is, under the flaps on every page of the book. Under each flap is an unexpected creature, and the result is a wonderful combination of ritual question and funny surprise answers that would appeal to anyone.

Ruth Hawthorn, "Befriending Pictures," in The Times Literary Supplement, *No. 4051, November 21, 1980, p. 1328.*

Here's a perky adventure that will keep toddlers entranced, a story illustrated by big pictures in bold and unexpected colors: a violet grand piano, a bed bedizened by covers of fuchsia and royal blue, etc. Sally the dog has eaten her supper but Spot's dish is still full. "Where can he be?" muses Sally and goes off to hunt. Children lift a flap, the door to a closet where Spot might be but he is not. A huge bear, eating honey, is there. Sally keeps looking, opening the door to a grandfather clock where a snake is coiled. She lifts the piano lid but finds only a hippo and a bird. By the time the maternal dog tracks down the playful hider, little readers will have had their fill of surprises. Author-illustrator Hill's lift-and-look creation beats most toy books in imaginative detail.

A review of "Where's Spot?" in Publishers Weekly, *Vol. 218, No. 24, December 12, 1980, p. 47.*

Small children seem delighted to look 'under the bed', 'in the box', 'behind the door' and so on, even when they know perfectly well what absurd alternatives are there to be found before the climactic 'Good boy, Spot. Eat up your dinner'. Smooth paint and positive shapes decorate a disarmingly simple idea executed with nicely judged humour.

Margery Fisher, in a review of "Where's Spot?" in Growing Point, *Vol. 19, No. 5, January, 1981, p. 3821.*

A perceptive, yet simple, illustration sets the scene and establishes the plot of ***Where's Spot?*** Sally, Spot's mother, has finished her dinner, while Spot's bowl is still full. Very young children will enjoy searching for him with her. . . . The large ink-and-watercolor illustrations are clearly delineated and abound with good humor. The book could be shared with a group, but its best use is with an individual child who can open all the doors. The flimsy binding and lack of end papers seem to indicate that it is not intended for libraries, which is unfortunate. Nevertheless, the clean layout and simple text are a refreshing change from the many complicated and busy pop-up books available for this age group.

Jean Hammond Zimmerman, in a review of "Where's Spot?" in School Library Journal, *Vol. 27, No. 7, March, 1981, p. 132.*

This is not a novelty item, but a solid story that young listeners can enjoy over and over. The art uses space, shapes, and hues to appealing effect, and the paper engineering is sturdy and simple enough for uncoordinated hands to manipulate. (p. 40)

Betsy Hearne, "The American Connection," in Signal, *No. 37, January, 1982, pp. 38-42.*

SPOT'S FIRST WALK **(1981)**

A bestseller since it appeared last December, ***Where's Spot?*** now has a companion toy book, Hill's sequel, which will surely be as great a favorite with the nursery crowd. The minimal text, in big print, is easy for tinies to follow as they listen to the story of the puppy's big day. Actually, the delightful paintings in bright colors need few words to tell what happens. Spot ambles off for a walk on his own and readers find what he does as they lift flaps on the pages. Ignoring the warning of a screeching bird, Spot opens an interesting door, to be hissed at by an angry cat. Then the puppy noses open a door leading into a garden and says, "What a nice smell," and hears busy bees say, "Thank you." Each page presents a surprise, some dandy and some discomfiting to Spot, all a joy to little readers who follow him until he's home again.

A review of "Spot's First Walk," in Publishers Weekly, *Vol. 220, No. 11, September 11, 1981, p. 72.*

Spot's First Walk makes a suitable first book, with its extra-large pre-primer type, uncomplicated but not empty pictures, and very basic easy-to-follow "story" which shows Spot leaving his mother behind and then investigating his immediate surroundings. . . . Spot's next-to-last discovery, inevitably but appropriately, is a bone, which he then trots home. The flaps here are more than a gimmick, they're an integral part of the concept.

A review of "Spot's First Walk," in Kirkus Reviews, *Vol. XLIX, No. 22, November 15, 1981, p. 1405.*

Eric Hill's new Spot book is technically less ambitious [than John Goodall's *Shrewbettina Goes to Work*], but it seems to me to be infinitely more successful. Here the devices—in this case all lift-up flaps—are material to the theme, not, as in Mr Goodall's book, imposed upon it. . . . Both scale and mood are maintained beautifully, and there is a perfect balance between the simple, strong drawings and the brief text—fifty odd words which could not be better or better presented. This is a model of how a first 'Reader' should be done.

M. Crouch, in a review of "Spot's First Walk," in The Junior Bookshelf, *Vol. 46, No. 3, June, 1982, p. 93.*

Bold, expressive illustrations highlight this easy reader. . . . Lifted flaps reveal some surprises along the way and help children share in the sense of discovery. . . . When he finally returns home, his mother questions him about what he has been doing. With the typical reply of an errant child, Spot replies, "Nothing." While the text is trite and overly cute (must a mother hen tell Spot to "Have a nice day"?), the overall tone is warm and appealing.

Lori Janick, in a review of "Spot's First Walk," in School Library Journal, *Vol. 29, No. 3, November, 1982, p. 69.*

Our greatest reading success of the holidays must beyond all doubt be Eric Hill's irresistible book, ***Spot's First Walk*** . . . I bought it for baby Ffion (sixteen months); but it has proved one of those rare books which become instant favourites for the whole family. My eldest daughter, seven-year-old Ceri, is a fluent reader, well beyond picture book stage. But she could not resist Spot, the most appealing of puppies—though naturally, she pretends she only reads it for the baby's benefit! Middle daughter Anwen (five) daunted by her sister's easy fluency, perhaps has been slower to launch out into reading on her own. ***Spot*** with its simple, easily memorised text and large bold print, has proved the perfect temptation. She reads it delightedly to little Ffion. As for Ffion herself, ***Spot*** is the one book—indeed the one plaything—of which she never tires. Joyously she greets the clear, uncluttered pictures of the lovable puppy, crying 'do(g)!' and 'woof!'. Soon she had mastered each flap; now she opens them excitedly, and makes appropriate noises for the creatures discovered underneath. Not for her do cats say *'miaow'*; they hiss, like the irate cat disturbed by Spot! It is only fair to admit that Spot has one more devotee in the family—yes, you've guessed, it's me!

Siân Victory, in a review of "Spot's First Walk," in Books for Your Children, *Vol. 17, No. 3, Autumn-Winter, 1982, p. 11.*

PUPPY LOVE (1982)

More like an extended greeting card, Hill's new book about the famous puppy may beat the record of his instant and lasting bestsellers, ***Where's Spot?*** and ***Spot's First Walk.*** On the inside of the front cover are facing hearts (one purple and one red) inscribed "to" and "from," an invitation to people of both sexes and all ages to send the tiny volume as a symbol of affection. The beguiling, colorful pictures hardly need the simple text. The message is clearly illustrated, as Spot shows he needs a kiss and a cuddle from his mom: whether he's alone or in a crowd, happy or sad, naughty or good as gold, Spot, like everyone, needs puppy love.

A review of "Puppy Love," in Publishers Weekly, *Vol. 222, No. 20, November 12, 1982, p. 66.*

AT HOME; MY PETS; THE PARK; UP THERE (*BABY BEAR BOOKS*) (1982)

Creator of the popular "Spot" books . . . , Hill will delight tinies anew with his set of ***Baby Bear Books,*** sturdy small board books featuring a friendly stuffed brown bear. The wordless volumes contain several bright, simply drawn, cheery scenes, with familiar objects that toddlers can easily recognize and name. On the cover of ***Up There,*** Baby Bear points toward the sky, making it clear he's going to show us some things we can see when we look up. Inside, a bird flaps by a gaily hued kite, balloons float merrily through the sky, a squirrel munches happily on an acorn atop a tree, clouds pelt raindrops on Baby Bear (who's equipped with a polka-dotted umbrella) and the sky clears, leaving a brightly shining sun and a rainbow over Baby Bear's house. (pp. 70-1)

A review of "Up There," in Publishers Weekly, *Vol. 223, No. 11, March 18, 1983, pp. 70-1.*

Small, square books with washable pages of heavy board, these have no texts; each is a compilation of brightly colored pictures that show more or less familiar objects in four different environments. ***At Home,*** for example, has pictures of the toy bear (who appears in every book) watching television, a chair, a table, a vase of flowers, a telephone, a curtained window, a mirror, a lamp, a clock, a towel, and the bear sitting on his potty. ***My Pets*** shows various animals; ***The Park*** has a bench, flowers, trees, a pond, playground equipment, et cetera; and ***Up There*** shows objects that are in the sky or, like a squirrel on a tree branch, that might be seen if one looked up. The books are useful for the very young child who likes to point to objects that are recognizable, but they are slight in coverage and at times garish in the use of color.

Zena Sutherland, in a review of "At Home" and other titles, in Bulletin of the Center for Children's Books, *Vol. 36, No. 9, May, 1983, p. 169.*

Pictures are bright and bold for identification and story invention, and the small size makes handling easy. Mid-one-year-olds who previewed the series enjoyed the look and feel of the books.

Margo Showstack, in a review of "At Home" and other titles, in Children's Book Review Service, *Vol. 11, No. 10, May, 1983, p. 97.*

Hill's simple cartoon-like drawings are executed in vibrant eye-catching colors against a white background. The illustrations are not detailed yet convey the sense of the object drawn. . . . Hill has a tendency to change from close-ups to long views of objects from page to page. Young children may have difficulty adjusting to this constant change in perspective. ***Up There*** depicts various objects associated with flight or the sky such as floating balloons and flags, falling leaves, kites, a helicopter and a rainbow. This particular theme is stretched a bit much and may need adult interpretation to make it understandable.

Marge Loch-Wouters, in a review of "At Home" and other titles, in School Library Journal, *Vol. 29, No. 9, May, 1983, p. 62.*

Best newcomers in 1982 [in the field of board books] are Eric Hill's ***Baby Bear Books*** and the Hamish Hamilton Playbooks. Baby bear is an appealing character, and the four wordless but effective titles offer bright pictures and plenty of interesting objects to talk about. There are amusing touches, and the themes of the books (***Up There,*** for example) get away from the usual preoccupations with eating, dressing and playing.

Valerie Willsher, "Board Books: 'At Home'" and other titles, in The Signal Review of Children's Books 1, *1983, p. 3.*

SPOT'S BIRTHDAY PARTY (1982)

Spot, the tail-wagging hero of ***Spot's First Walk*** (. . . 1981) and ***Where's Spot?*** (. . . 1980) is back and as energetic as ever in this charming book for nursery age children. Here he plays hide-and-seek with his friends at his birthday party. Doors open, a pillow is lifted, a shower curtain is pushed aside as Spot and the reader become quite literally involved in the seek. The text of simple words is printed in bold large letters. The illustrations are done in vibrant colors with sharp outlines on a white background; they convey expression and detail without clutter. Children will love the peek-a-boo aspects and the good humor of this very imaginative, very enjoyable book, which would be ideal for story hours.

Lisa Castillo, in a review of "Spot's Birthday Party," in School Library Journal, *Vol. 29, No. 8, April, 1983, p. 102.*

A third pop-up book about the engaging puppy Spot whose well-organised simplicity brings it right into the world of imagination of the very young, who should enjoy investigating by means of tabs and flaps the various surprises arranged to prolong the suspense until the climactic moment of the birthday party. The key to the success of these books is surely the unobtrusive humanisation, done solely by implication, which brings the puzzles into the child's experience.

Margery Fisher, in a review of "Spot's Birthday Party," in Growing Point, *Vol. 22, No. 1, May, 1983, p. 4081.*

[***Spot's Birthday Party***] follows the best-selling ***Where's Spot?*** and ***Spot's First Walk*** without quite achieving the calculated obviousness which made the earlier books such a success. This time it is Spot's birthday and during a game of hide and seek the now-familiar crocodile, bear, snake and monkey are discovered in cupboards, under carpets and behind curtains. They all have a smart remark for Spot (the snake says "Oh, hiss") but there is a certain lameness in the supposedly triumphant ending, with Spot being given his presents and simply saying "Thank you". Eric Hill's style seems to have become coarser, his colours are harsher and the subject entails an awkward anthropomorphism with Spot hiding his eyes and opening parcels. These are the sort of criticisms that are bound to be levelled at a follow-up to an established classic, but Spot is still lovable and the lift-the-flap formula has some life in it yet.

E. B., "In Brief," in The Times Literary Supplement, *No. 4190, July 22, 1983, p. 779.*

SPOT'S FIRST CHRISTMAS (1983)

Sally, Spot's mother, is trying to get ready for Christmas with Spot's "help." On each page a lift-up flap reveals that Spot is not helping at all. After a series of near mishaps caused by Spot's puppyish exuberance, he curls up in his basket and goes to sleep—and Sally glimpses Santa through the window. These books about the irresistible dog Spot have an instant and obvious appeal—the clear, brightly colored pictures are full of humor and portray two winning characters, the patient loving Sally and Spot himself, always full of energy, mischievous but never malicious. While the lift-up flaps will not withstand constant use, this will be perfect for Christmas preschool story hours.

Jean Hammond Zimmerman, in a review of "Spot's First Christmas," in School Library Journal, *Vol. 30, No. 2, October, 1983, p. 176.*

Eric Hill's books about the puppy Spot have consistently been the freshest first readers I've come across, and ***Spot's First Christmas*** . . . is up to standard. . . . [The] book is a joy.

Walter Clemons, "They Wish Us a Merry Christmas," in The New York Times Book Review, *November 13, 1983, p. 44.*

Eric Hill's latest 'lift the flap' book about Spot the puppy was clearly intended for the Christmas market and it will be popular with young readers; but for those familiar with his previous books, this one must come as something of a disappointment. ***Where's Spot?,*** the first of the series, remains by far the best, with its inventive theme, excellent drawings and careful colouring. The style becomes increasingly unpolished in the following books until in this one, line has become a rather crude shorthand. Spot and Sally are lumpish animals, the details are coarsely drawn and the colour is brash rather than bright. As the charm of the style has deteriorated, a tendency towards anthropomorphism has increased. Spot and Sally wrap presents and decorate a Christmas tree; Spot has a room with his name on the door; and Sally appears to be the householder. Anthropomorphism has a cherished place in children's literature, but it is regrettable that Spot's engagingly animal behaviour has been so submerged that he now seems merely a child in puppy form.

Gill Vickery, in a review of "Spot's First Christmas," in The School Librarian, *Vol. 32, No. 1, March, 1984, p. 37.*

The ingredients of the fourth lift-the-flap book about the yellow dog with the brown spots again promise success: bold, brightly coloured, explicit pictures; a minimal text (a grand total of sixty words) in large, clear letters; an easily recognised hero—Spot appears on every opening; a familiar background; and, above all, those tempting flaps that hide a surprise. As one would expect from a playful puppy, there are minor accidents—falling off step ladders, toppling the Christmas tree—and plenty to rouse canine grins. The under-fives will love it!

G. Bott, in a review of "Spot's First Christmas," in The Junior Bookshelf, *Vol. 48, No. 2, April, 1984, p. 60.*

GOOD MORNING, BABY BEAR; BABY BEAR'S BEDTIME (BABY BEAR BOOKS) (1984)

[***Good Morning, Baby Bear*** is] practically guaranteed to attract parents who share early reading with their tinies. Festive, extremely bright colors in the illustrations will catch the attention of small children and even the youngest should recognize the objects depicted. Beginning his day, Baby Bear wakes up; he smiles because the sun is shining. After a quick wash, he sits down to breakfast and a compliment from Mother: "What a clean Baby Bear!" After juice, milk and cereal, he's off to play with his toys and thus ends BB's very good morning. The introductory book and its sequel [***Baby Bear's Bedtime***] are colorful, durable, small enough for easy handling and bound so that the pages lie flat—definite assets.

A review of "Good Morning, Baby Bear," in Publishers Weekly, *Vol. 225, No. 15, April 13, 1984, p. 71.*

Ingenuous and chubby, Baby Bear stands in successfully for any and every infant as he splashily enjoys breakfast or bath, builds a tottering brick tower, listens to a bedtime story (with a toy bear in his arms). Justifiably recommended as books to share with babies as young as six months, these brightly coloured miniatures offer scenes to recognise, objects to identify and that universally acceptable toy, a teddy bear, to covet. Shapes and colours, bold and simple, make an immediate impact with their unfussy, pleasing style. (pp. 4293-94)

Margery Fisher, in a review of "Good Morning, Baby Bear" and "Baby Bear's Bedtime," in Growing Point, *Vol. 23, No. 2, July, 1984, pp. 4293-94.*

Mama Bear is a loving figure throughout, and a father is neither referred to nor shown. Very young children will enjoy these reassuring and cozy books, although they are not the best examples of the genre. The invaryingly cheerful tone and facial expressions lean toward monotony, as Hill lacks Rosemary Wells' or Helen Oxenbury's gift for putting real personality and life into very simple figures and events. Also, the bright colors are somewhat jarring, especially the frequent combination of hot pink with Baby Bear's orange fur. But, on the whole, these books will be popular where books for infants are in high demand.

Lauralyn Levesque, in a review of "Baby Bear's Bedtime" and "Good Morning, Baby Bear," in School Library Journal, *Vol. 31, No. 1, September, 1984, p. 104.*

SPOT GOES TO SCHOOL (1984)

[***Spot goes to School***] is an ultra-simple and wholly successful toy-book . . . in which flaps reveal the puppy's activities—playing on a seesaw, 'showing' his bone to the class, finding clothes in the Wendy house to adopt a new role. I am not sure, though, how the many children who already know Spot will view the change in his background. So far he has always moved naturally on the fringes of human life: now he has been taken to the more fantastic world of a humanised Zoo where his teacher is a bear and his fellow-pupils—crocodile, hippo, monkey, tortoise—are delineated in lurid, fanciful colour in a grotesque style. Personally I wish Spot had stayed in his more realistic world.

Margery Fisher, in a review of "Spot Goes to School," in Growing Point, *Vol. 23, No. 4, November, 1984, p. 4332.*

Likely to become an instant bestseller, in the company of Hill's earlier picture books, this one makes the most of Spot's biggest milestone so far. . . . The hour-by-hour activities in the classroom are illustrated in brightly colored, exuberant pictures with surprises for investigation under the fold-back parts on each page. The easy, breezy text and visuals combine to make an irresistible adventure for little boys and girls, particularly for those who are also about to begin their school careers.

A review of "Spot Goes to School," in Publishers Weekly, *Vol. 226, No. 18, November 2, 1984, p. 78.*

When asked by mom, "How was school, Spot?" he responds, "Great!"—the same reaction which will be elicited from children who read about Spot's first day at school. . . . Compared to the earlier stories, this new title lacks suspense under the flaps—it's as if a flappable Spot is being stretched too far. This flaw will be noticed more by the adults who read and reread these Spot stories to children, who will never tire of lifting flaps, no matter what the outcome. (pp. 71-2)

Nancy A. Gifford, in a review of "Spot Goes to School," in School Library Journal, *Vol. 31, No. 4, December, 1984, pp. 71-2.*

The world-renowned puppy in a flap-book performance that was [as teacher Frances Collinson reports] 'most enthusiastically received by my four-year-olds who had also just started school and could readily identify with him. . . . They have learnt the text and "read" it over and over again. . . . I have noticed that shy reserved children really enjoy flap books; the lifting of the flaps seems to enable them to lose themselves more easily in the book—they are in command of the situation, which gives them confidence.' The Spot books—this is the sixth and, after ***Where's Spot?***, possibly the best—are great favourites with very young children at home as well as being the prototype of the kind of book experience that helps children learn to read.

Nancy Chambers, "Picture Books: 'Spot Goes to School'" in The Signal Selection of Children's Books 1984, *Thimble Press, 1985, p. 4.*

SWEET DREAMS, SPOT (1984)

[Some] of the Spot books are flap books, others a puffy plastic which floats. ***Sweet Dreams, Spot*** is of the plastic variety. It

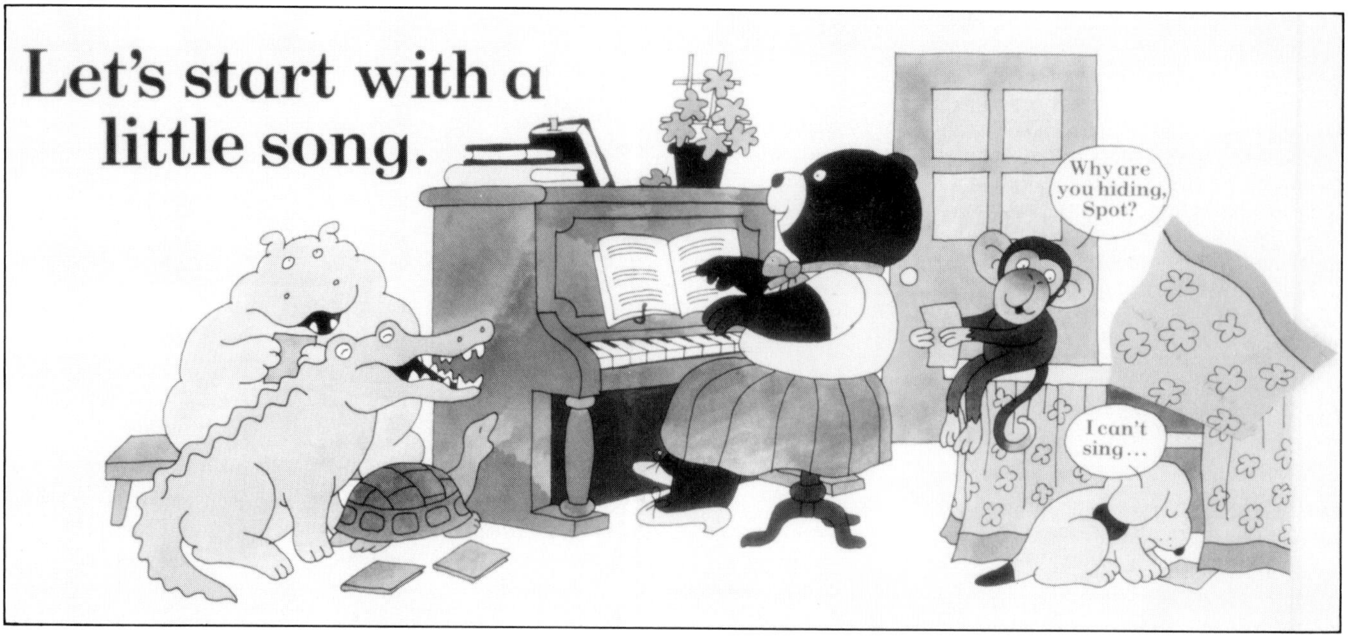

From Spot Goes to School, *written and illustrated by Eric Hill. G. P. Putnam's Sons, 1985. Copyright © 1984 by Eric Hill. All rights reserved. Reprinted by permission of the Putnam Publishing Group.*

has simple, clear illustrations and narrative as Spot puts away his toys, listens to a bedtime story, and curls up to sleep for the night. Content, language, and illustrations are all appropriate for young children. The content is on their level of understanding and is presented in a logical manner; the language is in a natural pattern, is simple without being simplified, and is not condescending; the illustrations are clear and uncluttered, following the story line accurately. (p. 198)

Joan Glazer, "Reflection," in Language Arts, *Vol. 62, No. 2, February, 1985, pp. 197-200.*

***SPOT GOES TO THE BEACH* (1985)**

The new lift-the-flap book featuring the energetic puppy will no doubt join Hill's previous picture stories on national best-seller lists. Spot's Dad is introduced here, in response to letters from fans asking why the father has been left out of the adventures so far. In the festive, boldly colored illustrations, Dad is reassuringly paternal, a real family dog. He escorts Mom and Spot to the beach where readers discover the little dog's secrets by lifting the flaps on each page. He buries his father in the sand, almost catches a fish, falls out of a rowboat but stays afloat in his rubber tube. Finally, Spot meets a pretty girl puppy who may share his capers in future Hill specials.

A review of "Spot Goes to the Beach," in Publishers Weekly, *Vol. 227, No. 22, May 31, 1985, p. 58.*

The full-color cartoon illustrations surrounded by plenty of white space depict the whole canine family on a cozy outing. Spot's antics are so childlike that kids and adults will easily identify with his adventures. The fragile flaps may preclude the book's use as a circulating item, but it will be a sure-fire hit with the preschoolers in story time.

Marge Loch-Wouters, in a review of "Spot Goes to the Beach," in School Library Journal, *Vol. 32, No. 1, September, 1985, p. 118.*

***SPOT AT PLAY* (British edition as *Play with Spot*); *SPOT AT THE FAIR; SPOT ON THE FARM* (British edition as *Spot at the Farm*) (*LITTLE SPOT BOARD BOOKS*) (1985)**

Rodney Peppé and Eric Hill are two tested favourites whose every endeavour goes down well. . . . ***Spot at the Farm, Spot at the Fair*** and ***Play with Spot*** . . . are "Little Spot" board books aimed at an even younger readership [than Peppé's Block Books] for their egregious canine and are a wow.

Both Hill and Peppé understand the simplicity demanded by a board book.

Victoria Neumark, "Young Ones," in The Times Educational Supplement, *No. 3617, October 25, 1985, p. 31.*

Three more irresistible books about lovable Spot. ***Spot at Play*** shows the caramel-colored puppy having fun with his animal friends. In ***Spot at the Fair,*** Spot and the same animal friends from the previous title enjoy the typical rides found at amusement parks. ***Spot on the Farm*** introduces common farm animals, as Spot helps to milk the cow, gather eggs and feed the pigs. These board books are small and the endearing illustrations are clear and brightly colored. Three guaranteed winners for very young children.

Anne Saidman, in a review of "Spot at Play" and other titles, in School Library Journal, *Vol. 32, No. 4, December, 1985, p. 74.*

***SPOT LOOKS AT COLORS; SPOT LOOKS AT SHAPES; SPOT'S FIRST WORDS* (*LITTLE SPOT BOARD BOOKS*) (1986)**

Spot is the star of a series of new board books which are colorful, imaginative, and delightfully simple. In each book, a word or concept is presented with a bold illustration and then used in a sentence accompanied by another bright picture. As in Hill's other books, sometimes Spot engages in dog-like activities such as fetching a shoe or playing with a toy; at other times he is more like a child, reading a book and sitting in a chair. The discrepancy doesn't intrude though, since Spot looks a bit like Snoopy, who also flip-flops back and forth between dog and child-like personae. These sturdy books are a welcome addition to any board book collection.

Janet E. Fricker, in a review of "Spot Looks at Colors" and other titles, in School Library Journal, *Vol. 33, No. 2, October, 1986, p. 161.*

SPOT GOES TO THE CIRCUS **(1986)**

An escaped ball leads Spot among the circus folks in his latest adventure. Some surprising twists—such as a ball not being a ball but a clown's nose—will be fun for the youngest viewers for whom *Spot* is a household word. Spot's father accompanies him to the circus, but it is Spot alone who follows his ball to the clown, lion, monkeys, and finally to his friend the seal. A dotted line traces the path of the ball so youngsters can easily follow along, too, as it disappears behind flaps disguised as balloons, lion chops, and even the parasol of a tightrope walking pig. One by one the animal entertainers display their antics as Spot's ball bounces on, until it lands appropriately on Seal's nose. "'That's a neat trick!'" says Spot and then shows us that he can learn a circus act himself. Spot's every wag has meaning, and Spot lovers will be right with him and behind every flap until he finds that pesky ball. Parents and others working with two-year-olds will welcome this circus book, which is also available in a Spanish edition, ***Spot Va al Circo.***

Elizabeth S. Watson, in a review of "Spot Goes to the Circus," in The Horn Book Magazine, *Vol. LXII, No. 6, November-December, 1986, p. 734.*

This new book about the adventures of Spot will be eagerly greeted by his fans. The clear, simple color illustrations of objects will be easily identified by toddlers, and the "lift-the-flap" sections are fully integrated with the text and illustrations. . . . Youngsters will delight in lifting the cleverly disguised flaps each time Spot believes he has found his ball. . . . The ending has a nice twist: the seal teaches Spot to balance the ball on the end of his *own* nose. Story hour participants as well as beginning readers will love to explore the big top with Spot.

Louise M. Zuckerman, in a review of "Spot Goes to the Circus," in School Library Journal, *Vol. 33, No. 4, December, 1986, p. 89.*

Tana Hoban

19??-

American author/illustrator of picture books.

Hoban is the creator of popular concept books designed to challenge young children to look at familiar objects from a new perspective and to appreciate the beauty around them. Featuring her simple yet skillful photographs of people, objects, and urban scenes, Hoban's varied works are noted for clearly and successfully presenting such concepts as size, shape, color, and language to an audience which includes learning disabled, emotionally disturbed, and bilingual children. Generally matching the difficulty of her black-and-white and color photographs to the age of her audience, which ranges from six months to the early primary grades, she utilizes either graphically simple shots or more complex, lively pictures which illustrate several concepts. Hoban employs compositional elements of color, balance, and texture to increase the aesthetics of both individual photographs and total book design, and she sometimes uses innovative methods to stimulate conceptual awareness. In *Look Again!* (1971), for example, she invites children to peer through a small square cutout on a white page and guess the identity of the item they partially see; the next page reveals the whole object, while the third page shows the object in its environment. In addition to her books, Hoban has also produced several filmstrips and short films.

Critics praise Hoban for the energy, imagination, and graphic skill with which she infuses her works. While reviewers find that some books require an adult to introduce them and that occasional photographs lack conceptual organization, they esteem Hoban as an exciting and gifted photographer who successfully translates her vision into insightful, enjoyable nonfiction books.

Recipient of several adult- and child-selected awards, Hoban won the Washington Children's Book Guild Nonfiction Award in 1982 for her body of work and a *Boston Globe-Horn Book* Special Award in 1985 for *1,2,3*.

(See also *Something about the Author,* Vol. 22 and *Contemporary Authors,* Vols. 93-96.)

© Daniele Fona

AUTHOR'S COMMENTARY

Nine years ago I heard of an experiment conducted by the Bank Street School in Manhattan that made a deep impression on me. Teachers had asked the children what they saw on the way to school. The children replied that they saw nothing, passed nothing, remembered nothing. Then they were given cameras. Looking through the small viewfinders at the same everyday places, the children discovered the river, the open markets, the construction going on in the streets and surprises all around them. With their new eyes they experienced a heightened interest, a new awareness and a new involvement. After hearing the outcome of this experiment I asked myself, "What is there, right where I'm standing that *I'm* not seeing?" To answer my own question, I began to examine the city with new eyes—things I'd never noticed before began to pop out at me.

I had lived and worked in the city for 30 years as a freelance photographer, but it took the children from the Bank Street School to make me see what I was missing. The little weeds surviving between the cracks in the pavement, a clump of grass around a fire hydrant, trash packed in multi-colored plastic bags and piled mountain high—these things were suddenly visible.

The way I have learned to focus on ordinary objects is the connection between children, my work, and me. Every concept I want to share with children is obvious in everyday life: shape, size, color, relationship, comparison and—emotion.

In my picture book of colors ***Is It Red? Is It Yellow? Is It Blue?*** there is a photograph of a small black fly on a green apple. Children may at first be interested only in the color but then with increasing awareness, may go on to make comparisons such as little fly/big apple, one fly/many apples, fly on apple/apple under fly, etc. In the eyes of a developing child there is something new to discover each time the book is opened.

Although I could contrive these situations I prefer the spontaneous moment. In ***Is It Red?*** I was photographing the bright yellow directions painted on a gray street surface when a woman in a green-striped skirt crossed directly in front of my camera. I could not believe how lucky I was . . . and it happens all the time.

I try in my books, to catch a fleeting moment and an emotion in a way that touches children and makes them want to respond. There is not one answer to any of my pictures. Through my photographs and through open eyes I try to say, "Look! There are shapes here and everywhere, things to count, colors to see and always, surprises."

Tana Hoban, "And Always, Surprises," in Early Years, *Vol. 10, No. 1, September, 1979, p. 6.*

GENERAL COMMENTARY

SAM LEATON SEBESTA AND WILLIAM J. IVERSON

The photographic presentations of Tana Hoban encourage a closer look at familiar, if unnoticed, phenomena. In ***Look Again!*** cut-out pages direct the reader's attention to the textures and designs of parts of seashells and small animals, while ***Where Is It?*** explores the posturing and movement of one delicate white rabbit. Admittedly, these books are not really fiction in that they contain little plot and characters are present only as subjects for photographs. Yet to the small child these are tantalizing ways of seeing into the outer world. They invite a closer look at outer reality. . . . (p. 260)

Sam Leaton Sebesta and William J. Iverson, "Realistic Fiction," in their Literature for Thursday's Child, *Science Research Associates, Inc., 1975, pp. 243-306.*

BARBARA BADER

Shapes and Things, photograms of familiar objects presented plain, without captions, was new, young, uniquely photographic—forty years later, a counterpart to Steichen's *First Picture Book*. The objects are at once recognizable and miraculous, tangible and illusory . . . , things and essences and pure form. . . . Tana Hoban followed it with ***Look Again!,*** and the photographic book took on fresh life.

Look Again! is a four-part perspective, magnifying pattern, texture, formal design, inviting a guess, assuring an answer . . . ; taking in the whole subject, its identity and its nature . . . ; turning over to its rear, its surroundings or its childlife . . . ; looking back on another fragment of its existence, now through the other end of the telescope. . . . One after another aspect of photography (and optics) is engaged, and one after another response to reality. The endpapers are a brilliant yellow, the title page has white block letters on black, the jacket puts the title letters in orange, an alert, and gives us, in a circle, the semblance of a peephole to the interior. A total concept and total, vital design. (p. 117)

Barbara Bader, "Photographic Books," in her American Picture Books from Noah's Ark to the Beast Within, *Macmillan Publishing Company, 1976, pp. 100-17.*

CHARLOTTE S. HUCK

Clear, beautifully designed photographs are used to illustrate the book ***Count and See.*** Tana Hoban has photographed objects that are familiar and meaningful to the young child, such as three school buses, six candles on a birthday cake, nine firemen's hats, a dozen eggs in their carton, fifteen cookies, and, amazingly, 100 peas in ten pea shells! A pair of young boys—one black, the other white—represent the numeral 2. The cover pictures an integrated group of seven boys and girls with balloons. The photographs are reinforced on opposite pages with the number as word, as numeral, and as model set represented by white dots. (p. 104)

A photograph, like a painting, can simply record an incident or, in the hands of a photo-artist, it can interpret, extend, contrast, and develop real insight. The most exciting photographic work for children's books is being done by Tana Hoban. Her book ***Look Again!*** does not present a narrative but helps the child develop his perception and sharpen his awareness of the world. . . . The book provides an exercise in seeing, a way of expanding the child's consciousness. Its total graphic conception is simple, yet superbly complex. (p. 120)

Shapes and Things, although it is completely wordless, suggests that young children might use form and shape as well as function to identify and classify familiar objects. The white-on-black photograms are so striking in their arrangement that the book might also be used to sharpen older children's perceptions of form as an element of art. (p. 539)

Charlotte S. Huck, "Picture Books" and "Informational Books and Biography," in her Children's Literature in the Elementary School, *third edition, Holt, Rinehart and Winston, 1979, pp. 92-155, 520-82.*

HARRIET QUIMBY AND MARGARET DENNEHY, S.C.

Among the books that have success [with bilingual children] are the concept books provided by Tana Hoban. Her clear, well-produced photographs in such works as ***Count and See*** (. . . 1972) and ***Push, Pull, Empty, Full: a Book of Opposites*** (. . . 1972) provide visual stimulation and the opportunity for children to verbalize difficult concepts in a setting with which they can identify. Her use of clear, primary colors in ***Is It Red? Is It Yellow? Is It Blue?*** (. . . 1978) add a further dimension to their experience. (p. 388)

Harriet Quimby and Margaret Dennehy, S.C., "Creative Connection: School Library Resources for the E. S. L. Child," in Catholic Library World, *Vol. 52, No. 9, April, 1981, pp. 387-88.*

ALLEN RAYMOND

"Tana Hoban has never failed on a book," says master storyteller and librarian Carol Hurst. "She seems to know her audience; I carry ten of her books with me as I visit classrooms and talk with teachers and parents."

This talented photographer/author, who also visits classrooms everywhere, could probably sit in your living room and develop the theme for one of her widely acclaimed photo-concept books. One's mind imagines her deciding the room could produce a book called "Legs," legs of the chairs, tables, couch, the people. Or perhaps the book would be called "Corners," corners of the room, the tables, the couch, the piano bench, the chairs. . . .

[Tana Hoban's] creativity shows in her books, and becomes even more evident as she discusses the painstaking detail that goes into each of her books, and into each photograph. "I can't remember how many shots I took of 'Walk' and 'Don't Walk' pedestrian signs before selecting the ones for my newest book, ***I Read Signs*** (. . . 1983)." The American Library Association's *Booklist* said of this book, and its companion, ***I Read Symbols,*** "This is Hoban at her best; simple and substantial" [see excerpt for *I Read Signs; I Read Symbols* (1983)].

Ms. Hoban might agree on the word, simple. Teachers will agree on the word, substantial. "I'm looking for a strong image. I would hope that image might be recorded in a child's

From Round and Round and Round, *written and illustrated by Tana Hoban. Greenwillow Books, 1983. Copyright © 1983 by Tana Hoban. All rights reserved. By permission of Greenwillow Books (A Division of William Morrow & Company, Inc.).*

memory bank, to be recalled in a flashback many years later.'' She aims for a ''simple graphic image; I want it to register immediately with the child. If my picture is good, the child won't have to filter out any extraneous images.''

The titles of her books explain the contents; one knows what to expect. (p. 22)

Tana Hoban carries a camera at all times. It's a 35mm camera, usually containing color film, although she had done some books in black and white. ''I don't carry two cameras, like some photographers—one with color film, the other with black & white. When I'm taking pictures,'' she continues, ''I like to think either in color or black & white—but not both.'' Her latest books have been in color, although the ones in black and white are considered just as striking, and just as effective in achieving their objectives. (pp. 22-3)

Tana Hoban's desire to keep her photographs simple has led to the use of her books by many teachers of the learning disabled, emotionally disturbed, or children with other learning handicaps. . . . [Her] photographs seldom show children. She'll show hands or feet, letting children guess whether the person is a boy or girl. She's not interested in showing ''cute little girls or boys.'' It's the *concept* that counts.

While her 20 books appear simple in concept, they're widely acclaimed for the ingenuity Ms. Hoban displays as she creates, in black and white photographs, for instance, easily understood explanations of collective nouns such as *group, flock, crowd* (***More Than One***, . . . 1981).

''My books are about *noticing things*,'' Ms. Hoban says.

We've noticed over 500,000 of her books have been sold, which is notice enough that teacher and parents like the concept. (p. 23)

Allen Raymond, ''Tana Hoban,'' in Early Years, *Vol. 14, No. 5, January, 1984, pp. 22-3.*

PUBLISHERS WEEKLY

A red alarm clock, a blue mitten, a yellow baby shoe and a purple flower are the first cheery photographs in ***Red, Blue, Yellow Shoe***—a book about color. ***Panda, Panda*** displays a real panda in a natural-looking setting, progressing from eating, drinking, rolling and climbing to yawning, resting and, finally, sleeping. Children will relate to both board books: the counting objects are toy-bright (some really *are* toys), and the panda's seemingly lazy pursuit of creature comforts is engaging. As with all of Hoban's acclaimed photo books, these are deliberately simple, and perfect for the very young.

A review of ''Red, Blue, Yellow Shoe'' and ''Panda, Panda,'' in Publishers Weekly, *Vol. 230, No. 22, November 28, 1986, p. 72.*

LINDA WICHER

Distinctive photographs of a distinctive animal make ***Panda, Panda*** appropriate for a wide age range. A panda is shown in a variety of engaging activities and poses. . . . Each picture is accompanied by a word in bold red type describing the activity. As usual with Hoban, outstanding photographs and design make this a special toddler book. The second title [***Red, Blue, Yellow Shoe***] is a simpler board book version of Hoban's ***Is It Red? Is It Yellow? Is It Blue?*** (. . . 1978). Photographs of objects familiar and engaging to babies and toddlers are centered on a white background, with the color name and a corresponding solid color dot below the picture. It's a standout in Hoban's distinctive style, and a must for all toddler collections.

Linda Wicher, in a review of ''Panda, Panda'' and ''Red, Blue, Yellow Shoe,'' in School Library Journal, *Vol. 33, No. 4, December, 1986, p. 90.*

SHAPES AND THINGS (1970)

Things to identify, *shapes* to perceive: like John Reiss' *Colors*, this is an apparently simple, actually subtle aesthetic exercise. Using photograms—in which three-dimensional objects are recorded on light-sensitive paper without a camera—Miss Hoban reconstitutes in white on black the everyday black-and-white: block forms are silhouetted; knives and forks have a silvery sheen, and through one spoon appear the letters of alphabet soup (that also spill over from endpapers to title page). Together the teeth of a comb, the bristles of a toothbrush, the squeezed outline of a toothpaste tube have a tactile presence; and in an assemblage of sewing articles, buttons and spools are contoured while the lace recalls an early photogram mistaken for the real thing. A pail and shovel are flat white on black—and on grains of sand like a star-flecked sky; in a spread of kitchen utensils a strainer is a dimity grid and the basketed eggs glimmer like glass decoys. The marvels mount—a mysteriously luminous shell, a lollipop glimpsed through speckled cellophane, the fierce skeleton of a fish. The images are both material and dematerialized, and the familiar yields a startling beauty.

A review of ''Shapes and Things,'' in Kirkus Reviews, *Vol. XXXVIII, No. 12, June 15, 1970, p. 637.*

Here is a denial of the old crack, ''There is nothing new under the sun.'' Here is a series of photographs that *does* ''open one's eyes to the understated beauty of pure shape.'' To the unexpected beauty of form—of design, of familiar things: combs and keys, hammers and paperclips, eggbeaters and beads. The world of shapes and things will never look the same again, thanks to Tana Hoban.

A review of ''Shapes and Things,'' in Publishers Weekly, *Vol. 198, No. 3, July 20, 1970, p. 70.*

This has no words, tells no story; yet it is a book through which a small child may wish to browse, alone or with a friend to share the pleasure of recognizing simple things by their shapes. . . . Some of the pages are almost blunt: a single apple. Some are arranged in patterns on a theme: tools, sewing things, kitchen utensils. Very attractive, useful for discussion, good for stirring perceptual acuteness.

A review of "Shapes and Things," in Saturday Review, *Vol. LIII, No. 46, November 14, 1970, p. 34.*

All in all, the book offers a very interesting treatment of common articles found in or around every home or school. . . . Used effectively, it could stimulate recognition, perception and even art appreciation. However, it needs a parent or teacher to introduce it to a child. . . .

Gail McGovern, in a review of "Shapes and Things," in School Library Journal, *an appendix to* Library Journal, *Vol. 17, No. 4, December, 1970, p. 35.*

LOOK AGAIN! **(1971)**

The first look—through a square hole centered in a white page—tempts, teases, bestirs: what to make of those nodes and filaments, those cloudy stars? To turn the page is to see the whole—the pinwheel head of a dandelion gone to seed. Then look again—overleaf is a little girl, cheeks puffed, lips pursed, blowing the winged seeds away. Elsewhere, vertical stripes become the brow of a zebra becomes the zebra banded from ears to hoofs; a pitted whorl becomes a spiral seashell becomes a child's head bent, shell pressed to ear. In each of the nine sequences (most dazzling, a peacock; cosiest, the halved pear that follows) perception enlarges from configuration to figure to firmament. No words come between the photographs and the child; the creator of ***Shapes and Things*** (1970) uses her camera eye to reveal and relate as nothing else can.

A review of "Look Again!" in Kirkus Reviews, *Vol. XXXIX, No. 4, February 15, 1971, p. 168.*

"Black-and-white photography" is too limiting a term when applied to Miss Hoban's art, for her searching camera picks up every nuance, from the pale gray of a dandelion wisp to the intense black of a sunflower's shadow on a hot day. . . .

Although aimed at the children's market . . . , [this book knows] no age limit.

Ann Sperber, in a review of "Look Again!" in The New York Times Book Review, *May 2, 1971, p. 38.*

Tana Hoban's books are hard to describe and easy to look at, such as ***Shapes and Things,*** in which she revealed new facets of familiar objects. In ***Look Again!*** she now gives children another rich visual experience; by enlarging a fragment of the picture on the opposite page she exhorts them to look again at everything they will see from now on. Your reviewer wished that the book had been printed in a bright color rather than in black-and-white, but it's still a book of magic.

A review of "Look Again!" in Publishers Weekly, *Vol. 199, No. 18, May 3, 1971, p. 55.*

"All nature is but art, unknown to thee," said the poet Alexander Pope. Photographer Tana Hoban believes that all too often the familiar aspects of things around us blind us to their "sublime simplicity" and beauty. There is more than just one way of seeing a thing, says Miss Hoban, so *Look Again!*. . . Her wordless photographic essay offers us a new look at the world we blithely assumed we knew. It's a stunning book.

Jennifer Smith, "To See, Test and Taste," in The Christian Science Monitor, *May 6, 1971, p. B5.*

A series of superb photographic studies provides the structure for an imaginative exercise in visual perception. An unusual format, the centering of a two-inch-square die cut on the blank white pages inserted between each sequence, achieves the effect of visual metaphor as the viewer sees first the isolated detail, then the specific object of which that detail is a part, and finally, on the verso, that object in relation to the general environment. The excitement of discovery provokes an immediate and personal response to the implicit question "what do you see". . . . The implications for aesthetic development are endless. It is a book to be enjoyed again and again because it is, like a subtle lyric, a concentration of experience. (pp. 396-97)

Mary M. Burns, in a review of "Look Again!" in The Horn Book Magazine, *Vol. XLVII, No. 4, August, 1971, pp. 396-97.*

COUNT AND SEE **(1972)**

As in ***Shapes and Things*** (1970) and ***Look Again*** (1971), Tana Hoban's photographs show you everyday objects in a way that seems to lift a film of familiarity from your eyes. The seven fingers extended from two chubby young hands (the other three are folded down) are more visually real than they would be in the flesh, the rough bumps between the twelve eggs in a carton protrude compellingly, the thirty rough-edged bottle caps in six groups of five (some topside up, some lined with cork, some dented) constitute an intriguing study in textures. And (in contrast) the 50 nails, arranged in seemingly random order within five differently shaped groups of ten, have a clean, serene beauty. Look and see.

A review of "Count and See," in Kirkus Reviews, *Vol. XL, No. 8, April 15, 1972, p. 472.*

Small children who have enjoyed the photographic visual delights of Tana Hoban's two previous books, ***Shapes and Things*** and ***Look Again,*** won't want to miss this instructive and entertaining learn-to-count book. In her photographs, Mrs. Hoban exposes new facets of objects familiar to a child's world—each photograph is accompanied by the number as word, as numeral and as model set. An imaginative, stylish book, a shining demonstration that learning can be fun.

A review of "Count and See," in Publishers Weekly, *Vol. 201, No. 18, May 1, 1972, p. 50.*

As in her other books, the author has uniquely used photography. To produce a simple—but very special—counting book, she presents familiar objects in such a way that the reader wants to "look again and again." . . . The texture of the photographs, the vivid capturing of small objects, and the graphic excellence of its design make the book outstanding in comparison with the many dismal, unattractive counting books in print.

Anita Silvey, in a review of "Count and See," in The Horn Book Magazine, *Vol. XLVIII, No. 4, August, 1972, p. 361.*

The illustrations are black-and-white photographs of things a child constantly sees about him—fingers, dustbins, buses, other children—but the young English reader may be bewildered by the fire hydrant that illustrates One. The book's idea is good and the pictures are well chosen and presented, but don't blame your pre-schooler if he prefers coloured filters and disappearing figures to the undoubted elegance of these photographs.

"Little Tots of Knowledge," in The Times Literary Supplement, *No. 3719, June 15, 1973, p. 687.*

One of the few counting books for the youngest that takes counting beyond the five fingers on two hands. Look closely and you spot striking photographs that make the familiar fresh and, more important, arrangements of grouped objects that show there's more than one way to see numbers. In concept and presentation, count this counting book Number One.

A review of "Count and See," in The New York Times Book Review, *August 11, 1974, p. 23.*

PUSH, PULL, EMPTY, FULL: A BOOK OF OPPOSITES (1972)

Clear and uncluttered, black and white photographs show pictures that illustrate opposites; the terms are used on facing pages, sometimes shown by separate pictures, sometimes by two parts of the same picture. Two boys rush "up" a flight of stairs, and they rush "down"—elephants are shown for "thick," and facing them are stilt-legged birds for "thin"—a hand holds a brick, another a feather, "heavy" and "light". Very simple, perfectly clear, and most attractive, this is a book that may well stimulate small children to think about other terms of comparison.

Zena Sutherland, in a review of "Push-Pull Empty-Full," in Bulletin of the Center for Children's Books, *Vol. 26, No. 3, November, 1972, p. 43.*

This disappointing concept book by the author of the highly acclaimed ***Count and See*** (. . . 1972) features 15 pairs of opposites which are not always well chosen. For example, an elephant would hardly be characterized as "thick" nor a flamingo as "thin." Moreover, a swan is not nearly "big" enough to stand comparison with a "little" duckling. The elephant and the duckling would have been a much more accurate juxtaposition. The concept of first and last is not clearly expressed by the picture of four youngsters in Indian file across a two-page spread. As usual, Tana Hoban's black-and-white photographs are competently executed, but they lack humor and excitement. Children are not likely to look twice at the dull pair of hands illustrating the ideas of left and right, or at the pictured front and back of an alarm clock and empty and full baskets of mushrooms.

Daisy Kouzel, in a review of "Push-Pull, Empty-Full: A Book of Opposites," in School Library Journal, *an appendix to* Library Journal, *Vol. 19, No. 3, November, 1972, p. 59.*

Some teachers, and often I am one of them, are allergic to animals in fancy-dress, and anyway prefer illustrations that are closer to children's own experiences. What we need then, is Tana Hoban's ***Push-Pull Empty-Full***. . . . It is illustrated with effortlessly classy black and white photographs: the eggs in "whole-broken" and the tortoise in "out-in" are particularly vivid. If you're giving marks to books for the discussion they spark off, then Tana Hoban is near the top of the class.

Mary Jane Drummond, "Take One Stage-Coach to the Tea Party," in The Times Educational Supplement, *No. 3411, November 13, 1981, p. 24.*

OVER, UNDER, AND THROUGH, AND OTHER SPATIAL CONCEPTS (1973)

Tana Hoban's fifth album in the last four years has less of the clear-cut immediacy which usually identifies her work: there are fewer close-ups and still lifes, and most of the concepts are acted out by children at play. Groups of two or three contrasting words (beside, below . . . around, across, between . . .) preface a series of photos, and this time it's left up to the child to match labels and pictures. It's a small variation on a good idea, but whether it's worthwhile to *Look Again* and again is another question.

A review of "Over, Under & Through," in Kirkus Reviews, *Vol. XLI, No. 3, February 1, 1973, p. 109.*

Since several photographs follow each set of two or three words, the distinctions are not always perfectly clear; some of the photographs illustrate more than one concept. The book may require some help in interpretation, therefore. (pp. 139-40)

Zena Sutherland, in a review of "Over, Under & Through," in Bulletin of the Center for Children's Books, *Vol. 26, No. 9, May, 1973, pp. 139-40.*

[Children] may need help understanding that many of the pictures illustrate more than one concept. However, both the photographs and the format, with the words printed large on broad yellow bands at the beginning of each section, are uncluttered and appealing.

A review of "Over, Under & Through," in The Booklist, *Vol. 69, No. 18, May 15, 1973, p. 907.*

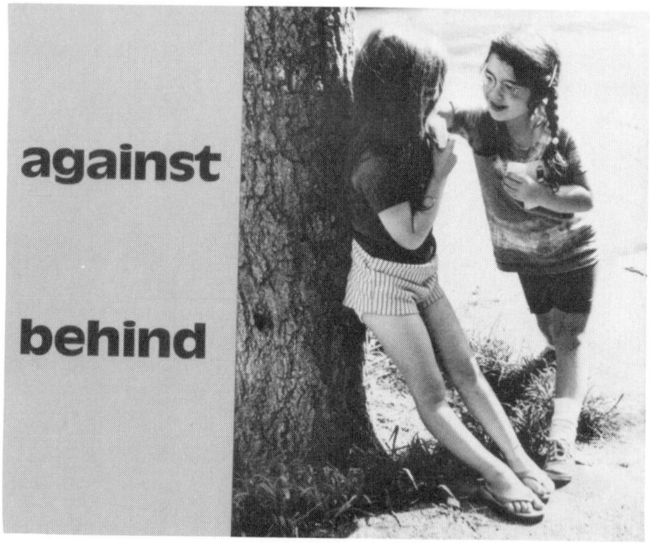

From Over, Under, and Through, and Other Spatial Concepts, *written and illustrated by Tana Hoban. Macmillan Publishing Co., Inc., 1973. Copyright © 1973 Tana Hoban. Reprinted with permission of Macmillan Publishing Company.*

WHERE IS IT? **(1974)**

A cottony, eastery bunny pantomimes "I wonder . . . Is it there? . . . Will I find it today? . . . There it is . . . Something special . . . for me," and after posing with eyes coyly covered, streaking across a lawn and sniffing behind a tree settles down happily beside his "something special"—a flower basket filled with cabbage and carrots. Performing rabbits must be rated a cliche even by two year-old standards; however, most of that audience will be happily oblivious to the staging and Tana Hoban executes an unpromising idea with clarity, directness and good taste. In the running for this season's bunny blue ribbon.

A review of "Where Is It?" in Kirkus Reviews, *Vol. XLII, No. 2, January 15, 1974, p. 51.*

Told in spare, poetic prose, the search lasts just long enough to match the attention span of two- and young three-year-olds. An Easter treat that will be popular throughout the year with parents searching for "first" books.

A review of "Where Is It?" in The Booklist, *Vol. 70, No. 17, May 1, 1974, p. 1003.*

A concise book for the very young with lovely, well printed photographs and large type, it does not dress animals in top hats to follow a story line as many photographic children's books do. It moves instead, with natural simplicity.

Karla Kuskin, in a review of "Where Is It?" in The New York Times Book Review, *May 5, 1974, p. 46.*

The photographs are excellent but repetitive, the captions often contrived; for example, one rear view is labelled, "There it is. Behind the tree," while another rear view is labelled, "Will I find it . . ." There's a modicum of suspense, and the fluffy white rabbit is appealing, but the whole is slight.

Zena Sutherland, in a review of "Where Is It?" in Bulletin of the Center for Children's Books, *Vol. 28, No. 1, September, 1974, p. 10.*

CIRCLES, TRIANGLES, AND SQUARES **(1974)**

Hoban's use of her camera to express basic concepts has become progressively more abstract and less dogmatic. Here she uses no words or obvious progression at all, but merely presents a series of pictures united by strong, geometrical compositions. In a few of the photos—of cut cookies, a house of cards, and a cross section of pipes—the shapes are determined by the subject matter; others—roller skating feet, a tugboat, a girl hanging by her knees—are more subtle and the shapes are imposed by the photographer. This could just as well be a lesson in basic photography or design as an exercise in geometrical form—in any case it's a real eye opener.

A review of "Circles, Triangles and Squares," in Kirkus Reviews, *Vol. XLII, No. 14, July 15, 1974, p. 736.*

Plane geometry moves from an abstract world into the real world of the child's own environment through the magic of the camera. Three basic shapes—circle, triangle, and square—are clearly delineated in white against the battleship-gray endpapers and then repeated through evocative black-and-white photographs, which demand full visual participation. How many circles, for example, can be found in the introductory picture of a small girl blowing bubbles against the dark wood of a door, a vagrant ray of light suggesting the roundness of the knob? Still more complex and fascinating is the subtle syncopation of shapes formed by four bicycles racked upside down on the roof of a car. An imaginative exercise for the development of visual awareness. (pp. 683-84)

Mary M. Burns, in a review of "Circles, Triangles and Squares," in The Horn Book Magazine, *Vol. L, No. 6, December, 1974, pp. 683-84.*

It is a more than plausible theory which holds that the mind's power of abstraction, made concrete by the words we use, forms delightedly around a nucleus of real examples of a new-found class. That theory is most persuasive when it is applied to the young, and this artist of the lens has given children at the edge of reading a little wordless treasury of the concrete, so sharply and wittily seen that the classifying urge should be beyond resisting. Circles? They are pipe bundles, eyeglasses, hoops, typewriter keys, baby buggy wheels. Triangles? They are a cocked paper hat, a director's chair, an elevated train structure, a cookie, a park swing, a house of cards. Here are real sets, vivid, unexpected and yet exactly as we know them. More than two dozen big black-and-white photographs fill this book with images of convincing meaning. It lies squarely (may we say) on the frontier of language and mathematics, without a word of text.

Philip Morrison and Phylis Morrison, in a review of "Circles, Triangles and Squares," in Scientific American, *Vol. 231, No. 6, December, 1974, p. 150.*

Often more than one shape appears in the photograph; because of this the book seems less pointed as a teaching tool than the Reiss book [*Shapes*]. . . . The photographs are of excellent quality, and while a picture that has several shapes is less explicit than a page of familiar objects that are all the same shape, there is an alternate value in letting the child search for and discover the squares, circles, and triangles that are not prominent.

Zena Sutherland, in a review of "Circles, Triangles and Squares," in Bulletin of the Center for Children's Books, *Vol. 28, No. 5, January, 1975, p. 79.*

DIG, DRILL, DUMP, FILL **(1975)**

In spite of a title that reminds us of ***Push, Pull, Empty, Full*** there's no particular conceptual organization to these photos of heavy machinery at work. In fact Hoban, who can usually be relied on to produce sharper, clearer compositions than these, never seems entirely comfortable with her subject, and her predictable uncaptioned views of dump trucks, cranes and loaders (the names are given in an appendix) don't add anything to what can be found in numerous other photo-picture books . . . ; certainly George Ancona's *Monsters on Wheels* (1974) packed a lot more horsepower.

A review of "Dig, Drill, Dump, Fill," in Kirkus Reviews, *Vol. XLIII, No. 20, October 15, 1975, p. 1176.*

Tana Hoban's camera catches heavy-duty machinery in powerful black-and-white action shots that will captivate children. Photographed in on-the-spot locations, the road rollers, fillers, diggers, and wreckers seem to rumble and roar as metal twists, cement mixes, and pavement crumbles. The eye of the camera captures a total feeling of what is happening, and children will enjoy supplying the sound effects.

Barbara Elleman, in a review of "Dig, Drill, Dump, Fill," in The Booklist, *Vol. 72, No. 5, November 1, 1975, p. 366.*

Large, clear photographs of various kinds of heavy machinery are presented without text or captions, although reduced pictures at the back of the book identify the machines and succinct descriptions are given. The pictures fill the page, so that the double-page spreads seem crowded, and the book is less appealing than it might be if the pictures were sequential or were grouped in any way.

Zena Sutherland, in a review of "Dig, Drill, Dump, Fill," in Bulletin of the Center for Children's Books, *Vol. 29, No. 8, April, 1976, p. 125.*

***BIG ONES, LITTLE ONES* (1976)**

Only a heart of ice can be indifferent to zoo babies, and there are several show stealers here, among them a duckling captured in mid-sprawl and a dignified zebra colt. Nevertheless, you've seen better animal portraits (if you still have Ylla's *Animal Babies,* take another look). As for the concept, big and little as a comparative "relationship," the idea isn't developed; it's simply reiterated through bear and cub, sheep and lamb, camel and baby camel, etc. On the scale of Tana Hoban's previous work, rate this little . . . though its diminutive appeal can't be entirely dismissed.

A review of "Big Ones, Little Ones," in Kirkus Reviews, *Vol. XLIV, No. 10, May 15, 1976, p. 588.*

A black-and-white photographic compilation depicts, without text, 14 sets of mature and young animals in natural activities. Including polar bears, hippos, lambs, elephants, horses, camels, and peahens, Hoban offers two full-page close-ups of each animal with a series of small identifying pictures at the end of the book. The presentation lacks the usual Hoban precision, and the effect is uneven; the baboons and ducklings are blurred and difficult to see against an indistinct background, and some of the compositions are lopped off. Yet the giraffes, zebras, and others are clear and bright; on the whole, children will find the pictures engrossing and the book a good starter toward identifying fellow creatures.

Barbara Elleman, in a review of "Big Ones, Little Ones," in The Booklist, *Vol. 72, No. 19, June 1, 1976, p. 1406.*

There are no words in this book of photographs, nor are they needed. . . . As a concept book, this has limitations, since it either presents old-and-young in a repetitive pattern or big-and-small in a restricted one; that is, all the big-small pairs are living creatures. However, taken simply as a wordless book that has photographs that show parents and children in the animal world (or maybe it's adults and babies) it has an appealing subject; the fact that young creatures resemble their progenitors is firmly established.

Zena Sutherland, in a review of "Big Ones Little Ones," in Bulletin of the Center for Children's Books, *Vol. 29, No. 11, July-August, 1976, p. 175.*

Two photographs for each grouping are included permitting considerable range in perspective: Thus, three peachicks are seen from a distance in relation to the mature peahen while on the companion page one small chick nestles close to the mother's wing—as much a study in texture and line as an informational device. An imaginatively conceived and vibrant book of animal families. . . .

Mary M. Burns, in a review of "Big Ones, Little Ones," in The Horn Book Magazine, *Vol. LII, No. 5, October, 1976, p. 491.*

***IS IT RED? IS IT YELLOW? IS IT BLUE? AN ADVENTURE IN COLOR* (1978)**

In her first book of color photographs, the author-photographer captures scenes from everyday life in vibrant hues. On the first page the six basic colors are identified in circles—red, yellow, blue, orange, green, and purple. The wordless book is simply designed and opens the eye to the marvelous world of color; each stark-white page contains one photograph which nearly fills it. In the bottom margin the predominant colors in the photograph are indicated by a row of corresponding circles; for instance beneath a picture of a cut watermelon are circles of red and green. The circles not only emphasize the color but make the viewer aware of the varied textures and shapes in the photographs; thus, a close-up of a grinning jack-o'-lantern becomes also an abstract composition of curves, triangles, and squares. The book is not a random hodgepodge of photographs—color, movement, and theme are subtly controlled. And far from being a mere exercise in color identification the book is a reminder of the beauty that is to be found in even the most ordinary objects—from stacks of plastic milk crates to a fallen maple leaf. (pp. 508-09)

Kate Mierzwinski, in a review of "Is It Red? Is it Yellow? Is It Blue?" in The Horn Book Magazine, *Vol. LV, No. 5, October, 1978, pp. 508-09.*

This can reinforce small children's familiarity with colors (some colors) but it isn't as provocative or open-ended as Hoban's earlier books, and it is weakened slightly by the fact that on a few pages a color is not picked up, i.e. no circle.

Zena Sutherland, in a review of "Is It Red? Is It Yellow? Is It Blue?" in Bulletin of the Center for Children's Books, *Vol. 32, No. 5, January, 1979, p. 82.*

A wordless concept picture book meant to teach basic colors to very young children does its work excellently for the most part. . . . Scenes become more complicated as the book progresses: a cluster of garbage bags features red, yellow, and blue; a big swirl lollipop has five colors in it, and stacks of bright plastic flowerpots have six. Confusion might come only in a scene or two where colors are muddy or unnamed: a stack of red, yellow, and blue packing crates also has some mossy green ones not alluded to; and what might an inquisitive viewer make of the pink balloon in the middle of a red-yellow-orange-blue color cluster? These are negotiable hurdles in an otherwise effective presentation. Imaginative, useful, and fun to look at.

Denise M. Wilms, in a review of "Is It Red? Is It Yellow? Is It Blue?" in Booklist, *Vol. 75, No. 9, January 1, 1979, p. 750.*

The six primary and secondary colors are the subjects of Hoban's latest thematic photo album, and they stand out here in smashing clarity. There's a spread of green apples and a facing one of oranges, there's a yellow leaf, a pumpkin, and a surprisingly sliced watermelon—but mostly these sharp, unadulterated colors occur in manmade objects, and it's a pleasure to report that plastic garbage bags, sunglasses, and flower pots have never looked so good. There's also much painted metal—a hydrant, a pipe, a rainbow of new cars, and just one confusing jumble of yellow street equipment—and, throughout, enough variety in scale and pattern and subject to keep viewers alert and responsive.

A review of "Is It Red? Is It Yellow? Is It Blue?" in Kirkus Reviews, *Vol. XLVII, No. 1, January 1, 1979, p. 3.*

***TAKE ANOTHER LOOK* (1981)**

This wordless photo-concept book, nearly identical in format to the author's ***Look Again!*** (. . . 1971), invites "another look" at nine familiar objects, from bread to umbrellas. A die-cut "porthole" covers each black-and-white photograph, luring preschoolers into the guessing game; the verso shows the same objects from an altered perspective. Similar in content to the earlier books, the photographs again demonstrate Hoban's attention to texture. The success of the sequences is not entirely uniform, but the most satisfying ones stretch the imagination to encompass the object's wholeness. A closeup of egg shells, for example, is lovely and mystifying; the final picture of the eggs themselves, cooking in a pan, comes as a delight.

Kristi L. Thomas, in a review of "Take Another Look," in School Library Journal, *Vol. 27, No. 7, March, 1981, p. 132.*

Perhaps the magic of Tana Hoban's ***Look Again!,*** a 1971 event, was not to be recaptured: that first glimpse, through a die-cut hole, of a fuzzy, starry, mysterious *something;* overleaf, the perfect head of a dandelion gone to seed; on the reverse, an intent black child, lips pursed, blowing. But if the drama of discovery is not to be replicated, one wonders what, here, prompted another go at the format altogether—for instead of a series of vivid, distinct triggering images (a zebra's stripes, the whorls of a snail shell, a peacock's fan of feathers), we have mostly less vivid, less distinct, guess-what allover textures and patterns—bread, a sponge, a grater—plus some less clear-cut equivalents of the first batch (e.g., a reptile's skin in lieu of the underside of a turtle) and just one bull's-eye: the spokes of an umbrella. What best conveys the difference, perhaps, is the head of the daisy here vs. the head of the sunflower in ***Look Again!***—the same thing, but less arresting in magnification *or* in toto. (That's also true of the center of the apple here vs. the center of the pear before.) There's still some pleasure in the encounter, of course, but less variety, imagination, or resonance. (pp. 279-80)

A review of "Take Another Look," in Kirkus Reviews, *Vol. XLIX, No. 5, March 1, 1981, pp. 279-80.*

This is not the first book to use the idea of a cut-out page that shows part of an object, inviting identification; however, it is a nice example of the type. The photographs—some enlarged—are clear, the objects familiar, and the format more than adequate for identification and for showing comparative size, so that no captions are necessary. . . . A nice concept book, this has a guessing game appeal. (pp. 194-95)

Zena Sutherland, in a review of "Take Another Look," in Bulletin of the Center for Children's Books, *Vol. 34, No. 10, June, 1981, pp. 194-95.*

Ten years ago the award-winning photographer began to use the art of the camera as a unique and original approach to picture books. In ***Look Again!*** . . . she created a series of visual questions and answers, first showing through a die-cut square a detail of an object, then a view of the object itself, and finally, overleaf, the whole thing in some sort of natural setting. The new book, though slightly smaller, is absolutely similar in purpose and in design. Again using black-and-white photographs, Tana Hoban stimulates perception by presenting ordinary objects in and out of context. Through die-cut openings—now round instead of square—one sees tantalizing glimpses of, for instance, a slice of bread, a lizard, an umbrella, a cat. Once more, imaginative photography serves, without words, as a simple introduction to aesthetics and as an aid to education through vision.

Ethel L. Heins, in a review of "Take Another Look," in The Horn Book Magazine, *Vol. LVII, No. 3, June, 1981, p. 292.*

***MORE THAN ONE* (1981)**

More Than One is a concept book illustrating collective nouns: group, herd, flock, stack, etc. Each page consists of one black-and-white photograph and ten words. The noun that Hoban is trying to illustrate is one inch high and bright blue, while the other nouns are of smaller, black type. All of the words on each page make up a list of all the words illustrated in the book. In some cases words in the list also apply to the illustrated word. Hoban's photographs, as usual, are well done. They

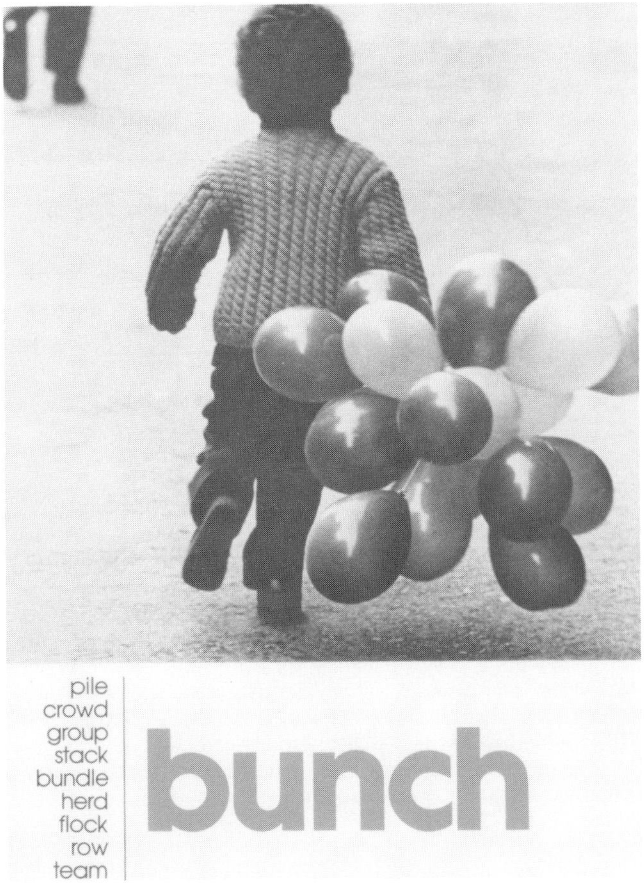

From More Than One, *written and illustrated by Tana Hoban. Greenwillow Books, 1981. Copyright © 1981 by Tana Hoban. All rights reserved. By permission of Greenwillow Books (A Division of William Morrow & Company, Inc.).*

include city and country scenes and will catch the eye and interest of children. The book, however, may be more beneficial if read aloud first. Hoban skillfully develops the subject matter, and while ***More Than One*** does not equal some of her earlier titles, it could be a useful addition.

Paula J. Zsiray, in a review of "More than One," in School Library Journal, *Vol. 28, No. 1, September, 1981, p. 109.*

Clever—and simple: beginning with the title. Each of the photographs illustrates "more than one"—in more than one way. Thus we see a *stack* of egg cartons and also, on either side, a *pile* of potatoes and onions. It wouldn't be wrong, either, to see the stack as *row* upon row of cartons—or to think of the loosely-piled onions as a *bunch*. What Hoban is dealing with—as dexterously as she has ever handled any concept—are ten collective nouns: *crowd, group, bundle, herd, flock, team,* in addition to the aforecited. . . . A lesson, then, of many sorts—and both enormously inviting (a *row* of zebras, a *bunch* of balloons, a football *team,* a *crowd* at the beach) and lots of fun to search out multiples in. (pp. 1156-57)

A review of "More than One," in Kirkus Reviews, *Vol. XLIX, No. 18, September 15, 1981, pp. 1156-57.*

The pictures have that visual energy typical of this well-known author: a row of four dazzle-painted zebras, a domestic herd of elephants, a group of children all jumping at once, a crowd of bathers at Coney Island and more. . . . The book declares itself to be at once a counting book, a word book and a shape book. It is a good book to be led through while you still hope to learn to read, and a fine one for new readers.

A review of "More than One," in Scientific American, *Vol. 245, No. 6, December, 1981, p. 47.*

A last-page explanation is necessary, as the concepts are more complicated than they first seem. The photography is not as sharp as in Hoban's other fine books. Good to hone the observations of the middle grades.

Ruth M. Stein, in a review of "More than One," in Language Arts, *Vol. 59, No. 3, March, 1982, p. 267.*

A, B, SEE! (1982)

An illustrious photographer and filmmaker, Hoban presents a magnetic picture book that should earn her more prizes than the many already awarded her works for children. The alphabet is the star of this show, the letters printed at the bottom of each page, black against white, with the one letter illustrated by photographed objects enlarged and in darker type. In contrast, the things grouped to feature each letter are reversed, stark white against black. There is a wide diversity of symbols in the photos that children will want to study again and again: "L" flaunts a dainty, casually folded strip of lace, a lock, a lollipop and two kinds of leaves. Everything about this creation is innovative, an impetus to really "seeing," as invited by the title.

A review of "A, B, See," in Publishers Weekly, *Vol. 221, No. 2, January 8, 1982, p. 83.*

Similar in composition and format to Hoban's earlier ***Shapes and Things*** (. . . 1970), this alphabet book has a slightly more utilitarian approach, developing letter and shape identification skills by using black-and-white photograms as sequential illustrations of the letters of the alphabet. The high-contrast pages are clean, clear and uncluttered, with the full alphabet appearing across the bottom border, one enlarged letter per page. The result is a book that both provides the fun of recognizing a common object in an unusual aspect and encourages an expansion of visual awareness: such ordinary things as leaves and lace transcend the page in their patterned clarity; jars and spoons glow with a luminous intensity; and a suddenly transparent pod of peas betrays its pregnant secret. Many of the photographed items are the same or very similar to those in the earlier work, but this is not to say that the latter is a rerun of the former. Relying on a similar design principle and photographic technique, the two are unique in concept and intent, and this newest addition to the Hoban oeuvre is a valuable expansion of the ABC genre.

Kristi L. Thomas, in a review of "A, B, See!" in School Library Journal, *Vol. 28, No. 7, March, 1982, p. 134.*

Here, we have the alphabet with one letter at a time printed large—and the objects on the page, as you may have guessed, all begin with that letter. It doesn't take from A (asparagus, apple, abacus, arrow . . .) to B to catch on; the self-reinforcing scheme is just the thing to build up small egos; the objects are mostly recognizable at age three or four (abacus is perhaps the most out-of-the-way)—or, in a few exceptional instances, so visually intriguing (a crab, a grater) that children will *want* to know what they are. And, though a page of diverse objects is the norm, there are other solutions too: most ingeniously, a page of question marks for the letter Q; three umbrellas in a row for U—and on the facing page, a single vase for V. Or, the enormously effective single, half-open zipper for Z. One might even become newly aware, because of the way the zipper intersects with the Z on that last page, that the enlarged letter has proceeded through the alphabet space. Altogether: a knockout.

A review of "A, B, See," in Kirkus Reviews, *Vol. L, No. 5, March 1, 1982, p. 271.*

Artistically arranged to provide rhythm and balance, the pictures are also exercises in object recognition and visual discrimination—intriguing puzzles to be solved rather than just lessons to be learned. Some objects are instantly recognizable; others demand somewhat sophisticated understanding; and still others require some mental agility to identify. Printed below each illustration is a complete alphabet . . . [that provides] both a handsome border and a unifying element of design. An exciting, original, and carefully conceived book.

Mary M. Burns, in a review of "A, B, See!," in The Horn Book Magazine, *Vol. LVIII, No. 3, June, 1982, p. 279.*

ROUND AND ROUND AND ROUND (1983)

A simple idea effectively executed. Hoban's crisp lesson on becoming aware of circular shapes is crystal clear in this album of apropos photographs. Sharp, well-composed pictures show, for example, a seal balancing a ball, with rings around the seal's neck echoing the ball's round shape. In fact, several of the pictures suggest both flat and spherical circular forms; and all the selections are aesthetic in both appearance and composition. One of the author's best.

Denise M. Wilms, in a review of "Round & Round & Round," in Booklist, *Vol. 79, No. 16, April 15, 1983, p. 1094.*

Hoban has given us another exquisite full-color photographic essay. Every page is a visual treat which encourages us to look closely and appreciate the beauty of ordinary round objects—a smokestack, a woodpile, concentric circles in a puddle. Though it doesn't measure up to ***Look Again*** or ***Take Another Look*** in inviting participation, the photographs are perhaps her best.

Arlene Stolzer Sandner, in a review of "Round & Round & Round," in Children's Book Review Service, *Vol. 11, No. 11, June, 1983, p. 108.*

The creator of such books as ***A, B, See!*** and ***Take Another Look*** . . . once again attracts readers visually—this time in a collection of vibrant full-color photographs set against a white background. Capturing everyday objects—green peas in a blue colander, wooden beads in a bowl, Swiss cheese on a roll—the photographer entices children to look at the familiar from different perspectives. Each photograph highlights something round, but further study may, in some cases, reveal other less obvious round items in the same picture. For instance, a girl wears tiny round earrings and a sweater with a round neckline while she blows a big, round bubble-gum bubble. Not all of the pictures have equal appeal and visual impact, but all of them invite perusal. With one photograph to a page, the book is striking and stimulating.

Nancy Sheridan, in a review of "Round & Round & Round," in The Horn Book Magazine, *Vol. LIX, No. 3, June, 1983, p. 290.*

This book is a vivid visual exploration of the concept of roundness in children's everyday environments. Circular concepts in shape and in motion are captured by colored photographs of balls, balloons, stacks of logs and orange halves. Roundness in nature provides such aesthetic experiences as dew pearls dripping off leaves or a cadre of dandelion puffs waiting to be blown way.

No merry-go-rounds for roundness of motion but more relevantly, wheels revolving, a cement mixer turning and a potter creating a bowl. The taste of round is a bowl of fresh green peas, the sound of round is rain falling into a puddle, while the touch of round is a bead or ball.

Hoban has the uncanny ability to capture the most action-packed sequences in her sumptuous photographs. Dramatically frozen, shots of a bubble-gum bubble about to burst, ice cream in a cone about to be licked, or a dog caught leaping through a hoop allow readers to speculate on the impending action.

Ronald A. Jobe, in a review of "Round & Round & Round," in Language Arts, *Vol. 60, No. 7, October, 1983, p. 897.*

I READ SIGNS; I READ SYMBOLS (1983)

These companion picture books are as basic as can be, and right on target as far as getting their message across to preschoolers. ***I Read Signs*** shows sharp, full-color close-up photographs of common signs (Come In We're Open, Walk, Don't Walk, Playground, Beware of Dog, etc.), encouraging preschoolers to recognize them and first-graders to test their budding reading skills. ***I Read Symbols*** follows an identical format, displaying some 27 road, street, and building symbols that youngsters will find it worthwhile to know. In both books the photography is excellent. Pictures are bright and clear and look exactly as they are to be found in the streets. This is Hoban at her best; simple and substantial.

Denise M. Wilms, in a review of "I Read Signs" and "I Read Symbols," in Booklist, *Vol. 80, No. 4, October 15, 1983, p. 359.*

Hoban's many picture books are well known for concepts demonstrated through striking photographs and minimum text. These two are deceptively simple. The 30 verbal and 27 symbolic street signs have been caught on location in close-ups with a minimum of background to give just a soupçon of milieu (city, sky or tree) or hint of meaning ("BEWARE OF DOG" on chain link fence). Design is bold; primary colors are emphasized. The familiar predominates; more unusual signs ("BIKE ROUTE," "LOW FLYING PLANES"; symbols for trail and deer crossing) add interest. ***I Read Symbols*** has an explanation of "What the Symbols Say" to ensure readers (or their parents) understand. Good for sharing with toddlers, for preschool concept awareness or for beginning readers.

Joanna Rudge Long, in a review of "I Read Signs" and "I Read Symbols," in School Library Journal, *Vol. 30, No. 3, November, 1983, p. 64.*

Spanking, bold, head-on images—that put other sign-displays in the shade. Once again, Hoban assumes that, for kids, things are interesting in themselves: in this case, street signs and the international language of symbols. Street signs are for reading here: WALK on one page, DON'T WALK opposite. (You can't see them both at the same time on the street.) BEWARE OF DOG, cagily, behind a chain-link fence; NO PARKING, FIRE LANE, smartly, on a row of stanchions; RAILROAD CROSSING paired with TAXI, NO LEFT TURN with (of course) KEEP RIGHT. Also, yes: COME IN, WE'RE OPEN to start with—and SORRY, WE'RE CLOSED at the close. Big as the signs are, in their color-photo-rectangles, it's a lot like looking at the TV screen—another dimension that will do no harm. The symbol book, by nature, is something of a conundrum—challenging youngsters to guess what the wiggly arrow or the big white H means, teaching them the symbols for ladies' room and men's room, acquainting them with the very idea of a symbol language. . . . Both are simple, instructive, and dazzling.

A review of "I Read Signs" and "I Read Symbols," in Kirkus Reviews, *Vol. LI, No. 21, November 1, 1983, p. 186.*

Tana Hoban, prize-winning photographer, once again gives her followers an "eye's worth." . . .

[These] photo displays are both art books and straightforward educational tools for children. The books seem to say to the child, "Let's take all those squares, triangles, and rectangles that we always see when we're driving, and just *look* at them, all by themselves." The result is an honest appreciation of signs for their color, shape, and content.

By studying both books, children are given the opportunity to become more observant of specifics of their environment, while gaining increased confidence in interpreting it. . . .

I Read Signs literally speaks for itself. It's those commonplace directives like "people working" and "pitch in." Again, the art resides in singling out these signs and bringing us face to face with their intrinsic, often surprising beauty.

Both books are good exercises in "nominating" familiar images. They earn their keep as effective learning tools—instructing the young reader in signs and symbols, while encouraging us to not let familiarity blind us to beauty.

Darian J. Scott, "Photos as Art and Education," in The Christian Science Monitor, *December 2, 1983, p. B10.*

I WALK AND READ (1984)

I Walk and Read sounds like Tana Hoban's earlier titles for the very young, ***I Read Signs*** and ***I Read Symbols.*** It even looks like them if you judge a book by its cover (which, with children's literature, most of us do). But in this instance, sounds and looks are deceiving. The contents of the package reveal an altogether fresh approach to the landscapes of language through which the author leads her early readers.

Miss Hoban is a first-rate color photographer whose vision of the urban and institutional settings that sprout signs was previously subordinated to the goal of instruction. The images in ***I Walk and Read*** are still calculated to heighten children's visual awareness of the words they first encounter in the urban out-of-doors. But here they also show us certain things about the streets that if *we* haven't noticed before, a small child probably has.

Yellow school buses and ice-blue police cars loom large as tanks. . . . A neon chicken, shoe and fish float magically in a lunar void at night. The image of a modern call box labeled FIRE faces the moniker on an old engine house on the opposite page, underscoring the contrast between the imperious iconography of today's signs and yesterday's decorative lettering. WET PAINT, OPEN SUNDAYS, PHONE, POST NO BILLS, MUSEUM ENTRANCE, EXIT ONLY, NO DOGS ALLOWED. We are surrounded by commands, broken here and there by a tradesman's whimsical graphic for ice cream or a mural painted on a stone wall.

The beauty of such a book for children is that for their first lessons in reading, it leads them to explore a larger world that they can touch and smell and see. For their parents, ***I Walk and Read*** brings home some important subliminal facts about language. Our initial exposure to language occurs not in the nursery but in public spaces. And our first encounter is with a series of reiterated messages largely based on a binary system of stop/go commands. Finally, words in their "natural," written, outdoor state are large; moreover, they possess weight, color and texture (they even sizzle if illuminated). And while they may appear startlingly abstract in composition, as some do here, they invariably convey information. They mean what they say. . . .

These are experiential facts well worth recalling, for later they are squeezed out of the deskbound reading programs in the schools. No wonder, then, that it often takes a writer or a poet who is privileged with the sensory intelligence of a child to repossess the concreteness of language for the rest of us.

Carol Brightman, in a review of "I Walk and Read," in The New York Times Book Review, *April 8, 1984, p. 29.*

Fans of Hoban should enjoy her new picture book. . . . This is a varied selection of color photographs. Common words and phrases such as *phone, wet paint,* and *U.S. Mail* are seen in their natural habitat. Some of the other pictures are more prob-

From A, B, See! *written and illustrated by Tana Hoban. Greenwillow Books, 1982. Copyright © 1982 by Tana Hoban. All rights reserved. By permission of Greenwillow Books (A Division of William Morrow & Company, Inc.).*

lematic. The neon restaurant sign, for instance, shines below a multiwindowed building, with no clue in the picture as to what it represents. The best photographs are the ones that display an inventive use of the words: *Repairs* is surrounded by a big neon shoe; the painted ice cream sign also features an array of mouth-watering delights. A logical progression for those who've learned a thing or two from Hoban's earlier works.

Ilene Cooper, in a review of "I Walk and Read," in Booklist, *Vol. 80, No. 18, May 15, 1984, p. 1343.*

Bold, attractive photographs lead young readers on a walk through city streets alive with bright signs that older eyes might take for granted. . . . The subjects and words in each picture will be easily recognized by most readers, but close-up shots of such familiar symbols as those for the Postal Service or for subway exits reverberate with new drama and fresh beauty. Another in Hoban's series of photo-documentaries for young children, the book continues her usual fine blend of technically skilled pictures, pleasing shapes, and a simple format. (pp. 457-58)

Ethel R. Twichell, in a review of "I Walk and Read," in The Horn Book Magazine, *Vol. LX, No. 4, August, 1984, pp. 457-58.*

Each of the visually powerful photographs presents a variety of signs, from paint to neon, in every location from walls to school buses, and about everything from food to street directions. Close-up shots of the signs are dramatically composed. Detailed images enrich the concept, resulting in little confusion of content or intent. However, the depth and significance of the photo interpretation of these signs may be missed by young children. (pp. 629-30)

Ronald A. Jobe, in a review of "I Walk and Read," in Language Arts, *vol. 61, No. 6, October, 1984, pp. 629-30.*

IS IT ROUGH? IS IT SMOOTH? IS IT SHINY? (1984)

Textures, yes—but also sizes of things, numbers and kinds and colors of things. Each of the natural-color photographs in this latest Hoban album illustrates several concepts. And it's up to the viewer not only to spot them, but to find the right words for them. The easy first picture shows five round shiny pennies . . . in a small-child's palm (five fingers, smooth skin) . . . on a board. The cropped, deadpan second is a close-up of a burst bubble-gum bubble—the essence of stickiness. There are other gooey things and prickly things, smooth and rough things; there's even, for wetness, a rain-spattered window. As usual with Hoban, there are contrasting and complementary pictures without any blatant thematic statement; and there isn't a picture—the piles of pretzels, the pebbly shore, the graffiti-ed truck—that isn't interesting, often story-telling, in itself. (See, for effortless impact, the small, sudsy brown hands in a bowl of shiny bubbles on the back cover.) A glorious addition to a great body of work, or vice versa. (pp. J61-J62)

A review of "Is It Rough? Is It Smooth? Is It Shiny?" in Kirkus Reviews, *Juvenile Issue, Vol. LII, Nos. 10-17, September 1, 1984, pp. J61-J62.*

There is no text in this concept book for young children, and no captions are provided for the excellent color photographs. That may be part of the reason that this is less effective than other Hoban books (***Is It Red? Is It Yellow? Is It Blue?*** or ***Take Another Look*** or ***Push-Pull, Empty-Full***) but it is primarily because, unlike those books, there are no sets of pictures used to establish contrast or show (as with color) differences. Here the pictures are handsome, but each is isolated, and the concept of texture is not always visually conveyed.

Zena Sutherland, in a review of "Is It Rough? Is It Smooth? Is It Shiny?" in Bulletin of the Center for Children's Books, *Vol. 38, No. 2, October, 1984, p. 27.*

Extraordinarily crisp, clean color photographs allow Hoban to call attention to textures. Viewers will find themselves tempted to reach out and touch things like a trio of shiny red apples on crinkled pink tissue paper or a spread of glistening beach stones. There are no words and none needed, for the concrete images will spark plenty to talk about between a child and anyone sharing the book with him or her. A simple idea executed with the requisite technical skill.

Denise M. Wilms, in a review of "Is It Rough? Is It Smooth? Is It Shiny?" in Booklist, *Vol. 81, No. 3, October 1, 1984, p. 248.*

Wonderful color photographs show objects with different textures in Hoban's textless concept book. Shiny apples, a scratchy beard, sticky marshmallows; pretzels, fish, rocks, sea shells, a porcupine, bubbles and other everyday objects are pictured, and they all work as superb discussion starters. In addition to presenting the concept of texture, the striking photographs will interest children in shape and color recognition, in counting, and in discussing the uses of the pictured objects. With this book, perfect for one-on-one sharing, Hoban continues in the fine tradition of ***Is It Red? Is It Yellow? Is It Blue?*** (1978), ***Take Another Look*** (1981) and ***Round & Round & Round*** (1983, . . .).

Lisa Redd, in a review of "Is It Rough? Is It Smooth? Is It Shiny?" in School Library Journal, *Vol. 31, No. 3, November, 1984, p. 109.*

1, 2, 3; WHAT IS IT? (1985)

AUTHOR'S COMMENTARY

[*Hoban received a 1985* Boston Globe-Horn Book *Special Award in the category of board books for* 1, 2, 3. *The following excerpt is from her acceptance speech.*]

I thank *The Boston Globe* and *The Horn Book* for . . . recognizing the importance of board books for babies. I believe that I worked harder and longer on these books than on any others that I have done. I shot many, many versions in order to find the simplicity and directness I always want for my readers, no matter what age. The book went through many changes as I worked it out, in our seventeenth-century atelier, overlooking the River Seine on the Ile St. Louis. My photographs in ***1, 2, 3*** are truly international. The book begins with an American cake in Rochester, New York. My daughter lives there, so a touch of Rochester is in all my books. The ABC blocks were my daughter's when she was little and now have been used by her children—my grandchildren. The five fingers and toes are also Rochesterian. The animal cookies were carried from New York to Paris in ample supply. The beautiful French flowers are my favorites—anemones. The oranges are Israeli, and I bought the beads in London.

Tana Hoban, "An International Picture Book," in The Horn Book Magazine, *Vol. LXII, No. 1, January-February, 1986, p. 37.*

Once there was a squarish book, of simple color photographs of familiar nursery objects, that endured for decades because it was so unequivocally and unsurpassingly a first book. These two squarish, heavy cardboard volumes (with rounded corners, on the side of the opening) are in that line of descent—the more outstanding (and rudimentary) because Hoban plumps a single object in bright primary colors—sock, sneaker, bib—in the middle of each page of ***What Is It?*** and the simplest, most natural of multiples—five fingers, four quarters of an orange—on each page of ***1, 2, 3.*** The latter, indeed, begins with a single candle on a birthday cake—this is a book for children at that age—and follows, in a cross-reference to ***What Is It?,*** with two sneakers. Many libraries of course steer clear of board books—and there'd be no place to put a pocket except on the back cover. But for display, or for the diversion of visiting tots, it's worth considering—while parents, caretakers, and kin will seize upon the books—especially ***1, 2, 3:*** a looking-and-learning knockout with its red numerals, number-words, and dots-to-count.

A review of "1, 2, 3" and "What Is It?" in Kirkus Reviews, *Juvenile Issue, Vol. LIII, Nos. 1-5, March 1, 1985, p. J-6.*

Not since Helen Oxenbury's set of baby board books has the simplest level of baby book been done so well. Where Oxenbury used illustration, Hoban, of course, relies on the camera. In each book she presents crisp, sharp photographs of everyday objects in a baby's world. . . . Large red dots beneath each picture [in ***1, 2, 3***] reinforce the number concept as they did in ***Count and See*** . . . ; in fact, this is a baby-oriented version of that modern classic. . . . Both books are superbly designed. Cardboard pages and binding are strong and sturdy; the pictures show vibrant primary colors associated with childhood; the hues mingle to give both works strong visual unity. Score another hit for this skilled artist.

Denise M. Wilms, in a review of "1, 2, 3" and "What Is It?" in Booklist, *Vol. 81, No. 14, March 15, 1985, p. 1059.*

Hoban, long distinguished for her photographic concept books, now offers two new board books, and the "chew and drool" group should be well satisfied with them. Both include sharp, clean photographs of brightly colored common objects. . . . In ***1, 2, 3,*** each page includes not only a photograph of an appropriate number of items (one to ten) but the numeral itself, the number spelled out and an equivalent number of dots, all in red. This allows for several different stages of learning. . . . Billed as "A first book for your baby . . . ," both of these would be excellent choices.

Martha L. White, in a review of "1, 2, 3" and "What Is It?" in School Library Journal, *Vol. 32, No. 1, September, 1985, p. 119.*

This superb counting book is intended for toddlers, ages twelve to twenty-four months. A perfect board book, ***1, 2, 3*** combines subjects, photographs, design, and color in the right manner for beginning counters. . . . The photographs are of excellent quality and color definition. You can count even the stripes on the zebra animal cracker! The careful craftsmanship extends to the back cover (traditionally the title page in board books) where three items—measuring cups—repeat the primary colors used on the front cover for the three blocks. Adults will be drawn to ***1, 2, 3*** as readily as children. Books like this one should be sold in six-packs! (p. 547)

. . . . .

Exceptional photography [in ***What Is It?***] depicts ten objects central to the toddler's world that call out to be named in a board book for the very young. One item is pictured on each page. The objects shown on facing pages are related to each other in some way—a bib and drinking cup, a spoon and alphabet soup in a bowl, a sock and small sneaker. Hoban has included one more element for youngsters with sharp eyes to catch and point out proudly; the front cover shows painted wooden blocks in a trainlike formation with a rubber duck and apple aboard, while the back cover has the "train" moving in the opposite direction, and the apple has been replaced by an orange for the return trip. Board books are the first book experience for many children, and examples of the genre that exhibit as much thought and care in their production as this one does are to be commended. (p. 548)

Elizabeth S. Watson, in a review of "1, 2, 3" and "What Is It," in The Horn Book Magazine, *Vol. LXI, No. 5, September-October, 1985, pp. 547-48.*

[*Twichell was the head of the 1985* Boston Globe-Horn Book *Award committee.*]

We have selected Tana Hoban's ***1, 2, 3*** . . . for a special award in the category of board books. Her clean, precise photographs of items immediately familiar to small children and the simple, but stylish layout stand out in a field which usually contents itself with mediocre materials. The book's durability, ease of handling, and bright, primary colors well deserve the warm welcome the book has already received. Although its youthful clientele may bite, gnaw, drool on, and drop the little book, it will defy their attempts to destroy it as well as delight their eyes and stimulate their quickening abilities to identify and count.

Ethel Twichell, in a review of "1, 2, 3," in The Horn Book Magazine, *Vol. LXII, No. 1, January-February, 1986, p. 37.*

IS IT LARGER? IS IT SMALLER? (1985)

Unsurpassed for her use of color photography in concept books, Hoban here presents a series of pictures in which there are sets of large and small objects that show contrasting size. Most of the photographs show items so clearly (a large and small goldfish in an aquarium; big beads and small ones) that the pair is immediately identifiable; occasionally (a child holding a rabbit) children may wonder what the big-small comparison is (ears, in this case) but it's always there, and the moment of searching may add a bit of game element.

Zena Sutherland, in a review of "Is It Larger? Is It Smaller?" in Bulletin of the Center for Children's Books, *Vol. 38, No. 8, April, 1985, p. 148.*

Is It Larger? Is It Smaller? exhibits the same skillful clarity and glowing color that have become Hoban's trademarks. But this is not just a technicolor version of her black-and-white animals-only size concept book (***Big Ones, Little Ones*** . . . 1976), for here Hoban features a variety of objects and activities familiar to young children and refines the concept by comparing as many as a half dozen objects of varying sizes, thus showing the relativity of the terms. The most successful photographs are close-ups, in part because distracting backgrounds are eliminated and in part because the question of perspective does not arise (young viewers might possibly be confused by the idea that a "small" boat in the background is actually larger than a "large" boat in the foreground). This is well within the tradition of Hoban's other well-crafted photo-concept books: a visually enriching exercise that will help children find words for the world in which they live.

Kristi Thomas Beavin, in a review of "Is It Larger? Is It Smaller?" in School Library Journal, *Vol. 31, No. 8, April, 1985, p. 79.*

Relative size is the concept unifying Hoban's latest collection of eye-filling photos. As always, her choice of subjects represents a wonderful conjuction of eye and mind.

See, for example, the rabbit's large ears against a little boy's smaller ones; the two large X's of a sawhorse picnic table with the four small X's of its benches stacked upside-down on the table; or the different measures of cake ingredients lined up in front of a partially-filled mixing bowl, being stirred. Often the motif is stated and echoed, as in the toy car beside a real Volkswagen being washed by father and son.

Other combinations are more and less obvious; but the simplest, most predictable groupings make striking pictures, and the subtlest (e.g., a row of icicles against a grubby background) bear longer gazing in their own right.

A review of "Is It Larger? Is It Smaller?" in Kirkus Reviews, *Vol. LIII, Nos. 5-10, May 15, 1985, p. J26.*

About 30 beautifully composed and eye-catching photographs appear here. . . . The organizing concept is absolutely clear, and the varied real world is seen so sharply that the single theme is enriched. . . . "This one is for my father," our author of a dozen such books writes in dedication, "who told me I was wonderful." How right he was!

Philip Morrison and Phylis Morrison, in a review of "Is It Larger? Is It Smaller?" in Scientific American, *Vol. 253, No. 6, December, 1985, p. 42.*

A CHILDREN'S ZOO (1985)

A strikingly designed book, this has bold, black pages, large, white words, and appealing portraits of 11 common zoo animals including pandas, seals, giraffes, and parrots. Pages feature crisp, spare, balanced design. Three appropriate descriptions (strong, shaggy, roars on the lion page) are slightly left of center and above the large, slightly right-of-center animal name; facing this left-page configuration is a full-color picture of the animal with a thin, white frame delineating it from the slick, dark background. The idea is remarkably simple, but as with much of Hoban's work, it is her precise vision and strong aesthetic sense that make the package seem exceptional. This will serve preschoolers well both for its subtly presented information and its enduring style. A chart on the last page explains where each animal comes from, what it eats, and in what type of environment it lives. (pp. 63-4)

Denise M. Wilms, in a review of "A Children's Zoo," in Booklist, *Vol. 82, No. 1, September 1, 1985, pp. 63-4.*

This is not intended to be a comprehensive listing of zoo animals, but the excellent color photographs show many of the creatures that are best known to children and that are popular recipients of zoo visits. The layout of the book adds to its visual appeal and gives information: . . . standing out in bold white type are the name of the animal and three descriptive words, so well chosen that most children would be able to guess ("red / blue / squawks" is clearly a parrot, and "striped / black and white / gallops" just as clearly a zebra) identity. This may not have been designed for the purpose, but (in addition to its more obvious attractions) it is an excellent catalyst for a discussion of descriptive adjectives.

A review of "A Children's Zoo," in Bulletin of the Center for Children's Books, *Vol. 39, No. 2, October, 1985, p. 28.*

A pleasing, small portfolio of familiar zoo animals. The omission of a gorilla or chimpanzee is puzzling, but never mind. Each animal is given splendid, full-color attention on its own black-framed page. Facing is its name in large, white print along with a three-word tag, "Big / white / growls" describes the polar bear, just as most young children would. These tags make nice riddles or beginnings for a child's additional description. . . . For the most part, the photographs are standard zoo fare, but a few are truly different and amusing. The pleasures of naming and describing are discovered and practiced early on in childhood, and Hoban's new photographic book adds to these delights like few others.

Anna Biagioni Hart, in a review of "A Children's Zoo," in School Library Journal, *Vol. 32, No. 2, October, 1985, p. 156.*

Large color photographs rimmed in white and set in black pages make this handsome presentation quite literally an album. . . . In nearly all cases the three descriptors consist of two adjectives and a verb, but the pattern changes unaccountably for the last two animals—a PANDA and a GIRAFFE. Here there is no verb to suggest activity of any sort; rather there is a third adjective. The final page of the book contains a chart of additional information about each animal set into three columns headed "Where Do They Come From?, Where Do They Live?, What Do They Eat?" Although the answers are brief, they will often be confusing for the very young children who are apt to be the chief audience. Usually the place of origin is the name of a continent, and occasionally that of a country (Asia, Antarctica, New Zealand, etc.). The generic phrases telling where the animals live will likewise need explanation of such terms as ice floes, the bush, and the Northern Wilderness. Food is listed as meat, fish and/or vegetation. The beautiful photographs and simplicity of design in the body of the book invite lingering enjoyment and will also encourage early word recognition.

Margaret Bush, in a review of "A Children's Zoo," in Appraisal: Science Books for Young People, *Vol. 19, No. 3, Summer, 1986, p. 37.*

SHAPES, SHAPES, SHAPES (1986)

In one of her more open-ended picture books, Hoban suggests on the first page some shapes to look for: arcs, circles, hearts, hexagons, ovals, parallelograms and illustrates them with small, simple drawings of the 11 shapes. On each of the following pages is a vibrant color photograph, bordered with white. Subjects vary from a construction site to a child's open lunch box, from a shoe store display to a manhole cover. Occasionally no single shape is clearly evident, an ambiguity that young children may find frustrating. As the book is wordless after the first page, there are no verbal leads or clues. The only continuity is provided by the title theme of shapes, which is broad enough to include almost anything. Hoban's attractive photographs earn high marks for composition and clarity. A handsome, though relatively unstructured, concept book.

Carolyn Phelan, in a review of "Shapes, Shapes, Shapes," in Booklist, *Vol. 82, No. 13, March 1, 1986, p. 1019.*

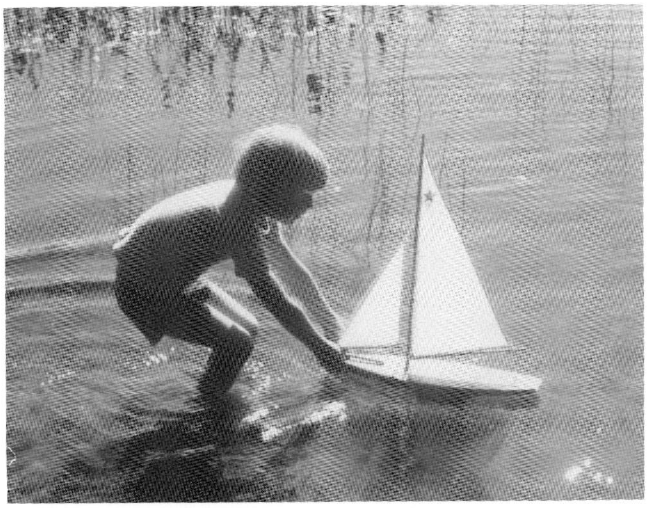

From Shapes, Shapes, Shapes, *written and illustrated by Tana Hoban. Greenwillow Books, 1986. Copyright © 1986 by Tana Hoban. All rights reserved. By permission of Greenwillow Books (A Division of William Morrow & Company, Inc.).*

Adults and kids of all shapes and sizes are in for a treat with this outstanding wordless book. Hoban's full-color photos have an astonishing clarity and glow to them. They include interesting and beautiful urban landscapes, portraits and still life. Children will have fun speculating about the photographs—or they can simply enjoy them, no comment necessary. Looking at this book for shapes is a little like looking at a Cézanne for shapes. Nevertheless, circles, stars, triangles and even fancier geometric figures like trapezoids are here in abundance. The 11 figures represented, as well as the photographs, reach well beyond Hoban's earlier books about shapes. This book has an impressive technical quality of photographic reproduction and fine artistic content. Do your eyes a favor, and don't miss this one.

Anna Biagioni Hart, in a review of "Shapes, Shapes, Shapes," in School Library Journal, *Vol. 32, No. 9, May, 1986, p. 76.*

As with other Hoban books, the scenes are sharp and well composed; all can be profitably examined again and again. Some have intrinsic interest, such as young musicians wearing sweaters with shapes on them or play kitchenware at the beach. Others heighten awareness of patterns, such as the holes in a stacking chair.

A beautiful, mind-stretching book. (pp. 786-87)

A review of "Shapes, Shapes, Shapes," in Kirkus Reviews, *Vol. LIV, No. 10, May 15, 1986, pp. 786-87.*

In an essay on the evolution of photographic picture books in *From Noah's Ark to the Beast Within* . . . , Barbara Bader speaks of Tana Hoban's first book, ***Shapes and Things*** . . . : "The objects are at once recognizable and miraculous, tangible and illusory, things and essences and pure form" [see excerpt dated 1976 in General Commentary]. During the past fifteen years the books created by the prolific prize-winning photographer have become ever more dynamic yet at the same time remain varied, ingenious, and appealing in subject matter. And when she began using color, it was not for showiness but for making specific graphic statements. The new book opens with "some shapes to look for"—for example, arcs, circles, hexagons, ovals, rectangles, and trapezoids. Then, all set in fascinating contexts, familiar and sometimes enticingly unfamiliar objects in uncaptioned pictures contain or exemplify various shapes. The photographs can be deceptive; looking like candid shots, they are actually meticulously planned compositions in which color and texture provide exciting contrasts, and such dramatic devices as truncation and juxtaposition heighten interest and arouse curiosity. There are elegant surprises on every page—a child launching a sailboat on still water; the superstructure of a bridge; a view of a partly demolished building; or two wonderful little boys wearing identical patterned sweaters, one playing a tambourine and the other a triangle. The handsome book can serve as a simple introduction to geometry, as an exercise in visual perception, and as an aesthetic, often poetic, experience. (pp. 340-41)

Ethel L. Heins, in a review of "Shapes, Shapes, Shapes," in The Horn Book Magazine, *Vol. LXII, No. 3, May-June, 1986, pp. 340-41.*

***RED, BLUE, YELLOW SHOE* (1986)**

Another sturdy and cheerful board book, this time devoted to colors, will find itself comfortably at home on the same book shelves where the author-photographer's ***1, 2, 3*** and ***What Is It?*** . . . are already well-thumbed friends. Choosing simple and familiar subjects, Hoban, as usual, gives each a presence which goes beyond the object itself. A blue mitten seems ready to enclose a small hand; a gray feather awaits the stroke of inquiring fingers. Placed carefully in the center of glossy, white pages, each object—for example, shoe, flower, and kitten—is accompanied by the clearly-lettered word for the color, leaving youngsters and obliging parents the task of identifying the item pictured. Highly sophisticated photography, skillfully capturing the grainy texture of an orange and the slickness of a maple leaf, and the durable pages add to the attractiveness of a book which demonstrates that the highest standards in layout and design can be given to the smallest picture-book devotees.

Ethel R. Twichell, in a review of "Red, Blue, Yellow Shoe," in The Horn Book Magazine, *Vol. LXII, No. 6, November-December, 1986, p. 735.*

With her customary clarity of concept and precision of photographic composition, Hoban has created a board book to equal ***1, 2, 3*** (*A First Book of Numbers*) and her other concept books for the youngest child. Each page contains one object, a familiar and attractively presented one, with a large dot in the featured color and the name of the object in large block print. Green is represented by a handsome maple leaf, gray by a feather in shades from light to dark, and black by an appealing but not sentimentalized kitten. The book itself is easy to handle, with rounded edges, and will serve for use in identifying the objects as well as the colors. Sturdy in every respect. (pp. 88-9)

Betsy Hearne, in a review of "Red, Blue, Yellow Shoe," in Bulletin of the Center for Children's Books, *Vol. 40, No. 5, January, 1987, pp. 88-9.*

***26 LETTERS AND 99 CENTS* (1987)**

Two books in one: a flip-over with an alphabet book at one end, a counting book showing coins used for amounts up to 99 cents at the other.

This is elegant simplicity at its best. Using the basic colors of a new box of kindergarten crayons. Hoban chooses brightly enameled upper-and-lower-case letters and figures whose forms resemble those taught to beginning writers. Each letter is accompanied by one easily recognized object (egg, goldfish, umbrella); coins representing each amount up to 30 cents plus 35, 40, 45, 50, 60, 70, 80, 90 and 99 cents are shown in as many as three combinations for a given amount. The organization of each page into four blocks gives the design rhythm, coherence and consistency.

The quintessence of first alphabet and money books, produced with grace and style.

A review of "26 Letters and 99 Cents," in Kirkus Reviews, *Vol. LV, No. 2, January 15, 1987, p. 139.*

Hoban's name is synonymous with creative and carefully crafted concept books for young children. This newest offering in arresting full color is really two books in one. ***26 Letters*** is a delightful ABC handbook. . . . Turning the book around reveals the even more creative ***99 Cents***. . . . Math concepts are extremely difficult to convey, while explaining nickels, dimes and quarters is harder still. An extremely inventive approach that will be hailed by parents, teachers and librarians.

A review of "26 Letters and 99 Cents," in Publishers Weekly, *Vol. 231, No. 6, February 13, 1987, p. 92.*

Hoban's clever design, providing two books in one, is highlighted with clear, bright photographs. . . . Interesting and challenging choices are presented to enhance vocabulary development of preschoolers [in ***26 Letters***]. . . . An exciting feature of ***99 Cents*** is the concept of monetary equivalency grouping which is introduced at number 5 and continues with increasing complexity. Teachers and parents can extend counting and grouping activities by creating additional coin combinations. Children will enjoy manipulating money, numbers, and letters to correspond to the photographs in this book. The combination of unique design, distinguished photographs, and superb layout adds up to a winner!

Gale W. Sherman, in a review of "26 Letters and 99 Cents," in School Library Journal, *Vol. 33, No. 7, April, 1987, p. 84.*

Milton Meltzer

1915-

American author of nonfiction and fiction and editor.

A prolific author best known for highlighting social struggles and historical figures with honesty, sensitivity, and enthusiasm, Meltzer is recognized for creating informational books which reflect his personal concern for justice as well as his respect for middle grade, junior high, and high school students. Noted as both an outstanding historian and a craftsmanlike writer, Meltzer is considered an author of conviction who presents his audience with well-rounded overviews of the history of discrimination. His thoughtful and thought-provoking books focus on historical events and personages that are often overlooked or glossed over in textbooks and other sources; to assemble his works, Meltzer often utilizes research materials previously accessible only to scholars. The majority of Meltzer's books center on black and Jewish history; others cover such subjects as world slavery, war, and the history of specific ethnic groups in America. He has also written biographies of such individuals as Samuel Gridley Howe, Lydia Maria Child, Langston Hughes, Margaret Sanger, and Dorothea Lange, all supporters of causes which helped to alleviate oppression. Addressing time periods which range from the ancient to the contemporary, Meltzer focuses on specific eras as topics for his social histories and as backgrounds for his biographies. Although his books are international in scope, Meltzer most often concentrates on the political and economic aspects of the United States. A unique feature of the works is Meltzer's extensive selection of primary sources, such as letters, diaries, newspapers, court reports, photographs, and political cartoons, which he combines with his narratives; many of the books also include bibliographies and indexes as well as glossaries and lists of related organizations. Writing in a straightforward style, Meltzer attempts to provide his audience with the opportunity to view humanity as both great and terrible, thus encouraging young people to make moral choices and, perhaps, to influence the course of history. He is also the author of a book of fiction, *Underground Man* (1972), a historical novel based on the memoirs of a young abolitionist which draws from sources similar to those Meltzer uses in his nonfiction.

Critics acclaim Meltzer for creating impressive works that illuminate both world and personal history while examining controversial, complex issues; several of his books are considered authority sources in their respective fields. Meltzer is also praised for the quality of his research and organization as well as for his success in bringing a sense of immediacy to the past. Although reviewers are divided in their assessment of his objectivity, most observers laud Meltzer for providing young readers with excellent introductions that both inform and stimulate.

Meltzer was nominated as a National Book Award finalist in 1969 for *Langston Hughes,* in 1975 for *Remember the Days* and *World of Our Fathers,* and in 1977 for *Never to Forget.* In 1976, *Never to Forget* won the Association of Jewish Libraries Children's Book Award and was selected as a *Boston Globe-Horn Book* Honor Book; it received the Jane Addams Award and the National Jewish Book Award in 1977. Meltzer won the Christopher Award in 1970 for *Brother, Can You Spare a Dime?* and in 1981 for *All Times, All Peoples;* in the same year, he received the Carter G. Woodson Book Award for *The Chinese Americans.*

Photograph by Catherine Noren. Courtesy of Milton Meltzer.

(See also *Contemporary Literary Criticism,* Vol. 26; *Something about the Author,* Vol. 1; *Something about the Author Autobiography Series,* Vol. 1; and *Contemporary Authors,* Vols. 13-16, rev. ed.)

AUTHOR'S COMMENTARY

[*The following excerpt is taken from an interview by Geraldine DeLuca and Roni Natov.*]

[Geraldine DeLuca]: We'd like to start by asking how you came to write so many books about oppressed peoples.

[Milton Meltzer]: That's something I wasn't aware I was doing initially. It wasn't until some ten books had been published that one reviewer observed that I was known for my books dealing with social issues, with the necessity for social change, and that I always took the side of the underdog. That's when it dawned on me it was what I had been doing, without any conscious plan. It obviously came out of some human necessity that I'm sure was shaped by my growing up during the depression of the Thirties. My parents were immigrants, my father a window cleaner, and my mother a factory worker. I grew up in Worcester, Massachusetts, finished high school in 1932 and got a scholarship to a new experimental college at Columbia (it no longer exists) which was designed to train undergraduates for teaching. It was a wonderful experience, but in my senior year I dropped out because the future seemed so bleak. The Depression had been going on for six or seven years and in spite of the New Deal, hope for work was very small, so I thought, what was the point of finishing? There were no jobs at all for teachers. Schools were contracting; budgets were being cut. I couldn't find a job. I was desperate to do anything. I went on relief—what we call welfare today—and stayed on relief for about six months. Then the W.P.A. Arts Projects began and I got a job on the Federal Theater Project as a staff writer, preparing educational materials, background on the plays, both contemporary and classical, that the project was producing in New York City theaters. They often brought students into the theaters to see W.P.A. plays, and sometimes the plays toured the schools. The job of our small unit was to provide teaching aids. I remember those few years as uproarious and wonderful. We were often on union picket lines, fighting to keep our jobs as Congress cut budgets again and again. I wrote a young adult book on all this—***Violins and Shovels***—which has some of my personal experiences in it. I guess growing up in hard times made me interested in this kind of material.

GD: When did you start doing research and writing history?

MM: Well, I didn't write books until I was in my late thirties. Until then I wrote for newspapers and magazines, radio, public relations projects. . . . Writing was my way to make a living. But I didn't think of writing a book until I got to that perilous time when I was nearing forty. Nothing is more ephemeral than yesterday's newspapers or last week's magazine and I began to wonder whether anything I did would last, even a little while. I came up with the idea for my first book, the ***Pictorial History of Black Americans,*** which I did with Langston Hughes. It appeared in 1956, just ahead of the public attention to civil rights issues. It was a great learning experience working with Langston. We became friends and eventually I did another book with him (***Black Magic: A Pictorial History of the Negro in American Entertainment***) published in 1967, soon after he died. One book led to another. The first several books were for adults. I didn't think of writing for children until one of my daughters suggested it.

GD: So it was then you began writing full-time?

MM: No. About 20 of my books were published while I was working at full-time jobs. I kept jobs until 1968. That final job, which lasted ten years, was as editor of a medical publication. I did my writing early in the morning, evenings and weekends. I managed to get one or two books a year done on that part-time basis. By 1968 my income from the twenty-odd books that were in print was sufficient to give up the salaried job. I much preferred to be doing my own writing full-time.

As it happened, 1968 was also the euphoric peak for writers of children's books. It was the last year of the Johnson administration and during his presidency the greatest amount of federal funding was poured into subsidizing book buying, through the public and school library systems. That meant decent royalties to those of us who were working in the field. Libraries didn't have to worry about budgets. So all of us, foolishly ignoring the fact that economics and politics have their ups and downs and that a different president, a different Congress or a crisis in the economy could radically change all that, thought that, in the future, when we got too old or tired to write anymore, we would be able to live on the income of our books that stayed in print. But when Johnson went out of office and Nixon came in, the federal subsidy program collapsed.

GD: What happened to your work then?

MM: The last few years have been disastrous for many writers of children's books. Inflation and the shrinkage of library budgets have put many of our books out of print.

[Roni Natov]: Is that what's happening to the *Women of America* series you edited?

MM: Yes, to some of the titles. There were 23 titles and about half were done in paperback too. Some of the paperbacks are in print but several of the hardcovers have been withdrawn. That's happened to some of my other books too. In some cases the paperback continues in print while the publisher stops reissuing the hardcover. In other cases both stay in print, as with my book on the holocaust, ***Never to Forget.***

GD: The hardcover sells to schools and libraries?

MM: Yes, but it also sells as a gift book to many parents who want their children coming of age to grapple with the subject.

GD: I think that would also sell as an adult book.

MM: It does, yes. It's won many awards which brought it to adult attention.

RN: Do you see yourself as uncovering areas of history that have been neglected?

MM: I've tried to show what you might call the underside of history. That is, how did a particular issue, a particular crisis in history appear to the anonymous people who were just as much makers of that history as the kings and queens and presidents and generals? One person who helped me do it better was John Anthony Scott who edited the Knopf series, the "Living History Library." (My ***Bread—and Roses, Brother, Can you Spare a Dime,*** and ***Bound for the Rio Grande*** were all written for that series.) Scott, a marvelous teacher, and the Knopf chief editor, Fabio Coen, came up with the idea for a series of books on American history that would go beyond the typical narrative history to convey the *quality* of that experience as it was lived and felt by the people who were part of it. Their notion was to imbed in the narrative the kind of documentary source material which is usually given to students only on a college level. Letters, diaries, journals, autobiography, memoirs, testimony given at trials or in public hearings, speeches, eyewitness reports, news accounts—these are among the sources for history voiced "in their own words."

For example, in ***Bound for the Rio Grande,*** the book on the Mexican War, I not only found documentary material about how the American soldier felt going into this war—which was a predatory, pro-slavery raid on another people's territory—but I also tried to document how the Mexican soldier felt. What was in his mind as he faced our troops? That war had interesting parallels to the war in Vietnam. I tried to show how people felt on both sides, what they thought, how they acted, the changes they experienced.

I like that technique so much I've used it in many young people's books. It works wonderfully. Readers, teachers, librarians like it very much and letters from readers tell me how meaningful it has made history for them.

RN: Did that interest in using sources that would give a more ordinary and personal point of view carry over into your biographies? Did it contribute to your interest in writing biographies?

MM: Well, with biographies of subjects remote in time it's harder to find that kind of material. If you're writing about someone long dead you can't do interviews with the subject or with survivors who knew the person. So you do the best you can by unearthing whatever documentary material is available.

For my recent adult biography—***Dorothea Lange: A Photographer's Life***—I had access to her letters and diaries. When Lange went out into the field to shoot, she kept notes on the situations she photographed as well as on the specific shots she took. That was rich material. But beyond that I interviewed over a hundred people who had known her: family, friends, professionals in the fields of art and photography. And there were also her own and her husband's oral histories to draw on.

In that book I attempted, probably more than in many biographies, to say as much as I could in the words of these people or in Lange's own words, while at the same time maintaining enough distance to incorporate my understanding of the intimate connections between her life and her work. Not everything people tell you is accurate or true, and you have to balance one source's view of the past against another's. You may find documentary evidence which corroborates or contradicts what someone says; two people may contradict each other: you have to make up your own mind about what's true. And if you're not sure, you have to tell the reader you really don't know, that this is just your guess or that you can't even make a guess. But first-person material is very important in that book.

GD: In writing for an adult, what kind of material do you include that you wouldn't include for a child?

MM: Off-hand, I think there are just two considerations when you're writing about a subject that you could just as well treat for an adult as for a youngster. One is sheer length. Almost every children's book has to be relatively short. Publishers figure that young readers, even if they are of high school age, are not likely to read five hundred pages on Madame X, but they will read two hundred pages. So you have to compress, which means being very selective. The second consideration is deciding if you are dealing with a concept or event that may be beyond young reader's normal experience. That doesn't mean omitting it. But you have to figure out how to bring it within their grasp. It's not done by talking down. In some cases, it's simply a matter of adding more information than you would if you were referring to the same event in an adult book.

This is where a good editor can be very helpful. As a writer, you may become so involved in what you're trying to say that you fail to realize you're sometimes too elliptical, too indirect. An editor can point out that a young reader wouldn't have the vaguest idea of what you're talking about and that you have to find a better way to clarify the point or situation.

GD: I found the explanations in ***Brother, Can You Spare a Dime?*** very helpful. There are basic facts about how the Depression came about that I had never really understood before I read your book.

MM: One of the interesting things about my young adult books is that most of them are used in colleges and read by adults, too.

RN: I think, also, that there has been a dearth of history books that use oral history and that actually clarify rather than just pile up facts as if history had no bias or point of view or narrative style. So I'm finding your books wonderful ways into subjects that I had difficulty feeling comfortable with in high school.

MM: Yes, young adult books of non-fiction, whatever the subject, are often helpful to adults who find history or science difficult or dull. They discover that a good children's book writer can make elements of many subjects clear and meaningful very quickly.

GD: How do you decide what personal material to include about a subject when you're writing a biography—either for adults or for children? How much of the personal life do you consider relevant?

MM: All of it that you can find out about is relevant of course. But you can't include everything. Selection is all-important, whether writing for children or adults. Some things are more important than others, they weigh more in the estimate of forces shaping character and behavior. There is no limit to what you can take up in a biography for adults, but censorship—or fear of it—sometimes affects work for younger readers. Margaret Sanger, for example, had relationships with men in which not only the sexual side was important but the intellectual exchange as well. In the biography of her I co-authored for young readers a dozen years ago we didn't pinpoint her personal sex life. We did discuss how her ideas were affected by such relationships, and of course we went into conception and birth control, dealing with them very simply and accurately. Yet some librarians and teachers objected even to this.

GD: Do you think that if you didn't need to be concerned about the conservative attitudes of the people who buy or don't buy these books that you would be inclined to include more of the personal lives of the people being written about? If these people were social and political rebels, as many of them were, shouldn't there be some recognition that their personal lives also broke with convention to one degree or another, that the two may go together?

MM: Well, the Emma Goldman biography (in the *Women of America* series) is quite explicit about the revolutionary's personal life. Many men were important in Goldman's life, and the author, Alix Shulman, deals with that plainly. But that book was published a few years after our Sanger book and already it was possible to say more. The publisher just wouldn't have accepted some of that material earlier. I'm sure, as you are suggesting, that there are still large numbers of teachers and librarians who can't or won't deal with this kind of thing, and who, for that reason, would not introduce the Margaret Sanger book, for example, into the classroom. They might be too nervous about students discussing the issue of birth control in class. They worry about kids going home and telling their parents the teacher gave them a book to read that deals with birth control. They may feel ill at ease themselves talking about the subject.

A related problem that I encountered while editing the *Women of America* series is that teachers and librarians are often reluctant to order a book about a person they're not familiar with. I was delighted that Crowell agreed that we weren't going to do "me too" books in this series. That is, we were not going to commission people to write the tenth biography of Eleanor Roosevelt for children or the sixth biography of Harriet Tubman. We wanted to find subjects who had, for the most part, never been treated before but who were just as important as those who had been. Women generally have been so grossly neglected that if we did do a subject who had been written about before, we would only do it if, in our considered opinion, the previous biographer had done a bad job. So almost all the books in the series are about women who had not had their lives told before. And what we discovered is that the books about the more obscure figures, no matter how well written, did not sell widely enough. (pp. 95-103)

RN: How did your work on the biography of Langston Hughes—whom you knew personally—differ from your work on other biographies where you were dealing more exclusively with secondary sources? How did your personal knowledge of Hughes affect the portrait that emerges in the book?

MM: My work on his life was very special because we had gotten to know each other over the last dozen years of his life and I had a very deep affection for him. The writing of the book was almost happenstance. I'd been asked to do four-page sketches of a number of figures of the past and present for John Wiley, the textbook publishers. This was during the sixties when a lot of publishers were reaching out to kids in ghetto schools. They wanted to find subjects that would be suitable for bright kids who were having trouble reading and present the material without reducing it to a childish level. So they asked a number of children's authors to write these pamphlets. I suggested, among other subjects, Langston Hughes. Writing the pamphlet was an easy thing to do. I wrote it without talking to Langston about it. When it was printed, I sent it to him and he was pleased with it. Then it suddenly dawned on me: why not try to write his life for young readers? (He had written two large volumes of his autobiography which covered his life only to the age of forty, by the way.) I hesitantly suggested the possibility to him, and without any delay, he said yes. He said I could talk to him about it as I went along, and he offered to read a draft.

So with that understanding, I got a contract and went to work on it. When I finished the first draft I showed it to him and he made some suggestions on matters of emphasis. Then while I was making revisions, he fell sick. Everyone thought it was a minor illness, but he was dead two weeks later. So he never saw the final draft.

When Langston died I had to put the book aside. I had no heart to work on it. But about six months later I picked it up again. In the course of doing the first draft, I had interviewed many of his contemporaries and younger people, too, some of whom were his literary proteges. He was wonderfully generous to young writers in helping them get a foothold in publishing. I went on interviewing people who had known him, going back to some a second time. So there's a lot of personal material in that book. A new opening took account of the fact that he died just after I had done the first draft. I think the feeling I had for him is there in the book.

My biography of Lydia Maria Child—***Tongue of flame***—is not that different in tone, however, because even though she died over a century ago, I came to love her. The few hundred letters I had to draw on when I was writing that book were marvelous evocations of what she was like. She was a wonderful human being—complex and humane and generous. You couldn't help loving her. So that feeling is in the book even though I never knew her.

GD: What makes you decide to write a book about someone?

MM: My first children's book, the life of Samuel Gridley Howe, called ***A Light in the Dark,*** came from two things. It developed out of my earlier work on the ***Pictorial History of Black Americans.*** That research revealed a vast untapped field of source material. There were thousands of marvelous people in our history, black and white abolitionists whom people knew nothing about. One after another these incredible vivid figures came to life as I worked on the book. I began to jot notes about people who would make good subjects for a full-scale biography and Howe was one of them. He was a complex, quixotic figure who grew up in Boston, went to Harvard Medical School, and as he was ending his training, in the 1820's, volunteered in the Greek War for Independence. That war has many parallels with the Spanish Civil War of the 1930's, which many of my contemporaries were involved with. It was one of the central experiences of those of us who came of age in the 1930's and here was Sam Howe who was involved in something very similar. Howe sailed to Greece and became a surgeon in the Greek fleet, fighting against the Turks, who had occupied Greece for hundreds of years. He was in action for seven years and had all kinds of extraordinary experiences. Later he married Julia Ward and pioneered in many aspects of social reform, as well as becoming a militant abolitionist.

When I told my young children something about Howe, one of them said, why don't you stop talking about Samuel Howe and write about him for kids? I thought about that and Crowell gave me a contract to do it. I had done adult books on Thoreau and Mark Twain, both for Crowell, so I went to the editor there and said I wanted to try my hand at a children's book. He turned me over to Elizabeth Riley, who was one of the great editors. I asked her if she had any hints on how to do it and she said, just go out and do it and if you have trouble, talk to us. So I went out and did it and I loved doing it. I was very excited about the whole process. The biography got good reviews, and they said, how about a second? So I proposed Lydia Maria Child. And that's how it began. (pp. 104-06)

Geraldine DeLuca and Roni Natov, in an interview with Milton Meltzer in The Lion and the Unicorn, *Vol. 4, No. 1, Summer, 1980, pp. 95-107.*

GENERAL COMMENTARY

JOHN A. WILLIAMS

Well, if you are the underdog you welcome any help you can get. What you get here is not bad at all. Each of these six books [***Thaddeus Stevens and the Fight for Negro Rights, In Their Own Words,*** and ***Time of Trial, Time of Hope*** by Milton Meltzer; *The Long Freedom Road* by Janet Harris; *Four Took Freedom* by Philip Sterling and Rayford Logan; and *The Unfinished March* by Carol F. Drisko and Edgar A. Toppin] gives the Negro some of the dimension, heritage and participation in American life that previously were denied, suppressed or ignored—the end result being the creation of an Afro-American without the roots or rights to share what other Americans take for granted.

Books of this type should be designed for both white and black readership. Negro colleges and schools have taught some smattering of Negro history for generations. White institutions rarely have got past "Little Black Sambo" and "Dr. Dolittle." The more the Negro learns about himself, the more he must become incensed at the reasons for and at the way his history has been suppressed or managed. To understand why the Negro now insists on his share of the American dream, the white American must read the same works the Negro reads—and those works could be called "the sub-history of America." Failing this, the agony must continue.

A good place to begin the journey to the underside of American history is with the books listed in this review. The remarkable fact about them is that there is no overlapping of material. Each deals with a specific time in American history or with a special aspect of the Negro in our society.

The Long Freedom Road, by Janet Harris, is the least exciting. . . .

When Mrs. Harris does go into the past, she perpetuates some of the dangerous untruths that have gained everyday credence. For example, the Civil War was indeed fought to save the Union, but it was *not* fought to free the slaves. They were freed because of military necessity. . . .

Milton Meltzer, on the other hand—in the three volumes in which he is represented—once with August Meier (***Time of Trial, Time of Hope***), once as an editor (***In Their Own Words***) and once as sole author (***Thaddeus Stevens***), labors in the valleys for the hard truths, not in the peaks where the air is so thin that truth and untruth have equal merit. The first two books are studded with the uncompromising statistics that delineate the Negro's second-class status—lynching, unemployment, migrations to the North and Negro soldiers. Meltzer's ***Thaddeus Stevens*** is not a saint, but an appealing part-time sinner. . . .

Placed in the proper institutions and in the proper hands, these six books should help to reap a harvest of racial harmony in the future. But one wonders why this could not have been so several generations ago, to avoid what we now have come to in race relations.

John A. Williams, "Up from Slavery," in The New York Times Book Review, *May 7, 1967, p. 5.*

BERNICE E. CULLINAN WITH MARY K. KARRER AND ARLENE M. PILLAR

Milton Meltzer followed the path to the terror and grief of the Nazi era through eyewitness accounts—letters, diaries, journals, and memoirs. However inadequate words, he says, language is all we have to reach across barriers to understanding. Letting history speak for itself characterizes all his work and provides accuracy and authenticity normally found only in primary sources. His technique brings a sense of immediacy to the past and recreates a feeling of the time.

Meltzer's more than thirty-five books reveal his love of the American story and his respect for the struggles of our forebears. . . .

Milton Meltzer believes that young people are interested in the past and that it is best discovered through letters, memoirs, journals, and other original documents. He feels it is unnecessary to fabricate stories about historical events since the truth itself is inherently intriguing. One need only read the letters and poems in ***Never to Forget: The Jews of the Holocaust*** to recognize the validity of his belief.

Bernice E. Cullinan with Mary K. Karrer and Arlene M. Pillar, "Historical Fiction and Biography: Profile, Milton Meltzer," in their Literature and the Child, *Harcourt Brace Jovanovich, 1981, p. 366.*

JUDITH WEEDMAN

In **"Beyond the Span of a Single Life,"** Milton Meltzer suggests that history is memory, a society's memory of itself and others. Children who read history acquire part of that memory. They come to know that people and places have changed and will continue to change, and in so doing they take a step out of childhood's natural egocentrism—to use a phrase of Penelope Lively's that Meltzer himself quotes, a step "aside from self."

Meltzer's books of history, sociology, and biography expand the range of children's and young people's knowledge in important directions. He is a passionate, partisan author. His theme is right and wrong—good and evil—in the relationships between groups of people. His topics are slavery, the Holocaust, terrorism, the Ku Klux Klan, Manifest Destiny, the Great Depression, human rights, and other contemporary and historical issues and events. . . . In each of his books, Meltzer shows a piece of the world and allows the reader to enter it and experience both the devastation of injustice and the heroism of those who battle it.

Never To Forget: The Jews of the Holocaust begins with the question "Why remember?" The answer is in the understanding that if a holocaust could happen once, it could happen again. The human ability to make moral choices is a central fact of the worlds Meltzer creates, and his books help to extend knowledge so that discriminations between good and evil may be made. ***Never To Forget*** traces anti-Semitism from early Christianity through the Crusades and Reformation to its modern version in Nazi Germany, and emphasizes the danger of public indifference and willingness to allow the government to decide moral values.

"Powerful" is a word that has frequently been used to describe Meltzer's books; its over-use is the result of its accuracy. ***Never To Forget*** becomes immediately personal as Meltzer tells of his own first awareness of German Nazism and the slogan "Jew perish!" That personal understanding carries the reader through the recounting of the almost incomprehensible events of the first half of the Twentieth Century. Meltzer combines chronological facts with selections from diaries, memoirs, court transcripts, and other contemporary and current sources, and makes sense of the material with his own insights into why people react as they do. Details give life to concepts. Quotations from concentration camp victims describing the mind's inability to understand what was happening illuminate generalizations about the difficulty of resisting a ruthless totalitarian power: "The people themselves pretended that the [crematorium] was a brickyard or a soap factory. This mass delusion lasted for four weeks." "One day we would believe our own eyes; the next day we would simply refuse to do so."

Brother, Can You Spare a Dime? uses newspaper accounts, cartoons and photographs, advertisements, and other contemporary sources, molded into the author's narrative and comment to recreate the world of 1929-1933 in the United States. The songs particularly—blues, ballads, songs of protest—are effective in bringing the reader into that world.

Meltzer has a keen sense for the detail that gives insight into the surrounding context, and the cadence of his sentences creates emotion. His opening paragraphs place the reader in the book, and create the emotional framework within which the text will continue.

> Half the people in America today are too young to remember the Great Depression of the 1930's. Their parents remember, and certainly their grandparents. Whether they were rich or poor, workers or laborers, they remember.

> Probably they never talk about it. People like to talk about the "good old days." They don't like to recall the bad days. Not when the days became weeks and months and years, and years and years. Years that made wounds that never healed.

In ***The Terrorists*** and ***The Truth About the Ku Klux Klan,*** Meltzer vividly describes the actions of fanatic groups who put their social goals above the law and even human life. He describes the kinds of people who are drawn into these groups and explores both what they hope to achieve and why they choose violent means to their ends. He argues passionately against the temptation to dismiss such groups as an unimportant lunatic fringe, citing newspaper editor Robert Cox's assessment that the tragic abuse of human rights in Argentina in the 1970s stemmed "largely from the failure of ordinary people to respond with revulsion when confronted with inhumanity." ***The Terrorists*** considers whether terrorist tactics can ever be justified; it presents the views of those who believe that certain limited forms of violence can in unusual circumstances be just, and the belief of some terrorists that the killing of innocent people is simply the consequence of commitment to righting serious wrongs. Meltzer questions whether even a worthy end can ever sanctify monstrous means and takes the stand that "Sacrificing the present to some vague and unpredictable future is a delusion. . . . The goal of life is life itself."

Meltzer's books frequently confront readers with the question of their own moral stands in the face of awareness of wrong. ***The Truth About the Ku Klux Klan*** contains a chapter on "What To Do." It confronts the issue of Klan members' First Amendment rights, and presents the positions both of those who feel that the danger presented by the Klan exceeds the danger of limiting their constitutional rights, and of those who feel that the greatest danger of all is the use of totalitarian measures in defense of democratic ideals. Meltzer lists actions outlined by the American Baptist Convention in 1980 which individuals and groups can take to express their concern about the Klan and its activities.

"Who Is Doing What?" in ***The Human Rights Book*** describes the work of the United Nations, the Helsinki Watch Group, Amnesty Internationl, the International League for Human Rights, and other governmental and nongovernmental groups. The chapter "What Can I Do?" takes the next step; it provides information on joining Amnesty International or other groups, asking libraries to buy and display human rights materials, writing to Senators and Representatives, and staying informed on issues and events.

Meltzer's biographies provide a particularly involving entrance into social history. Here the world he creates is that of an individual who was deeply involved in the affairs of his or her day. Lydia Maria Child, Thaddeus Stevens, Margaret Sanger, and Dorothea Lange are among his subjects. He selects telling incidents to illustrate how his subjects developed their ideals and how they acted upon them.

Thaddeus Stevens and the Fight For Negro Rights exemplifies Meltzer's ability to explain multifaceted issues simply. He combines the personal factors which shaped Stevens (his club foot, his alcoholic father, his helping his mother care for the sick) with the social conditions of the day. Meltzer shows clearly that the anti-slavery movement was neither totally idealistic nor monolithic; many who believed slavery was wrong also believed in white supremacy, and even Abraham Lincoln believed that colonization of Negroes in Liberia and Haiti was the best means of coping with this country's deeply entrenched racial prejudice, and linked the Emancipation Proclamation to plans for colonization.

Throughout the book, Meltzer conveys Stevens' passion and courage, showing him in his political role, then dramatically reminding us of Stevens as an individual, describing speeches given in Congress close to the end of his life when he was so weak that Congressmen had to crowd around his seat in order to hear him. Meltzer keeps the reader simultaneously in the current of national developments and in touch with the decisions of individuals.

Many of Meltzer's books are selections from source documents. ***In Their Own Words*** chronicles the lives of Black people from the arrival of the first slaves in the New World. ***Bound for the Rio Grande*** describes the years of the War with Mexico when the United States boundaries were considered to be "on the east . . . the rising sun, on the north .. the aurora borealis, on the west . . . the precession of the equinoxes, and on the south . . . the Day of Judgment." ***The Eye of Conscience*** is a gallery of the work of ten documentary photographers who used their art to convey and sometimes to change reality, accompanied by discussions of their work and lives.

In all his work, Meltzer draws for us a picture of individuals and groups acting out their values, influencing events, and in turn being affected by the events taking place around them. The person who reads his books sees a world in which ethical decisions are of the utmost importance. The experience of history and the present through Milton Meltzer's eyes allows readers to take that step aside from self and in so doing to expand their worlds. (pp. 41-2)

Judith Weedman, "'A Step Aside from Self': The Work of Milton Meltzer," in Children's Literature Association Quarterly, *Vol. 10, No. 1, Spring, 1985, pp. 41-2.*

ZENA SUTHERLAND AND MAY HILL ARBUTHNOT

Perhaps because ***Langston Hughes: A Biography*** (1968) is about a colleague and friend, it has an immediacy and warmth that Meltzer's other biographies do not have. Perhaps it is that the poet himself sheds light and grace. "Within a few years of his first book," Meltzer says, "he was the poet laureate of his people." Hughes' life and work were a testament to his belief that it was a proud thing to be black, his poetry more bittersweet than bitter. . . .

[His] travels, his involvement in causes, and his amazingly varied and prolific outpouring of magnificent prose and poetry are almost overshadowed by his passion for truth and justice. That is what Milton Meltzer has succeeded in conveying to the readers of ***Langston Hughes.***

The reader will want to explore Hughes' [works]. . . . (p. 467)

In an article on the distortions in children's history books, Milton Meltzer says:

> Biography is another way to re-create the past. The life of a Tom Paine, a Benjamin Banneker, a Sojourner Truth . . . lets the reader see history from inside, from the mind and heart of an individual struggling to reshape his own time. In history books, Wendell Phillips and William Lloyd Garrison are only a paragraph or a line, too often dismissed as irresponsible fanatics.

> Or there is a glancing reference to that other "fanatic," Thaddeus Stevens, painted darkly in the sky of Washington like some vulture hovering over the capital to pick the bones of Southern heroes ennobled in defeat.

Meltzer's ***Thaddeus Stevens*** (1967) destroys this picture and presents a mature and thoughtful biography of the Pennsylvania lawyer whose tenure in the national Congress was marked by bitter opposition from the South, particularly because of his battle against the fugitive slave laws. Thaddeus Stevens was a champion of public education and racial equality, his efforts on behalf of black people's civil rights continuing after the Civil War and through the years of Reconstruction. Meltzer's description of those years and of Stevens' leadership in the move to impeach President Andrew Johnson is direct and vigorous, one of the most valuable aspects of fine biography that does, indeed, see history from the viewpoint of "an individual struggling to reshape his own time."

Tongue of Flame: The Life of Lydia Maria Child (1965) and ***A Light in the Dark: The Life of Samuel Gridley Howe*** (1964) are, like the Stevens biography, imbued with enthusiasm for the causes to which the subjects were dedicated, yet they are not eulogistic in tone. Lydia Child founded the first children's magazine in this country, ran a newspaper, and was a pioneer in the fight against slavery. Howe was a pioneer in work for the blind and for prison reform, in programs to aid the mentally retarded, and provided help to fugitive slaves. Meltzer has let their amazing records speak for them, serving their reputations simply by recording their lives. (pp. 467-68)

The first of the three-volume survey of black history in America, ***In Their Own Words,*** contains material not previously known to many readers, drawn from letters, diaries, journals, autobiographies, speeches, resolutions, newspapers, and pamphlets of black people in slavery. It traces life on the plantation and conditions in the North in letters from escaped slaves in the free states, and tells of the day of Emancipation. In these excerpts, one can see Milton Meltzer's selectivity in showing the wide range of activity and writings of slaves and freed slaves. The three books are an excellent source of information on what living conditions have been for black people through American history. Each excerpt is short, some only two pages; occasionally a document is quoted in full. Each has an introduction by Meltzer and the source is identified at the close. The volumes cover three periods: 1619 to 1865, 1865 to 1916, and 1916 to 1966. Reissued as a single volume with some new material, the 1984 edition is entitled ***The Black Americans: A History in Their Own Words.***

Meltzer's books show his interest in social reform and its effects on the American people. ***Time of Trial, Time of Hope*** (1966) written with August Meier, describes the many problems and few victories of black people in the United States between the First and Second World Wars. The authors write with authority and from a broad viewpoint that includes political, economic, educational, and cultural problems as well as the role of labor.

Meltzer's book on the labor movement in the United States, ***Bread and Roses*** (1967), gives a vivid history of the struggles of the laboring class up to 1915. Using comments from contemporary sources, Meltzer documents the grim story of child labor, sweat shops, and defeated attempts to organize. As is true in all his books, the sources cited in ***Bound for the Rio Grande; the Mexican Struggle, 1845-1850*** (1974) give evidence of the author's meticulous research.

Meltzer's concern for any group that has suffered from prejudice is evident in his range of subjects: ***All Times, All Peoples: A World History of Slavery*** (1980); ***The Chinese Americans*** (1980); and ***The Hispanic Americans*** (1982). Several of Meltzer's books are concerned with the Jewish people: ***Never to Forget: The Jews of the Holocaust*** . . . discusses the treatment of Jews in Nazi Germany; Jewish life in Eastern Europe is described in ***World of Our Fathers*** (1974); and in ***Remember the Days*** (1974) Meltzer writes a brief history of American Jewry. The last two books were finalists for the now-extinct National Book Award; since that time, Meltzer has added ***The Jewish Americans: A History in Their Own Words 1650-1950. . . .*** (p. 497)

Zena Sutherland and May Hill Arbuthnot, "Biography: Milton Meltzer" and "Informational Books: Milton Meltzer," in their Children and Books, *seventh edition, Scott, Foresman and Company, 1986, pp. 467-68, 497.*

A LIGHT IN THE DARK: THE LIFE OF SAMUEL GRIDLEY HOWE (1964)

An amazingly good biography of the founder of the Perkins Institute for the Blind, pioneer in work with the insane, and vital man of many facets. That he has been confined too often to the shadows of the events in America prior to and after the

Meltzer's parents, Benjamin and Mary Meltzer. Courtesy of Milton Meltzer.

Civil War is herein corrected and he emerges as a most interesting personality.

Clayton E. Kilpatrick, in a review of "A Light in the Dark: The Life of Samuel Gridley Howe," in School Library Journal, *an appendix to* Library Journal, *Vol. 11, No. 1, September, 1964, p. 144.*

There seems to have been no humanitarian cause of the 19th century on which Samuel Gridley Howe did not take the unpopular stance. This is to say that he thought the blind could and should be educated; that the insane did not have to be equated with criminals; that slavery should be abolished; and that Negroes once freed, deserved equal rights. He also crusaded against education by corporal punishment and was one of the few Americans to take part in the Greek War of Independence. Younger readers will be most familiar with Howe through the stories of his work with Laura Bridgman, the deaf/blind girl he successfully taught at Perkins Institute in Massachusetts. His lifelong contempt for money and his undiminishing zeal for every idealistic cause will make him a subject for reader-identification at this level. This biography was carefully researched and written so that a life of adventurous ideas reads with as much verve as any career on the battlefield.

A review of "The Light in the Dark: Samuel Gridley Howe," in Virginia Kirkus' Service, *Vol. XXXII, No. 18, September 15, 1964, p. 961.*

[This is a] fine biography. . . . It is a feast of solid educational fare, spiced with adventure and entertainment. . . .

Howe is perhaps only vaguely remembered as a humanitarian whose wife wrote "The Battle Hymn of the Republic." For spotlighting him, for depicting him honestly and enthusiastically, Mr. Meltzer deserves our gratitude.

Robin McKown, in a review of "A Light in the Dark: The Life of Samuel Gridley Howe," in The New York Times Book Review, *November 22, 1964, p. 48.*

An excellent biography, candid in tone, written in a style that is informal yet dignified, and particularly lively because Samuel Howe was involved in so many great causes, controversial issues, and new programs. . . . A divided bibliography and an index are appended.

Zena Sutherland, in a review of "A Light in the Dark: The Life of Samuel Gridley Howe," in Bulletin of the Center for Children's Books, *Vol. XVIII, No. 11, July-August, 1965, p. 166.*

IN THEIR OWN WORDS: A HISTORY OF THE AMERICAN NEGRO, VOL. I: 1619-1865; VOL. II: 1865-1916; VOL. III: 1916-1966 **(1964-1967)**

AUTHOR'S COMMENTARY

The use of original sources—diaries, letters, news reports, testimony at public hearings, official papers, songs, speeches—as well as contemporary illustrations, is a giant step up and out of the textbook swamp. As a writer, I enjoy this kind of history more than almost anything else I have tried. Working with the living expression of an era, whether it be Colonial times, Reconstruction, the labor struggles of the 19th Century, or the terrible days of the Great Depression, you get close to reliving those experiences yourself. And the challenge of discovering a pattern in them and the meaning they held for millions who lived those lives, is endlessly exciting. Let the mill hand, the black abolitionist, the man on the Thirties breadline, speak in his own words to *our* children, to better prepare our children to help make this a freer and more peaceful world.

It is this kind of historical material, immediate and concrete, which provides an insight into humanity itself. You cannot calculate the meaning of an age by the use of formulas. General theses are necessary to understanding, but, as Herbert Butterfield warned, "they can only be harmful unless we keep in mind that jungle of life for which they provide the merest abstraction and diagram."

This kind of documentary history tells the young reader about the human cost of the past, by contrast with the source books providing the official record of government—state documents, judicial decisions, executive decrees—which may be indispensable references, but constitute history written largely by the people who came out on top. When I began working on ***In Their Own Words*** . . . four years ago, my goal was to let the young reader hear black voices speaking. Others had collected documents on slavery, but had omitted any testimony *from* the slave. Or they had told their version of Reconstruction without calling on the new freedmen to speak for themselves. Yet in letters, diaries, journals, autobiographies, speeches, resolutions, newspapers, and pamphlets, the living men, women, and children of the past could reveal to us their thoughts, their joys, their sufferings, their deeds. With the three volumes of ***In Their Own Words*** I hoped to open up the living stuff of history, to help young people see why things are as they are today. (p. 109)

For hundreds of years "American" history has really meant "white" history. It has grossly distorted a true account of what we are and how and why we came to be that way. Vincent Harding, a young black historian, has said: "Just as America can know no survival worth considering unless it finds a way of facing its black counter-image, so too our history is a tale told by fools if it does not incorporate the Afro-American experience with unflinching integrity. And if such open encounter between black and white American history should produce the same sense of insecure teetering on the edge of the unknown as we now experience in the human encounter, so much the better."

It would be foolish, nevertheless, to think that a book will work a miracle by itself; not even a library full of the very best books can do that. The racism and poverty that have damaged whites and blacks cannot be wiped out simply by pictures of Crispus Attucks dying at the Boston Massacre or Thurgood Marshall sitting on the Supreme Court bench. Good books help correct errors of fact, eliminate stereotypes, and can describe accurately the Negro's role in America's past. But what school can build self-esteem and forge interracial harmony while little or nothing is done outside its walls to eradicate the conditions that degrade American life.

What can writers do?

We can try to do more work, and more honest work, and to do it better. We can try to free ourselves from the old myths about our history. We can try to imagine how we might remold our society so that there would be no need for Vietnams and no cause for ghetto revolts. More than that, however, we must join hands with all who are struggling to convert the rhetoric of freedom and equality and justice into reality. (p. 111)

Milton Meltzer, "The Fractured Image: Distortions in Children's History Books," in School Library

Journal, an appendix to Library Journal, Vol. 15, No. 2, October, 1968, pp. 107-11.

To read ***In Their Own Words: A History of the American Negro, 1619-1865*** . . . is to understand how terrible and confounding is [Ed] Clayton's inclusion of the murderous Nat Turner as one of his hero's heroes [in *Martin Luther King: The Peaceful Warrior*].

In ***In Their Own Words*** Milton Meltzer has assembled biographical sketches and passages from the autobiographies of Negroes into a coherent and balanced account of slavery, from the beginnings of the American traffic in humans to the Emancipation. Perhaps there is some risk in making the guilt of white Americans so clear to youthful readers. We dislike those whom we have injured, and guilt makes us cruel. There will be some boys and girls who, after reading this volume, will encounter their Negro fellows with more shrinking and more intricacy than before. And yet, boys and girls must learn to live in the real world, and one of the realities they must learn is that, just as the Negro race won freedom from bondage, so the human race can win freedom from its inexpiable shame. (p. 55)

Donald Barr, "A Great Issue Confronts the Writer—And Haunts Us All," in The New York Times Book Review, *November 1, 1964, pp. 3, 54-5.*

With a few exceptions, books written for children and adolescents about race relations and the civil rights movement have been novels and biographies (often, secular hagiographies). One exception was the first volume in Mr. Meltzer's ***In Their Own Words*** series . . . ; it was a powerful evocation, made up of excerpts from the slaves' and freedmen's own accounts. The second volume, constructed in the same way, takes the story up to the stirrings of a serious movement for full dignity just before America entered World War I. It thus takes in the naivetés of the Radical Reconstruction and the terrors of the Southern Reaction. It has the quality which is indispensable in telling youngsters about such anger-misted and shocking episodes—the ring of authenticity. There is no better book for awakening and informing the conscience of a boy or girl on the issue of Negro rights.

Donald Barr, in a review of "In Their Own Words: A History of the American Negro, 1865-1916," in The New York Times Book Review, *January 23, 1966, p. 26.*

This final volume in a provocative documentation of three hundred years of Negro voices promises to reach out to teenage readers because it sparks and flames with the NOW, with the fire of revolution and renaissance.

A review of "In Their Own Words: A History of the American Negro, 1916-1966," in The Horn Book Magazine, *Vol. XLIII, No. 4, August, 1967, p. 489.*

For older readers, and perhaps the most celebrated non-fiction work published in America, is a three-volume set edited by Milton Meltzer titled ***In Their Own Words***. . . . ***In Their Own Words*** is highly recommended for older children and provides a rich and exciting approach to the history of the race. (p. 15)

Lee Bennett Hopkins, "Negro Life in Current American Children's Literature," in Bookbird, *Vol. VI, No. 1 (March 15, 1968), pp. 12-16.*

Although they are listed for the so-called juvenile market, there is nothing that should deter any interested adult from reading or consulting any of the three volumes. The only feature that distinguishes them from the average "adult" book is the size of the type face and the generous leading. Volume I offers David Walker's *Appeal* and Nat Turner's *Confessions* (the genuine article); and Volume II presents such atrocities as the cold-blooded murder of Charles Caldwell, while Volume III concludes with an interview with Fannie Lou Hamer, indicating no inhibitions on the author's part about "telling it like it is." The maturity of the content of the documents is matched by the candor and lack of condescension in the individual introductory paragraphs written for each excerpt. Insight and information are offered that cannot fail to be of interest to readers seeking to make a beginning of the inquiry so crucial to our epoch: "Who are we Americans and how did we get that way?"—the question posed by Lerone Bennett at a Negro History Week breakfast in New York in 1965. Meltzer weaves a narrative that informs as it entertains. The result is as impressive as Martin Duberman's *In White America* (a documentary drama) but more rewarding because so much more ground is covered. Each of the first two volumes deals with substantially the same periods as the two volumes of Herbert Aptheker's monumental *A Documentary History of the Negro People in the United States* (first published in 1951 . . .) to which they seem somewhat indebted. The Aptheker work remains essential for any serious student of American history. Meltzer's third volume, contrary to its title, terminates in 1964, and actually does not contain much about events in the sixties; it could nevertheless make invaluable reading for *both* a white parent and teen-age child in offering the former information about the times in which he grew up that was never covered honestly by the media, and the latter some questions to ask his social studies teacher about what is missing from the textbooks.

A review of "In Their Own Words: A History of the American Negro, Vol. 1, 1619-1865, Vol. II, 1865-1916, Vol. III, 1916-1966," in The Nation, *New York, Vol. 206, No. 23, June 3, 1968, p. 740.*

TONGUE OF FLAME: THE LIFE OF LYDIA MARIA CHILD (1965)

In her dedication to causes Maria Child's career seems a slightly milder version of Harriet Beecher Stowe's. This is not to say that she was any less fervent in her convictions or less active in promoting her causes, but her views were more open and less revolutionary in their implications. She was not a great thinker or writer but she was a courageous one. Her beliefs are portrayed here with their innuendoes and with their inconsistencies. . . . She particularly attacked the Northern business men who supported slavery in the South and the covert racism of the "free" states. In this respect the book has particular contemporary interest, for it shows the roots and ramifications of a problem which has only recently been admitted. . . . The book offers some delightful background details, including descriptions of Boston and New York during the mid-nineteenth century.

A review of "Tongue of Flame: The Life of Lydia Maria Child," in Virginia Kirkus' Service, *Vol. XXXIII, No. 6, April 1, 1965, p. 382.*

The author of ***In Their Own Words*** has provided teenagers with an outstanding biography of a little-known nineteenth-century woman writer, founder and editor of the first children's magazine, *Juvenile Miscellany*, and a fiery and tireless crusader for the abolition of slavery. In describing her activities as friend, co-worker, and advisor to many of the outstanding social reform figures of the time, Mr. Meltzer gives his readers a history of the period and the turbulent movements in which Maria Child took part. Read in the context of today's civil rights movement, this is a timely and exciting biography.

Sophia B. Mehrer, in a review of "Tongue of Flame: The Life of Lydia Maria Child," in School Library Journal, *an appendix to* Library Journal, *Vol. 11, No. 9, May, 1965, p. 116.*

From published works and private correspondence, Milton Meltzer, eschewing artificial devices, has re-created an indomitable woman of restless and compassionate intellect. Conveying in full measure the political and intellectual furor of the Civil War period, this is enlivened, highly satisfying scholarship.

Houston L. Maples, "Measures of Independence," in Book Week—New York Herald Tribune, *July 4, 1965, p. 9.*

Maria Child served so many causes and served them so zealously, a biographer less skillful than Milton Meltzer might easily depict her as one of those shrill women reformers who strode so militantly across the American scene in the middle of the 19th century. Mr. Meltzer falls into no such trap. Mrs. Child emerges as a gifted many-sided person who could commit herself totally and passionately to a movement without losing her independent view of it. And it is this view that, thanks to Mr. Meltzer, is so illuminating to the modern reader. Indeed, there could hardly be a better way to experience the cumulative effect of the slavery conflict, incident by incident.

"I sweep dead leaves out of paths and dust mirrors," Mrs. Child once said. Milton Meltzer has also dusted a mirror and he has done it well.

Jean Fritz, in a review of "Tongue of Flame: The Life of Lydia Maria Child," in The New York Times Book Review, *July 18, 1965, p. 22.*

An excellent biography, written in a mature style with an attitude that is more admiring than adulatory. . . . Well-researched, well-organized, and only lightly fictionalized. A list of source materials, a list of Mrs. Child's works, and an index are appended.

Zena Sutherland, in a review of "Tongue of Flame: The Life of Lydia Maria Child," in Bulletin of the Center for Children's Books, *Vol. XVIII, No. 11, July-August, 1965, p. 166.*

***TIME OF TRIAL, TIME OF HOPE: THE NEGRO IN AMERICA, 1919-1941* (with August Meier, 1966)**

An excellent new volume in this series [*Zenith Books*] about minority groups for young people which aims at promoting an understanding of the heritage of the particular minority for both members of that group and others. This particular volume begins with the return of Negro soldiers from World War I and ends with the threatened march on Washington in 1941 that culminated in the first Fair Employment Practices Commission fought for by A. Philip Randolph. It's the rare book of history that points out the problems of American Negroes in those years: problems of economic survival, court injustice, lynchings. Here are the bare facts, presented clearly and objectively without mincing of words.

A review of "Time of Trial, Time of Hope: The Negro in America, 1919-1941," in Publishers Weekly, *Vol. 190, No. 8, August 22, 1966, p. 106.*

A quite good description of the many problems and the few victories of the Negro people in the United States in the years between the first and second world wars. The authors write with authority and sympathy in a straightforward style. . . . The book considers political, economic, cultural, agricultural, educational, and other problems; the sections on the depression and on the organization of the CIO are particularly good. . . . (pp. 112-13)

Zena Sutherland, in a review of "Time of Trial, Time of Hope: The Negro in America, 1919-1941," in Bulletin of the Center for Children's Books, *Vol. 20, No. 7, March, 1967, pp. 112-13.*

***THADDEUS STEVENS AND THE FIGHT FOR NEGRO RIGHTS* (1967)**

The crusty mid-nineteenth century Congressman, a leader in Congressional reconstruction, receives solid treatment in this biography. . . . He emerges as a man of principles, neither a saint nor a fanatic, capable participant in the dirty and violent politics of the time. He himself said of the Thirteenth Amendment "the greatest measure of the nineteenth century was passed by corruption, aided and abetted by the purest man in America (Lincoln)." The analysis of people and events is illuminating, but occasionally dull and drawn-out. A useful supplement to Civil War study. Excellent bibliography of contemporary and current sources.

A review of "Thaddeus Stevens," in Kirkus Service, *Vol. XXXIV, No. 24, December 15, 1966, p. 1291.*

A timely, authoritative account of the career of a fanatical anti-slavery Congressman who served from 1833 until his death in 1867, and fought bitterly for Negro rights. Stevens' intolerance and acid wit are presented sympathetically yet objectively. The documentary style is enlivened by quotations from leading political figures of the day and supported by an extensive bibliography and adequate index. A welcome book on a much neglected early "civil rights" crusader.

Marilyn Goldstein, in a review of "Thaddeus Stevens and the Fight for Negro Rights," in School Library Journal, *an appendix to* Library Journal, *Vol. 13, No. 7, March, 1967, p. 138.*

School books often shun Thaddeus Stevens, but school children should not. It will be well worth their time and effort to read this thoughtful and provocative biography of a man whose influence on the Constitution and the political, economic, and historical life of the United States cannot be gainsaid. (p. 217)

Mary Silvia Cosgrave, in a review of "Thaddeus Stevens," in The Horn Book Magazine, *Vol. XLIII, No. 2, April, 1967, pp. 216-17.*

A mature and thoughtful biography of the Pennsylvania lawyer whose years in the United States Congress were marked by bitter opposition from the southern states. . . . The writing style is straightforward and the author's viewpoint objective: one of the most useful qualities of the book is that it gives information about the Reconstruction period.

Zena Sutherland, in a review of "Thaddeus Stevens and the Fight for Negro Rights," in Bulletin of the Center for Children's Books, *Vol. 20, No. 11, July-August, 1967, p. 173.*

Those persons among the clientele of the Negro History Bulletin, who are interested in the background of great historical characters as well as their deeds, are strongly advised to read and re-read Milton Meltzer's ***Thaddeus Stevens and the Fight for Negro Rights. . . .***

Milton Meltzer has given us a readable little account of Thaddeus Stevens' career. He has also weaved in much of the history of the period of Stevens' political activity. Although the author quotes extensively from the sources and from secondary works, the reader is not "plagued" by footnotes or references to notes at the back of the book. ***Thaddeus Stevens and the Fight for Negro Rights*** will probably fail to meet the test of rigid historical scholarship, but the average reader will be able to gain an appreciation of the life and works of one of the greatest precursors of "The Negro Revolution."

Joseph H. Taylor, in a review of "Thaddeus Stevens and the Fight for Negro Rights," in The Negro History Bulletin, *Vol. 30, No. 6, October, 1967, p. 23.*

***BREAD—AND ROSES: THE STRUGGLE OF AMERICAN LABOR, 1865-1915* (1967)**

Incisive and involving, this study of American labor documents living and working conditions during the period when millions left farms for the cities, found only factories, sweatshops and tenements, and suffered wage decreases with each succeeding depression. . . . With some attention to national economic problems and consideration of what early unions were and were not able to accomplish, it is a significant study with continuing implications. (The dictionary of labor terms is useful, the bibliography even indicates books available in paperback, and the reproductions include contemporary campaign posters, newspaper clippings and cartoons, and photographs.)

A review of "Bread—and Roses: The Story of American Labor 1865-1915," in Kirkus Service, *Vol. XXXV, No. 22, November 15, 1967, p. 1375.*

The concern of this compelling book is with the march of the nation's industrial workers out of conditions as destructive of health and self-respect as any that had prevailed on Southern plantations under slavery.

It is a one-dimensional story of battle by an infant labor movement against the forces of corporate greed in a period when all the institutions of government and polite society were on the side of the employer. The very fact that the book is episodic and often overdrawn adds to its usefulness in supplying a new generation of readers with some illumination on the atavistic hatreds and insecurities behind many of the seemingly irrational things unions do now that they enjoy large membership, huge treasuries and economic power sufficient to paralyze entire communities. . . .

Mr. Meltzer's pages, prickly with eyewitness accounts of unionism's birthpains in the sweatshops, the factories, the railroads and the mines, are a goad to revitalized activity in defense of industrial democracy and higher economic standards for those who remain on the outskirts of American affluence. . . .

Mr. Meltzer includes generous excerpts from John Reed's classic description of the 1914 massacre of strikers and their wives and children at the Rockefeller-owned coal mines at Ludlow, Colo. No less heart-rending is Ray Stannard Baker's report on the great 1912 uprising of the textile workers in Lawrence, Mass., under the slogan that gave the book its title, "We want bread and roses too."

All the bloody way stations on the road to labor's present strength are points of call for Mr. Meltzer. There are Homestead and Pullman and Haymarket Square, where a bomb explosion in 1886 killed seven Chicago policemen and labor's immediate hopes for an eight-hour day. Four anarchist leaders were hanged for the bombing, though there was no credible evidence of their guilt. . . .

Many will feel, with considerable validity, that Mr. Meltzer's book is oversimplified history—that none of the epic labor struggles he recounts could possibly have involved such a monopoly of guilt as emerges from page after page of workers' laments about the villainy of their employers. Still others may argue that, in any event, such an unrelieved picture of industrial oppression has scant relevance to this day when labor is often the aggressor and shows autocratic unconcern about the hardship its abuses of power inflict on the public.

But those who put forth such demurrers will find it hard to explain why other pillars of the community, through all the period of which Mr. Meltzer writes, were invariably certain that labor was ruining the country by its arbitrariness and its contempt for lawful process. No present executive of a giant corporation looks back with pride on what happened at Homestead or Ludlow; the fashion now is shamefaced dismissal of such episodes as skeletons to be buried with the vanished "robber baron" phase of capitalist expansionism. . . .

Mr. Meltzer's book will not tell young people all they need to know about labor. But it will give them a better understanding of the reasons for labor's undiminished belief that its unity is its only dependable source of strength, the rock on which rest both its material success and its capacity for survival.

A. H. Raskin, in a review of "Bread—and Roses: The Struggle of American Labor, 1865-1915," in The New York Times Book Review, *January 28, 1968, p. 26.*

Mr. Meltzer has managed to pack a lot of facts, including names, dates, and statistics, into an interesting presentation which clearly asserts the plight of laborers during the latter half of the 19th century. . . . There is special emphasis on the mistreatment of children and women and the severe hardships of immigrants. . . . [Equally] clear and emphatic is the point that the refusal of the unions to accept Negroes and immigrants vastly delayed trade union effectiveness. Drawings and photographs together with eyewitness accounts and the glossary add to the book's usefulness. This history will be most valuable to school libraries and collections backstopping school assignments.

Julia Russell, in a review of "Bread—and Roses: The Struggle of American Labor, 1865-1915," in School Library Journal, *an appendix to* Library Journal, *Vol. 14, No. 6, February, 1968, p. 95.*

[This book] provides a somewhat kaleidoscopic view of the plight of the worker and the more dramatic episodes that have characterized his struggle for a better life. . . . The most exciting chapters are devoted to such conflicts as the Railroad

Strike of 1877, the Haymarket Affair, the Homestead Strike, the Pullman Strike, the Textile Strike at Lawrence and the Ludlow Massacre. Drawing on carefully selected eyewitness accounts and skillfully weaving them into the narrative, the author makes everything come alive with telling effect.

Meltzer is an impassioned writer and he gives the impression of being very angry over the callousness and greed of management and the glaring injustices that confronted the worker. The author, who approaches the subject almost exclusively from the viewpoint of the embattled worker, has chosen his material judiciously and has marshalled it effectively. For the most part he lets the facts speak for themselves and they do carry a powerful message.

The absence of specific source citations, the very limited bibliography and the brevity of treatment (almost too sketchy in places) are blemishes in an otherwise excellent book. The dictionary of labor terms is helpful as are the many illustrations, and the author does achieve his purpose in producing a highly readable and fast moving account of the American worker as he lived and fought in an era when the odds were seldom in his favor.

Almont Lindsey, in a review of "Bread—and Roses: The Struggle of American Labor, 1865-1915," in The Social Studies, *Vol. 59, No. 6, November, 1968, p. 289.*

***BLACK MAGIC: A PICTORIAL HISTORY OF THE NEGRO IN AMERICAN ENTERTAINMENT* (with Langston Hughes, 1967)**

Black Magic is a big book, richly illustrated (although many of the photos, mere publicity stills, seem uninspired), and covering all the corners of what can be classified as theater and entertainment from the days of the arrival of the first slave ships through the Sixties, when black entertainers returned to Africa as cultural emissaries from America. ***Black Magic,*** then, also is an important adjunct of history. Many of the players on the Hughes-Meltzer stage are legendary—Blind Tom, the incredible prodigy from Georgia who made a fortune for his slave master; Thomas Dartmouth Rice, the original "Jim Crow" who traveled to London early in the nineteenth century; the famed Luca family which toured the North in the pre-Civil War years; Elizabeth Taylor Greenfield, the Mississippi songbird whose international career preceded Leontyne Price's by more than a century; and James A. Bland, the revered composer-performer ("Carry Me Back To Old Virginny"). The nineteenth century counterparts of Robert Hooks, Earle Hyman and James Earl Jones were Ira Aldridge and James Hewlett; "Black Patti" (Sisseretta Jones) and E. Azalia Hackley matched the flourishing careers of singers like Grace Bumbry and Gloria Davy, though, of course, without the respect for their artistry which the contemporary singers enjoy. With the onset of the popularity of the incomparable Bert Williams, black entertainers broke through into entertainment dominance in this country which—despite the usual restrictions, bigotry and double standards—they are unlikely to surrender in the foreseeable future. For those collectors of documents of Negro history in general, and of entertainment history in particular, ***Black Magic*** is a *must*. There has not been anything even remotely like it since Edith J. R. Isaacs' *The Negro in the American Theater,* first published in 1947. (pp. 96-7)

H. W. F., in a review of "Black Magic: A Pictorial History of the Negro in American Entertainment," in Negro Digest, *Vol. 17, No. 4, February, 1968, pp. 96-7.*

This is another rare instance of a published work fulfilling its promise. Not only is the book a tribute to the Negro performing artist, it is an eloquent statement about the human spirit's victory over suppression. . . . In it [Langston Hughes and Milton Meltzer] have reproduced rare photographs, playbills, program announcements, and other theatrical memorabilia from private and public collections across the country. That Langston Hughes was coauthor should override any possible criticism of pictorial examples of bigotry in the book . . . This splendid volume, together with Loften Mitchell's *Black Drama* . . ., will assure representative coverage in the field.

Edward Mapp, in a review of "Black Magic: A Pictorial History of the Negro in American Entertainment," in Library Journal, *Vol. 93, No. 4, February 15, 1968, p. 770.*

[***Black Magic***] is a truly impressive account of Negro entertainers in this country. . . . Together [the text and illustrations] cover virtually every Negro performer of consequence from Sam Lucas, a 19th-century minstrel, to Duke Ellington, the modern jazz master. The book, though, is not just a compendium or a volume of praise, but a sensitive and poetic evocation of the creativity and performances of Negroes in all phases of entertainment. It is a fitting testament to Mr. Hughes' devotion to Negro life and letters.

Alden Whitman, "End Papers," in The New York Times, *June 1, 1968, p. 25.*

As the title indicates, the illustrations are the main feature of this handsome book. The text is adequate but makes no pretense of any scholarly apparatus. The "Credits for Photographs," however, do constitute a kind of location list for the many photographs and facsimiles that give both pictorial and historical value to the volume. There is an index but no bibliography.

The scope of the book is extremely comprehensive. . . . To borrow the title of one of its chapters, the volume covers "Just About Everything." Thus it will not please the proponents of an "Afro-American culture," since the American Negro's success in the world of entertainment has been largely purchased at the price of doing "just like the white folks"—and if possible doing it even better (which has happened more often in the performing arts than in formal artistic creation). There is a lot about James A. Bland but not a word about the urban blues singer Bobby Bland; there are five "Kings" in the index—but not B. B. King, the "King of the [Urban] Blues."

The aim of the book is obviously to show that the American Negro has achieved success in terms of the white man's values. Taken on these terms, it is an impressive and comprehensive chronicle, a pictorial treasury that should be in every library.

Gilbert Chase, in a review of "Black Magic: A Pictorial History of the Negro in American Entertainment," in Notes: The Quarterly Journal of The Music Library Association, *Vol. 25, No. 2, December, 1968, p. 244.*

***LANGSTON HUGHES: A BIOGRAPHY* (1968)**

Langston Hughes was more than just a writer, more than just a Negro pioneer; he was a voice of the common man, and his biographer has done him ample justice in a stirring book. As is every black man's, Hughes's life was permeated with barriers, but he rose above them. As are few men's, Hughes's life was filled with movement and drama—a year in Paris, a trip through Russia with Arthur Koestler, six months as a war correspondent during the Spanish Civil War, and a lifelong love affair with the theater. Poems, plays, short stories, novels, histories, anthologies, translations and books for children are listed in a bibliography; what more can one say of a biographer than that he makes the reader want to read every one?

A review of "Langston Hughes: A Biography," in Saturday Review, *Vol. LI, No. 45, November 9, 1968, p. 71.*

A biography acceptable only by default, as there is little material in libraries on this most important Black writer. . . . After Hughes' untimely death in 1967, Meltzer was forbidden use of his papers by the executors of Hughes' estate—a fact which may explain the sketchy depiction of Hughes' later years. Accurate as far as it goes, this covers most of Hughes' work and includes bibliographies both of it and of studies on the author. But Hughes deserves better than the informal but plodding style which characterizes this pedestrian portrayal of him.

Bruce L. MacDuffie, in a review of "Langston Hughes: A Biography," in School Library Journal, *an appendix to* Library Journal, *Vol. 15, No. 5, January, 1969, p. 85.*

Enriched with numerous quotations and excerpts from Hughes's poetry, the biography not only records details of Langston Hughes's active, creative life from early childhood to death but also captures the spirit of the man and his work. The author, an able historian who twice collaborated on books of Negro history with Hughes, draws on his personal knowledge of the writer and that of Hughes's friends as well as on authentic source materials to portray the percipience and artistic integrity of the Negro poet.

A review of "Langston Hughes: A Biography," in The Booklist and Subscription Books Bulletin, *Vol. 65, No. 9, January 1, 1969, p. 498.*

The key to Langston Hughes, the most widely known of all black American writers, was the poet's deceptive and *profound* simplicity. Profound because it was both willed and ineffable, because some intuitive sense even at the beginning of his adulthood taught him that humanity was of the essence and that it existed undiminished in all shapes, sizes, colors and conditions. . . .

In ***Langston Hughes,*** the impressive new biography of the poet by Milton Meltzer, emphasis rightly is placed on the apparent simplicity of the man. . . . The enigma of Langston Hughes (for there remains one) is not raised for the speculation of the reader. From the always interesting events of the poet's life as recorded in this very readable book, one can move without nagging questions to the varied pleasures of the poet's works. And, to facilitate that, biographer Meltzer . . . has compiled a substantial bibliography of the poet's principal published works.

What seems so curious about the life of Langston Hughes as related in this biography and also in the author's published works, including the two volumes of autobiography *(The Big Sea* and *I Wonder as I Wander),* is precisely the determined façade of casual simplicity. In his lifetime, Hughes was swept up into the most dangerous political controversy of his generation and emerged from it scarcely scarred; he was innocently plunged into the tangled morass of a wholly Freudian family relationship; and he confronted and joyously overcame a cruelly racist and restrictive society. Yet he nowhere provides, even by implication, a personal philosophy, no record of inner struggle or turmoil, and then resolution, which would clue the reader to the source of his triumphant strength. Perhaps the mystique of "soul," which is currently fashionable as a concept but which was dear to Langston Hughes until his death in 1967, provides the answers the poet never gave.

"Langston Hughes' poetry has long been neglected by the dominant school of American literary criticism," Meltzer says. "Not all of his poetry, of course, deserves equal attention. Even at its best it was distant from the formal traditions the academic critics respect, and they chose to overlook it. Its seeming simplicity deceived them." Yes, and that also is true of the surface facts of his life.

Hoyt W. Fuller, in a review of "Langston Hughes: A Biography," in Book World—The Washington Post, *February 2, 1969, p. 12.*

Though Langston Hughes experienced poverty and suffered the usual indignities inflicted on his race, Charlemae Rollins in *Black Troubadour* (Stokie, Illinois, 1970) sees the poet as having a rather favorable environment. While some facts are included to indicate economic hardship, the suffering is made conducive to artistic success. The idea is that if you work hard, regardless of background, you will succeed. Milton Meltzer's ***Langston Hughes, A Biography,*** also written for teenagers, does not gloss over the poet's difficulties, nor does it see the American way of life with such blurry optimism. The physical and psychological brutality suffered by Hughes as a child is gone into, as are the conditions of the Black ghetto in Cleveland during the earlier part of this century. Later, as Meltzer indicates, during the era of McCarthyism, Hughes was cited as a communist (a charge never proved) for his "radical books." As a result of his having appeared before the "Un-American" Committee, he lost lecturing jobs. Not for epitomizing the American Dream is Hughes acclaimed in Meltzer's book, but rather for giving voice to social injustice, to the importance of the Black "soul," to the causes of the migrant workers and other deprived groups. (pp. 146-47)

Marilyn Jurich, "What's Left Out of Biography for Children," in Children's Literature: Annual of the Modern Language Association Seminar on Children's Literature and The Children's Literature Association, *Vol. 1, 1972, pp. 143-51.*

BROTHER, CAN YOU SPARE A DIME? THE GREAT DEPRESSION, 1929-1933 (1969)

The depression's rueful plaint is affixed to a graphic, sometimes scorching documentary history of "how it started and why, and what it felt like." The narrative begins in the easy-going '20's (not so easy for farmers or the persistently unemployed), picking up its first eyewitness account in ominous October 1929: Gordon Park losing his parttime job and leaving school. The crisis mounts: in one-industry towns the long-idle busy themselves with aimless activity (Waltham, Mass.) or tramp fruitlessly from plant to plant (Detroit); women without jobs are virtually without help; bankrupt schools shut down or shorten their terms, and children work in violation of the law (or take to the road); blacks are replaced by whites, often forcibly; professionals are "worth more dead than alive". . . . Mr. Meltzer points out that initially fewer than 200,000 were covered by unemployment insurance and emphasizes both the lag in providing relief and the demeaning way it was handled; he observes also that the depression "hardly nicked the old money." Reports on shelters and shantytowns, on farm activism and union apathy, lead into a cursory discussion of why protest remained peaceful, of why social consciousness rather than socialism was the outcome. Roosevelt's inauguration and quick action end the book but not, the author notes, the depression itself. As viewed by the victims and by writers as diverse as Anna Arnold Hedgeman and Edmund Wilson (and counterpointed by bland quotes from the mass media), the depression hits home, and hurts.

A review of "Brother, Can You Spare a Dime?" in Kirkus Reviews, *Vol. XXXVII, No. 1, January 1, 1969, p. 13.*

Robert Goldston's *The Great Depression* summarizes the politics of that era from Hoover to Willkie in the terms Roosevelt liberals used to describe them at the time. Milton Meltzer's ***Brother, Can You Spare a Dime?*** . . . aspires to tell "what happened to auto workers and wheat farmers, to sales clerks and secretaries, to teachers and doctors, to miners and share-croppers, to old folks and children, to white and black" between the Crash and the inauguration of Roosevelt. Both draw on the emerging photo-journalism of the day for illustration, but Meltzer relies heavily on eye-witness accounts of the time, while Goldston describes and interprets trends as if he were writing a newspaper feature story.

Both books are physically attractive but the Meltzer book is much better reading, and why shouldn't it be? Not only does it quote liberally from such masters as John Dos Passos, Edmund Wilson, Louis Adamic, Erskine Caldwell, John Steinbeck, but from scores of reporters and witnesses whose conviction made them momentarily eloquent. The selection is expert and wide-ranging. The most suspicious teenager cannot but recognize that (whatever has happened to these people since) they were speaking from the heart. Explanations are brief, clear, and free of journalistic jargon.

Caroline Bird, in a review of "Brother, Can You Spare a Dime? The Great Depression 1929-1933," in The New York Times Book Review, *March 23, 1969, p. 26.*

MARGARET SANGER: PIONEER OF BIRTH CONTROL **(with Lawrence Lader, 1969)**

On the sensible assumption that youngsters interested in Margaret Sanger are curious about birth control, this is as much an explanation of methods and a history of the movement as it is a biography—and therein lies its chief point of superiority over [Virginia Coigney's *Margaret Sanger: Rebel with a Cause*]. Much of the personal material is compressed in a way that dilutes it (to call her father "a local rebel" doesn't do justice to his views or behavior), or suppressed in a way that protects Mrs. Sanger's reputation (see the references to Havelock Ellis and the handling of long-time suitor and second husband Noah Slee). "Reserved" is the most affirmative descriptor for the treatment of Margaret Sanger as a person; not so the discussions of abortion and early birth control methods, of developments on both sides of the Atlantic and why they were different. There are sharp vignettes of movement figures and precise details on trips abroad and legislative fights at home that are absent from Coigney; also, at the close, an attempt to bring the various strands (investigation, implementation) up to date. The bibliography contributes to this effort and, in keeping with the reference potential of the book, there is a thorough index. Mr. Lader is the author of the standard adult biography but Mr. Meltzer's social science expertise carries the day. (Along with some intriguing photos also absent from Coigney.)

A review of "Margaret Sanger: Pioneer of Birth Control," in Kirkus Reviews, *Vol. XXXVII, No. 18, October 1, 1969, p. 1077.*

The life story of Margaret Sanger is especially timely now in view of the increasing attention to sex education in school curriculums and because of the freer role of modern women in 20th-Century life. . . . The superior biography by Lader and Meltzer is more complete [than Virginia Coigney's *Margaret Sanger: Rebel with a Cause*]. It provides straightforward, explicit information about the birth control methods available at various points in history. This makes the whole story of Margaret Sanger's crusades much more understandable, whereas Mrs. Coigney's book leaves a feeling of mystery and confusion. . . . Lader and Meltzer also used quotes from Mrs. Sanger, but the ones they chose are better able to convey why she worked so hard and sacrificed her personal happiness for the movement she created. Their book also vividly portrays Margaret Sanger's relationships with the famous people of her time, and fits the whole Planned Parenthood movement into the context of life in the 20th-Century.

Isadora Kunitz, in a review of "Margaret Sanger: Pioneer of Birth Control," in School Library Journal, *an appendix to* Library Journal, *Vol. 16, No. 4, December, 1969, p. 57.*

FREEDOM COMES TO MISSISSIPPI: THE STORY OF RECONSTRUCTION **(1970)**

The one solid, unassailable accomplishment of this book is to set forth the achievements of the black-supported Republican state government and black officeholders on the state and local levels between 1870 and 1873; as a history of Reconstruction, however, it is emotional and partisan, fuller of blame than of sober, discriminating assessment. Omitted from the impressionistic tableau are the very limitations to the Emancipation Proclamation that the Thirteenth Amendment rectified and the absolute necessity for Congress to give the blacks votes to gain ratification of the Fourteenth Amendment; much that was specifically motivated becomes a matter of amorphous pressures. Neither do even the most sympathetic studies of the period substantiate the claims made for black militance ("Thousands of new revolutionaries like the Gabriels and Denmark Veseys and Nat Turners of slavery times had fused into a powerful black fist to help crush their oppressors") or slave transformation "almost overnight into makers and doers," "into farmers and businessmen, students and teachers, lawyers and bishops, jurors and judges, sheriffs and senators." That socially and economically life changed very little for the majority is thereby obscured. Obscured also, in a quote, is the revolutionary nature of the expansion of government services beyond their prewar level. On the one hand more is made of Reconstruction than the facts justify; on the other hand, less. And the concentration on oppression, injustice and terror, inarguable per se, overshadows what explanations are offered for both the inception and termination of Reconstruction. There is much drama . . . , less enlightenment.

A review of "Freedom Comes to Mississippi: The Story of Reconstruction," in Kirkus Reviews, *Vol. XXXVIII, No. 19, October 1, 1970, p. 1114.*

A detailed study of reconstruction in one state, strong in presentation of background, especially that of changing policies emanating from Washington, but weakened by a deviation from chronological development and by a lack of objectivity in the tone. . . . A bibliography and an index are appended.

Zena Sutherland, in a review of "Freedom Comes to Mississippi: The Story of Reconstruction," in Bulletin of the Center for Children's Books, *Vol. 24, No. 10, June, 1971, p. 159.*

Milton Meltzer, one of our best writers in the field of black history, handles the Reconstruction story in ***Freedom Comes to Mississippi*** . . . with the spit and polish of a man with a message and the craftsmanship to get it told with dramatic impact. Instead of relating the story in the entire South, he concentrates upon what happened "when freedom came to Mississippi." From that, we may draw our conclusions about what happened to the South as a whole. The reader is introduced to a minimum number of people and events—but the point emerges, loud and clear: A century ago, freedom came to the black man, who experienced it for a few years—until the political bargain of 1877 between Republicans and Democrats left the whole business to be done over again a century later as the Second Reconstruction.

John K. Bettersworth, "After the War Was Over," in The New York Times Book Review, *July 25, 1971, p. 8.*

SLAVERY: FROM THE RISE OF WESTERN CIVILIZATION TO THE RENAISSANCE (1971)

A great deal has been written about slavery in the ancient world, but, unfortunately, some of the information is hidden away in scholarly books and journals often inaccessible. The merit of this short but authoritative work is that it makes available to the general reader many of the findings of scholars intent on their own special interests. Meltzer, widely known for numerous works on black history and social reform, writes directly and without sentimentality, making visible the entire pattern of slavery in human history, and in a manner which never fails to point up man's inhumanity to man. What emerges with especially graphic force is the life, the hopes and fears, of the slaves themselves. . . . [The] bibliography lists most important sources for those wishing to pursue the subject in greater depth.

Francis D. Lazenby, in a review of "Slavery: From the Rise of Western Civilization to the Renaissance," in Library Journal, *Vol. 96, No. 10, May 15, 1971, p. 1709.*

In a format suitable for junior-high readers to use for individual research or as a supplementary text in World History or institutional history courses, the book . . . presents a comprehensive survey of slavery from the beginnings of civilization in the Middle East through the Renaissance period. The extensive four-page bibliography . . . suggests additional sources for the teacher. Indexed. A unique contribution.

Mary M. Burns, in a review of "Slavery: From the Rise of Western Civilization to the Renaissance," in The Horn Book Magazine, *Vol. XLVII, No. 4, August, 1971, p. 395.*

[This is a] commendable volume. . . . The economic and political basis of slavery is developed and forms an excellent introduction for those readers concerned with the more recent racial basis of the "peculiar" institution. Profuse photographs of artifacts and works of art add to the attractiveness as well as to the clarity of the exposition. Mr. Meltzer has contributed a basic work in an area where almost no material exists on the junior-senior high school level, making this an essential item.

Janet G. Polacheck, in a review of "Slavery: From the Rise of Western Civilization to the Renaissance," in School Library Journal, *an appendix to* Library Journal, *Vol. 18, No. 1, September, 1971, p. 176.*

SLAVERY, VOLUME II: FROM THE RENAISSANCE TO TODAY (1972)

More complete and more searching than Pinney's *Slavery: Past and Present* (1971) this second volume of Meltzer's study . . . encompasses slavery as it existed, and in some cases still exists, in Africa, Arabia, China and under the Nazis, and also giving a remarkably detailed picture of the everyday existence of slaves in the Americas. As always, Meltzer is a careful historian who looks for the documentable truth behind prevalent generalizations—he gives the lineage of his statistics, citing Curtin's revised estimates of the volume of the Atlantic slave trade and, on such controversial topics as the extent of resistance among American slaves, he presents the opposing views of prominent historians. (Meltzer himself concludes that there is a good deal of evidence of widespread rebellion, both passive and active, but shows that there is room to doubt the scope of some of the more famous conspiracies, such as the Vesey uprising.) The attention given to cultural and economic differentials—the higher frequency of manumission in Cuba and South America, the practice of hiring out and, in some cases, of "breeding" slaves, the difficulty of eradicating the institution in countries where starvation may be the only alternative—and the generous use of quotations from primary sources make the narrative both more interesting and more illuminating than the ambitious scope might indicate. First rate.

A review of "Slavery II: From the Renaissance to Today," in Kirkus Reviews, *Vol. XL, No. 12, June 15, 1972, p. 681.*

After Columbus initiated the American slave trade which subjugated and massacred thousands of native Indians, Bartolomé de las Cases, a Spanish priest and somewhat misguided humanitarian, suggested the importation of Africans so that the natives would be spared. The story of Las Cases exemplifies an interesting thread of the history of slavery explored in this book: That history has not only involved the cruel, exploitative, the greedy, and the insensitive, but has also been sanctioned and supported by many "beautiful people"—Queen Elizabeth, Thomas Jefferson, the Cabots of Boston, and the Browns of Rhode Island all profited from the shedding of African blood. . . . One might question the author's bias in his discussion of forced labor in the Soviet Union and China, but generally he has refrained from biasing his material; using excellent scholarly sources, he balances his account by indicating different opinions on controversal questions. From the numerous depictions of human suffering presented in the book, a rather dim view of man's history—both past and present—emerges, and as the author states: "Wherever the weak—meaning the hungry, inarticulate, and ignorant—can be exploited for profit, prestige, or pleasure, slavery persists." (pp. 478-79)

Anita Silvey, in a review of "Slavery II: From the Renaissance to Today," in The Horn Book Magazine, *Vol. XLVIII, No. 5, October, 1972, pp. 478-79.*

This sequel to Meltzer's commendable ***Slavery: from the Rise of Western Civilization to the Renaissance*** . . . completes his comprehensive study of the institutions of slavery throughout the world and its history. . . . Meltzer's purpose "is to help the general reader to see the whole pattern of slavery in human history and how it has shaped the lives we are leading." He has admirably succeeded in reaching his goal. . . . His conclusion that slavery is essential to the world's economy holds forth little hope for its abolition, though almost every country in the world has laws preventing it. This is well documented. . . . An excellent overview of a distressing pattern in world culture which cannot be ignored.

Alice Miller Bregman, in a review of "Slavery II: From the Renaissance to Today," in School Library Journal, *an appendix to* Library Journal, *Vol. 19, No. 4, December, 1972, p. 68.*

***THE RIGHT TO REMAIN SILENT* (1972)**

A passionate, far ranging defense of the Fifth Amendment protection of the right to remain silent which goes back to the origins of its systematic violation during the inquisition (where the self-incriminating confession served as both the charge and the proof of guilt) and its gradual establishment as a principle of English common law through the struggles of political prisoners such as leveler John Lilbourne. Meltzer extends his examination of the right on through the nonpolitical applications of the Miranda and Esposito decisions, defending it as logical and necessary (though hardly sufficient safeguard) against the desire of the police to obtain a confession. Many will be surprised to learn that the much lauded Thomas More was a proponent of the inquisition, and Meltzer's defense of the rights of accused criminals strikes a note of welcome sanity (he does not deny the need for law and order, but suggests other methods of achieving it). Meltzer presents the historical evidence and often relies on his readers to draw the correct conclusions from excerpted testimony; still he covers a lot of ground and those who are able to keep up with him should be well rewarded.

A review of "The Right to Remain Silent," in Kirkus Reviews, *Vol. XL, No. 16, August 15, 1972, p. 954.*

The reader of this excellent and searching book will have a thorough understanding of the constitutional right that insures due process of law in trying the accused. Discussing actual cases of people persecuted because they claimed their privilege under the Fifth Amendment, the author shows how dangerous it is to take this stand as an admission of guilt. He reaches far back into ancient times as well to show how necessary it is to respect the right of the accused to remain silent.

A review of "The Right to Remain Silent," in Publishers Weekly, *Vol. 203, No. 3, January 15, 1973, p. 65.*

Well-researched, well-written and organized, a very competent and comprehensive survey of man's right to refrain from self-incriminating testimony. Meltzer describes in full the mechanics and principles of the Inquisition and of the slow accrual, in English law, of safeguards to the right to remain silent. . . . A bibliography and an index are appended.

Zena Sutherland, in a review of "The Right to Remain Silent," in Bulletin of the Center for Children's Books, *Vol. 26, No. 7, March, 1973, p. 110.*

***HUNTED LIKE A WOLF: THE STORY OF THE SEMINOLE WAR* (1972)**

The Seminole War is unique because it combined the goal of Indian removal with a campaign to recapture a large number of escaped slaves—many of whom had chosen a more benevolent bondage under masters from the Civilized Tribes. Meltzer describes the ways of the newly formed Seminole tribe (which was principally a southern offshoot of the Creeks) by calling on the observations of contemporary traveller William Bartram. But while the Seminoles were establishing a unique lifestyle and welcoming large numbers of former slaves—both as free neighbors and as bondsmen—Congress was beginning to debate the annexation of Florida because, as Henry Clay said, "It fills a space in our imagination." Some of the war's background, including Tecumseh's call to arms and the tactics practiced by the whites in obtaining treaties, will be familiar to those who've read about the Cherokees' removal from Georgia; and the rhetoric of the war's supporters, who renamed bloodhounds "peace hounds" and opined in congressional debates

Meltzer (left), with his brother Allan. Courtesy of Milton Meltzer.

that "we should not stop to inquire whether your war was *just* or *unjust* . . . We should hold it to be our country's cause . . .", has a tragically contemporary ring. As usual, Meltzer's strength lies in his conscientious crediting of his sources, his ability to select apt quotations from primary materials, and his talent for illuminating personalities without undue fictionalization. This dramatic, self-contained case study brings the researches of John K. Mahon (*History of the Seminole War,* 1967) and the earlier studies of Kenneth Porter on Seminole-black relationships before a popular audience.

A review of "Hunted Like a Wolf: The Story of the Seminole War," in Kirkus Reviews, *Vol. XL, No. 20, October 15, 1972, p. 1209.*

"'I have been hunted like a wolf and now I am being sent away like a dog,'" uttered Halleck, one of the last leaders of the Seminole resistance, after he had been captured. . . . The period of exploitation and conquest that was preface to Halleck's capture forms the bulk of the sober account beginning with the arrival of Columbus. . . . The story of the Seminoles' eventual subjugation is a sorry one, akin to similar stories from all parts of the country. Well-documented, it reveals how they were destroyed by greed, trickery, and the superior strength of a powerful government which completely disregarded their status as human beings. Photographs from several historical collections add to an understanding of the Seminole way-of-life, and a lengthy Bibliography lists the many sources consulted for the book. A substantial addition to the author's excellent examinations of social history in the United States. (pp. 606-07)

Beryl Robinson, in a review of "Hunted Like a Wolf: The Story of the Seminole War," in The Horn Book Magazine, *Vol. XLVIII, No. 6, December, 1972, pp. 606-07.*

Characterized by thoroughness of research and fairness of treatment, this book is an exhaustive study of the Seminole War. . . . This writer is blunt. . . .

This is an excellent treatment of a complex subject.

"Annotated Bibliography: 'Hunted Like a Wolf: The Story of the Seminole War'," in Books on American Indians and Eskimos: A Selection Guide for Children and Young Adults, *edited by Mary Jo Lass-Woodfin, American Library Association, 1978, p. 162.*

UNDERGROUND MAN (1972)

Josh Bowen's story is based on the "fragmentary and forgotten memoirs" of a Northern farm boy, briefly a preacher, who was later imprisoned for helping slaves escape from Kentucky. Meltzer draws also from court records, reminiscences of fugitive slaves and abolitionists, and other documents of the pre-Civil War period to create a narrative that is consistently suspenseful as well as historically accurate. Our first glimpse of Josh as a boy struggling for his father's acceptance gives him dimension as a character which makes his anti-slavery work later all the more compelling. Josh's accidental first encounter with a runaway, his subsequent dangerous and dramatic rescue missions, his years as a specially marked prisoner are thus true in both historical and fictional terms—and though it's the former aspect that provides the chief interest here, the two are smoothly meshed and discreetly balanced.

A review of "Underground Man," in Kirkus Reviews, *Vol. XL, No. 22, November 15, 1972, p. 1313.*

Adolescents and young adult readers of ***Underground Man*** may perceive that they have already experienced young Josh Bowen's America of the 1830's, through participating (if only via TV newscasts) in the social and civic disorders of the 1960's. In writing an absorbing story of a young Yank's adventures as a "nigger stealer" for the Underground Railroad, Milton Meltzer has written a contemporary novel. The cultural, political, moral and ethical issues that troubled young Joshua Bowen are those troubling today's youth. We hear them say so.

The familiar generation gap is dramatized in the opening chapters. It is not the expected brouhaha between a rebellious kid and his mean old man. Nowhere in the novel does Meltzer deal in stereotypes or resort to cliché situations.

There is the ubiquitous identity crisis. After the break with his father, Josh ponders who he is and what the purpose of his life. Was it not to pursue happiness, the basic right of every American? . . .

After serving a term in a Kentucky jail for "nigger stealing" Josh returns to New England and becomes an effective and popular speaker at Abolitionist rallies—but, once again, he finds that what he is doing does not fit what he is. He goes back to his "criminal" activity along the Ohio.

For a second time, Josh lands in a Kentucky jail; the jailer tells him that this time "it will take a whole army of nigger stealers to get you outa here." At first glance, this seems a most dismaying finale. But to turn the page and read the short Afterword is to learn the historic necessity for the "unhappy" ending. The author based his novel on the fragmentary, forgotten memoirs of a young man of another name, who was indeed set free—after 17 long years—by "nigger stealers" wearing the uniform of the Union Army.

Meltzer, historian of the Civil War era, moves through those times, and among those people, with authority and ease. There is satisfaction in ***Underground Man*** for those who read for "story" and an extra measure for the thoughtful who read between the lines. A fine novel.

Barbara Ritchie, in a review of "Underground Man," in The New York Times Book Review, *March 18, 1973, p. 12.*

Slavery and the abolitionist movement provide the background for this stiff historical novel. . . . Meltzer's nonfiction accounts of black history are much richer and tighter in their illumination of time and place. There is an absence of depth and intensity here due to his failure to develop the black characters fully as people instead of as types.

Rosalind K. Goddard, in a review of "Underground Man," in School Library Journal, *an appendix to* Library Journal, *Vol. 19, No. 8, April, 1973, p. 77.*

[The] sources cited in the author's postscript are evidence that Milton Meltzer has done the thorough research that distinguishes his nonfiction titles. . . . Spare in construction, the book has historical interest, dramatic appeal, and an aura of suspense and danger that emanates from the events rather than by the declaration of the author.

Zena Sutherland, in a review of "Underground Man," in Bulletin of the Center for Children's Books, *Vol. 27, No. 1, September, 1973, p. 14.*

BOUND FOR THE RIO GRANDE: THE MEXICAN STRUGGLE, 1845-1850 **(1974)**

Although still within the category of history written by the victor, the text does attempt with some success to present the dynamics of both sides. The narrative incorporates original documents of Anglo-American history with lucid commentary. There is a bibliography in addition to a chronology of important dates. While much background material generally available is given, there are several important observations which might be new, such as the sociological, political, and psychological forces which operated on both the Mexican and the American sides. All in all, a rare view of "America's first successful offensive war."

Carlota Cardenas Dwyer, in a review of "Bound for the Rio Grande: The Mexican Struggle 1845-1850," in Children's Book Review Service, *Vol. 2, No. 10, June, 1974, p. 88.*

History buffs will appreciate this factual, unbiased account of one of our history's least proud moments. Meltzer skillfully uses primary sources—diaries, letters, battle records, speeches, and the songs and literature of the time—to show what led to America's war against Mexico. Chronicles of early travelers vividly tell how the nation was divided over the treatment of the Indians and how later even highly trained West Pointers questioned the wisdom of this war of aggression. . . . Impeccably researched, this documented history is most valuable since it gives the point of view of the Mexicans as well as Americans and does not gloss over the savage treatment of Indians in the name of Manifest Destiny.

Edith F. Anderson, in a review of "Bound for the Rio Grande: The Mexican Struggle 1845-1850," in School Library Journal, *an appendix to* Library Journal, *Vol. 21, No. 2, October, 1974, p. 120.*

The author's previous works of nonfiction have already established him as one of the finest American historians for young readers. This volume demonstrates once again his skill at combining readable and enjoyable prose with an excellent choice and handling of original historical material. . . . Detailing the battles and military strategy of the first war which gave "West Point a chance to show the quality of its graduates," the author emphasizes the political and social upheaval caused by the war—the war's unpopularity, the desertions, the rivalry between Taylor and Polk. And in the conclusion he points to the Mexican War's grimmer offsprings—the Civil War and the political precedent involving presidents and their war powers. The numerous illustrations, the interspersed songs and poetry, the colorfulness of the first-hand historical accounts—all add to a superb analysis of the "most disgraceful war."

Anita Silvey, in a review of "Bound for the Rio Grande: The Mexican Struggle 1845-1850," in The Horn Book Magazine, *Vol. LI, No. 2, April, 1975, p. 160.*

[This work by Meltzer] in overall tones seems aimed at the junior high/high school level. Through clues of one kind or another, most of the sources for the quotations could probably be identified by someone willing to work at it. For the most part these clues are straightforward, such as "Henry Clay stated" or "Lieutenant Henry observed." Of course one still has to pick around a bit through the published statements of Clay or the observations of Henry in order to locate the source. But some of the clues are hopeless, such as "One Kentuckian wrote." I did not make a careful count, but Meltzer seems to have used roughly three to four different sources in each of the seventeen chapters, or perhaps fifty to sixty in all. He has done a craftman's job of weaving narration, quotation, and exposition into a readable whole. (pp. 461-62)

A skimpy four page bibliographic essay makes no pretense at identifying the contemporary sources quoted.

It is difficult to give a meaningful appraisal of the book. I am ambivalent about the unidentified contemporary quotations, but on balance, I like them, especially the skillful way they were selected and fit into the text. The whole book is easy reading, a tribute to the compiler-author. One would assume that he was a competent journeyman at writing. But from the dust jacket, it appears that he is a college history professor—who should have known better than to handle the subject without steeping himself in it more thoroughly. The book is flawed with numerous small errors inexcusable for a historian. One example only: on page thirty-three Meltzer wrote that in 1828 José Maria Sanchez visited "the Texas settlement that would become the city of Austin," and then quoted from Sanchez's description of the settlement of San Felipe de Austin. San Felipe is located on the Brazos River, about 100 miles east of present Austin, which was not founded until ten years after Sanchez's visit, and is on the Colorado River, not the Brazos.

In my judgment the book is a biased rehash of the old abolitionist and Whig antiwar sentiment. The chapters dealing with the background for the war are shallow castigations of American policy of the time. Other historians have berated Polk much more grandly and with better understanding. Naturally, all the contemporary material selected in the book is cut on the same bias. (p. 462)

Seymour V. Connor, in a review of "Bound for the Rio Grande: The Mexican Struggle, 1845-1850," in The Western Historical Quarterly, *Vol. 6, No. 4, October, 1975, pp. 461-62.*

THE EYE OF CONSCIENCE: PHOTOGRAPHERS AND SOCIAL CHANGE, WITH 100 PHOTOGRAPHS BY NOTED PHOTOGRAPHERS, PAST AND PRESENT **(with Bernard Cole, 1974)**

Reading this book is a little like those times in school when you went in for a session with the guidance counselor: the man meant well, but the points he made, even about important things, were so predictable, and the terms he used were so solemn, and he repeated himself so much, that you were never sure, by the end, whether you were more bored or more annoyed with him. Like the guidance counselor's, the language in ***The Eye of Conscience*** isn't the kind that's geared for having fresh perceptions, or even for presenting old perceptions in a lively way. It's a shame everything is so smothered, because the book presents good subjects for its audience: how photography helps affect social change, or mirrors social problems, and how the camera, when used daily and continually, is an instrument that tells us about our instincts and feelings.

The main focus in the book is on 10 photographers and their involvement with social problems (a photography "Profiles in Courage" is the general idea). The main trouble with the biographies is that the authors don't relate the individual photographer's character and motives to his pictures; the pictures just dangle alongside, like evidence. Social commitment is hammered in as the only thing to keep in mind. That commitment is important but, taken by itself, it's not why some people make memorable photographs.

It's surprising that the authors have so little sensitivity to the visual power of photographs; one expects that, since this teaching program is aimed at young people, most of whom have probably never taken pictures before, at least part of the course will be concerned with getting the audience interested in pictures—for their beauty, their eccentricity, their scaryness, for anything that makes them special. But Meltzer and Cole's assumption is that, if a career is noble and committed, the photographs automatically will be moving and important. They should have proved this—which isn't always the case here.

The profiles are on four classics (Timothy O'Sullivan, seen mostly in his Civil War days, Jacob A. Riis, Lewis W. Hine, Dorothea Lange) and six—not terribly well-known—contemporaries (William Mackey Jr., Martin Schneider, Fung Lam, Michael Abramson, Ira Nowinski, Morrie Gambi). Unfortunately, except for Schneider, these six don't represent distinctly different styles or attitudes—all are emotionally low-keyed, visually understated photographers. It's hard to have very strong feelings about their pictures; they don't make photography appear as an art of great visual complexity or emotional range. This is frustrating, because there are many alternate approaches to socially oriented photography (Henri Cartier-Bresson, Helen Levitt, W. Eugene Smith, Bruce Davidson, Donald McCullin, etc.); the chapters could have been very individual, instead of hard to tell apart.

And the book's implied meaning, that socially oriented photography is the kind that will most stimulate the young, is also questionable. Distinctive social photography takes more than sympathy (the failure of most attempts to repeat Lange or Cartier-Bresson says something). Anyway, the best art made by children, whether in photography or painting, rarely shows sympathetic awareness of people and their problems; children's art is private, it's derived more from spontaneous, instinctive reactions, usually to family and friends, and it's often close to fantasy. Meltzer and Cole, because they never clearly differentiate their Social Photography theme from their Be-a-Photographer theme, and because of the way they describe their subjects' lives, make it seem as if they want art to be the product of altruism. That's wishful thinking.

Sanford Schwartz, in a review of "The Eye of Conscience: Photographers and Social Change," in The New York Times Book Review, *August 25, 1974, p. 8.*

Little more than a picture book, the volume has no scholarly value. The essays are superficial and the quality of the illustrations is barely acceptable. Only libraries with large budgets and specialized interest in history of photography should consider purchase.

A review of "The Eye of Conscience: Photographers and Social Change," in Choice, *Vol. 11, No. 10, December, 1974, p. 1466.*

For children, magical associations may easily attach themselves to the camera, to the process of freezing and preserving on film a moment in time. The camera mysteriously catches images inside it; by a leap of the imagination, it may also seize something of the essence of what is photographed. (p. 179)

Photographs themselves play host to a child's curiosity, recording strange moments and new happenings. The visual presentation of a reality beyond the child's immediate experience, its transportation from *there* to the child through the medium of the photograph, must play upon his sense of wonder. Unlike most cartoons, which employ imaginary characters in a completely self-contained fantasy world, photographs invite the child to ask questions about the incomplete reality they present. Cartoons may induce excitement and exclamation but their narrative closure denies questions. The story a photograph tells, by contrast, is only implicit in its image; the story consists of the answers to the questions the child asks as his curiosity moves him to fill in the narrative gaps that a photograph suggests but does not reveal.

Such considerations are especially true of the documentary photograph. It places limitations on the extent to which the formal elements of composition can be emphasized. These elements—of line sharpness, focus, filtering, framing, mood, and the modulation of shadow—cannot be self-consciously displayed in photo documentation. They must be disciplined, limited, and given direction by the documentary intent, made to serve social and political ends. The statement of suffering or victimization must be direct, must be the controlling element in the photograph's composition. It is this directness, the photo's legibility as drama and history, that makes this kind of photography particularly attractive to children. For it focuses on people and hints at a larger story, encouraging questions that will complete the narrative suggested by the image.

The Eye of Conscience, a book of documentary photographs, is not written and edited expressly for children. But on the above grounds, and for other reasons as well, it may have an immense appeal for them. Many of the photographs in the book are of children. (pp. 179-80)

In these photos, children can see not reflections but *refractions* of themselves, for the photographed children are victims, orphans of social inequality. The photos may bring a child to sense his own relative impotence in a world where the balance of power lies with adults, his own helpless innocence before a potentially exploitative environment.

The book also taps a child's psychic life in less bleak ways. In the brief biographies preceding each photographer's work, the editors' prose and vocabulary are deliberately simplified in order to convey the social outrage and serious intent of the photographers: their hope that a visual documentation of suffering—more powerful, accessible, and immediate in impact than a purely verbal record—would yield reform. This stylistic posture unnecessarily romanticizes them, but it seems apt for children because it transforms the photographers' lives into stories of heroes who tried to do right:

> [Jacob Riis'] unrelenting struggle wiped out the horror of Mulberry Bend, brought light to dark hallways, cleaner water to tenement taps, desks to schoolrooms, settlement houses to slums, and improved conditions to factories. The camera was only the tool a humane man needed to express the misery and squalor he found in the slums.

The biographies, then, call upon a child's desire for a moral universe of Manichean simplicity—absolute evil pitted against absolute good. Because the photographers are presented as heroes, they appeal to a child's relatively untested powers of trust, to his will to believe in supermen, to his comparatively uncurbed sense of omnipotence.

In related fashion, the photographers' lives appeal to children on the level of sheer adventure. Here the photographers become moral swashbucklers abroad in dangerous territory. To take his photographs of the Civil War, Timothy O'Sullivan risked his life "amidst the excitement, the rapid movements and the smoke of the battlefield." Lewis Hine, also at great peril, hid his camera in a lunchpail and passed himself off as a fire inspector to get inside textile mills exploiting child labor. When Jacob Riis first came to the United States, he bought "the biggest revolver he could find. He strapped it outside his coat and paraded up Broadway, ready for the buffaloes and Indians he'd read about." Later, as a reporter, he witnessed street fights and gang warfare and photographed ominous locales like Bandits' Roost. Other newsmen called him the "boss reporter" and "The Dutchman." Landlords hated him because he exposed their practice "of jamming fifteen people into one or two rooms." For children, the text and the photos in combination are morality made animate with the photographer as romantic hero in a drama of man and magical machine against evil.

Several of the photographers' lives reflect in some measure their subjects' experience of suffering. O'Sullivan and his family were forced to flee the Irish potato famine of 1841. Dorothea Lange was lame from birth; she said it "formed me, guided me, instructed me, helped me, and humiliated me. . . . My lameness as a child and my acceptance, finally, of my lameness truly opened gates for me." Riis in his early poverty was forced to mine coal, cut timber, harvest ice, sell furniture, peddle flatirons, shiver in doorways, and sleep in stinking vagrants' rooms at police stations before he landed a respectable reporter's position at the *New York Tribune*. These experiences of the photographers add to the power of their photographs, enchance a child's understanding of the suffering they portray, and enlarge his sense of the photographers' conviction and the rightness of their course of action.

The victims in the photographs of O'Sullivan, Riis, Hine, and Lange are, of course, anonymous as individuals. Their collective pain is not; in retrospect, it is at least partly redeemed and dignified because it forms an integral part of crucial historical periods—the Civil War, the immigrant movement to American cities, the Great Depression, the decades of child labor and attempts at unionization.

Fung Lam's photographs of physically handicapped children differ markedly. The world of the handicapped child is an entirely private and hidden one, unconnected to events in the larger society. Because their stigmata are visible, undeniable, and permanent, we are tempted to deny them *any* future or responsibility in our rush to pity them; we may make victims of them when they are not. Lam's achievement is that his beautifully rendered photos break through this overlay of pity which hinders us from seeing handicapped children as human. He relieves us of the insistent victimization in the work of the other photographers. His photos are moments in the everyday life of the handicapped child: crippled children laughing together, hanging out on a porch, taking a first swimming lesson. Lam's photos are quietly lyrical, mute celebrations of ordinary life removed from history and the passage of time.

If Lam's photos fall outside history's compass, the other photographs in this book, because of their power as images, skew history by inflating the role of the photographer as an agent of social change. The editors in their text aggressively promote this distortion. Their viewpoint is uncritical, and they make no effort to set the documentarists in the perspective of other variables that led to reform. This further concentrates the power of the photographs, granting the photographers an Olympian presence in the flow of events.

But it is precisely this exaggeration that gives a child purchase on the notion of history itself. A child ten or eleven years old can see in the photographs other children of undeniably different social circumstances from his own. His curiosity stimulated and his feelings aroused, he can turn to the text or talk to someone who can help him fill in the gaps in the photographs' unclosed narrative. Perhaps, then, he senses the possibility of change. Because social arrangements are different for him, he may even sense that they could have been different for the photographed children, had people cared and acted sooner.

The photographs are thus subversive of comparatively linear, fact-oriented textbook history. For they provide a tactile link from the child-reader's present to the child-victim's past. The photographs join them in their common humanity through a demonstration, however vicarious, of their shared vulnerability before the threat of victimization. Paradoxically, through the example of the photographers' lives, they embrace a wider faith in the power of men to act. (pp. 180-82)

Ted Wolner, "Photography as Children's Literature," in Children's Literature: Annual of the Modern Language Association Seminar on Children's Literature and The Children's Literature Association, *Vol. 4, 1975, pp. 179-85.*

WORLD OF OUR FATHERS: THE JEWS OF EASTERN EUROPE (1974)

This survey of Eastern European Jewry was prompted by Meltzer's desire to investigate the background his immigrant parents never talked about. As Meltzer reads neither Yiddish nor Hebrew, the result is, predictably, a montage of impressions excerpted from such standard English works as Zborowski and Herzog's *Life is With People,* Charnofsky's *Jewish Life in the Ukraine,* I. L. Peretz' *Memoirs,* and I. B. Singer's novels. Yet the book—which ends up focusing on the 19th century *shtetl* of Russian-Polish Jews—possesses the virtue of eschewing sentimentality about that hard and dirty life. Meltzer also sketches with detachment the split between the Hasidic mystics and various opponents who wanted to merge Judaism with the Enlightenment, as well as the origins of the Bund and Zionism. A well made introduction for those who need a bridge to the standard works Meltzer introduces.

A review of "World of Our Fathers: The Jews of Eastern Europe," in Kirkus Reviews, *Vol. XLII, No. 24, December 15, 1974, p. 1313.*

A well-researched and lucid political, social, and economic history of Eastern European Jews from Medieval times to the outbreak of World War I. Numerous quotes from source material about shtetl [ghetto] life present a moving picture of the constant restrictions and frustrations that Eastern European Jews faced. Meltzer also does a very good job of chronicling the official approval and benign neglect which allowed violent anti-Semitism to flourish in these countries. An extensive bibliography and glossary of Yiddish vocabulary append the history.

Judith S. Kronick, in a review of "World of Our Fathers: The Jews of Eastern Europe," in School Library Journal, *Vol. 21, No. 5, January, 1975, p. 56.*

The major portion of this history is concerned with the Jews who settled in Poland around the seventeenth century. Their plight is depicted vividly through eyewitness accounts. This method is used throughout the entire history and makes for interesting and authentic reading. . . .

Despite their hardships, several East European Jews rose to fame because of the brilliant and determined use of their talents. Meltzer is careful to give brief biographical accounts of their accomplishments.

An index appended to the book makes for easy referral to important personages and events mentioned in this short history. It is another interesting account of a persecuted minority.

Sister Joseph Marie Anderson, S.S.N.D., in a review of "World of Our Fathers: The Jews of Eastern Europe," in Best Sellers, *Vol. 34, No. 19, January 1, 1975, p. 445.*

In the foreword to this special trip into a particular past, Milton Meltzer articulates what must be an almost universal experience: He tells us that, as a child and as a youth, he expressed no interest in where his immigrant parents had come from or what their life was like. Later, he began to search for his own roots as he became involved in writing history. What he has to tell young readers should fascinate them, no matter what their color or religion, because modern teenagers don't merely accept the present and take the past for granted. The rich and the poor Jews of 19th century Europe come to sturdy life in these pages; the author's research is thorough and his style is compelling, beginning with the first sentence: "Half the Jews of the world lived in Eastern Europe in the year 1800." Few will stop reading till they find out what happened to them.

A review of "World of Our Fathers: The Jews of Eastern Europe," in Publishers Weekly, *Vol. 207, No. 2, January 13, 1975, p. 60.*

REMEMBER THE DAYS: A SHORT HISTORY OF THE JEWISH AMERICAN (1974)

Where most books on the immigrant experience tend to concentrate on the accomplishments of notable individuals, Meltzer consistently relates the course of American Jewry to its European roots. Individuals do play a large part in the earlier stages of his narrative—up through the Civil War which was accompanied by a rise in anti-Semitism despite the pro-Union activities of many prominent Jews. However, with the arrival of large numbers of Eastern European Jews . . . , his scope broadens. Here, following a brief history of the pogroms, are sketches of the Lower East Side community—the sweatshop and the rise of unionism, the public schools which routinely "Americanized" at the same time as they satisfied the hunger for learning, the Yiddish theatre and the all-important socializing role of the *Jewish Daily Forward*. These are only glimpses, but telling ones of an era when the "pent-up energy" of many oppressed generations began to free itself. And, combined here with Meltzer's attempt to promote better understanding between blacks and Jews, they make an easy to read introduction, on a far higher plane of social sensitivity than most series-spawned celebrations of the melting pot.

A review of "Remember the Days: A Short History of the Jewish American," in Kirkus Reviews, *Vol. XLIII, No. 1, January 1, 1975, p. 22.*

Although no bibliography of sources is included, there is little doubt that this judicious and balanced survey of Jewish participation in American history is based on thorough research. Meltzer's writing is serious but not dry, his material well-organized, and his viewpoint broad, so that the problems of Jewish immigrants are seen as part of the whole immigrant problem, his account of Jewish activism in the labor movement seen against the background of the whole labor movement. The text discusses Jewish cultural life, discrimination, the life the immigrants fled and the conditions they found in the United States, Jewish contributions to causes and to public life, and support of Zionism in this country. An index is appended.

Zena Sutherland, in a review of "Remember the Days: A Short History of the Jewish American," in Bulletin of the Center for Children's Books, *Vol. 28, No. 10, June, 1975, p. 164.*

NEVER TO FORGET: THE JEWS OF THE HOLOCAUST (1976)

AUTHOR'S COMMENTARY

[In the following excerpt, Meltzer details his creation of Never to Forget: The Jews of the Holocaust *to show that nonfiction for young readers requires as much thought and artistic skill as fiction.]*

When John McPhee's book about the Alaskan wilderness was published, it excited national attention. One critic said that McPhee "is a journalist who writes of fact with that full measure of literary distinction that some associate only with fiction or poetry." *Coming Into The Wilderness* was praised for its author's "Balzacian zest for detail" and his "gift for portraiture that enables him to capture real people as memorably as any novelist does his imaginary one." Another critic said that McPhee "is above all a craftsman . . . a reporter who makes art. He writes pieces that are as complex as novels, as meticulous as scholarship . . . in prose that is humorous, elegant, economical."

Look at the subjects of the dozen other books that McPhee has published. He has written of "basketball and tennis, oranges and firewood, wilderness and city, physics and engineering, art and education, men who build bark canoes and those who build unique flying machines, people who dwell in New Jersey's Pine Barrens and who inhabit cabins on the tributaries of the Yukon River." Most of these are topics you might find in junior book catalogs in almost any season. In such a setting they would be indifferently treated as "information" books or "fact" books. (p. 110)

His books belong in the category The Literature of Fact, which is the title of a writing course he gives. . . . Why are they not catalogued as American Literature? Because no one has a proper name for his brand of factual writing. Everyone calls his work nonfiction—a frustrating label, for it says not what McPhee's books are, but what they are *not*. "Since 'fiction' is presumably made up, imaginative, clever, and resourceful, a book of 'nonfiction' must *not* be any of these things, perhaps not even a work of art. If the point seems a mere quibble over terms," [says Professor William Howarth, Professor of English at Princeton,] "try reversing the tables: are Faulkner's books on Mississippi 'non-history' just because they are novels?"

Now what is the main thing being said in all this praise of McPhee's work? It can be reduced to the three-word sentence already quoted: "He makes art." The verb "makes" is all-important. Art does not begin when the artist chooses his subject. It is what he does with it, what he *makes* of it, that counts. And here I pick up on another phrase quoted earlier: "McPhee is above all a craftsman." Which means he has superb technique. (pp. 110-11)

But some may discount what I am saying when it comes to writing nonfiction for young readers. They will assume that in children's books nothing is explored in any depth or with sensitivity and, therefore, that writers of nonfiction for children need only find the facts and type them up. Wolves are wolves, aren't they? Abe Lincoln is Abe Lincoln, the American Revolution is the American Revolution. Don't the facts speak for themselves? "But the facts *never* speak for themselves," the critic Jacques Barzun insists. "They must be selected, marshaled, linked together, given a voice." Fit expression, he goes on, is not "a mere frill added to one's accumulation of knowledge. The expression *is* the knowledge."

If the writer cannot find the language to express what he thinks he has to say, then whatever he is after is simply not there on the page. His work begins to exist only through his craft. Lacking craft, many books of nonfiction contain nothing but dead words, words which serve no purpose beyond the stale repetition of the most rudimentary kind of fact.

I hope I may be forgiven for what may look like an exercise in egocentricity if I now take apart a piece of my own nonfiction, showing what I tried to do and how I went about doing it, to illustrate what I have said. My example is ***Never to Forget: The Jews of the Holocaust.***

Why did I want to write it? The impulse came from a pamphlet reporting a study of American high school textbooks, which found that racism, anti-Semitism, and the Holocaust were either ignored in these influential books or dismissed in a few brief lines. Nor were college textbooks much better. It was appalling to realize that as far as young people's books were concerned, nothing of great consequence had happened.

By one of those remarkable coincidences, an editor at Harper & Row had read the same pamphlet at about the same moment, and concluded that Harper's must try to fill that hole. Knowing my other books on Jewish history, she approached me just as I was about to look for a publisher.

This was to be a book for young readers. I assumed that they would know little or nothing about the Holocaust and what gave rise to it, and this was to be a book for Gentile, as well as Jew. While writing about black history, I had learned that you couldn't deal with black Americans without dealing with white Americans. Black life and white life in America are profoundly affected by one another. Their experience is inseparable. So too with Jew and Gentile in the Holocaust. I knew the book couldn't be for Jews alone. It must be a book for the non-Jew too.

For a long time I read in the forbidding masses of source material. To include everything was manifestly impossible. I had to be concerned with selection, deletion, emphasis, proportion. I had to find a form and a voice that would enlarge the reader's experience, deepen it, intensify it.

I also had to catch the attention of my young readers. After several false starts, I came upon what felt like the right beginning—that day in 1930 when, as a high school boy and a Jew, I first saw the front-page news of Nazis in brown uniforms marching into the German parliament and shouting *"Deutschland erwache! Jude verrecke!"* ("Germany awake! Jews perish!") The preface decided upon, the focus now shifted to how to organize the facts and ideas scattered through my stacks of 3-by-5 slips. The thinking that goes into it! The fretting, the worrying, the doing and undoing, the snipping and patching, all to get the ordering of the parts right! Chronology—the simple and direct movement from point A in time to point Z—is the easy and tempting way, and of course I played with it. But chronological order can be terribly tiresome. The other kind of order is topical: I could arrange the history of the Holocaust by subjects. But then the book would read like a string of essays. This was history, after all—the passage of events through time. In the end, I combined the topical with the chronological. Each of the book's three main parts would stress one theme, while at the same time chronology would move the story forward.

The theme of Part One, covering five chapters, is anti-Semitism, with its development traced through time. Who were the Jews as a historical people? Why did anti-Semitism grow in Europe, and what part did the Christian church play in it? How did anti-Semitism change its character so that it turned from a religious issue into a racial one? Why did it take hold in Germany, and what part did it play in the rise of Nazism and Hitler's taking of power? The theme is carried from the ancient world up to the eve of the Second World War.

Part Two deals with the war itself and Hitler's use of it to seize the continent's Jews and destroy them. Eight chapters trace the step-by-step measures taken to that end.

In Part Three, I use five chapters for the single topic of the Jews' resistance to their fate. A conclusion I reached from my research was that everywhere there was oppression, resistance of some kind emerged. The Jews, counter to the old calumny, did not somehow murder themselves. Almost a third of the book—the action moving back and forth in time—traces the great variety of means by which the Jews carried out the watchword of their resistance: "Live and die with dignity!"

There is another aspect of the problem of form—its most important, I think—which accomplishes what nothing else could. Since I am not one of the Jews who experienced the ghettoization, the transport trains, the death camps, I could write about them only from a remote distance. To make the story immediately personal, it should be told in the words of people who did live it. Therefore, I drew upon original sources—diaries, letters, memoirs, eyewitness accounts, testimony given at hearings and trials, songs and poems. All these things I had culled in my preparatory study. Terrible and complex as the events were, I was convinced that if the readers could be made to feel it first hand, so to speak, they would be that much more able to understand. So the men, women and children who lived the experience speak of it directly to the reader in their own words.

With young readers as my primary audience, I wanted much of the testimony to come from boys and girls, or to be about them. There are 27 such documentary passages fitted into the narrative. For example, Inge and Lolo, two little Christian girls, innocently reveal to a neighbor how their teacher has poisoned their minds against the Jews. Erna, an Aryan schoolgirl, proudly sends her prize-winning classroom essay, "The Jews Are Our Misfortune," to be printed in *Der Sturmer,* and I give the text of her piece. Ernest, a Jewish farmer's son, is beaten up by kids in his rural school and then expelled by the teacher. When a six-year old Jewish boy refuses to give a passing band of Hitler Youth the *Heil Hitler* salute, he is stripped of his pants to show the passersby that this is a circumcised dog. On *Kristallnacht,* the home of 14-year-old Moses Libau is broken into by Stormtroopers, and he watches his parents terrorized and their belongings plundered. (pp. 111-14)

In writing true history, you are dealing not simply with the what and when of events, but also with the why and how. If you do not always have an easy time determining what happened and when, you are sure to have a much harder time finding out why and how it happened. For it brings you to the heart of what history is about—human behavior. That is the subject novelists deal with; it is just as much the subject for historians.

It is arguable whether history is any kind of guide, whether we have any lessons to learn from it. But even those who deny that the study of history is useful in a practical sense must accept the fact that it throws valuable light on human behavior—so illogical, so erratic, so unpredictable, and therefore so endlessly fascinating.

Studying the Holocaust and the behavior of human beings in that time, we can detect a kind of logic in what happened. Hindsight, of course. Could we learn enough from it to be able to predict its repetition in the future? Not, I think, where it might happen, or when, or to whom, but only that it *could* happen again. And, I am afraid I have to say, that it is all the more likely to happen again because it has *already* happened.

One idea that runs throughout ***Never to Forget*** is that we should not see the destruction process of the Holocaust as the work of a small band of arch criminals led by a Svengali who took control of the minds of the German people and forced them to carry out an insane policy. On the contrary. The Holocaust can be better understood if we regard it as the expression of profound tendencies of modern civilization. Central among these tendencies is the bureaucratization of power. Mankind has known oppression through millenia of enforced servitude, from the ancient world down through American slavery. But it was modern methods of bureaucratization that made possible the expenditure of human life on such a scale and with such absolute ruthlessness as that to which Auschwitz testifies.

Bureaucratization is not, of course, uniquely Nazi nor uniquely German in its nature. It is a phenomenon of the twentieth century. The Jews were first defined as vermin by the German state bureaucracy. It became a matter of finding the most efficient way of disinfecting the world of Jews. Having stripped the Jews of their humanity, the Germans saw no moral barrier to their annihilation. And for that goal, every section of German society gave its full cooperation. . . .

Nor did the Germans have to do it all alone. They found help whenever they needed it among the people of every nation they occupied; yes, in the ghettos and camps too. Among the Jews themselves were some who served the "master race" as police, spies, informers, and hangmen.

Here, then, is the dark side of human personality, seen in action in contrast with its opposite, the faith, the dignity, the courage of those who resisted destruction in so many different ways. Civilization itself, like human character, has both sides. (pp. 114-15)

The effect of the book, I hope, is to bring readers to think of man's nature as being neither good nor evil, but as containing both possibilities and that the greatest sin is indifference.

Now I come back to where I started—the possibilities of nonfiction writing for young readers. Does it have to be nothing but a pastiche of facts? Is there a function for the imagination? Is there room for ideas? for exercise of judgment? for the portrayal of character? for the illumination of human behavior? for the play of craftsmanship? Of course there is. Teachers, librarians, reviewers must look for literary distinction in nonfiction, ask for it, point it out when it exists, and criticize when it is missing. As writers, we must aim for it every time we sit down to the job. (p. 116)

Milton Meltzer, "The Possibilities of Nonfiction: A Writer's View," in Children's Literature in Education, *Vol. 11, No. 3, (Autumn), 1980, pp. 110-16.*

Milton Meltzer's book is an act of desperation—an act of piety and pity, wrath and love, despair and homage; but the motive force, the terrible sense of urgency which drives and animates it, is desperation. In an afterword, he notes that an authoritative study of American high school history textbooks, conducted nearly 30 years after World War II, revealed that "their treatment of Nazism was brief, bland, superficial, and misleading," that "racism, anti-Semitism, and the Holocaust were ignored or dismissed in a few lines," and that textbooks designed for colleges and universities were "not substantially better." "Darkness," said the historian Golo Mann, "hides the vilest crime ever perpetrated by man against man."

Yet how can it be otherwise? Hiroshima and Nagasaki are mere exotic names, if indeed they conjure up anything at all; it required the burning of American cities to call attention to the existence of our largest oppressed minority. . . . And if we are, seemingly, a nation of amnesiacs, the rest of the world is not noticeably more gifted at remembering.

Into this infinite void Meltzer sends his book levelling it without distinction—for none should or need be made—at teen-agers and young adults who came along after the fact, and at their elders who may have repressed or chosen to forget it. Within its small compass, he undertakes a task of intimidating scale: to convey some compelling sense of the experience of European Jewry in the Hitler years, culminating, of course, in the unprecedented slaughter of six million Jews. Not much more than a sketch is possible in a small book, yet what a full and resonant sketch it is. ("Definitive" studies, of course, abound, and are listed in a bibliography. Meltzer's intention is far more modest though it is uncompromising: he strives for a hard clarity of style and presentation that will span the divide between generations, and an unwavering concentration on essences unobstructed by the cumbersome and discouraging apparatus of scholarship.)

The progression is inexorable, unrelenting, beginning with the millennia-long historical background of anti-Semitism throughout Christendom and particularly in the Czar's Pale of Settlement in Eastern Europe and in pre-Hitler Germany. This was the context of discrimination, persecution, torment, pogrom—established by custom and law—in which the Nazis were able to formulate the diabolic design for the extermination of the Jews which bore the ambiguous, bureaucratic cover title: "The Final Solution to the Jewish Question." . . .

Six million massacred—men, women, children, babies straight from the womb. The imagination cannot encompass or fathom the horror; nor can the intelligence assimilate the magnitude and human meaning of those inert statistics. So Meltzer, with an intuitive eye for the illuminating image, event, moment, quickens and deepens his chronicle of catastrophe by brief, telling, heartbreaking and sometimes exhilarating passages from the records of survivors and of the dead; makes human what would otherwise be remote, stupendous, over-powering. (p. 25)

Nothing is evaded or scanted in this extraordinarily fine and moving book: not the vexed question of "why" the Jews "allowed" themselves to be destroyed (as if tanks and machine guns could be fought with bare hands), nor the abysmal existence of the sometimes brutal Jewish ghetto police and concentration camp trustees, nor the tormenting issue of the complicit role of some members of some of the Jewish Councils. Meltzer does not equivocate and he does not relent; he does not patronize or condescend or indulge—he respects his readers, whatever their age, and is therefore free to make moral and intellectual demands of them; he tells harsh truths harshly, and noble ones (the Warsaw Ghetto Uprising, the camp revolts, the magnificent Jewish partisans and resistance forces) proudly. He is never sentimental, bombastic, falsely romantic or heroic. His deeply felt and trenchantly written book is an act of mourning and a call to remember. For our own souls' sake it is indispensable. (p. 42)

Saul Maloff, in a review of "Never to Forget: The Jews of the Holocaust," in The New York Times Book Review, *May 2, 1976, pp. 25, 42.*

Extermination of a race by a ruler is not new; history records many mass murders, but the persecution and annihilation of the Jews in Europe during World War II burns fresh in our minds. As evidenced by the almost 100-title bibliography, anti-Semitism during that period has been studied, explained, analyzed, condemned, and commemorated in poem, song, sculpture, and art. An additional look at the horror seems sadistic. However, this penetrating account offers the *young* a glimpse at man's sometime cruelty to man.

Excerpts of diaries from survivors and from ghetto/prison ruins cause tortured souls to rise from the ashes to haunt the reader. . . . Only in one or two places does [the author] lose his objectivity, an understandable lapse in view of his closeness to the topic. Historically accurate, this volume should serve as a perceptive look at the ignominious side effects of war. An excellent chronology, bibliography, and index enrich some solid social studies material. With some teacher discretion, boys and girls from the sixth through twelfth grades could benefit from Mr. Meltzer's book.

Mrs. John G. Gray, in review of "Never to Forget: The Jews of the Holocaust," in Best Sellers, *Vol. 36, No. 5, August, 1976, p. 152.*

The mass murder of six million Jews by the Nazis during World War II is the subject of this compelling history. Interweaving background information, chilling statistics, individual accounts and newspapers reports, it provides an excellent introduction to its subject for American young people, whose lack of knowledge about the war and/or about anti-Semitism continually amazes people like the reviewer who lived through those times. . . .

The one deficiency of this background information is that readers are given the impression that Hitler controlled everything in Germany, including big business. It is much more likely that Hitler was encouraged by big business because, in addition to killing Jews, he also suppressed all labor union activity and all political opposition. (p. 16)

In relating information about the infamous German leaders and presenting first-person tales by anonymous victims, Meltzer exposes the myth of Jewish non-resistance. . . . Using recently discovered documents and the accounts of concentration camp survivors, Meltzer gives a stirring and important description of active and passive resistance that was marked by courage, confusion over tactics and passionate struggle for survival.

In his ***Never to Forget*** wrap-up chapter, the author makes it clear that the Holocaust must never be regarded merely as an aberration. (Unfortunately, the male pronoun is used to denote all of humanity in making this point.) He not only shows that "it can happen here" but that it *has* happened everywhere both before and after Hitler. . . . He also makes it clear that all humanity was responsible—individuals, churches, governments, along with the Germans who actually committed the murders—by not acting to prevent the Holocaust.

Readers will gain a greater understanding of history, of racism and of individual responsibility from this excellent book—and, hopefully, neutrality will be impossible. (pp. 16-17)

Lyla Hoffman, in a review of "Never to Forget: The Jews of the Holocaust," in Interracial Books for Children Bulletin, *Vol. 7, No. 6, 1976, pp. 16-17.*

The young people for whom this book was written will not remember the unbelievable horror that the world outside Europe felt, learning of the tragically successful story of Hitler's program to exterminate the Jews, but they may have read of the Holocaust. They will never have read a more moving and explicit documentation. . . . [Meltzer's] text is meticulously organized and written with an inexorable flow; it describes not only the persecution, pogroms, and death camps, but also the resistance workers of the ghettos, the camps, and the labor force.

Zena Sutherland, in a review of "Never to Forget: The Jews of the Holocaust," in Bulletin of the Center for Children's Books, *Vol. 30, No. 1, September, 1976, p. 14.*

Statistics alone cannot convey the extent of death and human misery suffered by the Jews of the Holocaust. They are so staggering as to be incomprehensible and beyond imagination. Milton Meltzer tries to give meaning to these statistics by relating the fates of many individuals and having others tell their own stories. . . . While no book can convey the Jewish suffering in its true dimensions, ***Never To Forget*** makes an excellent attempt. Written on a subject about which everyone should be knowledgeable, the book compels the reader to turn the pages until its conclusion. . . . While the author acknowledges that some sympathetic Gentiles did exist, he plays this point down (much to the detriment of the book) and prefers to let it appear that the Jews were universally disliked and left completely alone. In no way does this book exaggerate the horrors of the holocaust. In fact, it practically ignores the 'medical experimentation' done on human subjects in the concentration camps. Still ***Never To Forget*** will make the reader very uncomfortable and could conceivably cause nightmares. Recommended for older young adults only.

Nancy Aghazarian, in a review of "Never to Forget: The Jews of the Holocaust," in Young Adult Cooperative Book Review Group of Massachusetts, *Vol. 13, No. 1, October, 1976, p. 22.*

Meltzer interviews and quotes survivors of the infamous anti-semitic actions surrounding World War II, managing to effect a rare combination. He tells a specific real-life tragedy with such imagination and feeling that he turns statistics and documents into a piece of genuine literature. Occasionally Meltzer falls into the old trap of building up hatred for one people (this time, the Germans) while preaching against hatred towards another group (the Jews). But all in all, he did a marvelous job of walking a very fine line—telling the story fully and realistically without dwelling obsessively on barbaric behavior and cruelty.

Alleen Pace Nilsen, in a review of "Never to Forget: The Jews of the Holocaust, in English Journal, *Vol. 66, No. 6, September, 1977, p. 88.*

VIOLINS AND SHOVELS: THE WPA ARTS PROJECTS (1976)

The WPA gave Milton Meltzer his first writing job (in the Theater Project at a life-saving $23.86 a week), so this is an understandably glowing, nostalgic recollection of that agency's accomplishments. While not unmindful of the limitations of government-supported art and the problems of censorship, Meltzer recalls the tremendous strides made by young professionals given the chance to work full-time at their specialties; the program's role in helping talents like Jackson Pollack to survive; and any number of commercially unfeasible projects—the American Guide Series, the Index of American Design, retraining vaudevillians for children's theater—which flourished under its auspices. The defiant, underground opening of *The Cradle Will Rock,* the company of employees like Richard Wright and Nelson Algren, the vision of administrators like Hallie Flanagan who hoped to build a national theater, are heady memories; they're also a part of our cultural heritage that this compact personalized account will make available to yet another generation. That the worst economic crisis of our nation's history might be remembered as a relative boon to artists (giving them a freedom for which many paid dearly during the McCarthy era) is a multi-layered irony which Meltzer reinforces here with closing statistics on the "starvation diet" of the arts today.

A review of "Violins and Shovels: The WPA Arts Projects," in Kirkus Reviews, *Vol. XLIV, No. 16, August 15, 1976, p. 911.*

I think of ***Violins and Shovels*** as a *salutary* book. It is intended for young readers—but I think it could be read profitably by older ones who have neither the time nor the inclination to plow through the records in great detail. All will learn that, for a time, anyway, no government in history ever did what the Roosevelt Administration did: Make it possible for artists to live—neither well nor ill but in reasonable comfort, so that they might tend their arts and bring them to flower.

Readers will learn once more of the fundamental hostility toward the arts of legislatures and businesses. (I'm not exempting, even today, the foundations or corporations looking for Brownie points.) And they will learn exactly how little is required for an artist to survive and work.

Gilbert Millstein, in a review of "Violins and Shovels: The WPA Arts Projects," in The New York Times Book Review, *November 14, 1976, p. 42.*

A first-rate piece of reporting. . . . The text is dotted with vivid thumbnail sketches of famous figures from the art/theatre/music world . . . and with brief accounts of fascinating incidents from this little-known phase of our artistic history. Written in the same flowing style and with the same accuracy that characterizes Meltzer's histories, this is the only indepth treatment of the subject available for this audience. The fact that Meltzer worked in the New York WPA project and relates his personal experiences is an added bonus. (pp. 61-2)

Elizabeth McCorkle, in a review of "Violins and Shovels: The WPA Arts Projects, a New Deal for America's Hungry Artists of the 1930's," in School Library Journal, *Vol. 23, No. 4, December, 1976, pp. 61-2.*

The WPA projects in the 1930s have been much maligned. Commentators on that prolonged period of economic depression have often characterized the works projects as boondoggling. Or those projects have been ignored or merely referred to in a list of the new agencies of the federal government created in that terror-filled time.

Meltzer treats the WPA projects in a very different vein. He sees them as a vast social experiment in the arts. . . .

He writes from a background of personal involvement, incorporating interviews with many people and scholarly research. . . .

The book is vividly written, with much feeling as well as a great deal of social commentary on those times. This is social history of the first order.

A full account of other books to read on this period, an ample index, and several pictures add considerably to the value of this unique volume. It is highly recommended for social studies teachers and students.

Leonard S. Kenworthy, in a review of "Violins and Shovels: The WPA Arts Projects," in Curriculum Review, *Vol. 17, No. 1, February, 1978, p. 79.*

TAKING ROOT: JEWISH IMMIGRANTS IN AMERICA (1976)

While the vivid, first-hand memories of struggle and triumph—of William Zorach, Maurice Hindus, Mary Antin, Abraham Cahan, and others—are the backbone of this sequel to his documentary ***World of Our Fathers*** . . . , Meltzer isn't content with celebrating the success stories. These are the immigrant milieux of ***Remember the Days*** . . . reexamined in a harsher, sociological light: Meltzer focuses on the pressures toward Americanization that turned Mashkes and Yankels into Marys and Jims and on the process by which, in the words of historian Lucy Dawidowicz, "the freedom to make money became an obsession" for some. He shows how whole villages—and the attendant class conflicts—were often reassembled in American garment businesses, and he celebrates the success of Jewish socialists in organizing labor unions yet still questions whether the factory was in all ways a dramatic improvement over the sweatshop where, as in the factory the work was "more minute, more intense, and more monotonous." Similarly, the reminiscences of those who found public education a thrilling opportunity are balanced by the caution that the schools still failed to equalize opportunities for Jews or any other group. And nostalgia for the old *Daily Forward*—recalled here along with the Yiddish theater and Essex Street cafes—is tempered by a reminder that the Yiddish press developed its own brand of yellow journalism. Although others have drawn on much of the same sources (Karp's *Golden Door to America* . . . is the most recent and rich), Meltzer's succinct and intelligent commentary can serve, simultaneously, as a popular introduction to the era and a reexamination of the melting pot myths . . . and it could be an agreeable bridge to the more than 75 titles in his well selected bibliography.

A review of "Taking Root," in Kirkus Reviews, *Vol. XLIV, No. 17, September 1, 1976, p. 985.*

Extracts from personal diaries and first-hand recollections bring to life the existence of these new Americans. Although this book does not approach the scope or scholarship of Irving Howe's adult *World of Our Fathers* (. . . 1976), once again Meltzer presents a compassionate, vivid picture of a people and a time which will give greater insight into the Jewish culture and heritage.

Marilyn Kaye, in a review of "Taking Root: Jewish Immigrants in America," in School Library Journal, *Vol. 23, No. 3, November, 1976, p. 71.*

Promoted as a sequel to ***World of Our Fathers*** . . . , this is more complete than ***Remember the Days***. . . . Research is solid, but writing is very careless and it is frequently difficult to know precisely to whom or what the statistics cited are referring, or to assess their importance.

Barbara Wolfson, in a review of "Taking Root: Jewish Immigrants in America," in Booklist, *Vol. 73, No. 15, April 1, 1977, p. 1176.*

[***Taking Root***] is a worthy teenage substitute for Irving Howe's masterful study of the same subject. It makes an important contribution to the recent increased interest in ethnic studies and in the search for one's "roots." Although Meltzer has not specifically traced his own family history, he wrote "this story of the East European Jews because they are my people and I wanted to learn about them." His adept weaving into the narrative of eyewitness accounts and quotations from modern writers has indeed created a dramatic personalized account. Brief and easy to read chapters . . . poignantly fulfill his desire to depict "the quality of life, the delights and disappointments, the ambitions and fears, the labor and illusions" of these immigrants.

Although sympathetic and understanding, Meltzer's account is not a mere celebration of East European Jews in America. Taking cultural pluralism instead of the melting pot as his model for America, he is critical of those "native" and nativist Americans who either out of good will advise to "assimilate quickly or face a quiet but sure extermination" or from racism seek to exclude Jews and other "undesirable" ethnic groups from American life. He is also critical, however, of those Jews who sacrifice their ideals, values, and customs in their search for financial security and Americanization. While telling us about the anti-Semitic campaign joining Boston Brahmin, university professor, and KKKer against the nomination of Louis Brandeis to the Supreme Court, Meltzer also reminds us that a number of wealthy and conservative Jews suggested quietly that Woodrow Wilson withdraw the nomination for fear that the uproar would undermine their own privileged position.

Meltzer also shows us that class and cultural divisions are frequently stronger than ethnic unity. Thus German and Sephardic Jews finally helped East European Jews in America, but not before they failed to convince them to stop coming or to return to Russia. The Triangle Fire, which killed hundreds of men, women, and young girls, was a vivid reminder of the exploitation of working class Jews by Jewish clothing manufacturers.

Two aspects of the book make it particularly useful for students of high-school age. The excellent quotations make it easy for a student to identify with the experience of the speaker, and many excerpts could be the basis for interesting discussions about values. Secondly, each chapter is organized around a clear theme and an important historical question. Meltzer is not satisfied with simplistic interpretations. If emigration from Eastern Europe was the result of pogroms, why, he asks, did more than 300,000 Jews come from Austria-Hungary, where there were none? The schools failed to teach the immigrant children something of their own heritage, but how effective was the education they did try to impart? By raising such issues Meltzer encourages his reader to think critically and to see history as more than a collection of historical facts.

Although ***Taking Root*** is primarily concerned with Jewish immigration, it will be useful to all those interested in ethnic studies and in the problems faced by other immigrant groups at the turn of the century. (pp. 548-49)

Sanford J. Gutman, "In America," in Social Education, *Vol. 41, No. 6, October, 1977, pp. 548-49.*

[***Taking Root***] can be classified as a highly approachable and at times stimulating history for junior high and high school readers. Perhaps it can also be read in an introductory college course on immigrant or ethnic history. We say this because one gets a cursory view of some major areas of interest that can be explored in greater detail and complexity. Meltzer, very sympathetically, covers the motives for migration, the crossing, problems of arrival, mobility, Americanization, child labor, self-help organizations, cultural life, labor unions and nativism. The book is not carefully documented, and the general bibliography is of no assistance for one interested in tracing the specific memoirs, diaries, or letters he so skillfully includes within the narrative.

One is surprised at times that a text geared for young readers or historians contains insightful questions and quotations. It is less surprising, given Meltzer's interest in social reform, that he challenges common shibboleths about the melting pot. In reference to the fascinating 1890 guidebook of immigrants, a writer of the period (here his loose documentation frustrates) says that what America did for the immigrant was to substitute

Meltzer with his wife Hildy, daughters Jane and Amy, and son-in-law Philip McArthur. Courtesy of Milton Meltzer.

for "the ancient tradition of hospitality a system of heartless exploitation and of neglect. The determining factor in our hospitality has been the necessity for laborers—slaves if you will." Meltzer also offers some exciting success sketches that describe and attempt to explain how Jews took advantage of this substitution, and profited through intellect, determination, competitiveness and personal self-sacrifice. Surprise turns to dismay when he says that thousands of immigrant Jews managed to acquire East Side tenement properties. It is not enough to base this claim merely on a report by the muckraking journalist, Burton Hendrick, (1907) who stated that Harlem real estate was controlled largely by Jews.

In the chapter, "The Melting Pot Leaks," one looks for hints of leakage. Julia Richman, Jane Addams, and Horace Kallen are quoted as spokesmen for pluralism and the preservation of tradition. So at this level there was no melting pot. The author does not quote the resistance literature among East European Jews themselves, nor does he refer to the element within the Educational Alliance which challenged the Reform rabbis. If there were strong forces reducing ethnicity in its more glaring and embarassing forms, such as the school, settlement house, library, national Jewish organizations and synagogues, one wonders why the chapter is titled, "The Melting Pot Leaks." School effectiveness studies do not disprove the success of Americanization. Perhaps the chapter is more ideological in intention. Meltzer asks: "Apart from whether or to what degree this happened (melting of different peoples) was it a good idea? When it meant melting diversity into conformity with Anglo-Saxon characteristics?"

Meltzer hints at the movement for modern Jewish spiritual values but never mentions the Conservative movement. Secular Jewish schools and Zionism are referred to in passing in a chapter on the clash of cultures and the conflict of generations. This is a book of casual discussions and not a text that integrates, analyzes or concludes. The chapters on "Cahan and the Cafes" and "Actors and Poets" provide popular, almost stereotypical, identifications of leading figures. One is taken on a fast guided tour of the Lower East Side cultural spots. This is slightly compensated for by the original vignettes which are of value in themselves. The chapter on the rise of the United Hebrew Trades and the ILGWU, and the social reform impact of the Triangle tragedy are less sketchy. The final chapter, "The Door Closes," is a bold sketch of xenophobia and nativism in America from 1814 to 1930. Here the author concludes that the fear and perceived threat of heterogeneity and change during the period, as well as socio-economic unrest, resulted in hostility to Jews. By now this is a truism among historians and sociologists. That these lessons emerged at the time is questionable; more likely, the message of the time was that Jews must rely on their own organizations, e.g., the American Jewish Committee, the Congress and the ADL. The book has no conclusion, only an afterword, stating that the story is not yet complete until one shows the impact of the Holocaust, Vietnam, Watergate, etc., upon the immigrants who settled here.

This is a captivating narrative for young readers, and one which can give a sense of the conditions of life in the old country and of experiences and enterprises of immigrants arriving during the peak periods. It is attractive but not scholarly. The author does not ask sufficient questions of the reader or himself regarding what he reconstructs and weaves, and thus does not encourage a young potential historian to become engaged in a dialogue with the historian of the period. (pp. 181-83)

Arnold A. Gerstein, in a review of "Taking Root: Jewish Immigrants in America," in American Jewish Historical Quarterly, *Vol. LXVII, No. 2, December, 1977, pp. 181-83.*

***THE HUMAN RIGHTS BOOK* (1979)**

Meltzer has made another timely contribution to the collection of nonfiction works on topics not sufficiently emphasized in schools. ***The Human Rights Book*** begins with a short (156 page), thoughtful introduction to the subject of human rights at home and abroad. The remaining pages offer a bibliography, names and addresses of organizations working in the field, and documents issued by the United Nations and others dealing with human rights.

Readers learn that in 1977 there were serious violations of human rights in 116 countries. Meltzer describes some of the torture methods used and discusses a few of the countries with the worst records—Iran, Phillippines, Argentina, South Africa, the Soviet Union and others. There is a chapter on U.S. violations of political freedom by the FBI and the CIA and about U.S. political prisoners such as the Wilmington Ten, although Meltzer does not deal with the cruel treatment (including torture by isolation and many forms of degradation) routinely accorded to thousands of ordinary prisoners in U.S. jails. He does introduce differences in conceptions of what "human rights" means, including the different perspectives of socialist and capitalist nations. And he does point out that among the worst offenders using torture throughout the world are those who are "client" nations of the U.S. and dependent upon our official assistance.

This book belongs on all high school library shelves and would be a fine gift for any thoughtful young person.

Lyla Hoffman, in a review of "The Human Rights Book," in Interracial Books for Children Bulletin, *Vol. 10, No. 6, 1979, p. 18.*

With the strength and specificity that is missing from the Loeschers' *Human Rights* . . . , Meltzer takes a sober look at human rights violations in today's world. . . . Meltzer notes the socialist countries' emphasis on economic and social rights and the Third World's concern for the right to survival, but his chief interest is in totalitarian regimes' violation of the individual human freedom and dignity held precious in democracies. Torture and censorship get specific attention, as do the particular forms of oppression practiced in Argentina, Indonesia, South Africa, and the Soviet Union. Human rights violations here at home are seen chiefly as imperfections in practice, and the last word goes to [Columbia University philosopher Charles Frankel] on the basic virtue of our system. As for American companies' presence in South Africa and our government's support of dictatorial regimes in Iran, Nicaragua, and elsewhere, Meltzer attempts to air all viewpoints, pointing out flaws in official attempts at justification but also the claims of sometimes conflicting goals (such as arms limitations in our relations with the Soviet Union). With texts of several human rights documents appended, a valuable resource. (pp. 1150-51)

A review of "The Human Rights Book," in Kirkus Reviews, *Vol. XLVII, No. 19, October 1, 1979, pp. 1150-51.*

[Meltzer] offers a brief history of the human rights movement, a variety of examples of human rights violations worldwide, and a useful bibliography and appendix of related documents. For these reasons alone, his book is valuable. Further, while one might question anyone's ability to survey this topic in a single volume, Meltzer has provided a concise and clear outline of an issue so broad and complex that many find it overwhelming. The greatest value of the book may be as an entry point for more concentrated study. Such tools are rare in this field.

Keith B. Cooper, in a review of "The Human Rights Book," in Library Journal, *Vol. 104, No. 22, December 15, 1979, p. 2638.*

Milton Meltzer is certainly somewhat pretentious in calling this ***The Human Rights Book.*** While it is useful as an easily-read orientation to a complex and important global political and moral issue, it is hardly definitive. The text, only 156 pages long, begins with a graphic account of the brutal torture of the poet Reza Baraheni in the Iran of the Shah, and goes on to explore the meanings of "human rights," a phrase which means different things to different people. . . . Using the criteria that human rights must be universally seen as such and must be deliverable even in the poorest nations, the following minimum rights are established: the right not to be physically abused, due process with respect to criminal questions, protection in one's religion or irreligion, and protection of the family and its privacy. A survey of the current state of these elementary rights in Argentina, Indonesia, South Africa, and the Communist bloc makes clear that governments are quite capable of grossly violating even these basics in order to further their purposes. The foreign policy of the United States with respect to human rights is subjected to embarrassing scrutiny, but the difficult relationship between this and other fundamental foreign policy factors such as a secure defense, adequate supplies of oil and minerals, and foreign trade, is treated only superficially. An appendix contains the most significant human rights documents of the past thirty-five years, but, for the interested reader who wishes to become actively involved, the most valuable section will be the profile of organizations, ranging from the prominent Amnesty International to more specialized and less well known groups, which work in their own way to advance basic human rights.

It is an unfortunate comment that, at least in the foreseeable future, this book will never lose its timeliness. Note: This book was sent for review with the implication that it is a Young People's Book. It would, however, be of interest only to very mature adolescents.

Peter Haney, in a review of "The Human Rights Book," in Best Sellers, *Vol. 39, No. 11, February, 1980, p. 433.*

ALL TIMES, ALL PEOPLES: A WORLD HISTORY OF SLAVERY (1980)

Meltzer discusses slavery as a part of world history, showing how it developed from economic situations and desire for power. Using examples from Egypt, Rome, China, and other cultures, as well as the United States, he explains how slavery affected society and the life of the individual slave. Parallels are drawn between events such as the rebellions of Spartacus against Rome and Nat Turner in Virginia in 1831, with the result that readers will understand how slavery fits into the total picture of world history. Meltzer also discusses modern slavery in the African Muslim world and in labor camps. Meltzer writes in a beautifully clear style making a difficult subject understandable and interesting. . . . The book ends with an excellent list of fiction and nonfiction for further reading. There is little else that looks at slavery world-wide, and it is a fine introduction for readers younger than Meltzer's usual audience.

Jane E. Gardner, in a review of "All Times, All Peoples: A World History of Slavery," in School Library Journal, *Vol. 27, No. 2, October, 1980, p. 149.*

[Meltzer's] discussion of how we can get rid of slavery emphasizes laws against it and mentions that richer nations helping poorer nations "could make a difference too"—which doesn't come close to addressing the issues. As a history, though, this younger, easier summary clearly benefits from the author's having researched and thought out the subject for his substantial two-volume ***Slavery*** (1972). Here that information is neither condensed nor skimmed, but assimilated into a strong introduction that makes its points unemotionally with descriptions and examples.

A review of "All Times, All Peoples: A World History of Slavery," in Kirkus Reviews, *Vol. XLVIII, No. 20, October 15, 1980, p. 1358.*

Meltzer, fine historian and writer that he is, takes the pertinent facts and weaves them into a narrative that brings concepts and events within the range of the elementary student. His theme is in the title, supported by a close reading of historical patterns. The index and annotated bibliography add to the value. Why inject into so fine a work conflicting and confusing statements as the following: "It was Christopher Columbus who started the American slave trade" (p. 16), followed by ". . . they [the Europeans] also found slavery among the Native Americans when they sailed along the coasts of North and South America"? [Leonard Everett] Fisher's dark art matches the text in power. (p. 341)

Ruth M. Stein, in a review of "All Times, All Peoples: A World History of Slavery," in Language Arts, *Vol 58, No. 3, March, 1981, pp. 340-41.*

There is at least one historical un-truth in [this] book—giving "Hebrew" slaves credit for building the pyramids!

Of course, what most attracted my attention was [Meltzer's] treatment of the slave trade of Africans to various locations in the world. Meltzer does note that the trade of Africans was the first slave system in the world predicated on racism and hatred. Unlike other societies there was no opportunity for slaves to mix into larger society, without prejudice and discrimination. He also cites the fact that America's peculiar institution found unashamed support in the church (Catholic and otherwise), the government (and its slave-owning founding fathers) and society's upper crust. Meltzer does not, however, give enough detailed attention to the inhuman conditions of the Middle Passage and the savage treatment that Africans received upon their arrival in the U.S. Nor does he mention the motivation for separating families and forbidding Africans to keep their names and speak their languages. Children need to hear the grisly tales and understand the twisted mind-set that would conceive this particular brand of involuntary servitude and perpetuate it for so long. Meltzer does, however, mention Denmark Vesey and Nat Turner.

All in all, given the intent of the book as stated in the first paragraph, Meltzer does an adequate job of presenting a "world" history of slavery. However, since we, Africans in America, have been (and continue to be) the greatest victims of so heinous a system as slavery—American style, any discussion of that time must be from a frame of reference which sensitively takes into account the lasting effects of that time.

Dhamana Shauri, in a review of "All Times, All Peoples: A World History of Slavery," in Black Books Bulletin, *Vol. 7, No. 3, 1981, p. 67.*

***THE CHINESE AMERICANS* (1980)**

[Meltzer looks] at the problems, achievements, and living patterns of the Chinese men (and, at first, the very few women) who have come to the United States. Based on intensive and extensive research, carefully organized, written in a serious tone that forsakes objectivity only when the author protests prejudice, this is a beautifully knit and comprehensive book. It describes the life of the Chinese immigrant in towns, cities, and mining camps; the harsh distinction between the valor and diligence of railroad workers and the contumely with which they were treated; it explains the patterns of organized groups and family relations within the Chinese community, and cites the discriminatory legislation that made life so difficult and that fostered open persecution. The book concludes with a brief discussion of what life is like for Chinese Americans today, and includes a bibliography and an index.

Zena Sutherland, in a review of "The Chinese Americans," in Bulletin of the Center for Children's Books, *Vol. 34, No. 5, January, 1981, p. 98.*

When I received ***The Chinese Americans,*** my conditioned initial reaction was that it would probably be another poorly researched, poorly thought out and uncritical book about the history of Chinese in the U.S. To my pleasant surprise, I found the book quite good and thoroughly engaging.

Meltzer is not only a competent social historian with an impressive number of books to his name; he is also a very good writer who presents material in a way that is far from dry and boring. Instead of giving the usual chronology—*i.e.*, the immigration, what the Chinese did first, what they did second, and so on—Meltzer begins with the only bit of knowledge most non-Chinese Americans know about this neglected history. What did the Chinese build? Of course: The Chinese built the railroads. By dealing with the obvious Meltzer draws his readers into a fascinating reconstruction of this monumental project. The reader then quickly realizes, "Gee, I didn't know that." Meltzer goes on to discuss Chinese miners, farmers, fishermen and a number of other "I-didn't-know-that" occupations.

One chapter deals with where Chinese immigrants came from by discussing the history of relations between the West and China. Meltzer displays a fair knowledge of the difficult conditions within China which prompted much immigration, and he discusses the imposition of Western imperial powers upon the weak Manchu dynasty. Throughout, China is treated with understanding and respect.

The book's most effective chapter, "Pictures in the Air," examines the very difficult problems of cultural stereotypes of Chinese and Chinese Americans. Meltzer talks about his own childhood images and misunderstandings of Chinese and he writes frankly about learning the chant, "Chink, Chink, Chinaman sitting on a rail/Along comes a white man and cuts off his tail. . . ." He discusses how he came to realize that stereotypes distorted his understanding. Instead of moralizing about racism, the author carefully shows how stereotypes are all around us in the media, in jokes, in stories passed down for generations. This gives the reader concrete examples of racism in U.S. culture.

Two things bothered me. The first is relatively minor, but worth raising. A photograph shows a Chinese woman dressed in ornate holiday attire walking on a sidewalk. (Although it is not mentioned, the photograph was taken by Arnold Genthe in San Francisco before the 1906 earthquake.) The caption states that this woman had bound feet in "accordance to Chinese custom." First of all, the woman's feet are *not* bound, as evidenced by the type of shoes she is wearing and the fact that she is walking about unaided by an attendant. Secondly, Chinese custom did not dictate that all Chinese women have their feet bound. Binding became fashionable as a sign of femininity and beauty much as very high heels with pointy toes have again become fashionable in Western high fashion, but it was primarily the well-to-do whose feet were bound. Imagine a book on the U.S. with a photograph of a debutante ball captioned: "A rite of passage for U.S. women in accordance with Western custom." A more significant reservation I have is Meltzer's overuse of the word Chinese. It is difficult in such condensed histories to include the names of individual Chinese people. Nevertheless, constant referrals to a monolithic Chinese people do not help the reader to identify with individuals; they also encourage blanket statements about a whole people, such as "All Chinese are hard working." I have often been guilty of this same tendency when I want to make a general point; the solution is to be specific and give examples of actual situations. In order to give names to the people, a great deal of additional historical research in the field of Asian American studies is necessary.

It isn't often that a book for young readers is as well researched as this one. Meltzer manages to combine informed historical knowledge with a great deal of sensitivity for his readers and for Chinese Americans. The end product is a book with intelligence and feeling. It should be noted that this is a state-of-the-art book: it offers some of the best current scholarship, but it also means that current scholarship is far from where it should be, and a great deal more primary, nitty-gritty research is necessary to give names to the many faces and statistics that can now only be described as "the Chinese."

John Tchen, in a review of "The Chinese Americans," in Interracial Books for Children Bulletin, *Vol. 12, No. 1, 1981, p. 17.*

The low visibility of Chinese culture and contributions is driven home in Meltzer's opening gambit of asking who's missing from the official photograph of the completion of the transcontinental railroad. . . . The view of the Chinese today is not all rosy; Meltzer says that while a comfortable middle class has developed, there is still exploitation, often of Chinese by Chinese, that is abetted by government laxity in enforcing nondiscrimination laws. The author's personable style keeps his reportage moving nicely. Well-chosen detail and primary-source quotes drive points home effectively. A smooth introduction that probes harder than most at interlocking factors that shaped Chinese-American experience. . . . (p. 811)

Denise M. Wilms, in a review of "The Chinese Americans," in Booklist, *Vol. 77, No. 12, February 15, 1981, pp. 810-11.*

***THE HISPANIC AMERICANS* (1982)**

Meltzer gives us the most forthright treatment yet of the force behind Hispanic-American immigration: namely, the devastating effect on the Mexican, Cuban, and Puerto Rican economies of European colonialism and later US government and business practices. He shows how American sugar corporations and tax policy reduced Puerto Rico to an island of poverty; states that "The Mexican war was fought for no reason but to grab land that would expand slave territory"; and is tactful on the Cuban immigration: "Middle- and upper-class Cubans had the most to lose under Castro, so naturally they were the ones who wanted to emigrate." . . . Meltzer describes the wretched conditions of farm workers, somewhat alleviated by the union movement, that are better known to YA readers, and the effective slave labor system that traps illegals. He emphasizes that the Hispanic-American experience is not uniform: In New York, Hispanic-Americans have revitalized Jackson Heights, where newsstands sell papers from Bogota, Buenos Aires, Guayaquil, and Santo Domingo; yet in Spanish Harlem, an older Puerto Rican community, "the people live poorly." Their very numbers make their problem urgent: one in four New Yorkers is of Hispanic origin, as is 28 percent of the Los Angeles population and 40 percent of Miami's; and this group is growing nearly four times as fast as that of all others in the nation. To these facts and descriptions Meltzer adds an earnest chapter, similar to that in his ***Chinese Americans*** (1981), on the folly and evils of racial stereotypes and discrimination. He ends with the example of San Antonio's Chicano mayor, elected in 1981, and the hope that Hispanic-Americans can overcome the obstacles to organizing for political action. Essential.

A review of "The Hispanic Americans," in Kirkus Reviews, *Vol. L, No. 6, March 15, 1982, p. 351.*

In the first part of this book Meltzer describes the political, economic and social conditions in Puerto Rico, Cuba and Mexico that have made it necessary for many Hispanics to immigrate to the United States. He accurately describes the lack of employment opportunities in Puerto Rico, the "chronic problems of ineffective management" and "rigid bureaucracy" in Cuba and the poverty in Mexico. In the second part Meltzer gets carried away with the issues of discrimination and racism. He blames all the problems of Hispanics in the U.S. on the fact that people "have discriminated against one ethnic minority after another throughout the history of this country." He states that what Hispanic Americans are up against is much more than racism practiced by individuals: "It is institutionalized racism. . . ." Meltzer also discusses the complex and controversial issues of bilingual education and illegal immigration and, unfortunately, repeats the popular misconception that the "Spanish language spoken today among Puerto Ricans differs from that spoken among Chicanos or Cubans." (Would he state that the English language spoken today among Americans differs from that spoken among Englishmen or Canadians?)

Isabel Schon, in a review of "The Hispanic Americans," in School Library Journal, *Vol. 28, No. 8, April, 1982, p. 84.*

This is better balanced in coverage than *Coming to America from Mexico, Cuba, and Puerto Rico* by Susan Garver and Paula McGuire . . . and more analytical in exploring issues such as bilingual education; it is at times more sympathetic than objective, and provides a less extensive bibliography. Like the Garver and McGuire book, this has been carefully researched and includes a list of sources as well as an index. Like all of Meltzer's work, this is solid, thoughtful writing.

Zena Sutherland, in a review of "The Hispanic Americans," in Bulletin of the Center for Children's Books, *Vol. 36, No. 4, December, 1982, p. 74.*

The Hispanic Americans by Milton Meltzer is the one exception to the dismal picture [of Puerto Rico in children's nonfiction]. This book stands head and shoulders above the others because of its perspective. Although other books contain more detailed information, Meltzer tackles what others ignore: stereotypes, oppression and racism, among other issues. Not only are these issues identified but they are discussed in a forthright yet understandable way. One of the few books which runs counter to the "blame the victim" philosophy, ***The Hispanic Americans*** gives young people a sense of the exploitation suffered by Puerto Ricans under the U.S. flag, both here and in Puerto Rico. It also gives hard facts on such issues as unemployment and Operation Bootstrap, plus an accurate description of bilingual education and its support among Puerto Ricans.

Sonia Nieto, in a review of "The Hispanic Americans," in Interracial Books for Children Bulletin, *Vol. 14, Nos. 1 & 2, 1983, p. 14.*

THE JEWISH AMERICANS: A HISTORY IN THEIR OWN WORDS, 1650-1950 (1982)

[***The Jewish Americans: A History in Their Own Words*** is a] thoughtful and well-researched book. . . . From a soldier's account of a skirmish with the British in 1776 to a description of an American Jew's life on a contemporary kibbutz in Israel, a wide spectrum of experience is reflected, both American and specifically Jewish. A Jewish slave trader ordering his captain to be particularly "'careful of your vessel and slaves, and be as frugal as possible'" is counterbalanced by a rebel who joined John Brown's anti-slavery forces. . . . Almost every passage resounds with a will to survive, a passion for education, and a shrewd and ready wit. One finds greed and arrogance but also intense loyalty to causes—labor unions, women's rights or, above all, the retention of a Jewish identity. The author provides enough historical background to orient his readers, but it is the lively immediacy of his examples which will remain, as he wisely lets his witnesses speak for themselves. (pp. 531-32)

Ethel R. Twichell, in a review of "The Jewish Americans: A History in Their Own Words, 1650-1950," in The Horn Book Magazine, *Vol. LVIII, No. 5, October, 1982, pp. 531-32.*

Excerpts from letters, journals, books, documents, and assorted other sources provide a varied, firsthand look at Jewish experience in America from colonial times to 1950 when Holocaust survivors made their way to the U.S. The accounts range from the vivid to the mundane and cut across all classes—and thus offer a well-rounded composite that implicitly communicates the similarity of Jewish settlement with those of other ethnic groups. Yet Jewish ethnicity is not sacrificed and the perspective sheds light on negative elements such as discrimination and anti-Semitism. Meltzer offers commentary before each, helping to clarify context or define perspective by illuminating the times contemporary to the writing. Living history is inherently interesting for its focus on people rather than events, and that rule holds true here; this is a first-rate introduction to Jewish American history and a fine complement to the author's other examinations of various groups who helped build America.

Denise M. Wilms, in a review of "The Jewish American: A History in Their Own Words," in Booklist, *Vol. 79, No. 5, November 1, 1982, p. 372.*

Meltzer lets the Jewish Americans speak for themselves. They share with the reader the common experiences of their daily lives, including humor and tragedy, and relate their feelings about life in the United States. Included in the collection are familiar people such as Haym Solomon, Lillian Wald, Emma Goldman, Charles Angoff, Yuri Suhl and Alfred Kazin. Also incuded are a diary entry by a nameless Jewish peddler scratching out a living in 1842, a formal letter dated 1832 protesting an anti-Semitic remark by Henry Clay, and a passionate plea for women's rights by Ernestine Rose in an 1852 speech. The book is arranged chronologically and one wishes for more exact dating of some of the later entries (i.e., Suhl and Kazin). The introduction to each selection is pertinent, placing the individual in a historical perspective. The book has multiple curriculum uses and will be a welcome addition to any library. Interesting historical photographs and a comprehensive index add to the book's usefulness.

Amy Kellman, in a review of "The Jewish Americans: A History in Their Own Words 1650-1950," in School Library Journal, *Vol. 29, No. 5, January, 1983, p. 86.*

Any collection of brief excerpts—and particularly one like this, which runs from colonial times to the postwar era in fewer than 200 pages—is all too easy to condemn on grounds of omission. It does seem fair to point out, however, that the plan of the book allots only two selections to the 1945-50 period. . . .

In general, the experiences of those who define their Jewish identity through religious practice get short shrift here, though it must be said that the Jewish contribution to social justice and civil liberties is Mr. Meltzer's primary focus. Here he performs the highest function of the anthologist, including not just the names familiar from every textbook survey—Asser Levy, Ernestine Rose—but a tantalizing selection of readings, scholarly sources and memoirs.

Joyce Milton, in a review of "The Jewish Americans," in The New York Times Book Review, *February 20, 1983, p. 25.*

This excellent anthology shows the diversity of the American Jewish experience. . . . Because this is a small, although handsomely illustrated, volume, Meltzer omits much, most notably material on the variety of organizations created by American Jewry. While historians will appreciate the records Meltzer has culled from state historical societies, the author's general introductions and short selections are designed for a young audience. Consequently, while individual documents are suitable for the college classroom, the anthology as a whole is beneath most university students.

Pamela S. Nadell, in a review of "The Jewish Americans: A History in Their Own Words, 1650-1950," in Religious Studies Review, *Vol. 10, No. 2, April, 1984, p. 190.*

THE TRUTH ABOUT THE KU KLUX KLAN (1982)

The story of the Ku Klux Klan is a nightmare, and this book does a very fine job of examining and demystifying the bizzare history of a strange and dangerous cult. The author makes readers reflect on what the existence of the Klan means to all of us; it is growing now, and finding sympathizers throughout the world. Meltzer is one of the best social historians writing for children, and he somehow manages to maintain an admirable objectivity while listing in detail the atrocities done in the name of white supremacy. A final chapter on what can be done and a bibliography remind readers that the final challenge is left up to each individual. What we know about can't truly hurt us.

Terry Lawhead, in a review of "The Truth about the Ku Klux Klan," in School Library Journal, *Vol. 29, No. 3, November, 1982, p. 102.*

In this hard-hitting anti-Klan book, Meltzer looks at the origins of the organization and why it has risen to prominence four different times in our country's history. His basic theme—that the Klan stands for violence or the threat of violence—is brought home as he discusses some of the appallingly sadistic crimes (whippings, castrations, murder) perpetrated against those viewed as Klan enemies—blacks, Jews, and Catholics, to name the most prominent. One chapter, in which Meltzer lists a selective catalog of 50 Klan-connected incidents of violence since 1977, is especially moving because it is so starkly presented and stripped of emotions, arguments, and counterarguments. Statements such as, "They spill the same racist garbage their grandfathers did in the 1920's . . ." leave no doubt as to where Meltzer is coming from. Some of the solutions he seems to support, such as a law that would ban groups who teach and advocate violence, are controversial (that law was opposed by the ACLU); but in any case, he gives fair hearing to both sides on that question, and only rarely are his own views obtrusive throughout an excellent discussion of a provocative subject.

Ilene Cooper, in a review of "The Truth about the Ku Klux Klan," in Booklist, *Vol. 79, No. 9, January 1, 1983, p. 619.*

THE TERRORISTS (1983)

Always rational and objective in tone, Meltzer begins his study with an examination of the history of terrorism, from the assassins of ancient times onward. The book focuses on the western world but is not restricted to it; in covering the various terrorist movements of the past and present, it gives balanced coverage and adheres cohesively to the proposition that terrorism is a policy of intimidation, a policy usually used for political struggle, in which the advancing technology of the centuries has created new methods of violence rather than new concepts. The final chapter is on the moral issues involved in the use of force and violence in a thoughtful discussion of whether or not the end does justify the means. A serious book, carefully researched, organized, and written, this is more up-to-date than Robert Liston's *Terrorism* . . . and better written and balanced in treatment than [Jonathan Harris's *The New Terrorism*]. . . . A lengthy bibliography and an index are included.

Zena Sutherland, in a review of "The Terrorists," in Bulletin of the Center for Children's Books, *Vol. 37, No. 2, October, 1983, p. 33.*

Political terrorism without equivocation. . . . "How common is political terrorism? How far back does it go? Is it a worldwide phenomenon?" Beginning, expertly, by putting thoughts in the reader's mind, Meltzer proceeds first to define political terrorism: "the exploitation of a state of intense fear, caused by the systematic use of violent means by a party or group, to get into power or to maintain power.'' He also notes, importantly, that ''terrorism has become the weapon of many different ideologies (from extreme right to extreme left), religions, ethnic groups, nationalists.'' Then, he recounts the activites of terrorist groups from the 11th-century Muslim Assassins (whence of course, the word) through the French Revolution to: Russian anarchism (Bakunin, Nechayev, Herzen, Sophia Perovskaya and the assassination of Alexander II); ''Terrorism, American Style'' (the Reconstruction Klan, imported anarchism); the Irish ''Troubles''; the Irgun, and Palestinian-Jewish terrorism; the Palestinian-Arab terrorist network; Uruguay's Tupamaros and systematic terrorism; the Baader-Meinhof gang; Italy's Red Brigades; the Weather Underground; and spot outcroppings today. Again and again, Meltzer notes misgivings, miscarriages, splits—concluding the Irish chapter, for example, with a strong anti-Sinn Fein statement by Conor Cruise O'Brien (and incorporating into the Palestinian-Jewish chapter Weizmann's opposition). But he saves his strongest arguments for the finale—enlisting revolutionaries Emma Goldman and Alexander Herzen to testify against ''the end justifying the means,'' or ''sanctifying crimes by faith in some remote utopia.'' Brisk, knowledgeable, incisive.

A review of ''The Terrorists,'' in Kirkus Reviews, *Juvenile Issue, Vol. LI, No. 21, November 1, 1983, p. J213.*

Mr. Meltzer provides the reader with an interesting story of political groups who advocated the use of terror and violence for what they believed were legitimate ends.

Senior high school students should find Meltzer's method of presentation readable and stimulating for a number of reasons. First of all, the language is clean and straightforward. Secondly, Meltzer places each terrorist group within a historical and political context and attempts to explain their motives and goals without over simplifying. Third, although he discusses many disparate groups and individuals, he succeeds in showing their common error: the belief that acts of terrorism are justifiable means to achieve political ends. I should quickly note that this book is not a chronicle of good guys and villains, but rather a presentation of the dilemmas people confront in the presence of injustice and political wrong doing. . . .

The bibliography is adequate.

John Gasiorowski, in a review of ''The Terrorists,'' in Best Sellers, *Vol. 43, No. 11, February, 1984, p. 431.*

Some of the more interesting passages in ***The Terrorists*** are about women, particularly Sophia Perovskaya, one of those hung for killing the tsar in 1881. Unlike the stereotype of the terrorists, Sophia is sympathetic: ''She had the secret support of her mother, and the comradeship of young women who felt themselves joined together like a family.'' Though Sophia believed she stood for the people's interest, the tsar's death brought only ''further repression and reaction.''

Meltzer is a greatly respected writer of social history for young readers; his views are moderate. Yet his assertions about the terrorist activities of Americans, including the Pinkertons and the Klan, are not the kind that students are likely to read in American history textbooks today. Meltzer's belief that American support of authoritarian regimes in Latin America, Indonesia, the Philippines, and elsewhere has led to the growth of terrorism, though echoed in the editorial pages of our newspapers, is rarely heard in school libraries and classrooms. I recommend ***The Terrorists*** because it is absorbing, responsibly written, and exceptional among books written for teenagers. (p. 23)

Mary Lou Burket, ''Terrorism History,'' in New Directions for Women, *Vol. 13, No. 6, November-December, 1984, pp. 19, 23.*

***THE BLACK AMERICANS: A HISTORY IN THEIR OWN WORDS, 1619-1983* (1984)**

A fiercely arresting study of black American history in its original three-volume edition, ***In Their Own Words: a History of the American Negro, 1619-1865; 1865-1916; 1916-1966*** . . . , this revision is even stronger. Thirty pages of events between 1966 and 1983 have been added and material has been consolidated. While the wide episodic scope of the original books remains, the single volume is a tighter overview. One of the strengths of this title is its internal diversity. The eloquent ''well knowns'' from Gustavus Vassa to W. E. B. DuBois, from Langston Hughes to Maya Angelou are here alongside the ''regular'' people whose lives, too, comprise a part of black history. ***The Black Americans*** is a primary source history, utilizing letters, diaries, journals, speeches, newpapers, pamphlets and testimonies to give an almost collage-like picture of black history. The writing varies as does the language of each piece: there are poets, academic migrant workers and sharecroppers. Libraries owning the original three-volume edition may wish to consider the convenience of an updated one-volume edition; those who do not have the original will definitely want to consider this one.

Gale P. Jackson, in a review of ''The Black Americans: A History in Their Own Words 1619-1983,'' in School Library Journal, *Vol. 31, No. 4, December, 1984, p. 93.*

Emphasis in ***The Black Americans*** is on episodes that provide enlightenment about the lives and thoughts of its subjects. Because of the personal nature of the selections, the reader has a sense of ''being there,'' of viewing life through the eyes of participants; and of sharing the degradations, triumphs, burdens, and precedent-setting successes of both well-known and anonymous people.

The Black Americans is a valuable reference for junior high and high school students. Careful editing of the documents has made them readable without taking away their individuality; in addition, prints and photographs enhance the text and provide further insight into the Black experience. Unlike many collections of documents, this book has an excellent index making it possible for readers to locate people, events, and topics easily.

Helen Richardson, in a review of ''The Black Americans: A History in Their Own Words,'' in The Social Studies, *Vol. 76, No. 2, March-April, 1985, p. 95.*

This is Meltzer's condensation of his excellent three-volume ***In Their Own Words***. . . . Meltzer's introductions set each piece in context and help link them into a continuous history.

In shortening the work Meltzer again demonstrates his editorial skill, producing a book that is powerful, useful, and infectiously readable. His great service has been to make available historical documents previously restricted to use by scholars.

A review of "The Black Americans: A History in Their Own Words," in English Journal, *Vol. 74, No. 7, November, 1985, p. 91.*

***A BOOK ABOUT NAMES: IN WHICH CUSTOM, TRADITION, LAW, MYTH, HISTORY, FOLKLORE, FOOLERY, LEGEND, FASHION, NONSENSE, SYMBOL, TABOO HELP EXPLAIN HOW WE GOT OUR NAMES AND WHAT THEY MEAN* (1984)**

This is a potpourri of facts, with—in no discernible arrangement—a page or two devoted to each brief, topical treatment of names. It includes information about origins, meanings, legends, fads, customs, taboos, formal decrees about naming children, etc. Not weighty, and much of the material is in other, similar books for adults, but it's a good browsing book, and there's something in it to intrigue most readers.

Zena Sutherland, in a review of "A Book about Names," in Bulletin of the Center for Children's Books, *Vol. 38, No. 4, December, 1984, p. 71.*

Meltzer has redirected his talent from writing award-winning ethnic works to dabbling in onomastics. This title, targeted for casual readers, contains a haphazard assortment of miscellaneous information on surnames, given names and nicknames. Each entry, one or two pages in length, has a separate heading, a black-and-white cartoon [by Mischa Richter] and a few sentences about how names evolved and what they mean. An index and an appendix of famous names used in the text are included. While the cartoons may attract prospective readers, the meager content is insufficient to appeal to the intended age group. A much more comprehensive and better organized title is *The Guinness Book of Names* (Guinness, 1983) by Leslie Dunkling.

Cynthia K. Leibold, in a review of "A Book about Names," in School Library Journal, *Vol. 31, No. 4, December, 1984, p. 93.*

***AIN'T GONNA STUDY WAR NO MORE: THE STORY OF AMERICA'S PEACE SEEKERS* (1985)**

AUTHOR'S COMMENTARY

I was born during World War One—the war to end all wars, the war to make the world safe for democracy. A sign of how my parents felt—they were immigrants from Austro-Hungary—is a yellowed photograph I still have. It shows my older brother and me, runts trying to stand tall in army uniforms, with campaigner's hats on, and each of us clutching not a gun but a small American flag. I must have been three then, and my brother seven. We are smiling into the camera.

I was too young to absorb any discussion of the war by my elders. But soon, in my teens, I was reading the novels of disillusionment with the war—*All Quiet on the Western Front, A Farewell to Arms, The Enormous Room, Three Soldiers, Under Fire*. And non-fiction too—the tracts of the British pacifists, the exposes of the powerful war propaganda machine, the attacks upon the munition-makers, called the "merchants of death."

It was the time of the Great Depression, and many of us, born poor, struggling to get into college and remain there, but almost hopeless about ever finding a job once we graduated, were ripe for cynicism about the world the older generation was running for their benefit, not ours. We were convinced they had made a terrible mess of both politics and economics, bringing down upon us innocents both war and depression.

Still, when the newborn Spanish Republic was attacked by General Franco and his fascist allies, Hitler and Mussolini, those of us radicalized by the times swung passionately towards support of the battle to save democracy in Spain. Some pocketed their pacifism and volunteered for the International Brigades fighting to make Madrid the tomb of fascism. Others, often members of the traditional peace churches, abided by their deep beliefs while they did all they could to resist fascism at home and abroad by nonviolent means.

Franco won, and the Second World War began a few months later. My observation was that most Americans disliked Hitler and Mussolini for what little they knew of them, but few were eager to shoulder arms against them. When Hitler's armies overran Western Europe and then in 1941 invaded Russia it made folks at home nervous, but still not hot to shed blood. The Japanese attack upon Pearl Harbor changed the feeling overnight. I went into the Air Force, a 27-year-old now, and called an old man by my barracks mates, most of them 18 or 19. I spent 42 months in the control tower, helping to train fighter and bomber pilots. Then a few years of relative peace, interrupted by the Korean War. And not long after that the longest war ever for us—in Vietnam. Four major American wars in my lifetime—so far.

Which makes me think that for a country with a rather short history ours has done quite a bit of fighting. We have taken part in seven officially declared wars. And without the approval of Congress, we have sent our armed forces beyond our borders over 165 times. That comes close to one military intervention per year since the U.S. was founded.

At the beginning of this paper I mentioned some of the anti-war novels I read as a teenager. But did any of the books assigned us in school speak out against war? I can't recall any. They had plenty to say about war, but always to justify or even glorify it. Military heroes studded the histories and biographies but what book held up a peace-seeker as an example to follow?

My school years are ancient history. But are the books on the school library shelves much different today? What non-fiction titles there may be on anti-war themes are far outweighed by the others. I've tried to do something to begin correcting that imbalance. My new book, called ***Ain't Gonna Study War No More,*** is directed to young adults. It's the story of the peace-seekers in America, from colonial times to today. It goes into the various kinds of anti-war movements we've known, both religious and secular, and the remarkable men and women who've risked their jobs, their property, their personal safety and freedom, and even their lives to resist war.

I don't take up all this in abstraction. No—the book looks at all the real wars we've fought: the French and Indian, the Revolution, the War of 1812, the Mexican War, the Civil War, the Spanish American War, and the two World Wars, Korea, Vietnam, and Central America. How did these wars happen? What people resisted them and why? (pp. 21-2)

The peace-seekers are of many kinds. They have taken different paths to carry out their commitment. But there is a common core to their beliefs and acts. They denounce war because it destroys life, corrupts society and violates morality. And from that conviction they work to develop other means of resolving human conflicts and building social harmony so that peace might flower and endure. In other words, they do not simply oppose war: they try to make peace.

Most of the immigrants who came to America with pacifist principles belonged in their homeland to Christian sects that opposed war on religious grounds.

In the Sermon on the Mount, Jesus develops the ethic of nonviolence and love of enemies. "Blessed are the peacemakers: for they shall be called the children of God." And, he told Peter, "All they that take the sword shall perish with the sword" (Matthew 26:52). These last words are taken to mean that violence is futile in the long run. To meet violence with violence is only to perpetuate a cycle of violence that imprisons us.

Scholars believe the early Christians were probably the first individuals to renounce participation in war unconditionally. (p. 22)

It was late in the fourth century that the classic Christian idea of the "just war" was developed. It began with St. Augustine (354-430 A.D.). He held the traditional view that the individual Christian was barred from violence on his own behalf. But, he argued, defense of one's own community was a different matter. Even in this case the command to love one's enemies even in battle was a solemn obligation to Christian faith. An attempt was made to set up standards for deciding which wars were right and which wrong. Over the centuries the theory was developed and refined.

As many theologians now hold, the standards for a just war are seven: 1) War must be the last resort and used only after all other means have failed. 2) War must be declared to redress rights actually violated or for defense against unjust demands backed by the threat of force. It must not be fought simply to satisfy national pride or to further economic or territorial gain. 3) The war must be openly and legally declared by a legal government. 4) There must be a reasonable chance of winning. 5) The means used must be in proportion to the ends sought. 6) Soldiers must distinguish between armies and civilians and not kill civilians on purpose. 7) The winner must not require the utter humiliation of the loser.

It can be debated whether any war has ever satisfied all these reasonable conditions. (p. 23)

Throughout my book I focus on the dissenters from America's wars, the reasons they refused to fight, the punishments dealt out to them, the attempts after the blood stopped flowing to estimate whether the wars cost more in human life and treasure than the results claimed for them. Here different scales of values come into play, and these I discuss too. Usually by letting the advocates of the varying views speak for themselves. (p. 24)

As for those who think a modern war is possible that meets the criteria of the just war theory, there is this simple and often quoted declaration by Pope John XXIII in *Pacem in Terris:* "In this age of ours which prides itself on its atomic power, it is irrational to believe that war is still an apt means of vindicating violated rights."

Since those words were said the world has edged ever closer to the brink of a nuclear holocaust, an absolutely evil human-made catastrophe, beyond any experience in history. With a power rising out of the development of scientific knowledge and its technological use, man can destroy life itself, and make the earth uninhabitable.

With that unbearable prospect in mind, does it matter much if you or I or anyone else decides to become a conscientious objector? Not in the sense that our personal refusal to fight will prevent the killing of others. For before armies could be ordered into action the signal could be given for nuclear missiles to wipe out hundreds of millions of human beings. But the truth about modern war only underscores the need for nonviolent resisters to muster all their strength, intelligence and imagination to find practical ways to end the possibility of nuclear extinction. (p. 25)

[Happily] for the pursuit of peace, a sizeable part of the American public no longer stays silent when it sees its government make mistakes in foreign policy. They react to the danger of repeating past errors. They know American leaders can be guilty of intrigue, deception, secretiveness, lawlessness. They learned that dissent has its positive side and should never be crushed. It was only when dissent over Vietnam rolled high enough to reach into Congress and change many minds there that the policy of presidents was obliged to change. We rediscovered the old belief that the truth will make us free. We must continue to say how we see things, and speak out for what we believe. (p. 26)

Milton Meltzer, "Freedom and Peace: A Challenge," in Catholic Library World, *Vol. 56, No. 1, July-August, 1984, pp. 21-6.*

Meltzer's study of pacifism is a kind of alternative history of the U.S. that looks at the important wars from the point of view not of the generals and policymakers but of those individuals and organized groups who refused to fight. Moving chronologically from the revolutionary war to Vietnam, Meltzer traces the beginning of the modern peace movement in early religious groups, most notably the Quakers, and in various secular movements involved in direct, nonviolent mass action. He focuses on principled people of courage throughout history who were persecuted, sometimes even killed, for their pacifist beliefs. In clear, informal style and spacious format, his survey shows that the pacifists were frequently split over issues like the nonpayment of taxes, and over the concept of a "just" war, particularly on whether to fight in the war against slavery and in World War II against fascism. Concluding with a call for peaceful negotiation in Central America today, and for a halt in the arms race in the face of imminent nuclear disaster, Meltzer is openly partisan, urging readers to learn from history and courageously oppose the false heroism of war: "We can make a difference." An inspiring book, sure to stimulate discussion on its particular causes and on the nature of patriotism and glory.

Hazel Rochman, in a review of "Ain't Gonna Study War No More," in Booklist, *Vol. 81, No. 17, May 1, 1985, p. 1248.*

An extraordinary and important service to the cause of peace has been made by Milton Meltzer in presenting the history of civil disobedience. His account is illuminating, exciting and inspiring. It illuminates the theories, thoughts and deeds of generations of heroes who bravely rejected all violence or who rejected participation in particular wars they considered unjust. It excites readers by recounting how many young people suffered and sacrificed on behalf of peace principles. It inspires youth (and old folks like me) to take action against the death dealers of today. . . .

[The] book's usefulness goes beyond its being a superb resource for American History or Peace courses. It is uniquely valuable for thinking people *of all ages* who must come to terms with their own responsibilities and actions when faced by governmental power they deem mad, evil or irresponsible. I urge you to buy copies for your local library, local school—and local or long-distance young friends.

Lyla Hoffman, in a review of "Ain't Gonna Study War No More," in Interracial Books for Children Bulletin, *Vol. 16, No. 4, 1985, p. 19.*

In ***Ain't Gonna Study War No More*** . . . , Milton Meltzer provides a series of character sketches of historical figures opposed to war. While most of the persons identified as heroes and heroines in this volume are taken from United States history, passing references are made to figures from the ancient world and from other cultures. . . . Throughout the volume, the same message is conveyed—that conscientious men and women of principle have been found throughout history who have refused to participate in, or contribute to, the making of war even when severe consequences of fines, imprisonment, or even death have resulted.

Unfortunately, Meltzer makes little effort to balance his portraits of the pacifists and conscientious objectors. The difficult philosophical questions about duty to society and the common good when that society is threatened with extinction by force are either ignored or passed over as being largely irrevelant in face of an individual's determination that war is an unacceptable option. For the young reader of this book, the obviously intended impression is that war is an unacceptable option for the moral man or woman.

In his concluding pages, the author suggests that people in the United States are coming together to support the position that war is no longer acceptable. He cites the nonbinding House vote in favor of a mutual, verifiable nuclear freeze; the Roman Catholic bishops' draft pastoral letter opposing nuclear war; and a scattering of local referenda concerning a nuclear freeze. Typical of his one-sided approach to the issues, however, he completely neglects to mention the landslide re-election of President Reagan who carried 49 states on a platform arguing for increased defense spending and military preparedness as the best deterrent to an unwanted military confrontation with the Soviet Union.

The book deserves a "B" classification because it makes no real effort to provide both sides to an issue which has caused serious disagreement among highly moral thinkers over the centuries. When Saint Augustine is relegated to historical irrelevancy and Russ Ford, a 1982 draft registration resister, is portrayed as a model philosophical thinker, it should be clear that ***Ain't Gonna Study War No More*** is a polemic which should be taken as such by young readers and their parents.

Robert L. Spurrier, Jr., in a review of "Ain't Gonna Study War No More," in Best Sellers, *Vol. 45, No. 4, July, 1985, p. 158.*

Meltzer's many fans will get what they have come to expect from him: a serious, thought-provoking, and comprehensive treatise that is based on careful research, is logically organized, and is written in a temperate but forceful style that is built on the author's convictions but is tempered by moderation. . . . A bibliography is included, as is an extensive relative index.

Zena Sutherland, in a review of "Ain't Gonna Study War No More: The Story of America's Peace Seekers," in Bulletin of the Center for Children's Books, *Vol. 38, No. 11, July-August, 1985, p. 211.*

In his succinct appraisal of American history as war history, award-winning social reformer Meltzer gives direct testament here to the need to change the pattern by developing peaceful resolutions to conflict.

Meltzer brings to light many startling facts unavailable in history textbooks. Since the Revolution, no war ever fought by Americans has gone uncontested by some citizens. Draft resisters' flights to Canada did not begin during the Vietnam War; 60,000 evaders preceded them during the American Revolution alone. While discussing causes and conditions of American warfare until the present day in chronological chapters, Meltzer reveals the parallel struggles of the wide variety of peace activitists which America produced in every page. . . .

[Their] stories mesh together as examples of courageous action and vision. Meltzer states his forthright opinion, backed with historical facts, that the American government has promoted warfare to further its expansionist economic interests in world power, based on the mistaken idea that the U.S. has the right to declare "right" to the rest of the world's peoples. No nonpartisan treatment here: Meltzer concludes with an eloquent plea to all Americans, especially the young, to follow the honorable tradition of dissent in working against the nuclear arms race, accepting "the responsibility of the earth's survival." . . . Meltzer's clear, provocative interpretation will disturb many, frighten some, inspire others. In all libraries it should stand alongside more traditional histories as an impetus to young people's development of their own ideas, a challenge to actively confront their own future in a world on the brink. (pp. 199-200)

Cathi Edgerton, in a review of "Ain't Gonna Study War No More," in Voice of Youth Advocates, *Vol. 8, No. 3, August, 1985, pp. 199-200.*

Through the stories of American pacifists, Meltzer paints a succinct but accurate picture of the backgrounds of the military engagements in which the U.S. has been involved as well as the effect of war on American society. While many of the names and organizations may be unfamiliar to students, this book shows that the legacy of the anti-war activists is an important part of our history and our future. Numerous reproductions expand upon the text and offer visual information not readily found elsewhere. This is Meltzer at his best, and he covers the topic of conscientious objectors factually and with style, showing that dissent can be a positive means of effecting change in both our government and in society.

Joe Bearden, in a review of "Ain't Gonna Study War No More," in School Library Journal, *Vol. 32, No. 1, September, 1985, p. 147.*

DOROTHEA LANGE: LIFE THROUGH THE CAMERA (1985)

Meltzer conveys a remarkably vivid sense of photographer Dorothea Lange within the confines of writing for middle-graders. The significant events and acquaintances in her life are sketched in with just enough detail to make them meaningful and occasionally memorable. The same can be said for Meltzer's descriptions of Lange's work. The stories behind some of her most compelling photographs insure that the images laid out will not be forgotten by a new generation of viewers. There is respect and admiration for Lange, but not adulation, and her shortcomings—including painful ones such as her difficulty in being a good parent—are noted along with her greatness. . . . A striking, humane portrait of a sensitive, driven artist.

Denise M. Wilms, in a review of "Dorothea Lange: Life through the Camera," in Booklist, *Vol. 81, No. 22, August, 1985, p. 1668.*

Distilled from Meltzer's adult biography ***Dorothea Lange: a Photographer's Life*** . . . , this book is an excellent way to introduce Lange to younger readers. . . . Meltzer recounts Lange's drive to photograph the lives of the poor during the Depression, to inform and move viewers. He conveys her obsession with, and dedication to, documentary photography, for which she became famous. Although the book is brief, Meltzer brings Lange to life and shows her as an unusual and dedicated woman. . . . Perfect for book reports "due tomorrow." (pp. 136-37)

Anitra Gordon, in a review of "Dorothea Lange: Life through the Camera," in School Library Journal, *Vol. 32, No. 1, September, 1985, pp. 136-37.*

From a teacher's point of view, Dorothea Lange is a striking subject for biography because the story includes so much worth discussing with children. She walked with a limp as a result of childhood polio, but this handicap did not keep her from success. She was a woman who had the courage to choose her own career at a time when choices seemed very limited. She cared about social and economic concerns that are very similar to issues today. And she was a remarkable older woman, a producing artist involved in significant projects until her death from cancer at age seventy. (p. 791)

Milton Meltzer has produced a readable, balanced biography without fictionalization. It is an accomplishment to make biography simple without making it simplistic. The author succeeds here by using Dorothea Lange's own gifts, a feel for the essence of the subject and an eye for revealing detail. As an early offering in Viking Kestrel's "Women of Our Time" series, this book raises high expectations for the others. (p. 792)

Janet Hickman, in a review of "Dorothea Lange: Life through the Camera," in Language Arts, *Vol. 62, No. 7, November, 1985, pp. 791-92.*

MARK TWAIN: A WRITER'S LIFE (1985)

In a biography written with wit and style, Meltzer uses quotations from Twain as well as paraphrase and anecdote to communicate the exuberant comic spirit of the man. . . . In tracing Twain's self-education and career as printer, river pilot, journalist, and, finally, lionized writer, social activist, and lecturer, Meltzer discusses the circumstances in which the great books were written, and shows how early experiences haunted Twain's imagination and came to be worked into his stories. Though warm and admiring, the biography is far from adulatory; for example, in discussing *Huck Finn* as Twain's masterpiece, Meltzer sees it as a strong voice against racism and stupid conformity; but he says that Twain, like Huck, could not always rise above the bigotry of his day. Meltzer's candor is part of his respect for his subject and reader; his writing is simple and direct, without condescension, and will entice young people to read more of Twain for themselves. Includes photographs, a bibliographical note on the man and his work, chronology, index. (pp. 214-15)

Hazel Rochman, in a review of "Mark Twain: A Writer's Life," in Booklist, *Vol. 82, No. 3, October 1, 1985, pp. 214-15.*

Within the limited format of this biography series, Meltzer has done a creditable job of presenting some of the complexities of a true non-conformist. The liveliest passages, of course, are the subject's own: "It could probably be shown by facts and figures that there is no distinctly native American criminal class except Congress." The second half of the book seems more interesting than the first, as themes based on Twain's early experiences are picked up and developed into a perspective on his work. Overall, this is reliable background for those reading the still controversial adventures of Tom Sawyer and Huckleberry Finn. (pp. 73-4)

A review of "Mark Twain: A Writer's Life," in Bulletin of the Center for Children's Books, *Vol. 39, No. 4, December, 1985, pp. 73-4.*

Fine writing and good detail help to present Mark Twain in Meltzer's new biography. . . . There's a good integration of background information—what games children of that period played, what they read, the Civil War as the young Twain saw it. However, this ***Mark Twain*** seems a bit disjointed and doesn't always flow smoothly; there are several minor inconsistencies as well as disagreements with standard adult references (including Meltzer's 1960 pictorial biography [for adults, ***Mark Twain Himself***], from which the current work borrows liberally). There is no attempt to summarize Twain's life and literary impact, although the impact of *Huck Finn* on American literature is discussed. All in all, though, it's a readable account of an interesting personage that will be useful for reports and pleasure reading.

Ann W. Moore, in a review of "Mark Twain: A Writer's Life," in School Library Journal, *Vol. 32, No. 1, December, 1985, p. 104.*

In 1985 the world celebrates the return of Halley's comet and with it the 150th anniversary of Mark Twain's birth. Milton Meltzer has given us cause for further celebration with this fine biography of Twain. The author is obviously thoroughly familiar with his subject—having previously written ***Mark Twain Himself*** . . .—and holds him in great regard. Throughout the book the subject is referred to as Mark, a name he chose, rather than Sam. Meltzer plays out the facts of Twain's life in a style that makes them read much like one of Twain's own human interest pieces. Indeed, the author intersperses excerpts from letters, speeches, and books. These excerpts are brief and well chosen to give readers a glimpse of Twain's wit and his insight into human nature. The variety of his experiences and enthusiasms are detailed in a balanced account which, though full of warmth and affection, is not overly adulatory or romanticized. Although other fine biographies of Twain are in library collections, no other biography for intermediate readers is still in print. (pp. 71-2)

Elizabeth S. Watson, in a review of "Mark Twain: A Writer's Life," in The Horn Book Magazine, *Vol. LXII, No. 1, January-February, 1986, pp. 71-2.*

BETTY FRIEDAN: A VOICE FOR WOMEN'S RIGHTS (1985)

Betty Friedan's *Feminine Mystique* is credited with reigniting the fight for women's rights in the early sixties. This succinct profile of Friedan, a journalist, mother of three, and articulate spokeswoman for women's rights, looks at her midwestern background and at the developments that led her to write that hallmark book. As usual, Meltzer carefully sketches the context of the times, showing how Friedan's wish to keep some semblance of her journalism career, even as she mothered her three children, placed her at odds with prevailing attitudes. The impact of her book and Friedan's subsequent involvement in the women's rights movement (she was a founding member and first president of NOW) are also described. Meltzer's author's note talks about his interview with Friedan and how much he admires her accomplishments; nevertheless, the tone isn't adulatory. This is a straightforward introduction to a thinker whose insights undoubtedly have made the path easier for coming generations of women.

Denise M. Wilms, in a review of "Betty Friedan: A Voice for Women's Rights," in Booklist, *Vol. 82, No. 4, October 15, 1985, p. 339.*

Meltzer effectively covers the story of Betty Friedan's life. . . . Some of the simplifications are misleading, i.e., the implication that Carl Friedan courted Betty because he needed a place to live. Milton does stress throughout that Friedan has never been *against* men, but *for* equal rights for all people. There's some good information on how the National Organization for Women started and enough history for those seeking information on women's rights, but there is no index. A book that will give thoughtful youngsters much to ponder.

Deanna J. McDaniel, in a review of "Betty Friedan: A Voice for Women's Rights," in School Library Journal, *Vol. 32, No. 4, December, 1985, p. 92.*

A readable blend of personal and social history characterizes Meltzer's brief book. . . . The tone leans to admiration without adulation; the book offers perspective with its compact summary of the times that nurtured spontaneous consciousness-raising during the late 60s and early 70s. Black-and-white pencil sketches [by Stephen Mardesi] add to an accessible text.

A review of "Betty Friedan: A Voice for Women's Rights," in Bulletin of the Center for Children's Books, *Vol. 39, No. 6, February, 1986, p. 115.*

[This book] does a good job of detailing the turning points in Betty Friedan's life, including the anti-Semitism and social ostracism in high school that made her work all the harder to achieve academically and in extracurricular activities. Unfortunately, this section is marred by a sentence which, however unintentionally, attempts to win sympathy for Betty at the expense of others: "The girls from well-to-do families like her own lumped Jews with blacks and working-class kids who lived on 'the wrong side of town.'" The same point could have been made in a more sensitive manner. Similarly, the issue of race and class bias in the women's movement could have been discussed in more detail.

Carol M. Martin, in a review of "Betty Friedan: A Voice for Women's Rights," in Interracial Books for Children Bulletin, *Vol. 17, No. 2, 1986, p. 19.*

THE JEWS IN AMERICA: A PICTURE ALBUM (1985)

[Meltzer] compresses over 300 years of Jewish history into 169 pages, resulting in some generalities and simplistic conclusions. Conservative Judaism, the major movement in American Judaism, is described briefly as "moderately Orthodox and moderately Reformed." While the volume is called a picture album, the narrative clearly dominates over the black-and-white photos—some interesting, many standard. And for a treatment of American Jewry, there's quite a bit here about the oppressive history of Jews in Europe. Eyewitness accounts of such atrocities as a pogrom in Russia or the infamous 1911 Triangle shirtwaist factory fire in New York are heartfelt, but Meltzer dwells on the negative, ignoring much of what Jews have contributed to and gained from, America.

A review of "The Jews in America: A Picture Album," in Publishers Weekly, *Vol. 229, No. 17, April 25, 1986, p. 86.*

Not really a new title, but a re-working of Meltzer's earlier book ***Remember the Days*** . . . in a larger format, and with the addition of numerous photographs. Still, despite the format, this is less of an album than the title would indicate, and with a great deal of history compressed between the pictures. As in ***Remember the Days,*** Meltzer carefully chronicles the history of Jews in America. . . . The book closes with a thoughtful discussion of Zionism, Israel, and Jewish identity. To do justice to the Jewish experience in America requires more than one relatively slim volume. Still, Meltzer does a creditable job, helped immeasurably by the excellent photographs and his own customary skillful writing. A fine addition to any library.

Ruth Levien, in a review of "The Jews in America: A Picture Album," in School Library Journal, *Vol. 33, No. 2, October, 1986, p. 179.*

POVERTY IN AMERICA (1986)

A concise and informative overview of ***Poverty in America.*** Meltzer conveys complex concepts in easily understood terms. Beginning with a poignant appeal to consider what being hungry really means (not eating for several days because there is no food money), he then explains the definition of *poor* by various standards over the years, the history of the downtrodden in America, the pendulum swings of government's attempts to eliminate poverty, the perpetual existence of unemployment and the diversity of the peoples affected. He discusses those stymied by race, by age, by sex and by economic conditions. This well-researched volume supports, through statistics and documents by government, lay people, religious leaders, physicians and economists the premise that "what we do or fail to do about poverty matters to us all." Meltzer examines an idea, cites instances which illustrate a particular theory, then substantiates his thinking with numerous citings from authorities. Many programs are looked at in terms of their success or lack of success in easing poverty's pain, and diverse opinions are given as to why people are hungry and what should or should not be done to alleviate this condition. An extensive and accessible bibliography is provided, in addition to a helpful discussion of the techniques Meltzer used to research his book. A thorough index is provided also; by including easy subject accessibility and highlighting views of noted personalities, the book's usefulness is doubled. Black-and-white illustrations, strategically located, poignantly demonstrate the despair and humiliation of lives in poverty. Not only is this book well written, but also it imparts a vast amount of information in a concise and precise form.

Jane Campbell Thornton, in a review of "Poverty in America," in School Library Journal, *Vol. 32, No. 10, August, 1986, p. 104.*

Brief, graphic overview provides up-to-date statistics as well as a heartrending array of personal portraits describing poverty in modern America. . . . While not a comprehensive work, a detailed bibliography of additional book and periodical sources has been provided for those who need additional information. . . . Most school and public libraries will want to purchase this straight-talking, compassionate introduction.

Debbie Earl, in a review of "Poverty in America," in Voice of Youth Advocates, *Vol. 9, Nos. 3 & 4, August & October, 1986, p. 178.*

PATTY CAMPBELL

[***Poverty in America***] is a marvel of succinct writing that lays bare the multi-faceted shape of economic deprival and examines its causes. This is a book that should be prominently displayed in multiple copies right now in every library in America, and the fact that it does not appear in the American Library Association's list of Best Books for Young Adults is inexplicable.

In only 112 concise and readable pages of text Meltzer anatomizes the many complex aspects of poverty in America, documenting with anecdotes and with hard figures. . . .

Meltzer's tone is calm but compassionate, even when his statistics are shocking. Occasionally, however, his anger at the insanity of poverty surfaces:

> In one year the farmers of America grow twice as much food as our country can consume. But while millions go hungry, the government builds bigger barns to store the superabundance. Is it crazy? To let people go hungry, not because there's a shortage of food, but because they can't afford to buy it? . . .

The clarity and authority of ***Poverty in America*** make it an invaluable tool in the classroom and school library and a first purchase for public libraries. It is simple enough for junior highs and important enough for all ages. (p. 51)

Patty Campbell, in a review of "Poverty in America," in Wilson Library Bulletin, *Vol. 61, No. 8, April, 1987, pp. 51.*

***WINNIE MANDELA: THE SOUL OF SOUTH AFRICA* (1986)**

A biographical essay that accords the subject a justified measure of admiration without becoming adulatory, this traces Winnie Mandela's life story with just enough factual background on the South African apartheid situation to provide structure. Her commitment to freedom from oppression for Blacks, both through her own work and her efforts on behalf of her husband Nelson, are compacted into a brief but readable form, with quotations personalizing the factual information.

Betsy Hearne, in a review of "Winnie Mandela: The Soul of South Africa," in Bulletin of the Center for Children's Books, *Vol. 40, No. 2, October, 1986, p. 32.*

Meltzer could not interview his prime source—Winnie Mandela—who continues her struggle to liberate South African blacks, but through documents he brings us her words and actions in a lively, admiring chronology. The emphasis on Mandela's early life—her upbringing, schooling, romance with and marriage to Nelson Mandela—believably sets the stage for her working against great odds, becoming "a leader in her own right." Appealing, soft, even quiet drawings [by Stephen Marchesi] call out in hopeful counterpoint to horrifying descriptions of community ostracism, police violence and deadening prison life. Young readers may be surprised to learn today's oppression has been going on for so long, in a country where, in Meltzer's words, "every black is in prison."

A review of "Winnie Mandela: The Soul of South Africa," in Publishers Weekly, *Vol. 230, No. 18, October 31, 1986, p. 74.*

Meltzer used Mandela's autobiography, *Part of My Soul Went with Him* (Norton, 1985) and other written materials as sources for this biography in which he hoped to give readers a "sense of what this magnificent woman is like." Unfortunately, he has been unable to transfer the passion and human strength of Winnie Mandela's autobiography to this book, in which facts primarily about her adult life in South Africa are presented without context. Elementary school children will lack the background to understand the facts about South African politics or to relate them to Mandela's behavior mentioned in this book. Mandela is presented primarily as a speaker of words and an occasional defier of political repression, not as a thinking, feeling human being who interacts with others. Since her personality is not developed in the biography, children will have difficulty identifying with her and understanding the reasons for her political behavior. . . . This book adds neither empathy nor understanding to the image of Winnie Mandela that is presented by the American mass media.

Nancy J. Schmidt, in a review of "Winnie Mandela: The Soul of South Africa," in School Library Journal, *Vol. 33, No. 4, December, 1986, p. 106.*

***GEORGE WASHINGTON AND THE BIRTH OF OUR NATION* (1986)**

Unlike many biographies of the first president, this reaches beyond the symbolic leader to the man in context of his times, "a victim of both ignorance and prejudice" in his relations with Native Americans, a man who "treated his slaves more as property than as people." Yet Washington's qualities of leadership do emerge as almost superhuman at times; most of his mistakes seem to have been made from inexperience in undertaking new endeavors rather than from misjudgment. In general, Meltzer does a compact job of covering an enormously complex period, from life in the colonies through the military highlights of the Revolution to the establishment of a Constitution and formation of a new government amidst fierce factions. In spite of some uncharacteristic lapses of style, as in the abrupt transition from past to present tense when Washington sets out for Boston as commander-in-chief of the rebellion, Meltzer's is a competently written and carefuly documented book. . . . (p. 72)

Betsy Hearne, in a review of "George Washington and the Birth of Our Nation," in Bulletin of the Center for Children's Books, *Vol. 40, No. 4, December, 1986, pp. 72-3.*

Drawing upon extensive research, Meltzer does an excellent job of presenting young readers with a brief overview of Washington's life and career. In a highly readable, lucid, and straightforward manner, Meltzer makes clear the reasons, from Washington's childhood and youth, for his aristocratic views that later came to be tempered with "'integrity . . . most pure [and] justice . . . most inflexible.'" In addition, Meltzer surveys the American Revolution and clearly delineates Washington's role as a reluctant leader who rose above his own doubts and lack of experience to become an able and effective commander. . . . Meltzer includes a good selection of black-and-white reproductions of paintings, engravings, etc., depicting Washington and others, and some helpful maps. A discussion of books for further reading and a useful index complete this fine summary. The book is an excellent complement to Cunliffe and Morris' *George Washington and the Making of a Nation* (American Heritage, 1966; o.p.) (pp. 120-21)

David A. Lindsey, in a review of "George Washington and the Birth of Our Nation," in School Library Journal, *Vol. 33, No. 4, December, 1986, pp. 120-21.*

Milton Meltzer's writing skill is focused on the father of our country in this brisk, interesting, and nicely illustrated biography. Dispelling myths but reinforcing the central theme of Washington's contributions, Meltzer relates incidents from Washington's life as they fit into the events of the period. The author obviously feels that Washington well deserves his place in history and cites his accomplishments, selflessness, loyalty, and abilities. Failures and flaws, such as Washington's ideas on slavery, are touched on, but the treatment is primarily positive and respectful. . . . Surprisingly few biographies of George Washington are available for intermediate and older children; Meltzer's book is closest in content and reading level to *First in Their Hearts* (Walker) by Thomas J. Fleming but is more complete and slightly more critical. The volume is a fine addition to juvenile collections in the year of the Constitution's bicentennial celebration, when attention will be focused not only on the document but also on its authors.

Elizabeth S. Watson, in a review of "George Washington and the Birth of Our Nation," in The Horn Book Magazine, *Vol. LXIII, No. 2, March-April, 1987, p. 223.*

Zibby Oneal

1934-

(Born Elizabeth Oneal) American author of fiction, picture books, and nonfiction.

Oneal is regarded as a writer of remarkable literary skill and insight into human relationships. While she has also produced light fiction for younger children as well as a biography of the painter Grandma Moses, Oneal is best known for creating perceptive novels which explore the complex, conflicting emotions of adolescence. Unlike those in much of contemporary teenage fiction, her intricate plots stress inward growth and communication rather than outward circumstance. Oneal's books portray sensitive, intellectual heroines who contend with such difficulties as insanity, rejection, and the death of a parent. Often artistic, her protagonists find escape and healing through the self-expression and discipline of painting. By learning to accept the inevitable, these young women are able to move on with renewed self-confidence and hope. Oneal's stories deal with serious emotional situations while revealing the humor, warmth, and affirmation characteristic of all her works.

Critics praise Oneal for the candor and grace with which she handles delicate subjects as well as for her memorable characters, realistic dialogue, and vivid recreation of setting. While restrained in style, her language is also noted for its precision and figurative power. Some reviewers point out that the slow pace and descriptive narratives of her books may not attract all readers; however, most observers acknowledge that Oneal's superior craftsmanship and the authentic feelings she represents both illumine the understanding of her readers and add distinction to young adult literature.

Oneal has won numerous awards for her novels including The Christopher Award in 1983 for *A Formal Feeling* and the *Boston Globe-Horn Book* Award in 1986 for *In Summer Light.*

(See also *Contemporary Literary Criticism,* Vol. 30; *Something about the Author,* Vol. 30; and *Contemporary Authors,* Vol. 106.)

Photograph by Stephen Blos. Courtesy of Zibby Oneal.

AUTHOR'S COMMENTARY

[*In the following excerpt, Wendy Smith interviews Oneal and her Viking editor, Deborah Brodie.*]

Zibby Oneal's three young adult novels for Viking exhibit a depth and complexity of feeling rare in any kind of fiction. In a close working association with Viking Kestrel senior editor Deborah Brodie, Oneal has produced books that reflect the turmoil of adolescence, in rich metaphorical language and understated plots that chart interior progress rather than external events. Their partnership is a model of the fruitful writer-editor relationship.

PW met recently with the two . . . to learn more about how this dedicated pair work together. . . .

[***The Language of Goldfish***] dealt in a sensitive and unsensational manner with the attempted suicide of Carrie Stokes, a 13-year-old girl who subsequently learns to cope with the fears that had led her to this drastic act. ***A Formal Feeling*** . . . examined the emotional legacy of a death in the family, telling the story of 16-year-old Anne Cameron, who struggles to repress the anger and guilt she feels in the wake of her mother's unexpected death. . . .

In Summer Light probes just as deeply into the psyche of a young person as Oneal's two previous works did; yet its canvas is broader, the language subtler and the perceptions more profound than ever before. As Brodie remarks, "Zibby's stretched the young adult form about as far as it can go.". . .

The affection and respect the two women feel for each other is palpable; their description of their working relationship is punctuated by laughter, jokes and general high spirits.

Those high spirits were needed during the composition of ***In Summer Light,*** which took four years to write. "I didn't know where I was going for a long time," says Oneal. "I needed to get it centered and focus on what I wanted to talk about."

Oneal's third book had a curious start. "Actually, it was part of ***A Formal Feeling,***" Brodie remembers. "That's right," adds Oneal; "for a long time *Winter* and *Summer* were the working titles."

"I have a very vivid picture of the moment when the book split," Brodie recalls. "Zibby was working on a book and she sent me the manuscript, saying, 'It's kind of ready to be worked on.' There are certain moments you always remember in a working relationship and this was one of them. It was as though somebody had handed me an orange and said, 'This is a whole orange,' and I took it and split it. It was two books: one of them was all about summer and heat and sweat and light, and the other had ice and cold and winter. I wrote to Zibby and said, '*Winter* is ready to be worked on, and *Summer* needs more time. How would you feel about a two-book contract?' *Winter* became ***A Formal Feeling,*** and *Summer* was ***In Summer Light.''*** (p. 97)

The realization that ***In Summer Light*** was a separate book didn't solve all the manuscript's problems, by any means. "When Zibby's in an early stage, she can get so caught up in details," Brodie says. "How old is Kate, for example. That was a big question. I told her, 'She'll tell you how old she is. Just write, and afterwards we can change the details if we need to.'"

"I get too involved in a story to stand back and look at it," comments Oneal. "I don't know: Have I said enough? Have I not said enough? Is this going to be clear to anyone but me? Deborah is invaluable, because she looks at it with an objective eye. It's a collaborative process."

"The first stages are the hardest for Zibby," says Brodie. "Some authors write at white heat and then revise in great pain, whereas I think she painfully gets something down and then . . ."

"Revising, that's a cakewalk," interjects Oneal.

"You work hard at it," Brodie insists.

"Well, but by then I know where I'm going," replies Oneal. "To me, what's hard is the time I wonder where on earth I'm going, if anywhere! But Deborah's very good to work with on revisions, because she's so meticulous. It would kill me to have somebody go through it in a slapdash way and say, 'This is fine.' I want that very detailed sort of editing, because that means we're really communicating about the character and the situation. That's how I write, and that's how I want to be edited."

Though they do most of their work by mail and phone, Oneal thinks that "the times we have met and talked have been some of the best times for changes."

"This book was particularly tough," agrees Brodie. "But we had an 11th-hour meeting on ***A Formal Feeling,*** remember? Zibby was in town at Christmastime: we tried to go to the Plaza for a drink, and it was just mobbed with shoppers; we couldn't even get in. But we went somewhere else, and I said, 'This book is ready to go, I can put it in copy-editing tomorrow, but I'd like to ask you to look it over one more time and add a little more about Anne's anger.' Now, many authors at that point legitimately would say, 'You know, I'm just out of energy. It's a nice idea, but I just can't go on.' But Zibby took it back and made changes, and she didn't just tack them on in a new chapter or a new scene at the end; it was seamless."

"We had another good meeting on ***In Summer Light,"*** says Oneal. "There's a scene in the book where Kate comes down to the studio and says to Ian [the graduate student she's fallen in love with], 'Take me to Boston.' Well, that phrase came right from Deborah; she said that it would be more dramatic than Kate just saying she loved him. I thought it over and said, 'Yes, of course.' Very important things are added that are Deborah's suggestions."

"Zibby gives me too much credit," Brodie demures. "I'm not a coauthor by any means."

"No, but you're not just sitting there fixing the commas either," says Oneal.

"No," Brodie agrees. "I couldn't get up in the morning if that's all I did. I wouldn't be able to label everything that each of us contributed at certain stages. If I'm there, with the way we work together, the book might be stronger. But if I weren't there, there would still be a book: you can have a book without an editor, but you can't have a book without an author."

"Oh, I'm not arguing that there could be a book without an author!" Oneal says, laughing, but she's made her point that Brodie's contributions are greater than those of most editors. Brodie's own story of how the final manuscript of ***In Summer Light*** came into being shows that clearly.

"It was last January," she remembers, "and I was working at home in my daughter's room, because she has a big desk. I had the last three drafts spread out—one on the desk, one on the floor, one on the bed—and I was cutting and pasting, using the second draft as the master. I was working very intensely, because my time was so limited. And when I was finally finished and I got up to stretch, I looked out the window and I couldn't believe there was snow and ice! I was so full of the feeling of summer, heat and light." (pp. 97-8)

It infuriates both Oneal and Brodie that children's books are taken less seriously than their adult counterparts. "You come across it everywhere," says Oneal. "I will go to a party, and someone will learn that I write children's books and they'll say, 'Well, when are you going to write a real book?' A *real* book! As if there could be anything more satisfying than writing about this tremendously dramatic period of life. Adolescence is wonderful material for fiction, because there's so much going on in the way of changing and choices and learning new things. I don't really see how you could run out of things to write about."

Nonetheless, Oneal confesses, she has been thinking about writing an adult novel. "I'm very interested at the moment in the Brewers," she says, referring to Kate's parents in ***In Summer Light.*** "I feel as though I'm not through with them. But in a book for adolescents I couldn't go into the parents' relationship too much, because who cares? Kate's concerned with their relationship as it affects her future—is her mother a role model? is her father?—but she doesn't think about how they are together, what they mean to each other, or why this relationship has existed. It's not something anybody thinks about much at that age. But it interests me, so maybe I'm going to try and write a novel about it."

But Oneal resents even the faintest implication that a novel for adults would be more "serious" than her previous books. "I think our society doesn't value children very much," she says. "There's a lot of lip service given to the importance of children, but that's all it is—lip service. Anything involved with children somehow has less prestige: grammar school teachers don't make as much as college professors, pediatricians don't do as well as neurosurgeons."

"There's a lot to be done yet to have the whole field of children's books taken more seriously," Brodie declares. "I think it's coming, though, partly because of the demographics. More people are having their children later in life, and an older parent tends to take everything more seriously. Also, a lot of these women are upper-middle-class and very well educated; they pay more attention to books. I don't think we'll ever see the golden days of the '60s, with so much government money that you could publish anything, but we *are* in a resurgence."

However, Oneal, who had her children young (as did Brodie), deplores the tendency of older, more affluent parents to push their children into a cycle of ever-more-rapid achievement. As a teacher at the University of Michigan, she sees the result of all this aggressive goading and says, "My students are concerned only with grades. You can't interest them in the outside world. What their parents have done is put blinders on them."

One of the things she can do as a writer, she hopes, is to try to counteract this influence. "I feel a responsibility to make children understand that adolescence is a self-absorbed world—this may be why I always have islands in my books—but it's not a place you can stay forever. The movement away and out into the world, into concern for other people, has to happen; you aren't an adult until you make that move. Sure, explore your feelings, because if you're hung up on your problems you're never going to be able to move on. So work that out, but then get out into the world." (p. 98)

Wendy Smith, "Working Together," in Publishers Weekly, *Vol. 229, No. 8, February 21, 1986, pp. 97-8.*

WAR WORK **(1971)**

A World War II story. Anxious to do their bit for the war effort, Zoe and her sister Rosie are quite ready to help Joe Bunch when he announces that he has discovered an Enemy Agent. All three have seen a man put a note in a hollow tree, and their detective efforts make them even more sure that they are on the trail of a criminal. Although some of their suspects prove to be at worst engaged in Black Market activities, the children do help uncover a plot to blow up the local bomber plant. The book has good period detail, the writing style is competent, and the plot is occasionally improbable but never impossible; its weakness is that it is over-extended, the action slowed by dialogue and exposition that are tangential.

Zena Sutherland, in a review of "War Work," in Bulletin of the Center for Children's Books, *Vol. 25, No. 5, January, 1972, p. 77.*

This light story of three resourceful young people living in a Midwestern town during World War II should appeal to modern children who collect bottles and cans for recycling and who are growing up during a very different war—Viet Nam. . . . The story begins slowly but picks up suspense as the spy game becomes more real. The characters and their actions (e.g., sneaking out at night to spy from under the porch of their prime suspect, Miss Lavatier) are believable, and life on the home-front is effectively portrayed.

Ronna Dishnica, in a review "War Work," in School Library Journal, *an appendix to* Library Journal, *Vol. 18, No. 8, April, 1972, p. 138.*

THE IMPROBABLE ADVENTURES OF MARVELOUS O'HARA SOAPSTONE **(1972)**

Lemon and Iris Soapstone like pigs and their father wants to win a blue ribbon, and that's why they acquire Marvelous, who sleeps in the oven but worries the family by running away right in the middle of her christening ceremony. . . . Marvelous is retrieved but not until she's become violently attached to a huge cement dolphin which the indulgent Mr. Soapstone buys from the park to keep the pig from pining away. Soapstone almost loses patience when the statue must be hauled to the hog fair and Marvelous blows her chance for a blue ribbon by biting the judge who pokes her cement friend. . ., but the incident itself wins fame for pig and family. . . . The Soapstones are unpretentious folks (you can just hear them stressing that first syllable as they chew out the "cement" dolphin) and if Marvelous' friendship is pretty shallow next to that of Wilbur and Charlotte her adventures will provide a few laughs for those who like their humor as broad as the pampered pig's backside.

A review of "The Improbable Adventures of Marvelous O'Hara Soapstone," in Kirkus Reviews, *Vol. XL, No. 19, October 1, 1972, p. 1145.*

Slightly sophisticated, yet with something of the rattle-brain innocence of a Raggedy Ann story, ***The Improbable Adventures of Marvelous O'Hara Soapstone*** appeals particularly to a taste for the unconventional. Author Zibby Oneal and Illustrator Paul Galdone have spun a frothy spoof with daffy dialogue and unlikely encounters. . . .

The book's high point is a very funny and well-controlled christening scene. Then the pace becomes too frantic, the adventures fragmented rather than developed.

Dorothy H. Kelso, "Stories: Hard Fact and Deft Fantasy," in The Christian Science Monitor, *November 8, 1972, p. B4.*

TURTLE AND SNAIL **(1979)**

Oneal's low-keyed tone increases the enchantment of her I-Like-To-Read. . . . Although the other creatures in Snail's neighborhood invite him to join in their activities, he feels like an outsider. Trapped in a shell, he can't fly like Robin, shelter in a hole like Ant or hop like Grasshopper. He's desolate until he meets Turtle, who points out the advantages of a shell, and the two become bosom buddies. It's delightful to share their days . . . and to discover how their friendship is cemented by Turtle's reassurance as well as by the growing understanding between two who epitomize "To each his own."

A review of "Turtle and Snail," in Publishers Weekly, *Vol. 215, No. 22, May 28, 1979, p. 57.*

Five interrelated episodes of friendship between two animals, a turtle and a snail, who seem to have nothing in common except their shells. The theme is weak and unsupported by action. The daily events lead up to a pointless conclusion where turtle asks, "Do you remember when we laughed all day?" and receives the reply, "No." Oneal confuses young readers by delineating, in the second chapter, the food (flies and ants) that turtles actually eat, and then by describing, in the fourth chapter, a fanciful picnic during which the turtle and snail enjoy peanut butter sandwiches and lemonade. Vocabulary is simple and repetitive. . . . This is an unamusing book that doesn't come near the quality of Lobel's Frog and Toad adventures (Harper) or Hoban's *Stick-in-the-Mud Turtle* (Greenwillow, 1977).

Blair Christolon, in a review of "Turtle and Snail," in School Library Journal, *Vol. 26, No. 3, November, 1979, p. 68.*

***THE LANGUAGE OF GOLDFISH* (1980)**

AUTHOR'S COMMENTARY

I don't recall when I didn't want to be a writer. It has seemed to me the best and most exciting thing a person can do, for as long as I can remember.

My mother loved books, both for their content and because they are beautiful objects. Our house was full of them. She read aloud to us a great deal. I can remember finding it miraculous that she could look at the strange black marks on a page and see a story there. I planned to fill pages with black marks of my own as soon as I learned how to make them. Wanting to write goes back that far anyway.

Between the year I learned to print the alphabet and the year I saw my first book published quite a lot happened. The usual sorts of things mostly. I learned to ride a bike. I acquired a baby sister. I got through sixth grade, then eighth, then high school, writing all the time. In those days I mainly wrote stories having to do with love (which I didn't know much about), set in places I'd never seen. From time to time somebody would suggest that I try writing about something I knew. But what did I know? Nothing interesting.

In college I took writing courses, and once—just once—a professor praised a story. It happened to be a story about my sister and myself, about the day I realized that she was still a child but that I was not. This was something I knew about. I remembered the day, the sunlight on my sister's fine hair, her doll with its missing eye. I remembered the smell of the grass being cut and of strawberries being boiled into jam. Most importantly, I remembered how I *felt*. And so it turned out to be a pretty good story.

It would be nice to say that I learned something from that. I didn't, or only much later. *Then* I just went back to writing about love affairs in Hong Kong and collecting rejection slips.

It was only after I'd married, had two children, and had begun to write stories for them that I discovered what I both liked and could do. The first books came out of these stories created expressly for them. The latest ones I've written mostly for myself.

I found one day that a thirteen-year-old girl was on my mind. She began to haunt me. Thinking about her made me remember adolescence and what a difficult time that can be. Eventually I began to write about her, investing imagined events with remembered feelings, sorting things out for myself. This book turned out to be ***The Language of Goldfish.***

As my wonderful editor pointed out, it's a book about change. I hadn't seen that, but it makes sense that it should be. At the heart of adolescence is change, and change can be disturbing. Both ***The Language of Goldfish*** and ***A Formal Feeling*** are about people who resist change but learn finally to accept it. So, too, I now realize, was the story I wrote about my sister and me so long ago. . . .

There is a magnificent blindness involved in writing. You don't know exactly what you're doing until you've done it. At least I don't. I am convinced of that. Too often now people have pointed out things that clearly I have said but didn't recognize I was saying. I am always astonished when this happens, always grateful. It makes writing as wonderfully mysterious to me now as it was when stories were only strange black marks on paper.

Zibby O'Neal, in a promotional piece by The Viking Press, 1982. Reproduced by permission of Penguin Books Ltd.

This is an intelligent, meticulously crafted book on a theme that, though fascinating to young people, has not been well handled in YA novels. Thirteen-year-old Carrie, the middle child in an affluent and happy family, is full of fears about herself and her relations with other people. More precisely, she is afraid of becoming a sexual being—although the underlying sexual basis for her mental breakdown is suggested rather than stated. She sees her older sister growing away from her, becoming more interested in boys and in a separate social life. She is uneasy about the changes in her own body, frightened by the expectations that her parents and school have for her, intensely disturbed by the sensuality she perceives in an exhibit of Art Nouveau, upset when a trusted teacher casually refers to the importance of sex in human nature. She attempts suicide and then slowly, through therapy and through the creative stimulus of painting, begins to heal. *Why* she is so afraid is not explained. The carefully selected, precise details of Carrie's life, including realistic and compassionate character portrayals, establish a tension between external reality and the chaos of Carrie's mind. A serious but not dismal book, enlivened by flashes of humor, this draws out readers' empathetic response and enlarges understanding. It is remarkably good writing!

Linda R. Silver, in a review of "The Language of Goldfish," in School Library Journal, *Vol, 26, No. 6, February, 1980, p. 70.*

The Language of Goldfish deals with a somewhat touchy subject, the insanity of a child. Although written about and for a thirteen-year-old, it reminded me of nothing so much as Judith Guest's *Ordinary People,* and it is nearly as good, too. . . . The book operates on many levels; thus, [Carrie's] family's refusal to accept the seriousness of her illness reverberates in her friends' lack of understanding and her own unwillingness to understand why her beloved art teacher would leave her husband for another man. So too Carrie's eventual acceptance of growth and sexuality is marked by her first bra, her first dance class, her attempts at realistic drawing, her ability to accept her mother's refusal to acknowledge the reality of her breakdown. The story is believable and heartwarming. It offers reasonable hope, calm moments of joy, and the possibility of a future, without deviating from a serious appraisal of the problems today's young people face as they try to fit themselves into worlds they don't understand.

The book's technical strengths are many. The dialogue is very good, its terseness reflecting the teenage milieu. The symbols (the island, the bra, the dancing class, Carrie's development as an artist) are there for the reader to find but are never forced. The characters are neither fiends nor angels, just real people doing their flawed best in a flawed world.

I liked the book very much and wouldn't be surprised if it were considered for some of the more prestigious children's book awards. In fact, I'd be delighted to see it win. While the content is controversial enough to earn the book a B rating—after all, insanity is not yet quite out of the mental closet—the subject is handled so gracefully that most parents will want their children to have the insights Zibby Oneal offers.

Loralee MacPike, in a review of "The Language of Goldfish," in Best Sellers, *Vol. 40, No. 1, April, 1980, p. 39.*

[***The Language of Goldfish***] chronicles Carrie's emotional breakdown and attempted suicide. This subject matter is bound to attract some attention for its own sake, but it would be a mistake to include this novel in the wave of pop-sociological fiction about teen-age trauma. Certainly, its profile of an achieving daughter of a well-to-do family, panicked at the thought of competing socially with her more outgoing sister, would be recognizable to any clinician. And Carrie's attempts, as an art student, to translate her anxiety into studies of line and movement are entirely believable. For the most part, however, the people and events in Carrie's life are a bit flat and a bit hazy around the edges, which is entirely how she perceives them. In contrast, her inner turmoil, even during her dizzy spells when reality "slips sideways"—is conveyed in language that is poetic and precise.

No doubt many young readers will be drawn to this story because it promises to show "what it's like to go crazy." In fact, this promise is fulfilled, largely because the author has resisted the temptation to use Carrie's disordered thoughts as a vehicle for self-indulgent writing. But most readers will also see a good deal of themselves in Carrie. Her search for the magic island, which she can see in her imagination but no longer recognizes in reality, is a resonant metaphor for the lost illusions of childhood. This is a loss that sentimental people bemoan, but Mrs. Oneal reminds us that pretending is the work of childhood—and often very hard work at that. (pp. 52, 65)

Joyce Milton, in a review of "The Language of Goldfish," in The New York Times Book Review, *April 27, 1980, pp. 52, 65.*

In a perceptive novel which avoids clichés and exaggeration, evocative images create a sense of Carrie's inner experiences: the gaps in her consciousness, her whirling terror, and her longing for a safe place—a place like the island in the goldfish pond, a sanctuary of childhood. With strong characters, convincing scenes, and accurate, consistent dialogue, the author explores Carrie's journey and recovery and the remoteness of her affluent family. The story is not suddenly dramatic; Carrie's illness moves in an unpredictable, gradual downward spiral until the girl begins a cautious, tentative rebuilding of her life. Carefully crafted with delicacy and control, the book presents a moving portrait of a vulnerable child on the brink of young adulthood.

Christine McDonnell, in a review of "The Language of Goldfish," in The Horn Book Magazine, *Vol. LVI, No. 4, August, 1980, p. 416.*

The spare, simple style of writing is misleading: the depth of understanding shown for Carrie's disintegration is profound. The mood of depression and alienation is sustained through rich and unusual imagery, which changes as Carrie begins to grow again. The author's mastery of construction, characterization, and theme make this a book from which to teach creative writing. So many adolescents fear the encroaching demands of sexuality and responsibility. This speaks to them and to their friends, who should realize their needs.

Patricia Pearl, in a review of "Language of Goldfish," in Voice of Youth Advocates, *Vol. 3, No. 3, August, 1980, p. 35.*

This extraordinary work combines literary excellence with honest, compassionate exploration of the turmoil experienced by a youngster unable to cope with the changes in her life. Oneal's writing is crisp, sensuous, and insightful; characterizations are outstanding, and the plot is absorbing and credible. The heroine is seen as a basically "normal" child whose behavior is adaptive to a world she perceives to be threatening. . . . The role her art talent plays in the expression of her distress and as a barometer of her recovery is particularly interesting. Her therapeutic sessions are recorded in much detail, and the seemingly passive psychiatrist is sensitively depicted as he interacts with his patient. The reactions of members of her family and others involved in her life are realistic and create a vivid picture of the only intermittently supportive environment to which the teenager must return and adapt. (p. 342)

Barbara H. Baskin and Karen H. Harris, "An Annotated Guide to Juvenile Fiction Portraying the Disabled, 1976-1981: 'The Language of Goldfish'," in their More Notes from a Different Drummer: A Guide to Juvenile Fiction Portraying the Disabled, *R. R. Bowker Company, 1984, pp. 341-42.*

A FORMAL FEELING (1982)

With her mother dead for over a year and her father remarried, Anne Cameron reluctantly returns home to spend the holidays with a family she no longer feels part of. Operating in a kind of slow-motion haze, with grief and all its attendant emotions securely locked away inside, she views each change at home as a betrayal of the memory of a mother so talented, so disciplined and organized, and so lovely that no one could ever replace her. But familiar details of the place where Anne grew up and the stuff of daily life—a broken plate, choosing a Christmas tree, skating on a local pond—conjure up deeply buried memories of a less-than-perfect parent, disquieting images for Anne, who fears that by admitting her mother's imperfections she would be committing the ultimate betrayal. Oneal's pacing is slow and deliberate and her style highly descriptive—characteristics that may make this attractive to more experienced fiction readers—but the novel is filled with scenes of great emotional intensity, and Oneal . . . captures Anne's conflicting feelings with subtlety and perception.

Stephanie Zvirin, in a review of "A Formal Feeling," in Booklist, *Vol. 79, No. 3, October 1, 1982, p. 199.*

At first readers may suspect that Anne is just one of those pretty, accomplished, hollow teen-agers who agonize over having been merely runner-up in the tennis tournament, but Miss Oneal is a craftier writer than that, and the psychological climax (a freeing of painful memories by a physically painful skating accident) is both beautifully drawn and truly affecting.

Georgess McHargue, "Coming of Age," in The New York Times Book Review, *November 14, 1982, p. 48.*

The book is upper class, literary, cultured, and very intellectual. It is also thoughtful and insightful. The style, dialogue, descriptions, and action are both natural and beautifully controlled. Oneal writes very well, and her flawless style raises her somewhat conventional content above itself. This is clearly one of the best young adult books of the year.

Robert C. Small, in a review of "A Formal Feeling," in The ALAN Review, *Vol. 10, No. 2, Winter, 1983, p. 23.*

Despite the academic background, the atmosphere of the story is redolent of middle America; and although the texture of the narrative is tightly woven, the style—self-consciously descriptive and allusive—tends to be antiseptic. Centering on Anne's state of mind more than on her emotions, the novel not only lacks intensity but fails to attain the power of effective understatement. (pp. 173-74)

Paul Heins, in a review of "A Formal Feeling," in The Horn Book Magazine, *Vol. LIX, No. 2, April, 1983, pp. 173-74.*

The deftly varied narrative form adopted in ***A Formal Feeling*** gives a far greater impression of reality than the first-person device used in *My Brother the Thief* [by Marlene Fanta Shyer]. Using flashbacks and revealing the situation gradually, the author exercises an overall view with literary tact, so that we see matters mainly from the view of Anne, but with the opinions and emotions of her older brother Spencer, her father and her new step-mother broadening the scope of the book. . . . English readers who find it hard to accept the sometimes oppressive articulacy of American adolescents will be glad to find that this frank analysis of difficult family relationships has avoided both sentiment and didacticism.

Margery Fisher, in a review of "A Formal Feeling," in Growing Point, *Vol. 22, No. 2, July, 1983, p. 4102.*

Home for Christmas from her private school, sixteen-year-old Anne looks into her mirror at the end of chapter 1, and says, just to clarify matters: "Your mother has been dead for over a year. . . . Your father has remarried.'" We might be forgiven for thinking that here is another example of the tribe of teenage problem novels—but fortunately the resemblance ends there (apart from one character who 'chuckles'—but it is a momentary lapse).

A Formal Feeling . . . is so low-key that at times it seems to be in danger of stopping altogether. . . . Anne prepares for Christmas in a remarkably evoked midwestern U.S. campus town, but in an alien family atmosphere. Her elder brother, Spencer, is only prepared to help her so far: "'Well, this is a brave new world, my friend. You might try joining it.'" And it slowly dawns on her—and, because of the skill of the pacing, only a little more quickly on the reader—that her precise and talented mother might not have been as perfect as her memory insists. The fact that Anne's problems are more resolved than not at the end may be the inevitable result of the genre—but Zibby Oneal's restrained approach contrives to make the ending psychologically likely. ***A Formal Feeling*** is a formal book, requiring more patience and subtlety, perhaps, than its guise suggests.

Peter Hunt, in a review of "A Formal Feeling," in The Signal Review of Children's Books 2, *1984, p. 43.*

IN SUMMER LIGHT (1985)

AUTHOR'S COMMENTARY

[The following excerpt is taken from Oneal's acceptance speech for the 1986 Boston Globe-Horn Book *Award.]*

The landscape [of ***In Summer Light***] existed in my imagination long before I saw it for the first time. I recognized it at once. For me it was the landscape of fairy tale. When the prince comes riding to claim his princess, he rides through just such meadows of wild roses, through just such forests of dappled shade. At least that was the way I imagined it, always. How natural, then, that ***In Summer Light,*** born as it was of this magical landscape, should have turned out to be a fairy tale. (p. 32)

One day a friend and I were talking about the way that themes from certain tales reappear in present-day children's books in one disguise or another. I remember having a theory I was eager to argue for. While this might be true for some tales, I said, it wouldn't continue to be true for all. Surely certain tales—"Cinderella," for instance, "Snow White," "Rapunzel"—were no longer relevant to the present day. Surely these passive heroines, content to wait for their princes to arrive, had become anachronisms in the wake of the women's movement. How could these tales continue to interest modern girls, intent on careers and achievement? How could the themes found in these stories mean anything to them at all? It was at about this point that I faltered, as suddenly it occurred to me that, in fact, I had just written something suspiciously like "The Sleeping Beauty" myself.

One doubts the relevance of tales at one's peril, as I have discovered. It is foolish to argue with their wisdom, even if that wisdom seems, at first glance, hopelessly out-of-date. The tales clearly tell us that though young boys must go off to slay dragons in the pursuit of maturity, young girls must be content to sit and wait. To my astonishment, apparently I agreed. At least I had chosen to tell this ancient tale again, albeit unwittingly.

Suppose I were to tell you the story of ***In Summer Light*** in this way. Once upon a time on an island off the coast of Massachusetts there lived a famous painter and his wife. Now to this couple was born a daughter, and they named her Kate. All went well with them for a time, but then came the year that Kate was seventeen, and she fell into a curious state of lethargy. She began to languish there on the island, hedged all around by a thorny tangle of childhood memories. It was not from a jealous fairy's spell that Kate suffered. Rather it was from a thoroughly modern malady called mononucleosis, but the symptoms were much the same. Drowsy, dozing, full of lassitude, Kate rested, deep among the thorns and brambles of the family thicket. In time, of course, a prince arrived. He came riding one day to the place where Kate slept, not on a fine and spirited palfrey but in a car with broken-down springs. A graduate student from California, this prince had neither wealth nor title, yet he succeeded in awakening Kate. Much as I would have liked to deny it at first, I had to admit that the parallels were persuasive. Disguised in modern trappings, the old tale was there.

I had thought I was making use of a quite different model. Shakespeare's play, *The Tempest,* had been on my mind. I wanted to write about a powerful, arrogant, magical father and about his daughter's involvement with him. I wanted to talk about how a girl begins to move away from this intense childhood involvement; about how it is when, like Miranda in *The Tempest,* she is able to gaze for the first time on a man besides her father.

I wonder now whether the old tales about adolescent girls may not, themselves, be speaking of some such time. When Snow White and Beauty, Cinderella and Rapunzel gaze for the first time upon their princes, they are prepared to ride away. They are no longer the obedient and sequestered young girls they have been. Something has changed. We credit the prince with effecting the change, but I wonder whether his kiss is not meant to be more like an acknowledgment of something already accomplished. I wonder whether the change may not have occurred, in fact, earlier—during that time among the cinders or in the tower or deep in sleep. When at last the prince awakens these girls, they are ready to go with him. They have left childhood behind. So, too, it is with my Kate. By the time that she can name her feelings for her prince, she has moved beyond childhood preoccupations. She has left behind those things which prevent her becoming a woman. And she has done this while seeming to do nothing at all.

Passivity, then, is an illusion. Growing up is not a passive undertaking. If we do not see the process in tales—or only a metaphor for process—I do not think we are meant to assume that no effort has been expended, that no struggle has taken place. While boys journey off to seek their fortunes, the girls set off on a journey of another kind. It is a quiet, dreaming, inward journey, but who is to say that the dragons encountered are not equally fearsome or that the arrival at the destination has not been just as dearly won? Surely Kate has struggled by the time she wakes. During her long sleepy summer, she has fought a dragon or two. While doing nothing, she has done much. When at last her eyes are open, it is a young woman—not a child—gazing through them.

Fairy tales are shorthand. They are metaphors, models, myths. We carry them in our heads like patterns, and they tell us what we need to know about how humans grow and change and prosper. How very unsurprising, then, that we should sometimes turn to them when we have a story to tell, should sort among them for a pattern to fit our intention. That this should happen, as it did for me, unconsciously, seems only proof of how deep within us these patterns lie. Wanting to tell the story of an awakening, I turned intuitively to the oldest story of awakening I know. I could not have turned to it in any other way, prevented by all my rational arguments. Fortunately, I seldom write with both eyes open—fortunate because it is the closed eye, the dreaming eye, that leads me places I might never otherwise go. (pp. 32-4)

Zibby Oneal, "In Summer Light," in The Horn Book Magazine, *Vol. LXIII, No. 1, January-February, 1987, pp. 32-4.*

"There were peaches in a blue and white Chinese bowl and a cat almost the color of peaches stretched beneath the table." From the first sentence in her new novel, Oneal moves forward and takes the enchanted reader with her, into the summer months that 17-year-old Kate Brewer will never forget.

Kate languishes at her parents' home on a Massachusetts island. Trying to concentrate on an English term paper, she can't escape the idea of herself painted as a child by her famous father Marcus Brewer. The small Kate is merely part of the composition, like the peaches and the bowl and the cat. Born with Marcus's gifts, the young woman has long since given up painting. She doesn't yearn as she once had for her father's encouragement. Marcus in Kate's mind is a distanced figure, deferred to by his wife and daughters as a genius, who has no thought for anything but his creations.

The wounded daughter remains cool to her father, little sister, even her loving mother who tries to make Kate understand the driven man. That recognition comes later, after the arrival of Ian Jackson. . . .

The story is filled with wonders. It's about people who make us smile and cry; they live and breathe in all their faults and virtues. Oneal's exquisite prose leaves also the indelible memory of what the word "art" means. The novel surpasses her multiple prize winners, ***The Language of Goldfish*** and ***A Formal Feeling.***

A review of "In Summer Light," in Publishers Weekly, *Vol. 228, No. 5, August 2, 1985, p. 69.*

With this powerfully evocative coming-of-age story, Oneal tops her two previous award-winners (***The Language of Goldfish, A Formal Feeling***). She weaves a seamless spell around readers that never falters, even for an instant. . . .

Oneal uses words as deftly as artists use colors; the narrative is rich with meticulously crafted descriptions and metaphors. Teen-age readers who discover Oneal with this work will be treated to a beautiful piece of literature. (pp. 914-15)

A review of "In Summer Light," in Kirkus Reviews, *Vol. LIII, No. 17, September 1, 1985, pp. 914-15.*

It's hard to say which is more impressive in this literate, complex story—Oneal's use of language, imagery and color or the development of her finely drawn characters. . . . Artist that she is, Kate sees the world in colors; Oneal shows her audience Kate's world through her own use of color. A coming-of-age novel that is light-years above most others.

Trev Jones, in a review of "In Summer Light," in School Library Journal, *Vol. 32, No. 2, October, 1985, p. 186.*

Oneal writes evocatively of the artistic experience and incorporates scenes of pure joy (when Kate rediscovers her art) and sensitivity (when she and Ian sort out their feelings for each other) as she reveals Kate's confusion about her father, Ian, and herself. But through it all Kate remains a strangely unapproachable figure—her essence, her vibrancy, her vulnerability are too briefly glimpsed. Plot momentum is slowed by contrivances and descriptive passages—however richly contoured they are. Despite that, the novel is still beautifully written; its literary underpinning (Shakespeare's *Tempest*), is intriguing; and its portrayals of a father/daughter relationship and a young woman's struggle to carve a place for herself are not only intelligent and honest, but also ultimately affirmative. A moving book for the perceptive reader.

Stephanie Zvirin, in a review of "In Summer Light," in Booklist, *Vol. 82, No. 4, October 15, 1985, p. 330.*

For those YA readers who have already acquired a taste for quiet eloquently written books that explore complex human experiences of the mind and heart, ***In Summer Light*** will be a special literary treat of sustaining nourishment and illumination. . . . Like Willa Cather, Ms. Oneal is an author whose clear, vivid writing style transcends age categories and other classification boundaries. Superb.

Leigh Dean, in a review of "In Summer Light," in Children's Book Review Service, *Vol. 14, No. 3, November, 1985, p. 33.*

Zibby Oneal's heroines are cool, leggy and intelligent adolescent girls who struggle to unlock the repressed rage that blocks their growth to womanhood. Though the preoccupation seems narrow, the literary resolution grows more polished and mature with each novel. Miss Oneal's new book, ***In Summer Light,*** is also her most ambitious and coherent work to date. . . .

Miss Oneal uses an elegant dazzle of images to illuminate Kate's Oedipal conflict, while neatly sidestepping the boggy self-pity of so much adolescent fiction. Through Kate's rapt perceptions of light and color, both the prose and her character gain depth. And the parallels with *The Tempest* (there is even a little Caliban in the toadlike Frances, the cleaning woman's obnoxious daughter) enliven the plot, summoning echoes of meaning with a light, glancing touch. Even for a young reader who may be unfamiliar with the play, this is an excellent device because it puts Kate's silent war with her father at a bearable distance.

In Summer Light lacks the pathos of Miss Oneal's earlier book, ***A Formal Feeling,*** but it gains conviction from the quiet way in which Kate comes to recognize her mother's understated strength and the waning of her father's power. Best of all, it keeps the action focused on Kate's inward movement toward freedom. It is Kate, through her own clear sight and growing emotional generosity, who teaches herself the optimistic lesson of adolescence, even if the words are spoken by Ian: "Now and here aren't all that there will ever be."

As Kate takes the ferry away to the mainland and school, Prospero's island floats behind her, "fading into the middle distance." That's a sane bracing perspective on childhood for someone whose face is turning eagerly toward adult life.

Michele Landsberg, in a review of "In Summer Light," in The New York Times Book Review, *November 24, 1985, p. 21.*

MAUDE AND WALTER (1985)

Oneal's buoyant stories are a real treat for beginners, boys and girls who will twig to incidents in the lives of small Maude and her tall brother Walter. The book opens with Walter telling his sister to "go away." He's building a kite and can't be bothered with her. But Walter needs a tail for the kite and he's glad to accept Maude's offer of her long hair ribbons. He even lets her fly the kite, so they're pals until Walter pins a sign, "No Girls" on his tent. When the junior Machiavelli sees that, she "discusses" the matter and the sign then reads "Except sisters." There are other nifty short adventures . . . sparkling with color and wit.

A review of "Maude and Walter," in Publishers Weekly, *Vol. 228, No. 7, August 16, 1985, p. 70.*

The writing is more repetitious than need be for this level of beginning reader, but this fault is made up for by the genuine feeling between this brother and sister, be it impatience or affection, which never seems forced or smarmy. The amusing two-color drawings [by Maxie Chambliss] with their realistic expressions and kid-like postures, help reinforce that real-life feeling.

Nancy Palmer, in a review of "Maude and Walter," in School Library Journal, *Vol. 32, No. 4, December, 1985, p. 110.*

A number of appealing picture books have been published recently, dealing not so much with a single central event as with the relationship between a pair of characters. They often appear as chapter books, divided into three or four separate adventures instead of one longer story. Arnold Lobel's classic *Frog and Toad* stories have had something to do with the evolution of this genre, but a number of fine stories have come out more recently. And now Oneal, acclaimed for her novels for older readers, throws her hat into the ring as well. . . .

Oneal's book is funny, believable, and tender at the same time. . . . Like the best of the "relationship" books, this one goes beyond specific brother-and-sister issues. It's a warm, heartening depiction of friendship.

A review of "Maude and Walter," in Kirkus Reviews, *Vol. LIII, No. 24, December 15, 1985, p. 1398.*

What a riot! In four short vignettes, Oneal captures the feeling of petty squabbles and sweet resolutions between brothers and sisters. . . . ***Maude and Walter*** has a lot of zip, is fun to read, and fun for young readers to read themselves.

Margo Showstack, in a review of "Maude and Walter," in Children's Book Review Service, *Vol. 14, No. 5, January, 1986, p. 49.*

GRANDMA MOSES: PAINTER OF RURAL AMERICA (1986)

[Oneal's book] gracefully conveys the central focus of the subject's life and work. In this case, the strength and independence of Anna Mary Moses' personality emerge long before the art for which she became famous. Her country childhood and hard life as a farm wife simply set the stage for the serving of a talent that had simmered many years. Oneal's style is graceful and richly spiced with Grandma Moses' own pithy comments. Illustrated with reproductions that exemplify the succinct descriptions of Moses' paintings.

Betsy Hearne, in a review of "Grandma Moses: Painter of Rural America," in Bulletin of the Center for Children's Books, *Vol. 40, No. 2, October, 1986, p. 34.*

Oneal's biography is brief, but it covers the artist's life from birth (near Albany, N.Y., in 1860) to her death in 1961. Moses is seen as an independent person who managed to squeeze creative moments into a busy life as a farm wife and mother of ten. . . . The brevity of the text doesn't allow for much depth or detail. Fictionalization is minimal, but the text is uneven and occasionally choppy. Lack of color reproductions will deprive children of the full enjoyment of Moses' charming works. Despite these flaws, this is an adequate biography for middle grade readers and older slow readers.

Nancy Kewish, in a review of "Grandma Moses: Painter of Rural America," in School Library Journal, *Vol. 33, No. 2, October, 1986, p. 180.*

Jack Prelutsky

1940-

American poet, translator, and editor.

One of the most popular contemporary poets of humorous verse for children, Prelutsky is noted for his irreverent style, technical versatility, and keen awareness of juvenile likes and dislikes. Well known for his droll animal sketches, spine-tingling ghoulish jingles, and eccentric characters whose exaggerated peculiarities often include gross eating habits, Prelutsky tends to stress the baser instincts of human nature in his picture books. His rhyming, rhythmic stanzas combine traditional form and literary devices with clever wordplay, colloquial expressions, and surprise endings. Formerly a professional singer, Prelutsky reveals his musical training in the sensitivity to language sounds, patterned repetition of words, and strong metric beat that characterize his works. In addition to macabre and slapstick ballad-type tales, Prelutsky writes occasional lines of lyric beauty, modern epigrams, and short collections about major holidays. He has also translated German and Swedish children's poetry into English.

Likening him to Shel Silverstein, Ogden Nash, Lewis Carroll, and Edward Lear, critics praise Prelutsky for his nearly faultless rhythm, wry wit, and virtuosity with words. Although a few reviewers express concern about the possible negative influence of his more wicked characters on young readers, many credit Prelutsky with winning early converts to poetry through his exuberant rhymes and outrageous nonsense.

Several of Prelutsky's books have received adult-selected awards.

(See also *Something about the Author,* Vol. 22 and *Contemporary Authors,* Vols. 93-96.)

Courtesy of Greenwillow Books

AUTHOR'S COMMENTARY

Once there was a teacher who had charge of thirty-three open and eager young minds. One Monday morning, the teacher opened her curriculum book, which indicated that she should recite a poem to her students. She did, and it came out something like this:

Blah blah the flower,
blah blah the tree,
blah blah the shower,
blah blah the bee.

When she had finished her recitation she said, "Please open your geography books to page one-hundred-thirty-seven."

On Tuesday morning, the teacher (a wonderful person who happened to be rather fond of poetry) decided, on her own initiative, to read another poem to her class. This poem, which was somewhat longer than the first, came out something like this:

Blah blah blah blah blah blah hill,
blah blah blah blah blah blah still,
blah blah blah blah blah blah mill,
blah blah blah blah daffodil.

Then she said, "Please open your history books to page sixty-two."

She went on like this for the entire week, and by Friday, the children (who knew what was coming when she opened her book of verse) began making peculiar faces and shifting restlessly in their seats. The staunchest aesthetes in the group had begun to lose interest in flowers, bees, and hills etcetera. Many of the children were harboring strange feelings about poetry. They began saying things about poetry to themselves and to each other. Here are some of the things that they said:

"Poetry is boring."
"Poetry is dumb."
"Poetry doesn't make any sense."
"Poetry is about things that don't interest me."
"I hate poetry."

Once there was another teacher with a class of thirty-three young students. She was also a wonderful person with a fondness for poetry. One Sunday evening, she opened her curriculum book and saw that a unit of poetry was scheduled for the next day's lesson. "Hmmmmmm," she mused. "Now what poem shall I share with them tomorrow?" After giving it some careful thought, she settled on a poem about a silly monster, which the poet had apparently created out of whole cloth, and which she thought might stimulate her pupils' imaginations.

"Hmmmmmm," she mused again. "Now how can I make this poem even more interesting?" She deliberated a bit more and, in the course of memorizing the poem, came up with several ideas. The next morning, this is what happened:

"Children," she said. "Today is a special day. It is the first day of silly monster week, and to honor the occasion, I am going to share a silly monster poem with you." She held up a small tin can, and continued. "The monster lives in this can, but I am not going to show it to you yet, because I would like you to imagine what it looks like while I'm reciting the poem."

She then recited the poem, and upon reaching the last word in the last line, suddenly unleashed an expanding snake from the can. The children reacted with squeals of mock terror and real delight. Then they asked her to recite the poem again, which she did. Afterward, she had them draw pictures of the silly monster. No two interpretations were alike. The drawings were photographed and later presented in an assembly as a slide show, with the children reciting the poem in chorus. She shared a number of other poems during "silly monster week," always showing her honest enthusiasm and finding imaginative methods of presentation. She used masks, musical instruments, dance, sound effects recordings, and clay sculpture. The children grew so involved that she soon was able to recite poems with no props at all. At the end of the week, these are some of the things her students said about poetry:

"Poetry is exciting."
"Poetry is fun."
"Poetry is interesting."
"Poetry makes you think."
"I love poetry."

(pp. 322-23)

Jack Prelutsky, "Through the Eyes of a Poet: Poetry Doesn't Have to Be Boring!" in Through the Eyes of a Child: An Introduction to Children's Literature *by Donna E. Norton, Charles E. Merrill Publishing Company, 1983, pp. 322-23.*

GENERAL COMMENTARY

ELAINE MOSS

Impact is . . . what Jack Prelutsky achieves with his relentlessly repetitive, remorselessly grinding verses for ***The Terrible Tiger***. . . . Listeners begin to shudder deliciously, and at the same time to wonder whether this haughty beast may not get his come-uppance—which happens when he swallows the tailor and his scissors. . . . Immediately the terrible tiger becomes an object of sympathy and when, duly stitched up, he lopes off into the jungle murmuring, to reassure himself, his boastful refrain; the Terrible Tiger is terribly lovable. In ***Circus*** . . . , the rhythm of Prelutsky's verses swings with the trapeze artist, honks with the seals and jangles with the juggler. . . .

Elaine Moss, "The Unclassified Appeal," in The Times Literary Supplement, *No. 3826, July 11, 1975, p. 771.*

VIRGINIA HAVILAND

[***The Pack Rat's Day and Other Poems*** is a] gay picture book of verses superb for reading aloud with their bouncy rhythms, entertaining alliterations, and verbal wit. . . .

. . . . .

Rollicking hyperbole and movement [in ***Circus***] give a high-spirited view of sights and sounds of the circus. Tongue-twisters abound. . . .

More fun with words characterizes poems about animals in ***Toucans Two and Other Poems*** (1970), while words with strong rhythms and alliterative dexterity create horrendous images in ***Nightmares: Poems to Trouble Your Sleep*** (. . . 1976). (p. 15)

Virginia Haviland, "Rhymes: 'The Pack Rat's Day and Other Poems'," in Children & Poetry: A Selective, Annotated Bibliography, *edited by Virginia Haviland and William Jay Smith, second edition, The Library of Congress, 1979, pp. 14-15.*

ALETHEA HELBIG

Jack Prelutsky's verse is spotty . . . ; he has been turning out a lot of it lately, to the detriment of originality and spontaneity. His ***The Headless Horseman Rides Tonight: More Poems to Trouble Your Sleep*** (. . . 1980) repeats his ***Nightmares*** (1976). Like ***The Snopp on the Sidewalk*** (. . . 1977), which brazenly puts such never-never-land creatures as grobbles, the gibble, the meath, and the lurp in real-life situations, and ***The Queen of Eene*** (. . . 1978), about a queen and her zany, mixed-up friends, the verses are overdone, contrived, and monotonous. Prelutsky's work appears consciously aimed at the fourth grade silly set, and some pieces are hardly better than what the kids themselves might do. (p. 40)

Alethea Helbig, "The State of Things: A Question of Substance," in Children's Literature Association Quarterly, *Vol. 5, No. 2, Summer, 1980, pp. 38-45.*

X. J. KENNEDY AND DOROTHY M. KENNEDY

A formalist, and rather a specialized one, is Jack ("Blood and Guts") Prelutsky. Prelutsky's work, always strictly written to meters and rhyme schemes, has been criticized for its alleged morbidity, yet its very formality helps indicate that it is meant in fun. Casting evocations of vampires, ghouls, and walking mummies into the rollicking measures of Swinburne, Kipling, and the popular balladeers, Prelutsky spellbinds the listener, not only with Gothic imagery, but with assonance and alliteration, leaving no doubt that his terrifying creatures aren't really going to do the reader any harm. . . . (pp. 78-9)

X. J. Kennedy and Dorothy M. Kennedy, "Tradition and Revolt: Recent Poetry for Children," in The Lion and the Unicorn, *Vol. 4, No. 2, Winter, 1980-81, pp. 75-82.*

BERNICE E. CULLINAN WITH MARY K. KARRER AND ARLENE M. PILLAR

Jack Prelutsky weaves a gruesome spell in his poems in ***Nightmares: Poems to Trouble Your Sleep*** . . . (1976), in which a grisly ghoul waits patiently beside a school to feast on girls and boys. (p. 110)

[***Nightmares***] is a hit with children, who squeal with delight at the eerie spooks. (p. 245)

[Rhythm] helps to create and then reinforce a poem's meaning. In ***Circus*** . . . (1974), Jack Prelutsky adjusts his rhythms to the subject:

Over and over the tumblers tumble
with never a fumble
with never a stumble,
top over bottom and back over top
flop-flippy-floppity-flippity-flop.

But the tumblers pass, and are followed by the elephants, whose plodding walk echoes in the new rhythm:

> Here come the elephants, ten feet high,
> elephants, elephants, heads in the sky.
> Eleven great elephants intertwined,
> one little elephant close behind.

and the rhythm plods along in the way elephants walk. (p. 254)

In ***Toucans Two and Other Poems*** . . . (1970), he quips about animals in a mischievous way that enables readers to see them or think of them in never-before ways. In ***The Pack Rat's Day and Other Poems*** . . . (1974), Prelutsky describes the habits of the Pack Rat. He uses tongue-tangling nonsense with strong rhythm and rhyme to describe fanciful creatures in ***The Snopp on the Sidewalk and Other Poems*** . . . (1977). (p. 286)

In ***Rolling Harvey Down the Hill*** . . . (1980), Jack Prelutsky is his usual hilarious self. This funny collection is about a group of boys—Lumpy, Tony, Will, Harvey, and the narrator—and their misadventures. They smoke in the cellar, eat worms, break a window, and scare girls. A delightful gang! (p. 287)

Bernice E. Cullinan with Mary K. Karrer and Arlene M. Pillar, in their Literature and the Child, *Harcourt Brace Jovanovich, Inc., 1981, 594 p.*

DONNA E. NORTON

The kingdom of immortal zanies could be the description of the characters and animals who live within the poetry written by Prelutsky. Within the pages of ***The Queen of Eene,*** children will find such preposterous characters as "Pumberly Pott's Unpredictable Niece," peculiar "Mister Gaffe," "Poor Old Penelope," "Herbert Glerbertt," and the "Four Foolish Ladies" Hattie, Harriet, Hope, and Hortense. The humorous world of animals is contained in the poems in ***Toucans Two and Other Poems.*** The humorous experiences of a boy and his four friends are found in ***Rolling Harvey Down the Hill.*** In ***The Sheriff of Rottenshot*** eccentric characters include Philbert Phlurk, Eddie the spaghetti nut, and a saucy little ocelot. ***The Baby Uggs Are Hatching*** has poems about such oddly named creatures as sneepies and slitchs. The humor of an unbelievable situation, rhyming words, and rhythm are found in **"Pumberly Pott's Unpredictable Niece"** [from ***The Queen of Eene***]. . . . (p. 335)

Poltergeists, zombies, and giants are some scary subjects found in Jack Prelutsky's ***The Headless Horseman Rides Tonight.*** These poems . . . suggest the world of the dark sepulcher, the ghostly moor, and the darksome dominion. (p. 345)

Jack Prelutsky's humorous animal poems encourage bodily interpretation of animals of various sizes, speeds, and agility. His ***A Gopher in the Garden and Other Animal Poems*** . . . contains some very enjoyable poems. (p. 350)

Adults have used the nonsensical, humorous situations found in Prelutsky's poems in ***The Queen of Eene*** to stimulate humorous dramatizations. . . . The final poem in this book, **"Gretchen in the Kitchen,"** has been used for spooky witch scenes at Halloween. The quarts of curdled mud, salted spiders, ogre's backbone, and dragon's blood provide a setting appealing to children who are preparing to be spooks, witches, and black cats.

Another Prelutsky poem that stimulates Halloween dramatizations is **"The Ghostly Grocer of Grumble Grove"** . . . who lives near Howling Hop. The spectacle of a cauliflower poltergeist juggling thinly sliced apples, sausages skipping on ghostly legs, and cornflakes fluttering through the air while being supervised by a ghostly grocer is conducive to creating many animated conversations and surprising happenings. (p. 351)

Donna E. Norton, "Poetry," in her Through the Eyes of a Child: An Introduction to Children's Literature, *Charles E. Merrill Publishing Company, 1983, pp. 318-67.*

A GOPHER IN THE GARDEN, AND OTHER ANIMAL POEMS (1967)

From epigram to extended, entangled word-play, from tyrannosaur ("just can't be found here anymore") to the multilingual mynah bird ("can say most any word he's heard"), a collection to capture the most difficult audience. This is one that worked even in galleys, and the illustrations [by Robert Leyden Frost] have the same grave, slightly surprised wit. We see this as a teaser at class visits, a show-stopper at assembly programs—it's in the line of Lewis Carroll and way above most juvenile whimsy.

A review of "A Gopher in the Garden and Other Animal Poems," in Kirkus Service, *Vol. XXXV, No. 14, July 15, 1967, p. 805.*

Fewer than two dozen short poems are contained in this very funny picture book, but these few poems are delightful. Mr. Prelutsky writes clever, funny poems with definite child appeal and a lovely use of words. These verses bring to mind poems by Shel Silverstein, Ian Serraillier, John Ciardi, Eve Merriam—the best of the contemporary poets of nonsense for children.

Phyllis Cohen, in a review of "A Gopher in the Garden, and Other Animal Poems," in Young Readers Review, *Vol. IV, No. 3, November, 1967, p. 16.*

Occasionally, like a harpsichordist proud of his trills, Mr. Prelutsky gets carried away with the sheer rhyming rhythm of it all. But mostly he gives a pretty fair tour for those who are willing to sing-song it once more with the inevitable Yak and his friends.

Melvin Maddocks, "Verse Like Rain on a Pond," in The Christian Science Monitor, *November 2, 1967, p. B5.*

In one of the gayest of picture books the poet offers almost two dozen nonsense rhymes about the world's more exotic and amusing animals, beginning with the "long-extinct tyrannosaur." He sustains the fun without a letdown in easy, delightful rhymes and rhythms, and with words that call for reading aloud and chanting in response by young listeners. Who could resist "Yickity-yackity, yickity-yak, / the yak has a scriffily, scraffily back . . ." or **"The Giggling Gaggling Gaggle of Geese"**?

Virginia Haviland, in a review of "A Gopher in the Garden and Other Animal Poems," in The Horn Book Magazine, *Vol. XLIII, No. 6, December, 1967, p. 744.*

THREE SAXON NOBLES, AND OTHER VERSES (1969)

The verses are generally longer [than those in ***Lazy Blackbird and Other Verses***] and not as light or bright or limber . . .—this is no match for ***Lazy Blackbird*** in this or any other season, and, with a couple of exceptions, too stiff and obvious to make a mark on its own.

A review of "Three Saxon Nobles and Other Verses," in Kirkus Reviews, *Vol. XXXVII, No. 18, October 1, 1969, p. 1060.*

Mr. Prelutsky's earlier title, ***A Gopher in the Garden and Other Animal Poems*** (. . . 1967), offered a more substantial collection of poems than this book; the light and humorous verses presented here, however, read easily and contain enough nonsense to amuse five-, six-, and seven-year-olds.

Barbara H. Gibson, in a review of "Three Saxon Nobles and Other Verses," in School Library Journal, *an appendix to* Library Journal, *Vol. 16, No. 6, February, 1970, p. 75.*

***LAZY BLACKBIRD, AND OTHER VERSES* (1969)**

Suppose it's bed-time, and the 4-6-year-old has miraculously slowed down to 40 miles an hour, and is clean, fed, nightied or pajama'd. Sit in an easy chair, take the should-be-sleepy one on your lap, and explore ***Lazy Blackbird and Other Verses*** with him or her. . . . [This is a] singularly engaging bit of whimsy. Jack Prelutsky's deft, childlike nonsense verses are rewarded by the solemnly enchanting childlike pictures of Janosch. A useful starter for bright, colorful, lively, nonsensical dreams.

Neil Millar, "Angelic Children—and Others," in The Christian Science Monitor, *November 6, 1969, p. B3.*

[There are] 11 verses which comprise this small but alluring book. Mother Goose-ish in tone, the verses are uneven in quality. . . . Youngsters in the primary grades should have a great deal of fun with this one.

Euple L. Wilson, in a review of "Lazy Blackbird and Other Verses," in School Library Journal, *an appendix to* Library Journal, *Vol. 16, No. 4, December, 1969, p. 43.*

***THE TERRIBLE TIGER* (1970)**

[Here's] a perfect book to read out loud to your child, with a built-in guarantee that he will be able to quote it back to you after one reading—at least, he'll learn to roar the terrible tiger's terrible song.

A review of "The Terrible Tiger," in Publishers Weekly, *Vol. 197, No. 9, March 2, 1970, p. 82.*

Prelutsky's terrible tiger will be a source of merriment for children, as he carnivorously cavorts around the countryside, downing a grocer, baker, farmer, and—unfortunately for himself—a tailor. The resourceful tailor snips his way out of the tiger's belly, in the process freeing the other captives, then stitches the tiger up again with a mild reprimand for his rudeness. But, once repaired, the incorrigible beast makes an unrepentant exit, roaring and gnashing his teeth at the tailor. Readers know that his life style hasn't been radically altered by the encounter. . . . Prelutsky's rollicking verse in a cumulative story pattern is ably complemented by [Arnold] Lobel's comical, grey and yellow pictures. . . .

Diane G. Stavn, in a review of "The Terrible Tiger," in School Library Journal, *an appendix to* Library Journal, *Vol. 17, No. 2, October, 1970, p. 124.*

***TOUCANS TWO, AND OTHER POEMS* (1970; British edition as *Zoo Doings, and Other Poems*)**

Jack Prelutsky thinks pictures and Jose Aruego pictures thoughts and ***Toucans Two*** is twice the book for it. . . . **"Toucans Two"** and **"Zoo Doings"** will trip your tongue, **"The Zebra"** will trick your eye, and **"Oysters"** . . . well, "Oysters / are creatures / without / any features." Quintessence of animal, essence of fun.

A review of "Toucans Two and Other Poems," in Kirkus Reviews, *Vol. XXXVIII, No. 18, September 15, 1970, p. 1032.*

Toucans two, a kudu, and a zebu we do view, all in verse and amusing, too. Prelutsky presents 17 delightful animal poems. . . . The humor of the rhymes is suggestive of that of Ogden Nash, and each one is based on a factual observation—how a snail moves, what beavers do, what a dromedary looks like, etc. Though the brief poems are appealing to all ages, the reading level is better suited to older children. The book as a whole offers great fun for a read-aloud and amusing diversion for independent readers.

Ginger Brauer, in a review of "Toucans Two and Other Poems," in School Library Journal, *an appendix to* Library Journal, *Vol. 17, No. 2, October, 1970, p. 124.*

Jack Prelutsky is a young New Yorker with a gift for witty or humorous jingles. . . .

Most of the verses offer no more light or meaning than a riddle; but they're often neat and comical, and they rhyme and scan pleasantly. The pictures, in a parallel spirit of deadpan nonsense and semi-nonsense, cheerfully or irascibly illustrate the animals involved.

Perhaps the title poem is a fair sample. . . . Fun to say aloud, fun to sing-song either solo or with an older companion.

And it is plummed with nice, fat words like "hippopotamus" and "philosophical."

Neil Millar, in a review of "Toucans Two and Other Poems," in The Christian Science Monitor, *November 12, 1970, p. B4.*

The verses are of the kind that one makes up for the delectation of one's nearest and dearest. They are technically better than most and they play prettily with words and fancies, but they seem scarcely to deserve a wider public than the family circle.

M. Crouch, in a review of "Zoo Doings, and Other Poems," in The Junior Bookshelf, *Vol. 35, No. 5, October, 1971, p. 309.*

***CIRCUS* (1974)**

The greatest show on earth has never inspired equally spectacular children's books and even Jack Prelutsky's tributes to flip-floppy tumblers, a monkey band ("out of rhythm and time and tune"), eight balancing bears, a wiggling, wriggling, jiggling juggler, and all the other "splendidly arrayed" performers in the great parade lacks the spontaneous splashy wit and new twists of his ***Toucans Two***. . . . However, they are high flying show stoppers compared to the tired ballyhoo we're used to, and if none of the subjects step out of their ancient roles, that's all part of the circus mystique. (pp. 106-07)

A review of "Circus," in Kirkus Reviews, *Vol. XLII, No. 3, February 1, 1974, pp. 106-07.*

Circus is a circus in verse, meant to be read OUT LOUD. Read in silence it loses a lot of its animation. Jack Prelutsky's interest in music is obvious in his rhythms and repetitions and pace. Each verse is about a different circus act. . . . Unfortunately, some of the verse leaves me wishing that it was less ordinary and its rhyme less forced.

Arnold Lobel's full color pictures help to make the verbal circus work. There would be a lot missing without them. . . .

The book gives me a taste of the circus. All that's missing is the sawdust and popcorn under my feet.

Judi Barrett, in a review of "Circus," in The New York Times Book Review, *March 31, 1974, p. 8.*

Although this hasn't the sense of fun that has distinguished earlier Prelutsky books, the combination of subject appeal, extravagant descriptive verse, and the colorful ebullience of the illustrations should captivate the read-aloud audience. Almost every exciting circus act is portrayed: the human cannonball, the trapeze artist, the clowns and jugglers, the performing animals (with one nice set of paired verses from the lion and the lion tamer), and all the razzle-dazzle of the circus parade.

Zena Sutherland, in a review of "Circus," in Bulletin of the Center for Children's Books, *Vol. 27, No. 11, July-August, 1974, p. 184.*

With hyperbole rampant on every page, a carnival atmosphere pervades the book. . . . Like noisy fanfares, the rhythmic verses and splendid illustrations introduce an array of traditional circus features. . . . Ideally, the book is for reading aloud. Most of the poems, which are full of extravagant alliteration and tongue-twisters, are longer than one might expect to find in a picture book; and it will probably require an adult to roll them trippingly off the tongue. (pp. 369-70)

Ethel L. Heins, in a review of "Circus," in The Horn Book Magazine, *Vol. L, No. 4, August, 1974, pp. 369-70.*

THE PACK RAT'S DAY AND OTHER POEMS (1974)

Librarians who have had story hour success with Prelutsky's previous collections of animal rhymes will find more read aloud material here, but we expected something sharper from the author of ***Toucans Two*** and ***Gophers in the Garden.*** Unfortunately the bland docility of some of the subjects is too often paralleled in Prelutsky's form ("Sheep are gentle, shy and meek. / They love to play at hide-and-seek. / Their hearts are softer than their fleece / And left alone they live in peace") and the jocular warnings of some of his endings are far from novel. . . . Still Prelutsky does come up with some light verbal nonsense here, as in our favorite about the cow who "chooses to moo as she chooses" and "chew(s) just to chew as she muses," and his ear for funny sounds and eye for amusing features are evident in spots throughout.

A review of "The Pack Rat's Day and Other Poems," in Kirkus Reviews, *Vol. XLII, No. 12, June 15, 1974, p. 633.*

This is silly stuff in the Belloc tradition. . . . The forgettable verses—"Sheep are gentle, shy and meek . . ."—are offset by memorable nonsense about the cow who "chooses to chew as she muses," which makes for good tongue-tangling, and, best of the lot, the pack rat himself.

Helen Gregory, in a review of "The Pack Rat's Day and Other Poems," in School Library Journal, *an appendix to* Library Journal, *Vol. 21, No. 2, October, 1974, p. 107.*

Humorous verse for children often appears to be deceptively simple, and these new poems about animals come from a young writer who possesses a rare dexterity with words. . . . Children will make a game of alliterative nonsense like "The widdly, waddly walrus / has flippery, floppery feet". . . . Much less complex than the poems in the previous book ***Circus,*** which was a brilliant display of words and pictures, the fifteen new verses are terse and direct. . . .

Ethel L. Heins, in a review of "The Pack Rat's Day and Other Poems," in The Horn Book Magazine, *Vol. L, No. 6, December, 1974, p. 698.*

NIGHTMARES: POEMS TO TROUBLE YOUR SLEEP (1976)

Whether or not they trouble your sleep, Prelutsky's ogre's gallery makes other monster poems turn pale. The company numbers thirteen from Will o' the Wisp to Bogeyman and includes loose-jointed skeletons who will set tongues dancing "with the click and the clack / and the chitter and the chack / and the clatter and the chatter / of their bare bare bones" and a grisly schoolyard ghoul who'll make mincemeat of your funnybone. The all-stops-open rhythm swings along with never a break or groan, and [Arnold] Lobel, disguised as Edward Gorey for the occasion, falls into the spirit of morbid glee. The whole performance is as polished as a vampire's incisor.

A review of "Nightmares: Poems to Trouble Your Sleep," in Kirkus Reviews, *Vol. XLIV, No. 12, June 15, 1976, p. 690.*

A series of twelve tongue-in-cheek poems about the gruesome subjects of folklore and superstition, such as a haunted house, a vampire, and a werewolf. Using traditional verse forms and pulling out the poetical stops, the author molds stanzas bristling with rhyme, repetition, alliteration, and onomatopoeia. . . . The reader is buttonholed and drawn into the knowledge of terrifying revelations. . . . But there is a kind of black humor in many of the verses. In **"The Ghoul"** the horror of "Fingers, elbows, hands and knees / and arms and legs and feet— / he eats them with delight and ease, / for every part's a treat" is mitigated by the mildness of such expressions as "with delight and ease" and "for every part's a treat." (pp. 513-14)

Paul Heins, in a review of "Nightmares: Poems to Trouble Your Sleep," in The Horn Book Magazine, *Vol. LII, No. 5, October, 1976, pp. 513-14.*

[***Nightmares***] is the book that tells children what they always wanted to know about vampires, trolls and witches but were afraid to ask. The descriptions of victims being gulped, gobbled and clubbed senseless appalled me and will no doubt satisfy the boldest child's appetite for the ghastly. . . .

There's considerable Gothic claptrap in Prelutsky's poems and shades of Poe in his heavy use of rhyme. Reading them aloud, one forgives their flaws.

Nancy Willard, in a review of "Nightmares: Poems to Trouble Your Sleep," in The New York Times Book Review, *October 3, 1976, p. 32.*

The sub-title "Poems to trouble your sleep" promises certain qualities which are not fully redeemed in the performance. Mr. Prelutsky writes a neat poem, competent, technically versatile, well-suited to reading aloud, but frightening? No. The contrivance is always in evidence. One never gets the feeling that this has been put down in the terror of the moment.

M. Crouch, in a review of "Nightmares," in The Junior Bookshelf, *Vol. 43, No. 3, June, 1979, p. 160.*

Without doubt *the* most successful book of the year for us if we judged by the number of children ranging from seven to fifteen who chose this out of all the books in our office. It proves in the most delicious way that it's fun to be frightened. Very highly recommended.

A review of "Nightmares, Poems to Trouble Your Sleep," in Books for Your Children, *Vol. 15, No. 2, Spring, 1980, p. 22.*

THE SNOPP ON THE SIDEWALK, AND OTHER POEMS (1977)

Marvelously funny and original poems guaranteed to tickle a giggle out of readers. Prelutsky's Carrollesque verses on improbable monsters like ("lying on the sidewalk like a gray old ragged mop") beg to be read aloud. Like the best of Shel Silverstein, the rhythm and rhyme are deft and the tongue-tangling nonsense wonderfully daft.

Marjorie Lewis, in a review of "The Snopp on the Sidewalk and Other Poems," in School Library Journal, *Vol. 23, No. 8, April, 1977, p. 56.*

Jack Prelutsky's rousingly rhythmic ***The Snopp on the Sidewalk*** . . . gives us as obnoxious a pack of monsters as a child could want, all bent on devouring humanity and one another (except for the snopp, an inert blob that utters monosyllables). Prelutsky's nonsense drew approving chuckles from a 12-year-old, even though I had the same reservations about it that I have about much of Dr. Seuss: its setting in a world remote and abstract, its heavy reliance on coinages:

> The blatt, though flat, was also fat.
> The snatt, not flat, was fatter.

(p. 31)

X. J. Kennedy, "The Flat, Fat Blatt," in The New York Times Book Review, *May 1, 1977, pp. 31, 33.*

Skillfully employing alliteration, metaphor, repetition, and portmanteau words within the framework of traditional rhymed verse forms, the poet has conjured into reality a menagerie of imaginary beings. . . . Some, like the "Snopp," are enigmatic; others, like the "wozzit in the closet," have unusual dietary preferences; all are worthy descendants of such literary luminaries as the Jabberwock, the Pobble, and the Quangle Wangle. Despite the pseudo-macabre situations, the tone of the twelve poems is gleefully ghoulish without being gruesome. . . . A delectably bizarre gathering of marvelously outrageous nonsense.

Mary M. Burns, in a review of "The Snopp on the Sidewalk and Other Poems," in The Horn Book Magazine, *Vol. LIII, No. 5, October, 1977, p. 550.*

Jack Prelutsky, master of the neat and nimble jingle, offers us a slim, tough—and ultimately scary—volume which begins gently: **"The Snopp on the Sidewalk,"** the title poem, is a melancholy mop-like creature, taciturn and still. It needs nothing but company.

The gibble, on the other hand, bristles with rage and predatory hunger; but it is too small to do much damage with its ambitious teeth. The monumental meath is harmless for another reason: he has no teeth. Wrimples, which make things go wrong, can be disposed of by any competent dewrimpler; but not so the ravaging wozzit: wozzits lurk in closets, chomping everything within reach—if wozzits exist.

For children who like to be deliciously scared, the book could be great fun. It isn't intended for the sensitive chicks to whom preying is fearful and fear is pain.

Neil Millar, "Cherry Blossom Haiku: Delicate Petals of Concentrated Verse," in The Christian Science Monitor, *November 2, 1977, p. B6.*

Middle-graders will find these monsters less chilling than those of ***Nightmares,*** more mischievous than malevolent. "The gibble is glum and big as a thumb," while the wozzit in the closet swallows slippers and chews shoes. Things get too contrived and downright silly when the frummick and the frelly spread jingleberry jelly. Some of the creatures sound like escapees from reading exercises. "The flime devoured the floober / and the flummie dined on flime. . . ." . . . [Poetically] inferior to ***Nightmares.*** (pp. 951-52)

Ruth M. Stein, in a review of "The Snopp on the Sidewalk and Other Poems," in Language Arts, *Vol. 54, No. 8, November-December, 1977, pp. 951-52.*

IT'S HALLOWEEN (1977)

"I saw a ghost / that stared and stared / And I stood still / and acted scared. / But that was just / a big pretend. / I knew that ghost . . . (new page) . . . it was my friend!" His ***Nightmares*** tamed for beginning readers, Prelutsky settles into the spirit of the holiday—reveling in all the fearsome props, obligatory for the occasion, that never really scare anyone over three. Prelutsky's rhythms, too, are milder here—all the better, of course, for easy access, and they're catchy at the most rudimentary level. . . . [The] collection makes a lively warm-up for the big night—and a tempting lead-in to Prelutsky's more devilish entertainments.

A review of "It's Halloween," in Kirkus Reviews, *Vol. XLV, No. 17, September 1, 1977, p. 930.*

Thirteen poems designed to spice up the festivities that ghouls and ghosts love most. All verses are brief and range in scare-ability from the "Bony bony bony bones" of a **"Skeleton Parade"** to the rousing chorus of "Trick or treat, / trick or treat, / give us something / good to eat" from a poem titled **". . . or Treat."** Prelutsky again exhibits his rare talents for catering to juvenile taste in subject matter here in his least horrific title.

Judith Goldberger, in a review of "It's Halloween," in Booklist, *Vol. 74, No. 4, October 15, 1977, p. 382.*

A gathering of thirteen light-hearted verses celebrates for beginning readers the deliciously frightening aspects of Halloween. Although a few seem constrained by the format, the majority demonstrate the inventive use of words and agile rhythms characteristic of the poet's style. And some poems—like the "goblin as green / As a goblin can be / Who is sitting outside / And is waiting for me"—could be appreciated both in and out of season. The illustrations [by Marylin Hafner] . . . highlight the contrast between the real and the imagined, thus providing an appropriate visual extension for the simple text. A piquant and ingenious treatment of a familiar subject.

Mary M. Burns, in a review of "It's Halloween," in The Horn Book Magazine, *Vol. LIV, No. 2, April, 1978, p. 182.*

THE QUEEN OF EENE (1978)

Prelutsky is an incomparable creator of absurd poetry, witty works that are equal blends of the macabre and the hilarious. . . . Kids will lose no time memorizing the rhyming tales about "The Queen of Eene" who brushes her teeth with onion juice and wonders why no one visits her and the book's other eccentrics, like "Herbert Glerbett." . . .

A review of "The Queen of Eene," in Publishers Weekly, *Vol. 213, No. 1, January 2, 1978, p. 65.*

This is a wicked, irreverent, splendid book of 14 verses, with admirable scansion. . . . The pleasure both poet and artist [Victoria Chess] take in their work is evident on every page. I especially like The Visitor, a doglike, leering wad of fur with Dracula eyes who came for a day and "smeared my head with honey / and filled the tub with rocks."

Natalie Babbitt, in a review of "The Queen of Eene," in The New York Times Book Review, *April 23, 1978, p. 32.*

Prelutsky's poems about a series of peculiar people are merrily ghoulish, stylishly nonsensical. . . . There's no relationship among the poems, they simply form a gallery of oddities described in verse that has rhyme, rhythm, and humor that are well controlled. . . . Great fun. (pp. 16-17)

Zena Sutherland, in a review of "The Queen of Eene," in Bulletin of the Center for Children's Books, *Vol. 32, No. 1, September, 1978, pp. 16-17.*

Here Prelutsky presents fourteen separate poems featuring dolts and noodles worthy of a Lear or Carroll or Nash. Prelutsky's wildly imaginative characters can blind one to his ability with language. He pulls out all of the stops, using internal rhymes, onomatopoeia, alliteration, assonance, and almost anything else you can mention. Chess' drawings on wash are as controllably mad as the writing.

Ruth M. Stein, in a review of "The Queen of Eene," in Language Arts, *Vol. 56, No. 6, September, 1979, p. 688.*

THE MEAN OLD MEAN HYENA (1978)

The hyena is given to practical jokes: he paints the zebra plaid, makes the elephant sneeze, ties the ostrich in a knot, and shaves the lion's mane. His grating, heckling chorus, "I'm the mean old mean hyena, / there is no hyena meaner," rings between the verses as he gets into trouble and out again. . . . This masterful villainy . . . is well-sustained nonsense to tickle its young readers.

Helen Gregory, in a review of "The Mean Old Mean Hyena," in School Library Journal, *Vol. 25, No. 2, October, 1978, p. 138.*

Prelutsky's nasty anti-hero pulls a briar-patch ploy when the other animals seek revenge for the tricks he's perpetuated. . . . While the mischief will appeal to young listeners, there's an even greater appeal in the rhyme and rhythm of Prelutsky's verse, with its humor and use of refrain, alliteration, and internal rhyme. (pp. 124-25)

Zena Sutherland, in a review of "The Mean Old Mean Hyena," in Bulletin of the Center for Children's Books, *Vol. 32, No. 7, March, 1979, pp. 124-25.*

[***The Mean Old Mean Hyena***] is a book by which children are delighted and about which adults are not too sure. I suppose what it takes is a sense of humor and a realization which children have that, even though these animals have been given the gift of speech by Mr. Prelutsky, after all, they really are animals living in the wild and don't abide by our civilization and rules. The Hyena is indeed mean, a dreadful, ugly, cruel beast, and, worst of all, he's clever. . . . This book is not for the faint-hearted. It is done in rhyme, is very catchy and fun to read out loud. . . . Even though the "bad guy" wins in this story, I didn't mind too much.

Barbara Ann Kyle, in a review of "The Mean Old Mean Hyena," in The Babbling Bookworm, *Vol. 7, No. 5, June, 1979, p. 2.*

ROLLING HARVEY DOWN THE HILL (1980)

Fifteen contemporary poems describe the mischievous antics of five apartment-house buddies. The large gray-and-white illustrations [by Victoria Chess] depict the five as taunting, teasing terrors. Mean Harvey antagonizes his four friends to such an extent that they roll him down the hill. Many youngsters will empathize with these ornery kids, but others may be tempted to copy their worst pranks. I have mixed feelings about this book and thus cannot recommend or not recommend purchase.

Margaret M. Nichols, in a review of "Rolling Harvey down the Hill," in Children's Book Review Service, *Vol. 8, No. 12, Spring, 1980, p. 112.*

Five boys: Tony, who is clumsy and wears glasses; Lumpy, who picks his nose and wipes it on the narrator's shirt; Willie, who eats a worm one day (but only after cleaning it off); Harvey, a cheat, bully, and braggart; and "I" hang out together in a vacant lot. Their adventures are told in small boy phrases, packaged in rhythmic cadences that only sporadically fulfill the promise of the marvelous title and the author's own previous successes. Little is original; the lads smoke and choke, hate girls, break a window with a baseball, etc. But once, Harvey ties them all to trees, pulls down their pants, and leaves them there. Which precipitates the title adventure (a gem) and suitably wraps up a cautionary warning to all the Harveys of the world as, pushed beyond endurance, the boys roll Harvey down the hill for three pages of stanza and refrain that will surely invite loud and glorious participation. Pictures show appropriate kids with a touch of ugliness that—like the events themselves—treads a thin, uneasy line between funny and not-so-funny.

Marjorie Lewis, in a review of "Rolling Harvey down the Hill," in School Library Journal, *Vol. 26, No. 8, April, 1980, p. 115.*

Prelutsky's droll verses do a nice bit of storytelling as they introduce a forthright narrator's buddies and then sketch out their eminently boyish pastimes and misadventures. . . . This is fresh, funny, and quite in tune with scampish concerns.

Denise M. Wilms, in a review of "Rolling Harvey down the Hill," in Booklist, *Vol. 76, No. 15, April 1, 1980, p. 1132.*

Excessive niceness isn't a hang-up for Jack Prelutsky. . . . [***Rolling Harvey down the Hill***] isn't poetry, but rollicking light verse. Boys should enjoy finding their secrets mirrored, and girls, glimpsing the seamy side of boys, should be confirmed in their feelings of superiority.

X. J. Kennedy, in a review of "Rolling Harvey down the Hill," in The New York Times Book Review, *April 27, 1980, p. 47.*

In these 15 singsong rhymes . . . , Prelutsky makes an effort to show the kids as they really behave away from grownup censors (or, perhaps, as they did behave in film and fiction a couple of generations ago). . . . For similar scruffy kids unmoved by more innocent matter, this might have the appeal of recognition; but Prelutsky's naughty ideas are as stale as his rhythms.

A review of "Rolling Harvey down the Hill," in Kirkus Reviews, *Vol. XLVIII, No. 11, June 1, 1980, p. 711.*

THE HEADLESS HORSEMAN RIDES TONIGHT: MORE POEMS TO TROUBLE YOUR SLEEP (1980)

Like his phosphorescent **"Spectre on the Moor,"** Prelutsky's droll verses have "dread allure." . . . [In] all there's a dozen dire denizens of the dark and deep and you betcha they're gonna getcha. . . . Prelutsky's rhymes are as lethal, lithe, and literate as ever. . . . (p. 62)

Pamela D. Pollack, in a review of "The Headless Horseman Rides Tonight: More Poems to Trouble Your Sleep," in School Library Journal, *Vol. 26, No. 9, May, 1980, pp. 62-3.*

This companion to Prelutsky's noteworthy ***Nightmares*** . . . caters to similar horror predilections with similar relish. The poems introduce a dozen creepy, deadly creatures, always with an eye to their lethal stalking powers. **"The Mummy"** starts off—and typifies—the baleful images in this gallery: "Inside its stone sarcophagus / beneath the pyramid, / it moves its cloth-enshrouded hands / and pushes back the lid." . . . The poems are tightly crafted, rolling easily along with beguiling or sonorous rhyme. One called **"The Banshee"** is Poe-like in its solemn cadences. Definitely for reading aloud come Halloween, or any other time that calls for good, bone-chilling fun.

Denise M. Wilms, in a review of "The Headless Horseman Rides Tonight: More Poems to Trouble Your Sleep," in Booklist, *Vol. 76, No. 19, June 1, 1980, p. 1426.*

Despite the grim threat of his title, . . . Jack Prelutsky isn't all that serious. An encore to his earlier collection ***Nightmares***, this new book evokes a dozen of childhood's best-loved creatures—such as the mummy, zombie and abominable snowman—in rhymes so rollicking that no kid who can endure an amusement park spookhouse is likely to take them for dangerous. . . .

Like many post-Poe spinners of horror tales, Mr. Prelutsky leans hard on fuzzy adjectives ("ghostly," "ghastly," "hellish," "awful"); still, he's a spellbinder. (p. 51)

X. J. Kennedy, "The Poets Speak," in The New York Times Book Review, *November 9, 1980, pp. 50-1, 62.*

The poems are all very regular in form, generally a ballad style, sometimes a bit slickly engineered, but certain to be effective if read aloud with a little relish, particularly as some young readers might find themselves labouring with vocabulary such as "primordial", "labyrinthine" and "sarcophagus"—however essential they may be for the horror-buff.

Chris Waters, "Space and Suburbia," in The Times Educational Supplement, *No. 3545, June 8, 1984, p. 50.*

There is no mitigating strain of humour, no fairy tale triumph of good over evil. The nightmarish impact of the pictures [by Arnold Lobel] and the directness of the verses could hardly fail to alarm many young readers. The rhythms and vocabulary lend a terrifying realism to creations which an adult mind could marshall into perspective but I am far from convinced that we should shrug off the effect of these ghoulish rhymes on children quite so readily.

G. Bott, in a review of "The Headless Horseman Rides Tonight," in The Junior Bookshelf, *Vol. 48, No. 5, October, 1984, p. 210.*

RAINY RAINY SATURDAY (1980)

Decidedly differing in mood from the author's macabre poems in his recent books ***Nightmares*** and ***The Headless Horseman Rides Again*** . . . , the fourteen humorous sets of verses about childhood experiences seem to owe their inspiration to Stevenson. "I took some wood and wire / and I built a little boat, / then I put it in the bathtub / to see if it would float." Four of the selections point out how to overcome the necessary inconvenience of staying indoors on a rainy day; others consider such activities as somersaulting, whistling, and cleaning one's room; while still others celebrate such joys as eating spaghetti and drinking chocolate milk. Simple in language, adroit and unhackneyed in rhyme, uncomplicated but precise in diction, the poems are bouncy in expression and childlike in mood.

Paul Heins, in a review of "Rainy Rainy Saturday," in The Horn Book Magazine, *Vol. LVI, No. 5, October, 1980, p. 533.*

Mixed in with the younger poetry on a non-fiction shelf, including Prelutsky's own spirited offerings, these 14 rhymes about ordinary rainy-day activities would seem pretty commonplace. . . . As made-to-order exercises for beginning readers, though, they might help pass a small part of a rainy day. The ode to spaghetti, though no more original in concept than the rest, puts some bounce into the dull day; and, conversely, the entry that begins "Sometimes I simply have to cry, / I don't know why, / I don't know why" can hit a nerve with its echo of a certain rainy-day mood.

A review of "Rainy Rainy Saturday," in Kirkus Reviews, *Vol. XLVIII, No. 20, October 15, 1980, p. 1355.*

Prelutsky sacrifices some of his usual flair and humor to write more sedately and simply for the beginning independent reader. The poems are childlike in concept and appeal. . . . While these don't have the barbs or wit of Prelutsky's poems for older readers, they have some of the same appeals of rhyme and rhythm, and the combination of subject appeal and simple vocabulary makes them appropriate for the intended audience.

Zena Sutherland, in a review of "Rainy Rainy Saturday," in Bulletin of the Center for Children's Books, *Vol. 34, No. 4, December, 1980, p. 78.*

IT'S CHRISTMAS (1981)

[This] collection of light poetry is on a variety of Christmas themes, with a fairly even division between presents and observances. The verses are bouncy, often comic, written from the child's viewpoint. Nothing of great moment here, but a pleasant selection.

Zena Sutherland, in a review of "It's Christmas," in Bulletin of the Center for Children's Books, *Vol. 35, No. 2, October, 1981, p. 36.*

Like ***It's Halloween*** (1977), this collection of rhymes is tame Prelutsky, touching the usual bases (Santa Claus, carols, school play) in a conventionally sprightly manner. Still, there's enough snap to keep the rhymes rolling. Prelutsky squeezes much fun from holiday rituals gone awry: Dad suffers so many minor injuries chopping down a Christmas tree that he vows to buy one next year; a little girl wonders if she forgot to stamp the unreceived Christmas cards she sent out two weeks ago; and another girl rushes out with her new sled to find that the snow has melted overnight. Often you know just what's coming, but Prelutsky keeps bounding merrily along without switching to automatic. . . .

A review of "It's Christmas," in Kirkus Reviews, *Vol. XLIX, No. 19, October 1, 1981, p. 1234.*

The poems in Prelutsky's Read-Alone are easy and fun for beginners to tackle. . . . The rhymester's frisky style even takes the sting out of disasters like . . . the elaborately wrapped package from Auntie Flo that contains underwear. Most boys and girls will like best of all a wishful kid's letter to "Dear Santa". . . .

A review of "It's Christmas," in Publishers Weekly, *Vol. 220, No. 23, December 4, 1981, p. 50.*

THE SHERIFF OF ROTTENSHOT (1982)

Just the thing to cure the glooms in any weather, Prelutsky's preposterous verses rise to new heights of nonsense on pages fittingly illustrated by [Victoria] Chess's weird humans and animals. Meet Jogalong Jim, the sheriff of Rottenshot: "He was short in the saddle and slow on the draw, / but he was the sheriff, his word was the law." More lines describe fat, inept Jim who owes his position to the fact that nobody but him lives in Rottenshot. The book abounds with more gems, including the saga of a cycling centipede: ". . . she rates awards, she merits medals, / working all those centipedals." So does Prelutsky for his rhyming feats especially for the echoic poem about the saucy little ocelot who likes to toss a lot, fuss a lot, is cross a lot, wants to be boss a lot.

A review of "The Sheriff of Rottenshot," in Publishers Weekly, *Vol. 221, No. 6, February 5, 1982, p. 387.*

Another inspired cast of human and animal weirdos munches its way through bizarre, ghostly, and fatal diets; or perks away at feats of fiendish or cantankerous contriving ("I know this does not work for you, / but ah! it works for me," says individualist inventor Philbert Phlurk, while Kermit Keene ends up swallowed by the "something monstrous, moist, and mean" that emerges from his transforming machine); or expires with flamboyant originality (sneezer Cecil Snedde finally sneezes his head right off); or simply bumbles about exhibiting its exuberantly described peculiarities. Prelutsky's verses, unlike most such, end with a bang, not a fadeout, and his jubilant rhythm and sound are echoed in [Victoria] Chess' zingy miscreations.

A review of "The Sheriff of Rottenshot," in Kirkus Reviews, *Vol. L, No. 4, February 15, 1982, p. 202.*

Sixteen rollicking nonsense poems characterized by flawless and contagiously recitable meter, sharp, economical characterization and always a clear, focused central idea or kernel joke. And punch lines that punch. Within the special genre of contemporary nonsense verse, there are none better than these, reminiscent of Ogden Nash and John Ciardi. The centipede on the velocipede, and Ed, who courted Nettie Cutt, and "got a cottage in Connecticut," "Philbert Phlurk . . . inventing things that didn't work"—all are genial, jolly and silly and make their home in a grab bag of word games, sound games, rhyme games and diverse prosodic high jinx. . . . This is an ebullient, thoroughly successful book with no pretensions other than to give lightsome fun, which it does . . . with never a hitch. (pp. 138-39)

Peter Neumeyer, in a review of "The Sheriff of Rottenshot," in School Library Journal, *Vol. 28, No. 7, March, 1982, pp. 138-39.*

The wry, slightly askew look to Chess' people and animal figures is just right for the absurd note struck by Prelutsky's dotty rhymes. They hum along with nary a miss, introducing a hodgepodge of daffy types whose doings are guaranteed to raise a chuckle, at least. The verses' economy and effortless humor are enviable whether spinning a wacky story . . . or simply playing around with rhythms. . . . Guaranteed to please both the crowd and the solitary browser.

Denise M. Wilms, in a review of "The Sheriff of Rottenshot," in Booklist, *Vol. 78, No. 14, March 15, 1982, p. 962.*

It is difficult to maintain a quality level of nonsense and humor throughout a whole book. In ***The Sheriff of Rottenshot*** . . . , Jack Prelutsky does a creditable job. His work indicates a knowledge of children and of what they think is funny. There are people eating strange mixtures, fumble-bumbleness, globby and weird animals, things that go backward, people who do the opposite of what is expected, name calling, and plays on words. Pieces like **"The Spaghetti Nut,"** which plays on words with awesome cleverness, and **"The Ghostly Grocer of Grumble Grove,"** which has a certain lyric beauty, are verses that seem perfect material for anthologists.

Ardis Kimzey, in a review of "The Sheriff of Rottenshot," in The New York Times Book Review, *April 25, 1982, p. 37.*

IT'S THANKSGIVING (1982)

Like Prelutsky's ***It's Halloween*** and ***It's Christmas,*** this consists of jog-trotting rhymes concerning standard holiday topics—including the modern one of the after-dinner football game on TV. The least expected but still mild ending comes in **"I Went Hungry on Thanksgiving."** The reason—"my new braces hurt so much." There's a rhyme about the parade seen (the last line reveals) on TV; a straight one about **"The First Thanksgiving"**; another set at school ("Our teacher gives us projects / that we work on every day, / we make Indians and Pilgrims / out of paper, paste, and clay. . . ."); still others set at the dinner table; and a final one about too many turkey leftovers. . . . [Though] there are no delights here, the sheer predictability of form and content (suitable perhaps to this most predictable of holidays) might be an advantage to beginning readers.

A review of "It's Thanksgiving," in Kirkus Reviews, *Vol. L, No. 5, March 1, 1982, p. 274.*

A collection of poems about Thanksgiving has rhyme, rhythm, and humor as well as a variety of topics. . . . This isn't great poetry, but it has a bouncy quality that's appealing and it's useful new material for the holiday. (pp. 35-6)

Zena Sutherland, in a review of "It's Thanksgiving," in Bulletin of the Center for Children's Books, *Vol. 36, No. 2, October, 1982, pp. 35-6.*

Again Prelutsky has succeeded in distilling the essence of an important American holiday into poetic forms that will be appreciated and enjoyed by children. The twelve poems cover aspects of Thanksgiving that are within the child's realm of experience. . . . An example of the wit and charm of the poems can be seen by the lines of **"If Turkeys Thought."** "If turkeys thought, they'd run away / a week before Thanksgiving Day, / but turkeys can't anticipate, / and so there's turkey on my plate." A perfect addition to any collection serving children preschool through grade 4. Highly recommended.

James A. Norsworthy, in a review of "It's Thanksgiving," in Catholic Library World, *Vol. 54, No. 5, December, 1982, p. 225.*

THE BABY UGGS ARE HATCHING (1982)

It is difficult to decide which awful creature in the collection of poems is the most delightful—the Ugg, perhaps? or maybe the Nimpy-Numpy-Numpity? No, it is probably the Quossible. . . . The author's talent . . . seems to lie squarely between that of Edward Gorey and Shel Silverstein. . . . The catchy rhythms, humorous drawings [by James Stevenson], and deliciously alarming subjects make a splendid book.

Ann A. Flowers, in a review of "The Baby Uggs Are Hatching," in The Horn Book Magazine, *Vol. LVIII, No. 5, October, 1982, p. 527.*

Prelutsky, in a dozen breezy, lilting poems, creates twelve wildly improbable creatures and Stevenson matches them with wildly silly and totally engaging drawings. Children should enjoy the rhyme, the rhythm, the alliteration, the nonsense words and the comic pictures of, for example, **"The Sneezy-snoozer."** (p. 51)

Zena Sutherland, in a review of "The Baby Uggs Are Hatching," in Bulletin of the Center for Children's Books, *Vol. 36, No. 3, November, 1982, pp. 51-2.*

Here are 12 astonishing creatures in rollicking nonsense verse by a master of this difficult genre. Jack Prelutsky makes traditional meters and rhyme schemes sound newly invented. In his hands the whole thing seems as easy as if all he had to do were conjure up opening lines and the rest had come of its own. . . .

I'll tell you my favorites first: The ravenous, bouncy, spring-green, eponymous Uggs, bursting out of their shells, gobbling up everything, including—shudder—their mothers. The huge, grinning Quossible, with fiery antennae, 18 pink-and-white striped legs and an alarming diet too. The leonine blue-green Smasheroo, who puts ordinary everyday tantrums to shame. The Slithery Slitch in his limousine, "a monster glorious, great and grand." The ducklike Creature in the Classroom, with lavender shoes, a pair of pink legs and one pink hand (all that's left of the teacher) sticking out of its spacious bill. The boulder-eating, lava-drinking Grubby Grebbles. And the highly adaptable Flotterzott, who does a neat trick with its skin.

The others are a shade less outrageous but also original and a lot of fun. Which brings me to why giving such nonsense verse to children makes very good sense: It's a powerful antidote to the stuffy, predictable poetry that still gets force-fed to them. It can legitimize their own monster-creating capacities. Last and best, they'll love it.

Doris Orgel, in a review of "The Baby Uggs Are Hatching," in The New York Times Book Review, *November 21, 1982, p. 43.*

Seven grotesque monsters—plus the Sneepies, the Sneezy-snoozer, the Grebbles, and the totally inoffensive rabbittish Flotterzott—have their essential natures detailed in nonsense verses that tickle the ear and twist the tongue. I gathered that the consistently hostile behavior of the comically offensive monsters who snatch things, smash things, eat people, eat each other and their mothers, wreck classrooms and gobble teachers, and glorify ugliness, avarice, and grumpiness, was meant to create a harmless, constructive outlet for very angry children. I applaud the fresh use of language and the vigorous though minimal pictures. What I can't condone is the complete anti-loving-caring-living message of this book. (pp. 42-3)

Leigh Dean, in a review of "The Baby Uggs Are Hatching," in Children's Book Review Service, *Vol. II, No. 5, January, 1983, pp. 42-3.*

KERMIT'S GARDEN OF VERSES (1982)

What's the best-known fantasy of all time? The Muppet Show, of course. Well, maybe not, but the Muppet fantasy is surely up there with Oz, Disney and the Hobbits as multi-media fantasy worlds widely enjoyed by children and adults alike.

The central figure in the Muppet world is, of course, Kermit the Frog, and it's a Kermit's-eye view we get in this delightful little collection of Muppet verse. Jack Prelutsky has done an outstanding job of capturing the Kermit charisma in simple rhymes—poetry that works so well it's pure pleasure to read it aloud, or even to yourself. Most of the poems are Kermit's homages to or assessments of his fellow performers on the Muppet Show, although a few are more autobiographical and reflective. . . .

I wouldn't trade this ***Garden*** for a ream of speculative verse or all the Rysling anthologies laid end to end. Three cheers—the spirit of poetry lives on in simple children's verse such as this.

Neal Wilgus, in a review of "Kermit's Garden of Verses," in Science Fiction Review, *Vol. 14, No. 4, November, 1985, p. 37.*

ZOO DOINGS: ANIMAL POEMS **(1983)**

The animal verses from three of Prelutsky's books, ***A Gopher in the Garden, Toucans Two*** and ***The Pack Rat's Day,*** are gathered in this single volume. Clever wordplay, these verses are like jellybeans: gobbled quickly as a snack, they offer little in the way of long-lasting nourishment. The rhymes are well constructed, but silly, without being either rib-ticklingly funny or elegantly witty.

Holly Sanhuber, in a review of "Zoo Doings: Animal Poems," in School Library Journal, *Vol. 29, No. 8, April, 1983, p. 116.*

The subjects are appealing, the verse bouncy and lilting, with strong rhymes and meter. Although not new, the poems are witty, and the book can also be used for reading aloud to younger children.

Zena Sutherland, in a review of "Zoo Doings," in Bulletin of the Center for Children's Books, *Vol. 36, No. 9, May, 1983, p. 175.*

The poet invites the reader to look, laugh, and linger at all manner of creatures—forty-six of them in all. From aardvark to zebu, Prelutsky's animals and antics alike excite the reader to browse through the pages looking past cages for the no loafer of a gopher, "speedy cheetah," "Yickity-yak," and "huge hippopotamus." A humorous pace is sustained throughout. Well-turned phrases make plain animals seem exotic and cause the reader to go along with the play in a zoo that includes bees, oysters, and the "long-extinct tyrannosaur."

Prelutsky's zoo visit, actually a revisit, is a gathering of his best poems from earlier books. It is however, a special poetry invitation, one that all will accept and cherish. (pp. 1022-23)

Marlene Ann Birkman, in a review of "Zoo Doings," in Language Arts, *Vol. 60, No. 8, November-December, 1983, pp. 1022-23.*

IT'S VALENTINE'S DAY **(1983)**

The trouble with Valentine's Day as the latest occasion for a Prelutsky collection of easy-reader holiday rhymes is the also-limited subject-matter: nobody does much but send valentines—and valentine doggerel sounds a lot like what Prelutsky's been writing for the whole series. Still, if much of this is predictable, it's also comfortably familiar and kid-like. . . . [For] a finale, a smidgin of real Prelutsky: "I only got one valentine, / and *that* was signed / LOVE, FRANKENSTEIN."

A review of "It's Valentine's Day," in Kirkus Reviews, *Juvenile Issue, Vol. LI, Nos. 13-17, September 1, 1983, p. J-158.*

He's done Thanksgiving, Christmas and Halloween, so Valentine's Day is a natural next stop on Prelutsky's holiday hit parade. Hallelujah! The 14 poems here range from the genuine joy of **"It's Valentine's Day"** ("and you just made / the morning shine— / you said you'd be / my valentine") to the giddy goofiness of **"I love you more than applesauce"** or **"Jelly Jill loves Weasel Will."** Some work better than others, but the feelings will all hit home somewhere—be they the guilty pleasure of the boy who devours his mother's valentine chocolates, the confused elation of the girl who receives her best valentine from a boy she can't stand, the fear of not getting anything in the class valentine box or the horror of being kissed on the cheek by a *girl*. The rhymes are generally simple but clever. . . . Stupid stories and/or sentimental mush frequently characterize Valentine's Day material; a small valentine to Prelutsky who gives us instead, "I only got one valentine, / and *that* was signed / Love, Frankenstein." (pp. 79-80)

Nancy Palmer, in a review of "It's Valentine's Day," in School Library Journal, *Vol. 30, No. 4, December, 1983, pp. 79-80.*

Prelutsky, as always, is careful about rhyme and meter; his poems are light and humorous, occasionally barbed, and full of situations and actions that will be familiar to young readers—like having to make a paper heart smaller and smaller when you cut it freehand. Not impressive, but entertaining, especially for those readers who react with embarrassed giggles to the sentimentality of Valentine's Day.

Zena Sutherland, in a review of "It's Valentine's Day," in Bulletin of the Center for Children's Books, *Vol. 37, No. 6, February, 1984, p. 116.*

IT'S SNOWING! IT'S SNOWING! **(1984)**

Prelutsky must invent poetry in his sleep to keep furnishing his amazing number of books annually. They can never be too many, though, for children who respond to every line. Winter pleasures and woes are the themes of this charmer. . . . Among the comic verses are several lovely meditations. . . .

A review of "It's Snowing! It's Snowing!" in Publishers Weekly, *Vol. 225, No. 6, February 10, 1984, p. 194.*

This seasonal romp could shape classroom excitement come first snow or raise drooping spirits come the inevitable winter blahs. Seventeen short, vivid poems zero in on the spirit of play with staccato verses. . . . While some rhymes are sing-song, there is a kind of exuberance that carries the lot, along with some clever twists. . . . (p. 1346)

Betsy Hearne, in a review of "It's Snowing! It's Snowing!" in Booklist, *Vol. 80, No. 18, May 15, 1984, pp. 1346, 1348.*

Whether the subject is the intricacy of one snowflake or a romp through a winter landscape where "the air is a silvery blur," these poems speak with immediacy and wit of the child's experience. Using colloquial language and rhythms, Prelutsky moves from concrete, everyday images . . . to a wider world, and then back again; as in the wry, dreamy poem, "My sister would never throw snowballs at butterflies" ("she only throws them at me''); or in the dark humor of **''The Snowman's Lament''** . . . with its funny use of rhyme and assonance. . . .

Zena Sutherland, in a review of ''It's Snowing! It's Snowing!'' in Bulletin of the Center for Children's Books, *Vol. 37, No. 10, June, 1984, p. 190.*

From **''One Last Little Leaf''** to **''The Snowman's Lament''** the course of a season is marked by the natural phenomena and human activities of winter. The tone is quite different from the macabre humor of ***Nightmares*** or ***The Snopp on the Sidewalk*** . . . ; the fragile symmetry of the single flake is emphasized rather than the menace of the storm. The humor derives from an implicit recognition that the pleasures are worth the discomforts—dripping nose, itchy ski pants, heavy shoveling. An easy-to-read format and large print suit the facility of the rhyme and accessibility of the imagery. Where more challenging vocabulary is introduced, contextual clues help the beginning reader appreciate the music of such words as *withered, kindred, serenades,* and *intricate.*

Charlotte W. Draper, in a review of ''It's Snowing! It's Snowing!'' in The Horn Book Magazine, *Vol. LX, No. 5, September-October, 1984, p. 603.*

WHAT I DID LAST SUMMER (1984)

School is over, and in this poem of epic proportions (primary-grade style), Prelutsky's hero tells exactly what he did during summer vacation. Most of the happenings are things with which kids can easily identify—going to the museum, eating too much at a county fair, having a yucky cousin come to visit. The singsong poems are amusing for the most part, but occasionally Prelutsky gets a bit highfalutin for his audience. His description of the Fourth of July celebration is particularly flowery (''Great torrents cascaded in red, white and blue . . .'').

Ilene Cooper, in a review of ''What I Did Last Summer,'' in Booklist, *Vol. 80, No. 16, April 15, 1984, p. 1196.*

Is there a kid alive who has never had to write this book? It's doubtful, and the teachers who cruelly assign it year after year hardly deserve the goofy, rollicking, comically real poetry Prelutsky turns in here. . . . Prelutsky tosses off rhymes which—though not his hottest stuff—still read with ease and humor. . . . Not a crucial addition, but fun.

Nancy Palmer, in a review of ''What I Did Last Summer,'' in School Library Journal, *Vol. 30, No. 9, May, 1984, p. 99.*

Conventional responses to conventional summer-vacation situations, in mundane verse: lesser Prelutsky (in the ***Rainy Rainy Saturday*** vein) but a passingly agreeable easy-reader exercise. . . . [It's] the August torpor, and the August doldrums, that score here. . . .

A review of ''What I Did Last Summer,'' in Kirkus Reviews, *Juvenile Issue, Vol. LII, Nos. 6-9, May 1, 1984, p. J-35.*

THE NEW KID ON THE BLOCK (1984)

To quickly take the measure of Prelutsky's new collection of humorous verse, his claim to parity with America's best in the class, you might skim the index of first lines, concentrating on the letter I. . . . Prelutsky's a natural rhymester. He has a keen sense of what tickles kids. His rhymes are infectious, his verses ineradicable. . . . He slips into nonsense without your hardly knowing it: ''Nine mindless mice, who paid the price, / are thawing slowly by the ice, / still sitting on their tricycles / . . . nine white and shiny *micicles.*'' . . . But the pair-up with [illustrator James] Stevenson is the coup here: both have an offhand drollery that knows no age distinctions. A fat, squat book, full of jolly rhymes and juicy drawings, that's fun just to have around.

A review of ''The New Kid on the Block,'' in Kirkus Reviews, *Juvenile Issue, Vol. LII, Nos. 10-17, September 1, 1984, p. J-76.*

[***The New Kid on the Block*** is] a collection that consists primarily of humorous poetry, much of it flagrantly nonsensical. Prelutsky's writing, dependable in its scansion and rhythm, has an appealing lilt and a communicable sense of the fun of word play. This isn't great poetry, but it's good poetry for the most part (a bit jingly here and there) and it's the kind of poetry that may capture the attention of children who have not been poetry lovers.

Zena Sutherland, in a review of ''The New Kid on the Block,'' in Bulletin of the Center for Children's Books, *Vol. 38, No. 2, October, 1984, p. 34.*

Undeniably a winner with children, Prelutsky has much of the verve and irreverence that Shel Silverstein and Dennis Lee have, with a somewhat more relentless metric scheme—the kind of rhyme and rhythm that live forever in jump-rope and playground chants. Most of the 100-plus poems here are mini-jokes, wordplay, and character sketches . . . , with liberal doses of monsters and meanies as well as common, garden-variety child mischief. . . . The reading aloud of **''Bleezer's Ice Cream''** might infect an entire classroom to add its own list of flavors; the hungry **''Flotz''** may turn into a common excuse for the disappearance of punctuation marks from papers that were turned in perfect. **''Today Is Very Boring''** could well become every parent's answer to summer complaints. Even at his most mechanical, Prelutsky is brisk; at his most inventive, as in **''Happy Birthday, Dear Dragon,''** he bubbles with unflinching energy right over into children's best and worst moments.

Betsy Hearne, in a review of ''The New Kid on the Block,'' in Booklist, *Vol. 81, No. 4, October 15, 1984, p. 310.*

A poetry stew! Seasoned with chuckles, giggles, ''micicles,'' rages, and ''slines,'' this collection of 107 poems offers unexpected links to the possibilities of everyday living: a rollicking celebration of delights in the sounds of language. **''Eggs!''** and **''Ballad of a Boneless Chicken''** are particularly flavorful morsels.

Characteristic of his previous poems, Jack Prelutsky creates the reality of the impossible with a fast, rollicking pace, pleasing rhyme scheme, and repetitive patterns of words and sounds. He revels in the sounds of names: Floradora Doe, Minerva Mott and Archie B. McCall. Clever twists give ordinary situations an unexpected element of surprise: being caught in a revolving door, a girl as the neighborhood bully, and an alley cat with one life left.

Ronald A. Jobe, in a review of ''The New Kid on the Block,'' in Language Arts, *Vol. 62, No. 2, February, 1985, p. 191.*

'You need to have an iron rear to sit upon a cactus, Or otherwise, at least a year of very painful practice'. Briskly cantering rhythms, oddball rhymes, a hint of risky coarseness, ruefully grotesque illustrations . . .—these are all elements to capture the eye and ear of children from seven or so ready to take at least a temporarily irreverent attitude to the pressures of family and neighbourhood. There is dashing nonsense here (**'Forty performing bananas'**, **'A wolf is at the Laundromat'**) but far more verses defining areas of complaint (of miserly relatives or teasing school fellows), of momentary distaste (**'New York is in North Carolina'**, **'Floradora Doe'**) and of simple pleasures (**'Yubbazibbies'**, **'Gussie's Greasy Spoon'**). Children who enjoy [Michael] Rosen should find plenty of fun here but I think a few may notice a certain monotony of technique and approach.

Margery Fisher, in a review of "The New Kid on the Block," in Growing Point, *Vol. 25, No. 2, July, 1986, p. 4656.*

MY PARENTS THINK I'M SLEEPING (1985)

Prelutsky turns his rollicking poetry talents to the problems and thoughts of bedtime. Unlike his ***Nightmares*** (. . . 1976), the night visions in these 14 poems are lighthearted rather than scary. **"A Spooky Sort of Shadow"** is really just a brush and comb; the monster in **"When I'm Very Nearly Sleeping"** can be frightened away by a bedside light. [Yossi] Abolafia's drawings . . . reinforce the book's domestic, comfortable tone. A literary dessert for collections that, like the narrator of the poem **"Chocolate Cake,"** have "got an empty space."

Kathleen D. Whalin, in a review of "My Parents Think I'm Sleeping," in School Library Journal, *Vol. 32, No. 4, December, 1985, p. 81.*

Most of the selections, which are often humorous but less often witty, have to do with wakeful nights, some spent in happy under-the-covers reading and others spent in coping with night fears. These should have the appeal of everyday (or everynight) life experiences and they are adequately written, but few of the poems are Prelutsky at his best.

A review of "My Parents Think I'm Sleeping," in Bulletin of the Center for Children's Books, *Vol. 39, No. 5, January, 1986, p. 94.*

Sometimes humorous, sometimes thoughtfully quiet, the poems reflect an interesting range of reactions to the night and are more subdued, more suitable for bedtime reading, perhaps, than the earlier ***Nightmares: Poems to Trouble Your Sleep***. . . . While some of the selections may seem a bit limper than the poet's usual crisp, fresh fare, the book will probably still find an audience with Prelutsky fans.

Karen Jameyson, in a review of "My Parents Think I'm Sleeping," in The Horn Book Magazine, *Vol. LXII, No. 1, January-February, 1986, p. 68.*

RIDE A PURPLE PELICAN (1986)

A rollicking, rambunctious collection of rhymes by the author of the popular and acclaimed ***The New Kid on the Block.*** Prelutsky's nonsense verse is simple and tongue-twisting by turns as he carries his readers along on fantastic flights of fancy "from Seattle / to the city of New York." Kids will enjoy the stops along the way to visit "Timble Tamble Turkey," "Jilliky, Jolliky, Jelliky, Jee" and "Hannah Banana," or pronounce such locales as Saskatoon, Albuquerque or Cincinnati. . . . This is a fine and funny introduction to poetry for the very young. Kids will want to climb on board for another trip, and soon.

A review of "Ride a Purple Pelican," in Publishers Weekly, *Vol. 230, No. 4, July 25, 1986, p. 183.*

Prelutsky has caught the rhythm and spirit of nursery rhymes in 29 short poems about drum-beating bunnies, bullfrogs on parade, Chicago winds, giant sequoias and other wondrous things. Many of these easy-to-remember poems are filled with delicious sounding American and Canadian place names. . . . Highly recommended.

Ann L. Kalkhoff, in a review of "Ride a Purple Pelican," in Children's Book Review Service, *Vol. 15, No. 2, October, 1986, p. 15.*

With this book of new rhymes, readers will discover a modern-day alternative to Mother Goose. Twenty-nine wonderfully rhythmic chants introduce such colorful characters as Hannah Banana, who "walked on her hands from Montana to Maine," and Minnie and Moe, who "went to Chicago / to see the wind blow." Prelutsky's rhymes are rich in language, story, humor, and sensory content. But the joy of this book is not just the rhymes—it's also [Garth] Williams' glorious, brightly colored pictures, which bring the words to life.

Constance A. Mellon, in a review of "Ride a Purple Pelican," in School Library Journal, *Vol. 33, No. 3, November, 1986, p. 82.*

Almost every one of these bouncy rhymes hosts a reference to a city or region in America. . . . Some of the poems have a tongue-twister element, which will add to the fun, and almost always there's the child's-eye view: "When Molly Day wears yellow clothes, / finches flutter by her toes, . . . / but when she wears her suit of gray, / no one follows Molly Day." . . . In modes of the silly (Timmy Tatt with his watermelon hat) or the sublime (a white cloud swan over Saskatchewan), this combo of veteran illustrator and seasoned rhymster will have youngsters chanting aloud with parents and teachers.

Betsy Hearne, in a review of "Ride a Purple Pelican," in Bulletin of the Center for Children's Books, *Vol. 40, No. 5, January, 1987, p. 96.*

Johanna (Heusser) Spyri

1827-1901

Swiss author of fiction and short stories.

The following entry presents criticism of Spyri's *Heidi*, published as *Heidis Lehr und Wanderjahre: Eine Geschichte für Kinder und auch für solche welche die Kinder lieb haben* [*Heidi's School and Wander-Years: A Story for Children and for Those Who Love Children*] (1880).

Spyri is recognized as Switzerland's most beloved and enduring writer for children. The author of more than forty books featuring lively, likable youngsters growing up in the Swiss Alps, she is best known as the creator of *Heidi*, the story of a high-spirited orphan girl whose loving ways change the lives of her misanthropic grandfather, a taciturn goat boy, his impoverished family, and a wealthy city family. *Heidi* is considered a classic of children's literature as well as one of the most popular stories to originate in a foreign country. Spyri's first full-length book, it is the only one of her works still to be read today. Spyri wrote *Heidi* to tell her young son about her active childhood in a large and happy family. A devout Christian, she underscores her book with several sections on the virtues of childlike simplicity and innocence, belief in God, and the healing power of nature. In addition to revealing her understanding of how children think and behave, the story introduces readers to the natural surroundings Spyri loved and the customs of the Swiss people. *Heidi* is usually acknowledged as the first juvenile written in German that was both realistic and entertaining. Its success caused succeeding Swiss writers to imitate Spyri's naturalistic subjects, countryside settings, sincere style, and concern for the social and religious questions of the day. When it was first translated into English in 1884, *Heidi* was acclaimed as a refreshing change from the overly sentimental and often morbid stories of the time. Swiss and German readers saw thirteen editions in ten years; many translations, editions, and dramatizations later, *Heidi* continues to be read by children, despite controversy that the strong religious teachings and submissive acceptance of social conditions are outdated.

For more than a hundred years, critics have lauded *Heidi* for its memorable characterizations, vivid recreation of the Alpine out-of-doors, inclusion of humorous incidents and dialogue, and poignant description of childhood feelings. Reviewers credit its longevity to the authenticity and appeal of Spyri's uninhibited heroine and the successful transformation of an unfamiliar landscape into a place as well-loved and recognizable as home. Although some observers object to the book's sentimentality and didacticism, most acknowledge that *Heidi* is a masterpiece of literary craftsmanship and a tribute to the land and people of Switzerland.

(See also *Something about the Author*, Vol. 19.)

MARIAN EDWARDES?

Madame Spyri, like Hans Andersen, had by temperament a peculiar skill in writing the simple histories of an innocent world. In all her stories she shows an underlying desire to preserve children alike from misunderstanding and the mistaken kindness that frequently hinder the happiness and natural development of their lives and characters. The authoress, as we feel in reading her tales, lived among the scenes and people she describes, and the setting of her stories has the charm of the mountain scenery amid which she places her small actors. (p. 9)

Marian Edwardes? in an introduction to Heidi *by Johanna Spyri, David McKay Company, 1922, pp. 9-10.*

ADELINE B. ZACHERT

There are not many children's books that measure up to the high standard set by teachers, librarians, and thoughtful parents, and which are also enthusiastically approved by the children. Among such standards, Johanna Spyri's ***Heidi*** easily takes high rank. It has been a prime favorite for many years. Before children's rooms in public libraries claimed it for their shelves, and so helped greatly to popularize it, before reading for pleasure came to be recognized as a legitimate classroom activity requiring a collection of the choicest children's books, the English translation of ***Heidi*** had been introduced to many children in the form of Christmas and birthday gifts.

For more than a quarter of a century Johanna Spyri's books have appeared on the approved lists of best books for children.

Moni, the Goat Boy, has become almost as popular as ***Heidi; Rico and Wiseli*** is read eagerly by the fortunate children who know Heidi and Moni. In more recent years Gritli's children, Cornelli and Rosele, have been added to the group of delightful child characters created for us by Frau Spyri in her sunny, genuine stories of child life in the Swiss Alps.

Johanna Spyri knew children, she knew how they think and act, for she was one of a large family of children, and so had ample opportunity to acquire an insight into children's minds and hearts. Coupled with this opportunity of knowing children, Frau Spyri had the advantage of being reared in a happy, cultured home and in a literary environment. The art of vivid portrayal of child life was hers by heritage and training. Her mother, Meta Heusser, was a popular writer and poet. Her father was a well-known and greatly beloved physician in the canton of Zurich. The hospitable home of the Heusser's attracted the literary and other intellectual people of the time. Johanna Spyri's early life is clearly felt in all her books. She knew child life and she knew how to tell about it. Her stories give an impression of reality. The characters stand out as personalities. The sunny tempered Heidi, the stolid but dependable Peter, the patient Clara, as well as all adult characters never once fail to be true to type, to think and speak and act as real people.

It is not surprising, therefore, that children everywhere know and love these little Swiss boys and girls who were introduced to them through Frau Spyri's books. But of all the children Heidi and her associates are best beloved.

The grown-ups approve of ***Heidi*** because the story gives our American children delightful pictures of child life among the Swiss mountains, because it is a genuine story of a happy little girl, the kind of child who in real life would make an ideal playmate for children. The story produces a realization of the freshness of mountain breezes, of colorful flowering meadows, which invite to a new enjoyment of the great outdoors. It makes the right kind of emotional appeal to children; there are incidents which awaken sympathy, foster kindness, stimulate a sense of justice. The reading of the story establishes a knowledge of human nature, a clearer understanding of human motives, an accurate and kindly judgment of people and events. All this is accomplished easily and naturally without any obvious drawing of morals. Such a book is eminently good for children.

However, children do not always like what is good for them. The reason ***Heidi*** is a great book is that children as well as adults read it with interest and like it. (pp. v-viii)

Adeline B. Zachert, in a preface to Heidi *by Johanna Spyri, edited by Adeline B. Zachert, The John C. Winston Company, 1924, pp. v-x.*

JOSEPH WALKER McSPADDEN

Johanna Spyri has been called the Louisa May Alcott of German literature. Yet this comparison does not quite do her justice, as her range of characters is much more extensive than that of the New England author. Spyri has produced a wonderful gallery of child portraits, dealing particularly with Swiss life and customs. (p. 45)

Her first short stories met with such general favor that she was emboldened to begin a longer work, ***Heidi.*** This was several years in preparation, and appeared in 1880. . . . From the outset this delightful story won friends—first among the Swiss and German children and then in ever-widening circles until it penetrated into every country in Europe, and finally reached America. To-day ***Heidi*** is so well recognized as a classic of childhood that it is hard to think of the book as being less than a half century old. Like all her succeeding train of stories, its charm lies in its simplicity and understanding of boy and girl life. On the title-page of ***Heimatlos*** [alternate German title for ***Heidi***], which ran into several editions, she placed a dedicatory note that it was written for those who loved children as well as for the children themselves. This remained her creed in her succeeding work, and explains in a measure why her stories have been read with equal interest by older readers.

By the year 1890, ***Heidi*** had run through thirteen editions in Germany, and was being translated into other tongues. Still almost bewildered by her rapidly mounting fame, Johanna Spyri did not allow her head to be turned by it. She remained the retiring woman of her earlier days. She is spoken of as having lived a singularly pure and beautiful life. Hers was a Christian character, which permeated both her life and her books, as none who is familiar with either can dispute. At this time her health began to fail and for several years she was an invalid, but this increased rather than diminished her tide of authorship. Other popular books coming from her busy pen include ***Rico and Wiseli, Gritli's Children, The Little Alpine Musician, Veronica, Uncle Titus, Arthur and Squirrel,*** and numerous shorter stories. It is said that no German child's Christmas is complete without another book by the author of ***Heidi.*** She has become an institution. (pp. 48-51)

A very important characteristic of the Spyri stories is that every one of them, whether long or short, teaches some sweet and useful lesson. In this respect lies the Swiss author's great strength, and it places her far above the New England writer [Louisa May Alcott]. This is why, also, Johanna Spyri appeals to the universal human heart as do few other writers of children's literature. (p. 52)

[Turn] to ***Heidi*** and the others of her immortal books. Here she stands revealed as one who loved children and understood them as few are permitted to do. And thus it is that she will live for all time through her books. They convey a message as sweet, pure and wholesome as the breeze which blows continually from the summit of her beloved Alps. (pp. 53-4)

Joseph Walker McSpadden, "Johanna Spyri, the Author," in Recollections of Johanna Spyri's Childhood *by Anna Ulrich, translated by Helen B. Dole, Thomas Y. Crowell Co. Publishers, 1925, pp. 45-54.*

HELEN B. DOLE

Johanna Spyri has long been recognized as one of the world's favorite writers for children. . . .

Heidi is known and loved everywhere, by grown people as well as by children. Written first to amuse Mrs. Spyri's own little son, the story is in a sense a true one, for it recalls many of the experiences and impressions of the author's own childhood. The author practically *transfers* her own memories, so that the reader feels he too has really known Heidi and the beautiful country in which she lived. (p. iii)

Helen B. Dole, in an introduction to Heidi: A Little Swiss Girl's City and Mountain Life *by Johanna Spyri, translated by Helen B. Dole, Ginn and Company, 1927, pp. iii-iv.*

MAY HILL ARBUTHNOT

[***Heidi***] continued the fine tradition of *Hans Brinker* by introducing American children to children of other lands through a delightful story. . . . It is a long book . . . , with pages of solid reading. Still, children read it, and many college students say it is one of the books they reread in childhood in spite of the fact that they belonged to the generation which also had *The Good Master* and *The Trumpeter of Krakow*.

Heidi uses the most popular of all themes—a variation of Cinderella, the unwanted, neglected child who comes into her own—but there is a convincing quality about ***Heidi*** which many of the modern Cinderellas lack. The child is full of the joy of living. She skips and leaps and she falls in love with an apparently grouchy old grandfather, the goats, and the mountains, all with equal vehemence and loyalty. When she is torn away from them by force and deception and sent to live in town as a companion to the invalid child, Clara, she suffers acutely. Still she manages to make friends, to secure kittens and a turtle for Clara, and to send out shy tendrils of affection in many directions. In the town she learns to read and gets her first religious instruction. This is of a kind that will offend no religious group today since it is built on a faith in God and on the ability to draw strength and wisdom from communion with God, in prayer and thanksgiving. This is a deeply religious book, yet children read it all. Probably because the emphasis is reassuring, it gives both faith and hope. Homesickness for her mountains and her loved ones almost destroys Heidi, and not until she is restored to them does she recover. From the security of her life in the mountains she is able to reach out to the town friends and help them, too. Clara is brought to the mountains, and there the good milk from the goats, the clear, fresh air, Grandfather, and Heidi cure her. The little invalid walks for the first time in her life, and Heidi keeps her mountains and her town friends, too.

Spyri's birthplace in Hirzel, Switzerland.

No child who has read and loved ***Heidi*** will ever enter Switzerland without a feeling of coming home. . . . Nothing about Switzerland will ever seem alien to the child who has read ***Heidi***. In every old man he will see Heidi's grandfather; in every village, Heidi's Dorfli. This is what books about other lands should do for children—leave them feeling forever a part of that country, forever well disposed toward the people. In good stories of other people, they have no sense of oddity, no feeling of irreconcilable differences, but a desire to know these people so like themselves.

To accomplish this, a book about other lands must be completely authentic and sincere. ***Heidi*** has both these virtues because of the experiences and character of the author, Johanna Spyri. . . . Nothing in the book is labored or superficial. Heidi is as wholesome and real as her mountains. Every child reading this book will wish for a bed of straw just like Heidi's, up in the loft, looking out on the mountain peaks under their glittering crown of stars. (pp. 413-14)

May Hill Arbuthnot, "Other Times and Places: Early Books about Children of Other Lands," in her Children and Books, *Scott, Foresman and Company, 1947, pp. 412-14.*

PUBLISHERS WEEKLY

[***Heidi***] is a popular book for reading aloud. Like most good books for children it has a tremendous amount of suspense. It also shows a sharp observation of children. Heidi is not a goody-goody child. She means well, but she is always in difficulties.

The little girls and boys (though it is primarily a girls' book) who read ***Heidi*** probably understand very well such things as her dismay when the mountain wildflowers or the fresh white rolls she has innocently collected and stored in her pockets wither and spoil, and her cheerful lack of concern at the trouble she continually gives her elders. They understand why she refuses to confide in the kind grandmother who is willing to help defend her against the humorless Fraulein Rottenmeier and her alibi when she fails to say her prayers ("If all the people in Frankfurt are praying at once, God couldn't possibly hear me"). When the goatherd, Peter, has to climb down the steep mountainside on a hot summer day to retrieve the articles of clothing that Heidi has shed along the path, chances are that the young readers' sympathies are all with Heidi. Adults cannot fail to understand the emotions of the older characters. Heidi, for all her charm, is a disrupting influence in their peaceful lives.

There is a touch of quite modern psychology here and there, too, as when the doctor suggests that Heidi walks in her sleep because she is homesick and unhappy, and that she can be cured if she is sent home to her beloved Alps.

The author shows great understanding of the older child, Peter, as she shows his growing affection for Heidi and then his increasing jealousy when her fine city friends come to visit her, a jealousy which culminates in his act of destroying Klara's wheelchair by pushing it down the mountain. Almost the only old-fashioned element in the book are the heavy doses of rather simple-minded religion that are ladled out to Heidi by her elders every few chapters. (p. 320)

"'Heidi;' or, The Story of a Juvenile Best Seller," in Publishers Weekly, *Vol. 164, No. 4, July 25, 1953, pp. 318-21.*

ANNE EATON

It is probable . . . that no other book of [the 1870's and 1880's], showing a background foreign to English and American young readers had such a success or has implanted itself so firmly in youthful memories as did ***Heidi***. . . . [With] its snow-capped mountains, its free outdoor atmosphere, its happy children, simple pleasures and warm affection between the characters, it is still delighted in by boys and girls. The reason for this is that Heidi herself is so honest, so genuine in her enjoyment of the life in her grandfather's cottage that every detail of that life is glowing and memorable. One feels forever after that there can be no bed like a mattress stuffed with hay and laid opposite the open wooden shutter of a window facing a whole world of mountains and stars. Was there ever anything that seemed more delicious to the imagination than the hot, creamy goat's cheese with which her grandfather spread her thick-crusted bread? Heidi's adventures are small but spirited. The real accomplishment of this book is that it renders a hitherto alien scene not only familiar but beloved, it makes clear, not the hardships, but the deep and satisfying pleasures of peasant life. (p. 191)

Anne Eaton, "Widening Horizons, 1840-1890: A Broader Field," in A Critical History of Children's Literature *by Cornelia Meigs and others, edited by Cornelia Meigs, Macmillan Publishing Company, 1953, pp. 189-98.*

ELIZABETH ENRIGHT

[Heidi] is 75 years old this year; and since she shows none of the usual signs of aging and fading she may reasonably be considered an immortal. . . . Her name is almost a household word. . . .

Heidi, the dark-haired girl who wore all the clothes she owned to save her aunt the bother of carrying them, is just as vigorous and as interesting to children today as she was to their grandparents.

Why is it? In an era when so much children's literature was burdened with dead dialogue and moral content, the freshness of this story must have come as a breath of mountain air; today, Heidi holds her own with carefree heroines of any of the best modern children's books because she is real. Through all the grind and clatter of awkward translations her character continues to ring true. She is good-natured and sensible, never dull. Escaping from the aunt, she intelligently takes off her dresses, shoes and stockings (knitted); and in her petticoat, barefooted, hops nimbly up the rocks with Peter the goatherd and his flock. And Peter is real, so are the goats.

The author . . . did not escape some of the literary conventions of her day. In the fiction of that period one of the principal characters always had to be an invalid (a few years earlier one of the principal characters, preferably a child, always had to die), somebody else had to be rich, and another, or others, had to be very poor. All these requirements were filled in ***Heidi;*** but the invalid, fortunately, gets well and walks on her own two feet; the rich people spend their money wisely by giving everybody presents, and the poor are suitably benefited and grateful. And over and above the action of the characters tower those other mighty characters, the mountains, with their fiery snowfields and high pastures all jeweled with rock-roses and gentians. For a child who has never seen it, a new land is created: high, airy, exciting. His inward ear can hear that world of bells and brooks; his imagination's eye can scan the deeps or see the eagle in the air.

Reading about Heidi and Peter eating their lunch on the mountainside is enough to make anybody hungry, and many a child has developed a sudden taste for cheese after reading this book. And then what could be cozier to think about, to imagine oneself in, than that little bed of hay under the eaves? There Heidi and the reader look through the round window at a thousand stars, just as if, as Clara says, one "were driving in a high carriage straight into the sky." One can hear the great soft roaring of the wind in the old fir trees by the hut. . . .

As a child, I remember, I never felt comfortable about the Alm-Uncle. He seemed to me too forbidding and austere, and I did not really like him after his conversion to kindliness. I seem to have missed the point that he had been a gay blade in his youth, loving wine and high-living, squandering his money and at last retiring to the Alm-hut, stung by the criticism of his neighbors, to live a life of solitary misanthropy. I suppose, being a child, that I viewed such reckless behavior by an adult as pure wickedness, whereas now I can look on his derelictions with a tolerant eye. I used to feel that Fraulein Rottenmeier, the governess-housekeeper, was entirely evil; now I see that she was a humorless fool with an unhealthy passion for authority. Perhaps she was the daughter of a Prussian officer. Who knows?

About Heidi I had no misapprehension. I recognized her as a girl like myself: better, more sensible and generous, praying oftener (much oftener), but nevertheless a real child whom I would have liked for a companion, and whose marvelous playground I wished had been my own.

After her marriage Johanna Spyri lived for many years in Zurich, but she never lost her longing for the mountain valleys with their bells and birds, and probably it is just this quality, this longing to relive, by describing, the brightest morning-moments of childhood, that gives the story its share of authentic power. Reading it we can almost know what it was like to see the snowfields catching fire, or hear the night wind combing through the firs.

Elizabeth Enright, "At 75, Heidi Still Skips Along," in The New York Times Book Review, *November 13, 1955, p. 42.*

NOEL STREATFEILD

Heidi was published in 1880, and it was written in German, for Johanna was a German-speaking Swiss. From the beginning ***Heidi*** was much talked about, for apart from the charm of the story, it was the first good, well-written book for children ever written in German. (pp. iv-v)

Heidi is as popular with Swiss children now as it was when it was first published. For although there is more moralizing in it than children are accustomed to today, the story lived, for Heidi herself is such a darling and has such a vivid personality, as indeed has the grandfather and most of the other people in the book. But why the book holds the great place it does in the hearts of all Swiss children, is perhaps because Heidi, like themselves, so loved the glorious countryside of her native land. Maybe that is one of the reasons too, why children all over the world have loved ***Heidi***. . . . (p. v)

Noel Streatfeild, "About This Book," in Heidi *by Johanna Spyri, translated by Joy Law, Franklin Watts, Inc., 1959, pp. iii-v.*

BETTINA HÜRLIMANN

[*The following excerpt was originally published in German in 1959.*]

Johanna Spyri was a friend of C. F. Meyer . . . and other Zürich intellectuals and she was anxious to write good books without consciously talking down to her child readers. It is for this reason that her books . . . are *Volksbücher* rather than books expressly for children—with the exception, of course, of ***Heidi*** which became an attraction for children all over the world through the portrayal of its young heroine, its sensitive treatment of homesickness and its superb descriptions of Swiss scenery.

Johanna Spyri's success soon became a clear danger for the future of children's literature, for it provided a fixed recipe for children's writers to copy in the same way that *The Swiss family Robinson* had done earlier in the century with its curious mixture of adventure, precept, and instruction. . . . These new tales created their effects from real life, a thing which few German books were doing at that time. Above all, religious and social questions figured in these tales and they were based on the actual experience of Johanna Spyri, who was the daughter of a country doctor. Almost everything she describes could actually have taken place. Even the rural elements played a bigger part here than in the corresponding German publications. The result was that the Swiss writers pounced on the salient features and would not let go of them. What in Johanna Spyri had been new and unique now became a general Swiss style, only a little modified or changed. (pp. 251-53)

Of all Switzerland's literature in the nineteenth century, ***Heidi*** is the export that has lasted the best. . . . (p. 254)

Bettina Hürlimann, "Towards a History of Children's Books in Switzerland," in her Three Centuries of Children's Books in Europe, *edited and translated by Brian W. Alderson, The World Publishing Company, 1967, pp. 246-55.*

LUCIA BINDER

[***Heidi*** can] be classified as one of the few humorous realistic children's books of [its] time; despite all the adverse criticism it receives today and despite all negative forecasts it still remains on the list of widely read children's books. This success is not only a result of its sentimental appeal but also to a great extent of its humorous descriptions of country and people. Goatpeter in his simplicity, the gossip-mongering villagers, the self-important governess and the wordy, unctuous explanations of "Mr. Candidate" make the reader smile. There are also some comical situations in ***Heidi:*** when the strict governess enters the study importantly to restore discipline and takes flight before a few young kittens, etc. . . .

[There are] warm-hearted understanding smiles in [this] romantic-idyllic Swiss children's book. (p. 14)

Lucia Binder, "Humor in Children's Books," in Bookbird, *Vol. VIII, No. 4 (December 15, 1970), pp. 8-14.*

MARY F. THWAITE

Towards the end of the nineteenth century Switzerland was to become known in many lands through the transmigration of ***Heidi***. . . . ***Heidi,*** one of [Johanna Spyri's] earliest books, proved overwhelmingly the most popular. Love of children and love of her native land are expressed in the author's many stories, but they are also much affected by the contemporary emphasis on sentiment and pathos. Homeless, orphan, or otherwise unfortunate children predominate. Sorrows and trials are overcome by goodness, and happiness usually prevails at the end. In some ways ***Heidi*** is typical of its time, but the little heroine's story is unfolded with so much true feeling and vivid description that it transcends its limitations. How clearly the Alpine scenes are depicted, where Heidi lives at first a simple and happy existence with her grandfather! Sent away to the city the child becomes lonely, sad, and ill, but she does not complain. At last all comes right. Heidi goes back to her beloved Alps, with new friends she has made, and radiates love and friendship to make everyone happy. Religious faith and sincere emotion animate this charming story, which has the sharp contrasts that young readers love. Most of Johanna Spyri's books are now forgotten but Heidi lives on, endearing herself and her mountain home to new generations of children everywhere. (pp. 264-65)

Mary F. Thwaite, "Children's Books Abroad: 'Heidi'," in her From Primer to Pleasure in Reading, *revised edition, The Horn Book, Inc., 1972, pp. 225-74.*

KLAUS DODERER

Heidi is still so popular in West Germany that year after year, during the annual read-aloud contest, many of the eleven- or twelve-year-old participants—especially girls—continue to choose it for their selections. Since 1966 there has been a Johanna Spyri Foundation (home office, Zurich); its archives not only collect ***Heidi*** editions from all over the world but also preserve documents on the life and work of the writer. ***Heidi*** must certainly be as well known to the American child as it is to the Swiss, the Austrian or the German youngster. (p. 12)

Although the figures around Heidi are given individual treatment by Johanna Spyri, they exist only in their relationship to her. The author's own moral and religious views assign Heidi the function of turning disrupted relationships back in the right direction and thereby creating harmony in her world. She accomplishes all this by virtue of her naive, unspoilt innocence; she is a figure out of the religious-based *Heimatsroman* (pastoral novel) of the nineteenth century, which pictured a world that was intact as a consequence of natural living. Sin was a consequence of rejecting the community, and inner salvation was wealth.

It's interesting to note that a novel containing so many social elements defines poverty and wealth within a religious-moral context. In ***Heidi,*** the person who lives by faith and practices love-thy-neighbour is fulfilled because he lives within a closely knit community. Johanna Spyri invites her readers to conclude that such a state can more easily be realized in a poor mountain village than in the atmosphere of a city, where people are superficially richer but live cut off from each other. She implies that one should come to terms with existing social conditions, that one should accept poverty as being willed by God, and by seeking refuge in inner wealth, overlook the unfair economic conditions among people.

Obviously no one wants to part with the bright happy child of nature, who changes her surroundings for the good and shows innate worldly wisdom. But when we consider the dubious philosophy underlying Heidi's existence, we must ask ourselves whether this book is still suitable for today's readers. How relevant to our children is a novel that gives a realistic picture of the social conditions of the second half of the nineteenth century, but in addition pushes aside the problems of that era, even stands them on their heads. (The poor man is rich because it's easier for him to reach God?) Is there a religion for which this book's faith can still serve as a model, a faith that is simple but at the same time so all-encompassing that it ultimately leads people into an uncritical acceptance of secular matters? And what benefit can today's reader derive from a sentimental novel whose high esteem for the isolated mountain world can't help but create antipathy toward our technological surroundings? Johanna Spyri's ***Heidi*** should therefore be consigned to literary history. (pp. 12-13)

Klaus Doderer, "German Children's Classics," in Bookbird, *Vol. XII, No. 1 (March 15, 1974), pp. 8-16.*

MARGERY FISHER

The story of Heidi has always been popular even though the religious and moral message of the book is expressed more directly than present-day taste allows. Some modern editions in fact seek to spare children by cutting the long moral passages; this throws too much emphasis on the carefree aspect of Heidi's character and life, and her time in Frankfurt comes to seem almost like a term of imprisonment. In fact the gaiety, freshness and vigour of the mountain scenes show us only one aspect of the child; her serious consideration for other people, her instinct for the good and true side of life, her innocent power to combat the dark moods of her elders, are just as important and need to be seen clearly in the context in which Johanna Spyri set them. Heidi is no less a real child because her story is used to illustrate certain matters of principle and to serve an educational purpose. However, the two sequels written by one translator of Heidi [Charles Tritten] do not really succeed in extending her function into the grown-up world; it is as a child that this character is understood. (pp. 137-38)

Margery Fisher, "Who's Who in Children's Books: Heidi," in her Who's Who in Children's Books: A Treasury of the Familiar Characters of Childhood, *Holt, Rinehart and Winston, 1975, pp. 137-38.*

JACK ZIPES

Heidi is a conservative product of the nineteenth century which has been kept very much alive in the twentieth. Spyri, a devout Christian, projects a vision of a harmonious world which can only be held together by Judeo-Christian ethics and God himself. Briefly, her story concerns a five-year-old orphan, Heidi, who is sent to live on top of a Swiss mountain with her grandfather, a social outcast. After three years, her aunt, who works in Frankfurt, comes to fetch her so that she can become a companion to a rich little girl who is crippled. Both the aunt and the rest of the Swiss village think it will be better for Heidi, for they have a low opinion of the grandfather and feel that Heidi needs to be educated. For the grandfather, who has come to love Heidi deeply, this is a devastating blow, and he becomes more of a misanthrope. In Frankfurt, Heidi turns a wealthy bourgeois household upside down with her natural ways, which are contrasted with the artificial and decadent ways of the city people. Nevertheless, she endears herself to the grandmother, Klara the cripple, the businessman father, and their servants. Only the governess and teacher cannot grasp her "wild" ways. Eventually, Heidi becomes homesick for the mountains, and Klara's grandmother tells her to have faith in God, who will always help her. Indeed, as Heidi begins to wane, God interferes in the person of the doctor, who advises the businessman to return Heidi to the grandfather. When Heidi is sent back to the mountains, the grandfather is ecstatic and becomes convinced that it was an act of God which brought about the return of his granddaughter. In this sense, Heidi is God's deputy and reconciles the grandfather to the rest of the community. (pp. 165-66)

[***Heidi***] concerns the experiences of a little girl, who is made into some kind of an extraordinary angel, a nature child with holy innocence, incapable of doing evil, gentle, loving, and kind. At first, she does not comprehend the world, but as she grows, everything is explained to her according to the accepted social and religious norms of the day. Here it is important to see the pedagogical purpose of the narrative and its dependence on the traditional *Bildungsroman*. Heidi learns that the world is static and directed by God. Although she is disturbed that her grandfather and relatives are poor and must struggle merely to subsist, the grandmother in Frankfurt brings her to believe that God wants it that way and that material poverty is insignificant when one considers the real meaning of richness: to be rich means *possessing* faith in God and behaving like a good Christian—that is, making sacrifices to benefit the wealthy and looking forward to paradise in the world hereafter. While the simple, pious community of the Swiss village is contrasted with the false, brutal life in the city, Spyri does nothing to explain the real contradictions between city and country. The hard life in the Swiss mountains becomes idyllic. There the people are pure and closer to God. The world of Switzerland caters to the escapist tendencies of readers who might seek release from the perplexing, difficult conditions of urban life. Heidi, too, is a figure of the infantile, regressive fantasy which desires a lost innocence that never was. Since *natural* equals *Christian* in this book, there is no way in which children can comprehend what really is a natural or socially conditioned drive. Nevertheless, Heidi . . . has taken on a classical existence that has become more lifelike than that of real Heidis, and she continues to serve as a (dubious) model for young readers. (pp. 166-67)

Jack Zipes, "Down with Heidi, Down with Struwwelpeter, Three Cheers for the Revolution: Towards a New Socialist Children's Literature in West Germany," in Children's Literature: Annual of the Modern Language Association Seminar on Children's Literature and The Children's Literature Association, *Vol. 5, 1976, pp. 162-80.*

BOB DIXON

[***Heidi*** is] still a 'classic', after nearly a century, very widely read and still going strong. More than that, Heidi's a kind of female Little Lord Fauntleroy, if that isn't too much to imagine, and she brings the little-ray-of-sunshine idea of girls right to the fore. The story says that it's much better to be up on the mountain in God's good sun and fresh air, with toasted cheese and goat's milk for food, and hay to sleep on, than to live with good, rich people and their (largely nasty) servants in Frankfurt. God looks after everything and Heidi is His skipping for joy, or brave little suffering angel, who melts the crusty heart of an old recluse. Everything is homely and cosy and everything turns out marvellously in the end, even though God does leave the rich people, through their charity, to supply certain unexplained wants amidst the idyllic mountains. It makes you weep.

Heidi is a link between books which are realistic, however much reality is manipulated, and stories which are clearly aimed at fantasy. (p. 13)

Bob Dixon, "Sexism: Birds in Gilded Cages," in his Catching Them Young 1: Sex, Race and Class in Children's Fiction, *Pluto Press, 1977, pp. 1-41.*

Illustration by Gustaf Tenggren from the Riverside Bookshelf edition of Heidi, *by Johanna Spyri. Copyright 1923 by Houghton Mifflin Company. Reprinted by permission of Houghton Mifflin Company.*

PHYLLIS BIXLER KOPPES

That Johanna Spyri's ***Heidi*** . . . is a children's classic few would deny. . . . The reasons for ***Heidi***'s continued status as a classic, however, may not be so apparent. Usually, critics credit Spyri's characterization of Heidi and portrayal of setting: Heidi is ''wholesome,'' ''good-natured and sensible, never dull,'' and above all she is ''real,'' as ''real'' as her mountains and goat-milk cheese. On the other hand, Spyri's classic strikes many twentieth-century readers as too didactic and sentimental: Heidi quotes the Frankfurt grandmother's pious wisdom several times too often, and the adults around Heidi are a bit too gushing in their appreciation of ''their happy child.'' No doubt, it was reasons such as these which led Alice Jordan to exclaim, ''And Heidi—who can say just why that little Swiss girl lives so vividly in many hearts?'' The following literary analysis seeks to provide answers to this question. Through an examination of Heidi's placement within the traditions of the *exemplum* and the pastoral romance, this article offers some reasons why the book has survived and probably deserves to survive as a children's classic. This primarily generic approach helps weigh the book's admitted didacticism and sentimentality against the congruence of theme and structure which gives to the work much of its power.

Northrop Frye's assertion that just *value* judgments of literature depend on appropriate *categorical* judgments, that we cannot tell how *good* a thing is until we know *what* it is, is particularly applicable to ***Heidi,*** which can only superficially bear the label of realism sometimes suggested for it. The book nowhere approaches psychological realism, for example. Heidi may be a memorable literary creation, but she, like her friends, is not given enough personality traits to become more than a character type. The ''realism'' of Spyri's setting is similarly questionable: the book may make its reader want to buy a ticket on Swiss Air, but reflection suggests that a hayloft bed might be too cold and that goatmilk cheese every day might become tiresome.

If ''realism'' is inappropriate to describe the literary mode of ***Heidi,*** equally so is ''fantasy.'' Heidi has a marvelous effect on those around her, but she does so without magical apparatus; her mountains suggest those in picture postcards; but they belong more to Switzerland than to J. R. R. Tolkien's desideratum for fantasy, ''Faerie.'' Like many other children's classics confusingly labeled ''realistic,'' ***Heidi*** functions somewhere between realism and fantasy; it presents a fictional territory Laura Ingalls Wilder also explored and located when she combined the fairy-tale formula for timelessness with a specific, historical time reference in the opening sentence of her first book: ''Once upon a time, sixty years ago.'' This realm is that ''neutral territory, somewhere between the real world and fairy-land, where the Actual and the Imaginary may meet'' which Nathaniel Hawthorne identified as the world of the romance as opposed to that of the novel. In this kind of fictional world, as Richard Chase has pointed out, character often becomes ''somewhat abstract and ideal,'' and ''astonishing events may occur'' which have a ''symbolic or ideological, rather than a realistic, plausibility.'' Thus Heidi embodies the ideals of empathetic sensibility and natural simplicity, and the ''astonishing'' effect she has on most persons around her demonstrates the power of these virtues. She is precisely the child whom the Frankfurt housekeeper wanted as a companion for her invalid charge but, ironically, did not recognize in Heidi: ''such a creature as I have read about in books, a girl, you know, born in the fresh mountain air, one who walks through life scarcely touching the ground beneath her feet''. . . . ***Heidi,*** then, is not a realistic novel but a romance, more specifically a pastoral romance since the ideals it portrays are those often celebrated in the Western pastoral tradition. The tradition to which it more immediately belongs, however, is that of the *exemplum*.

Like the romance, the *exemplum* is a literary form devoted to the portrayal of ideals—ideals of conduct, of virtue, or, especially in the evangelical tradition which influenced ***Heidi***, of salvation or conversion. Frequently in this tradition, we find the child who is converted and then through preaching or example helps convert others, especially adults. The concept of the child as a model for adult conversion has a Biblical basis. In the Gospel of Matthew (XVIII.1-14), for example, when his disciples asked him, "Who is the greatest in the kingdom of heaven?" Jesus set a child among them and said, "Except ye be converted, and become as little children, ye shall not enter into the kingdom of heaven." In nineteenth-century literature for adults as well as for children, this religious concept underwent a Romantic secularization and stressed other beneficent effects children could have on adults. Through his innocence and vulnerability, for example, the child could give new meaning to the life of a misanthropic adult. Such a child is Eppie in George Eliot's *Silas Marner*, which has as its epigraph a quotation from Wordsworth's "Michael": "a child, more than all other gifts/That earth can offer to declining man,/ Brings hope with it, and forward-looking thoughts" (11.146-48). Cedric Errol has this effect on his irascible selfish grandfather in Frances Hodgson Burnett's *Little Lord Fauntleroy* (1886). Often, the child helps "save" others by becoming the focal character of a family or small redemptive community; examples include little Diamond in George MacDonald's *At the Back of the North Wind* (1871) and Mary in Burnett's *The Secret Garden* (1911).

Spyri's ***Heidi*** clearly belongs to this *exemplum* tradition. Most of Part I is devoted to Heidi's "conversion." Consistent with the Romantic secularization of the evangelical child, she is not portrayed as sinful; on the contrary, her natural simplicity and sensibility are used to measure the artificiality and repressiveness of urban life. She exposes the social pretensions of the housekeeper Miss Rottenmeier and the French maid Tinette, for example, and her efforts to repress her naturally strong emotions prove unhealthy. Heidi does have to learn, however, to confide her sorrow to God and to wait for him to answer her prayers in his own way; the grandmother of the invalid girl Clara must give Heidi the religious instruction her grandfather on the mountains neglected to give her. And even as she is a test for Frankfurt, Heidi is being tested there. It is not just her faith that is being tested; she is undergoing a test, like those found in fairytales, to reveal her true nature. Heidi ultimately reveals herself a genuine "Alpine rose" . . . which, like the flowers she had earlier brought home in her apron, dies when cut from its roots in the mountain soil. . . . Her wan appearance and nocturnal sleepwalking indicate she must be returned to her mountains; and she returns "converted," confident that God answers prayer for those who faithfully wait.

Upon her return, Heidi "converts" her grandfather, that "old dragon" . . . so long "at odds with God and men". . . . Before she was taken, against his wishes, to Frankfurt, she had given him new reason to live. Now, she is ready to reconcile him to God and men. Reading him the story of the prodigal son, she tells him "it's never too late" to return to God. . . . When, to the astonishment of all, she and the "Meadow Nuncle" appear in the village church the next Sunday, the pastor acknowledges the accomplishment of the little preacher of the mountain meadow. "Neighbor," he says to the repentant man, "you went to the right church before you came down to visit mine". . . . (pp. 62-5)

Having "converted" her grandfather, Heidi is ready, with his help, to bring about marvelous changes in others who visit them on their mountain. First she revives the sinking spirits of Clara's doctor; compensating for the loss of his daughter, she helps him to recover from his grief. Next, she works "a miracle" . . . with the goatherd Peter; after his schoolteacher has given up on him, Heidi teaches Peter to read. Finally, when the invalid Clara comes from Frankfurt, Heidi convinces her that she can walk, first by leaning on Heidi and Peter and then by herself. By the end of the book Heidi is the center of a small community of persons whose lives she has changed in some way—not only her grandfather, Peter, Clara, and Clara's doctor, but also Clara's father and grandmother who arrive to give thanks for the "miracles," and Peter's mother and grandmother whose lives have been brightened by Heidi's company and who have received gifts from the wealthy Frankfurt family because of her intercession.

This analysis of Spyri's classic as a series of tests and miracles suggests that it has as much in common with a saint's legend as with a realistic novel of child life, that it is holding up for the reader's wonder an example of the testing and power of virtue rather than depicting for the reader's imitation specific ways children do or ought to behave. Moreover, these conversions and miracles give structure to the work. Each of the work's two parts has a tripartite division. The first two sections of Part I, the first set on the mountain and the second in Frankfurt, are devoted to Heidi's conversion. In the third section she returns to convert her grandfather. In Part II, the structural character of the three marvelous changes is underscored by the three seasons in which they occur: the doctor pays his visit and is healed in the fall; Heidi teaches Peter to read during long winter evenings indoors; and Clara's new health and strength comes in the spring. An analysis of ***Heidi*** as religious *exemplum*, then, demonstrates that the book does not just "tell" the reader its meaning in explicit statements of religious piety. Like any respectable work of literature, ***Heidi*** "acts out" its meaning: through characters and plot which have "symbolic" and "ideological" rather than "realistic" plausibility, the book presents a repeated enactment of the archetypical experience of rebirth.

The setting of ***Heidi***, also, of course, contributes to the book's symbolic portrayal of the experience of rebirth. Heidi's inability to thrive in the city, the Alpine setting for the healing of the city dwellers, and Spyri's use of the seasonal cycle to underscore the repeated pattern of rebirth make it clear that the book's miracles are brought about by Nature as well as by Heidi herself. Like Burnett's *Secret Garden* which it resembles in characters, plot, and themes, Spyri's classic belongs to the tradition of Western pastoral as well as to the *exemplum*. Like Shakespeare who depicted the repentance, forgiveness, and rebirth of courtiers in the forest of Arden, Bohemia and Prospero's island, Spyri portrays the renewal of several characters in the Alps. And like Rousseau and Wordsworth, who idealized the child as a pastoral figure in *Emile* and *The Prelude*, she portrays a child as the special agent of Nature's healing powers.

Like most modern pastorals, Spyri uses the city instead of the more traditional court to represent Art in the pastoral dichotomy of Nature versus Art. She stresses the artificiality of life within the Frankfurt household, the complicated set of manners and language demanded by its social status and hierarchy of masters and servants. These artificial constraints on behavior are paralleled by the physical constriction of the house and the city itself; outside her windows Heidi can see only more walls and windows; from the church steeple she can see only more of the city. Cut off from views of "sky and earth," she feels like a bird "shut up in a cage".... In contrast, the "peaceful cottage" Heidi shares with her grandfather on the mountain lies under a "canopy of twinkling stars"... which Heidi can see from her hayloft bed. In their perch in Nature, Heidi and her grandfather enjoy the simple satisfaction of life's most basic needs—food, shelter, companionship. Their social manners are honest expressions of their feelings. When Heidi's grandfather brings her to visit Peter's mother and grandmother, he will not stay to exchange verbal pleasantries he does not mean, but he will return later to make their cottage less vulnerable to the wind and cold. Heidi does not hesitate to examine "closely everything that was to be seen" within the cottage, and she is neither reproved for this curiosity nor for her frank questions about the grandmother's blindness. In this Alpine retreat, life is supported by Nature, and Nature is modified by only the simplest of human arts—primarily the carpentry and the animal and herb lore practiced by Heidi's grandfather.

The two settings of the book, therefore, represent the contrasting modes of life usually portrayed or suggested in the pastoral romance; in the city, life is dominated by Art, and in the mountains it is dominated by Nature. Moreover, Spyri's alternation between these settings, like her series of conversions or miracles, helps give structure to her work even as it underscores her pastoral message, her preference for Nature over Art. The usual sequence of settings in pastoral romances—such as Shakespeare's, for example—is from city or court to rural retreat and then back to city or court. In the first part of her book, Spyri reverses this pattern since her main character is not an urbanite seeking renewal through Nature but rather a Nature child testing and being tested by the artful life of the city; Heidi leaves her Alpine retreat for a visit to Frankfurt and then returns. But in the second part of the book, Spyri dramatizes the more usual pattern of the rural retreat; some Frankfurt persons visit Heidi's mountain and are physically or psychologically healed. All of this part, however, is set in the mountains; the city visitors eventually leave, but Spyri does not follow them; she leaves the reader with Heidi in the mountains. This emphasis on the rural setting reinforces Spyri's pastoral theme: the good life lies in Nature.

The pastoral contrast of Nature with Art is expressed in the book's structure not only through its two contrasting settings and modes of life but also through the spectrum of character groups representing each one. On the Art or urban side, at least two groups can be distinguished. At the extreme are the French maid Tinette and the housekeeper Miss Rottenmeier, both so tied to the city's artificial codes of behavior that the Nature child Heidi is incomprehensible to them. Spyri expresses her disdain for their position by laughing it out of order; both, but especially Miss Rottenmeier, are objects of ridicule. Though he is less hostile to Heidi, the children's tutor probably also belongs to this group since he is similarly ridiculed for his pedantry. These three characters represent the extreme urban position also in that none shows an interest in visiting the mountains. The butler, Sebastian, occupies a slightly less rigid position. He twice leaves the city to travel as far as Mayenfield and Ragaz..., and he tries to make Heidi's life in Frankfurt more bearable. Then there is the group of urban characters who are ultimately responsive to the reviving effect of Nature. Most obviously, this group includes the Doctor, who experiences the first healing visit to Heidi's mountain, and the invalid Clara, who learns to walk there. When we meet him, Heidi's grandfather has already made his retreat to the mountains; however, since his earlier travels, military experience, and unfriendly reception in his home village have made him pessimistic about human society, Grandfather also can be placed with this group of urbanites who are receptive to Nature's reviving touch. Finally, Clara's father and grandmother belong to this group, though they themselves do not undergo a change during their brief sojourns in the natural world. The fact that they do not, however, is significant. By presenting two sophisticated urbanites who are sensitive, kind, and good even before they visit the mountains, Spyri avoids a simplistic condemnation of urban life in her idealization of rural life.

In addition, Spyri also avoids sentimentalizing her idealization of Nature by including a humorous character who represents its extreme even as the ridiculous Miss Rottenmeier, Tinette, and the tutor represent the extreme of the Art side. Goat Peter is a Caliban who dramatizes the brutish potential of Nature unmodified by Art. Like Caliban, Peter is described as an animal or a "savage"..., and he is kept in line or "tamed"... mainly by force or threats. Moreover, like Caliban, Peter seems one "on whose nature/Nurture can never stick" (*The Tempest*, IV. i. 188-89). Though he can talk, Peter expresses himself mainly non-verbally, through grins, frowns, angry gestures, and beating his goats. The odd behavior of "this simple son of the Alps"... prompts Clara's grandmother to ask if there is "something wrong with this boy's upper story".... Peter has convinced himself and his teacher that he cannot learn to read, but with Heidi's encouragement and the threat of Grandfather's stick, he finally does so.

Unfortunately, Spyri does succumb to sentimentality in her portrayal of Peter's mother and blind grandmother. The two women bear the curses of poverty and blindness with a grace and exemplary piety that while ostensibly idealizing the virtues of the simple life, ultimately exalt the poverty itself. Particularly painful is the grandmother's self-abasing gratitude for the gifts of charity the wealthy Frankfurt family gives her: "How can there be such people in the world, to go and bother about a poor old thing like me?".... Without question, the portrayal of poverty and the isolated acts of charity that go with it represent the most serious sentimental failing in Spyri's book.

Spyri's idealization of innocence does not, however, involve a comparable sanction of ignorance. Though Heidi's ignorance of social and natural ills such as affected manners and physical blindness is shown to be more praiseworthy than otherwise, she cannot remain untutored in the ways of heaven and the world. She needs religious instruction to understand the test she is undergoing in Frankfurt, and she must learn to read and write. Her grandfather, who after all relies on the simple arts of carpentry and nature lore, eventually recognizes this and moves down to the village during winter so that Heidi can attend school. Similarly, Spyri avoids a sentimental idealization of childhood itself in her portrait of an ideal child; since neither Clara nor Peter has both her innocence and oneness with Nature, Heidi is shown to be exemplary rather than typical. Moreover, it is precisely because she is exemplary and because she lies at the very center of an artfully structured work that she is a memorable literary creation. By acquiring the religious and secular learning needed for even a simple life in the mountains, Heidi ultimately combines the best qualities of Art and Nature. She is both the link between the two sides of the pastoral dichotomy—it is because of her that urbanites and mountain dwellers meet and become friends—and the agent through which Nature can work its miracles of healing and rebirth.

Johanna Spyri's ***Heidi*** is unmistakably flawed by sentimentality and didacticism, but a children's book, like an adult book, can survive ineffective parts if it has an effective or affective whole. . . . After one has finished reading ***Heidi,*** one may forget the irritation of long-winded speeches and perhaps even the embarrassment of the sentimental portrait of Peter's grandmother. Something pleasing about the work as a whole, however, is likely to remain; for the book's meaning is reflected in its underlying structure. Plot, character, and setting all work together to show that child-like simplicity and Nature's life-giving powers can bring about the archetypical experience of rebirth. (pp. 65-71)

Phyllis Bixler Koppes, "Spyri's Mountain Miracles: 'Exemplum' and Romance in 'Heidi'," in The Lion and the Unicorn, *Vol. 3, No. 1, Spring, 1979, pp. 62-73.*

SHEILA A. EGOFF

When Johanna Spyri's ***Heidi*** was translated into English in 1884, the English realistic novel for children, and particularly for girls, was barely struggling out of its cocoon of home and hearth, and the narrow settings of gloomy Victorian houses and dingy London streets. Heidi brought a breath of fresh air into children's literature which had been lacking since *Little Women* had been published almost twenty years before. Its freshness lay not only in its physical setting of the Swiss Alps but also in its portrayal of believing, loving relationships between the old and the young, the whole and the maimed. In tune with the prevailing ideas of childhood, Heidi conquers her problems through her innate, childlike qualities of simple goodness and perception. Yet Heidi's feeling of aloneness as she leaves her grandfather's mountain cottage for a wealthy town life is equally movingly described. The sense of alienation that she suffers has now become a major trend in modern children's literature but, unlike the modern writers, Spyri developed her theme without showing the traumatic effects on a child's life of such a disruption. But then Spyri and her contemporaries probably ascribed a tougher quality to children than do their modern counterparts. (p. 279)

Sheila A. Egoff, "The European Children's Novel in Translation," in her Thursday's Child: Trends and Patterns in Contemporary Children's Literature, *American Library Association, 1981, pp. 275-96.*

Title page of Heidi, *by Johanna Spyri. Illustrated by Jessie Willcox Smith. David McKay Company, 1922. Courtesy of David McKay Company, a Division of Random House, Inc.*

MALCOLM USREY

Heidi does not now, and did not when it was published, represent an innovation or breakthrough in children's literature, in the way that Beatrix Potter's *The Tale of Peter Rabbit* or Louise Fitzhugh's *Harriet the Spy* did when they were published. Yet ***Heidi*** is a book of enduring interest and significance.

Heidi belongs to a group of novels for both children and adults that can be called "convert-and-reform" novels. A popular theme in late nineteenth and early twentieth century fiction for children and adults, the conversion and reformation of an adult by a child perhaps occurred first in George Eliot's *Silas Marner* . . . , in which Eppie lead Silas away from his miserly love of gold and his anti-social behavior to his being again an active participant in his community and its institutions—just as Heidi leads her grandfather back to Dörfli. (p. 232)

The reformation and conversion of Heidi's grandfather is the major plot of ***Heidi,*** and it is around his reformation and conversion that Spyri builds both the grandfather's and Heidi's characters, making Grandfather something of a Byronic hero and Heidi a child of nature, a natural child in the vein of Rousseau's ideal child, Émile. Further, this major plot is closely related both to the three sub-plots of the novel and to its natural setting, especially to the vigor and beauty of the Swiss Alps.

Nearly all of the antagonists in the convert-and-reform novels for children and adults owe something, directly or indirectly, to the legendary Germanic Faust, and more specifically, to the Byronic hero—the romantic sinner the poet Byron had specialized in describing. In most of the children's stories, the heroes are only faint and barely visible facsimiles of the Byronic original. The sins or crimes of Byronic heroes are dark and hidden, much too awful to be stated; they can only be hinted at, while the sins of the adults in children's convert-and-reform novels are never hidden and never dark. For instance, Rebecca's aunt, Miranda Sawyer, in *Rebecca of Sunnybrook Farm* is simply a sour and cruelly, brutally frank maiden lady, who is finally won over, but little changed, by the sunny disposition of her ward and niece. And Cedric Errol's grandfather in *Little Lord Fauntleroy* . . . is merely selfish, egocentric, and hypocritical, and his sins are hidden only to his grandson. Only in the novel for adults, [Augusta Evans Wilson's] *St. Elmo,* do the sins of the antagonist approximate those of heroes in the true Byronic tradition. With one exception—Heidi's grandfather.

The Byronic hero has several characteristics. He has often committed some dark crime, which can only be hinted at; he has or has had wealth and position. Living in isolation, he seems to detest his fellow human beings; he seems to have an affinity for religion, but cannot perceive himself as worthy of it; and he lives simply and close to nature, which he admires and often identifies with.

In the first chapter of ***Heidi,*** when Dete is taking Heidi up the mountain to live with her grandfather, she suggests that Uncle has apparently committed some heinous crime or crimes in his youth. Dete tells Barbie, her friend from the village of Dörfli, the gossip about Uncle. Dete explains, "It was said that he had deserted from the army at Naples, so as to avoid some trouble about killing a man—not in battle, you understand, but in a brawl". . . . Like the crimes of the Byronic hero, Uncle's crime is unclear, and what Dete tells is only conjecture and gossip.

Dete also tells Barbie that Uncle had once been well off and adds more about his crimes:

> He had one of the best farms. . . . He was the elder son. . . . But old Uncle wanted nothing but to ape the gentry and travel all over the place. He got into bad company, and drank and gambled away the whole property. His poor parents died, literally died, of shame and grief when they heard of it. His brother was ruined too, of course. He too himself off, dear knows where, and nobody ever heard of him again. Uncle disappeared too. He had nothing left but a bad name.

The Byronic hero comes to detest other people. He lives alone because society condemns him, refuses to understand why he has sinned, and fails to be forgiving of his sins. Uncle's reaction to the Dörflian's unforgiving condemnation of him is similar to that of Byron himself when England rejected him after the public learned of some of his escapades, which he echoed in his drama *Manfred*. Dete explains to Barbie why Uncle has chosen to live alone on the mountain above Dörfli. After the parents of Heidi, Uncle's son and daughter-in-law, die, Dete says,

> People said it was Uncle's punishment for his mis-spent life. They told him so to his face, and the Pastor told him he ought to do penance to clear his conscience. That made him more angry than ever, and morose too. He wouldn't speak to anyone after the Pastor's visit, and his neighbours began to keep out of his way. Then one day we heard that he'd gone to live up on the mountain and wasn't coming down any more. He's actually stayed up there from that day to this, at odds with God and man. . . .

The self-righteous piety of the Dörflians and their judgmental condemnation of Uncle send him to the mountain to live alone, and Spyri indicates that, similar to Byron's Manfred, Uncle is more or less justified in his actions, thus preparing readers for Uncle's acceptance of Heidi and revealing that Uncle is perhaps not as sinful as gossip suggests. This justification for Uncle's action lays the groundwork for his later conversion and reformation, for his rejoining society, and for the affirmation of his religious faith and belief, all with Heidi's help. In this way, of course, he is quite unlike the Byronic hero, who never rejoins society and never reforms.

But just as the Byronic hero is often identified with an aspect of nature, so does Spyri make the big hawk of the mountains a symbol of Grandfather. Grandfather's explanation to Heidi about why the bird croaks loudly is his way of explaining why he has chosen to live alone, away from the Dörflians. He says, "He's jeering at all the people who live in the villages down below and make trouble for one another. You can imagine he's saying, 'If only you would all mind your own business and climb up to the mountain tops as I do, you'd be a lot better off.' The old man spoke these words so fiercely that it really reminded Heidi of the croaking of the great bird". . . .

The Byronic figure lives not only in isolation but also, simply and close to nature. That Grandfather lives close to nature is obvious; his little hut on the mountain is made of natural materials, and is no more than

> a biggish room which was the whole extent of his living quarters . . . [with] a table and a chair, and . . . [a] bed over in one corner. Opposite that was a stove, over which a big pot was hanging. There was a door in one wall which . . . was a large cupboard with . . . clothes hanging in it. There were shelves . . . [for] shirts, socks, and handkerchiefs, . . . plates, cups, and glasses, while on the top one where a round loaf, some smoked meat, and some cheese. Here, in fact, were all the old man's possessions.
>
> (pp. 233-35)

Although Uncle is in his seventies, he is strong and vigorous, and it seems that he has absorbed something of the tenacity, strength, and endurance of the shrubs and trees, and of the wind, cold and heat, of the mountains he lives among.

Even if the Byronic hero is inclined to be a religious or spiritual person, he also seems to believe his sin or sins are of such a nature that he cannot seek and have forgiveness; and, apparently, Heidi's grandfather feels something similar. When Heidi tells him that "we'll never forget God again," Grandfather asks, "And when someone does forget?" Heidi replies, "That's very bad." Then Grandfather says, "half to himself, 'If God forsakes a man, that's final. There's no going back then.'" Heidi quickly assures him that one's forsaking God is not final. . . . That Grandfather sees himself as a man who can be forgiven is significant in his conversion and reformation. Under Heidi's guidance, it is the major step in his reconciliation with God and man.

The conversion of Grandfather begins as soon as Dete brings Heidi to the hut of her grandfather, for Spyri makes Heidi one of the most appealing children in nineteenth-century fiction. Heidi is irresistible, innocently frank and naive, but above all, totally natural. Heidi's grandfather, not nearly as evil as Dete and the gossipers have made him out to be, is perhaps predisposed to like people; and his liking for people, along with Heidi's appealing nature, makes the relationship of Heidi and Grandfather remarkable.

The change that Heidi works in her grandfather begins gradually, and works to its climax when Heidi reads to her grandfather the story of the prodigal son. Afterwards, in his recognition of his sin of having forgotten God, Grandfather prays and weeps. (pp. 235-36)

In the beginning, however, it is Heidi's candid honesty and naturalness that appeal to Grandfather and make him learn to love her—and that later makes him susceptible to the religious teaching Heidi acquires in Frankfurt under Grandmamma Sesemann and then conveys to him. Her naturalness, along with her innocence, frankness, and honesty, charm Grandfather. Soon after Dete leaves her on the mountain, Grandfather asks her what she wants to do. Without guile, Heidi replies, "I want to see what is inside the hut". . . . When Grandfather tells her to come into the hut and to bring her clothes, which she has taken off coming up to the mountains, Heidi tells him she will not want them any more, and he asks why. Heidi's words are simple and direct, and her simile reveals her naturalness when she answers, "I want to be able to run about like the goats do". . . . Spyri makes Heidi's naturalness even more evident throughout the second chapter, as she makes herself at home in the hut and its immediate surroundings and on the mountain. Nothing frightens or intimidates her, not her gruff grandfather, nor the goats, the wind, nor sleeping alone in the loft on a mattress of hay.

One instance is a particularly strong affirmation of Heidi's naturalness. A wind storm descends on the mountain hut on Heidi's first night there. Afraid that Heidi may be frightened by the wind and the noise, Grandfather climbs the ladder and looks down on the peacefully sleeping child, who is at one with the world she has come to. Appropriately enough, Spyri does not sentimentalize the scene, but strongly conveys the impression that Grandfather's conversion has begun. (pp. 236-37)

Similar to the innocence and naturalness of Rousseau's Émile and Wordsworth's Lucy, the innocent and natural charm that Spyri embues Heidi with is a fresh and innovative chapter in the development of children's literature. . . . Heidi, the innocent and natural child, is the precursor of one of the most innocent and charming children in literature, little Lord Fauntleroy. . . . It is likely that Heidi is the first completely and disarmingly natural child of any consequence in children's literature—with the possible exception of Tom Sawyer, who may be charming and natural, but who lacks Heidi's innocence. Elsie, in Martha Farquharson's *Elsie Dinsmore,* seems totally lacking in naturalness, and she is hardly a child of nature. Furthermore, she is never as at home in this world as Heidi is, being one of those piously priggish children of nineteenth century literature with a one-way ticket to heaven firmly in hand. Elsie is, however, close to Heidi in her religious convictions, though Heidi never spouts her religious creeds as patronizingly and sanctimoniously as Elsie does. Given her personality and the time of the story, Heidi's assimilation of the attitudes towards God and religion that she learns from Grandmamma Sesemann is as natural as her becoming an integral part of her mountain environment.

Heidi's naiveté and naturalness create some humor in the otherwise dark episode when she goes to live in Frankfurt in the Sesemann household, to be a companion to Clara. In contrast to the appeal of her innocence and naturalness on the mountain with her grandfather, they are less appealing in Frankfurt, at least in the eyes of Miss Rottenmeirer, the Sesemann housekeeper, through whose eyes we see Heidi for much of her time in Frankfurt. Though Heidi is just the kind of child she wants for Clara, as Rottenmeirer says, "a real child of nature, hardly touched by this world at all" . . . , Rottenmeirer ironically does not recognize Heidi as the "child of nature" she wants.

The Frankfurt visit has several important functions in the novel. It contrasts the city with the country, making the city appear cold, hard, and forbidding; everywhere Heidi looks, she seems to see only stones, bricks, and mortar when she longs to see naturally growing trees and grass. Once, the sound of a carriage in the streets makes her think of the wind in the fir trees behind her grandfather's cottage.

In spite of the light humor that plays in and out of the Frankfurt interlude, the entire episode indicates all the more fully how natural and how much a part of nature Heidi is. Out of her natural element, and like the flowers she picked on the mountain that faded and wilted, Heidi becomes desperately homesick, and she loses weight, cannot sleep or eat well, and even begins to sleepwalk. Spyri makes clear that it is not the fault of Clara, Mr. Sesemann, or Grandmamma Sesemann that brings about her decline, though Rottenmeirer may have contributed to it.

Another function of the Frankfurt interlude is to give Heidi a chance to learn to read and write and to find out about God and religion, all in a natural way. The tutor, Usher, fails completely in teaching Heidi to read. But Grandmamma Sesemann, using natural methods to teach both reading and religion, is wonderfully successful. Without the Frankfurt interlude, Heidi might not have learned to read, might not have learned about religion, and therefore, could not have finished the task of converting and reforming her grandfather that Spyri sets for her.

With a naturalness befitting the character of Heidi and the time of the novel, the conversion and reformation of Grandfather are an integrated part of the story, in spite of some critics' views. Phyllis Bixler Koppes thinks ***Heidi*** "unmistakably flawed by . . . didacticism . . . " [see excerpt above dated 1979], and Jack Zipes denigrates the social and religious creeds of the novel . . . , as he perceives them, perhaps with some justification [see excerpt above dated 1976]. But even though some adults find the religious didacticism somewhat tiresome and unpalatable, children probably pay little attention to it; in any case, millions of adults still subscribe to Grandmamma Sesemann's religious beliefs, which may help account for the continued sales and popularity of the novel. And neither Koppes nor Zipes seems to recognize that such treatment or handling of religion in children's stories of the time was standard; furthermore, they do not seem to consider or remember that the didacticism of ***Heidi*** is not as stultifying as—at least no more overt or direct than—the didacticism of most stories and novels for children of the time. When compared with its contemporaries, the religious and social didcticism of ***Heidi*** is relatively mild; ***Heidi,*** along with *Little Women* and *Tom Sawyer,* may mark the beginning of a relinquishing of obvious and patronizing didacticism in children's literature.

In addition to the main plot of conversion and reformation, there are three sub-plots in ***Heidi,*** and all are strongly related to the main one. All three deal with "the relationships between the old and the young, the whole and the maimed," . . . as Sheila Egoff so aptly phrases it [see excerpt above dated 1981].

The first sub-plot deals with Clara Sesemann's invalidism, resolved when she comes to spend several weeks on the mountain with Heidi and Grandfather. Under the patient care of Grandfather, with his ministrations of good, wholesome, natural foods and the warm sunshine, fresh air, and finally, with the wreck of her wheelchair, Clara gains strength and health, and with Grandfather, Heidi, and Peter's help, she learns to walk.

The second sub-plot deals with Grannie, the goatherd Peter's blind grandmother, who suffers from a lack of adequate food, the cold in winter, and the poverty that she, her daughter, and grandson live in. Her best medicine is the happy and cheerful

Heidi, who, with help from Grandfather and the Sesemanns, alleviates some of the causes of Grannie's illnesses. And though Grannie remains blind, she is much better physically at the end of the novel than at the beginning.

The third sub-plot deals with Dr. Classen, the Frankfurt physician and friend of Mr. Sesemann and Heidi. During Dr. Classen's visit to Heidi and Grandfather, he largely recovers from the grief caused by the recent death of his daughter. He finally determines to live permanently in Dörfli in a house, half of which he will share with Heidi and Grandfather.

These three sub-plots not only point up the natural generosity of Heidi, heighten her innocence and kindness, and give her much of the quality of a fairy tale heroine that several critics have rightly noted; they also help to exemplify dramatically the character of Grandfather. Further, through Heidi's contact with the people of these sub-plots, she in turn brings Grandfather into contact with other people, helping to make him a part of the community, and showing him as a good and kind man. While these sub-plots may seem separate from the main convert-and-reform plot, they are integral, if somewhat sublimated, to it.

As Heidi's own naturalness suggest, nature is one of the most pervasive concepts in Heidi. The site of Grandfather's hut on the mountain is a glorious one. . . . (pp. 237-40)

Spyri uses the hawk as a symbol for Grandfather and his isolation, and she uses the mountain flowers that wilt after Heidi picks them to foreshadow and to symbolize Heidi's declining health in Frankfurt. On her first day with Peter on the mountain, Heidi picks her apron full of flowers. Later, as she presents them to Grandfather, she discovers they "had all faded and looked like so much hay." Heidi wonders what has caused them to wilt and die, and Grandfathers answers. "They wanted to stay in the sun and didn't like being shut up in your apron". . . .

On seeing for the first time the sun set on the snow-capped peaks of the Swiss Alps, Heidi thinks they are on fire. Grandfather's explanation of what happens Heidi finds very satisfying. He says, "It's the sun's way of saying goodnight to the mountains. . . . He spreads that beautiful light over them so that they won't forget him till he comes back in the morning". . . . So it is with Heidi; she spreads her beautiful light on Grandfather so that he won't forget her when she goes to Frankfurt; and so it is with Grandfather in his relationship with Heidi. When she goes to Frankfurt, she won't forget him either.

Humankind's recognition of the relationship between nature and religion is an ancient one. Spyri suggests such a relationship when the Pastor tells Grandfather that the mountains have served as a church for him, preparing him for his return to the church in Dörfli. . . .

Nature, in the form of the sun and fresh air, helps to heal Clara. When she first comes to the mountains, she discovers that the sun and fresh air help her appetite. "'Isn't it queer,' she said to Heidi. 'As long as I can remember I've only eaten because I had to. Everything always tasted so of cod-liver oil, and I used to wish I didn't have to eat at all. And here, I can hardly wait for your grandfather to bring my milk'". . . .

Although the mountain air and sunshine work their goodness on Clara, it is left to Dr. Classen to express the importance of the mountains and all they imply, after he has recuperated from his depression during his first visit on the mountain with Heidi and Grandfather. As he leaves to return to Frankfurt, he thinks to himself, "This is certainly a wonderful place for sick minds as well as bodies". . . .

Johanna Spyri's ***Heidi*** is a work of fiction for children that makes extensive use of a number of conventions that were relatively new, if not altogether new, to children's fiction at the time of its writing: for one, the Byronic figure, for another, nature, as backdrop, as healer of both spiritual and physical ills, and as symbol and metaphor in a story of the conversion and reformation of an adult through an innocent and natural child. (pp. 240-41)

Johanna Spyri's ***Heidi*** may not have been an important innovation or breakthrough in children's fiction, but for a hundred years, it has been a distinguished and widely read children's book. It is indeed a touchstone. (p. 241)

Malcolm Usrey, "Johanna Spyri's 'Heidi': The Conversion of a Byronic Hero," in Touchstones: Reflections on the Best in Children's Literature, Vol. 1, *edited by Perry Nodelman, Children's Literature Association, 1985, pp. 232-42.*

Tasha Tudor

1915-

(Born Starling Burgess) American author/illustrator of picture books, illustrator, reteller, and editor.

Tudor is noted for creating picture books and illustrated anthologies for preschoolers and primary graders which reflect her love of nature and her nineteenth-century lifestyle. Her varied works include realistic stories, holiday tales, fantasies ranging from the mysterious to the comical, craft books, pop-up books, and collections of prayers, graces, folktales, bedtime stories, and Mother Goose rhymes; Tudor frequently features members of her three-generational family in these books, as well as the animals and artifacts of her New England farm. Originally published in miniature format, her earliest works were popular as Christmas stocking-stuffers and helped to establish a devoted following of appreciative children and nostalgic adults. Tudor's commitment to the values of an earlier day—integrity, hard work, enjoyment of the out-of-doors, and an appreciation of the beauty inherent in handmade, homemade products—are evident in her books, which stress the positive, gentler aspects of the American heritage and teach such subjects as the alphabet, counting from one to twenty, and the months of the year. In simple, unpretentious prose or verse, Tudor conveys the pleasures of country living, warm relationships with family and friends, and traditional holiday activities, all with the conviction of personal experience and observation. Her joyous, old-fashioned, delicate pencil and watercolor illustrations exhibit the floral borders, soft pastel colors, and representational style associated with Kate Greenaway, to whom Tudor is often likened.

In addition to lauding the realism, charm, and excellence of her meticulously designed drawings, reviewers praise Tudor for her ability to capture the child's interests, evoke happy memories, and anticipate the delight of her audience through her books. Although some critics find her works overly sentimental and irrelevant to the concerns of contemporary readers, the majority agree that Tudor's winning portrayals of family unity, holidays, and the changing seasons hold an enduring appeal for readers of all ages.

Two of Tudor's works have been designated Caldecott Honor Books—*Mother Goose* in 1945 and *1 Is One* in 1957. She was awarded the Regina Medal in 1971 for her body of work and has also won several other awards, mainly for her illustrations.

(See also *Something about the Author,* Vol. 20 and *Contemporary Authors,* Vols. 81-84.)

Photograph by Bill Finney

GENERAL COMMENTARY

ILSE L. HONTZ

Tasha Tudor has given children a very special ray of sunshine—that of pictures which like the kind South Wind, carries the imagination of children into history, into the human heart, into the joys of family life, into love of friendship itself. . . .

Colors and lines, forming images, telling a story, give children a language which expresses what they themselves so often feel but cannot express. Raising a child with the beautiful is giving him a hand to hold. Tasha Tudor has given children this very special hand. Her subtle and soft colors are there when needed, as a kindly mother, to whom children can run and settle into a secure lap, feeling the reassurance of loveliness.

In the world of illustration, children are permitted to dream, to go beyond the concrete, to cry, to laugh, to feel the emotions of peoples and to enjoy a peaceful heart. Without the world of color and its music, the world is incomplete.

Nothing is too beautiful to give as a present. Tasha Tudor has given children a gift, a gift of colors, of mood, of joy—to hold close and cherish forever. (p. 351)

Tasha Tudor's being speaks through her illustrations. Upon entering ***Take Joy!*** children can admire the many glimpses into the red and white, old-fashioned farmhouse in New Hampshire which is surrounded by stately old trees, guarding our Tudor family. In **"The Legend of the Lucia Queen"** the illustration depicting this legend could be the picture of one of the Tudor children. The delicate border and corner design with its Christmas goodies of gingerbread man and toys, can be a complete illustration of its own, but remains in the background to permit Lucia Queen to reign.

Through ***Becky's Birthday,*** children are permitted to tiptoe quietly into the life of the Tudor family and participate in all the excitement and warm family feeling offered here.

Every border and page is unique with wonderful and new surprises. When Sally ". . . hears spring as the robins sing, . . ." in ***First Delights,*** we find that Sally has her kerchief tied *behind* her ears in order to be certain to have the full benefit of the sounds of spring.

The delights of humor which are Tasha Tudor's, spread to all children. One has to be alert, however, and quick to catch all the nuances offered. Humor plays hide and seek and tag, and children delight in finding and capturing it. In ***Wings from the Wind,*** an anthology of poetry, the chapter heading, **"Nonsense"** presents the frog and mouse completely absorbed in the dance at hand, and mousekin holds her tail to make certain it does not drag. Oh, yes, and have you ever seen a cow in a hammock, with her tail dangling over the edge? Tasha Tudor has created this perfectly normal and logical situation to accompany **"A Nonsense Song"** from ***Wings from the Wind.*** (pp. 351-52)

All children need a release from the serious. They need to laugh; they need an occasional handful of nonsense, and Tasha Tudor has given children this opportunity.

How delicious a smile can be when we observe the cat playfully tugging at the end of the Devil's tail in ***Tasha Tudor's Favorite Stories.*** Children will gather basketsfull of chuckles over the margin sketch for **"The Emperor's New Clothes,"** from ***The Tasha Tudor Book of Fairy Tales,*** where the rook tries to emulate the peacock as far as his dark, dull colors and short tail will let him. And Rumpelstiltskin, perched on top of the T, how contentedly he waits for the Queen's child!

Each page, each line is very well thought out. Every detail is important to the whole. In going over the pages one discovers new joys; ones that can be recalled over and over again. The picture of **"Sleeping Beauty"** in ***The Tasha Tudor Book of Fairy Tales,*** is exquisite with its delicate pink roses, encircling the sleeping princess, and is in complete harmony with the mood of the story. The child, if he looks carefully, will find at the very bottom left hand corner, alas! three sleeping white doves.

Tasha Tudor radiates a deep appreciation of family life, animals, nature. She brings another world of peacefulness into our consciousness. Children may walk across a rainbow of color to arrive in Tasha Tudor land of gentle folk and beast. The Tudor family lives "Where Time Stands Still." . . . Her children were raised on a 400-acre farm. There is, indeed, a pioneering spirit in Tasha Tudor's being. Her children, Seth and Tom, and Bethany and Efner help with the household. The family produces all its own food and is completely self-supporting. Tasha Tudor may weave clothes for herself and her family with wool from their own sheep. It is colonial living at its most beautiful. The Tudors form a close and special family where everyone, including the dolls and pets, play an important role. Children are permitted, through Tasha Tudor's artistry, to feel the warmth of the family unit and are deeply enriched by this experience.

Robert Louis Stevenson's ***A Child's Garden of Verses*** is embroidered with Tasha Tudor's grace. In **"Auntie's Skirts"**

> Whenever Auntie moves around
> Her dresses make a curious sound;
> They trail behind her up the floor,
> And trundle after through the door.

Tasha Tudor's black and white sketch recalls immediately the era from which the poet speaks. And immediately after, we are transported to yellows, greens, soft browns in **"Where Go the Boats"** and joyously sail to far away places.

Mr. E. B. Hills, a collector of works by our artist, has pointed out the many implications and overtones to be found throughout all her works. He recalls especially "I shall not want" in ***The Twenty-Third Psalm*** where the dominant is the child at table with her bowl and cup and a loaf of bread only partly consumed. In the borders, birds, squirrels, and a dog are feeding their young, a bird and a chipmunk are enjoying the bunches of grapes on the vines; bees are making honey. Grain field and dairy are represented. There are a nest of eggs, a heap of vegetables, a glass of jelly, a pail and a basket for gathering fruits. Three puppies are nursing, a fourth, his wants satisfied, lies snuggled at its mother's chest.

Kenneth Grahame's **"Christmas Carol"** in ***Take Joy!*** as performed by the carolers is guaranteed to bring approving smiles from children. How eager and happy these mice are to spread the joys of Christmas!

One can almost say that Tasha Tudor is a poet with her art. She creates an atmosphere of discovery. Children love to feel, to explore. A poet creates visual images through his carefully thought out words and phrases. Tasha Tudor goes beyond that in creating the desire to "feel." There are the smells of roasted turkey, freshly made Christmas tree gingerbread, maple syrup and fudge. The soft ears of the dogs to be fondled; the delicate fragrance of daffodils to savor in ***First Delights;*** real dollhouse furniture to play with; tiny tea cups to fill and lift, real lichens to find—these and all manner of good things are lovingly presented by an artist who loves children and pets and picnics and who paints from her close contacts with them.

Walter de la Mare wrote: "Only the rarest kind of best in anything can be good enough for the young," and Tasha Tudor has given this best to children throughout the world. (pp. 352-54)

Ilse L. Hontz, "Tasha Tudor," in Catholic Library World, *Vol. 42, No. 6, February, 1971, pp. 351-54.*

SISTER JULANNE GOOD

[The following excerpt is taken from a speech delivered by Sister Julanne Good, Regina Medal Award chairman, on April 13, 1971.]

Looking at the work of Tasha Tudor, one sees repeatedly three dominant, forceful concepts: charm, excellence, and tranquility. Miss Tudor's exquisite use of soft colors and imaginative details creates for the reader a world of gentle charm and delicacy. Her graceful blending of a nineteenth-century style with the realism of the story reflects a talent which is difficult to duplicate. She is able to highlight the precise moment of a happening, or the feeling of a character and reproduce these intangibles in the expression on the face of a child or in the beauty of nature. Her technique is natural and expressive, revealing a creative and imaginative personality.

The quality of Miss Tudor's work has a lasting appeal in our realistic 1971 world. Today we salute the excellence in the work of a woman who has shown her talent, both through the printed word and visual art in providing high standards in the field of children's literature. She is in agreement with Walter de la Mare that "only the rarest kind of best in anything is good enough for the young." Tasha Tudor has striven to present nature in its freshness, and to show its eminent place in creation. She has given us a clean, bright, and beautiful world through her pictures which are stamped with her own individuality. Miss Tudor is truly gifted in the art of illustration and its relationship to the text.

In contrast to present day society, Miss Tudor continues to bring calm and tranquility to the child. Soft and warm colors draw the young child into a world of love and balance. In her pictures the child sees the authentic settings artistically illustrated. The peace of the picture is in harmony with the quiet mood of the text. Miss Tudor is capable of raising the child's awareness to the beauty—the calm of a changing season. (pp. 614-15)

Sister Julanne Good, "Regina Medal Presentation," in Catholic Library World, *Vol. 42, No. 10, July-August, 1971, pp. 614-15.*

PATRICIA CIANCIOLO

The watercolor and pencil illustrations by Tasha Tudor are realistic in style, although they reveal the artist's nostalgic attitude toward nineteenth-century Americana. In her beautiful and quaint alphabet book, ***A Is for Annabelle,*** Ms. Tudor uses an old-fashioned, delicately illustrated doll. In ***Becky's Birthday,*** the story of a little farm girl of bygone years celebrating her tenth birthday, the artist-author depicts the happy events and surprises of the day in a realistic, and yet nostalgic manner, with charming and pleasing watercolor paintings, as well as with black-and-white pencil sketches. The wonderful candle-lighted, flower-bedecked birthday cake at the evening picnic party in the pasture by the river would bring pure delight to modern young readers. (p. 33)

Patricia Cianciolo, "Styles of Art in Children's Books," in her Illustrations in Children's Books, *second edition, Wm. C. Brown Company Publishers, 1976, pp. 33-57.*

PUMPKIN MOONSHINE **(1938)**

The Kate Greenaway of today, with a New England rather than an Old England flavor, gives her small readers another small book. Here's a natural for Hallowe'en in the story of how Sylvie Ann goes hunting the biggest pumpkin in her grandmother's field—and then has to roll it back to the house—with catastrophic results. . . . Old fashioned charm. A reissue of a 1938 book which appeared originally in stocking size format.

A review of "Pumpkin Moonshine," in Virginia Kirkus' Service, *Vol. XXX, No. 14, July 15, 1962, p. 620.*

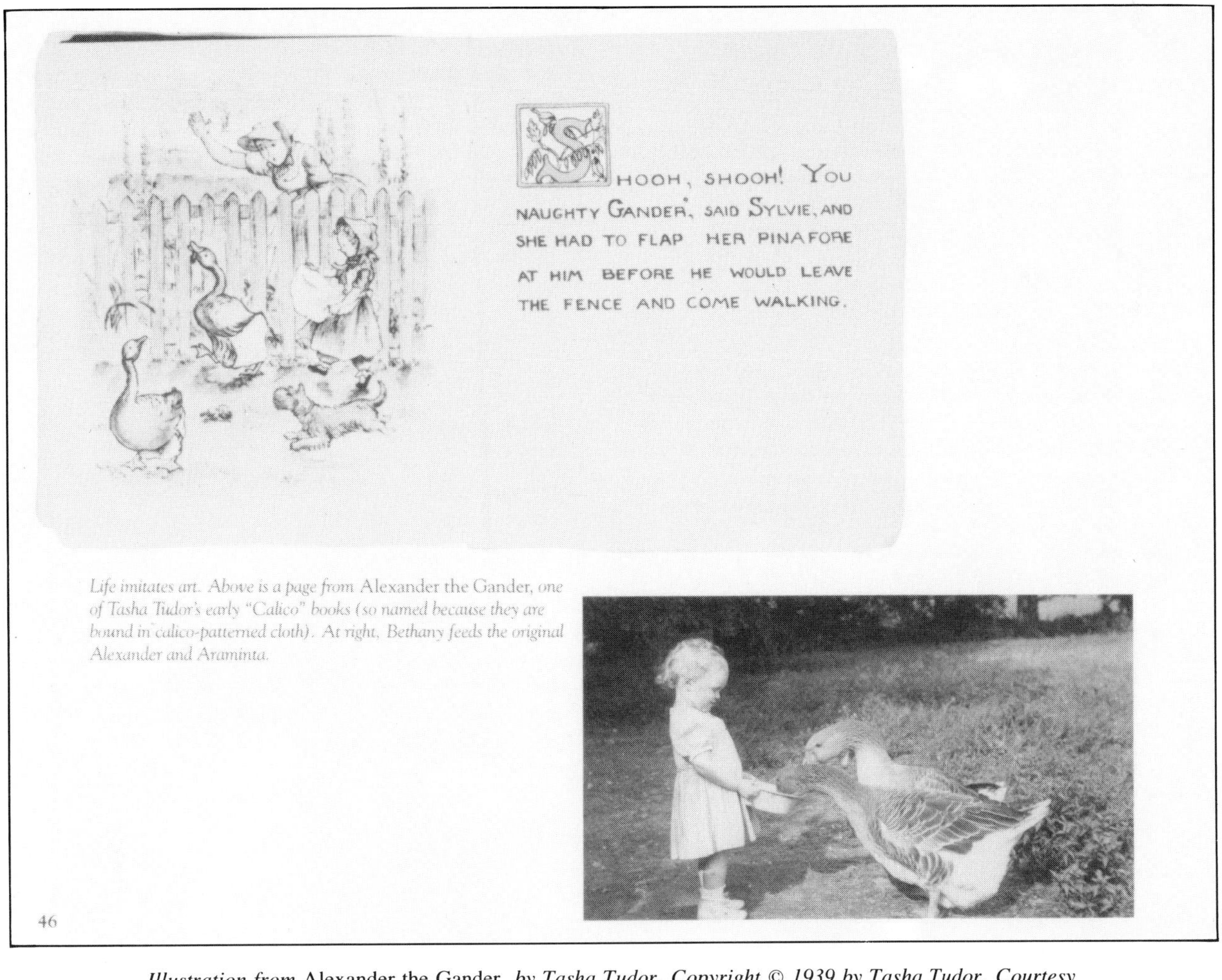

Illustration from Alexander the Gander, *by Tasha Tudor. Copyright © 1939 by Tasha Tudor. Courtesy of David McKay Company, a Division of Random House, Inc. Photograph by Nell Dorr.*

ALEXANDER THE GANDER **(1939)**

A reissue of a 1939 title. When his mistress stopped to chat with Mrs. Fillow, Alexander noticed the delicious-looking heliotrope pansies in the garden; he soon found a chance to get into the garden, where he feasted on vegetable seedlings. Just as he was about to have the pansies for dessert, he was seen by Mrs. Fillow, who shooed him away. His owner brought him back "to apologize for doing such naughty things," and Mrs. Fillow pardoned him; then they all had a friendly meal together. The illustrations are pretty and pastel, the story—although slight and just a bit sweet—has simplicity and some humor.

Zena Sutherland, in a review of "Alexander the Gander," in Bulletin of the Center for Children's Books, *Vol. XV, No. 11, July-August, 1962, p. 184.*

THE COUNTY FAIR **(1940)**

A third Sylvie Ann book, about getting ready and going to the County Fair and coming home triumphant with prizes. Sylvie Ann and her brother Tom decided to exhibit their best possessions—Alexander the Gander, a calf, and a jar of strawberry jam. The lovely rural vistas, clear little figures, and animals are as fine color work as any this artist has done. Another gem of a tiny book, pocket-sized like the others, perfect for the children's room collection of miniatures.

Irene Smith, in a review of "The County Fair," in Library Journal, *Vol. 65, No. 18, October 15, 1940, p. 880.*

As in the two preceding miniature volumes by Tasha Tudor, ***Pumpkin Moonshine*** and ***Alexander the Gander,*** the very simple story is told as much by the pictures as by the text. . . .

Pumpkin Moonshine tells a better story than either of the later books, but all three of these little volumes have the same charm of clear and lovely color, the same pleasant out-of-door atmosphere and the same delightful drawings of children and farm animals. Children who have been to county fairs and those who have not will enjoy the pictures of exhibits, the dashing horses of the merry-go-round and the drawing of Sylvie Ann, Tom and their father, bringing Alexander and Buttercup home in the farm wagon when the fair is over.

Anne T. Eaton, "At the Fair," in The New York Times Book Review, *November 3, 1940, p. 10.*

A TALE FOR EASTER **(1941)**

Although she works in the softest of colors, Tasha Tudor has captured in her beguiling picture books, ***Pumpkin Moonshine*** and ***The County Fair,*** much of the abundance and heartiness of old-fashioned farm life. Now in this new book she made some of her loveliest drawings, pictures which have the same fragile beauty of early Spring evenings.

It does not even pretend to be a story; it is rather an evocation of those days before Easter which the fortunate will always remember as having a quivering anticipation, a newness of life which makes Christmas seem almost garish by comparison. Here is a little girl's first vague awareness of the approaching day, taking shape with the fitting of a new dress, with Hot Cross buns, with conferences with the chickens about the egg supply, and as "you can never tell what might happen on Easter," there are dreams of all the young things of woods and pasture, waiting with sleek coats and bright eyes for Easter morning. As slight and simple a thing as the first narcissus, the book has the same unforgettable air of joy.

Ellen Lewis Buell, "A Picture Book,' in The New York Times Book Review, *March 30, 1941, p. 10.*

A charming little book concerned with the days before Easter, as fragile in content as it is in appearance. With drawings of rabbits, chickens, ducks, and lambs, delicate both in line and color, the author has caught that intangible feeling of expectancy with which children greet special days.

A review of "A Tale for Easter," in The Booklist, *Vol. 37, No. 16, May 1, 1941, p. 412.*

A jewel of prettiness, this little book is light in the hand, tidy in size, gentle in spirit. Its water-color pictures are not imitations of Kate Greenaway, but bring her to mind by making one happy in the same way. "You never can tell what might happen on Easter," begins the tale, in Hilda Scott's clear calligraphy, and many things do—even dreams of little fawns that if you have been especially good take you riding up, up over the misty, moisty clouds. Waking up on Easter is quite as good. It is a tiny book to be kept at hand for any Easter.

"Other Books Chosen for Honor," in New York Herald Tribune Books, *May 11, 1941, p. 10.*

Tasha Tudor's ***A Tale For Easter*** is an old friend to keepers of children's book lists. . . . The simple story of preparations for the holiday, a little girl's Easter Eve dream and the surprises of Sunday morning is really secondary in interest to the illustrations, which are typically Tudor: detailed, old-fashioned, rural New England settings, birds and bunnies and baby animals, all very prettily pastel. Sugar-coated? Yes. Sentimental? Definitely. Wasp? Entirely. But if you're looking for a book to put in the Easter basket that's as springtime as crocus and cottontails, this is the one.

Judy Noyes, "Rabbit Roundup," in The New York Times Book Review, *April 15, 1973, p. 8.*

SNOW BEFORE CHRISTMAS **(1941)**

From its very first words "Over the hills and far away," this little book sparkles with the enchanting beauties and homely fun of winter time in an old New England country house. The water-color illustrations are less delicate than those in ***A Tale for Easter*** . . . but equally lovely.

A review of "Snow before Christmas," in The Booklist, *Vol. 38, October 1, 1941, p. 38.*

In this, perhaps the loveliest of the little Tasha Tudor books, the story is definitely subordinate to the illustrations. Seth and Bethany and Muffin and the mice live in the old house and play in the snow and wait for Christmas to come. But oh! the color and warmth and beauty of that living and playing and waiting! This small book is too fragile for ordinary wear and tear. (Or is it? *Peter Rabbit* and *Tailor of Gloucester* and the Kate Greenaway books are fragile too.) But the joy of ownership and of handling on the library picture book table is something that will last life-long.

Siddie Joe Johnson, in a review of "Snow before Christmas," in Library Journal, *Vol. 66, No. 17, October 1, 1941, p. 847.*

From Mother Goose: Seventy-Seven Verses *with pictures by Tasha Tudor. Henry Z. Walck, Inc., 1944. Copyright 1944 Henry Z. Walck, Inc. Reprinted by permission of Henry Z. Walck, Inc./David McKay Co., a Division of Random House, Inc.*

Here, in a brief text and many delightful pictures, we find an old-fashioned country Christmas as seen through a child's eyes. The snowy roads and hills, the frozen brook, the moonlight throwing blue-gray shadows on the gleaming crust, make the New England scene very real. . . .

The pictures are charming in color and spirit, and Tasha Tudor has succeded in capturing that feeling of anticipation in which, for the child, lies the joy of the Christmas season.

Anne T. Eaton, "Country Christmas," in The New York Times Book Review, *December 14, 1941, p. 10.*

DORCAS PORKUS **(1942)**

There are now four stories about Sylvie Ann and her friends, beginning several years ago with ***Pumpkin Moonshine,*** the Halloween story which is still the best loved of Tasha Tudor's books. If we add ***Snow Before Christmas*** and ***A Tale for Easter*** to the list, we find all the seasons represented in these small, appealing volumes with their exquisitely colored illustrations.

Dorcas Porkus was a pig whom Sylvie Ann and Tom were trying to bring up as a pet, with a collar and company manners. However, a tempting mud-puddle, and a well-meant but ill-timed attempt on the children's part to restore their favorite to cleanliness, created considerable commotion. For Dorcas Porkus, suddenly deciding that the last thing she wanted was a bath, dashed through an open door straight into the middle of the church quilting bee. Dire disgrace for the children resulted, but Mrs. Bartram, the minister's wife, cheered them greatly the next Sunday when she gave them peppermints and assured them that the quilting bee was the liveliest she had ever attended.

As always in Tasha Tudor's books the story is simplicity itself, yet it has lively action and eventfulness in line with a little child's interests. The drawings on every page add distinction and atmosphere and make the setting very convincing. The sunflower and Black-eyed Susans seem really to blossom, and we see serious Sylvie Ann and well-intentioned Tom against the gracious golden green of a Summer landscape. These little stories are never dull nor perfunctory, for the artist-author has touched them with the magic of the changing seasons, of Spring meadows and falling snow, of firelight and candlelight, cozy kitchens and shady orchards, all homely delights which belong by right to childhood and contribute to its joy. (pp. 10, 39)

Anne T. Eaton, "Sylvie Ann's Pig," in The New York Times Book Review, *October 25, 1942, pp. 10, 39.*

***THE WHITE GOOSE* (1943)**

The many boys and girls and older readers who have taken pleasure in Tasha Tudor's charming little books. . . , in which the artist-author has captured the joy of childhood in each of the year's seasons, will welcome this delicate moonlit addition to the list.

The little white goose flies away on a moonlight night; finding white feathers in the pathway, Robin follows them down to the marsh where he sees a magical sight. Then, like a breath, the happening and the tale are over.

Tasha Tudor has put real beauty into the drawings and she handles her story with a light and delicate touch. The tale is so slight it seems like a footnote done in moonlight to the author's other books. Children from 6 to 8 will enjoy it all the more if they make the acquaintance of one of the daytime stories as a companion piece.

Anne T. Eaton, "Marsh Magic," in The New York Times Book Review, *October 10, 1943, p. 6.*

***MOTHER GOOSE: SEVENTY-SEVEN VERSES* (1944)**

This is a lovely little Mother Goose, quite off the beaten track, not only in its selection but in its small format, scarcely larger than a squarish stocking book. The illustrations by Tasha Tudor have a Kate Greenaway quality, and the reproductions are excellent, giving a feel of original pastels and wash drawings. There are 77 rhymes in the collection,—more than half of them are the indispensables; the balance includes some that we think of as counting rhymes, rounds, familiar sayings and some that are rarely seen except in complete editions.

A review of "Mother Goose," in Virginia Kirkus' Bookshop Service, *Vol. XII, No. 20, October 15, 1944, p. 479.*

An enchanting book of Mother Goose rhymes, both the familiar and some quite unfamiliar, with inimitable illustrations in color and in black and white. Perfect in flavor and spirit for the young child and delightful from the adult standpoint.

Dorothea Dawson, in a review of "Mother Goose," in Library Journal, *Vol. 69, No. 19, November 1, 1944, p. 938.*

Tasha Tudor's place in contemporary illustration is established, and in the hearts of children quite as firmly. Her work has Victorian fragrance but is not Victorian in spirit: her pictures have charms like those of Kate Greenaway but greater reality. The page of this book is larger than the "pocket" or "stocking" size by which she is best known: there is a rhyme on each, with a picture either in warm, tender coloring or in soft grays. Each of these fulfills the first great requirement of Mother Goose pictures: you can tell at a glance, without glancing at the text, which rhyme it illustrates. For the characterization is perfect, and sometimes one feels she has seen deeper into the character than many of her predecessors.

A review of "Mother Goose," in New York Herald Tribune Weekly Book Review, *November 12, 1944, p. 12.*

Another "Mother Goose" is out this season, dear little new ***Mother Goose,*** such a pleasant size for small hands to hold, charmingly illustrated by Tasha Tudor in her own quaint and characteristic fashion. . . . There is a New England flavor to many of the landscapes and details of interiors. Jack Horner explores his Christmas pie beside a wonderful colonial fireplace, and surely that is a New Hampshire farm doorstep where little Miss Muffet sits with the ducks and the Halloween pumpkin. A book to linger over and to treasure.

Frances C. Darling, in a review of "Mother Goose," in The Christian Science Monitor, *November 27, 1944, p. 12.*

Tasha Tudor's beautiful pictures bring to the well-loved verses a fresh, bright interpretation. Whether in color or black-and-white, they reflect order and rhythm in the simple arrangement of forms, with pictures of a young child on almost all the well-designed pages.

Constantine Georgiou, "Picture Books and Picture Storybooks: 'Mother Goose'," in his Children and Their Literature, *Prentice-Hall, Inc., 1969, p. 94.*

Tasha Tudor deserves praise for including among the 77 verses in her ***Mother Goose*** some little known and extremely beautiful rhymes. Unfortunately, her illustrations convey nothing of the magic inherent in the verses. She manages warm, touching bits of observation throughout the book, but they barely survive the oppressive flood of sentimentality. Poorly designed pages and soupy, garish full-color pictures combine to deliver the rhymes a graceless *coup de grace*. (p. 192)

Maurice Sendak, "Mother Goose's Garnishings," in Children and Literature: Views and Reviews, *edited by Virginia Haviland, Scott, Foresman and Company, 1973, pp. 188-95.*

***LINSEY WOOLSEY* (1946)**

Children like mischief whether performed by small animals or other children, but this poor little lamb has to take terrible punishment before he learns the path of virtue. The Tasha Tudor pictures have a quaintness reminiscent of Kate Greenaway, but I've always had a feeling that adults like them better than children do.

A review of "Linsey Woolsey," in Virginia Kirkus' Bookshop Service, *Vol. XIV, No. 23, December 1, 1946, p. 591.*

[***Linsey Woolsey*** is] a delightful little book. . . . [The] pictures are in colors, just the sort that only Miss Tudor can paint in soft tints and full of quaint and delightful details of houses and farmyards to illustrate the story of Linsey Woolsey's antics. . . .

Frances C. Darling, in a review of "Linsey Woolsey," in The Christian Science Monitor, *December 10, 1946, p. 16.*

***THISTLY B.* (1949)**

Gently beautiful story of Thistly B. and his canary-wife. They chose the dolls' house for their home, and the tiny bathtub was their nest. They belonged to Efner and Tom Tom who provided suitable materials for the nest and watched with interest while the babies hatched. Both story and pictures are as delicately charming as the author's ***Tale for Easter*** and ***Snow before Christmas.***

Elizabeth Sussdorff, in a review of "Thistly B.," in Library Journal, *Vol. 74, No. 16, September 15, 1949, p. 1334.*

The lovely small color books by this artist provoke from little girls of eight or so words like "adorable, darling, precious." The new one will be greeted by the same exclamations. For the first time since a long-ago story by Helen Ferris we have a tale of canaries. . . .

Children, dolls, birds and flowers are painted with this artist's usual sunny charm.

Louise S. Bechtel, in a review of "Thistly B.," in New York Herald Tribune Book Review, *November 13, 1949, p. 6.*

Tasha Tudor's books make the nicest kind of Christmas present for little boys and girls. . . . The details of the doll's house and the drawings of Tom and Efner are especially attractive.

Mary Gould Davis, in a review of "Thistly," in The Saturday Review of Literature, *Vol. 32, No. 50, December 10, 1949, p. 37.*

THE DOLLS' CHRISTMAS (1950)

Two very old dolls belonged to two little girls, and all four had the great luck to own Pumpkin House, a marvelous dollhouse big enough for large dolls. It is probably the best dollhouse ever put into a book (of course, next to Queen Mary's and to the once-loved *Rackety Packety House*). The story is about the dolls' dinner party at Christmas and the marionette show that followed. Every detail is told and drawn in a way to enchant small girls—the dolls' Christmas tree, stockings, dinner guests. My only complaint about this charming book is that it is not twice as long. But there is enough to set off many a small doll owner on plans for the same sort of Christmas party. All the pictures are in full color, in the familiar Tudor style, and will enchant the many homes that collect her little books.

From The Dolls' Christmas, *written and illustrated by Tasha Tudor. Henry Z. Walck, 1950. Copyright 1950 Henry Z. Walck, Inc. Reprinted by permission of Henry Z. Walck, Inc./David McKay Co., a Division of Random House, Inc.*

A review of "The Doll's Christmas," in New York Herald Tribune Book Review, *November 12, 1950, p. 16.*

The Dolls' Christmas has more of a story than do some of Miss Tudor's books, and little girls from four to eight will delight in the account and detailed pictures of the party given by Sethany Ann and Nicey Melinda. Their home has something new in doll houses—a conservatory with tiny potted plants in it. There is little doubt that the dolls and one of the mothers are part of the author's own family.

Jennie D. Lindquist and Siri M. Andrews, in a review of "The Dolls' Christmas," in The Horn Book Magazine, *Vol. XXVI, No. 6, November-December, 1950, p. 478.*

All the pictures are endlessly interesting, but the most interesting of all is the one of the marionette show. The faces of the watching children, the backs of the little ones who sit on the bench, the tiny stage with the familiar figures of Red Riding Hood and the wolf make it one of the most rewarding of all Tasha Tudor's unusual drawings. Her text in this is longer than in most of her books. Little girls will love it, and their elder sisters will appreciate the art that gives both dolls and children such beauty and such reality.

Mary Gould Davis, in a review of "The Dolls' Christmas," in The Saturday Review of Literature, *Vol. XXXIII, No. 49, December 9, 1950, p. 43.*

AMANDA AND THE BEAR (1951)

For the cult, another bright little picture book, based on the true story of a little girl who kept a bear cub as a pet. Adam, the bear, became a part of the Davenport family, attending tea and having the run of the house. Of course, as a bear, Adam indulged in behavior often startling to humans—awakening guests, frightening maids, etc., so he is finally banished to the zoo. Neat, pretty full-color Nineties pictures for a predictable Tudor market.

A review of "Amanda and the Bear," in Virginia Kirkus' Bookshop Service, *Vol. XIX, No. 15, August 1, 1951, p. 386.*

FIRST PRAYERS (1952)

A charming small book, one to give to a child to read now and perhaps to keep and look at for many years, even when old and gray. Illustrated in tiny relief and soft pastels are familiar prayers, evening solicitations and morning thanks, the Lord's Prayer, a verse from a New England sampler, old English and German praises, hymns—"Now the Day is Over", psalms—the twenty-third, and graces to say at meal times. Thoroughly pleasing. We hate even to be commercial about it, but watch it for gifts.

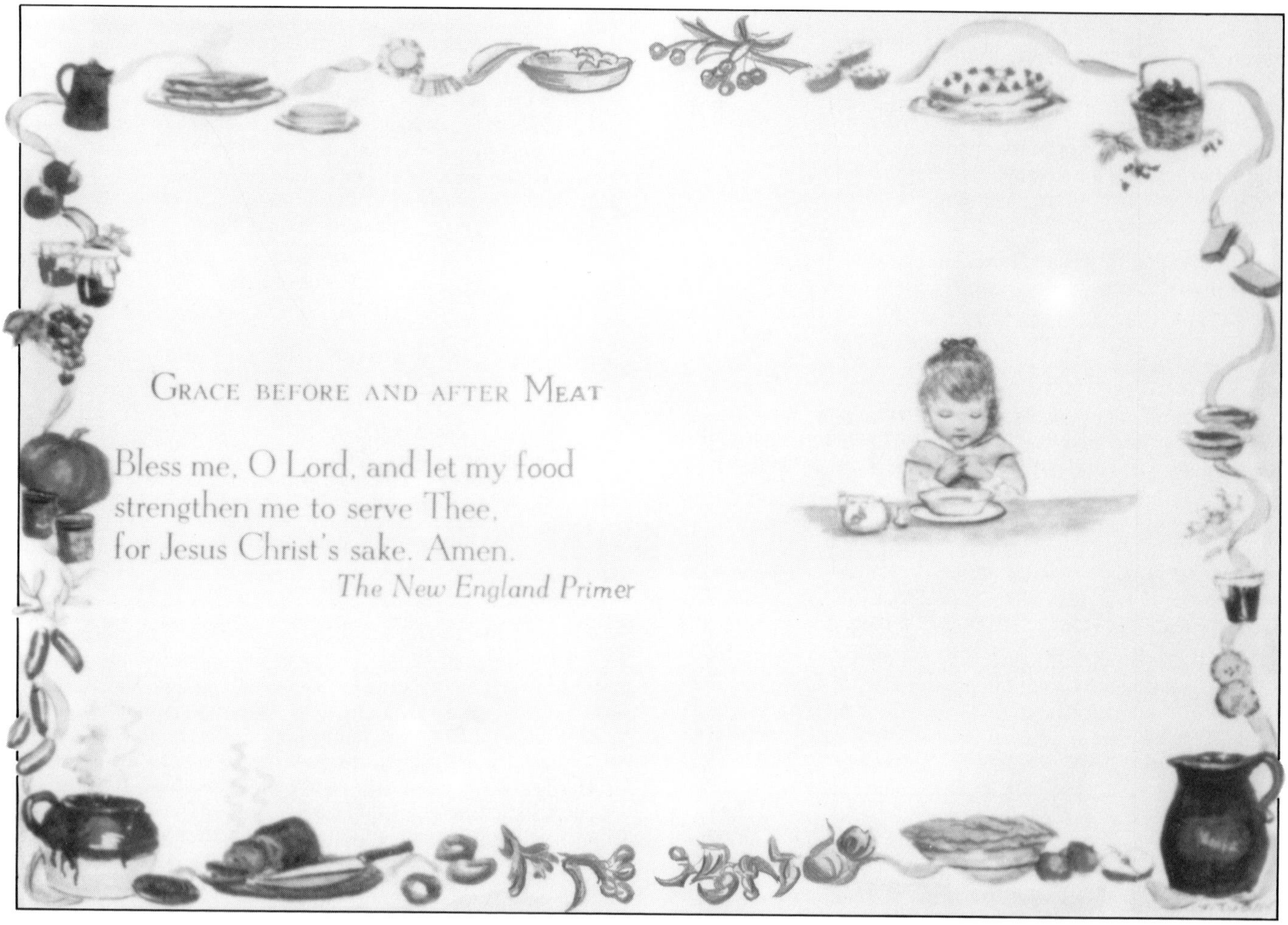

From First Prayers, *illustrated by Tasha Tudor. Henry Z. Walck, Inc., 1952. Copyright © 1952 by Henry Z. Walck, Inc. Reprinted by permission of Henry Z. Walck, Inc./David McKay Co., a Division of Random House, Inc.*

A review of "First Prayers," in Virginia Kirkus' Bookshop Service, *Vol. XX, No. 18, September 15, 1952, p. 600.*

This charming collection of favorite prayers and graces, including some less familiar but equally lovely, will encourage the small child to begin his devotional life early. Parents will be delighted with its dainty appearance and especially with the author's choice of exquisite color pictures and delicate marginal decorations that are just right for this tiny book. . . . Recommended for the child's own collection.

Mildred M. Gantt, in a review of "First Prayers," in Library Journal, *Vol. 77, No. 18, October 15, 1952, p. 1819.*

Twenty-four prayers, hymns (without music) and graces have been collected in ***First Prayers*** and have been given a charming setting of flowery borders and softly pretty pictures in Tasha Tudor's appealing style. Some of these selections are as familiar as the Twenty-third Psalm; others, less well known, such as the sixteenth-century "God be in my head, / and in my understanding" will bring to the child a new awareness of God's presence in everyday life. That is the basic theme underlying this collection expressed with dignity.

Ellen Lewis Buell, "A Child's Devotions," in The New York Times Book Review, *December 14, 1952, p. 24.*

EDGAR ALLAN CROW **(1953)**

Tasha Tudor's latest beguilingly illustrated book-to-read-aloud is delightfully inconsequential. It is about a crow named Edgar Allan. Captured from his nest when young, he comes to live with, and plague, a family of humans until, when older, he simply becomes useful by catching all the cutworms in the garden. Complete nonchalance is conveyed in a pat text and those small, calm Tudor pastels.

A review of "Edgar Allan Crow," in Virginia Kirkus' Bookshop Service, *Vol. XXI, No. 22, November 15, 1953, p. 737.*

A IS FOR ANNABELLE **(1954)**

Without apologies, this is a delectably old-fashioned kind of alphabet book. In delicate pastels, pretty as they come, one goes through the alphabet with two little girls and their discoveries about an old fashioned doll with elegant clothes and accessories. A real doll house forms the appropriate setting for this lovely creature. And everything but "X" has its place, in jingles that make no pretense to do more than rhyme. For Tasha Tudor fans—and for old fashioned grandmothers and great aunts to give the littlest ones.

A review of "A Is for Annabelle," in Virginia Kirkus' Bookshop Service, *Vol. XXII, No. 21, November 1, 1954, p. 725.*

Two lucky little girls of today can go to a chest on the hall table and take out Annabelle, a grandmother's doll, with all her treasures: costumes, bonnets, gloves, slippers of long ago, the precious little fan, watch and zither, the parasol, umbrella and Paisley shawl. Each object makes a letter of a rhymed alphabet as the children try them on. Is that an old filigree holder we see on the nosegay? Does her "posy" hold all of those lovely old-fashioned flowers that circle each page with such grace? Even the roses are chosen from grandmother's time.

Other little girls, from about four (on and up, especially up to grandmothers and doll collectors) will gather, on inevitable second looking, affection for the little girls who show their joy in these treasures. They even own an extraordinary old doll carriage in which Annabelle can take the air. Thanks to Tasha Tudor for the prettiest book of all she has made, for letting us share her own wonderful Annabelle and her own characterful small daughter.

A review of "A Is for Annabelle," in New York Herald Tribune Book Review, *November 14, 1954, p. 4.*

In the delicate penciled lines and water-colors which her name evokes for her many devotees Tasha Tudor draws an alphabet around the wardrobe of Grandmother's doll, Annabelle. . . .

Though this beautiful oblong book is too fragile for baby fingers, it will appeal to those old enough to respect their ABC's.

Sarah Chokla Gross, "Alphabet Annabelle," in The New York Times Book Review, *November 14, 1954, p. 38.*

This darling book is for grandchildren and their grandmothers. The author has contrived to make two generations as one, for Annabelle, Grandmother's doll, is as important today as is the Hitchcock chair on which she sits in one of the lovely illustrations.

This book offers one very good way for little girls to become acquainted with all twenty-six letters of the alphabet, even with the X which has no rhyme.

Rae Emerson Donlon, in a review of "A Is for Annabelle," in The Christian Science Monitor, *December 9, 1954, p. 17.*

FIRST GRACES **(1955)**

Companion volume to the favorite ***First Prayers,*** this, while equally enchanting in format, has, perhaps, less wide an appeal. The use of grace before meals is today much less general than formerly. But for those to whom the idea has acceptance, this selection of twenty prayers of thanksgiving is excellent. One could wish that at least one Jewish grace had been included, but perhaps that is laboring the point when the number is limited— and the probable market primarily Protestant.

A review of "First Graces," in Virginia Kirkus' Service, *Vol. XXIII, No. 22, November 15, 1955, p. 836.*

In Tasha Tudor's very pretty pocket-size book, the short verses or brief prose graces are chosen with fine taste. Small children to whom you read or teach them will find that the many pictures, half in full color, contain storytelling incidents taking little boys and girls around the year. We see them outdoors and in, sometimes celebrating holidays. It is a charming gift for those before six, and a fine year-round prize book for kindergartens in Sunday schools.

Louise S. Bechtel, in a review of "First Graces," in New York Herald Tribune Book Review, *December 11, 1955, p. 8.*

---

1 IS ONE **(1956)**

Ten rhymes and forty sets of Tudor drawings get right down to the tiny and the fanciful things children like, and count, from one to twenty. "1 is one duckling swimming in a dish . . . 2 is two sisters making a wish" and so it goes. The pictures in soft greys and full color, with border decorations of delicate flowers, make the kind of counting book one is apt to keep and treasure for many years.

A review of "1 Is One," in Virginia Kirkus' Service, *Vol. XXIV, No. 22, November 15, 1956, p. 839.*

A picture book seven by nine inches, reminiscent of "gift books" of the turn of the century, is the dainty ***1 is One*** of Tasha Tudor. There is a soft blurry sweetness about the flower-wreathed pages (alternate ones are in full color or gray) that is very appealing to many people. Tiny bluets, columbine, field flowers, arbutus, roses, berries, fruits and violets are drawn with loving care, one kind making a wreath for each double page. Children and birds and beasts illustrate a jingle that sing-songs the numbers from one to twenty. We find some charming, like the little mouse accompanist on the toadstool, but most are a bit too charming.

A review of "1 Is One," in New York Herald Tribune Book Review, *November 18, 1956, p. 5.*

Beautiful, quaint pictures in color and black and white by the author make this an outstanding picture book. The colored vignette is lovely. The purpose, other than to please with its art, is to teach the numbers from 1 to 20. Recommended for preschool children.

Juanita Walker, in a review of "1 Is One," in Library Journal, *Vol. 3, No. 5, January, 1957, p. 18.*

Some of the pictures are quite pleasing, although all tend toward the sentimental. The book is more useful as a picture book of familiar objects than as a counting book, since extraneous objects are often introduced in a way that becomes confusing, and as the numbers become larger the objects become smaller and more difficult to distinguish.

A review of "1 Is One," in Bulletin of the Children's Book Center, *Vol. X, No. 6, February, 1957, p. 83.*

Placid loveliness adorns this small book that matches mathematical language with symbols from one to twenty. Twice emphasizing the tens concepts, ***1 is One*** uses graceful shapes

From 1 Is One, *written and illustrated by Tasha Tudor. Oxford University Press, 1956. © Oxford University Press, Inc., 1956. Reprinted by permission of David McKay Co., a Division of Random House, Inc.*

and simple, accurate terms, along with artistically alternating color and black-and-white drawings.

Constantine Georgiou, "Picture Books and Picture Storybooks: '1 Is One'," in his Children and Their Literature, *Prentice-Hall, Inc., 1969, p. 75.*

AROUND THE YEAR **(1957)**

The quaint and careful, delicately colored paintings which have charmed Tasha Tudor's followers in earlier books mark each month of the year. Here, the pleasantly old-fashioned character of her work now appears in an almost Currier and Ives vein. "January brings us . . . coasting, Taffy pulls and apple roasting." Two double spreads illustrate each month while simple rhymed lines describe it. For children to whom the calendar is still a confusing complexity, this will fill a need. Period and pastoral, this is a nostalgic view of country children of long ago . . . around the year.

A review of "Around the Year," in Virginia Kirkus' Service, *Vol. XXV, No. 19, October 1, 1957, p. 735.*

The delicate old-fashioned drawings, the pastel colors, the quaint children, the pleasure in animals and flowers that characterize Tasha Tudor's work have been heightened in this calendar of the year. Each month is represented by an outstanding occasion pictured in loving details of children, flowers, and animals, and described in simple rhyming couplets.

Frances Lander Spain, in a review of "Around the Year," in The Saturday Review, *New York, Vol. 40, No. 51, December 21, 1957, p. 39.*

The scenes [in ***Around the Year***] are all rural and although the text is written in the present tense, the activities as described and pictured are those of a past generation. A book of more nostalgic appeal for adults than of present meaning for children.

Zena Sutherland, in a review of "Around the Year," in Bulletin of the Children's Book Center, *Vol. XI, No. 6, February, 1958, p. 64.*

AND IT WAS SO **(1958)**

The author has chosen some Biblical passages, illustrating and adapting them for the understanding of very young children. The drawings are a translation of the text into characters rather than being literal illustrations: for example, the words "Then children were brought to Him that He might lay His hands on them and pray,'' are not self-explanatory nor are they illuminated by the illustration, which shows a mother and three children walking. Probably the book will prove useful in nursery groups within a religious education program.

A review of ''And It Was So,'' in Bulletin of the Center for Children's Books, *Vol. XIII, No. 3, November, 1959, p. 55.*

BECKY'S BIRTHDAY (1960)

A story of nostalgic enchantment is this account of ten-year-old Becky and her birthday. In a period where children are glutted by material reassurances of parental affection, the story of a country birthday made memorable by gifts of flowers, a hay ride, and homemade ice cream is not only romantic, it is refreshing. Tasha Tudor's illustrations are soft and evocative of a less harsh time in which experience was less mechanized and more in harmony with the rhythm of nature. A poetic recapitulation of what is one of the most significant anniversaries in a person's life, the celebration of having lived one decade.

A review of ''Becky's Birthday,'' in Virginia Kirkus' Service, *Vol. XXVIII, No. 15, August 1, 1960, p. 619.*

As long as birthdays roll around, especially those very precious ones between five and twelve, children will look forward to their own with a very special anticipation, and parents and friends will give them books about these happy events. Tasha Tudor in offering one provides a very different sort of pleasure from the slap-happy, jolly nonsense of Dr. Seuss in his book of last year, *Happy Birthday to You*. Her book is a gentle, serene account of the delights offered Becky on her tenth birthday. It was a most magic birthday, one with a turn-of-the-century flavor that many a little girl of the sixties will long to share. From the preparations, driving to the village to market, freezing ice cream, and gathering wild flowers until the evening picnic party in the woods, in a setting worthy of the storied ''wood near Athens,'' every moment adds to her happiness. This kind of book is a specialty of Tasha Tudor who pictures sweetly in soft water colors an idyllic country life, drawing on her experiences with her children.

Margaret Sherwood Libby, in a review of ''Becky's Birthday,'' in New York Herald Tribune Book Review, *September 11, 1960, p. 9.*

[A] delightful story. . . . The quaintness of the author's illustrations may not attract young tomboys, but most domestically inclined little girls with imagination will find both story and illustrations enchanting. Unfortunate that format is that of a picture book for younger children.

Elizabeth Mitchell, in a review of ''Becky's Birthday,'' in Library Journal, *Vol. 7, No. 3, November 15, 1960, p. 4229.*

Tasha Tudor is [an] illustrator of children's books whose work has undeniable charm. She has always reminded me of a rather plush perversion of Kate Greenaway, although she lacks Miss Greenaway's asperity and authenticity. In ***Becky's Birthday,*** written and illustrated by Miss Tudor, the illustrations are stronger in color and firmer in line than usual, but the coy charm which carries the illustrations becomes cloying and sentimental in her written work. The quaint nineteenth-century charm is about as authentic as a set of Rock Maple Colonial from Eaton's Fourth Floor. The family togetherness, the theme of ***Becky's Birthday,*** is straight out of the *Ladies Home Journal*. (p. 209)

Elizabeth Kilbourn, ''Turning New Leaves (2),'' in The Canadian Forum, *Vol. 40, No. 479, December, 1960, pp. 209-10.*

The events of Becky's tenth birthday—from breakfast greetings and spanks to a magical picnic by the river at dusk—carry a child's feeling of delight in little pleasures which are made big because of family affection and sense of festival. The pictures, half of them in the author's typical soft water colors, and the spelled-out details in the text reveal a period picture of New England farm life in horse-and-buggy days, including the fun of freezing ice cream, picking sweet corn, and honoring Queen Becky with home-contrived favors more exciting than the usual gifts.

Virginia Haviland, in a review of ''Becky's Birthday,'' in The Horn Book Magazine, *Vol. 36, No. 6, December, 1960, p. 509.*

A pleasant rural flavor permeates the story of Becky's tenth birthday—somewhat sentimental and dated, but evocative of the pleasures of an old-fashioned family celebration. The illustrations are delicate in pastel or black and white.

Zena Sutherland, in a review of ''Becky's Birthday,'' in Bulletin of the Center for Children's Books, *Vol. XIV, No. 5, January, 1961, p. 88.*

BECKY'S CHRISTMAS (1961)

[A] sequel to ***Becky's Birthday.*** Now ten, Becky is happily looking forward to an old-fashioned Christmas and busily making presents. Rather sentimental, but not saccharine, and with many pleasant details of rural life and a mingling of Christmas customs of several derivations. A nice period holiday story, with good family relationships and good attitudes implicit in the sharing of work and doing things for others.

Zena Sutherland, in a review of ''Becky's Christmas,'' in Bulletin of the Center for Children's Books, *Vol. XIV, No. 4, December, 1961, p. 67.*

[***Becky's Christmas***] tells of the exciting preparations for and the wonderful celebration of Christmas in Becky's farm home. . . . An aura of anticipation and joy and a sense of family sharing shine through both the story and the pleasing drawings in color and black and white.

A review of ''Becky's Christmas,'' in The Booklist and Subscription Books Bulletin, *Vol. 58, No. 7, December 1, 1961, p. 232.*

[In ***Becky's Christmas***] Tasha Tudor pictures in words and soft naïve illustrations, a rural New England celebration a couple of generations ago, beginning with ''the smell of Christmas cakes baking and the first snow on the far mountains'' and ending with a bang-up family gathering. It all sounds delightful—merry, warm and loving—yet it does seem odd that in such a traditional and enthusiastic family no one, apparently, thought of going to church.

Ellen Lewis Buell, in a review of ''Becky's Christmas,'' in The New York Times Book Review, *December 3, 1961, p. 68.*

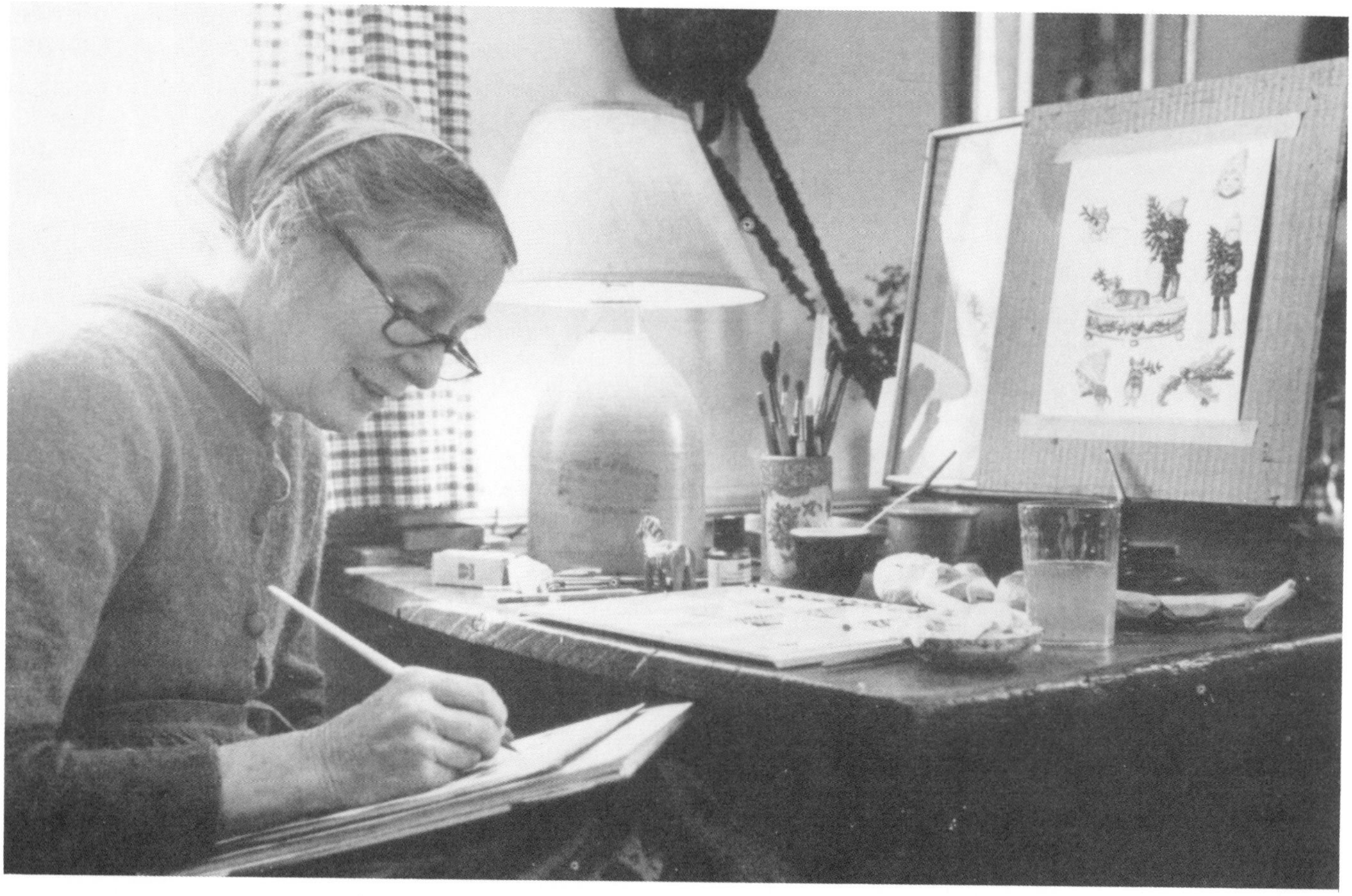

Tudor at her desk. Photograph by Pete Main.

If you were a child at the turn of the century and happened to live in the country, this will fill you with nostalgia, for it recaptures all of the fun of the preparation for Christmas at that time. . . . Children who ask you to tell about the olden days will enjoy this, and all little girls of 8-10 will delight in reading about the mystery of the present which Becky's family was making for her and of her happy surprise on Christmas morning. Recommended.

Elsie T. Dobbins, in a review of "Becky's Christmas," in Library Journal, *Vol. 86, No. 22, December 15, 1961, p. 36.*

TAKE JOY! THE TASHA TUDOR CHRISTMAS BOOK **(1966)**

An inviting collection of Christmas thoughts, poems, stories, carols, lore, and legends, generously illustrated with tenderness and reverence in full-color and black-and-white pictures. A final section of the book describes the Tudors' own celebration of Christmas for which preparations begin almost as soon as the ornaments from the Christams before are put away. Of special interest to children who enjoy homely, old-fashioned pleasures, parents and grandparents wanting to preserve family Christmas traditions, and to Tasha Tudor fans of all ages.

Ruth P. Bull, in a review of "Take Joy!" in The Booklist and Subscription Books Bulletin, *Vol. 63, No. 11, February 1, 1967, p. 585.*

THE TASHA TUDOR BOOK OF FAIRY TALES **(1969)**

[A] collection of fifteen favorite fairy tales, simplified for the youngest listeners. Perrault, Hans Christian Andersen, the Brothers Grimm—and some folk tales from other sources have been told with a view to those things Tasha Tudor has made her own—the everyday views of woods and fields and homes. Old favorites are here:—Sleeping Beauty, Rumpelstiltskin, Puss in Boots, Thumbelina, Jack and the Beanstalk, Red Riding Hood, Cinderella. But Tasha Tudor couldn't bear unhappy endings so rescues Red Riding Hood and her grandmother from the stomach of the wicked wolf—but is willing to let Rumpelstiltskin come to a deserved end! Charming—if excusably sentimental—illustrations in full color, with Tasha Tudor's exquisite attention to minute detail, will keep small spectators entranced. Surely popular.

A review of "The Tasha Tudor Book of Fairy Tales," in Virginia Kirkus' Service, *Vol. XXIV, No. 21, November 1, 1961, p. 969.*

The foreword states: "These stories, newly retold, blend wit and sparkle and soaring imagination with the delightful artistry of Tasha Tudor." This wit, sparkle, etc. I do not see. The stories are shortened and softened. Rapunzel suffers by the complete expungation of her twins—who were the natural result of the Prince's nightly climb to her tower. Why? Hans Christian Andersen's stories are brashly retold, or shortened. Why? To make more room for oversweet pictures? We have known Tasha Tudor as an illustrator and writer for some time.

This year she has a reissue in larger form of a favorite story, ***Alexander the Gander,*** and a Christmas book with another publisher. Why do this inferior book?

Alice Dalgliesh, in a review of "The Tasha Tudor Book of Fairy Tales," in Saturday Review, *Vol. 44, No. 45, November 11, 1961, p. 41.*

In a large and glorious volume luxuriously crammed with princes, fairy godmothers and promises of happy living ever after, Tasha Tudor has collected her favorite, less grim tales. She has illustrated them with full-page romantic water colors and slipped tiny everyday details in margins and corners and around her "Once upon a time" beginnings.

P. M., in a review of "The Tasha Tudor Book of Fairy Tales," in The Christian Science Monitor, *November 16, 1961, p. 4B.*

CORGIVILLE FAIR **(1971)**

In the time-ago village of Corgiville, "west of New Hampshire and east of Vermont," the population of cats, rabbits, corgis ("enchanted" small dogs the color of foxes), and boggarts (toy-like "trolls") turn out for the annual country fair. The plan of young Caleb Brown, a corgi, to ride his goat Josephine in the Grand Race, is almost foiled by rival Edgar Tomcat who feeds Caleb a soporific hot dog and stuffs Josephine with mince pies and cigars. But Caleb's resourceful buddy Merton Boggart gets the groaning Josephine going by feeding her the rockets for his fireworks display. "The results were spectacular!" Caleb wins the race, leads the grand parade, starts off the Virginia Reel with Miss Corgiville ("much to his embarrassment and pleasure"), and applauds Merton's closing fireworks display. It's the kind of village that you enter through a covered bridge and the kind of story where everyone wins prizes and no apologies are offered or expected for gratuitous whimsy. (Why are the corgi described as enchanted? What are the ball-and-stick-constructed boggarts doing in a place like this?) Mrs. Tudor's pictures are of course executed in quaint and loving detail.

A review of "Corgiville Fair," in Kirkus Reviews, *Vol. XXXIX, No. 20, October 15, 1971, p. 1117.*

There's a very pungent part of America to be found in the late summer when you head into livestock land—it's the county fair—that heady attack on the senses where fat gray geese and prize Guernseys vie for your attention with home preserves, handicrafts and the harvest best of the vegetable kingdom. But if you've never been to one—seen the pony pulls or walked the dusty midway—you can still have second best; you can go to the fair at Corgiville.

"West of New Hampshire and east of Vermont" lies Tasha Tudor's special bit of ruralism named for the dogs that live there. Though Christmas and the fair are the most exciting events of the year and the town is Corgied by such upright citizens as the Bigbee Browns (he's in town government and raises racing goats), all is not so quiet as the delicate, pastel pictures or your rememberance of the author's ***The County Fair*** of 1940 might have you think.

For one thing, there are also cats, rabbits, and boggarts who live in Corgiville and boggarts are extremely resourceful. . . . In short, boggarts are not to be trifled with, yet that is just what Edgar Tomcat did. . . . Of course, come race time wonderful trouble ensues. . . . Both text and illustrations provide a myriad of details to pleasure and wink over—there are the various town residents presented with just a touch of caricature, the country story with a pin-up Corgi calendar, the whispered suspicion that Edgar is betting "with money!" (not too surprising really since he is disposed to loud clothes and noisy singing) and then the blue-ribbon, ferris-wheeling, once-a-yearness of the fair itself with its fireworks finale of an "American flag done in Catherine wheels and supercharged torpedoes."

All told, it's a generous harvest of Mrs. Tudor's living, feeling and observing—a bounty of imaginative, delicate watercolors for as exuberant an aggregation of Americana as you'll find on land or paper.

Ingeborg Boudreau, "Americana, City-Style and Country-Style," in The New York Times Book Review, *November 28, 1971, p. 8.*

An occasionally amusing bit of Americana New England style. . . . The intricately detailed, pastel-colored pictures are better than the text and successfully evoke a small New England farming village, town hall, church supper, and, of course, fair, with its tents, barns and rides, machinery, exhibit, food and patent medicine stands, peep show, etc.

Constance S. Roupp, in a review of "Corgiville Fair," in School Library Journal, *an appendix to* Library Journal, *Vol. 18, No. 4, December, 1971, p. 4181.*

The preparations and the attractions and events of the Fair . . . are delineated in a lively story and appealingly detailed watercolor paintings which depict the New England scene and evoke a feeling of anticipation and the atmosphere of the glorious day. The book possesses the charm and much of the quaintness of Tudor's earlier work but has more vitality.

Aileen Howard, in a review of "Corgiville Fair," in The Booklist, *Vol. 68, No. 9, January 1, 1972, p. 395.*

Quaintly pretty pictures of an old-fashioned village peopled by animals (top-clad males and children, females modestly full-skirted) are a background for a story with a minimal plot that, like the pictures, is embellished with many details. . . . Fairs and animals have an unquenchable appeal, but this story is weakened by over-extension and dependent on the quaintness of the situation rather than on storyline or humor.

Zena Sutherland, in a review of "Corgiville Fair," in Bulletin of the Center for the Children's Books, *Vol. 25, No. 7, March, 1972, p. 116.*

The story is neatly illustrated by large-scale spreads crowded, Scarry-like, with bustling figures, behind which an idealised landscape stretches prettily. A touch of rustic idiom in the text helps to counteract the mildly sentimental and whimsical flavour of the book.

Margery Fisher, in a review of "Corgiville Fair," in Growing Point, *Vol. 12, No. 2, July, 1973, p. 2190.*

TASHA TUDOR'S SAMPLER **(1977)**

Three of Tudor's quaint holiday tales, first published separately—which would seem a more appropriate format for a seasonal goodie. Most insipid is the first story, ***Waiting for Easter,*** about the dream of a wee fawn, little lambs, ducklings, etc., that "you" will have on the night before—"But . . . only

There was the Big Tent, where vegetables, fruit, preserves, flowers, and fancywork were shown. There was the Poultry Shed, the Goat and Guinea Pig Barns, the Ginger-Beer Stand, the Peep Show, and the Merry-Go-Round, with a calliope and
dashing wooden goats with flowing beards. There were runaway pigs and lost puppies, and tabby cats selling cotton candy. There were boggarts with patent-medicine remedies and old corgis with trained fleas. IT WAS WONDERFUL!

From Corgiville Fair, *written and illustrated by Tasha Tudor. Thomas Y. Crowell Co., Inc., 1971. Copyright © 1971 by Tasha Tudor. All rights reserved. Reprinted by permission of Harper & Row, Publishers, Inc.*

if you have been good and can find the dust on daffodils with your eyes tight shut.'' That leaves most of us out. Though still mincing, the Halloween story (from 1938) has a pinch of old-fashioned humor and genuine coziness: ***Pumpkin Moonshine*** (you might call it Jack-O-Lantern) is what a good little girl named Sylvie Ann wants to make—and does, but not till the pumpkin she finds in a field rolls away (Bumpity Bump Bump!) down the hill, through the barnyard and ''right into Mr. Hemmelskamp who was carrying a pail of whitewash!'' ***The Dolls' Christmas,*** all about the preparations Laura and Efner make for the Christmas tree, dinner, gifts, etc., of their lavishly housed dolls Sethany Ann and Nicey Melinda, is the only one of the three cast in then (1950) modern dress—but Tudor can't resist putting everyone into ''old-fashioned clothes'' for the climactic marionette performance. Ruffles and lace, for other adults who equate children's holidays with sweets and nostalgia.

A review of ''Tasha Tudor's Sampler,'' in Kirkus Reviews, *Vol. XLV, No. 10, May 15, 1977, p. 538.*

Tasha Tudor is here represented with reprints of three exceedingly slight stories. . . . Little girls of a previous generation loved the cozy domesticity of these tales and the delicacy of Tudor's illustrations, but they have not aged well and their only appeal today will be to nostalgia buffs. Most children will find the stories dull, with little relevance to their own interests and activities.

Margaret Maxwell, in a review of ''Tasha Tudor's Sampler,'' in School Library Journal, *Vol. 24, No. 1, September, 1977, p. 117.*

A TIME TO KEEP: THE TASHA TUDOR BOOK OF HOLIDAYS (1977)

Nostalgic memories of days long ago shimmer across the pages, as Tasha Tudor reminisces about her family's early New England festivities. Twelfth Night charades, Valentine's Day cards, maple sugaring, Easter egg trees, maypoles, Fourth of July picnics, Halloween pumpkins, Thanksgiving turkeys, and Christmas crèches are remembered in brief narrative and depicted in soft delicate watercolors. Twinings of pines, grasses, and herbs border the pictures, which are filled with the Corgis, cats, looms, marionettes, wheel-barrows, cider presses, lanterns, and fascinating minutiae found in the artist's own home. This glimpse into yesterday will be a book to keep for years to come.

Barbara Elleman, in a review of ''A Time to Keep: The Tasha Tudor Book of Holidays,'' in Booklist, *Vol. 74, No. 8, December 15, 1977, p. 686.*

A nostalgic trip into the past when holidays were treated with excitement and non-commercialism. This beautifully illustrated large-sized book will make an ideal gift for all seasons. The customary family togetherness depicted may inspire families of today to establish their own traditions and perhaps adopt a few from the Tudor family, who still observe holidays as described in detail in this delightful book.

Margaret M. Nichols, in a review of ''A Time to Keep: The Tasha Tudor Book of Holidays,'' in Children's Book Review Service, *Vol. 6, No. 6, Winter, 1978, p. 54.*

Nostalgia is Tasha Tudor's middle name. No fan of hers will be surprised or disappointed by this charming account of family doings. Despite the subtitle, ***Book of Holidays,*** this is really a book of seasons, punctuated by holidays. Delicate watercolors, intricately framed in flowers, pussy-willows or ribbons, depict a very large family rejoicing in ''every season . . . under the heaven.'' The family is dressed for the rural 19th century. Someone must be busting blood vessels offstage cooking and cleaning, washing and weeding; but we see only happy, relaxed faces. The children are delighted to help with sugaring and harvesting; and the parents seem under no stress. They labor quietly, slowly, like Nature itself. Appropriate quotations—''Welcome be thou, faire fresshe May''—assist the grandmotherly text, ''On May Day the children left May baskets at our neighbors' doors. And we danced around a Maypole.''

At first glance I decided "It's a fraud!" No one family could do so much. And this family is much too neat to convince me. No one ever frowns, spills or quarrels. According to the book, however, it's all true! Not only did the artist do these neat things in her childhood, and with her own children. She does them today with her grandchildren!

In the light of this information, ***A Time to Keep*** takes on a downright sinister hue. It becomes dangerous, threatening, like the Walton television series. Exposed to it, a modern child is bound to ask "Why don't we live like this?"

Economic, sociological answers will not satisfy; for what will arouse wonder and envy is not the material, natural abundance of the pictured life style, but its quiet joy and gentle activity. "Be ye perfect as your heavenly Father is perfect" is the enticement of this lovely book. Many parents may brush it off brusquely; "It's unreal!" Others may well be enticed to try once more, with feeling, to make of their childrens' childhood a time to keep.

Anne Crompton, in a review of "A Time to Keep: The Tasha Tudor Book of Holidays," in The New York Times Book Review, *February 5, 1978, p. 26.*

Tudor takes readers through the year with detailed vignettes illustrating all the conventional holidays. Conventional the holidays may be, but the special way that three generations of the author's family celebrate them add a full measure of good humor and enjoyment. It is hard to choose a favorite among a birthday cake floating down a river, the dolls' Valentine tea, and meringues in the shape of toadstools—but then children won't have to choose as they race through these enchanting pages. (pp. 79-80)

Merrie Lou Cohen, in a review of "A Time to Keep: The Tasha Tudor Book of Holidays," in School Library Journal, *Vol. 24, No. 8, April, 1978, pp. 79-80.*

From A Time to Keep: The Tasha Tudor Book of Holidays, *written and illustrated by Tasha Tudor. Rand McNally & Company, 1977. Copyright © 1977 by Checkerboard Press, a Division of Macmillan, Inc. Reprinted with permission of Checkerboard Press, a Division of Macmillan, Inc.*

This is a book to keep and use around the year for years! Delicate watercolor paintings in the representational style so typical of Tasha Tudor offer young readers a nostalgic glimpse of some holiday traditions celebrated by Tasha Tudor's family during her childhood in New England. . . . The quotations—taken from such sources as the Old and New Testaments and the works of such personalities as James Whitcomb Riley, Christina Rossetti, Thomas Jefferson, Hans Christian Andersen, Plato, and Shakespeare—capture the spirit of each season or holiday and convey the traditional values Tasha Tudor so obviously admires and wants to share with her readers.

Patricia Jean Cianciolo, "Me and My Family: 'A Time to Keep'," in her Picture Books for Children, *revised edition, American Library Association, 1981, p. 62.*

TASHA TUDOR'S BEDTIME BOOK **(1977)**

Fond relatives of little children have made Tudor's books best sellers for generations. They surely will do the same for this anthology. The artist's sweet touches personalize the many full-color paintings . . . and invest the classics collected here with extra facets. . . . The stories are mostly familiar ones. . ., but there are several rarely heard delights here as well, to perk up the story hour.

A review of "Tasha Tudor's Bedtime Book," in Publishers Weekly, *Vol. 213, No. 1, January 2, 1978, p. 65.*

There is a slapdash look to Tudor's illustrations for these familiar stories and poems; even her trademark cats and corgis could use a grooming. There's nothing new here and much that should have been left out of a supposedly soothing bedtime anthology—particularly the tear-jerking **"Babes in the Wood"** ("The babes died peacefully in each other's arms.") and **"Snow White . . ."** pictured inside a see-through glass coffin.

Merrie Lou Cohen, in a review of "Tasha Tudor's Bedtime Book," in School Library Journal, *Vol. 24, No. 8, April, 1978, p. 72.*

A BOOK OF CHRISTMAS **(1979)**

[Tasha Tudor's pop up ***Book of Christmas*** consists of] six three-dimensional tableaux that fall flat. "Joyous" baking, cooking, and tree trimming, depicted in dingy colors, give way to a no-surprise advent calendar with 24 windows opening wide on a cute mix of tots, teeny animals, and heavenly cherubs blowing horns. Plus, a solid gold seraph points the Magi and sundry miracle seekers to the manger.

Laura Geringer, "A Litter of Runts: Christmas Books '79," in School Library Journal, *Vol. 26, No. 2, October, 1979, p. 116.*

Tudor's dainty, old-fashioned paintings and stories have earned her millions of fans during her long career. Few will pass up her new Christmas offering, a three-dimensional book overflowing with tiny joys, pictured in soft pastels. . . . An Advent calendar is a special feature of the production, with numbered squares on a full spread that challenge readers to find and open each on its appointed day. Tudor also provides information on how Christmas is celebrated in many lands, plus excerpts from Luke and Matthew, describing the birth of Christ.

A review of "A Book of Christmas," in Publishers Weekly, *Vol. 216, No. 18, October 29, 1979, p. 83.*

A Book of Christmas is entirely modern, a 'Three Dimensional Book'—which is contemporary jargon for 'pop-up'. In technique it is less ingenious than its Victorian forerunners, but the drawing is, to modern eyes at least, infinitely better and the interpretation more authentic. A brief text tells a little about Christmas and its origins. The pop-ups show jollity at home, a coaching scene (this is also an Advent calendar), Christmas customs in different countries, and three scenes from the first Christmas, in which the angel leaps across the sky, the wise men move sedately across the page on their camels, and children worship at the stable while plump cherubs make music on the roof. A pretty book. (pp. 16-17)

M. Crouch, in a review of "A Book of Christmas," in The Junior Bookshelf, *Vol. 44, No. 1, February, 1980, pp. 16-17.*

THE SPRINGS OF JOY (1979)

Glimmering watercolors on each page celebrate the joys and wonders of the natural world as discovered by little boys and girls and by the inimitable artist herself. In a foreword, the author-illustrator—who has long been an odds-on favorite of readers young and old—says that she chose the excerpts here to record a few things that bring her intense joy. Undoubtedly countless readers will luxuriate in her pastoral scenes, Tudor's interpretations of "other men's flowers"—the thoughts of Wilde, Patmore, Wordsworth, Thoreau, Shakespeare, Dryden, Elizabeth Barrett Browning and other immortals.

A review of "The Springs of Joy," in Publishers Weekly, *Vol. 216, No. 20, November 12, 1979, p. 58.*

Chosen for their reflection of the philosophy, goals, and innermost concerns of [Tasha Tudor's] life, the selections complement full-color paintings that are beautifully reproduced in the pale, shimmering shades, expressive details, and wistful nostalgia long associated with the artist. The sometimes excessive botanical borders that Tudor uses are mostly gone, allowing a clear focus and providing a sweep to the pictures. The children that canoe in the pond, run with lambs, jump in the hay, gather eggs, contemplate the moon, and share a moment with a corgi portray a life-style even more subtly and evocatively than the biographical text of Bethany Tudor's *Drawn from New England*. . . . A book for sharing.

Barbara Elleman, in a review of "The Springs of Joy," in Booklist, *Vol. 76, No. 11, February 1, 1980, p. 772.*

TASHA TUDOR'S OLD FASHIONED GIFTS: PRESENTS AND FAVORS FOR ALL OCCASIONS (with Linda Allen, 1979)

True, many of Tudor and Allen's 30-plus gift projects can be found in other crafts books; but nowhere else can one find patterns that convey more of the handcrafted personal touch that is part of the spirit of giving. Stuffed animals, a variety of apparel for all ages, mobiles, plus 15 very traditional recipes (Halloween candied apples, fudge, and toffee, among others) are all gathered together in this very suitable "gifts for all seasons" book. Illustrations are tasteful and directions are clear enough for almost any beginner who understands the rudiments of sewing and knitting. Appended: common metric equivalents and conversions.

Barbara Jacobs, in a review of "Tasha Tudor's Old-Fashioned Gifts," in Booklist, *Vol. 76, No. 10, January 15, 1980, p. 694.*

As quaintly and sweetly as ever, Tasha Tudor now offers directions for 36 "presents and favors for all occasions." Sixteen of these are recipes for food (mostly candy), and the rest vary greatly in kind and difficulty. Paper hats and cardboard tube "snappers" are easy to make; patterned two-color mittens and patchwork pillows are more difficult. Some of the more old-fashioned gifts are a miniature band box which, say the authors, could hold clothes of a beloved doll or a hoard of beautiful buttons; and, a "pocket," whose use is not explained but which appears in an illustration to be like the one lost by Lucy Locket. Directions are clear and diagrams aid construction. The co-author and co-illustrator, whose name is not in the title, is Linda Allen, who has done about half of the watercolors and pencil sketches which abound in this book. Her art is imitative of, but inferior to, Tudor's. The purpose of this fluffy, nostalgic book, stated in the introduction, is to inspire readers to make their own gifts and to be creative. There are other books which accomplish this more effectively; one of them is *Family Book of Crafts* by Hellegers and Kallem (Sterling, 1973).

Carolyn K. Jenks, in a review of "Tasha Tudor's Old-Fashioned Gifts: Presents and Favors for All Occasions," in School Library Journal, *Vol. 26, No. 7, March, 1980, p. 144.*

THE LORD IS MY SHEPHERD: THE TWENTY-THIRD PSALM (1980)

Parochial schools, church libraries, and general collections wanting to add religious materials will find this illustrated King James version of Psalm 23 a gentle expression of faith. Tudor's homespun watercolors of a small child kneeling for prayers, meditating in the fields, playing with animal friends, and glorying in the stars are deftly portrayed. Wrapped in vine-and-leaf borders, the pastoral scenes, liberally scattered with rabbits, turtles, chipmunks, and dogs, provide a serene backdrop for a book that children and adults will enjoy together.

Barbara Elleman, in a review of "The Lord Is My Shepherd: The Twenty-Third Psalm," in Booklist, *Vol. 77, No. 9, January 1, 1981, p. 625.*

The drawings done in Tudor's usual style are not equal to her best work. In addition, her pictures do not illuminate the text and in a couple of instances do not clearly relate to the text. For example, the phrase "Thou anointest my head with oil" is illustrated with the child hugging her dog. The total effect is facile, and the cozy, warm approach serves only to reduce the meaning and power of King David's poem.

Jane E. Gardner, in a review of "The Lord Is My Shepherd: The Twenty-Third Psalm," in School Library Journal, *Vol. 27, No. 6, February, 1981, p. 58.*

Chris Van Allsburg

1949-

American author/illustrator of picture books.

Van Allsburg is considered one of the foremost contemporary creators of surrealistic fantasies for children as well as an exceptionally talented illustrator. Noted for inventing sophisticated tales of enchantment that stimulate and linger in the imagination, he presents young readers with picture books which intermingle reality with illusion and feature inexplicable worlds, enigmatic characters, and straightforward, understated texts. A professional sculptor and drawing instructor, Van Allsburg characteristically utilizes carbon pencil and conté crayon to create illustrations which reflect his fascination with massive shapes, manipulation of perspective, and use of light-and-shadow effects. His earliest books, *The Garden of Abdul Gasazi* (1979), which concerns a lost dog found by a magician, and *Jumanji* (1981), about an eerie board game, won immediate acclaim for their originality, mysteriousness, and monochromatic artistry; with his next book, *Ben's Dream* (1982), Van Allsburg depicts an imaginary journey around the world in black-and-white line art. He added an emotional dimension to his highly structured compositions by creating pastel paintings in full color for two works which deal with leaps in time—*The Wreck of the* Zephyr (1983), about a flying ship, and *The Polar Express* (1985), about a trip to the North Pole on Christmas Eve. With *The Mysteries of Harris Burdick* (1984), a collection of unrelated, often bizarre pictures in black and white accompanied by brief captions, Van Allsburg designed a book through which his readers become the storytellers by attaching their own meanings to the illustrations.

Critics often praise Van Allsburg for transcending the boundaries of traditional picture book creation. Likening him to such artists as Claude Monet, René Magritte, and Edward Hopper for his haunting, dreamlike scenes and symbolic figures, observers applaud Van Allsburg for his ability to portray evocative atmosphere and mood, his technical proficiency, and the excellence of his compositions. Although reviewers point to implausible storylines and inaccurate forms while questioning the suitability of the books for a read-aloud audience, they agree that Van Allsburg is a master of modern myth and a consummate artist.

***The Garden of Abdul Gasazi* was a Caldecott Honor Book and received the *Boston Globe-Horn Book* Award in 1980; it was also placed on the International Board on Books for Young People (IBBY) Honor List in 1982. *Jumanji* won the Caldecott Medal in 1981 and was designated a *Boston Globe-Horn Book* Honor Book in 1982. *The Mysteries of Harris Burdick* won the *Boston Globe-Horn Book* Award in 1985. *The Polar Express* won the Caldecott Medal and the *Boston Globe-Horn Book* Award in 1986.**

(See also *CLR,* Vol. 5; *Something about the Author,* Vol. 37; and *Contemporary Authors,* Vols. 113, 117.)

Courtesy of Houghton Mifflin Company

GENERAL COMMENTARY

BARBARA McKEE

Chris Van Allsburg has, to date, written and illustrated six children's books viewed as exemplary works of surrealistic fantasy. Much praise has been rightly given to his ability to create striking illusions through dramatic use of scale, to the detail and precision of his renderings with their skillful use of value changes and subtle manipulations of surface quality, and to the concrete stability and the sculptural appearance of his objects frozen in space. Van Allsburg's books have won several major awards. . . . Although he has created only six books, Van Allsburg has received the Caldecott Medal two times—for ***Jumanji*** and for his latest book, ***The Polar Express*** . . .—a distinction unprecedented in the history of the award. But although the books have received extraordinary recognition from the beginning, there is no doubt that Chris Van Allsburg is an artist who has been developing and learning his craft.

Van Allsburg states that for him the joy of being an artist lies in the challenge of solving particular technical problems and in creating impossible worlds. In ***Jumanji,*** for instance, he has succeeded in manipulating perspective and arranging objects in space to present a world in which we can look down on a carpet and at the same time look up at the bottom of a chair resting on that carpet. In the same book we view a park from above and, simultaneously, see the trees in that park drawn as if we were on the ground looking up at them. These space-stretching manipulations create impossible worlds in which we believe because they are so well laid out and carefully constructed. Yet recurring incongruities appear in his early work, which on first viewing we are inclined to overlook or interpret as deliberate but which remain disturbing to the internal balance of the illustrations. When compared to the harmony and accuracy of the other elements of his drawings, many of Van Allsburg's human figures display distortions—exceeding those used to create the surreal effect of the whole—that do not always seem attributable to artistic intention. The viewer is, in fact, sometimes left with a sense of confusion in attempting to reconcile the beauty of the rest of the drawings with the awkwardness of the human figures. Most of these problem figures occur in ***The Garden of Abdul Gasazi*** and gradually give way to increasingly convincing characters, more of a piece with their surroundings than they are in the earlier works.

Alan, the main character in ***The Garden of Abdul Gasazi,*** has a thicker and more geometric torso than he needs to fit in with the sculptural quality or the perspective of his world. By the time he is shown suspended in midfall down Abdul's garden steps, the articulation of his head and torso is contrived, and he appears distorted rather than strange or haunting. When the convention of perspective is pushed too far, its internal balance is lost and its artificial logic, which allows the viewer to suspend disbelief, is violated. This is what happens when Gasazi appears at his door to greet Alan. The coherence of the work is disrupted by the extreme foreshortening of the figures. Realistic touches, such as Alan's stomach bulging over his belt, can't make the enormous bulk of his legs believable. The distortion of Gasazi's head and neck are much too out of keeping with the rest of the picture to seem justifiable as artistic convention or interpretive distortion.

The figures in ***Jumanji*** are more accurately observed and executed. They are more successful because they constitute a larger part of their picture format. With the exception of the man hunched over a map, who presents a flattened back, these large, cropped figures are quite stylistically perfect; the much smaller full figures, especially those of the Budwing boys, are again overly geometric.

Like the successful figures in ***Jumanji,*** the children in ***Ben's Dream*** . . . are proportioned normally and mark the beginning of an important new subtlety in Van Allsburg's interpretation of humanity. Observe Margaret's pursued lips as she notices the black rain clouds and Ben's face, half in shadows as he comes home to an empty house and then falls asleep over his book. His shock as he wakes to find himself and his house afloat is more evocative than that of the frightened children in ***Jumanji.*** The depiction of his face, flooded by sunlight as he is wakened, is truly beautiful, the eyes open but gazing fixedly inward at his dream rather than at the girl before him. Though executed in a different medium, this small drawing is important as an early reference to Van Allsburg's most moving human portrayal, which later appears in "Oscar and Alphonse" from ***The Mysteries of Harris Burdick***. . . . Only once does the finesse of these drawings falter: the stiff figure of Margaret as she stands watching Ben ride away on his bike seems unreal.

In ***The Wreck of the Zephyr*** . . . Van Allsburg's landscapes have greatly evolved; they are frozen in time, yet vibrant and blooming in this new pastel medium. With the addition of color we see a new side of Van Allsburg's sensibility. In the best of these drawings color provides a wonderful and poetic counterpoint to the tightly ordered structure so integral a part of the artist's vision. There is a perfected balance between linear composition and color, and a delicate play of light and shadow pervades the drawing of the boy and sailor talking on a dock while two boats hover overhead. This picture is at once a delight to the intellect and the senses. Many of the figures in this work avoid the woodenness of their predecessors—they are yet another indicator of a new stylistic freedom. There appears just the tiniest upward curve in the line of the narrator's left shoulder as he is shown passing by the ***Zephyr*** wrecked on a hillside far above the sea. In art this is the sort of nuance that makes a figure come alive. The boy sailing his boat across the second illustration is a vital streak of colored motion, though in several of the following drawings his back is overly flattened and his head appears to be much too round. Van Allsburg almost loses control of the narrator's figure in the last drawing by his insistence on an expanded perspective and by the inaccuracy of the figure's bent leg, which, as drawn, originates from the figure's middle instead of the hip joint.

This movement away from delineation of details toward a more atmospheric diffusion of forms seen in ***The Wreck of the Zephyr*** is continued in ***The Mysteries of Harris Burdick.*** This softening lends a psychological depth to the interiors seen in "Uninvited Guests" and "The Third-Floor Bedroom" and a sense of greater mystery to the land and seascapes of "Another Place, Another Time" and "Captain Tory." In "The Harp," Van Allsburg's most breathtaking and complicated landscape, appears one of his smallest figures, which, despite its scale, is so alive that the viewer can almost feel him straining to see the harp in the distance.

In this book we also find a more representative use of a variety of figural and facial types. The face of the woman in "Just Desert" is a beautiful translation of a sinister ritual mask. Her

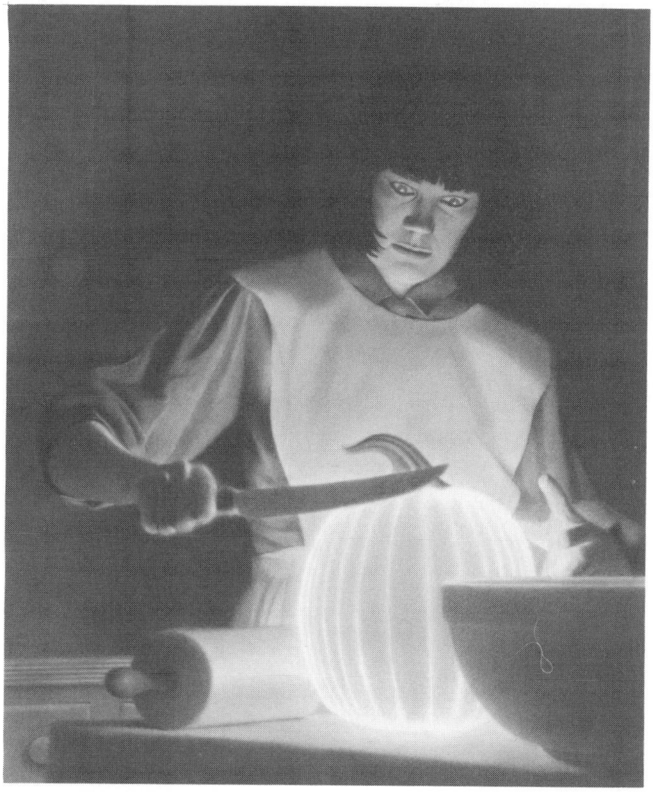

From The Mysteries of Harris Burdick, *written and illustrated by Chris Van Allsburg. Houghton Mifflin, 1984.*

eyes rolling down are a perfect opposite of the artistic convention of the beatific upward gaze. "Oscar and Alphonse" reveals a young girl, framed in sunlight with a glowing presence and an emotional reality that make her, by far, the most alive of all Van Allsburg's characters. She possesses physical as well as inner beauty, her face diffusing into light, hair floating gently in an imperceptible breeze.

From the beginning we sense that Van Allsburg's latest award-winning book, ***The Polar Express,*** is a special work. Van Allsburg has chosen unusually somber colors for these pastels yet has imbued them with an amazing warmth. The chocolate, rich world of the dining car reveals figural poses familiar from previous Van Allsburg books. The porter pushing the urn is a successful rework of Gasazi; the boy's turned head beside him is a color version of Ben. Perhaps the loveliest touch in this scene is the twisting, violet clad body of a boy leaning over his seat back to share secrets with the smiling child behind him.

The drawings in this book are a testimony to Van Allsburg's ability to use color and texture with great psychological as well as artistic power. The seemingly frozen moonlit night is, in reality, warmed by the inner glow of his blue and violet-red pastels. Even the eerie, green dream light which illumines the child's first glimpse of the North Pole has a welcoming warmth. In a scene reminiscent of Monet's cathedral paintings, a rose-colored tide of elves floods a city scape overlaid with shimmering flecks of blue snow. As Santa flies overhead the same elves look like hundreds of candle flames flickering below him. The children's surprise, sadness, and comforting concern as they discover the Christmas bell's loss contain an emotional depth paralleled in Van Allsburg's work only by the girl in "Oscar and Alphonse."

There seems to be something in the creation of standing male figures which sometimes thwarts Van Allsburg's attempts to depict mythic monumentality. The figure of Santa holding up the harness bell is not nearly as believable as the upturned face of the child beside him. The flatness of Santa's figure and the misplacement of his whip arm in the following pastel are minor failures of form in this remarkable book which radiates a gentleness new to Van Allsburg's work.

Van Allsburg shares his sensibility for creating a surreal environment, frozen in time and powered by a strategic choice of unusual perspective, with Edward Hopper, one of the artists he admires. Hopper has similar difficulties in some of his paintings in bringing the nature of his figures into line with their surroundings. Another admired influence, Rene Magritte, also creates surreal environs peopled with wooden, often primitive figures. Unlike Van Allsburg, Magritte is less likely to painstakingly model every inch of his painting in order to articulate his strange, compelling vision. In Magritte's work one senses a humor and deliberateness in the primitive quality which is less evident in Van Allsburg's polish. The meticulousness with which Van Allsburg works over his surfaces makes his humor less intellectually playful than Magritte's. The figures of Balthus, yet another artistic influence on Van Allsburg, are sculptural and display unusual proportioning, but Balthus's figures have an inner life of a more emotional nature than that of Van Allsburg's characters.

Van Allsburg in his latest works seems to be resolving the earlier technical problems in presenting believable human figures in the framework of his expanded perspective, though inconsistencies still appear. In his latest works the awkwardness of figure execution is disappearing and is being replaced by a deeper psychological interpretation of character. (pp. 566-71)

Barbara McKee, "Van Allsburg: From a Different Perspective," in The Horn Book Magazine, *Vol. LXII, No. 5, September-October, 1986, pp. 566-71.*

LYN ELLEN LACY

When Chris Van Allsburg's ***Jumanji*** came out in 1981, the book was hailed in reviews as a masterpiece of light and dark and a diabolical exercise in eye-fooling angles. The artist himself was called a consummate draftsman whose extraordinary multiplicity of gray tones displayed a subtle intelligence beyond the call of illustration. That Van Allsburg created such a startlingly realistic-looking setting for a world in which the utterly impossible happens results from use of artistic perspectives that force the audience to join in as participants. The mood is ominous from beginning to end and reality is imitated solely through incredible mastery of black-and-white drawings. This twilight fantasy, as ***Jumanji*** has been called, has very dramatically given children a new way to see the inner world of an imagination gone berserk.

The element of surprise in stories is another of Van Allsburg's contributions to children's literature. Like Sendak, he delights primary-age youngsters by requiring that they listen carefully to the words and look closely at the pictures to get the point. Van Allsburg's ***Ben's Dream*** and his 1980 [Caldecott] Honor Book, ***The Garden of Abdul Gasazi,*** have ambiguous twists at the end implying that the plots are indeed more than just dream sequences. For his first full-color book, ***The Wreck of the Zephyr,*** the author-illustrator suggests, just as in ***Jumanji,*** that the fantasy adventure need not be entirely over just because the book itself is closed. The only text for his 1984 book ***The Mysteries of Harris Burdick*** is in the introduction found before a collection of totally unrelated illustrations with mysterious captions that leave interpretation to the viewer—"in hopes that children will be inspired by them to tell stories" of their own, said Van Allsburg. In the 1986 Award winner, ***The Polar Express,*** the first gift of Christmas from Santa is lost by the young hero of the story, only to be found at the end underneath the Christmas tree that morning. And the sleigh bell's sweet sound can only be heard by those who truly believe. Mystery, suspense, and magic are marvelously combined in all these Van Allsburg titles to exploit the storyteller's age-old tactic of surprise.

As illustrator for his own tales, the artist included details in both pictures and text that hint that what follows is not as it may seem. In ***Gasazi,*** flowered wallpaper and the landscape painting hanging over the sofa as Alan takes a nap are suggestive of the garden and bridge in the next illustration, when the boy embarks on his excursion into the traumatic land of magic with Fritz the dog. An open geography book sets the stage for a flood in ***Ben's Dream.*** In ***Jumanji,*** the solemn blank stare of a toy dog and a dollhouse with dark empty windows and an open door like a startled face mutely accuse Judy and Peter: they have not only made a mess of the house, but they now appear likely to make things even worse. The topiary garden (inspired by a visit to the famous "Green Animals" garden in Portsmouth) from ***Gasazi***'s book cover is pictured on the lid of the game box in ***Jumanji;*** the magical flying boat from ***Zephyr*** is shown mounted on the wall above a bed in ***Harris Burdick;*** the white bull terrier pops up in all the books after Fritz's debut in ***Gasazi;*** and a toy locomotive in ***Jumanji*** turns up as a full-sized steam engine in ***The Polar Express.*** Most droll is the self-portrait of Van Allsburg himself that appears in illustrations for ***Zephyr, Express,*** and ***Harris Burdick,*** like Alfred Hitchcock's brief signature appearances in his own movies. (pp. 111-12)

Lyn Ellen Lacy, "Light and Dark: 'The Little House', 'Where the Wild Things Are', and 'Jumanji'," in her Art and Design in Children's Picture Books, *American Library Association, 1986, pp. 104-43.*

ZENA SUTHERLAND AND MAY HILL ARBUTHNOT

It would not be a great exaggeration to say that Chris Van Allsburg was like a meteor erupting into the field of children's books; his first book, ***The Garden of Abdul Gasazi*** (1979) was cited as a Caldecott Honor Book, an ALA Notable Book, as one of the best books of the year on four standard lists, and as the winner of two awards. Van Allsburg's focus on sculpture in his academic studies was reflected in the bold carbon pencil drawings that achieve a stunning solidity and chiaroscuro virtuosity, solid in their mass and architectural forms. Although he used different techniques (conté pencil and conté dust) for his next book, the sense of mass and the play of light and shadow are also outstanding in ***Jumanji*** (1981) which was awarded the Caldecott Medal. The sense of architectural form is in ***Ben's Dream*** (1982) but there is more play with perspective in the drawings that make heavy use of parallel lines; in ***The Wreck of the Zephyr*** (1983) the artist moves to pastel paintings that are vastly different from his other work, yet have the same virtues of strong composition and bold use of mass. Van Allsburg's remarkable mastery of controlled, dramatic light is most evident in ***The Mysteries of Harris Burdick*** (1984).

Zena Sutherland and May Hill Arbuthnot, "The Twentieth Century: Chris Van Allsburg," in their Children and Books, *seventh edition, Scott, Foresman and Company, 1986, p. 158.*

BARBARA BADER

[Chris Van Allsburg] is probably best regarded as a popular phenomenon. A master of theatrical effects and suave magic-realism, he delivers visual shocks and thrills and a single Romantic message—about how kids are wiser, in their credulity, than grownups: the old poet's notion of the loss of imagination with the loss of innocence, moved up to the age of the knowing child and the obtuse parent.

Jumanji has a superlative jacket—as a poster and a trailer—enhanced by omitting Van Allsburg's name (deemed unnecessary: distracting and self-evident?). A comparison with [Arnold Lobel's] *Fables,* similar in format, points up the excellence of the interior design, too: type of a darkness and weight and character to set off the infinitely modulated grays, the molded forms and precisionist textures of the Conté pencil drawings.

Through use of perspective, scale, and lighting, the drawings make the banal look eerie, as when the bespectacled boy and pigtailed girl—with (anachronistic) toys abandoned at their feet—sit down to play the game. They telegraph the children's reactions to the ensuing disorder in dumb show—the boy's stupefaction ("He couldn't believe his eyes") at the sight of the lion on the piano, the girl's gasp on seeing the monkeys in the kitchen. They pitch the onlooker into the picture space, and the pictured forms at the onlooker, in a razzle-dazzle of 3-D cinematics and baroque *trompe l'oeil. . . .* (pp. 298-300)

The terror, though, is of a neutral, painless sort—unthreatening alongside, say, Hansel and Gretel. There's no real mystification, by comparison with the likes of Arthur Yorink's *It Happened in Pinsk.* As an imaginary construct, the whole thing is formulaic: The children have only to say the magic word *JUMANJI* to dispel the danger, sending the diamond-spotted snake back into the flower-spotted upholstery. And, in the dénouement, an unthinking adult remark lets us know that the hazardous game will go on—whereupon we see two new children bearing it away. The illustration, manipulative and matter-of-fact, leaves nothing to the imagination either. What can be said for it, as can also be said of certain high-impact poster imagery, is that it stays in the mind. (pp. 300-01)

Barbara Bader, "The Caldecott Spectrum," in Newbery and Caldecott Medal Books: 1976-1985, *edited by Lee Kingman, The Horn Book Incorporated, 1986, pp. 279-314.*

ETHEL L. HEINS

Unquestionably, Chris Van Allsburg's work heralded a virtuosity as unique as his instantaneous success. His sculpturesque figures and architectural forms and his tonal range of grays in concert with black and white all add emotional force to his illustrations. And when he burst into full color with ***The Wreck of the Zephyr,*** one saw intensified the characteristics of his work—beauty of composition, confident drawings, a striking use of light and shadow, a sense of clarity and solidity, and the intriguing ambiguity of illusion and reality. (p. 328)

Ethel L. Heins, "A Decade of Children's Books: A Critic's Response," in Newbery and Caldecott Medal Books: 1976-1985, *edited by Lee Kingman, The Horn Book Incorporated, 1986, pp. 323-42.*

THE WRECK OF THE ZEPHYR (1983)

AUTHOR'S COMMENTARY

[The following excerpt is from an interview by Selma G. Lanes, author of Down the Rabbit Hole: Adventures and Misadventures in the Realm of Children's Literature *and* The Art of Maurice Sendak.]

Few stars in the firmament of children's books have risen so meteorically as Chris Van Allsburg. . . .

The accomplishment is all the more remarkable for having been achieved in black-and-white (a noncolor scheme having long been considered the kiss of death in a children's picture book)—and by an artist who considers himself primarily a sculptor, although he has been teaching drawing at the Rhode Island School of Design since 1977.

Now . . . [comes] Van Allsburg's first work in full color. . . . What lured an artist, whose black-and-white work has been shown at the Whitney Museum of American Art and in two one-man exhibitions at the Allan Stone Gallery in New York, to abandon the stark palette that, in his hand, has achieved almost rainbow richness?

"For me, the joy of being an artist is the challenge of solving particular technical problems," Van Allsburg says. "Obviously, when you use color, whole new vistas open up. For one thing, there are emotional qualities you can achieve with color that are far more elusive in black-and-white. On the other hand, there were certain surrealistic effects I could get in black-and-white that are impossible once color is introduced." (p. 38)

To create the art for ***Zephyr,*** Van Allsburg selected pastel over paint because, he says, it seemed a more natural choice for someone whose forte is drawing. "In ***Zephyr,*** I used Rembrandt

From The Wreck of the *Zephyr, written and illustrated by Chris Van Allsburg. Houghton Mifflin, 1983.*

pastels—crayons as thick as a finger—for broad passages,'' he explains, ''and well-sharpened pastel pencils for the details.'' This necessitated working on a larger scale than before: his original art has undergone a 60% reduction for clear and detailed reproduction in the Houghton book. ''If I had thought color drawing would be easier in pastel than other alternatives,'' Van Allsburg says, ''I've since learned from colleagues—and experience—that that medium is just about the hardest one I could have chosen.'' (pp. 38-9)

Selma G. Lanes, ''Story behind the Book: 'The Wreck of the Zephyr','' in Publishers Weekly, *Vol. 223, No. 14, April 8, 1983, pp. 38-9.*

At the edge of a cliff, high above the sea, rested the wreck of a small sailboat. By way of explanation, an old man tells a fantastic tale. Many years before, a boy, proud of his extraordinary skill at sailing, defiantly took his boat the *Zephyr* into a fierce storm. Struggling against mountainous waves, he was knocked unconscious and eventually washed up on an unfamiliar island, where he saw boats riding wondrously—not upon the water but above it. A local sailor kindly offered to set him on a homeward course, but the boy begged to stay and learn the magical art of navigating through the air. Reluctantly, the man consented; but although the two cruised for hours, only the older sailor—not the young one—could turn the *Zephyr* into a flying craft. Late that night, however, the boy stole out to his boat, and sailing into open water, he finally made it rise high above the waves. Then, propelled almost as much by the boy's hubris as by the fair wind, the *Zephyr* glided through the dark sky—until the wind suddenly shifted and the sailboat fell to the ground. In ***The Garden of Abdul Gasazi*** and ***Jumanji*** . . . the unique tonal range of various grays in concert with black and white add great interest and dramatic power. The new story depends heavily on the virtuoso illustrations. Although the book is illustrated in full color, it displays recognizable hallmarks of the artist's work: beauty of composition, striking contrasts of light and shadow, and especially the fascinating ambiguity of illusion and reality. The confident forms and the colors—clean and sharp yet constantly modulating—carry an unusual emotional impact, while the paintings themselves convey a sense of clarity, solidity, and force. (pp. 295-96)

Ethel L. Heins, in a review of ''The Wreck of the Zephyr,'' in The Horn Book Magazine, *Vol. LIX, No. 3, June, 1983, pp. 295-96.*

Ever since he made his debut in 1979 with ***The Garden of Abdul Gasazi,*** Chris Van Allsburg has had a position all his own as a poet of displacement or, in other words, of the world turned upside down.

Whether with Conté dust and Conté pencil or, as in his new book, with pastel, his illustrations begin by setting up a world that is unmistakably and palpably our own. Everything in it is solid, precise and as it should be. Overtones of high art there may be—from Balthus to Winslow Homer and Magritte, one might say—but the point of departure is the epitome of everyday experience.

The text likewise is a model throughout of plain good sense. We accept the narrator as laconic, exact and wise, in the great tradition of 19th-century American narration. As for the children, they are adventurous rather than disobedient, and resourceful without being implausibly courageous.

And it's just as well, given the number of bizarre and unpredictable things that happen to them. Never were children better at keeping their heads. If a magician claims to have turned their little dog into a duck, they address the problem as best they can. If their house takes off on a tour of the world in which all the great monuments turn out to be under 50 feet of water, they take it all in without squawking. If a board-game brings them into all too close contact with a lion, a python, a rhinoceros, a monsoon rainfall and a volcano in eruption, they just keep on playing and hope that the game will end happily.

In ***The Wreck of the Zephyr,*** Mr. Van Allsburg tells of a very young sailor who puts out to sea in impossible weather, just to show off. Nature bangs him on the head with the sailboat's boom and sees to it that the boat gets carried impossibly far inland. From that point onward, text and image could not be more happily mated. We are carried into a world where sailboats can be made to fly through the air and the seasoned navigator can always find a safe harbor.

We believe it, and we also believe in the boy as an archetype of the will to succeed and the wish to be recognized as "the greatest sailor of all." What happens to him in the end is too good a secret to reveal here. Suffice it to say that whereas in Mr. Van Allsburg's earlier books we never really leave the enclosed world of childhood, this one ends with a 60-year leap in time that is most subtly and elegantly contrived. There is a new richness of color in ***The Wreck of the Zephyr,*** and some of the images of flight are worthy of Magritte himself. But the text is as spare, as sober and telling as ever. It would be difficult to imagine a better book of its kind.

John Russell, in a review of "The Wreck of the Zephyr," in The New York Times Book Review, *June 5, 1983, p. 34.*

Van Allsburg has created a dreamlike story that mixes fantasy with reality. Yet this kind of fantasy deviates sharply from the type more commonly found: children's books featuring such things as magic crayon worlds, talking cows, bicycling monkeys, and tea-partying animals. ***The Wreck of the Zephyr*** is far more sophisticated and somewhat mystical in content.

While the story itself falls short in plausibility, Van Allsburg's full-color pastel paintings create their own exquisite story. The soft delineation of sea, sky, and sailboat gives the book an airy, timeless quality.

Cynthia B. Marquand, "Dreamlike Tale with Exquisite Illustrations," in The Christian Science Monitor, *June 29, 1983, p. 9.*

The explanation of a ruined hull so far from the sea cleverly conceals the personal involvement of the narrator. Remarkably his subtle tale captures the eternal searching for past dramas, glories and pleasures.

The powerful illustrations go beyond just capturing the essence of the story by exuding a magical feeling as the ghost ships skim above the waves. Each oil-painted illustration is a work of art in itself.

The old man is not the only person who dreams of the future by wishing back on the past. Child readers will want to share their remarkable experiences too! (p. 900)

Ronald A. Jobe, in a review of "The Wreck of the Zephyr," in Language Arts, *Vol. 60, No. 7, October, 1983, pp. 899,--,-900.*

In this joyous celebration of change and mystery, a visitor enquiring about a wrecked boat found far inland is offered an alternative to the obvious explanation of storm-movement in the fable of a sailor-boy. . . . In gloriously spacious scenes in a fine range of pastel and deep colours the pictures set an atmosphere of airy magic against normal land and sea-scapes; darkness and light, implied movement, the boy's visible excitement, take us from the plain statements of the text to the boundless world of the imagination.

Margery Fisher, in a review of "The Wreck of the Zephyr," in Growing Point, *Vol. 23, No. 2, July, 1984, p. 4292.*

Mystery, magic, and ambiguity permeate Van Allsburg's work. High above shore lies a wrecked sailing boat. Was it thrown there by a stormy sea—the explanation offered by villagers—or does the truth lie in the supernatural tale of a lame sailor? His story of a boy obsessed with becoming the 'greatest sailor of all' has the timeless quality of myth. . . . Which story is real? Is reality what is, or what we imagine? In Van Allsburg's pastels, sea and air become possessed of an eerie life of their own, producing surreal images of dislocation. Powerful though these images are, they reflect only what the uneven text tells us—restricting, not extending, the imagination. Though this may not be a true picture book, it is still one whose themes prompt intense debate.

Elizabeth Hammill, "Picture Books: 'The Wreck of the "Zephyr"'," in The Signal Selection of Children's Books 1984, *The Thimble Press, 1985, p. 12.*

THE MYSTERIES OF HARRIS BURDICK (1984)

Harris Burdick calls on a publisher and leaves a set of drawings, each suggesting a story plot in one sentence; then he vanishes, leaving the publisher haunted by the weird scenes, disquietingly realistic pictures of impossibilities. This is the gist of Van Allsburg's new epic, displaying yet again his incomparable artistry. The drawings are his, of course, graphic black-and-white views shot with light, that challenge readers to write the mysteries envisioned by fictional Burdick. The emotions conjured up by the book are extreme and lasting. In one instance, we are mesmerized by "Missing in Venice," an ocean liner forced into the canal "even with her mighty engines in reverse." The sight of the enormous vessel shouldering aside Venetian buildings chills the blood. Readers who have progressed beyond the banal pick-your-plot stories will welcome the artist's prod to inventiveness.

A review of "The Mysteries of Harris Burdick," in Publishers Weekly, *Vol. 226, No. 10, September 7, 1984, p. 78.*

In ***The Wreck of the Zephyr*** . . . , Van Allsburg added color to his tantalizing art. Here, he works again in his signature velvet black and white, and the pictures are nothing short of spectacular. The only thing missing is a story (or more correctly, stories), which the reader is left to provide. . . . While some may find this just an excuse for handsome artwork, others will see its great potential for stretching a child's imagination. Although the book could be used in countless ways, primarily it will make storytellers of children. They will need little prompting once they set their eyes on Van Allsburg's provocative scenes. An inventive, useful concoction. (pp. 135-36)

Ilene Cooper, in a review of "The Mysteries of Harris Burdick," in Booklist, *Vol. 81, No. 2, September 15, 1984, pp. 135-36.*

Conventionally, the method of the visual or literary artist is to present his vision more or less fully formed. The living work is completed as readers/viewers cross the barrier into the artist's world to share that vision. In this exciting new work, Van Allsburg dares to ignore these boundaries. Instead, he offers 14 glittering fragments, invitations to grow the flower from the seed. . . . [The] minimal information from each "missing" story is intense and provocative, with subtle references to Van Allsburg's earlier books. . . . [Each] illustration is so unlike the others that examples are misleading: the only common thread is magical wonder. The tight, realistic forms and hard edges of earlier fantasies are softened in these conté drawings, as if seen through a mist. The angles of perspective are more subtle, but no less powerful. Using less pattern and detail, the pattern of form is more dominant, with gradient shadows and sensitive atmospheric effects. Van Allsburg's use of contrast is masterful; one squints at the light from his windows. Layered in mystery, this extraordinary book will stun imaginative readers of all ages. It takes the breath away.

Nancy J. Horner, in a review of "The Mysteries of Harris Burdick," in School Library Journal, *Vol. 31, No. 2, October, 1984, p. 152.*

Like mirror images which recur and repeat themselves into eternity, these mysteries have a delightful way of multiplying as we lose ourselves in Chris Van Allsburg's latest picture book. . . . Using conte crayon to effect fine gradations of black and white, Van Allsburg enhances the mood of mystery. He creates feelings of intimacy and shared secrets through skillful handling of light on strongly modeled forms which seem to reach out to us at the same time they draw us into and beyond the picture plane. While each illustration stands on its own as a separate mystery, the design of the book (the charcoal black end pages, the rhythmic layout of the text and pictures, and the dark and spooky values of the black-and-white drawings enlivened by the pumpkin orange cloth cover) pulls the individual pages together into a whole that is much greater than the sum of its parts.

Van Allsburg's creation of these secret worlds and his sense of playfulness will reach out to children of all ages, just as the stunning images do. The book is a natural for language arts classrooms—Van Allsburg's suggestion that children write their own mysteries will be impossible to turn down. The only danger is that in hurrying to write their stories, children will forget to take time to look, to savor, to think about the book's visual sumptuousness, and to consider the greatest mystery—how does Chris Van Allsburg continue to be an innovator in the art form of the picture book, and whatever will he do next? (p. 87)

Barbara Kiefer, "Critic's Choice," in Language Arts, *Vol. 62, No. 1, January, 1985, pp. 86-7.*

While I was excited about ***The Mysteries of Harris Burdick*** . . . , I wasn't sure it would be successful with children. Oh, me of little faith. Chris Van Allsburg knows what he's doing.

I'm a fortunate bookseller in that I have children in the store most of the time. I'm a convenient kiddie-drop while parents are at the post office or the grocery store. That's fine with me. On their first drop-in most of these children head for the book version of the latest movie madness—***Gremlins*** (Western), for instance, when that film was playing. During their second time in, I do a little shepherding. I thrust a book into their hands that I think they should know about and say something like, "Here, look at this one and tell me what you think of it." Everybody wants to be a critic.

I tried this approach with ***The Mysteries of Harris Burdick,*** first with a pretty child of about nine or ten. She looked at it for only a minute, then ran out of the store, coming back quickly with her mother to explain that this book was perfect for her brother. She showed her mother the illustration of Archie Smith, Boy Wonder, which carries the line " 'Is he the one?' " Mother agreed and bought the book. Does the girl's brother have visits from little white lights?

After word got around that the bookshop had this crazy book, children arrived on bicycles, alone and in packs. They'd take ***The Mysteries of Harris Burdick*** down and sprawl on the floor to become mesmerized by whatever page reached out and grabbed them. With a child alone you can almost see the hair rising off the scalp. With a group there is very little conversation, perhaps an occasional, barely audible "weird." I have from time to time asked, "What do you think is pulling that ship into the canal?" or "What do you think is happening in the third floor bedroom?" The replies are so filled with astral forces and kinetic energy that I'm quickly left in the lurch of an older generation.

The Mysteries of Harris Burdick invites children to use their own imaginations, and they are accepting the invitation. I'm sure they also discuss the book at home because parents come in to buy it. Thank you, Chris Van Allsburg. (pp. 351-53)

Robert D. Hale, "Musings," in The Horn Book Magazine, *Vol. LXI, No. 3, May-June, 1985, pp. 350-53.*

The Mysteries of Harris Burdick neatly evades the question of what part illustrations play in books for older children by throwing it straight back at the reader. The book consists of fourteen haunting pictures, each embellished only by a title and a quotation. They allegedly constitute a "portfolio", left thirty years ago as a sample with a publisher, never matched with the full stories and never claimed by their mysterious author. There is something slightly but harmlessly odd about this; the fuzzy soft-focus monochrome drawings make such a range of recently fashionable references (Wyeth, Hopper, Parrish, Magritte) that it is hard to believe that they date from the 1950s. But their surreal implications raise interesting echoes: a clapboard house lifts off like a rocket, a liner looms up jammed down a Venetian canal, a seated nun levitates in the aisle of a Romanesque cathedral, and the reader is implicitly required to reconstruct the stories that inspired them. It is a clever do-it-yourself outfit, rather like a game of literary Consequences. How much mileage there is in it is another matter; but it may stand as a tribute to the eternal ingenuity of publishers determined to plug an awkwardly shaped gap.

Roy Foster, "Space for Words," in The Times Literary Supplement, *No. 4324, February 14, 1986, p. 174.*

THE POLAR EXPRESS **(1985)**

AUTHOR'S COMMENTARY

[*The following excerpt is taken from Van Allsburg's Caldecott Medal acceptance speech of June 29, 1986.*]

It seems strange now, considering my susceptibility to the power of the printed word, that I'd been reading for more than twenty years before I thought about writing. I had, by that time, staked out visual art as my form of self-expression. But my visual art was and is very narrative. I feel fortunate that I've become involved with books as another opportunity for artistic expression.

Over the years that have passed since my first book was published, a question I've been asked often is, "Where do your ideas come from?" I've given a variety of answers to this question, such as: "I steal them from the neighborhood kids," "I send away for them by mail order," and "They are beamed to me from outer space."

It's not really my intention to be rude or smart-alecky. The fact is, I don't know where my ideas come from. Each story I've written starts out as a vague idea that seems to be going nowhere, then suddenly materializes as a completed concept. It almost seems like a discovery, as if the story was always there. The few elements I start out with are actually clues. If I figure out what they mean, I can discover the story that's waiting.

When I began thinking about what became ***The Polar Express,*** I had a single image in mind: a young boy sees a train standing still in front of his house one night. The boy and I took a few different trips on that train, but we did not, in a figurative sense, go anywhere. Then I headed north, and I got the feeling that this time I'd picked the right direction, because the train kept rolling all the way to the North Pole. At that point the story seemed literally to present itself. Who lives at the North Pole? Santa. When would the perfect time for a visit be? Christmas Eve. What happens on Christmas Eve at the North Pole? Undoubtedly a ceremony of some kind, a ceremony requiring a child, delivered by a train that would have to be named the Polar Express.

These stray elements are, of course, merely events. A good story uses the description of events to reveal some kind of moral or psychological premise. I am not aware, as I develop a story, what the premise is. When I started ***The Polar Express,*** I thought I was writing about a train trip, but the story was actually about faith and the desire to believe in something. It's an intriguing process. I know if I'd set out with the goal of writing about that, I'd still be holding a pencil over a blank sheet of paper.

Fortunately, or perhaps I should say necessarily, that premise is consistent with my own feelings, especially when it comes to accepting fantastic propositions like Santa Claus. Santa is our culture's only mythic figure truly believed in by a large percentage of the population. It's a fact that most of the true believers are under eight years old, and that's a pity. The rationality we all embrace as adults makes believing in the fantastic difficult, if not impossible. Lucky are the children who *know* there is a jolly fat man in a red suit who pilots a flying sleigh. We should envy them. And we should envy the people who are so certain Martians will land in their back yard that they keep a loaded Polaroid camera by the back door. The inclination to believe in the fantastic may strike some as a failure in logic, or gullibility, but it's really a gift. A world that might have Bigfoot and the Loch Ness monster is clearly superior to one that definitely does not.

I don't mean to give the impression that my own sense of what is possible is not shaped by rational, analytical thought. As

From The Polar Express, *written and illustrated by Chris Van Allsburg. Houghton Mifflin, 1985. Copyright © 1985 by Chris Van Allsburg. All rights reserved. Reprinted by permission of Houghton Mifflin Company.*

much as I'd like to meet the tooth fairy on an evening walk, I don't really believe it can happen. (pp. 421-23)

The application of logical or analytical thought may be the enemy of belief in the fantastic, but it is not, for me, a liability in its illustration. When I conceived of the North Pole in ***The Polar Express,*** it was logic that insisted it be a vast collection of factories. I don't see this as a whim of mine or even as an act of imagination. How could it look any other way, given the volume of toys produced there every year?

I do not find that illustrating a story has the same quality of discovery as writing it. As I consider a story, I see it quite clearly. Illustrating is simply a matter of drawing something I've already experienced in my mind's eye. Because I see the story unfold as if it were on film, the challenge is deciding precisely which moment should be illustrated and from which point of view.

There are disadvantages to seeing the images so clearly. The actual execution can seem redundant. And the finished work is always disappointing because my imagination exceeds the limits of my skills.

A fantasy of mine is to be tempted by the devil with a miraculous machine, a machine that could be hooked up to my brain and instantly produce finished art from the images in my mind. I'm sure it's the devil who'd have such a device, because it would devour the artistic soul, or half of it anyway. Conceiving of something is only part of the creative process. Giving life to the conception is the other half. The struggle to master a medium, whether it's words, notes, paint, or marble, is the heroic part of making art. Still, if any of you run into the devil and he's got this machine, give him my name. I would, at least, like to get a demonstration.

An award does not change the quality of a book. I'm acutely aware of the deficiencies in all of my work. I sometimes think I'd like to do over everything I've ever done and get it right. But I know that a few years later I'd want to do everything over a third time.

This award carries with it a kind of wisdom for someone like me. It suggests that the success of art is not dependent on its nearness to perfection but its power to communicate. Things can be right without being perfect. (pp. 423-24)

Chris Van Allsburg, "Caldecott Medal Acceptance," in The Horn Book Magazine, *Vol. LXII, No. 4, July-August, 1986, pp. 420-24.*

Critics and spellbound readers recognize Van Allsburg as an innovator who always pushes beyond the known frontiers in conjuring up marvels. His new book matches in daring and wonders ***The Garden of Abdul Gasazi, Jumanji, The Mysteries of Harris Burdick*** and his other prize winners. Here a boy of about five years relates happenings on Christmas Eve when he joins the children on a train traveling to the North Pole. Although the narrator may ask Santa Claus for any gift, he chooses only a bell from the reindeers' harness. Back home on Christmas morning, the boy understands the symbolism of faith in the magic bell, recorded in the author's sweet-wistful denouement. Imbued with haunting airs, the paintings are in darkly eerie colors, pierced here and there by flashes of white from the moon, snowflakes and the lamps in windows of brooding buildings.

A review of "The Polar Express," in Publishers Weekly, *Vol. 228, No. 4, July 26, 1985, p. 166.*

It's the ending that carries the message of this Christmas story: "Though I've grown old, the bell still rings for me as it does for all who truly believe." . . . Whether the read-aloud audience gets the message or not, they will probably enjoy the several appeals of a story that has Santa Claus and a journey in it; along with older readers-aloud, they will surely appreciate the stunning paintings in which Van Allsburg uses dark, rich colors and misty shapes in contrast with touches of bright white-gold light to create scenes, interior and exterior, that have a quality of mystery that imbues the strong composition to achieve a soft, evocative mood.

A review of "The Polar Express," in Bulletin of the Center for Children's Books, *Vol. 39, No. 2, October, 1985, p. 39.*

Given a talented and aggressive imagination, even the challenge of as cliché-worn a subject as Santa Claus can be met effectively. . . . This is a personal retelling of the adult storyteller's adventures as a youngster. . . . The telling is straight, thoughtfully clean-cut and all the more mysterious for its naive directness; the message is only a bit less direct: belief keeps us young at heart. The full-page images are theatrically lit. Colors are muted, edges of forms are fuzzy, scenes are set sparsely, leaving the details to the imagination. The light comes only from windows of buildings and the train or from a moon that's never depicted. Shadows create darkling spaces and model the naturalistic figures of children, wolves, trees, old-fashioned furniture and buildings. Santa Claus and his reindeer seem like so many of the icons bought by parents to decorate yards and rooftops: static, posed with stereotypic gestures. These are scenes from a memory of long ago, a dreamy reconstruction of a symbolic experience, a pleasant remembrance rebuilt to fulfill a current wish: if only you believe, you too will hear the ringing of the silver bell that Santa gave him and taste rich hot chocolate in your ride through the wolf-infested forests of reality. Van Allsburg's express train is one in which many of us wish to believe. (pp. 164-65)

Kenneth Marantz, in a review of "The Polar Express," in School Library Journal, *Vol. 32, No. 2, October, 1985, pp. 164-65.*

There's always been an element of mystery in Van Allsburg's books, and this one is no exception. . . . The story unfolds alongside deep-toned, double-page paintings as full of mystery as the story itself. Darkened colors, soft edges, and the glow of illuminated snow flurries create a dreamlike adventure that is haunting even as it entertains. An imaginative, engrossing tale of Christmas magic. (pp. 271-72)

Denise M. Wilms, in a review of "The Polar Express," in Booklist, *Vol. 82, No. 3, October 1, 1985, pp. 271-72.*

A few years ago, the young sculptor Chris Van Allsburg decided to go outside his field and write a book. More accurately, he decided to draw a children's book and write a suitable accompanying text. The result was ***The Garden of Abdul Gasazi,*** quickly hailed as one of the best children's books of 1979. The simple story is nicely told; the illustrations are stunning. The book won two awards and was on three lists of notable books.

In 1981, Mr. Van Allsburg wrote and drew another book—and ***Jumanji*** won four awards, including the Caldecott Medal. That is, of course, the top prize a picture book for children can get. In two years Mr. Van Allsburg had reached the crest.

Three more books have followed, all well received, but none so ecstatically as the first two. That's a common pattern among American writers: a brilliant start, and then a long slide to competence. It's not going to be Mr. Van Allsburg's pattern, however. His new book, ***The Polar Express,*** represents another crest. As a story, it's not as exciting as ***Jumanji,*** but the pictures may be the best he's done. . . .

[The] plot is the same as in most of Mr. Van Allsburg's books, and also in Mary Poppins, Wordsworth's poetry and so on—the loss (for most people) of the quite literally magical experiences of childhood.

As story, that idea is much more adventurously expressed in ***Jumanji,*** and more humorously, too. But as picture book, ***The Polar Express*** is magic indeed. Mr. Van Allsburg is a master of light. The windows of the train on the long ride north are beautiful, glowing, mysterious, even breathtaking. The lights of the city at the North Pole—a fine baroque city—are, if possible, still more appealing. There is nothing cute here, rather there is something I would have to call majestic. Nor is Mr. C. cute, or even fat and jolly. He is to most Santa Clauses as a real angel, say, in Milton, is to the plump cherubs of the candy box. The one disappointment is the rendering of the elves, who look a little too much like teen-age boys in stocking caps and pointed shoes.

Most of Mr. Van Allsburg's books have been in black and white. This one is in color. The publisher has done it extraordinary justice. And as for Mr. Van Allsburg, he handles it so well as almost to make you wonder why he bothers with sculpture.

Noel Perrin, "The Sleigh Bell Rings," in The New York Times Book Review, *November 10, 1985, p. 46.*

As in so many of the earlier books, like ***The Garden of Abdul Gasazi*** and ***The Wreck of the Zephyr,*** Mr. Van Allsburg works effectively combining the sinister and the sentimental, but it would take a poet-sociologist to explain precisely why these dark, moody sculptural pastels somehow evoke feelings of glad tidings and joy.

Christopher Lehmann-Haupt, in a review of "The Polar Express," in The New York Times, *December 2, 1985, p. C16.*

THE STRANGER (1986)

Farmer Bailey thinks he's hit a deer while driving his truck, but in the middle of the road lies a man, an enigmatic stranger. He goes home with Farmer Bailey, his memory apparently gone. Weeks pass at the Bailey farm; the stranger seems happy to be around them, and helps with the harvest. Oddly, while trees to the north of the farm turn red and gold with the arrival of fall, Bailey's land seems to be in a state of perpetual summer. One day, the stranger sees geese flying south and knows that he, too, must leave. Not long after that, the leaves at the farm change color and the air turns cool. And every year since, summer lasts a week longer at the Bailey farm than anywhere else. Van Allsburg's story is strangely melancholy, and his straightforward writing is uncannily dry, in contrast to the vivid green and golden landscapes of his paintings. The mood and suspense in this book make it compelling—a chance to see the artist take a slight incident and create a truly mysterious event.

A review of "The Stranger," in Publishers Weekly, *Vol. 230, No. 13, September 26, 1986, p. 77.*

Van Allsburg's aptitude for odd stories edges toward obscurity here. . . . There are carefully planted clues as to the stranger's identity, but they are a bit obscure for young listeners. The full-color illustrations, framed in white, evoke an old-fashioned New England landscape at the end of summer; some are remarkably peaceful in tone, others slightly spooky by virtue of brooding colors, unexpected perspectives, or the stranger's peculiar expressions. Children who can figure out what is going on (when the doctor tells Mrs. Bailey to throw away the thermometer, for instance, because the mercury is stuck at the bottom) could be intrigued; others may pass this one up for the artist's fantastical but more specific ***Jumanji*** or ***The Polar Express.***

Betsy Hearne, in a review of "The Stranger," in Bulletin of the Center for Children's Books, *Vol. 40, No. 3, November, 1986, p. 59.*

The Stranger is a down-homey modern myth about the phenomenon of Indian Summer, but the opening owes less to the folktale than to *The Twilight Zone*. Farmer Bailey, rapt on an end-of-summer day in his 1940s pickup, suddenly hits something: the next page shows a young man's body, dramatically foreshortened and stretched out at eye-level in the evening shadows. . . . The text scatters clues to the stranger's identity (Jack Frost); but the moment of recognition is cleverly given over to the electrifying illustration alone. Characteristically, the bold simplifications of Van Allsburg's warm pastels look back to American regionalist paintings of the 1930s and '40s—especially to Thomas Hart Benton and Grant Wood. The story is too low-keyed for most children, although several compositions provide suspense with their unorthodox points-of-view, out-of-frame action, and play with effects of light. Here the interweaving of fantasy and reality is more complex than in Van Allsburg's earlier books, and the effects more subtle; but the surface pleasures of color and form are still enticing.

Patricia Dooley, in a review of "The Stranger," in School Library Journal, *Vol. 33, No. 3, November, 1986, p. 84.*

Chris Van Allsburg's magnificently illustrated books have been receiving awards since 1979. . . . Text and pictures have dazzled readers as Mr. Van Allsburg has moved from rich and muscular black-and-white drawings to a cool palette that sometimes suggests the Pointillist masterpieces of Georges Seurat. . . .

The story [of ***The Stranger***], beautifully told with Mr. Van Allsburg's characteristic simplicity, may prove deeper and more intriguing for young readers than his earlier tales. Part of the book's charm is that everyday human life is presented as wondrous. It seduces and satisfies the supernatural visitor. And the visitor's magic, rather than being sinister or unnatural, is part of nature itself.

But the warmth and intimacy of the illustrations are perhaps the most exciting new elements here. For the first time, we are brought close to Mr. Van Allsburg's characters and their feelings. The innocent facial expressions of the stranger, the blissful smile of the farmer's little daughter as she looks up at

From The Stranger, *written and illustrated by Chris Van Allsburg. Houghton Mifflin, 1986. Copyright © 1986 by Chris Van Allsburg. All rights reserved. Reprinted by permission of Houghton Mifflin Company.*

the stranger, the ecstatic dance of the two while the farmer and his wife make music—these are almost without precedent in the artist's other books, which are more cerebral and more remote.

How marvelous that this master painter and storyteller has added a new dimension to his consistently original and enchanting body of work. His fans are certain to embrace this fascinating, yet sublimely comforting book.

Anne Rice, "Jack Frost's Amnesia," in The New York Book Review, *November 9, 1986, p. 58.*

In this book Chris Van Allsburg has used a warmer, more autumnal palette than in ***The Polar Express***. . . . The light in these pictures has the bright, crisp quality and long shadows of summer's end. To achieve the glowing colors of trees and fields, he has used an impressionist, almost pointillist technique. Some of the individual pages have the quality of the mystery found in ***The Mysteries of Harris Burdick***. . ., particularly those of the stranger eyeing the soup ladle and the little girl peeking through a crack in the parlor door. The author-illustrator has woven a thread of fantasy in and around his realistic illustrations to give the reader, once again, a story that stays in the imagination. (p. 742)

Hanna B. Zeiger, in a review of "The Stranger," in The Horn Book Magazine, *Vol. LXII, No. 6, November-December 1986, pp. 741-42.*

The jacket art of this book is riveting; a young man with an astonished look in his eyes is watching as soup is being ladled from a large tureen into a soup dish. The painting is a bold, full-color, super-real portrait. What makes this picture so arresting is the strange juxtaposition of the young man's amazed gaze and the utter homespun familiarity of the scene. Chris Van Allsburg is interested in not only what we see, but what we often take for granted and what we fail to see. His texts, as well as his art, hint at mysteries. . . . Children, and their parents, who appreciate the private gesture in the art and the unspoken word in the text—together with Van Allsburg's many fans—will find this stark, lean picturebook most satisfying.

Leigh Dean, in a review of "The Stranger," in Children's Book Review Service, *Vol. 15, No. 5, January, 1987, p. 49.*

Gabrielle Vincent

19??-

Belgian author/illustrator of picture books.

Vincent is well known as the creator of a series of picture books for preschool and elementary-age children about Ernest and Celestine, a paternal, loving bear and childlike mouse who share a warm and empathetic relationship. Focusing on such familiar childhood experiences as losing a beloved toy, planning parties and outings, overcoming jealousy, and initiating independence, the works spotlight the duo's everyday pleasures as well as their creative and optimistic solutions to various financial struggles. To convey the ideas and feelings of her stories, Vincent uses simple texts written entirely in dialogue and employs a variety of illustrative approaches, layouts, and perspectives. She illustrates her books with soft watercolor and line pictures which present detailed domestic and outdoor scenes and expressively portray facial expressions and body actions. Vincent's anthropomorphic characters—all bear adults and mice children who are dressed in an old-fashioned French style—are placed in an original, timeless setting. In addition to several titles that combine text and illustration, Vincent has created two wordless books, *Breakfast Time, Ernest and Celestine* (1982) and *Ernest and Celestine's Patchwork Quilt* (1982). She has also published several picture books about Pic-Nic, a tenderhearted koala, which have not yet been translated into English.

Vincent is praised for creating expertly designed books which successfully convey emotion through their artful graphic style and understated texts. Although she is occasionally faulted for excessive anthropomorphism, Vincent is especially appreciated for her characterizations: Ernest as fatherhood personified and Celestine as an endearing blend of temperamental and adorable traits. Considered classics by many reviewers, the books display Vincent's understanding of childhood while providing gentle reassurance to her audience through the mutually supportive friendship she describes.

Courtesy of Editions Duculot

AUTHOR'S COMMENTARY

To all who love the books I have drawn:

All my work is done for you . . . and I am saving many other surprises. You wish to know me better. You would be pleased if I would accommodate you. Know well that this touches me greatly. But I beseech you not to ask me to leave my table continually. Protect my pleasure in drawing. Protect my private life. Rejoice in your ability to peruse the books' pages. Everything is contained therein. I don't have a great deal more to say. From my table I send all of you my very friendly thoughts.

Gabrielle Vincent, in a promotional letter of October 13, 1986, Duculot, Publishers. Translated for this publication by Gale Research Co.

GENERAL COMMENTARY

JUDY TAYLOR

An extraordinary privilege has come my way this year. I have had a chance to look at and to dwell upon a wide range of picture books published in the U.K. in 1982. (p. 13)

The greatest delight of my picture-book year has been the arrival in this country of Ernest and Celestine, the endearing and heartbreaking couple in Gabrielle Vincent's books. It is almost too rich a pleasure to have all four books in one year but at least it gives me the opportunity of looking at them together—and the first four do belong together.

The drawing is masterly, a line here and there changing the mood from joy to sorrow, a brush stroke softening the fold in a sheet, the cover on a chair. The texts are spare and beautifully complement the pictures from a position of airy space beneath each frame. The design of the books shows a definite pattern, progressing from the simple full-page frames of ***Ernest and Celestine,*** the occasional vertical double frames of ***Bravo, Ernest and Celestine!,*** the introduction of horizontal and four-to-a-page frames in ***A Picnic for Celestine,*** to the quite complicated design of ***Smile Please, Ernest and Celestine!,*** where the text is suddenly placed inside each frame, there are four, six and nine frames to a page, and the traditional pattern of the previous books is broken with the two spreads of 'photographs'.

These are books for sitting down and looking at; they are not read-aloud books because the text and pictures have to be seen together. Everything to do with them gives endless opportunity for speculation, discussion, investigation. Just what is the relationship between Ernest and Celestine? Why are all the adults in the books bears and all the children mice? Are there more stories to come? I do very much hope so. (pp. 13-14)

Judy Taylor, "My Picture-Book Year," in The Signal Review of Children's Books 1, *1983, pp. 13-16.*

***ERNEST ET CÉLESTINE ONT PERDU SIMÉON* [*ERNEST AND CELESTINE*] *ERNEST ET CÉLESTINE, MUSICIENS DES RUES* [*BRAVO, ERNEST AND CELESTINE!*] (1981)**

In these picture books, two continental figures make an American debut. Ernest, a cuddly and presumably adult bear, is roommate to Celestine, a demure and spirited young mouse. ***Ernest and Celestine*** finds Ernest replacing Celestine's ruined toy bird at great trouble, finally making one to hang on their Christmas tree. In celebration, the duo hold a great party for Celestine's friends. ***Bravo*** . . . finds them in dire financial straits. Celestine cajoles Ernest into playing his violin on the street; second day out, they find that her vocal accompaniment makes them a hit. The illustrations are watercolors full of whimsy and warmth, which, with the text, convey a great sense of mutual appreciation and pleasure shared. Because the text is entirely written in uncluttered dialogue, eyes are pulled to the detailed illustrations. The books are translated from the French, and their origin is apparent in the character's environment and dress. The tales take place in some pleasant indeterminate past (at least pre-automobile). Perhaps because so much is not expressed by words in ***Ernest and Celestine*** it is more difficult to enjoy. In any case, the pair's sparkle and warmth will make both good companions for young readers.

Carolyn Noah, in a review of "Bravo, Ernest, and Celestine!" and "Ernest and Celestine," in School Library Journal, *Vol. 28, No. 7, March, 1982, p. 141.*

Shades of Ernest Shepard in the expressive, lightly brushed watercolors—and a pair of cohabitants, wee mouse Celestine and fatherly bear Ernest, whose affinity is the more affecting for being conveyed all in pictures. The text is also uncommonly

From Ernest and Celestine, *written and illustrated by Gabrielle Vincent. Greenwillow Books, 1982. Copyright © 1981 by Duculot Paris-Gembloux. Translation copyright © 1982 by William Morrow and Company, Inc. All rights reserved. By permission of Greenwillow Books (A Division of William Morrow & Company, Inc.).*

effective all in dialogue—which suggests that Vincent may have had her eye on A. A. Milne altogether. In the first story, ***Ernest and Celestine*** (#1 because it does more to establish the relationship), the two go for a walk in the snow and Celestine loses her toy bird Gideon. "It's all your fault, Ernest!" says the disconsolate Celestine, tucked in bed, to the solicitous Ernest, fatherhood personified in a floor-length red bathrobe (while in the room—it's a memorable scene altogether—Gideon's doll carriage stands empty and Celestine's togs are strewn about the floor). . . . ***Bravo, Ernest and Celestine!*** is a less subtly interwoven, more situation-bound affair—with, unfortunately, more slapdash pictures. (The detail tends to be just stuff; the proportions less carefully calculated—even as between Ernest and Celestine. . . . Their success [as street musicians] is gratifying because you identify with the pair—but Ernest's initial diffidence and later stage-fright give the story its only internal vibrations. One could recommend ***Ernest and Celestine*** without ***Bravo*** . . . except that children would probably feel cheated. (pp. 343-44)

A review of "Bravo, Ernest and Celestine!" and "Ernest and Celestine," in Kirkus Reviews, *Vol. L, No. 6, March 15, 1982, pp. 343-44.*

Direct speech is . . . used successfully in ***Ernest and Celestine*** and ***Bravo, Ernest and Celestine!*** These are tender little stories about the friendship and mutual support of a bear and a mouse (a father and daughter, or perhaps a grandfather and granddaughter?) The gentle water colours by a new Belgian author and illustrator, Gabrielle Vincent, are reminiscent of both Beatrix Potter and E. H. Shepard. I found the stories gripping and attractive, but something in ***Ernest and Celestine*** struck a wrong note: Celestine loses her baby doll (in the shape of a bird) in the snow and is heart-broken. Ernest stays up all night sewing together a new one, and Celestine is happy again. Could a favourite toy be replaced in this way any more easily than a favourite person?

Kicki Moxon Browne, "On the Right Wavelength," in The Times Literary Supplement, *No. 4121, March 26, 1982, p. 346.*

A notable new talent makes an appearance in ***Ernest and Celestine*** and its sequel. . . . [The artist makes] a careful decision about the proportion of words to pictures. The text, brief as it is, has found another formal limitation as well—it consists entirely of dialogue; and who could guess, from 'Come on, Gideon, Ernest is taking us for a walk' or 'Are you going to help me with the dishes?' that the benevolent father-figure is a bear or that piping Celestine is a mouse, deeply attached to her foster-father but rather more so to her rag-bird. An adventure in snow in the first book, a money-making enterprise in the second—the two episodes are developed from the words spoken by bear and mouse, each one giving a lead, emotional or factual. Using a small range of colour—brown and blue wash, with sepia line—the artist preserves animal forms unaltered but through facial expression and movement, with judiciously chosen costume, tactfully humanises the animals so that Celestine's devoted care of her toy or Ernest's anxious care for her are totally clear and acceptable. The craftmanship of the pictures is outstanding. In each picture carefully chosen details (of furniture, costume and so on) are subordinated to the central figures, which express the particular feeling in each scene and so carry the story along on a succession of beautifully delineated moods. These picturebooks from France, elegant, tender and subtly comic, set a new standard in their kind.

Margery Fisher, in a review of "Ernest and Celestine" and "Bravo, Ernest and Celestine," in Growing Point, *Vol. 21, No. 2, July, 1982, p. 3917.*

[***Ernest and Celestine***] will have the universal appeal of a true classic. The illustrations, in delicate colour, are charming. Each is worth close study for its carefully drawn detail, and imaginative touches. There is only a line or two of caption under each picture. The whole story is unfolded with such sympathy that even these are scarcely needed. Gentle, loving Ernest, and his care for diminutive Celestine are woven into a heart-warming story.

A. Thatcher, in a review of "Ernest and Celestine," in The Junior Bookshelf, *Vol. 46, No. 4, August, 1982, p. 136.*

It isn't surprising to find a world where adults are all bears and their children all mice in picture books. We need not become unsettled by this biological improvisation. As long as some kind of authority figure is central to the plot, the combination of creatures who express childhood by being little and adulthood by being big works satisfactorily. Demure, defenseless mice are ideal for the former role and lumbering, well-padded bears for the latter.

In Gabrielle Vincent's ***Ernest and Celestine,*** a family circle is suggested simply by the fact that one character, Ernest, is given the assignment of watching out for the interests of little Celestine. Ernest is a bear and Celestine a mouse, but they are never specifically referred to in those terms in the text. . . .

By allowing pictures to carry the story line, Vincent avoids sentimentality. The anguish over the doll's loss and the triumphant mood of the party are conveyed with an appealing understatement. Just three words—"A green beak?"—combined with a picture are all we need to understand the happenings in one scene. The illustration shows Ernest leaning on the counter of the toy store and the bear-clerk trying to make sense of his request for a peculiar-looking bird doll. This is the pattern throughout the book: fragments of naturalistic conversation in perfect coordination with a series of narrative-packed drawings.

Vincent's style is loose and sketchy, with many objects arranged in what looks like haphazard positions. Clothes, toys, brooms, baskets, and rugs are scattered throughout the picture space to create lived-in interiors rather than rooms with fixed decors. A feeling of liveliness is enhanced by the use of incomplete contour lines that change in thickness as well as color. The relationship between mouse and bear is tender and relaxed, and Vincent's graphic style captures this quality in its deceptive casualness.

Donnarae MacCann and Olga Richard, in a review of "Ernest and Celestine," in Wilson Library Bulletin, *Vol. 57, No. 3, November, 1982, p. 234.*

***ERNEST ET CÉLESTINE VONT PIQUE-NIQUER* [*ERNEST AND CELESTINE'S PICNIC*] (British edition as *A Picnic for Ernest and Celestine*); *ERNEST ET CÉLESTINE CHEZ LE PHOTOGRAPHE* [*SMILE, ERNEST AND CELESTINE*] (British edition as *Smile Please, Ernest and Celestine*) (1982)**

Children who have already met Ernest, a fatherly bear, and the mouse-child Celestine . . . will be pleased to find there are now two more stories of this appealing pair. If Celestine's spirits are easily dampened, Ernest's solutions are direct and simple. In ***Smile, Ernest and Celestine,*** Celestine rummages through Ernest's drawer and finds a folder of old photographs. Although many show Ernest with other children, she finds none of herself. Ernest explains to the glum Celestine who the children are: then both dress up and hurry off to the photographer's. Result: a special album, "Photographs of Ernest and Celestine." In ***Ernest and Celestine's Picnic,*** a rainy day threatens their planned outing. Celestine is predictably disheartened until Ernest suggests that they pretend it's a lovely day and have their picnic anyway. Off they go in boots and rain gear and settle down under a tarp to have their lunch. A huffy property owner arrives, is warmed by their hospitality and helps make the rainy-day picnic a truly grand adventure. . . . [The] stories are noteworthy on two counts. Children will readily understand Celestine's downers and relish their satisfying resolutions. They will be taken, too, by the first-rate watercolor illustrations; expanding the brief texts, they reflect concrete domestic details, the action of the stories and every nuance of the volatile Celestine's emotions. Celestine is sometimes pouty and not always good, but happy or dour, she is always endearing. (pp. 60-1)

Janet French, in a review of "Ernest and Celestine's Picnic" and "Smile, Ernest and Celestine," in School Library Journal, *Vol. 29, No. 4, December, 1982, pp. 60-1.*

Vincent's appealing duo is back again, and Ernest proves once more that he is the nicest father figure a mouse child could ask for. . . . [In ***Ernest and Celestine's Picnic,*** the scenes] of the two suiting up, walking to the picnic site, and relishing their food under a makeshift canopy are quite beguiling. It's no surprise that their determined good cheer leads them to new friends at a nearby estate and the promise of another picnic come better weather. . . . [In ***Smile, Ernest and Celestine,*** the] lightly sketched and washed scenes capture anew the warmth of the previous titles. . . . It's apparent that Vincent has a mainline connection with childhood behavior and concerns. Celestine's outbursts have undeniable verité, while Ernest's devout fathering is a cherished ideal. Stories and pictures are inseparable, with mouse child and bear masterfully drawn to reflect the nuances of emotional expression suggested by the stories' simple plots.

Denise M. Wilms, in a review of "Ernest and Celestine's Picnic" and "Smile, Ernest and Celestine," in Booklist, *Vol. 79, No. 8, December 15, 1982, p. 569.*

The two latest Ernest and Celestine books enchant chiefly for Gabrielle Vincent's many fine small-girl studies of the little mouse Celestine. The mouse face, with its huge eyes, is at once distancing, so that Celestine's naughtiness and spoilt sulking can be enjoyed without too much guiltiness, and cuddlesomely attractive, without being tied to human characteristics of one type and time. As for the rest of her, it is all human and very exactly observed, often in a series of frames without words. The Belgian dress—pinafore at home and frilly best clothes—gives a quaint old-fashioned appearance which at points recalls John Goodall's Edwardian mice. There are beautiful water-colour interiors full of homely and untidy details, and impressions of street scenes and countryside, with a strong use of white space. In ***Smile Please,*** naughty Celestine opens Ernest's locked drawer while he is out, finds his photos, nearly gets caught, and makes herself very unhappy. Child-like, she gives herself away eventually in her jealousy of the other girl-mice in the photos. . . . Her furtive actions and subsequent sulking-fit are wonderfully lifelike.

In ***A Picnic for Ernest and Celestine,*** after their preparations, the picnic day dawns rainy. Once more, Celestine sulks, and Ernest gives in in a positive way—they have a pretend picnic. . . . This plot is more attractive, and the outdoor scenes show how like in quality Gabrielle Vincent's draughtsmanship can be to that of Caldecott (compare, for instance, the pair's happy dance, umbrellas raised, with the frog and the rat in the *Wooing,* taking tea with Mrs. Mouse). Again, there is the fine portrayal of a child, eager and expectant then sulkily immovable. But surely the English publishers, at least, should provide *some* clue in later books as to *why* a bear should be bringing up a girl mouse single-handed! Even a childreader must find this incongruous.

M. Hobbs in a review of "Smile Please, Ernest and Celestine!" and "A Picnic for Ernest and Celestine!" in The Junior Bookshelf, *Vol. 47, No. 1, February, 1983, p. 13.*

[Like the first books in this series] these sequels are illustrated with delicately-tinted drawings that have the liveliness of line and the humor that make Ernest Shepard's work distinctive. The paintings are not imitative, however, and they capture to perfection a child's mobile face, for Ernestine is more a child than a mouse. . . . The relationship between the protagonists is never made clear, although Ernest's role is parental. . . . [The stories] have a nice balance of brisk pace and gentle humor in their minimal texts, and the illustrations are deft in draughtmanship and echo the affectionate tone of the writing. (pp. 137-38)

Zena Sutherland, in a review of "Ernest and Celestine's Picnic" and "Smile, Ernest and Celestine," in Bulletin of the Center for Children's Books, *Vol. 36, No. 7, March, 1983, pp. 137-38.*

Two new books about Celestine, the diminutive mouse-child, and Ernest, the large resourceful bear, are based on much more substantial narratives than those in the initial volumes. . . . With very brief texts, effectively translated from the French, both books rest on strong pictorial storytelling; irresistible, pellucid watercolor paintings on interestingly composed pages clearly delineate the childlike narratives and define the characterizations of the anthropomorphic animals in their cozy domesticity. (pp. 163-64)

Ethel L. Heins, in a review of "Ernest and Celestine's Picnic" and "Smile, Ernest and Celestine," in The Horn Book Magazine, *Vol. LIX, No. 2, April, 1983, pp. 163-64.*

There have been four books published this year that feature Ernest, a large brown bear, and Celestine, a young mouse, who share a home. For me, their creator is the find of the year. All the books are superb, but I think my favourite is [***Smile Please, Ernest and Celestine!***] which is not as simple as the few words per page might lead you to think. The text is entirely in speech, much of it being Celestine's interior monologue as she discovers, first, a packet of photographs of Ernest as a child and then, upsettingly, another set showing other mouse children with her beloved guardian. Gentle, eloquent water colours portray the special relationship between the pair, and the books manage to be touching without being sentimental. They are best read silently—indeed, they encourage silent reading—when text and illustrations interact to produce a resonance that stays with the reader long after the books have been put back on the shelf. (pp. 7-8)

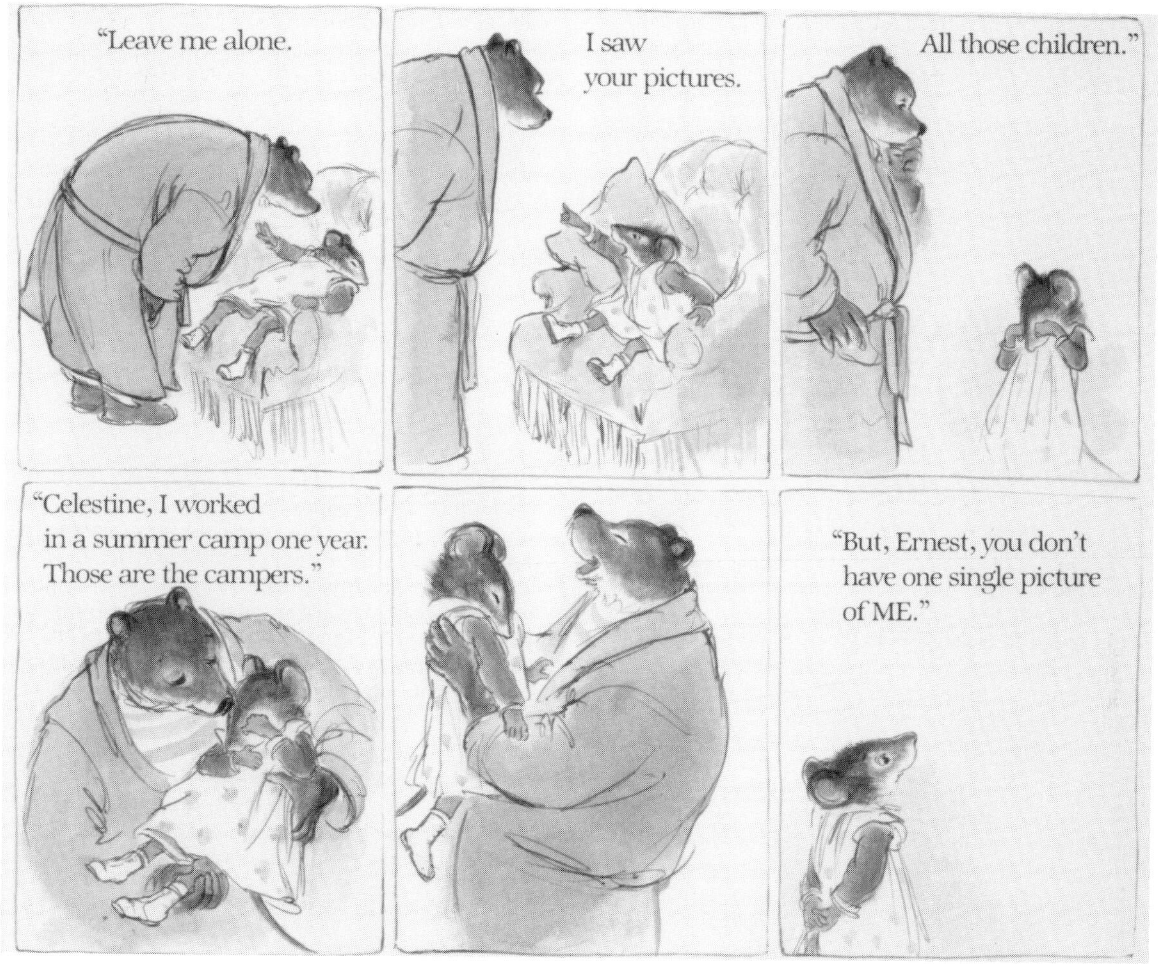

From Smile, Ernest and Celestine, *written and illustrated by Gabrielle Vincent. Greenwillow Books, 1982. Copyright © 1982 by Editions Duculot, Paris-Gembloux. Translation copyright © 1982 by William Morrow & Company. All rights reserved. By permission of Greenwillow Books (A Division of William Morrow & Company, Inc.).*

Jill Bennett, "Picture Books for Learning to Read: 'Smile Please, Ernest and Celestine!'" in The Signal Review of Children's Books 1, *1983, pp. 7-8.*

LA TASSE CASSÉE [BREAKFAST TIME, ERNEST AND CELESTINE]; LE PATCHWORK [ERNEST AND CELESTINE'S PATCHWORK QUILT] (1982)

These two wordless additions to the Ernest and Celestine books bring this endearing duo to a slightly younger audience than the previous, larger ones that came with slim texts. In ***Breakfast Time,*** little Celestine mouse knocks her breakfast bowl onto the floor where it breaks. Ernest bear moves to clean up the mess, but Celestine pushes him off to do the job herself in a typical display of childlike independence. Ernest, meanwhile, beams at the results. In the second story, Ernest stitches a quilt from a book of fabric samples. The lovely result makes Celestine slightly jealous, and she wants one for herself. Ernest obliges, and that night Celestine cuddles under her bright new bed cover. The smaller formats have not shortchanged the stories: Vincent's deft lines and pale washes are as charming as ever. The series' themes of resourcefulness and gentle family love continue to be born out with humor and grace.

Denise M. Wilms, in a review of "Breakfast Time, Ernest and Celestine" and "Ernest and Celestine's Patchwork Quilt," in Booklist, *Vol. 82, No. 2, September 15, 1985, p. 141.*

Families should smile as they continue to enjoy the warm friendship between the bear, Ernest, and the mouse, Celestine. Soft pastel watercolors shine with a joy of simple life. . . . ***Patchwork Quilt*** conveys an appreciation for friends making something together and sharing. Both are delightful and have more plot than many other wordless books; wonderful expression in the simple faces make up for the lack of words. Common household items and familiar everyday activities make these two books perfect for expression of early childhood language development and learning sequencing. Earlier ["Ernest & Celestine" picture books] . . . have been extremely popular; these two will be no different.

Susan McCord, in a review of "Breakfast Time, Ernest and Celestine" and "Ernest and Celestine's Patchwork Quilt," in School Library Journal, *Vol. 32, No. 3, November, 1985, p. 78.*

Smaller than earlier Vincent books, [***Breakfast Time, Ernest and Celestine***] is a brief, wordless story that is very clearly told by the illustrations. . . . Deft use of line, soft colors, and a clear sequence of ideas make the book as appealing as it is comprehensible.

A review of "Breakfast Time, Ernest and Celestine," in Bulletin of the Center for Children's Books, *Vol. 39, No. 5, January, 1986, p. 98.*

Like ***Breakfast Time, Ernest and Celestine, [Ernest and Celestine's Patchwork Quilt]*** is a small, square book with no text, and the pictures have the same visual appeals. The story, however, may be less clear to young children unless they are observant enough to notice the differences in the beds of the protagonists, a crucial factor in the action.

A review of "Ernest and Celestine's Patchwork Quilt," in Bulletin of the Center for Children's Books, *Vol. 39, No. 6, February, 1986, p. 119.*

NOËL CHEZ ERNEST ET CÉLESTINE [*MERRY CHRISTMAS, ERNEST AND CELESTINE*] (1983)

A charming picture book from France, it is the fifth in the series about Ernest and Celestine, but with no lack of invention. To label Ernest as a bear and Celestine as a mouse would be to restrict them unfairly, for Celestine is obviously any child and Ernest a loving uncle, or father, and the relationship between them is one of affectionate tenderness. This is all that matters, for these two have an innocence and goodness all their own.

In this book Celestine persuades Ernest to give a Christmas party, although they have no money to buy decorations, presents or even food. But with loving invention all these things can be found or made. All the children in the neighbourhood are invited to enjoy the simple pleasures and games and Ernest as Father Christmas. Only one child is contemptuous of the festivities, but no one cares about *him!*

The illustrations by the artist-author in delicate watercolour, are rich in fascinating and loving detail, as though the artist herself rejoiced in creating the happiness of the mouse-children who appear in them.

Here is the kind of large book that is studied over and over again, new details being constantly pointed out by small fingers. Surely this series of picture books could become a nursery 'classic'. And *all* these books are fun!

E. Colwell, in a review of "Merry Christmas, Ernest and Celestine," in The Junior Bookshelf, *Vol. 47, No. 5, October, 1983, p. 203.*

Family affection could scarcely be more gracefully demonstrated than in the pictured life of paternal bear Ernest and his tiny mouse charge. The exquisite arrangement of images in framed blocks, the muted colours and touching postures reconciling sizes and species, the neatly personalised guests at the party and the message that a little resource and skill can make an occasion happy without spending a lot of money—these are some of the points that distinguish this fifth instalment of a currently popular continuing story.

Margery Fisher, in a review of "Merry Christmas, Ernest and Celestine," in Growing Point, *Vol. 22, No. 4, November, 1983, p. 4172.*

Most children's books aimed at the Christmas market base their commercial appeal on some form of the religious, pre-religious

"See, Ernest,
I told you
you could draw."

From Merry Christmas, Ernest and Celestine, *written and illustrated by Gabrielle Vincent. Greenwillow Books, 1984. Copyright © 1983 by Editions Duculot, Paris-Gembloux. Translation copyright © 1984 by William Morrow and Company, Inc. All rights reserved. By permission of Greenwillow Books (A Division of William Morrow & Company, Inc.).*

or sub-religious sentiment which prevails at this time of year. Occasionally, one of these books comes off, and this year that book is ***Merry Christmas, Ernest and Celestine.*** Any primary teachers who have not yet met this pair should indulge themselves at once with a copy (after which they will not be able to do without the four earlier books either). If the message of Christmas is 'love conquers all' then there can be imagined no more joyous and tender celebration of that message than Ernest and Celestine's party, and like all great picture books there are no age limits on its appeal. While the youngest children will revel simply in the pictures of the happy partygoers, older ones will feel for poor Max, too big to be comfortable at the little ones' party, but drawn in despite himself and learning to be both bigger—and smaller. Adults may share my perplexity that Gabrielle Vincent's beautiful children, with their grace and innocence, their plunges into despair and their lightning recoveries, their bursts of temper and affection and—most noticeably—their carefully drawn children's *feet,* need to wear mouse masks and tails. Why, in such a celebration of childhood, should the children be . . . mice? Don't let it worry you. It's a must for the primary Christmas tree. (pp. 347-48)

Sue May, in a review of "Merry Christmas, Ernest and Celestine," in The School Librarian, *Vol. 31, No. 4, December, 1983, pp. 347-48.*

[***Merry Christmas, Ernest and Celestine*** shows] that the most familiar story-type *can* be made to live and breathe again. Ernest and Celestine dragging the fir tree back from the woods, constructing cheap Christmas presents from scrap paper, and ransacking the dustbins for old clothes to furbish up as party costumes, have the genuine, throat-catching, irresistible Christmas magic, and ***Merry Christmas, Ernest and Celestine,*** with its beautiful domestic interiors, and its triumphant story of a party that succeeds against the odds, stands a good chance of being read all the year round.

Myra Barrs, "But Once a Year," in The Times Educational Supplement, *No. 3520, December 16, 1983, p. 20.*

[As in ***Ernest and Celestine*** and ***Ernest and Celestine's Picnic***], Vincent has created a touching story of friendship between a fatherly bear and a child-like mouse. . . . Celestine is as beguiling and conniving as ever, and she convinces Ernest that they can have a Christmas party without spending money. . . . Animated softly-colored illustrations of various sizes, appearing one, two or more per page, clearly show the love between the bear and the mouse. What is missing in color consistency (Ernest's Santa suit varies from red to pink to orange) is made up for in Vincent's endearing characters, all of whom are imbued with personalities of their own. Ernest and Celestine are a pair that will add holiday spirit to any occasion.

A review of "Merry Christmas, Ernest and Celestine," in School Library Journal, *Vol. 31, No. 2, October, 1984, p. 175.*

In a new book about the two unlikely companions, tender concern and gentle affection gladden the work of preparing a special Christmas party. . . . In appealing watercolors, the warm interior of Ernest's kitchen is brought to life with its comfortable clutter of hanging laundry and scattered toys while deft pen strokes capture expressions of weariness, joy, bashfulness, and compassion on the small mouse faces. Ernest and Celestine's loving companionship is the glowing heart of the book about which revolves an entrancing band of mice sharing a joyous Christmas celebration. (pp. 747-48)

Ethel R. Twichell, in a review of "Merry Christmas, Ernest and Celestine," in The Horn Book Magazine, *Vol. LX, No. 6, November-December, 1984, pp. 747-48.*

***ERNEST ET CÉLESTINE AU MUSÉE [WHERE ARE YOU, ERNEST AND CELESTINE?]* (1985)**

With ***Where Are You, Ernest and Celestine?*** Gabrielle Vincent adds to her growing list of winning books about Ernest, a gentle bear, and his precocious mouse-ward, Celestine. Varying in theme and format (some are wordless), the series devotes itself to the trials and tribulations in the relationship between the caring duo. This book . . . continues the exploration. . . .

[The] new book brings Ernest and Celestine to a museum—the Louvre in Paris, no less. Ernest applies for a job there, but will only accept the position if Celestine can accompany him daily to work. He doesn't get the job. Nevertheless, they spend the day enjoying the splendid art in the museum. So engrossed is Ernest in the art that he momentarily loses track of Celestine. Happily, they are reunited. Yet Celestine is worried that Ernest is more fond of the paintings than of her. The concern is temporary, for Ernest sets her mind at ease by saying: "There is nothing I like better than you, Celestine!"

Surely, the real charm here, as well as in the rest of the series, is in Miss Vincent's fresh and simple watercolor illustrations. The clean design, with a light sepia line around all the pictures, is particularly suited to these pleasant ink sketches. The contrast of the whiteness of the paper to the warm washes in the pictures enhances the book's calm and gentle spirit. The typeface and its position never intrude upon the mood of the pictures; indeed, all the design elements work toward the successful marriage of story and pictures.

The illustrations I find most appealing are the interior scenes of the museum, taking one through room after room, giving just the right feeling of a museum visit. The rhythm of wide views to distance to close-ups to medium shots is timed exquisitely so that the pacing serves not only to move the reader along but also to convey the particular experience of being inside a museum. This is first-class picture-book making.

Consider the two facing pages that form a panoramic view of one of the larger galleries. In the left corner we see Ernest conversing with a guard. To the far right we see Celestine looking straight up at a row of masterworks. In one fell swoop we are treated to the breadth of the room, the stillness, the quietness, as well as the profound effect art can have on its viewers, dwarfing them as it does both Ernest and Celestine. What a marvelous spread!

In this age dominated by the films of George Lucas and Steven Spielberg, much of the current work for children in all media is laden with gimmicks and flash and a slickness that, to my mind, is cold and unfeeling. This superficiality can be seen in movies, television and, most assuredly, in current picture books. Miss Vincent's success lies in her attempt to engage and move readers rather than manipulate or overwhelm them. I heartily applaud her for that.

Yet, as refreshing and reassuring as these illustrations are, a few problems remain here, and in the series as a whole. There is a flaw in the unities. The ambiguity of the animal characters and their human surroundings is sometimes confusing. This is most clearly seen in the museum itself. When we first enter the Louvre we see statues in the likeness of bears, we meet the bear director, we see visitors, all of whom are bears. Fine; perhaps this is the Bear Louvre. Yet the paintings are all quite human—images taken from actual works, such as the Mona Lisa.

Also, the very naturalism I admire goes a bit too far, I fear, into the realm of the literal in the plot, text and dialogue. The anecdotal nature of the story is so very human that I begin to lose the sense of the characters Ernest, the bear, and Celestine, the mouse. This problem runs through the entire Ernest and Celestine series. What would enhance and enrich the themes—here the anxiety of separation—would be a deeper rendering of the pair. As is, Ernest and Celestine are too bland; there is a distinct danger that they will be overly cute and generalized. Specific individuals lead us to universal themes, not the other way around.

Certainly there is a long tradition of anthropomorphism in children's books, but the most successful examples are the ones that retain, in some measure, an element of the animal in the character portrayed as well as a unique personality infused by the creator. Take the "Little Bear" series by Else Holmelund Minarik, illustrated by Maurice Sendak, or the works of Beatrix Potter. True, Ernest and Celestine are symbols of a parental figure and a child, but before we can get to any universal truths we must first care about *this* Ernest the bear and *this* Celestine the mouse. They both, I believe, could use a little more "animal" and a little less "human."

Making a picture book is a terribly difficult thing to do and perhaps these points will be construed as nitpicking. But taken together they form a discernible fault in an otherwise wonderful book.

Arthur Yorinks, in a review of "Where Are You, Ernest and Celestine?" in The New York Times Book Review, *March 30, 1986, p. 23.*

Vincent's delicate line and airy wash are always a pleasure; when impressionistically applied to the generous spaces and famed paintings of the Louvre, the result is delightful. The lost/found drama, always good for enthralling the youngest, is treated with warmth and humor, and given extra point because Ernest has wished to work in the museum but only on condition that Celestine be allowed to come with him.

Perfect to share with a small child or a small group.

A review of "Where Are You, Ernest and Celestine?" in Kirkus Reviews, *Vol. LIV, No. 8, April 15, 1986, p. 637.*

Another appealing addition to the French picture books about Ernest the bear and the tiny mouse, Celestine. It is a worthy successor to the popular ***Merry Christmas, Ernest and Celestine***. . . .

The two look round the galleries together—and so does the reader for there are many tiny paintings on the pictured walls, easily recognisable for the adult. 'The 'Mona Lisa' smiles like Celesine,' says Ernest tenderly. . . .

Sentimental? Maybe, but young children need affection and reassurance. A picture book of this calibre becomes a loved possession and—who knows—some children will recognise a famous painting they have seen in these pages when they visit France.

E. Colwell, in a review of "Where Are You, Ernest and Celestine?" in The Junior Bookshelf, *Vol. 50, No. 3, June, 1986, p. 107.*

A beautiful picture book in which the pictures give a feeling of space and elegance. It really does look like an Art Gallery.

The sort of book that gets "AH's" as you turn the pages.

Sit with a little one and feel their joy, as well.

Larry Thomson, in a review of "Where Are You Ernest and Celestine?" in Books for Your Children, *Vol. 21, No. 3, Autumn-Winter, 1986, p. 10.*

Cynthia Voigt

1942-

American author of fiction.

One of the most respected authors for young adults to emerge in the 1980s, Voigt is recognized as an accomplished storyteller who creates well-developed characters, interesting plots, and authentic atmosphere. A thoughtful writer, she examines such serious topics as child abandonment, verbal abuse, racism, and coping with amputation. She is best known for her "Crisfield" novels—*Homecoming* (1981), *Dicey's Song* (1982), *A Solitary Blue* (1983), *The Runner* (1985), and *Come a Stranger* (1986)—which are set in an imaginary town on the Eastern Shore of Maryland and focus on the family and friends of Dicey Tillerman, a resilient yet sensitive teenage heroine. Voigt displays characteristic insight into human nature in these works by exploring the complex family relationships of her protagonists and the personal growth achieved through their struggles. While most noted for her realistic fiction, Voigt has also written *The Callender Papers* (1983), a gothic mystery in which a Victorian adolescent discovers the secrets of her heritage; *Building Blocks* (1984), a time-travel story for middle graders in which a son learns to understand his father by becoming friends with him as a boy; *Jackaroo* (1985), a medieval fantasy in which an original socioeconomic setting is the background for the story of a female Robin Hood; and *Stories about Rosie* (1986), a picture book in which the Voigt family dog has humorous adventures.

Reviewers appreciate Voigt's fluent and skillfully executed writing style, compelling topics, and vividly detailed descriptions. Although they sometimes find her stories slow paced, critics consider Voigt's themes universal and meaningful to young adults. They especially praise her expertise in fashioning memorable characters and rich relationships in which both adults and children grow in understanding.

***Homecoming* was nominated in 1982 for the American Book Award. In 1983, *Dicey's Song* received the Newbery Medal and was a *Boston Globe-Horn Book* Honor Book. *A Solitary Blue* was both a Newbery Honor Book and a *Boston Globe-Horn Book* Honor Book in 1984; *The Callender Papers* won the Edgar Allan Poe Award the same year. Voigt has also won other adult- and child-selected awards for her works.**

(See also *Contemporary Literary Criticism,* Vol. 30; *Something about the Author,* Vols. 33, 48; *Contemporary Authors New Revision Series,* Vol. 18; and *Contemporary Authors,* Vol. 106.)

AUTHOR'S COMMENTARY

[*The following excerpt is from an article based on Dorothy Kauffman's interview with Voigt on October 26, 1984.*]

Like many contemporary women, Cynthia Voigt . . . must constantly juggle the roles of wife, mother, and teacher. Theoretically, her day is constructed so that her husband Walter and two children, Jessica and Peter, go off to school at eight o'clock, and she has the remainder of the morning, till noon, to write. . . .

Photograph by Walter Voigt. Courtesy of Cynthia Voigt.

Reality, however, must have its own way, so Cynthia's daily schedules end up as cluttered as ours—what with shopping, family responsibilities, class preparations, the grading of papers, and participating in conferences—and those four hours devoted to writing get nibbled at constantly.

Cynthia herself compares modern life to a Gordian knot and her answer to the situation is something "sharp, quick, and definitive," as Alexander the Great's. In Cynthia's case, this sharp, quick, definitive response is the process of writing.

Reviewers and readers readily agree that Cynthia's characters are clearly drawn; her writing is sophisticated and volatile; her word choice is precise; her ability to establish intense emotional levels is keenly developed. (p. 876)

It is writing itself which permeates the person of Cynthia Voigt. She openly recognizes the importance of writing in her life and admits when she is not writing, she tends to "screw up in everything else. I get very grouchy." It is the writing—the making of something—that helps order her world.

Cynthia's tenacious belief in the worth of her writing convinced her to keep going for over two decades. She decided she wanted to be a writer in ninth grade. "But deciding you want to do it and getting somebody to buy something you've written is a long time. I was thirty-seven when I sold my first book."

Cynthia, like many other writers, states, "I don't know where I get my ideas." She can report that the idea for ***Homecoming*** began at the grocery store. "You always see kids in cars in grocery store parking lots. One day I saw these kids in cars and thought, 'What would happen if . . .?' I went home and wrote it down. A year later I wrote the story."

The impetus behind ***Tell Me If the Lovers Are Losers*** occurred one night when she was having dinner with several friends. Though she did not wear glasses at the time, as they passed around each other's glasses and looked through them, she found she could not focus through a pair of really thick ones. Knowing the owner was a basketball player, she asked, "How do you play basketball with these?" He responded, "No problem." But he did recall a similar incident in high school where a "wonderful, dead-eye shot basketball player" got glasses and could no longer play. "I thought, 'Wow!' and that was the basis of the story."

Both ***Dicey's Song*** . . . and ***A Solitary Blue*** grew out of the work of ***Homecoming.*** By the end of ***Homecoming,*** she knew ***Dicey's Song*** was next. ***A Solitary Blue*** developed as soon as the character of Jeff was thought out.

Dreams are sometimes the sources for stories, so writers say. Well, Cynthia's story of ***The Callender Papers*** originated that way. Though she admits that most of her dreams written down do not get anywhere, a dream formed the foundation for this mystery. "I'm prone to Gothic dreams and at the time I felt I needed to work on plotting. A Gothic novel needs a plot. Write this one!"

The origin for ***Building Blocks*** resided in her own home; she had only to recognize its presence. Her son Peter, who was quite young at the time, frequently played with the large, lightweight cardboard building blocks familiar to most two-year-olds. One night Walter constructed a rather large fortress with them. The next morning when Peter and Cynthia came downstairs, there it was! Peter (also known as Duffle) reacted immediately and crawled into the inviting structure. "There are stories where you go through a door. As Duffle crawled in, I thought, "'What would happen if . . .?'"

Cynthia's most recent title, ***The Runner,*** is another Tillerman story that she knew from the beginning of the series she would write . . . "once I figured out what I was doing with [the characters]." The next book that will be published is ***Jackaroo,*** a book she refers to as "my Zorro book."

When asked to identify the reason her stories are set in the East and much of the state of Maryland, her response is multilayered. Cynthia grew up in Connecticut, went to boarding school and college in Massachusetts, lived in Pennsylvania for a while, and is now living in Annapolis, Maryland. Essentially, then, her books reveal an autobiographical geography. "I think what it comes down to is there are some parts of the world that just strike you as extremely lovely. If I were a sculptor, somehow I'd want to express this; if I were a painter (which I'd love to be), I'd want to paint them. What I want to do is wrap my words around them."

Cynthia values the "everyman-kind-of-state" quality that Maryland has. "It is rural and urban. It has a southwestern sense of sky. It has both mountains and water but is not distinguished like Colorado with its mountains and pure air. You can find a lot of things in Maryland."

Until now, most of her stories are set in actual places. An exception to this is ***The Callender Papers*** where the setting is purely fictional, but "it's supposed to have the feel of the Berkshires." When Cynthia creates settings, she finds she has to draw maps, "and, as my students will tell you, I can't draw maps. Frequently I'll find that what I want to do can't work in the map I've drawn, so if I change it I have to change everything because I have to visualize it." Working with real settings is much preferred to made-up ones." Although this is true, Cynthia admits that ***Jackaroo*** . . . and ***Izzy, Willy Nilly*** . . . are also set in fictional locations.

This tendency to lay the foundation for story in reality extends to other aspects of Cynthia's writing too. She states she feels much happier when part of the story is based on fact. "My parents moved to Sewickley, Pennsylvania, and lived there until recently. It's a real town." Consequently, the settings in ***Building Blocks*** are true—the town, the cemetery, the caves, and the Ohio River (which really is much cleaner now than it was twenty years ago.) "I've been in those caves. But on hindsight, I can't figure out why I was down there. There was one place, just about a sacrificial slab, and you had to get down on your back just to get across the slab. I went down there with my boyfriend who said he knew the caves. Years later I found out . . . he didn't."

Because her settings are most frequently actual places, and because her characters are termed "original," "intriguing," and "outstanding" by reviewers who recognize Cynthia's ability to create believable, "real" people, one wonders where these characters originate.

"In some cases a character may be part of myself, but not really." To the extent that Dicey is the kind of kid Cynthia would have liked to have been and that Gram's the kind of lady she would like to be, the characters may be a kind of wish fulfillment. In some ways, Cynthia admits, the character of Sammy is similar to her son, but she quickly adds, "Only similar." Her characters take on their own lives—sometimes by a gesture or a telling point—and then they fill out into persons of their own.

Cynthia describes her connection with her characters as "pulling out a thin piece of torte," or "like with kids in a class. You have an insight that will enable you to connect even though you can't really explain who they are. You can't pin them down as to who they are, but you can connect with who they are, talk to them and see what they're trying to communicate. It's that narrow sliver connection from which you intuit outwards. I think that's how most of my characters are connected and absolutely different."

Characterization is alluring for Cynthia, as a writer, teacher, and individual. "I really like the question of 'who people are.' It's a fascinating question because people don't duplicate. They're like snowflakes. You can't ever really know them. But you can learn things about them. Characters are wonderful. Aristotle said characters are easiest. I agree. I really like my characters. . . . [I] would not be surprised if they'd all come and knock on my door and tell me I've done it all wrong."

Perhaps because, as Aristotle said, plot is hardest and because Cynthia agrees, she finds herself wrestling with plot. The outlined plot for ***Homecoming*** was a series of dates and a map of red dots. ***A Solitary Blue*** was envisioned as two long discussion/storytelling chapters with a third chapter that was to be epigrammatic in nature. She had a rhythm of storytelling with an epilog-prelude-commentary pattern in mind. It was the editor who reconstructed the material, especially the beginning of the story.

Cynthia purports that stories, for her, have a shape and declare their own terms. "My job is to figure out what they are. A story never really says 'Yes.' It's like Socrates' daimon: it never says it's true. But when it says 'No,' you know you'd better listen. I can't be sure when a story is ringing true, but I know when it's ringing false. This happens when I put too much of myself in it."

In terms of plot, Cynthia admires the writing of Dick Francis, who writes convincing, clever, complex, cantilevered plots. She also declares that "nobody had done a Sherwood Anderson trick for me. In the beginning of *Winesburg, Ohio*, he says it's like a door opening and suddenly there he was and he could do it." The plumb line against which Cynthia measures her own writing, however, is Shakespeare. "Measure yourself against Shakespeare. Most of us come out in the satisfactory category—which is not bad at all."

Winning the Newbery Medal was both "wonderful and appalling" for Cynthia. For her, the Newbery award is somewhat like Olympus, yet simultaneously the opposite. "For the Olympics there is training with a stop watch. A literary award, on the other hand, is chancy. You can't measure the achievement, for there is no sense of having earned it. With literary awards, it becomes a matter of with whom you stand, not where."

Winning awards does not get Cynthia to the typewriter. After winning the Newbery, it was four months till she got down to writing again.

What does push Cynthia to the typewriter is her own personal desire to write. "I write for children because I want to write. I don't consider myself a good storyteller, and I have no burning stories to tell. I have no solutions to the problems of the world. I think there are solutions for individual people and individual circumstances. My writing is my way of saying, 'Have you looked at it this way?' I do it. I enjoy it." She confesses, "It's a razzle-dazzle kind of fun to have a story come out and do well. That's wonderful. But it's only when you're up there working when it's actually real: that's what the whole thing is rooted in, and that's the only thing that actually counts." (pp. 876-79)

Dorothy Kauffman, "Profile: Cynthia Voigt," in Language Arts, *Vol. 62, No. 8, December, 1985, pp. 876-80.*

GENERAL COMMENTARY

JOANNA SHAW-EAGLE

Homecoming follows four children through the difficulties of finding a new home after their "momma," overwhelmed by poverty, had abandoned them. Their father, never married to their mother, left years before. They managed, under Dicey's leadership, to make their way from Connecticut to Crisfield, Md., to their wonderful, eccentric "Gram." ***Dicey's Song*** is about their adjustment to their new home and to their mother's death.

However, ***Homecoming*** has its detractors because of its 312-page length; it has been criticized for "dragging" in the middle (it was cut down from its original length by one-third). Both [***Homecoming*** and ***Dicey's Song***] are marketed . . . for the 10- to 13-year-old age group, but mature audiences seem to enjoy them as well. . . .

Voigt tells it the way it is—what it's like to live close to the bone. She is a serious writer on serious themes. Her characterizations have dimension and depth. The reader really cares about the characters. Dicey is an example; her name is especially important, and it sums up the book; "dicey" is the British slang expression for chancy, risky.

The plot is well developed, fast paced, with some suspense. The book deals with the pain of losses—death, separation, poverty—but also with responsibility, friends, wisdom, happiness, survival. It's about insecurity but, above all, love and happiness through *family*.

Mrs. Voigt is divorced from her first husband, . . . but her obvious happiness with her present family of four radiates from her and can also be seen, one feels, in the book.

Although the New York Times has called her work "strong stuff for young readers" [see excerpt for *Homecoming* dated May 10, 1981], Voigt believes books should deal with bottom-line situations. "They're milder than Grimm's Fairy Tales," she emphasizes, "and there's always pain in great literature."

"Kids are really tougher than adults," she adds, "but we tend to forget this in an affluent society that lets kids indulge themselves."

Her books are not autobiographical, but the recurring themes of water and music are distinctively hers. Both books are set near the shore—Provincetown, Mass.; Bridgeport, Conn.; as well as Maryland. Dicey tries doggedly to repair a boat so she can sail. . . .

Dicey's Song, as the title implies, is also full of music: the children singing together; little sister Maybeth's singing and piano lessons; Maybeth's piano teacher becoming a family friend; Dicey's friend Jeff strumming his guitar. Voigt sees music as a symbol of happiness through family. . . .

She says, "I was no scholar in college, and was arrogant about what I thought. I was an independent thinker, like Dicey."

Perhaps it's these qualities that make her books so special: They depict problem solvers who are young, dealing with their problems in unusual, resourceful ways, and as part of a family who love one another very, very much.

Like Cynthia Voigt.

Joanna Shaw-Eagle, "Cynthia Voigt: Family Comes First," in The Christian Science Monitor, *May 13, 1983, p. B2.*

ANN MARTIN-LEFF

If you haven't yet discovered Cynthia Voigt, sprint to the nearest bookstore or library. Captivating stories, richly drawn characters with all the idiosyncrasies of real people and a fine-tuned understanding of the complexity and importance of family relationships—these qualities make her books unusually rewarding for adults and teens alike. ***Homecoming*** and its sequel, ***Dicey's Song*** . . . , feature a remarkable female adolescent with more courage and smarts than most adults. ***A Solitary Blue*** . . . begins when 7-year-old Jeff comes home from school one day to find a note from his mother: she's left home. Jeff expends his remaining psychic energy trying to please his uncommunicative, unemotional father. As father and son slowly—*very* slowly—build a relationship, Jeff makes some disturbing discoveries about his mother during a summer visit with her. Another impressive book from a superb writer.

Ann Martin-Leff, in a review of "A Solitary Blue," in New Directions for Women, *Vol. 14, No. 3, May-June, 1985, p. 20.*

LANCE SALWAY

Together, ***Homecoming*** and ***Dicey's Song*** are a remarkable achievement, and these long, enthralling books are particularly welcome at a time when novels for children seem to be getting shorter and less substantial. Just as Dicey herself seems to echo the spirited heroines of earlier American children's books, so the epic structure and long, detailed plots of Cynthia Voigt's novels recall an age when books were rich enough and long enough to get lost in. (pp. 20-1)

Lance Salway, "Fiction: 'Dicey's Song'," in The Signal Selection of Children's Books 1984, *The Thimble Press, 1985, pp. 20-1.*

KIRKUS REVIEWS

Voigt has a gift for writing books that are impossible to put down, not because of breathtaking plots but because her characters so involve the reader in their inner lives. [***Izzy, Willy-Nilly***] is a penetrating look at some real people. Izzy is a winner.

A review of "Izzy, Willy-Nilly," in Kirkus Reviews, *Vol. LIV, No. 11, June 1, 1986, p. 872.*

ZENA SUTHERLAND

To add to Cynthia Voigt's pleasure in winning the 1983 Newbery Medal for ***Dicey's Song,*** there must have been a special satisfaction in knowing that the authors of five Honor Books that year included such stellar names as Jean Fritz, Virginia Hamilton, and William Steig as well as two outstanding newcomers, Paul Fleischman and Robin McKinley. The book is a sequel to ***Homecoming***. . . . The first book had more dramatic action, but ***Dicey's Song*** is much more cohesive, a beautifully balanced and developed story of individual growth and interpersonal support. The characterization is consistent and perceptive, the setting solidly established, and the plot elements are firmly knit by a writing style smooth enough to compensate for the occasional lag in pace that comes with iteration. It undoubtedly surprised few of Voigt's readers that her novel ***A Solitary Blue*** was an Honor Book in the following year. (p. 160)

Zena Sutherland, "Newbery Medal Books," in Newbery and Caldecott Medal Books: 1976-1985, *edited by Lee Kingman, The Horn Book Incorporated, 1986, pp. 153-66.*

HOMECOMING **(1981)**

When four children are deserted by their mother in a shopping-mall parking lot, they begin a long journey on foot to find a home. Led by the oldest child, resourceful 13-year-old Dicey, the children encounter a series of ups and downs in their quest, which culminates in a reasonably happy and satisfying ending. The characterizations of the children are original and intriguing, and there are a number of interesting minor characters encountered in their travels. While the scope and extent of their journey has an element of unbelievability about it, the abundance of descriptions that detail their efforts to survive and keep going help achieve a semblance of reality. The only real problem with the story is that it's just too long, and despite the built-in suspense of the plot, the on-going tension suffers in the multitude of crises.

Marilyn Kaye, in a review of "Homecoming," in School Library Journal, *Vol. 27, No. 8, April, 1981, p. 144.*

Despite flaws, the alarmingly hostile characterization of most adults, an overly long ending, this is a glowing book. Its disturbing undercurrent of hostility and cynicism is counter-balanced by the four's obvious love and loyalty to one another, and by the capability, cleverness and determination that characterize all the survival episodes on the road and the homemaking scenes in Maryland.

The bleak fundamentals of the children's situation may be strong stuff for many young readers, but for those who have the resilience to take it, the accomplishments of this feisty band of complex and, in contrast to the adults, sympathetically conceived kids makes for an enthralling journey to a gratifying end.

Kathleen Leverich, in a review of "Homecoming," in The New York Times Book Review, *May 10, 1981, p. 38.*

The children—aged six to thirteen—are carefully individualized, and the author reveals with subtlety and perceptiveness the psychological stress on each of them. She has a good command of language and moves easily between descriptive passages and dialogue. Throughout the book the children try to understand why they have been left in such a situation and what they should do about it. Although the outcome is not wholly convincing, the account of the events leading up to it is imaginative, thought-provoking, and worked out to the finest detail. (p. 439)

Karen M. Klockner, in a review of "Homecoming," in The Horn Book Magazine, *Vol. LVII, No. 4, August, 1981, pp. 438-39.*

The dangers and people encountered along Route #1 symbolize almost everything met in life, too much to expect in just thirteen short years. And this is possibly the book's major weak point, but not enough to detract from a first adolescent novel that is rich in character development, sensitive to atmosphere, and woven from many lives, the threads of which the author never loses sight. The jangling highways contrast with the smooth flow of ocean river, and bays—Dicey's metaphoric dream, attained through her practical wits and the personalities of unforgettable siblings. A book for sharing. (p. 56)

Ruth M. Stein, in a review of "Homecoming," in Language Arts, *Vol. 59, No. 1, January, 1982, pp. 55-6.*

Homecoming is an unusually long and detailed book, but it is an absorbing one. . . .

The dangers the children meet, the people they encounter, their struggle to find even basic food and shelter, hold the reader's interest so firmly that they will surely demand to know 'what happened next'.

A story of this calibre involves the reader in both heart and mind. It is perhaps overlong in its account of the first part of the children's journey, but the characters are so convincing in their faults and virtues and their humanity that this is forgotten.

A moving story of a search for what everyone desires, a home.

E. Colwell, in a review of "Homecoming," in The Junior Bookshelf, *Vol. 48, No. 3, June, 1984, p. 147.*

Cynthia Voigt's story of the epic quest of four abandoned children to return "home" is as timely as the "CBS Evening

News'' broadcast of March 31, 1983, that covered the story of a Memphis mother who allegedly had abandoned her four children because she could no longer stand to see them go hungry, as timeless as Homer's Odysseus striving to return to Ithaca, and as primally evocative as the fearful wanderings of Hansel and Gretel in the forest of the cannibal witch. Little wonder so many readers find ***Homecoming*** compelling. Voigt has taken an unpleasant reality of contemporary America and endowed it with fairy tale and epic qualities. The story of Dicey Tillerman and her brothers and sister is the story of Hansel and Gretel and the saga of Homer's wily hero. (p. 45)

Recently, I discussed ***Homecoming*** with scores of students, grades 10 through 12, who attended the annual English Festival sponsored by my university. I told them that Voigt had structured her novel on two classic stories and that to nudge their memories I would give them two ''keys''—lists, really—so that they could locate and discuss incidents in the contemporary story that paralleled episodes in those earlier tales. The first key was (1) children deserted by impoverished parents, (2) a trail of flints, (3) a trail of crumbs, and (4) a cannibal witch. The students immediately recognized these as significant components of ''Hansel and Gretel.''

Homecoming's fairy tale substructure is set up early in the novel. The unemployed Liza, unable to cope with the poverty facing her brood, is taking them to her aunt's. However, in the parking lot of a busy shopping mall, the distracted mother wanders off from her children. As the Tillermans restlessly await their mother's return to the old car, Dicey orders James to keep the younger children occupied by telling them their favorite story, ''Hansel and Gretel''. . . . This episode, of course, immediately serves to link Liza's desertion of her children with the forest abandonment of Hansel and Gretel by their impoverished parents; and the link is soon subtly underscored as the hungry Tillermans, searching for their mother, wander through the mall, ''a fairyland of colors and sounds''. . . . The second prominent reference by Voigt to the Hansel and Gretel tale takes place on the trek to Bridgeport. Recall that, in the fairy tale, when Hansel and Gretel are abandoned in the forest for the first time, they find their way back home by following a trail of shiny flints that Hansel had dropped to mark the path. Similarly, as the Tillermans trudge along Connecticut Route 1, they are able to supplement a dwindling food budget by picking up coins that careless shoppers have dropped alongside the road. . . . (pp. 46-7)

These initial parallels were quickly ferreted out by the Festival students. Not so with Voigt's version of the ''Hansel and Gretel'' bread-crumb episode, which my high-school readers vehemently maintained did not even exist in the novel until I reminded them of Mr. Rudyard and his dog. In the fairy tale, the two children are led into the forest for a second time and again abandoned by their father. This time, unable to find flints, Hansel had dropped a trail of bread crumbs, which the birds promptly ate. Without a trail, brother and sister become lost and are captured by the witch, who cages the boy to fatten him up for the pot. (p. 47)

[In ***Homecoming***] the Tillermans' meager food budget is exhausted, and they are forced to seek jobs. Here their luck appears to run out, for they meet the demented Mr. Rudyard. The first thing that strikes Dicey as they approach his house is that its ''yard was a three-sided cage''. . . . Rudyard decides to keep the children as slaves, puts them in a field to pick his crop, and stations his dog, a large brute ''with a huge slavering mouth'' to guard them. The farmer pointedly warns the runaways, ''I keep him hungry''. . . . Obviously, he is implying that if they try to escape, the dog will devour them. But escape they do, and here a trail of crumbs is their salvation. As the Tillermans flee their captor, the dog follows, but in fleeing, the children inadvertently scatter the lunch that Rudyard has brought them—a mound of buttered biscuits. The fugitives are able to make good the break because the hungry dog stops to eat the trail of biscuits instead of pressing the pursuit. . . . (pp. 47-8)

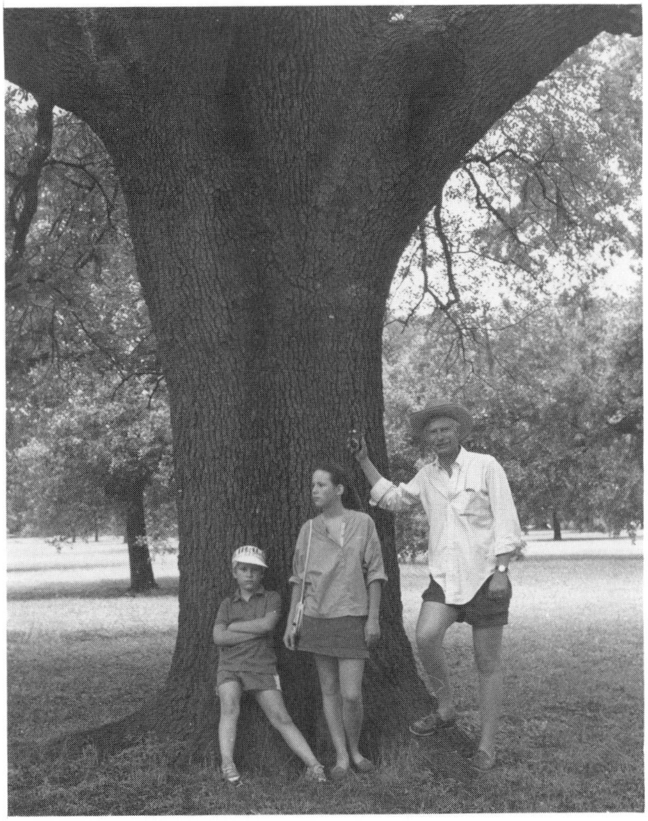

Voigt's son Peter, daughter Jessica, and husband Walter. Courtesy of Cynthia Voigt.

Voigt, more overtly this time, replays the confrontation with the cannibal witch when Dicey first meets her grandmother. Abigail already has received a letter from Eunice telling her that the Tillermans are heading for the farm. When Dicey shows up, the old woman, pretending not to know the girl's identity, warms up a can of spaghetti, and the child sits with her to eat. Abigail—probably trying to scare off the girl or maybe to test her courage—asks: ''You like my spaghetti?'' Dicey answers, ''No.'' Then, the old woman begins: '''It's easy to fix. You know what I sometimes think?' Her grandmother looked straight at her, her mouth chewing. 'I sometimes think people might be good to eat . . . Especially babies . . . Or children. Do you have brothers and sisters?''' (p. 48)

With the exception of the Rudyard incident, the Festival students found all of these ''Hansel and Gretel'' allusions easy to identify. This was not the case with the Odyssean parallels in the novel, because many of the discussion groups were less familiar with the epic quest than with the adventures of the fairy tale protagonists. So, to guide discussion of the *Odyssey* substructure of ***Homecoming,*** I used a ''key'' composed of character names that might be somewhat familiar even to those who possessed only a passing knowledge of the epic: (1) Odysseus, the wily wanderer, (2) Polyphemus, (3) Lotus-eaters, (4) Aeolus, (5) Scylla, (6) Circe, (7) Penelope. Even without a complete grasp of the epic, the students found these Homeric "echoes" a productive topic, if for no other reason than that they are so extensive in the novel. For instance, Dicey, obviously, is a contemporary rendition of Odysseus, a fact betrayed by the names and the traits of both characters. "Odysseus" means "child of anger" . . . a name equally appropriate to Dicey. Grandmother Tillerman describes the environment in which her children grew up as one of suppressed rage at a domineering, bellicose father. Abigail confesses of herself, "I was angry—most of my life," and of her family, "anger and shame were sitting [always] at the table with us". . . . This is why her own children fled from home and why Dicey's mother never would marry the children's father. She simply refused to submit to any man the way her own mother had submitted to her husband. In a sense, quick-tempered Dicey and all of the Tillermans are "children of anger." Indeed, the name "Tillerman" is also significant. It alludes not to one who tills the land; rather it seems to signify one who mans the tiller of a ship—especially so in Dicey's case, because one of the characteristic traits that she shares with Odysseus is a fascination for the sea.

The parallels between the epic and the novel become even more precise. Book IX of Homer's poem tells how Polyphemus, the cyclops, traps the hero and his men in a cave and begins to devour them. They escape by blinding the creature's one eye. In the opening chapter of ***Homecoming,*** Dicey eludes a huge security guard at the shopping mall after giving him a phony name, as Odysseus does with Polyphemus. Like Homer's blinded giant, the big man chases the slippery hero. She hides while the guard shines "his flashlight out over the parking lot, like one bright eye." He uses "the beam like a giant eye, to peer into the shadows". . . . But like the cyclops, his "eye" is blind and the girl escapes.

Later in the Rockland Park episode of ***Homecoming,*** Voigt offers her readers another revamped portion of Book IX of the Greek classic. In Homer's story his hero tells of a visit to the land of the Lotus-eaters. When his men eat the lotus, they no longer care about returning home. Indeed, the narcotic effect of the plant dims all memory of home and of loved ones. In the novel, the children—especially James and Sammy—are extremely reluctant to leave the quiet safety of Rockland and return to the hazards of Route 1. The park seems to have the same tranquilizing effect on the teenagers, Louis and Edie. When Dicey asks these runaways what they do when they are not camping in the park, Edie murmurs: "I can't remember . . . Nothing before [now] is worth remembering"; and Louis quips, "we pluck the lotus". . . . (pp. 48-9)

In Book X of the *Odyssey,* Odysseus recounts his visit with Aeolus, keeper of the winds. To speed the hero's return to Ithaca, Aeolus imprisons the violent sea winds in an ox-hide bag, which he stows in the Greek's ship, so that his voyage will be a smooth one. Underway, however, Odysseus' crew—thinking the bag contains treasure and intending to steal it—open the sack, unleashing a storm that drives them back to Aeolus' island. The enraged keeper of the winds refuses the wanderers any more assistance. In Voigt's version, the Tillermans meet Windy in New Haven. The college student "feasts" the children, as Aeolus does the Greeks. As the youngsters sit in a diner gobbling food, "Windy's voice blew over them, smooth and steady". . . . After the meal, he takes Dicey and her family to the dorm rooms that he shares with Stewart and persuades his roommate to drive the Tillermans down to Aunt Cilla's the following day. During the night, however, James steals twenty dollars from Stew's wallet. When the theft is discovered the next day, Dicey makes her brother return the money. The girl feels "as if a big black cloud had just covered the sun". . . . Fortunately, Voigt's Aeolus gives this crew of contemporary wanderers a second chance. Windy smooths over the unpleasantness and gets Stewart to take the children to Aunt Cilla's anyway. Incidentally, the "Aunt Cilla" sojourn in ***Homecoming*** . . . is an expanded parallel to a brief passage in Book XII of the epic, which describes how Odysseus loses six of his crew to the monster Scylla, who snatches them from off the deck as he sails past. At Aunt Cilla's house located, appropriately, on Ocean Drive, Dicey almost loses her "crew." Though hardly monstrous, Father Joseph and Cousin Eunice almost succeed in snatching her brothers and sister from the girl after the authorities discover that Liza Tillerman is a hopeless mental case.

Book X of the *Odyssey* contains the story of Odysseus' yearlong stay with Circe. The enchanting sorceress turns his men into beasts with her magic. Later, however, albeit forced to do so by the hero's threats, she helps the men on with their journey. In ***Homecoming,*** Circe's magic isle is transformed into a traveling circus. In Part 2, chapter 6 of the novel, the circus folk rescue the fleeing children from Mr. Rudyard. Because the circus is going to be passing close to Crisfield on its rounds, Will, the owner, allows the Tillermans to travel with the show. At night, they sleep with Claire, a tall, striking redhaired animal trainer. In her trailer, Sammy delights in nestling down for sleep amidst the woman's "pile of terriers". . . . During the day, the younger children are thrilled by the magic of the circus; indeed, they even become a part of it. Sammy, for instance, literally is transformed. Dressed in a spangled costume, he participates in Claire's animal act.

Homer draws his epic to a close as Odysseus finally returns to Ithaca and to his faithful Penelope, who has kept his house intact and who for years has resisted a horde of beseiging suitors. Odysseus disperses and kills the crowd of greedy swains. After his long journey, he finally claims his own. The concluding chapters of ***Homecoming,*** in contrast, are not so simple. As Dicey, herself, says several times, things get very "contradictory". . . . To be sure, Abigail Tillerman is Penelope. She has kept house and land intact; and while her husband was alive, she had clung to him faithfully.

On the other hand, because husband and children could not live together in peace, she drove out her own children, much as Odysseus drives out the suitors. Indeed, those children have not fared much better than the suitors; one has never been heard of again, one has wound up in a mental institution, and one has been killed in battle. Now, enter Dicey and her sister and brothers. Dicey, who throughout the novel has been portrayed as a contemporary Odysseus, wants the farm for herself and her family. Suddenly, the grandchildren become the suitors of Penelope as they woo Abigail in an attempt to persuade her to let them stay. But the parallels shift again. In the epic, Penelope had put off selecting a husband from among the suitors by telling them that she could not marry until she had finished weaving the pall for Laertes. At night, she secretly undid the work that she had woven that day. In ***Homecoming,*** Dicey and the children adopt Penelope's ruse of the never-ending task. They decide that as long as they continue a never-ending series of jobs for themselves around the farm, Grandmother will not send them away. Identities shift again for a final time as Abigail eventually does accept the children. Like Odysseus, Dicey and the Tillermans have come home.

At this juncture, both teacher and student alike well may wish to pause to question the significance of this apparent confusion. Has the artist lost control of her material? No. The shifting epic parallels and the contradictions that haunt Dicey are the logical product of the conflicting needs and emotions pulling at Voigt's characters. Dicey, for instance, covets the sailboat that she discovers in one of the farm's outbuildings. Little wonder, the craft embodies the spirit of adventure and independence that is so much a part of her personality. Yet she also desperately wants a permanent home for herself and her brothers and sister. Moreover, the heroine seems to intuit that she needs the guidance of a strong, mature woman in order to become one herself, and she certainly realizes that she needs Gram to help shoulder the burden of raising the younger Tillermans. Abigail, on the other hand, fears that burden, appalled by the prospect of raising (or failing) a second flock of children. Yet without her grandchildren she is as incomplete as the mutilated nameplate on her mailbox that reads "llerma" instead of "Tillerman." No, the fingers that draw together the final threads of this rich tapestry are as deft and skillful as when they began the work.

There is one final question about the work that does merit consideration, however. Ironically, it was asked me by a colleague, an old friend who had read ***Homecoming*** with much pleasure and who had heard of my approach to the novel. She demanded, "Okay, *if* that stuff is in the book, *why* is it there?" Although a bit hostile, this is a fair question and one my Festival students might have asked had time permitted. So here is a partial answer. The stories of Hansel and Gretel, Odysseus, and Dicey convey a theme as primordial as the dawn of mankind itself, yet as fresh as E.T., the extraterrestrial being. The theme is, of course, that of the "lost child." Why did my friend like ***Homecoming*** so much? Why do parents and offspring alike love the movie? Why, over the years and the centuries, have countless readers been fascinated by the fairy tale and epic? Because whether 14 or 40, 15 or 50, at some time in our lives (and perhaps more than once), we all have been the lost child. The young teenager who has outgrown the familiar and comforting certitudes of childhood—just as surely as her body has outgrown last year's clothes—is the lost child. In the midst of what we conveniently term "midlife crisis," the 50-year-old executive who looks backward with amazement to ask, "What have I been doing with my life?"—is the lost child. Like E.T., most of us spend a good portion of our lives trying "to phone home," to assuage the fear and loneliness of that lost child within us. Stories like the *Odyssey* and ***Homecoming*** aid us in this process. As we respond to them, we live out our fear, at least subconsciously; and, in doing so, perhaps we come to realize that we are not alone and that what has been lost also can be found again.

Does Cynthia Voigt know all of this? I cannot say, but I know that the "child" who crouches inside the woman's body knows. (pp. 49-52)

James T. Henke, "Dicey, Odysseus, and Hansel and Gretel: The Lost Children in Voigt's 'Homecoming'," in Children's literature in education, *Vol. 16, No. 1 (Spring), 1985, pp. 45-52.*

TELL ME IF THE LOVERS ARE LOSERS (1982)

An eastern college for young women of high ability is the setting for an unusual teenage novel about three disparate freshmen who come together as roommates in 1961—Ann Gardner, cosseted daughter of a well-to-do couple, is an apologetic, nonaggressive conformist; Niki Jones, product of a broken marriage, is headstrong, hyperactive, and fiercely competitive; and Hildegarde Koenig, only girl in a large farming family, is a taciturn innocent of sorts, possessed of a single-minded morality and purpose. Volleyball becomes their common ground as Hildy, who has an almost mystical impact on her teammates, coaches and leads the freshmen toward the championship. Vivid imagery vies with effectively subtle understatement in a thoughtful multiple-character study written in the third person but filled with introspection, primarily from Ann's perspective. Characterizations—not only major but supporting ones—are consistently and distinctively individualized while interactions and mutual influences are developed naturally, making this both provocative and rewarding for older, more perceptive high school age readers.

Sally Estes, in a review of "Tell Me If the Lovers Are Losers," in Booklist, *Vol. 78, No. 14, March 15, 1982, p. 950.*

[***Tell Me If the Lovers Are Losers***] is heavy going. . . . After a sluggish start, . . . there is lots of volleyball action as that sport becomes the center of the girls' lives their first semester. The story offers a good look at adjusting, coping and competing to win. But it is thick with philosophy as each girl presents her background and view of life. The girls talk like very intelligent college students. The author also gives midwestern Hildy a prim, precise and stilted voice that does not register as true or representative of the region. Nothing special is done with the time period. One can come to know these roommates, but there is much to go through to get there.

Joe McKenzie, in a review of "Tell Me If the Lovers Are Losers," in School Library Journal, *Vol. 28, No. 9, May, 1982, p. 88.*

The forging of the [volleyball] team is the real story here, and it's a compelling, immensely satisfying one. A collection of six disparate and, in many respects, disagreeable young women grows through stress and self-discipline from anarchy and infighting, past tolerance and mutual respect, to devotion and loyalty.

As with Mrs. Voigt's previous novel, ***Homecoming,*** the theme of this book is bonding. No problem in that, but ***Tell Me If the Lovers are Losers*** suffers (and to an even greater extent) from the same excesses that marred the earlier work: exaggeration of character and the sacrifice of the theme to improbable theatrics. No literary or thematic purpose is served by the melodramatic ending; on the contrary, the book is considerably diminished. And readers would be more inclined to accept the characters if their personalities were drawn in subtle shadings instead of in caricatures.

Mrs. Voigt is a wonderful writer with powerfully moving things to say. Her books, however, overcompensate for what she apparently feels are excessively subtle conflicts and an atmosphere that is too rarified for the general reader. When she dispenses with contrivances and sensationalism, her characters and scenes come alive in their own unique and exciting way.

Kathleen Leverich, in a review of "Tell Me If the Lovers Are Losers," in The New York Times Book Review, *May 16, 1982, p. 28.*

[There] is no doubt that [Voigt] is an exceptionally fine writer who offers her YA readers much more than most writers do. This means that reading her work requires effort: the characters and ideas are unusual and thought-provoking.

The title comes from a Carl Sandburg poem, "Cool Tombs," and it has nothing to do with romantic love; neither does this book. Instead, Voigt is concerned with attitudes toward life. Her main characters embody the varieties of attitudes, and YAs who too are identifying their own attitudes will be stimulated by Voigt's work.

[Claire Rosser], in a review of "Tell Me If the Lovers Are Losers," in Kliatt Young Adult Paperback Book Guide, *Vol. XVII, No. 6, September, 1983, p. 20.*

DICEY'S SONG (1982)

[***Dicey's Song***] details Dicey's settlement into adolescence and a new life with Gram. Dicey finds it hard to relinquish the reins of control and responsibility over her siblings and equally hard to adjust in school, where she feels—and is—apart from her peers in wisdom and experience. The story is a perceptive exposition of two strong personalities, Dicey and Gram, neither of whom is perfect but both of whom learn powerful lessons in reaching out and accepting love. Dicey lowers her defenses enough to accept the friendship of schoolmate Mina, a girl who is much like herself, and learns, when she and Gram go to Boston to be with her dying mother, that adulthood doesn't necessarily bring all the answers. The vividness of Dicey is striking; Voigt has plumbed and probed her character inside out to fashion a memorable protagonist. Unlike most sequels, this outdoes its predecessor by being more fully realized and consequently more resonant. A must for those who've read ***Homecoming*** but independent enough to stand alone. (p. 50)

Denise M. Wilms, in a review of "Dicey's Song," in Booklist, *Vol. 79, No. 1, September 1, 1982, pp. 49-50.*

The strong characterization of ***Homecoming*** . . . is one of the most trenchant facets again, in this story of the four children who live with their grandmother on the Eastern Shore of Maryland. . . . This is much more cohesive than ***Homecoming,*** in part because the physical scope is narrower, in part because the author has so skillfully integrated the problems of the individual children in a story that is smoothly written. Dicey learns how to make friends, how to accept the fact that she is maturing physically, how to give and forgive, how to adjust—in a touching final episode—to the death of the mother whose recovery she had longed for. A rich and perceptive book.

Zena Sutherland, in a review of "Dicey's Song," in Bulletin of the Center for Children's Books, *Vol. 36, No. 2, October, 1982, p. 38.*

[***Homecoming***] centers on the children's survival; the sequel focuses on their growth. And ironically, although the first volume ends with their grandmother's eventual acceptance of them, it is tense with rejection and deprivation; while the second, which ends with the death of their catatonic mother in a mental hospital, teems with restorative life. . . . [Worries] flow in and out of the backwater area with a soothing rhythm—syncopated with knitting sweaters, baking cookies, sharing paper routes, and family singing—which eases the hurt of their earlier rejections and allows them to endure their mother's death. The writing is fluent, the tone consistent, and the characters distinct and likable. One wants life to be good to them, but there remains a niggling feeling that all of this, including indefatigable Dicey, just might be too good to be true. (p. 654)

Nancy C. Hammond, in a review of "Dicey's Song," in The Horn Book Magazine, *Vol. LVIII, No. 6, December, 1982, pp. 653-54.*

Dicey's Song is a gentle melody of an early teen's search for purpose in a life that is no bargain. . . .

Loving and caring are the theme of ***Dicey's Song.*** To her credit, Mrs. Voigt does not lay it on too heavily. . . . There's an undercurrent of juvenile cruelty throughout, sometimes unspoken, sometimes sotto voce disdain and sometimes flailing fists. The Tillerman kids are ragtag and a little different.

This touching work ends on a triumphantly sad note. Death, however long expected is life's hardest lesson in letting go. For Dicey, Momma's passing is the antithesis of Gram's fundamental truism that reaching out and holding on are what life is really all about. How Dicey handles this ideological conflict is a beautiful moment.

Robert J. Flynn, in a review of "Dicey's Song," in Best Sellers, *Vol. 42, No. 10, January, 1983, p. 408.*

More and more we hear the term "qualitatively different" used in reference to educating gifted and talented young people. This indicates that added quantity alone is not sufficient to meet the needs of this group of exceptional children. (p. 33)

This article will examine the qualitative differences that are found in one book. Cynthia Voigt's ***Dicey's Song***. . . . The plot and characters of the story have appeal to young people with a wide variety of interests, reading tastes, and abilities.

Although the story has broad appeal, ***Dicey's Song*** is eminently appropriate for gifted readers. As I searched for literary examples to use in a course I taught on "Library Services to Gifted and Talented Youth," I saw in a new light qualities of this book, which I had grown to know intimately when I was a member of the 1983 Newbery Committee. Gifted young people, along with all other humans, have specific needs in both the cognitive (intellective) and the affective (emotional) domains. Books may meet the challenge in one of these areas while not qualifying in the other. ***Dicey's Song*** bridges the gap and manages to stimulate the intellect, while at the same time it satisfies the psyche in ways especially suitable for the exceptionally able reader. . . .

The first clue that ***Dicey's Song*** meets the criteria for gifted readers lies in the title. Some titles immediately give the reader a clear expectation of what is to come, e.g., *Alexander and The Terrible, Horrible, Awful, No Good, Very Bad Day* (Viorst). The meaning of others, such as *Julie and the Wolves* (George), becomes apparent as soon as the reader is immersed in the story.

Dicey's Song tantalizes. The title appears to be simple. Yet the author, in a flexible manner, has woven into the story the possibility for several interpretations or approaches. Each reader must analyze and synthesize information, be fluent in generating possible explanations, elaborate on at first simple ideas, and then must evaluate his or her own conclusions to decide why the book has been named as it has. Of the numerous songs referred to in the text, none stands out clearly as Dicey's. Yet any single one, or perhaps all of them collectively, form the "song" of the title. Music is obviously an important factor in Dicey's life—it is so important that she tells her friend Mina that music is a quality by which she judges people, despite Mina's insistence that a person cannot *be* music.

Gifted readers will find themselves led into fluent thought about the significance of the title. Dicey herself gives a clue to meaning on another level when reflecting that life should be simple like a song—sung straight through without the complexities that seem to be impinging on her. Or perhaps Dicey's song is the unraveling and development of her own character and personality, an as yet unfinished song.

The astute reader will be led to the realization of another and more subtle meaning for this simple, yet provocative title. Consider the cadence, the flexibility and fluency of Voigt's writing. Both are essential ingredients of literature for the gifted. When the mood is angry, bothered, or unsettled, Voigt's words form a melody in the staccato mode. Sentences are abbreviated and breathless; repetition is used for emphasis. "Dicey waited. Gram's mouth was straight and her eyes stared vacantly at the envelope. Dicey waited." . . . On the other hand, the cadence of the writing switches to legato when the mood is reflective or calm; sentences are longer and more fluid. As we see in this paragraph, the entire text, with its carefully crafted changes of tempo, is an elaborate song—Dicey's song:

> The children were settling in, just as fall was settling in, over the farm and the water, into shades of brown: the harrowed soil, the dried summer grasses, the broken stalks of corn, and the long golden bars of sunlight from a sun settling closer to seven now than eight.
>
> (p. 34)

Through the music used in the book, Voigt has taken simple themes and elaborated on them. Nancy Polette, in her *Picture Books for Gifted Readers,* states that "elaboration is . . . expanding upon an . . . idea in order to make the original more interesting or workable." . . . This is precisely what Voigt has done with her music. The average reader may let the musically related themes pass by unnoticed—gifted readers will find them a challenge.

Jeff, Dicey's guitar-playing friend and the protagonist of Voigt's ***A Solitary Blue,*** a companion book to ***Dicey's Song,*** stimulates thought through the folk songs he plays and sings. In folk songs, according to Alan Lomax, a well-known collector of American folk songs, people express their dreams, their fantasies, their desires, and their fears. Voigt has carefully chosen each song to do just that for her characters. The reader must be flexible in interpretation as the writer has been in selection of various songs for various reasons.

"When First Into This Country a Stranger I Came" is sung several times throughout the book. This song plays more than one role, although the title itself carries an obvious meaning for Dicey. Noting and analyzing the circumstances of each of its appearances, then synthesizing this information, will add understanding of the characters involved; use of this song is an example of the author's taking a simple idea and elaborating on it.

"Pretty Polly" has a theme that is similar to that of Dreiser's *An American Tragedy*. It has its place, according to Lomax, as one of the best of American murder ballads. The singing of this song produces a conversation between Dicey and Jeff which, if the reader knows that ballad, relates to one of the undercurrents of the story. The ballad is about a young woman who, like Dicey's mother, was deserted by her man when she was with child and dies tragically.

"Amazing Grace" is the family song for Dicey. Although the words speak to the saving of a soul coming home, they also are reminiscent of the long journey made by Dicey and her siblings: "Thro' many dangers, toils and snares, I have already come. . . ." A song Dicey remembers as a favorite of her mother's, "The Water is Wide, I Cannot Get Over," tells much about her mother's life, her initial hope for happiness followed by disappointment in love. The story can be read without understanding the choice of songs, but the deeper level of meaning is there to entice a curious thinker to probe.

The originality of a book for the gifted may come in a variety of forms. "And they lived happily ever after" is a satisfying, if common ending to a book. However, this happens to be the first sentence of ***Dicey's Song.*** And the last sentence? "So Gram began her story." A most original beginning and ending which provide structure to the book. A reader who can deduce why these sentences are where they are will understand the essence of the book, which starts with an ending in the children's lives and progresses with them to a beginning. The reader can then elaborate upon this idea and follow it as it develops consistently throughout the text.

Setting and imagery can be mundane. ***Dicey's Song*** not only escapes this pitfall, but instead presents a highly original symbolic relationship between setting and imagery. This skillful crafting alone places the book with literature suitable for the gifted reader. . . . Elements of the Chesapeake Bay country, the marshes, the mist, the wind, the water, the sun, and the brown earth are intertwined with descriptions of characters and events. "Worry was like the mist along the marsh, it rose up from the floors of the house." . . . An example above likens the changes in the children's lives to the changing seasons. Again, a unique pattern is set and elaborated upon for the gifted child to discover and emulate.

Two symbols occur and recur throughout ***Dicey's Song,*** bringing strength and unity to the text. The symbols are not intrusive—only careful analytic thinking can reveal their importance or even their occurrence. The symbols, the boat and the tree, appear early in the book. The children's lives and the boat both appear "broken" in the beginning; as the story progresses, each moves toward a restored state, although neither is completely repaired at the book's end. But the function of the boat is not so simple, and fluency on the part of the reader is called for if all of its roles are to be discovered. And the tree—Dicey sits under it as the story begins: seasons and the children's lives are paralleled by changes in the tree. Near the end, Gram likens the tree to families and how they grow.

The last name of the family, Tillerman, has itself a variety of meanings and may set the reader to generating possibilities for its choice. Certainly, its relationship to guiding the boat comes immediately to mind, but this is the most simplistic suggestion. But, other than their name, Voigt gives no easy-to-locate descriptions of her major characters. . . . Incidents, not explicit descriptions, tell the reader details of Dicey's, James's, Sammy's, Maybeth's, and Gram's personalities. Gram's visit to Sammy's school as "the Lone Marble Ranger" for example, reveals, all at once, her individuality, her caring, and her sense of humor. No black-and-white descriptions are given to stifle the imagination of the reader in discovering each person.

The gifted reader who pays close attention to detail will find Voigt, a teacher of senior English, using punctuation in an extremely flexible and original manner. Commas and periods are not reserved for their traditional roles, they are used to make the text stop and go. Commas, rather than periods or semi-colons, separate sentences when fluency is essential to mood and meaning. "Gram didn't like taking charity, Dicey knew that because Gram said so." . . . Also, periods placed in mid-sentence signal readers to stop. ". . . the bell rang. Ending class." . . . A connection to the style of e.e. cummings will be made by any reader who has encountered his poetry or may encounter it in the future. Gifted readers are often gifted writers as well. ***Dicey's Song*** has much to offer the young person who has learned the rules of correct English structure and is now ready to break them.

Because ***Dicey's Song*** offers writing that is flexible, fluent, original, and elaborate, it demands analysis, synthesis, and evaluation. The reader is forced to be active, rather than passive. ***Dicey's Song*** is "qualitatively different"; it possesses qualities different from many other books for young people—qualities which meet the cognitive needs of gifted and creative youth.

Two aspects of the affective domain loom as important to the young gifted reader: the formation of values and the finding of peers who have outstanding abilities. (pp. 35-6)

A major point seen in ***Dicey's Song*** is the progress toward development of a value system. First Dicey must learn to value, must take the risk of valuing the relationships around her. Then comes the difficult task of organizing a value system. The reader must participate with Dicey in this, for Gram has told Dicey that reaching out (to people), holding on, and letting go are all essential, but she has not told Dicey how to reconcile the conflicts of these values. Dicey ponders how one can hold on and let go at the same time. No clear-cut answer is given, but Dicey does manage to some extent to organize and live in accordance with the value system she develops.

Another aspect of the affective domain is the development of a positive self-image, self-confidence, the understanding of one's own abilities and what they mean. One way in which young people come to terms with their giftedness and realize they are not alone or unique in the opportunities and difficulties it creates is to meet others like themselves. Sometimes this can happen in real life and sometimes in literature. (p. 36)

The U.S. Office of Education (USOE) defines the gifted as youth who have demonstrated or have potential ability for high performance in one or more of the five areas: (1) general intellectual ability; (2) specific academic aptitude; (3) creative and/or productive thinking; (4) leadership abilities; (5) visual or performing arts. Joseph S. Renzulli, a chief spokesperson for the education of the gifted, adds another characteristic which he believes is essential for true giftedness: task commitment. He believes above-average ability, creativity, and task-commitment must exist, in concert, for a child to be gifted.

On occasion the behavior of gifted children is misinterpreted: sometimes their intellectual curiosity and boredom with routine is seen as a lack of respect for authority. Or their higher-level thought processes may lead them to seem, or in fact to be, inattentive to instructions. The unusual gifts of some young people may go unnoticed because they deliberately attempt to hide them in order to be accepted by their peers.

Dicey's Song has three young people, Dicey (13), James (10), and Maybeth (9), who could be identified as gifted by USOE's definition. Depicting three children, all gifted, yet totally different from one another, in one book has many advantages. First, it is apparent to the gifted reader and to others that there is no such thing as a "gifted child," but that gifted children have diverse interests and many ways of exhibiting their giftedness. The three youngsters' interactions and appreciation of each other's gifts are a facet of this story not to be found when a solitary gifted child is depicted. Another unique feature of the gifted children in ***Dicey's Song*** is that they are not from an advantaged background. Finding peers in literature with whom to identify is especially difficult for the disadvantaged gifted child.

Perhaps Dicey's greatest gift is leadership. Alone, she took hold of her family and led them on the journey to Gram's house. She is able to plan and follow plans through; certainly she fits Renzulli's model, for she exhibits not only intellectual ability and creativity, but definite task commitment. The work accomplished on her boat to get it into shape for sailing is only one example of her capability to define a task and stick to it. She never shirks her responsibility, and is astute at perceiving the needs of her siblings and reacting to them.

Once at Gram's her brothers and sister look to her for guidance in forming a new family unit. Academically, Dicey does not make all A's as James does, but her paper for Mr. Chappelle in English demonstrates her high ability in writing. Dicey is the gifted child who cannot comprehend the boredom of a requirement to learn to cook and sew in Home Ec. when she has been sole provider for her family for many days. She is a good role model, since her self-confidence and self-sufficiency are not destroyed when her English teacher accuses her of plagiarizing her sensitively written portrait of her mother.

James's giftedness lies in the areas of general intellectual and specific academic ability. But, unlike Dicey, he does care what others think. He masks his ability by rewriting a highly original paper on the Pilgrims, turning in one like everyone else's. Although he is part of a class of gifted students, James realizes he is different. His contribution to the family comes from his wide reading and understanding of issues. He is able to solve problems in ways that others cannot because of the knowledge his curiosity has forced him to accumulate. The outstanding vocabulary James possesses is a clear sign of his giftedness.

Maybeth is considered retarded—certainly she is a slow learner. Her musical ability, on the other hand, is far from ordinary. Her piano teacher finds her his most exciting student in ten years, and Maybeth sings better than anyone in her musical family. A young person like Maybeth, who may fit only one or two of the categories of gifted in USOE's definition, is no less "gifted" than those who fit all categories.

An examination of the value system that is built up in the book and of the three gifted children who grow and develop in it, providing peers for the reader, demonstrates that ***Dicey's Song*** is qualitatively different in the affective as well as the cognitive domain.

Dicey's Song, then, provides a starting point for those who have not examined children's literature in terms of its suitability for gifted readers, and an additional example for those who have. Both the intellectual and the emotional needs of gifted children are met in this book, which challenges while it reassures. (pp. 36-7)

Eliza T. Dresang, "A Newbery Song for Gifted Readers," in School Library Journal, *Vol. 30, No. 3, November, 1983, pp. 33-7.*

It is good to be able to concur wholeheartedly with those who chose ***Dicey's Song*** for the 1983 Newbery Award. It is well-written, thoughtful, imaginative and haunting. The chief characters are interestingly unusual (the more so for English readers) but in many ways, their experiences will strike a chord, not least with those who find themselves "outside", because they are not merely content to accept passively society's values today. . . . There is so much to this book—utter veracity in the people, rich humour, pathos, the beauty of the Southern Maryland seasons, contrasted with Dicey's memory of Cape Cod, the vivid minor characters. A splendid story. (pp. 146-47)

M. Hobbs, in a review of "Dicey's Song," in The Junior Bookshelf, *Vol. 48, No. 3, June, 1984, pp. 146-47.*

THE CALLENDER PAPERS (1983)

[***The Callender Papers*** is] an engrossing mystery. Jean Wainwright, almost 13, has been raised by her loving and wise Aunt Constance, headmistress of a girls' school in Cambridge, Mass., who has instilled in Jean the value of rational thinking. This is put to the test when the girl accepts a summer position from taciturn Daniel Thiel, a trustee of the school. Her job, once she arrives at Thiel's secluded home in the Berkshires, is to sort through his wife's (Irene Callender) family papers, immediately immersing Jean in the lives of Callenders past and present. Connections become apparent between the puzzle surrounding Irene's death and her child's disappearance, and the tangled provisions of rich Josiah Callender's will. Taken in by the charms of Irene's brother, Jean learns that appearances can deceive, and that all actions have consequences, brought home to her when she discovers the secrets of the Callender clan. Once again, Voigt proves herself a masterful storyteller, combining strong characterizations with crystal-clear insights into human nature. (pp. 86-7)

A review of "The Callender Papers," in Publishers Weekly, *Vol. 223, No. 10, March 11, 1983, pp. 86-7.*

Less ambitious than Voigt's other novels, this conforms to an established juvenile-fiction genre, but it is a superior example of its type. Written in the first person with a touch of period primness, it's the story of Jean Wainwright's 13th summer in 1894. . . . [Jean] exhibits a direct good sense and alert intelligence that win regard from all parties, and from readers as well. Readers may suspect all along what Jean discovers only at the end—that she herself is the Callender heir, Mr. Thiel is her father, and Enoch, spoiled and discontented, is responsible for his doting sister's death. But knowing that doesn't lessen the suspense or the satisfaction to be found in this engaging, aptly plotted, character-centered identity-mystery.

A review of "The Callender Papers," in Kirkus Reviews, *Vol. LI, No. 6, March 15, 1983, p. 308.*

This is a highly enjoyable and stylishly written Gothic mystery. . . . Voigt occasionally comes dangerously near to permitting Jean, the narrator, to be too stupid to be believed—always a risk in the atmospheric had-I-but-known type of mystery—but through her deft prose and Jean's real youth and innocence, she brings it off successfully.

Robin McKinley, in a review of "The Callender Papers," in Children's Book Review Service, *Vol. 11, No. 12, Spring, 1983, p. 128.*

Fluent but never terse, the author compounds the mystery with a multitude of details and digressions, some of which border on melodrama. And Jean, so young in years, may strain the reader's credulity with her mature, self-possessed first-person account, which occasionally dips into fairly complex moral, and even philosophical discussions.

Ethel L. Heins, in a review of "The Callender Papers," in The Horn Book Magazine, *Vol. LIX, No. 4, August, 1983, p. 458.*

Bright readers will probably guess the secret of Jean's own birth as well as the villain's identity—but this needn't spoil the fun.

As in her Dicey Tillerman books, Cynthia Voigt gives us a spunky young heroine forced into precocious independence and resourcefulness, as well as adults who'll victimize kids if allowed. Although this genre novel is entertaining, interesting and well-written, it does not, and does not pretend to, offer the sensitively drawn, richly memorable real-life characters and situations that made its predecessors so rewarding.

Miriam Berkley, in a review of "The Callender Papers," in The New York Times Book Review, *August 14, 1983, p. 29.*

A SOLITARY BLUE (1983)

AUTHOR'S COMMENTARY

Some books grow out of others, like shoots out of a felled tree. ***Dicey's Song*** grew out of ***Homecoming.*** As I finished ***Homecoming,*** I knew what "the next one" would be. ***A Solitary Blue*** grew out of ***Dicey's Song*** in that same fashion. As I wrote about Jeff in Dicey's story, where he had a certain purpose to serve, I found myself thinking about his particular story, what had happened to him, how he had come to be where he was, and who he was. That story wanted telling. I wanted to try telling it. This was so clear to me that when I said to my mother, "You know what the next one will be" and she answered, "Of course, about the story Gram tells the children"—well, I was completely surprised. I have no intention of telling the birthday party story; I have no idea how Bullet got out of going to that birthday party.

But Jeff's story, I knew how that would go, what his life had been like, and why Dicey was so important to him. In writing the book, I ran into some interesting problems. One was the problem of how to cover so much time. Most of the things that happen to Jeff happen slowly, step by step. The book covers ten years of his life. This clearly constitutes a problem in writing—to reflect the long length of time without misrepresenting the rhythm of the story, to show the major events but keep clear their place in the whole context. Another interesting problem was to introduce the Tillermans from the outside, from somebody else's point of view, to think about them as subordinate characters whom my main character would meet, and have impressions of. I had to think of how my imaginary family would look through the eyes of my imaginary character. That problem was simply fun to work on because it is always fun (and often illuminating) to try to perceive through someone else's eyes.

So I have now a felled tree with two shoots coming off of it, or a felled tree, a felled shoot, and a shoot off of it, and I am beginning to wonder seriously what the next one will be. I am sharpening my metaphorical ax. My daughter has told me what she thinks. "You've got to write about Jeff and Dicey," she said. This time I am not at all surprised.

Cynthia Voigt, "On the Writing of 'A Solitary Blue'," in Language Arts, *Vol. 60, No. 8, November-December, 1983, p. 1026.*

When Jeff Greene was seven, he came home from school to find a note from his mother, Melody, saying that she was leaving home to help "little boys like you who don't get enough to eat and are hungry every night when they go to bed." Charged to be his mother's "best assistant," he was careful to make everything just right for his remote, undemonstrative father for fear he too would leave. Only his father's friendship with a fellow academic, Brother Thomas, brightens the emotionally bleak next five years for Jeff. At age 12, a severe case of pneumonia (brought on, in part by his father's neglect) brings Jeff back in touch with his mother. All too soon, however, Melody begins to repeat her familiar patterns of betrayal. As his pathetic desire to please her wears off, Jeff begins to see how much she has hurt him and his father. After an emotional confrontation with Melody, Jeff begins to see himself less as the "solitary blue" heron that had caught his imagination in the South Carolina sea islands. Written in a purposefully detached style, early sections of the book read like a journalistic case-study of child neglect. The confrontation with Melody, which would seem to be the climax, comes quite early in the book, and further chapters, while necessary to show Jeff's ultimate resolution of his relationship with his parents, are choppy, episodic and disconnected. The last section, in which he meets Dicey Tillerman and her family (from ***Dicey's Song*** . . .) is unnecessary and dull. While well-written (the character of the father is outstanding), the book ultimately disappoints: Melody is a monster, and Jeff's feelings are never clearly portrayed. The theme of a child abandoned by his mother will be interesting to some, but many will lose interest in later chapters. (pp. 139-40)

Gloria P. Rohmann, in a review of "A Solitary Blue," in School Library Journal, *Vol. 30, No. 1, September, 1983, pp. 139-40.*

Voigt's novel is a lengthy portrayal of fractured family relationships and of love—how it perseveres and nourishes, and how it heals the deepest of wounds. . . . As with ***Dicey's Song*** . . . , the story is full-bodied and carefully drawn. Characterizations are thorough, and there is an emotional depth that is compelling; this is richly resonant—perhaps the best Voigt venture yet.

Denise M. Wilms, in a review of "A Solitary Blue," in Booklist, *Vol. 80, No. 1, September 1, 1983, p. 92.*

Jeff resolves his mixed heritage by deciding to go into ecology: "No, not saving the world or getting back to the good old prehistoric days, not that," he tells his father. "But responsible management of it, somehow . . . with computers too. . . ." This doubly simplistic resolution is disappointing, and Voigt's lack of sympathy for Melody's postulated type is a problem from the start. However, Jeff's own feelings at every stage are compellingly real and affecting; the growing closeness between him and his father is moving and subtly developed; and his own emotional development and growing character (that old-fashioned term is the only word for it) brings out Voigt at her best, as well. (p. J-179)

A review of "A Solitary Blue," in Kirkus Reviews, *Juvenile Issue, Vol. LI, Nos. 13-17, September 1, 1983, pp. J-178-79.*

In *Bleak House,* Charles Dickens gave us Mrs. Jellyby, who took such a charitable interest in far-away Borrioboola-Gha that she failed to notice when her own wretched children were falling down the stairs.

Cynthia Voigt has created a contemporary version of Mrs. Jellyby, an equally appalling mother-philanthropist. . . .

The reader guesses from the beginning of this beautifully written story that the mother is a washout—guesses too that the father's still waters run deep. The book has a natural suspense. One wants to see the boy discover the truth about his parents for himself. There is an "I could have told you so" satisfaction in seeing him betrayed once again by his mother, pleasure in watching the development of his new friendship with his responsible father. Professor Greene's repressions and inhibitions begin to seem like virtues compared with Melody's treacherous "I love you's". (p. 34)

The story is slightly damaged by the appearance of a flock of new characters at the end, but nothing can undo the artistic thoroughness of this study of a boy in pain. (p. 35)

Jane Langton, in a review of "A Solitary Blue," in The New York Times Book Review, *November 27, 1983, pp. 34-5.*

The reader is strengthened and rewarded by an immediate identification with Jeff. Few writers are so poignantly able to reveal the gradual realization of inner strength, resolve, and growth as does Cynthia Voigt. Surely and subtly, she reveals Jeff's depth of character which has evolved as a result of the long, solitary hours in his life. Jeff is astutely aware of his environment and the people in it. He is caught by the power of music, finds emotional release in wandering miles of solitary beaches, and is moved by the magnificent solitary blue herons standing motionless. It is only gradually, as the author allows him to reflect on his situation, that his abilities and talents are realized. As he learns to appreciate his father, their communication improves and he is able to gain a perspective on his life.

Readers leave the story knowing all will be well and may come to regard their own lives with the same self-confidence in their own abilities and decisions. (pp. 1025-26)

Ronald A. Jobe, in a review of "A Solitary Blue," in Language Arts, *Vol. 60, No. 8, November-December, 1983, pp. 1025-26.*

[The relationship between Jeff and his father] makes the novel sparkle. As father and son reveal their deep hurt and take risks, they grow in a love for each other.

There are flaws in the novel. Some events (e.g., the will toward the end) are a little hard to accept. And some of the characters seem to cloud the central issues of the novel. Dicey Tillerman and her clan are interesting, but I had a sense that there were too many of them and Jeff felt compelled to help them all.

Voigt's daughter Jessica with Rosie. Photograph by Walter Voigt. Courtesy of Cynthia Voigt.

There were times, too, when I had to check to see how old Jeff was because he was acting much older than he really was. Nonetheless ***A Solitary Blue*** is a strong, sensitive, and well written portrayal of the relationship between love and risk.

Paul B. Janeczko, in a review of "A Solitary Blue," in Voice of Youth Advocates, *Vol. 7, No. 1, April, 1984, p. 36.*

BUILDING BLOCKS **(1984)**

In an interesting time-travel story, Voigt posits a boy of twelve who, living in 1974, finds himself in the bedroom of another boy and realizes that this ten-year-old child of the depression is his father. Brann's means of entry is falling asleep within a big construction of blocks that have been handed down in the family. What is unusual here is not the encounter but the subtlety with which Voigt uses it to help Brann see why his father has turned out to be the quiet, self-effacing man he is, and how the man's strengths have been masked by his meek ways. An excellent story of a father-son relationship, this is a smooth blending of realism and fantasy.

Zena Sutherland, in a review of "Building Blocks," in Bulletin of the Center for Children's Books, *Vol. 37, No. 8, April, 1984, p. 158.*

When Brann was born, he was supposed to be named Thomas. Then his father saw him and suddenly decided he must be called Brann—with two *n*'s. This is one of the few times the diffident Mr. Connell has ever taken a stand. . . . A well-crafted story, this will appeal to readers on a number of levels. It contains high adventure, perceptive observations, and strong characterizations. The transition in time, a plot element that is often the weakest part of such stories, is handled well here. The only disappointment is Mr. Connell's failure to remember Brann from the past, though his naming of his son indicates that their time together is buried somewhere in his subconscious. Had he remembered, the story could have come full circle even if Mr. Connell did not fully understand the implications of the meeting. Now Brann's knowledge gives him the upper hand, which leads to his pat resolution of the family's problems. This aside, Voigt has written a full-bodied work showing that she has as much to say to younger readers as she does to young adult audiences.

Ilene Cooper, in a review of "Building Blocks," in Booklist, *Vol. 80, No. 18, May 15, 1984, p. 1350.*

Manipulating time to solve intergenerational relationships has become a noticeable trend in otherwise realistic novels. In Brann's story the action set in the past is more significant than that in the present. Furthermore, the plot bears a double burden in establishing credibility for the time-warp mechanism. A sense of intrusion rather than of assimilation undermines the structure of the novel. Fortunately, the author's gift for imagery and sensitivity to character development enables her to evoke a feeling for the Depression and an appreciation of the boy who grows into manhood without becoming embittered or vicious. Thus, the changed relationship between father and son is both touching and believable. (p. 471)

Mary M. Burns, in a review of "Building Blocks," in The Horn Book Magazine, *Vol. LX, No. 4, August, 1984, pp. 470-71.*

The author is sympathetic to both parents though the story is told through Brann's eyes. . . . Though the transition back in time is awkward, the scenes of Brann with his young boy father are beautiful and will leave the reader wishing to return to a parent's youth. The story suggests in a very subtle way that there are good reasons why parents are not all they could or should be. A child's compassion for parents is important.

Elizabeth Sachs, in a review of "Building Blocks," in New Directions for Women, *Vol. 15, No. 2, Spring, 1986, p. 13.*

THE RUNNER (1985)

In a Tillerman family story set a generation before ***Dicey's Song*** . . . , 17-year-old Bullet (he named himself) is an unusual hero in young adult fiction: a strong, hard loner prejudiced against "coloreds." He runs 10 miles a day, everyday, and he is Maryland state champion, but only cross-country. He is angry most of the time, fighting his cold, despotic father, who has already driven away Bullet's vulnerable sister Liza (Dicey's mother). In his determination that nobody will "box him in," Bullet denies his finer feelings, until his killing of Liza's dog in a hunting accident shocks him into facing his grief and responsibility. He sees how much he is like his father, and that his mother, Abigail, is trapped in a cruel marriage, her pain intensified in the cross fire between father and son. It is 1967 and in the high school the burning issues are Vietnam, the draft, and integration. Although he refuses to become politically involved, Bullet overcomes his prejudice partly through a challenging relationship with a clever and intelligent black runner, Tamer. On his 18th birthday Bullet enlists, knowing that it is not for any heroic ideal, but to be free of his father and to choose the box that fits him best. The book ends with Abigail's fierce anguish on hearing of his death. There are serious flaws in this ambitious novel: for example, it jars to have Tamer say (and more than once) that he is "a civilized man." The rhythmically repetitive style is overdone and there are sometimes four adjectives where two would do. But Bullet is presented with dramatic intensity, not only in the assertive confrontations, but also in the quieter moments. Like the teacher who reaches Bullet through the poetry of Housman, Voigt is raising—without didacticism—important ideas of courage and personal integrity and "being young at a difficult time in time."

Hazel Rochman, in a review of "The Runner," in Booklist, *Vol. 81, No. 14, March 15, 1985, p. 1052.*

The Runner is about connections—severed, denied, sustained, treasured. . . . Told through the eyes of Bullet, the coming-of-age story is written in the third person. The technique, meant to distance the reader, is a subtle reflection of Bullet's purposeful disconnection from his feelings and his relationships with others. Cynthia Voigt has once again succeeded in crafting a powerful, intensely moving novel with a singular and memorable main character. In an outstanding, unforgettable work of fiction she makes the reader feel deeply the painful disintegration of this family and the tragic brevity of a boy's life. (pp. 321-22)

Ruth Nadelman Lynn, in a review of "The Runner," in The Horn Book Magazine, *Vol. LXI, No. 3, May-June, 1985, pp. 321-22.*

In Samuel "Bullet" Tillerman, the central character in her new novel ***The Runner,*** Cynthia Voigt has created a young tragic hero. Silent, unyielding, Bullet keeps to his principles and goes after his personal goals with no compromises—not with circumstances and certainly not with other people. His tragic flaw, if you will, is the classic one of hubris. He thinks he can remain above it all. Bullet, for whom honesty and doing one's best are the motivations for everything, desperately wants his friends to share the same aspirations. Yet he refuses to try and convince others to set those goals. When his friends fail to be as good as they can be, he wants "not to care."

Bullet is a brilliant high school runner with not only the strength and reflexes of a talented athlete but the doggedness it takes to turn talent into victory. . . . He always wins. Bullet's running is the frame on which Voigt builds her story, the energy which impels it. Sometimes running is all that keeps Bullet himself going.

Through school crises, family warfare, through tests that shake his character to its foundation, he keeps running. . . .

Besides running, the other anchor in Bullet's life is his mother Abigail. As strong and stoic as Bullet, she bends but never breaks under her husband's tyranny. She and Bullet have a relationship of mutual respect, trust, and certainly love, although neither seems able to express it. "He could read her and she could read him, which was the closest they came to talking." Much is communicated through silence in the Tillerman household.

The atmosphere inside the farmhouse helps build our sympathy for Bullet. Outside his own home, however, he's less likeable, more exasperating. With his classmates, he is often arrogant and inscrutable. (Bullet has never heard of peer pressure.) The high school has recently been integrated, but Bullet will have nothing to do with "coloreds," as he calls the black students. Although he almost single-handedly halts a racial brawl at the school when he attacks the white bully who's started it, his action is prompted not by any liberal principles but by his disdain for messiness. "The last thing he wanted to put up with was a riot. That wasn't even clean fighting."

Voigt handles Bullet's racial prejudice and his gradual enlightenment deftly by working in a black runner, a newcomer to Bullet's track team. His name is Tamer Shipp and he slowly gains Bullet's respect, not because he seeks it but because he wants to be as good as he can be. Tamer and Patrice . . . together convince Bullet that a man's worth depends on his character, not his race.

All of which is to say that Voigt sails ***The Runner*** through some heavy seas, but always with a steady hand. She's never preachy, her story never contrived for didactic purpose. All she gives us here is plausible and engaging. Her scenes of high school life—assemblies, classes and, above all, the cafeteria—are perfectly drawn, her little river town of "Crisfield" and the country around it lovingly rendered. . . .

Those who have read the earlier Tillerman novels will also know what becomes of Bullet. Those who meet him here for the first time will not be surprised at his fate. Bullet is certainly a prickly character; if we met him in, say, the high school lunch room, he might seem cold and aloof. We might even "want not to care" about him. Voigt's accomplishment is to make us care about Bullet, and care deeply.

Alice Digilio, "What Makes Bullet Run?" in Book World—The Washington Post, *July 14, 1985, p. 8.*

Much of the novel's contrived plot turns around issues of race. Bullet—clear about his dislike of "coloreds" and his unwillingness to get involved in anything except running—nonetheless stops a potential riot between Black and white students after a Black athlete is severely beaten by white students. Bullet next refuses his coach's request to help this same Black student—Tamer by name—with his running. When Bullet discusses this incident with his after-school boss Patrice, he is shocked to learn that Patrice is part Black; "I thought you were just tan," says Bullet. (To add some melodrama, we learn that Patrice was a resistance fighter in his native France during World War II and was tortured by the Nazis.) Bullet, who has always liked and respected Patrice, suddenly sees the light and agrees to help Tamer.

The convoluted plot proceeds through a major school brouhaha in which the editor of the school paper is dismissed because he writes about Tamer's beating and through various musings on the war in Vietnam. . . .

The plot is overwrought, the style dense and offputting and the portrayal of Black characters is simple and one dimensional. Patrice is a super-understanding and compassionate mentor. Tamer (who got the name because his mother hoped he would be tamer than his brothers) is a cardboard character. Twenty years old with a wife and child (you know those colored people) and returning to high school after dropping out, Tamer is the super Black athlete who can only run successfully after Bullet helps him. Though Tamer is the focus of racism, he never shows any emotion about it.

The novel is about Bullet, the runner, who is an unusual but interesting young man. The issue of racism complicates Bullet's life as it does for all in this country, but the author has failed to reflect this in her portrayal of her Black characters.

Kathleen E. Goodin, in a review of "The Runner," in Interracial Books for Children Bulletin, *Vol. 16, No. 8, 1985, p. 16.*

Cynthia Voigt fans are in for a puzzling experience. Her fourth book about the Tillerman family (though they hardly featured in the third) centres on a character who had been long gone when the sequence opened. . . .

Should new readers start here then? If they do, they will find some powerful writing. Cynthia Voigt improves with every novel and she is now well into her stride. . . .

The strength of the book is partly in the many details it illuminates in ***Homecoming*** and ***Dicey's Song.*** On finishing ***The Runner,*** I immediately re-read the first two novels and was struck by the remarkably complete picture Cynthia Voigt must have had of several generations of Tillermans, before she worked on any part of it. The weakness lies in the excessive value she places on emotional restraint and being "one's own man". Too many of the characters that we are encouraged to admire are laconic; the talkers are the untrustworthy ones. But Bullet could do with a bit more communication—anyone who gets close to him is frightened by his failure to connect.

Physically he is an instrument for running, tuned to concert pitch. Emotionally he can't even manage a scale. One feels for Bullet, but I would worry even more about any young reader who found him attractive. A moving character but a disastrous role-model.

Mary Hoffman, in a review of "The Runner," in The Times Educational Supplement, *No. 3643, April 25, 1986, p. 28.*

Cynthia Voigt offers a disturbing picture of the American teenager. I found myself struggling to overcome an initial resistance to her book—perhaps it was that dreadful jacket design—but in the end I felt myself privileged to have read it. We may not like her prickly, self-sufficient hero but we can't ignore him. (p. 119)

Because Cynthia Voigt writes with great power, she compels us to a committed interest in a character whom we can pity but certainly cannot love. She breaks all the old conventional rules of the adolescent novel, and forces us to follow her in the investigation of this strange, remote, inaccessible young man in his loneliness and vulnerability. Hers is a book which could only have been written in America, not only because the vividly painted scene is essentially American, but because so frank and open an exposure of a central character's strengths and weaknesses conflicts with the innate reticence of every English writer. (pp. 119-20)

M. Crouch, in a review of "The Runner," in The Junior Bookshelf, *Vol. 50, No. 3, June, 1986, pp. 119-20.*

JACKAROO **(1985)**

Cynthia Voigt moves into the romantic/medieval milieu in a tale that uses the theme of the defender of the poor, and she does it with great success. In a feudal society, the Lords rule, or misrule, with impunity, and for many years there has been legend of Jackaroo, the masked rider who appears to help the poor and oppressed. Clever, confident, courageous, Gwyn the Innkeeper's Daughter assumes the role of Jackaroo when she finds the legendary clothes and mask hidden in a cupboard. Then she knows that there has been a long line of Jackaroos, that he's not a legend—and that anyone who assumes the role may have to pay a price. The end of this carefully structured story may bring a surprise or two to readers, but few are likely to be astonished by the late blooming love affair that the independent and indomitable heroine had not expected. This is a good adventure story, and a believable one; the writing style and characterization are capably controlled, but what gives the book a deep matrix for them is Voigt's full conception of the society and its socioeconomic system.

A review of "Jackaroo," in Bulletin of the Center for Children's Books, *Vol. 39, No. 1, September, 1985, p. 19.*

Cynthia Voigt has put together a combination of setting and character that spells a surefire formula for teen-age readers.

Her new novel, ***Jackaroo,*** takes place in a mythical land with medieval trappings, while the heroine is a teen who's more molded by today's feminist views than the dictums of the Middle Ages. Putting this up-to-date miss into an archaic atmosphere makes for lively reading. The heroine shuns the medieval hoe-and-hut routine, opting for life Robin Hood style.

Even though the principal character is a girl, the novel has appeal for male readers, too, because there's a hero (silent and strong—naturally) who stands in the background, ready to emerge in the nick of time. . . .

The reader soon recognizes that Gwyn is not only an independent young woman and a hard worker, but, more important, a compassionate being. And her caring at a time when many find it inconvenient to care foreshadows the unfolding events. The reader is hardly surprised when Gwyn finds the dusty attire of the long-gone Jackaroo hidden in the top of an old cupboard. And, of course, the costume fits.

Fortunately, the author does more than simply stitch together a series of exciting events. Readers can't help but tune in to Voigt's slices of wisdom, so deftly woven into the story fabric. When all seems smooth for the heroine, suddenly she is falsely accused of not caring for her lord's little son, a deed punishable by death. Both family and friends watch as the lord's sword is put to her throat. No family member rises to her defense, in speech or action, even though all know she's innocent. They simply stand by, watching, waiting, unwilling to risk their own well-being.

As expected, the heroine clears her name and goes free. But from then on, nothing is ever the same within the family fold. Gwyn continues to love her family. And they continue to love her. But now there's a chink in that chain of family love. "Betrayal" blares loudly within each conscience, though no one voices it.

Through this incident, Voigt lets her readers know that love must carry the seal of loyalty, otherwise it's love that's hollow.

Assuredly, the author knows her audience: She's aware that a dilemma among teens today is finding meaningful friendships. So Voigt shows how the heroine drops the criteria of looks, wealth, and conformity to search for companions who view the world as she does, whose standards and values mirror hers.

Throughout, Voigt keeps her story flowing in a smooth style. And readers will appreciate the fast pace of the prose. Some teens, however—those who like to glean factual tidbits even when reading fiction—might prefer the story more firmly anchored in a medieval time frame. Although the author draws on the lords and nobles, peasants, hovels, gallows, and the darkness of illiteracy found in the Middle Ages, her scenes are nevertheless fantasy. A more authentic setting would have ushered teen readers through the back door into a fascinating historical period.

Hattie Clark, "Adventures of a Spunky Medieval Heroine," in The Christian Science Monitor, *November 1, 1985, p. B1.*

An intense and elegantly written historical adventure-romance. . . . ***Jackaroo*** will stimulate the imagination and make readers marvel at Voigt's creative genius. She presents a carefully designed, mystery-filled plot which once again illustrates her abilities as a master storyteller. Characters are somewhat reluctant to reveal themselves—but this is a most appropriate style for a tale of dangerous and uncertain times. ***Jackaroo*** will cause readers to pause and consider the process of legend making and the changes that take place in the retellings of legendary deeds.

Karen P. Smith, in a review of "Jackaroo," in School Library Journal, *Vol. 32, No. 4, December, 1985, p. 96.*

Voigt is best known in YA circles for her Newbery winners ***Dicey's Song*** and ***A Solitary Blue***, and the related stories ***The Homecoming*** and ***The Runner***. These novels have shown her deft hand with plot and character, and in ***Jackaroo*** she carries these skills into new territory in a fine strong fantasy. The setting is the usual feudal village in a time resembling the Middle Ages, but Voigt renders it with uncommon vividness: the ceaseless round of domestic tasks, the limited diet and the limited world view, the chasm between lords and common folk, the joyful release of a feast day, and the colorful revelry of a country fair. (p. 50)

The story of how [Gwyn] uses wit and courage to save herself and her people makes an adventure as deeply satisfying as a timeworn fairy tale. (p. 51)

Patty Campbell, in a review of "Jackaroo," in Wilson Library Bulletin, *Vol. 60, No. 7, March, 1986, pp. 50-1.*

Jo March who, as her creator Louisa May Alcott records, loved to stride around in russet leather boots as the daring Roderigo would have applauded a noticeable trend in recent years—the emergence of the swashbuckling female. A logical extension of the strong feminine characters in realistic fiction, these iconoclasts are a welcome addition to the scene—providing action, not merely decoration, to tales of derring-do. Cynthia Voigt's Gwyn is the latest example of a multidimensional personality developed through a moving and engrossing story set in a time reminiscent of the late feudal period. The daughter of a well-to-do innkeeper, she is reliable, thoughtful, and, unlike her sisters, wary of an arranged marriage with a local villager merely because he could offer security. Yet, she is aware that times are hard, that single or widowed females are the most vulnerable to those who prey upon the weak. . . . Playing the role [of Jackaroo] . . . demands a stiff payment, as [Gwyn] soon learns, but it brings rewards as well, chief among them being the knowledge that Jackaroo is an idea as well as a reality and that love between a man and woman does not necessarily mean loss of individuality. As in all of Cynthia Voigt's books, the style is fluid and consistent with the personalities of her characters; the setting is evoked through skillfully crafted description; the situations speak directly to the human condition. What is most notable, however, is the skill with which the social and political structures are described without interrupting the flow of the plot. This is a fully realized country—so convincingly delineated that it seems as if it had once existed only to be rediscovered by a master storyteller.

Mary M. Burns, in a review of "Jackaroo," in The Horn Book Magazine, *Vol. LXII, No. 2, March-April, 1986, p. 210.*

IZZY, WILLY-NILLY **(1986)**

Before, Izzy's life had been colorful as a pretty, popular cheerleader, but grayness swallows her up after a car accident results in the amputation of her leg. Her trio of girlfriends are too uncomfortable to be around her, but the void of their friendship is filled by unattractive, blunt Roseamund, who bounds into her life, providing bolstering support. It's Roseamund's persistence that helps Izzy over the hurdle of returning to school. Several expedients effectively convey Izzy's stages of reaction: the miniature Izzy visualized in her head that does back flips expresses her true feelings; the way denial is demonstrated by Izzy not looking at the empty leg space until 30 pages after the doctor tells her he has to take it off; the cool reserve of the black therapist which makes her "examine" herself. As with other Voigt characters, the perspective is from within. Readers see the mental anguish and self-pity through Izzy's eyes. Consciously, the pace is slow, as is the healing process, and the tone is ponderous throughout. The story is about learning to balance: physically as Izzy maneuvers herself on crutches and emotionally as she sorts out her friends and a new self-identification as Isobel. Work on the school paper, the prospect of a prosthesis and Roseamund's staunch support start to mend her crippled life. No one will be able to finish this story without understanding the psychological trauma an amputee faces. The message is not *Willy Nilly*.

Julie Cummins, in a review of "Izzy, Willy-Nilly," in School Library Journal, *Vol. 32, No. 8, April, 1986, p. 101.*

Voigt shows unusual insight into the workings of a 15-year-old girl's mind. . . . Just as Voigt's perceptive empathy brings Izzy to life, other characterizations are memorable, whether of Izzy's shallow former friends or of her egocentric 10-year-old sister. In this refreshing change from her Crisfield novels, Voigt provides not only a highly satisfying read, but one of the notable books of the season.

A review of "Izzy, Willy-Nilly," in Publishers Weekly, *Vol. 229, No. 17, April 25, 1986, p. 79.*

From the first sentence ("Isobel? I'm afraid we're going to have to take it off") to the last ("The little Izzy balanced there briefly and then took a hesitant step forward—ready to fall, ready not to fall"), this is a single-minded analysis of a girl's adjustment to amputation of part of her leg after an automobile accident. There is occasional relief, as in Voigt's perceptive description of family interaction at Thanksgiving, but almost immediately she returns to repetition of the problem: "He couldn't know how it felt to be a fifteen-year-old girl with part of a leg amputated and my whole life changed." Parts of the first-person narrative work vividly as scenes; other parts are over-explained and expository. Izzy's former friends all desert her, which isn't quite convincing; a class misfit comes through for her in an excellent, well-rounded characterization. Izzy's family is a mixture of individuals and stock figures. Overall, this could have been cut to good effect, but readers will probably pursue it from interest in Izzy's disability and the parts of the narrative that show instead of tell.

A review of "Izzy, Willy-Nilly," in Bulletin of the Center for Children's Books, *Vol. 39, No. 9, May, 1986, p. 179.*

Though drunk driving seems initially to be an issue here, Voigt chooses not to pursue it. Friendship is a more developed theme, but the author deals most distinctly with the notion of preconceptions and self-conceptions. While not burdening readers with clinical details, she conveys a keen understanding of the physical practicalities involved in coping with a handicap and of the strength needed to reevaluate and redirect oneself. She shepherds Izzy's recuperation slowly but honestly, brings her full circle from Izzy to the new Isobel without sentimentality, and leaves her a new person at the close of the novel "ready to fall, ready not to fall."

Stephanie Zvirin, in a review of "Izzy, Willy-Nilly," in Booklist, *Vol. 82, No. 17, May 1, 1986, p. 1305.*

There's a stimulating moment late in the book when Izzy's brothers, minor characters, surprise her by returning home from college and filling the kitchen with motion, talk, and masculine presence. It's as if someone had suddenly opened a window and let in the wind. The scene is intentionally vibrant, but why, we ask, is the rest of the book so static?

The answer lies with Izzy, a supremely well adjusted girl who accepts a date with a boy who gets drunk and drives them both into a tree. Though the boy is unhurt, one of Izzy's legs is eventually amputated.

The story is not as sensational as it sounds. It has the stock characters of a hospital story—good doctor, devoted parents, and an especially well-drawn loyal friend—but Voigt concentrates on Izzy, focusing less on her Terrible Tragedy and more on the rocking of Izzy's assumptions about her life. "I don't think I ever wanted to be more than nice," Izzy tells us, and for her this has had a particular, valid meaning. It is no longer, of course, enough.

Unfortunately, Izzy is just too restrained, too understanding, to carry this long, deliberate novel. At story's end she is "more than nice"—there is, as she puts it, a "richness in me"—but surely an intelligent young woman does not have to be maimed to achieve such subtle wisdom about her friends, her family, herself. (p. 22)

Mary Lou Burket, "Teen-Agers and Troubled Times," in Book World—The Washington Post, *May 11, 1986, pp. 17, 22.*

Best young adult novel of the season, and perhaps of the year, is ***Izzy, Willy-Nilly*** by Cynthia Voigt. Baldly stated, the plot sounds syrupy: a young girl loses her leg in a car crash and grows in maturity from experiencing her own and other people's reactions to her deformity. Yet in Voigt's skillful hands, the story is spare and clean, with compassion but no sentimentality.

Central to this accomplishment is the kind of character she has put at the heart of the story. Izzy is a nice girl and an uncomplicated jock, a cheerleader, one of the in-crowd at school. Although she is a kind person with decent impulses, Izzy is not much given to introspection about her own or other people's feelings. . . .

Then Roseamund Webber appears at the door of her room. Badly dressed, with an awkward figure and impossible frizzy hair, Roseamund is a good-hearted intellectual who says exactly what she thinks—and regrets it later.

Voigt develops this offbeat relationship with subtlety and humor. The other people around Izzy react to her loss in a variety of ways that are grounded in their characters, and as she learns to understand them and herself, her strength grows and deepens. There have been many YA problem novels about dealing with a handicap, but ***Izzy, Willy-Nilly*** transcends the genre to be more than a book about a girl learning to live without a leg. It is a book about a girl learning to live.

Patty Campbell, in a review of "Izzy, Willy-Nilly," in Wilson Library Bulletin, *Vol. 61, No. 3, November, 1986, p. 49.*

***STORIES ABOUT ROSIE* (1986)**

Newbery Medalist Voigt has turned her attentions, for the first time, to a picture book audience. Inspired by her own dog named Rosie and the Voigt family, the author gives readers a dog's eye-view of an idyllic existence. The family's job "was to take care of her. Rosie's job was to be happy." Rosie runs away from home, but when she's tired, she allows the family to take her back; she knows better than to bark at anyone inside the house, even if it's an intrusive bat; in Maine, when the whole family wants to see a deer, Rosie finds one, and it remains her secret. This is a funny, realistic look at an energetic dog, and Voigt seems to know just what makes Rosie bark. . . . ***Rosie*** is a lightweight, just-right book for dog fans everywhere.

A review of "Stories about Rosie," in Publishers Weekly, *Vol. 230, No. 13, September 26, 1986, p. 82.*

Four episodes show Rosie's adventures both inside and outside of her home. . . . Even though they are told from Rosie's point of view, which should be amusing, the stories fall flat due to the stilted sentences, which dampen what little action there is. (The exception is the episode involving the bat, which is the funniest of the four.) Readers never get to know Rosie's family at all, as their behavior is inconsistent throughout. Black-and-white line drawings [by Dennis Kendrick] alternate with [his] watercolors; they contain more action than the plot itself, which is too slow to be acceptable for early primary grades. Readers who have a dog will smile in recognition at Rosie's antics, but that's not enough to sustain interest in the book. Stick with Margaret Graham's "Benjy" books (Harper).

Kathleen Brachmann, in a review of "Stories about Rosie," in School Library Journal, *Vol. 33, No. 2, October, 1986, p. 167.*

The four stories here are not terribly thick on plot. . . . The style is very simple, however, and funny as well, with the humor of Rosie's knowledge versus the humans' easily keeping the text afloat. . . . Good practice fare for young readers.

Betsy Hearne, in a review of "Stories about Rosie," in Bulletin of the Center for Children's Books, *Vol. 40, No. 4, December, 1986, p. 78.*

***COME A STRANGER* (1986)**

Less cohesive and involving than Voigt's previous Crisfield novels, this is the story of Mina Smiths, the strong black girl readers first met in ***Dicey's Song.*** Ever since being the only black at an all white ballet camp one summer in Connecticut, 13-year-old Mina has been questioning her blackness: straightening her hair, reading "white" books, playing up to white classmates. The next summer at the camp, she finds none of her white friends want to room with her (why this wasn't a problem the first summer is not clear) and that her body has grown too awkward for ballet, prompting the director to ask her to leave. This seems unrealistic, serving only to illustrate the director's racism; many of the characters suffer from this kind of one-dimensional stereotyping. Mina's search for identity takes her to the young married minister, Tamer Shipp (first met as Bullet's competitor in ***The Runner***), with whom she falls in love. Aware of her love, but too respectful to embarrass her with it, Tamer talks to Mina about God, racial identity, his pretty but sad wife, and his pain over the death of Bullet in Vietnam. Their discussions, like the story, raise interesting questions, but are static, overly prolonged, and occasionally forgotten midstream. Tamer and Mina played dramatic supporting roles in previous books, but here they are unable to sustain a dull story.

Roger Sutton, in a review of "Come a Stranger," in Bulletin of the Center for Children's Books, *Vol. 40, No. 2, October, 1986, p. 40.*

[Mina Smiths] takes center stage in this addition to the Tillerman saga and holds it with energy and spirit. The story takes her from age 10 to 15, following her from a youthful dancer, full of herself and her ambitions, to a wise and realistic young woman. . . . There is little plot here, but the story moves well, with the theme, Mina's changing view of the world and her place in it as a young black woman, carrying it in a rich current. The events are seen through Mina's eyes, as are the characters who, nonetheless, emerge with strong identities of their own. . . . It is her relationship with the Tillermans and with Tamer which brings the story to its climax, as Mina finds a way to complete the circle, bringing a measure of peace to all. Voigt tells her story smoothly, getting inside of Mina's perceptions easily and believably. To catch the resonance of the story, it would be helpful to have read the earlier books about the Tillermans, although, except for minor lapses in character description and incident, this does stand well on its own. Voigt permits readers to know her characters in a way they rarely know people in real life.

Christine Behrmann, in a review of "Come a Stranger," in School Library Journal, *Vol. 33, No. 2, October, 1986, p. 184.*

This is a finely crafted novel where nothing is written for effect or carelessly. Each word and phrase is important, and the passages about Mina's growth and awareness are beautiful. . . . A fine, rich "growing up" novel.

Leila Davenport Pettyjohn, in a review of "Come a Stranger," in Children's Book Review Service, *Vol. 15, No. 3, November, 1986, p. 34.*

Mina grows before our eyes, profiting from each experience, into an independent yet warmly loving young woman, deeply involved with her closely-knit community. . . . Although Mina's family is almost too obviously the vehicle through which the author's own thoughts on race and acceptance are voiced, Mina's engaging personality is believable, and her story fills in still another part of the absorbing saga of the Tillerman family.

Ethel R. Twichell, in a review of "Come a Stranger," in The Horn Book Magazine, *Vol. LXII, No. 6, November-December, 1986, p. 749.*

The strengths and weaknesses of women—of all humanity—are beautifully illustrated in Doris Buchanan Smith's *Return to Bitter Creek.*

But it is in Cynthia Voigt's new book, ***Come a Stranger,*** that the image of women is most strikingly portrayed. Wilhemenia Smiths is a young black woman who must come to terms with her blackness, her womanness, but, most importantly, her "personness." In spite of Mina's own strength, intelligence, and integrity, it is her mother's sense of self-worth and personhood that allows the entire family the solid foundation on which to grow and develop. For in Raymonda Smiths we see the image of woman—of the human being—we hope all people can become: a person who listens quietly, responds intelligently and loves fully, accepting all people realistically yet charitably, seeing life as it is and as it has the potential to be, and making a difference in her own life and in the lives of those around her.

Frances Bradburn, in a review of "Come a Stranger," in Wilson Library Bulletin, *Vol. 62, No. 5, January, 1987, p. 61.*

Robert (Atkinson) Westall

1929-

English author of fiction, short stories, and nonfiction and editor.

Westall is regarded as a versatile and talented writer of emotionally charged, fast-paced narratives for young adults. Winner of two Carnegie Medals, he is esteemed as a powerful and uncompromising prose stylist who expresses sharp insights into adolescent character and feelings. A controversial author, Westall is viewed by some observers as an angry, sardonic, and pessimistic novelist obsessed with violence, and by others as the creator of frank, realistic works that underscore his personal aversion to cruelty and brutality. Westall's books exhibit a variety of fiction subgenres: realistic fiction (*The Machine-Gunners,* 1975); ghost story (*The Watch House,* 1977); time-travel adventure (*The Devil on the Road,* 1978); short stories (*Break of Dark,* 1982); science fiction (*Futuretrack 5,* 1983); and historical fantasy (*The Cats of Seroster,* 1984). Sometimes considered demanding reading, his novels and short stories often center on psychological and supernatural situations, raise questions about guilt, inhumanity, chance, courage, and the validity of war, and stress the importance of myth and appreciation of the past. Several of Westall's works contain complex plots in which he sets human relationships against psychic phenomena and occasionally juxtaposes real and historical events. Other characteristics of Westall's fiction include the use of authentic English idiom and setting, fluidity, humor, and above all, excitement. Westall is best known for his first book, *The Machine-Gunners,* which presents a compelling, unsentimental account of the Second World War as experienced by a group of English teenagers. Compared to William Golding's *Lord of the Flies* for its accurate depiction of adolescents operating without adult supervision, the novel continues to receive mixed reviews for its presentation of violent behavior and obscene language. The success of *The Machine-Gunners* prompted a sequel, *Fathom Five* (1979), a spy story in which Westall uses the same time period and many of the same characters, and *Children of the Blitz* (1985), a compilation of biographical and autobiographical childhood war reminiscences.

Critics praise Westall for the breadth of his originality, the strength of his writing, and the perception of his characterizations. He is also acclaimed for successfully combining reality and fantasy and for creating exceptional ghost and horror stories. Although he is faulted for an excessive use of violence, swearing, and sexual references as well as for thin plots, weak structure, and demeaning portrayals of women, most reviewers acknowledge that Westall respects the sophistication and depth of his audience while continuing to expand the boundaries of young adult literature.

***The Machine-Gunners* received the Carnegie Medal and a Guardian Commendation in 1976 and became a *Boston Globe-Horn Book* Honor Book in 1977. *The Devil on the Road* won a Carnegie Commendation in 1979, while *The Scarecrows* was awarded the Carnegie Medal and was designated a *Boston Globe-Horn Book* Honor Book in 1982.**

Courtesy of Robert Westall

(See also *Contemporary Literary Criticism,* Vol. 17; *Something about the Author,* Vol. 23; *Something about the Author Autobiography Series,* Vol. 2; *Contemporary Authors New Revision Series,* Vol. 18; and *Contemporary Authors,* Vols. 69-72.)

AUTHOR'S COMMENTARY

[The following excerpt is from an abbreviated version of a talk first given to the Youth Libraries Group on October 7, 1978.]

Ever since I wrote ***The Machine-gunners*** (and in spite of the fact that my last three books have been fantasies) people keep consulting me about realism in children's books. Rather as if I'd been appointed high priest and was being asked to read the entrails. There is not much career-structure for high priests who fail to read entrails, so I'd better come clean with what I think.

Certainly there is a great hunger for childhood-realism at the moment. The feel of a stream running through your toes; the feel of a faceful of gravel when your best friend has just pushed you in the gutter. Like Laurie Lee's breathtaking dive into infancy, *Cider with Rosie. . . .*

Vivid stuff. Adults love it; it reawakens their child-within. But when I read it out in school, children are curiously unmoved. The reason isn't hard to find. Lee's sensations are those of a child; his language is that of a highly sophisticated adult and,

I feel, deliberately so. The child-within-the-author is hygienically cut off from the adult-author-writing. (p. 34)

Lee is on the side of the adults, plundering the child's world on their behalf. This is nostalgia; it takes a gap of thirty years *really* to enjoy a faceful of gravel.

But, to be fair, Lee wrote his book for adults; it was those same gleeful adults who have tried to foist the book on to children. The trouble is, that same temptation to send up children sits on the shoulder of every children's author; because before an author can get to the children, he must first please adults: editors, critics, parents, librarians. And so many of them are hooked on nostalgia.

Nostalgia is the enemy of children's realism. (p. 35)

Perhaps all the best books start by being written for only one child, and that child very close to you. They start when the child-within-the-author turns to the real child and says, "Come away with me and I will show you a place you otherwise will never see, because it is buried under thirty, or three hundred or three thousand years of time." (p. 36)

That is why I wrote ***The Machine-gunners.*** No thought of publication: it lay over a year in manuscript before I even bothered to have it typed up. I wrote it only for my son, then twelve. To tell him how it felt to be me, when I was twelve. As I read it out to him, chapter by chapter, we were, for the first and last time, twelve-year-olds standing side by side. He had "come away" with me. Twelve spoke to twelve, without interruption.

By the time I wrote my second book, my first was being published. It was not just Chris looking over my shoulder, but my two beloved editors: helpful, sympathetic, tolerant, but with definite views of their own, and definitely not twelve years old. Then publication day, and ***The Machine-gunners*** was favourably reviewed as an adult novel by the literary gent from *The Times* (a sort of pat on the back that most children's authors absolutely and hypocritically adore). The crowd looking over my shoulder as I wrote got bigger and bigger. And then ***Machine-gunners*** won the Carnegie, and it felt like the whole world was watching; for a month I couldn't write at all. The burden of all their expectations was totally flattening. My target figure had grown from one to thousands; how could I please them all?

To my shame, I tried. Crawlingly and contemptibly, though unconsciously, I tried. The amount of swearing in my books dropped; the intellectual content, the scholarship and research grew. I began writing books for the children of publishers, librarians and the literary gent of *The Times*. . . . Now that I am at last conscious of what I was doing, I look round and see so many "good" children's books written for the same bloody audience. Books that gain splendid reviews, win prizes, make reputations and are unreadable by the majority of children. I recall hearing somewhere that twenty per cent of people in this country own eighty per cent of the property. In the same ghastly way, their children own eighty per cent of children's books.

Now I feel the only way back to freedom is for me to write a really *dreadful* book—not one that's perverted or full of sex and violence, but simply one that will get me dragged to the head critic's study and given six of the best. So I'll know again whose side I'm on: the eighty per cent of kids who, like my own son, might enjoy ***Machine-gunners*** but wouldn't get past the first three pages of ***The Wind Eye*** or ***The Watch House.***

It's not going to be hard to get caned. Once you get back to real childhood-realism, there are so many unsuitable topics. Because real children have got such grotty interests.

As an art teacher, I take classes sketching down by the river. I want them to draw the things that please the adult me: the yacht basin, mossy stumps sticking out of the water, the play of sunlight on ripples. But they are interested in death, and even the nicest river is full of death. (pp. 37-8)

I remember the age—like Laurie Lee I too had my dead cat—a place of knee-trembling pilgrimage for six months, till some well-meaning adult cleared the bones away. I could not bear to make such a pilgrimage now. I would empathize with the dead cat too much—I own five, or five own me. Cats are persons to me now. Death is personal too. I know that one day, in the not too distant future, I will die too, and I don't like being reminded.

But to a child, death has no immediacy. Children think they will live forever; dying is for grandpa and grandma—one of *their* duties, like giving sweets on demand, going bald or wrinkled, smelling funny and wearing old-fashioned clothes. Duties which render them as comfortably alien a species as the giraffe. So a child can afford to be detached and fascinated by death.

But if I put such thoughts in a children's book, I would be accused of being a morbid and heartless corrupter of the young. Because we adults are upset by children's real thoughts, we regard them as being unsuitable material for children's books. Only one book, to my knowledge, has been allowed to speak to children on this topic in depth, with official approval . . . , and that is William Golding's *Lord of the Flies*. And that was written as an adult book, and only allowed to drift into children's ken when the initial shock of it had been anaesthetized by ten years of adult familiarity. Yet once a child has read *Lord of the Flies* he is willing to discuss it at exhausting length, even many years later. It is the one book that seems to speak to every child's condition.

How many more of the best children's books have come drifting down from the adult world? *Billy Liar, The Loneliness of the Long-distance Runner*? Why can't we children's writers write stuff that good?

Because it wouldn't be suitable for children. You don't even have to go as far as death to find taboos in the children's book world. We need go no further than the loo. (pp. 38-9)

And I haven't even mentioned the worst words yet. Neither has four letters. They are "class" and "politics".

Surely, surely, I hear the voices braying, we can keep *class* and *politics* out of children's books? It'll come to the little dears soon enough.

Too late, missus. It's in the books already. Only trouble, it's all *your* sort of politics, which you've managed to kid yourself is no politics at all. Tory politics, establishment politics. (p. 40)

There is politics in ***The Machine-gunners.*** But again, it is largely the acceptable politics of the war against Hitler. Chas doesn't like coppers and headmasters, but what twelve-year-old does?

There is one difference; Chas's dad doesn't like coppers either, even though he is strictly an honest man. I am proud of creating him, because so often in children's books, the workers are either baddies (Jed Stowe the village no-good and poacher, with no job and seven filthy kids) or entirely establishment-loving goodies, often a bit comic (like Gowther Mossock and his wife). The idea of the intelligent workingman, who is honest, but honestly bitter and critical of our society, *is* a comparative rarity. I can think of few in English children's books (Alan Garner's *Stone Book* sequence is an honourable exception). . . .

Yet in reality they do exist; and in realism they should.

But there is yet worse to come.

The adult psychopath; and I'm not talking about Jed Stowe the poacher. I suppose I would define psychopathy as a lack of empathy with living things. Children have to learn this, slowly and painfully. (p. 41)

What do we writers do about this problem? Usually we invoke Jed Stowe the poacher, or an evil slant-eyed Chinese, or in films a Mexican bandit who punctuates his killings with insane laughter. But if you want realism in children's books, this really will not do. The devils are among us, among those most respected. Like Winston Churchill, who allowed the fire raid on Dresden that killed a hundred thousand refugees when we had clearly won the war. Or Harry S. Truman, who allowed Hiroshima when he could have burnt off Mount Fujiyama instead, with equal effect in ending the war. Children are not fools. I am glad to relate that, in 1947, the sixth form at Tynemouth High School found both men guilty in a mock trial and sentenced them to life imprisonment.

And so, to sum up, thanks to a subtle chemistry that takes place, usually unconsciously between the reasonably successful writer and the establishment which is beginning to absorb him, a lot of realism and vitality is drained from children's books, and replaced with nostalgia and a body of opinion acceptable to the establishment. Naturally, the children reject them, and go to those adult writers who are allowed to handle the basic realities of blood, decay, hate, shit and death. (pp. 42-3)

We must look for the hot-line to the reader. . . . It lies, I think, in children's love of inevitable catastrophe. (p. 44)

But what about that even deeper source of reality, the hot-line to the *subject*?

For me, long after all my research is done, this is where my books start, where they draw their first infant breath. The moment I touched the German machine-gun in the Imperial War Museum; the moment I gently touched St. Cuthbert's tomb in Durham cathedral; the moment I roamed the empty rooms of the real Watch House, fingered the skull in its glass case; the moment I first felt a motorbike kick forward under my bottom, the books came *alive*. (p. 45)

[I] am besieged by people who passionately explain to me what ***The Machine-gunners*** is about—and all their answers are different.

But perhaps that is the way realism is. As Eliot said, his poems meant something different to each person—they meant what each person thought they meant. And I must warn you that Eliot also said that mankind cannot bear too much reality. (p. 46)

Robert Westall, "How Real Do You Want Your Realism?" in Signal, *No. 28, January, 1979, pp. 34-46*

GENERAL COMMENTARY

BOOKS FOR YOUR CHILDREN

Without doubt . . . the best new writer for young teenagers, a man with an instinctive understanding of the emotional and moral dilemmas that teenagers are grappling with is Robert Westall.

He achieved instant fame with his first novel ***The Machine Gunners***. . . . ***The Machine Gunners*** like so many stories for older children at present is set in the last war. It tells of a group of children who come into possession of a machine gun which they rescue from a crashed German bomber and set up for use when they think that the Germans have landed. His two subsequent novels ***The Wind Eye*** and ***The Watch House*** . . . are also set in the North East of England. ***The Wind Eye*** is an unusual combination of a closely observed family, emotional problems between parents are picked up by children, and an almost fairy tale fantasy involving the legend of St. Cuthbert associated with the Farne Islands. The Watch House is in fact an actual place in Tynemouth, a relic almost from the days of Grace Darling when local seamen performed heroic feats of rescue. Maybe following the phenomenon that ghosts, particularly poltergeists, are well known to appear to teenage girls, Robert Westall makes the central character of this story a girl, but it will appeal equally to both sexes, adults as well as teenagers. The spook that haunts the Watch House has a purpose which is beautifully worked out in a story which again weaves real life emotional tensions with lingering echoes from the past.

". . . . . . and onto Science Fiction," in Books for Your Children, *Vol. 13, No. 2, Spring, 1978, p. 21.*

ERIC HADLEY

[Robert Westall's] first book ***The Machine Gunners*** was a distinguished exploration of life in wartime England. Its strength derived not simply from the authenticity of the detail, which it has in abundance, but also from the complex and often ironic presentation of the relationship between child and adult values—particularly the way their confrontations are coloured by and, at the same time, throw light upon the larger conflict in which they're set.

His two books since then—***The Wind Eye*** and ***The Watch House***—although they've both been acclaimed, seem to be a diversion of the talent he revealed in that first novel. Although the contemporary world is now present and sharply observed in the shape of two heroines bruised, damaged and rendered hypersensitive by the collapsed marriages of their trendy parents, the real centre of interest has shifted into the world of the 'supernatural'—the fashionably irrational (***The Watch House*** even has an exorcism). The energy has moved into the creation of brooding and charged 'atmosphere' and what one is left admiring is the apparently inexhaustible changes Westall can ring on the production of the delicious 'frisson' at the 'unspeakable' lurking on the edge of our lives.

I found myself 'absorbed' and 'swept along' by those later Westall novels. . . . (pp. 57-8)

Eric Hadley, "The Scrubbed Pine World of English Children's Fiction," in The Use of English, *Vol. 31, No. 2, Spring, 1980, pp. 56-65.*

ANNE WOOD

The part books can play in helping children analyse their feelings as a way of coming to terms with experiences should never be overlooked. Many very good novels for fluent older readers by authors such as Robert Westall, for example ***The Wind Eye*** and his latest novel ***The Scarecrows*** . . . , deal with broken and breaking family relationships in quite sensational stories but do so sensitively. Robert Westall is very concerned with the way in which young people can be frightened by their own very strong emotions. In ***The Scarecrows*** Simon Wood had passionately identified with his late father an army officer and hero. His violent reactions to his mother's second quite different husband, a very talented nationally recognised cartoonist, is the springboard for this often violent book. It demands a reading age of 14+ and is powerful reading at any level. Hopefully any young person for whom it came too close for comfort would put it down and find it again later at a moment when some of the sting had gone out of their first raw feelings. . . . Robert Westall is himself a very experienced teacher of adolescents and is not afraid to handle violence both emotional and physical in his books. Nevertheless it would be a wise teacher who read ***The Scarecrows*** carefully before recommending it in the same breath and to the same child as confidently read and enjoyed ***The Machine Gunners***. . . .

> *Anne Wood, in a review of "The Wind Eye," "The Scarecrows" and "The Machine Gunners," in* Books for Your Children, *Vol. 16, No. 2, Summer, 1981, p. 19.*

JOHN ROWE TOWNSEND

[***The Machine-Gunners*** (1975)] is a powerful story, crowded with character and incident; it also shows an interest in violence which many have found disconcerting. Violence—physical or psychological, overt or suppressed—is in fact a major ingredient of Westall's novels. In ***The Wind Eye*** (1976) an unlikeable Cambridge don has his whole view of life crushingly destroyed. In ***The Scarecrows*** (1981), Simon Brown loathes his stepfather and resents his mother's marital happiness; and it is obviously his own fury and malice that bring to life the Scarecrows, grown from clothes left in the nearby ruined mill by the participants in a long-past, murderous triangle of passion.

Westall indeed gives the impression of being an angry writer; of detesting his own middle-class characters and, it would seem, his feminine ones. He writes with bitter insight about internal conflicts, family tensions and teenage passions; and he has a particular gift for psycho-fantasy, for exploring the borderlines between the real and the supernatural. At full strength he is a novelist of disturbing brilliance. (pp. 336-37)

> *John Rowe Townsend, "Since 1973 (i): Older Fiction," in his* Written for Children: An Outline of English-Language Children's Literature, *second revised edition, J. B. Lippincott, 1983, pp. 329-40.*

DAVID REES

Robert Westall's ***The Machine-Gunners*** won the Carnegie Medal in 1975 which is perhaps a little surprising since in that same year Nina Bawden produced her masterpiece, *The Peppermint Pig;* but it is nonetheless a good story: amusing, exciting, with some memorably caricatured people, as salty as a seaside picture postcard. However, the seeds of later decline were sown here, in this first novel. The plot, in the last fifty pages, becomes increasingly improbable; macho characteristics, guts rather than integrity, are extolled, and there is too much emphasis on incidents of unpleasant violence:

> Clogger raised his boot and kicked Boddser in the ribs three times. It made a terrible noise, like a butcher chopping a leg of lamb. Then he kicked him three times more, and three times more. Boddser was much more sick now. When he looked up, his eyes had changed. He looked as if he understood something he had never understood before. . . .

Also the unpleasant attitudes about class (later to surface in ***Fathom Five***) are already present. The paragraph in ***The Machine-Gunners,*** which describes the plight of a bombed-out Council House family, is an example, and one a responsible editor should have questioned:

> The family were scurrying around like ants from a broken nest, making heaps of belongings they had salvaged, and then breaking up the heaps to make new heaps. Chas watched them as if they were ants, without sympathy, because they were a slummy kind of family; a great fat woman in carpet slippers and a horde of boys of assorted sizes; hair like lavatory brushes, coarse maroon jerseys that wouldn't fasten at the neck and boots with steel heelplates.

Not only do these attitudes become more prominent in the subsequent books, but the quality of the writing deteriorates too. The plots become increasingly thin and improbable—the supernatural elements are little more than stage props; and the characters, more often than not, are stereotypes or collections of mannerisms: one thinks particularly of Bertrand in ***The Wind Eye*** or Prudi, Arthur, Timmo and the two priests in ***The Watch House,*** or Derek in ***The Devil on the Road.*** The dialogue is often unconvincing—you can't create North of England speech simply by flinging the odd "bairn" or "hinny" into every third line and turning all the "I's" into "Aah's." Most irritating, too, is that Westall's writing can be garrulous, with nothing under the surface; confused by sentences in which verbs are never given a subject; marred by cliché; and hyperbolic language that is inaccurate, distasteful, or completely absurd:

> The female camp-followers had cleavages you could have ridden a horse down.
>
> (***The Devil on the Road***)

> Bertrand used the same back-handed flick to the nose. He felt the nasal bones break under his hand like Hong-Kong plastic.
>
> (***The Wind Eye***)

> I caught him smack on the nose; it made a *lovely* mess. He was a big kid; meaty slabs of yobbo muscle.
>
> (***The Devil on the Road***)

Macho attitudes increasingly replace detailed observation of the behavior of real people. Timmo's hand, in ***The Watch House,*** we are told "felt hard and bony and much more reassuring than Pat's. There was so much vitality in Timmo." Madeleine, in ***The Watch House,*** is criticized for careless driving and for being aggressive and unpleasant; whereas John, the central character of ***The Devil on the Road,*** who is as unpleasant and aggressive, and who drives a motor-bike far too fast, is treated very sympathetically. What is sauce for the gander is evidently not sauce for the goose. Madeleine becomes acceptable only when she reverts to a more traditionally feminine role—happily baking goodies in the kitchen. No such change occurs in John; reckless behavior on the road, violence, and rudeness are presumably virtues in men. John—with his big biceps and all the women wanting to seduce him—is more like a *Playgirl* fantasy than a real person. Girls in ***The Devil on the Road*** are portrayed as little more than sexual objects, and even the sprightly, forceful Johanna is most praised when most a stereotype, running around after John, cooking his meals, and tidying up.

Macho man is always extremely uneasy about his sexuality and about his role in the world; machismo is a facade that covers inferiority complexes of all sorts and huge chips on the shoulder. He needs to dislike a lot of things in order to reassure himself that he functions adequately, and Westall's heroes indeed dislike a wide variety of human behavior: the upper classes, bosses of all sorts, intellectuals, university dons, middle-class people from southern England, working-class people less well off than themselves, unfeminine women, foreigners, and homosexuals. The socio-political attitudes expressed in ***Fathom Five,*** a sequel to ***The Machine-Gunners,*** as far as foreigners are concerned, are not far removed from those of W. E. Johns in the *Biggles* stories, with Mr. Kallonas being compared to a "Wop boxer;" the Maltese seen as criminal; and the Chinese chattering "frantically to each other like a cage of canaries." Macho man also needs to face his dislikes with an impressive show of physical force since it is usually all he has to offer. The violence in Westall's novels is particularly disturbing because of the author's implied attitudes to it. Violence seems to be admired, is seen as a sign of toughness and integrity. ***The Machine-Gunners,*** in this respect, is every bit as bad as its successors:

> He was very silent and very hard. He was the junior team scrum-half and had once played a whole match after losing two front teeth: spitting blood thoughtfully before putting the ball in the scrum, and scoring two tries.

Thoughtfully? And consider the implications of the word "satisfying" in this:

> Clogger moved like greased lightning. His steel toecap caught the first minion on the knee, leaving him writhing in the gutter. His fist caught the second full on the nose, drawing a satisfying stream of blood.

Satisfying to whom? This together with the clichéd simile "like greased lightning" and the hackneyed "writhing in the gutter" reduces the prose to the level of a comic or Richard Allen's obnoxious *Skinhead.*

In ***The Devil on the Road*** homosexuals are insultingly called "poufs" and are seen as predators:

> Was he a pouf, getting ready to take advantage of my drunken state? No, he wasn't a pouf. Girl like Susan wouldn't stay married to a pouf. Besides, I wasn't the type. Poufs like pretty-boys and I was as ugly as sin.

In an article called "Hetero, Homo, Bi or Nothing" that appeared in *Is Anyone There?* (a collection of essays and stories edited by Rosemary Sutcliff and Monica Dickens) Westall naïvely sees homosexuals as people who listen to Vivaldi, discuss poetry and play backgammon, while heterosexual men drink, discuss football and women. He shows no compassion for gay people, but he expresses a lot of sympathy for the heterosexual boy who's labelled a "pouf" by his mates. The fear of being called a "pouf" he sees as responsible for the lack of tenderness in young people—a simplistic piece of reasoning by any standards.

Westall's novels certainly won't help teenagers to feel tenderness; they're much more likely to leave young people disturbed and uneasy. They raise to the category of virtue far too many questionable human tendencies. John, in ***The Devil on the Road,*** is one of the nastiest central characters in recent teenage fiction, yet he's seen as a hero. He gets very soft about cats, but never about humans. He's a rather short-tempered, intolerant isolate who doesn't mind hitting people or dogs, even if he claims he's sorry to do so: to be sure, he is attacked by an Alsatian, but the description of his counter-attack is gloating, sick—

> I hit it a couple of left hooks, hard enough to drop any guy. No effect at all, except the sound effects of a Russian peasant being devoured by wolves. I kicked it in the guts. That discouraged it a bit, and it dropped on all fours, still having my gauntlet for breakfast. I kicked it again, in the ribs with every ounce I could put behind my Belstaff Roadrider. It made a sound like a big bass drum, and became merely one very thoughtful Alsatian. . . .

(pp. 115-19)

Westall's portrayal of relationships between men and women is often without gentleness. To macho man, women are for sex or doing the domestic chores; Johanna, John says, certainly knew how to look after her men. Macho man usually prefers talking to his own sex because it's safer, and he's more interested in proving he's as "male" as his peer-group than in entering a relationship which requires an ability to give, to love, to be tender. If Ted Hughes, in "Myth and Education" is correct in saying that great works of imaginative literature are hospitals where we heal, and that bad works of literature are battlegrounds where we get injured, then Westall's novels, particularly ***The Devil on the Road,*** fall into the second category.

I think a major problem with Westall's books is that the untrustworthy aliens, the chinless upper-class wets, the nagging working-class mums, the tarts with hearts of gold, the outdated slang ("jeepers") and the immature, cocking-a-snook-at-authority gleefulness of some of the attitudes, are found in TV comedy programs and old-fashioned boys' magazines, not in real life. But Westall's work is extremely fashionable, constantly praised by teachers and critics. Copies of ***The Machine-Gunners*** are found far more frequently in schools in Britain than any other recent novel for children set in the Second World War. Westall . . . is thought of by many people in the children's literature establishment as a major author. Perhaps his status has to do with what I see as defects being regarded by a great many people as real strengths. Westall must be very reassuring to the traditionalists who expect men to be tough and unsentimental, interested in motor-bikes and other suitable masculine toys; who feel women's proper place is beside the kitchen sink; who think of the Second World War as the last time "real" values were allowed proper scope; who may not object to breasts and swear-words in the teenage novel but who feel uneasy if there is any genuine exploration of teenage sexuality; who think that modern liberal tendencies are damaging the fabric of society; who regard the quality of the writing as less important than the "right" attitude.

The Scarecrows was also awarded the Carnegie Medal; Robert Westall is only the second author to have received this honor twice. It's a somber book, but, despite the illustrious award, it is not much of an improvement on its predecessors. It tells the story of Simon Wood, aged thirteen, driven almost to insanity because of the intense jealousy he feels about his mother's second marriage. He hears about a very unpleasant murder that happened a long time ago in an old mill house near where he lives, and he becomes aware of the spirits of the three people who died—the miller, his wife, and the wife's lover. The three dead people appear to him as scarecrows, and he realizes he could use them in his attempt to turn his mother against her new husband. There are clear echoes in this story of *The Owl Service*—the triangular relationship in modern times being manipulated by the triangular relationship that occurred in the past—and of *Marianne Dreams* by Catherine Storr, in which Marianne invests the stones she has drawn in her picturebook with a malevolent life of their own: they advance on the house just as Simon seems to invest the scarecrows with a kind of power, so that they also move threateningly on the house in which he lives.

There is some moderately effective writing in this novel, particularly in the descriptions of the mill and its garden. . . . Yet there are some extremely poor passages too. As usual, Robert Westall cannot handle the big, dramatic moments except by analogy, using a cluster of uneasy similes. Here is the destruction, in the last chapter, of the mill:

> There came a crack that made him turn. Then a series of sounds like sheet lightning. A whole snapped beam of timber, sharp as a lance, speared upward through the roof, sending a patch of tiles up into the air like birds. The windows burst out in hails of shining silver like snowflakes.

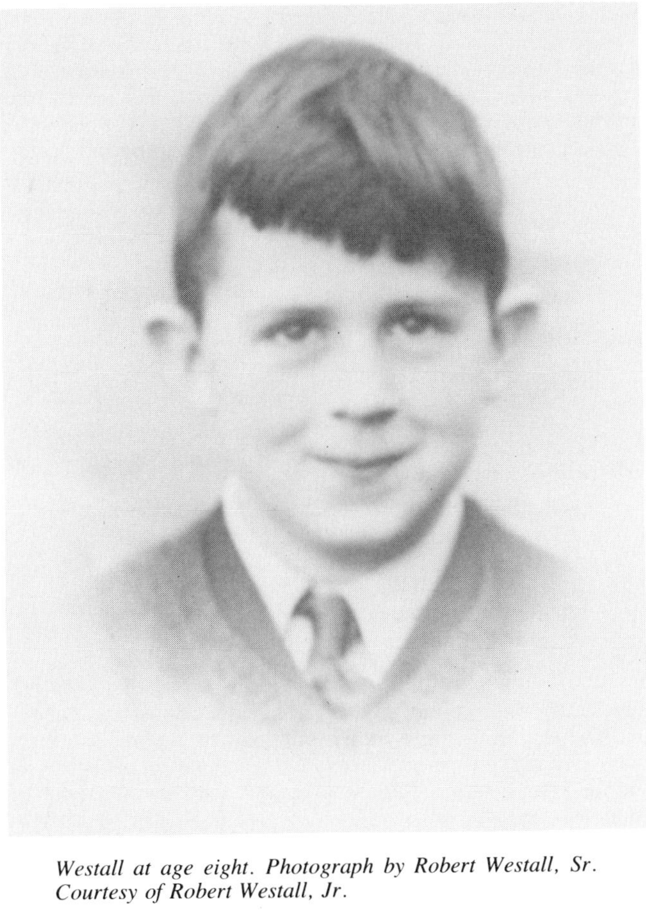

Westall at age eight. Photograph by Robert Westall, Sr. Courtesy of Robert Westall, Jr.

Lightning, a lance, birds, snowflakes, all in five lines! And can lightning have a *sound*? Do snowflakes really look like shining silver? What, one may ask, are "hails of shining silver"? Then there is the awkward sound of "upward" too close to "up". This kind of writing is not the literary excellence one would require of a Carnegie Medal Winner.

The story itself seems to me more of an exercise in *grand guignol* than the creation of a genuinely felt experience. Also, too much is left unexplained, or seems improbable. Why do the sightseers and the TV camera crews walk so carefully around the scarecrows? How—and why—is Tris la Chard capable of seeing into Simon's mind? Why does he have such an unlikely name? (It has some resonance that is not made clear.) Tris and Simon don't always think, or speak, convincingly for thirteen-year-olds. They sound, at times, a lot older. The adults—Mum and Joe Moreton—are more real, drawn more fully.

Most of Robert Westall's prejudices are still with him. There are derogatory references in ***The Scarecrows*** to homosexuals and it is time someone pointed out to Westall that gays in England like being called "poufs" about as much as American blacks like being called niggers. Just as bad is the continuing obsession with class. The speech and behavior of the upper middle-class people at the art gallery preview of Joe Moreton's drawings is simply not believable; coming from the pen of an experienced author the result is embarrassing.

Of course children need to read about the nastier aspects of life: a diet of nothing but talking rabbits and Nancy Drew will equip no one for anything. But when it comes to the Second World War, rather than ***The Machine-Gunners,*** I would give them Nina Bawden's *Carrie's War* which stresses inner integrity, not physical prowess; and for violence, rather than ***The Devil on the Road,*** I would give them Leon Garfield's *Black Jack,* in which Tolly Dorking's hitherto undiscovered strengths see him through—he is a hero who is physically weak, indeed puny, but capable of really caring about people, even his enemies. For teenage relationships—loving, affectionate, sexual, considerate—those in Jill Chaney's novels are superior to almost any other author's creations, though she is totally ignored by the establishment. Her male characters are particularly successful—rounded, credible, complex human beings—too successful perhaps: they don't fit into the slots society expects. Gary in *Mottram Park,* like John in ***The Devil on the Road,*** is a motorcycle enthusiast, but Jill Chaney shows that owning one of these machines is not just a way of proving you're a man by charging down village main streets at eighty miles per hour.

Machismo in teenage books, it seems to me, should be recognized and deplored. An emphasis on guts, big biceps, a good fighting fist, cleavages, manly men and little feminine women, on rejecting life-styles different from the hero's or the author's just because they *are* different, is no way to help young people to be complete human beings. This emphasis does not help them to grow up; it positively hinders the process.

There are, of course, aspects of Robert Westall's work other than male machismo that may be thought worthy of comment. ***The Wind Eye, The Watch House*** and ***The Devil on the Road*** are time-slip tales with elements of the supernatural, but compared to the work of other authors in this genre—Alan Garner, Penelope Farmer, Penelope Lively—Westall's writing here, too, seems second-rate, the fantasy elements more of a vivid, theatrical backdrop than something genuinely felt and conveyed compellingly to the reader. A comparison of ***The Devil on the Road*** with Penelope Farmer's *Year King* is revealing; in both novels there is sex, violence, a rural setting, a male hero who owns a motorcycle, time-slip—but in every way *Year King* is the finer book, particularly in its portrayal of the central character: Lan is a complex, interesting, credible young man, not a fantasy creation of big biceps and loud mouth. Both books are in some ways inheritors of the "blood and thunder" adventure story tradition that nineteenth-century writers for young people employed so often—indeed one might say that all Westall's books follow this tradition. In the nineteenth century, too, violence was sometimes handled brilliantly, sometimes poorly—R. M. Ballantyne's *Coral Island* is an example of a book in which the author, like Westall, seems to enjoy violence, and it therefore repels the reader instead of engaging his attention. On the other hand, R. L. Stevenson in *Treasure Island* and J. Meade Falkner in *Moonfleet* create fights and scenes of danger and excitement that are totally absorbing: the blood spills and the wounds are terrible, but there is no sensational mucking about in the blood and the guts. Robert Westall could perhaps write much more persuasively if only he would stop associating such matters with spurious "manly" virtues—Stevenson and Falkner never made this mistake. (pp. 119-24)

David Rees, "Macho Man, British Style—Robert Westall," in his Painted Desert, Green Shade: Essays on Contemporary Writers of Fiction for Children and Young Adults, *The Horn Book Inc., 1984, pp. 115-25.*

PETER HOLLINDALE

The quiet terraced house in Northwich, where Robert Westall has lived for many years, seems far removed from the embattled war-torn Tynemouth of his celebrated first book, ***The Machine-Gunners.*** But that sense of distance in space and time is not our experience in the book itself. The achievement of that extraordinary novel is its power to abolish the gap between then and now, and bring the Second World War to vivid, near-at-hand physical life for later generations of young readers. It is the work of a writer for whom the past is reachable, and time is important. (p. 2)

Robert Westall divides his novels into two kinds, the naturalistic-comic and the 'spooky', and ***The Wind Eye*** is undeniably spooky. Although it may have surprised the critics at first, it is the 'spooky' strain in his writing which has proved to be the dominant one. 'I doubt whether I shall do any more naturalist-comic books. They were the two I wrote for Christopher, to show him how it was to be me. That purpose is now served and is gone.'

Perhaps the two parts of Robert Westall's writing are less distinct than the categories make them sound. ***The Machine-Gunners*** and ***Fathom Five*** arose from the desire to let one period of childhood history exchange experience with another, and it is this selfsame interest that attracts him to ghost stories. Even Chas McGill, the machine-gunner himself, has a ghostly meeting with an earlier generation in the title-story of a more recent book, ***The Haunting of Chas McGill and Other Stories.***

> There is a freedom in ghostliness. You break the boring surface of life and let the underside come out. If everyday life is a flat plane, the ghostliness gives depth and height. It's a new dimension. It's also a way of bringing in time. I am fascinated by time, and I think time-slips are very useful. On the whole children don't read historical novels any more. They don't want to know what the seventeenth century said to the seventeenth, but they become quite interested in what the *twentieth* century might have to say to the seventeenth. I feel able, with research, to let the twentieth century talk to the seventeenth, and to see the seventeenth as an observer.

Sometimes the distant centuries can prove too close for comfort, as Jack Webster, the hero of ***The Devil on the Road,*** discovers to his cost. Jack is a very modern hero, independent, self-reliant and clever, whose idea of summertime undergraduate freedom is to set off on his motor-bike and commit himself to Chance. When he finds himself drawn into the seventeenth century, not by Chance but by unsuspected witchcraft, he needs all the resources of his twentieth-century intelligence to understand and survive the encounter. The final irony is that he needs a charm learned in the seventeenth century in order to escape its clutches. It is the unnerving mixture of remoteness and nearness, of alien threat and intimate beckoning, that characterizes the meeting of past and present in this as in several of Robert Westall's novels.

Much of the creative process goes on beneath the conscious level, and Robert Westall is guarded about extracting precise meanings from his books. He values mystery and uncertainty. It is the books' refusal to yield all their secrets that causes them to go on living after the last page is turned. Perhaps the most enigmatic of his books is ***The Scarecrows***. . . . The scarecrows have origins in reality. They were the work of a farmer who was a scarecrow artist, creating a new and striking group each year in a field on Salisbury Plain. One of these groups was seen by Westall during a drive, and struck him so deeply that he photographed it. Years later, coming across the photograph in a drawer at home, he found in it the cue for the unwholesome, menacing, yet somehow pitiable trio of his book. The scarecrow apparitions become intensely important to the boy Simon, during a holiday when he is sunk in bitter resentment and hostility at his widowed mother's remarriage. Somehow Simon and the scarecrows are entwined, but how?

> Simon's relationship with the scarecrows is a mystery to me. Things happen in my books that I don't understand. I know they're valid because I pull at them and they don't come apart, but I haven't calculated them. People try to corner me and ask if it was all in Simon's mind. Did he move the scarecrows himself? Are they a symbol of his unconscious or are they outside forces? I have to say that I don't know and don't want to know. Once I gave a final verdict it would become like a dead butterfly pinned to a cork board. While I haven't done that it's alive. I hate obscurity which is there merely to baffle the reader or to be impressive, but you can use obscurity to set up a thing which is dynamic and goes on living.

The Scarecrows is a memorable book, full of disturbing echoes and suggestions, with a tragedy of hate attempting to replay itself among new people in another generation. In this book too the supernatural is intimately linked with the mysteries of time.

Time and the generations are an essential part of Robert Westall's everyday life, not only his books. After many years as a teacher he has taken early retirement and is now an antique dealer. (pp. 2-3)

All the same, his many years as a teacher are not lightly put aside. . . . A great part of his teaching career was spent in Northwich, the last seven years in a newly established sixth-form college. The sixth-form age-group is one for which he feels particular affection, and he is very conscious of the pressures that bear on them in the contemporary world. They emerge vividly from his description—clear-headed, hard-working, utilitarian and pragmatic in their attitudes to learning, determined at all costs not to seem like schoolchildren. He feels a responsibility towards them, as a schoolmaster naturally so, but also as a writer. . . . 'There is always a wanting to help—not to tell them how to behave but to show them what's coming. Warnings, really.'

In his two roles as antique dealer and as teacher it is possible to see a reflection of the doubleness that makes his work so compelling, and allows him to handle disturbing themes and situations with such sure judgement. Always there is a sense of the past and of risk—many of his stories could be thought of as dangerous conversations through time—and they are shaped by an artistic integrity that rules out neatly packaged interpretations. Yet there is also something of the caring teacher, who is able to present moral challenges and encourage doubt and openness and exploration without ever destroying the final defences of moral necessity, and who can dramatize the grimmest ordeals for his heroes and heroines without dismantling ultimate faith and hope. It comes as a surprise to hear that his recent powerful science-fiction novel, ***Futuretrack 5,*** was turned down by one publisher because it appeared too despairing. Despite its uncompromising close, the nerve, intelligence and glorious bloody-mindedness of its hero offer constant promise of eventual release from the technocratic tyranny he challenges. That final perimeter of unbroken hope is there in all Robert Westall's excursions into past and future, and so is the moral concern. He feels that the freedom to explore moral questions is something he owes to the supernatural.

> I like ghosts because they can make morality a live issue. It's almost impossible in the present day to bring explicit morality into a book. I wouldn't dream of daring. I've been too much caught up with today's children. But somehow with ghosts the morality creeps back. You can talk about good and evil, provided you talk in a context of ghosts. I suppose I present moral questions in an anarchistic way. Most of my writing is mildly anarchistic. I like to leave fresh doubts in people's minds: doubts about whether the rigid structures are always right. I'm not foolish or brave enough to want to blow the whole structure up, but I do like to see it wobble.

Perhaps the most rigid structure of all is humanity's conviction of its own superior biological status, and this also Robert Westall has called in question. It is cats in particular who stand in his books for rival qualities and powers. His love of cats . . . will come as no surprise to his readers. Cats are frequent presences in his stories, sometimes as enigmatic couriers between one generation and another. In his recent historical fantasy ***The Cats of Seroster***—a book many years in the making but a new departure in his published work—it is the cats with their beauty and dignity and mysterious telepathic gifts who wield decisive power in a mean and bitter human conflict. The power is carried further still in his forthcoming novel ***Urn Burial,*** set in a kind of 'alternative world' where different species have gained the ascendancy. Here it is the cats who are the most advanced species, with *homo sapiens* several rungs down the ladder. 'I've tried to reduce man right down. Without saying that man is worthless, I am suggesting that man is puny. I dislike books where a human being comes into contact with other races or species and immediately becomes the centre and king-pin and hero.'

Characteristically, the message is disturbing and provocative without being destructive or hopeless. Robert Westall's books are written for readers who are still forming their attitudes to life, still malleable, still open to change. It is one reason why he is committed to writing for teenagers, and finds them a more challenging audience than adults. In the teenage years a book is potentially more than simply entertainment. It can make a difference to your view of the world. To Robert Westall this matters a great deal. 'I don't want fame. I hate public appearances. But power, the power that comes from what the books are doing, is very important. I have a desperate hope to write something that will, however minutely, change the way that people see things.' (pp. 3-4)

Peter Hollindale, "A Freedom in Ghostliness: Interview with Robert Westall," in British Book News Children's Books, *December, 1986, pp. 2-4.*

THE MACHINE-GUNNERS (1975)

AUTHOR'S COMMENTARY

[The first essay in this section is a letter from Mrs. P. S. Jones and seven other children's librarians from the London Borough of Bromley. Westall's response is featured in the second excerpt. For a further expansion of the issues discussed, see the entry dated January, 1977 for The Machine-Gunners.]

Once again we are in disagreement with the Committee's choice for the Carnegie Medal. We were distressed to find that violence and bad language should now be so acceptable, and indeed are sufficiently praiseworthy to be awarded a medal.

It was stated that it was the members' express wish that the Carnegie Medal should be awarded to a book definitely written for children and not for a more mature readership. It would seem that the Committee did not have this in mind when they selected ***The machine-gunners***. . . . The book has much bad language which is accepted as everyday speech by the children in the story, and the descriptions of the violence are altogether too vivid. Surely these traits should be discouraged in children, and not acclaimed nationwide. The plot itself *was* fast moving and exciting, but . . . "totally credible"?

Isn't it time that the medal was again awarded to a *real* children's book as it was originally intended?

Mrs. P. S. Jones and others, "Bad Language Honoured," in Library Association Record, *Vol. 78, No. 10, October, 1976, p. 497.*

I was interested to read Mrs. P. S. Jones's letter . . . criticizing my book ***The Machine-gunners*** for bad language, violence and incredibility of plot. It expresses a point of view that should be taken seriously and answered.

Bad language: The first reaction of one of my pupils who read the book was "Cor, sir, you weren't half *polite* in those days". From schoolmasterly observation I would have said that swearing among 11-year-olds has now reached saturation-point—every second word. Oddly enough, it seems to wear itself out in succeeding years—sixth formers hardly ever swear, at least within earshot of teachers. This, of course, refers to boys' behaviour among themselves—not at home, or, one presumes, in libraries.

Had I been a dedicated corrupter, I would have despaired of this sphere. The work is already done.

Swearing can be seen as part of the male adolescent's toughness ethic. Unlike shoplifting . . . , it is not criminal. Unlike smoking, drinking and riding mopeds too fast, it is not lethal either. So swearing only concerns me to the degree with which I want adolescents to empathize with my characters. Alas, any boy who does not swear today gets himself regarded as a freak or Establishment lackey. And who wants to read books about freaks and Establishment lackeys? So I allowed the boys in my book *minimal* swearing.

Violence: My descriptions of violence were nothing like as nasty as those in *The Lord of the Flies* which 14- and 15-year-olds are now studying for O level. Violence is one of adolescents' main interests today. Anybody who has tried a classroom debate on Northern Ireland will tell you that boys (at least) want to hang, shoot or burn the lot. It is an interest that needs addressing, and, ironically enough, in ***The Machine-gunners*** I tried to address it from the pacifist angle. If I have a voice in the book, it is that of the war-weary air-gunner Rudi, who is about as militaristic as the good soldier Schweik. The hero of the book, Chas, as a result of using violence loses his best friend, his gang, his most precious possession (the machine-gun) and his good name. Was there anything else *for* him to lose? Surely my whole theme is violence does not pay? Or is Mrs. Jones one of those who thinks we should not even *mention* violence "in front of the children"? That, to me, in our present situation, would be nothing less than rank cowardice. How can you condemn violence without mentioning it?

As to the unlikelihood of the plot, may I remark how many men in their 40s have mentioned to me what they got up to in the war. One wrote from Australia: "We found an unexploded 3.7" AA shell in the ruins of Coventry, and smuggled it through the city, strapped to the crossbar of my bike, with an old coat thrown over the top."

My doctor told me: "A Spitfire crash-landed on our public-school playing field in Lancashire. We got a whole suitcasefull of cannon shells, which we hid under the beds in our dormitory. The staff knew they were somewhere, but by smuggling them from place to place we kept them till the end of the war."

And so ad infinitum. Actually, there could be a splendid non-fiction book made, about 40-year-olds' recollections of what went on during the last war. A nice title might be ***The children of the Blitz*** [see title entry dated 1985]. Unfortunately, I haven't got the stamina to research it. I think it would make ***The Machine-gunners*** look like a vicarage teaparty. (p. 39)

Robert Westall, "Defence of—and by—Author Robert Westall," in Library Association Record, *Vol. 79, No. 1, January, 1977, pp. 38-9.*

Tyneside, 1940. A raiding German Heinkel is brought down in a wood. Local lad Chas McGill, fourteen or so, finds the wreckage and sees sticking from the ruined stern an undamaged machine-gun. At first the chance to pinch such a prize is motivated by nothing more than the craze for collecting bits of Jerry litter. But then an idea grows: why not spirit the gun away to some secret nest from where it is possible to let fly at hit-and-run bombers? Chas's bit for the war effort.

In ***The Machine-Gunners*** Robert Westall describes in unsparing detail the result of that dangerous thought. Chas is no angel, Tyneside then (as now) is a tough place to live, and the devastation wreaked by night is a cruel aid to brutalized sensibilities. Soon Chas has gathered about him an incongruously talented squad of contemporaries and one pathetic adult with a giant's strength, handy for building earthworks, but with a child's mind which prevents his betraying to harassed officials the deadly plan.

As the plot develops through twists and turns as unexpected and cliff-hanging as a thriller's, the episodes are morticed together with scenes from Chas and his squad's family and community life. These incidents are entirely necessary for an understanding of story and character. But at the same time they add up to a vivid, three-dimensional picture of that time and place: the battered streets, the refugee families, the weary nights and days, the shortages, the acts of courage, love, and decent neighbourliness, and the moments of desperation, cowardice and stupidity too.

There will inevitably be those who will wonder about offering ten or eleven year olds a book so uncompromising in language and incident as this. They might take note of the controlling element of humour which throughout redeems this story from any hint of maundering pleasure in the hellish horror it in part depicts, just as that same humour—ironic, sardonic, sometimes surgically brutal, but always in the end compassionate—relieved those who lived through the evil of the times.

Best of all in this book is Chas himself. Cunning, irreverent, disrespectful of pompous authority, healthily unimpressed by the bogus and dishonest. Tyneside breeds the race. Mr. Westall gets beneath his carapaced skin and touches the nerves inside. He reveals Chas's native intelligence and his resilience. It is this dimension of the book which makes it not just the best book so far written for children about the Second World War, but turns it into a metaphor for now.

Aidan Chambers, "War Efforts," in The Times Literary Supplement, *No. 3836, September 19, 1975, p. 1056.*

I can think of few writers who have put on paper as successfully as Robert Westall has done in ***The Machine-Gunners*** the sheer muddle of [the Second World War] and the day-to-day difficulty, for civilians at least, of deciding what was important. This book has a remarkable authenticity of atmosphere. It would be wrong to recommend it as anything but a story but if young people want to know what the war was really like, this book should go some way towards telling them. (p. 2707)

Robert Westall tells his story in a no-nonsense fashion, setting the scene with a light, pointed use of local idiom, cutting in moments at an early warning post, in an air raid shelter, at school, in the McGill's kitchen or Nicky's lonely bedroom, always with due attention to personality. The action of the story is dependent, ultimately, on character. Because Chas is what he is, or McGill his strict, responsible father, or Rudi with his gambling streak or the shrewd schoolmaster Liddell, certain events happen that cause more events, until the final moment when muddle and mistake come to their dangerous yet almost farcical climax. For the timing and tempering of the narrative, the free flow and the relevance of the dialogue, for the controlled humour and perception in the drawing of character, this is a notable first book. (p. 2708)

Margery Fisher, in a review of "The Machine-Gunners," in Growing Point, *Vol. 14, No. 4, October, 1975, pp. 2707-08.*

The cunning, initiative and courage which [the boys] show in carrying out their plan under the noses of the adults, as well as those of a suspicious rival gang, are totally convincing and most admirably recounted by the author, whose insight into the boy mind places him in the William Golding league. (pp. 55-6)

No better junior novel than this has appeared for a long time, and it is a 'must' for every school library serving boys and girls from eleven up to any age. Indeed, adult readers would learn a great deal from it. (p. 56)

Robert Bell, in a review of "The Machine Gunners," in The School Librarian, *Vol. 24, No. 1, March, 1976, pp. 55-6.*

The children, alternately tough as nails and audaciously funny, are delightfully individualized characters and Westall's writing is smashing throughout. Other adults might not be ready to share Mr. McGill's not so grudging admiration of his son's guts, but Westall leaves one free to draw a grimmer moral from the children's ingenious imitation of a grownup game. Seat-of-the-pants suspense with a premise that recalls *Lord of the Flies* and might provoke the same kind of debate.

A review of "The Machine Gunners," in Kirkus Reviews, *Vol. XLIV, No. 18, September 15, 1976, p. 1046.*

On reading the letter from Mrs P. S. Jones and seven children's librarians [see excerpt in Author's Commentary for *The Machine-Gunners*] one is instantly prompted to inquire how they would define a child. They seem to assume a cut-off age at around the end of primary school; in which case, what is to be the reading matter of those young people who are thereby denied further claim to childhood and must presumably wade straight into adult literature as "a more mature readership"?

In ***The Machine-gunners,*** Robert Westall has written about the age-group who happened to be what most of us would accept as children in wartime England—a period which has fascinated every subsequent generation, and which inevitably brought all ages into vivid contact with violence, fear and hatred. Mr Westall has said that one of his aims in writing a book is not just to portray life, but to put the reader into a situation that is "live", so that the dilemmas of the story are as real for him as for the protagonists. He feels that children need an element of the "horse's mouth" in their fiction as well as myth, and this cannot be achieved if reality is doctored (by the toning down of juvenile aggression, for example, or the omission of bad language).

As to Mrs Jones's doubts as to the credibility of the plot: quite apart from Robert Westall's own experience, he has apparently received letters and comments in response to the book from contemporaries whose anecdotes confirm that there is nothing exceptionally hair-raising about the exploits of Chas McGill.

Although ***The Machine-gunners*** will undoubtedly appeal most to children of secondary school age, it has been successfully read (unabridged) to at least one class of top primary children, who were inspired to pursue the theme as a project. Surely a piece of writing so perceptive and sympathetic towards children and adults alike, conveying a locality and era with such immediacy and humour, is worthy of formal recognition. The fact that it is at the same time "fast moving and exciting"—and eminently readable—must make it in the best sense a *real* children's book and, as such, it is heartening to find it awarded the Library Association's Carnegie Medal. (p. 38)

Rachel Boyd and others, "Defence of—and by—Author Robert Westall," in Library Association Record, *Vol. 79, No. 1, January, 1977, pp. 38-9.*

Things certainly crash down into bathos [in ***The Machine-Gunners***], as they could only do in a world of petty tyranny and officialdom where adults are largely pompous, vindictive, and ineffective. Teachers, police, and Home Guards go through their mindless routines, jealously guarding their preserves and frequently working against each other. As for the kids, they are cunning, tough as nails and, when occasion demands it, wholly ruthless. Even the nervous, sensitive boy whose parents were killed in the war reaches manhood on the last page. . . . That Westall is preoccupied with the violence in everyone is a possibility, but he throws scant light on the way people keep it in check, unless they do so by barrages of swearing and naked insults. The prize for violence must go to Clogger, a Glaswegian evacuee who takes on Boddser the head of a rival gang:

> "Had enough?" asked Clogger. Boddser nodded silently.
>
> "Aye, ye've had enough for now. Enough till ye get home and blab to your mother that I'm still in Garmouth, and where I'm living, and that Chas knows all about it. You know where the machine-gun is now, don't you? *And* your precious mother'll run straight to the police."
>
> Boddser's eyes flickered. Clogger had read his thoughts exactly.
>
> "They'll send you away to Borstal," he managed to mumble. "All of you."
>
> "If you tell them."
>
> "Try and stop me!"
>
> "Ah will!" Clogger raised his boot and kicked Boddser in the ribs three times. It made a terrible noise, like a butcher chopping a leg of lamb. Then he kicked him three more times. Boddser was much more sick now. When he looked up, his eyes had changed. He looked as if he understood something he had never understood before. . . .

It is as if Robert Westall had never liked Boddser, a sneak and bully of the Flashman variety, but there is a kind of ecstasy of violence here that is more than merely retributive. Quite clearly, what we are asked to admire in ***The Machine-Gunners*** above all else is physical toughness. (p. 77)

David L. James, in a review of "The Machine-Gunners," in Children's literature in education, *Vol. 8, No. 2 (Summer) 1977, pp. 76-8.*

THE WIND EYE **(1976)**

The author of a highly praised first novel must inevitably be faced with a difficult decision when he starts work on a second book. Should it be the mixture as before, a mixture proved to be popular and successful? Or would a complete change of direction be preferred, in order to avoid the inevitable critical comparison with its predecessor? Robert Westall has wisely settled for the latter course. . . .

Although the plot and characters of ***The Wind Eye*** bear no resemblance to those of his previous book, the ingredients of Robert Westall's new mixture have long been the staple constituents of English children's fiction. Take one academic, articulate family consisting of an austere professor, his capricious second wife and three children from their previous marriages; place them in a remote holiday cottage overlooking the Farne Islands on the Northumbrian coast; add the legend of St Cuthbert, still a force to be reckoned with in that part of England, together with the discovery of an age-old boat that can transport its occupants back into the time of the saint; stir briskly with dashes of vivid local colour, authentic dialogue and uncomfortably realistic family tension, and the result is that familiar dish: the family holiday-adventure-time-fantasy.

But, Robert Westall is too skilled and perceptive a writer to remain content with such a well-tried-recipe, and the family's experiences in and out of time are not used simply to provide exciting adventure, though the book has plenty of this. Robert Westall is primarily concerned with his characters, with the conflict between them, and with the way in which their attitudes and behaviour are changed, for better or worse, as a result of their experiences. By the end of the book, each member of the family has come to terms with themselves and with their relationship with each other; the benign influence of St Cuthbert has crossed the centuries and touched them all. ***The Wind Eye*** is a many-layered book, and it succeeds admirably on each level. Whether the book is viewed as exciting time fantasy or as a perceptive study of family behaviour, the reader is kept in thrall until the final page. And, above all, it reinforces Robert Westall's reputation as an exciting and stimulating new writer for the young.

Lance Salway, "Fantastically Familiar," in The Times Literary Supplement, *No. 3900, December 10, 1976, p. 1547.*

This is a book of extraordinary power. The blending of present and past is controlled with complete mastery. The modern children and their parents, and the conflicts within the family group, are drawn most convincingly. Perhaps the best of a very good book is the way in which the setting, which is hardly described at all, plays its vital role in the action. Wise, often funny, sometimes deeply moving, this book might have a formative influence on those children who can meet its formidable technical and emotional demands. (p. 123)

M. Crouch, in a review of "The Wind Eye," in The Junior Bookshelf, *Vol. 41, No. 2, April, 1977, pp. 122-23.*

Westall's merciless and unequivocal argument for the sort of unseen reality that the Cuthbert legend represents is unduly heavy and not likely to disarm other, unconverted Bertrands; but his plotting will keep them in thrall. The bickering parents are unpleasantly real enough to win identification with their offspring, and the compellingly evoked coastal locale makes the bridging of centuries there seem entirely natural.

A review of "The Wind Eye," in Kirkus Reviews, *Vol. XLV, No. 20, October 15, 1977, p. 1104.*

An intriguing time-shift story has a solid contemporary base and is at the same time a perceptive story of the adjustment to stepparents of three children who have an affinity that transcends their divided loyalties. . . . Westall's characterization is firm, particularly astute in drawing the petulant, egocentric Madeleine and her relationships with other family members. The plot is tightly constructed and nicely meshes realistic and fantastic aspects, and the story has good pace and a compelling narrative flow. (pp. 103-04)

Zena Sutherland, in a review of "The Wind Eye," in Bulletin of the Center for Children's Books, *Vol. 31, No. 6, February, 1978, pp. 103-04.*

THE WATCH HOUSE **(1977)**

The Watch House, set in the Robert Westall country of ***The Machine-Gunners,*** concerns Anne, who has been dumped like a lost parcel on Prudie, her mother's old nanny, during a family break-up. She becomes interested in the Watch House where the Garmouth Volunteer Life Brigade was founded and does its training, and plays billiards, and where there is a museum. The past begins to catch up with the present when Anne goes to dust the display cases there, and through her two unsettled ghosts begin to work towards their final enmity against each other. She is searching for a solution to her own problems, and because she takes the ghosts seriously they are able to feed on her, becoming a visible force until in the end one is exorcised under the putting green and the other finds quietude.

It is a fast-moving, action-packed story written in a racy style; the dialogue is sharply observed and makes the necessary genuflections towards a little bit of sex, a little bit of violence and a bit more of the occult (there are several hypnotic trances). . . . [The] trouble is that too many of the characters look and sound like caricatures; there are two fathers, one Catholic and the other C of E, who are like a religious Morecambe and Wise show; there is Timmo and Pat, a Professor Branestawm with his young assistant; Anne's parents, her mother spoilt and flighty, her father big, golden hearted; and even a shaggy dog and a Gallower pony, who perform their expected roles in the story. Anne is the only character who is not caricatured: and, curiously enough, she is the least well-known of all.

There seems to be a lack of respect between the author and his characters, and because the story does not evolve from the interplay of relationships between them, it has to do all the work on its own. In fact, the story is made to do too much work. After the exorcism, the Catholic father is seen trying to invest it with a deep, inner meaning. But too many of the mortices and tenons show through its craftsmanship for it to be capable of bearing such a meaning.

Ralph Lavendar, "Sea Scapes," in The Times Educational Supplement, *No. 3258, November 18, 1977, p. 40.*

The combination of genuine adolescent problems and the ghost story is a curious paradigm of the dilemma of the older-children's book. Even the best authors have foundered on the reefs of paradox where psychological reality and psychological fantasy sit rather uncomfortably.

Robert Westall's ***The Watch House*** is another attempt to blend the two, and after his Carnegie Medal winner ***The Machine-***

Gunners, it is rather disappointing. There is great potential in the twist—a ghost who is himself haunted—and more in that the ghosts' powers both reflect and derive from the heroine's uncertainty and loneliness. . . . Unfortunately, after a strong beginning, where both relationships and mysteries are hinted at, much of the plot is expedient rather than organic, the characters more pointmakers than people, and Westall's version of Tynemouth, Garmouth, has become little more than a collection of postcard pictures.

Thus, at first, when Anne is dumped by her rather overdrawn bitchy mother with the old people, Prudie (a collection of mannerisms) and Arthur (a gem of a cameo), there are subtle connections established with the history-riddled watch house of the lifeguards, and its frightened ghost. But once she has re-lived the ghost's traumas, watching shipwreck and murder, the mechanics begin to dominate; the ghost's Morse messages, the amateur hypnotism, and the jumbled exorcism at the end are all not far short of both the routine and the ludicrous. None the less, much of the horror is genuinely chilling—as when Anne finds herself on the pier at nightfall with both ghosts; and many of the incidents shrewdly conceived—the two priests playing their blasphemous fog-bound tennis. Overall, ***The Watch House*** seems to be an unrealized achievement, the draft of a good book; rather too ready to fall on the obvious simile, and the next happy ending.

Peter Hunt, "Haunting the Haunted," in The Times Literary Supplement, *No. 3949, December 2, 1977, p. 1408.*

The price of admission to ***The Watch House*** is high in terms of effort and patience demanded, but for those readers who can manage the challenging vocabulary and major doses of British slang and dialect, the rewards are numerous and varied. Westall is a wordsmith of consumate skill in the tradition of Stevenson and Kipling; his characters are believable, unique, and multi-dimensional; and he has important things to say about values; responsibility, and relationships. Most other books of the same genre seem absolutely pallid by comparison.

Chuck Schacht, in a review of "The Watch House," in School Library Journal, *Vol. 24, No. 8, April, 1978, p. 99.*

As in ***The Wind Eye*** Robert Westall uses a real landscape, this time lightly disguised, as the setting for a story of great power, in which human relationships are set against, and perhaps give the motive force to, psychic phenomena. ***The Watch House*** is a great ghost story, one of the best ever, but it is much more. (p. 163)

[The story] is much too good to spoil with advance relevation. Enough to say that here is magnificent story-telling, shrewd observation of human behaviour, suspense and thrills, and pervading humour. Robert Westall reinforces his claim to be the most original writer of children's books to appear in this country in the last five years. (pp. 163-64)

M. Crouch, in a review of "The Watch House," in The Junior Bookshelf, *Vol. 42, No. 3, June, 1978, pp. 163-64.*

THE DEVIL ON THE ROAD (1978)

Where Robert Westall differs from other exponents of a 'Time' theme is that he allows a greater degree of participation in the past. Others may be content to let their time explorers be witnesses to past events; John Webster, in this remarkable story, is right up to his neck in them.

Westall's son Christopher, for whom Westall wrote The Machine Gunners *and who later served as the model for John in* The Devil on the Road. *Photograph by Robert Westall, Jr.*

Through the operations of Lady Chance, John finds himself set up as caretaker and odd-job-man in a Suffolk barn. The barn had been a manor-house in the seventeenth century—the book is a marvellous exercise in local history and archaeology—and, through the agency of a time-cat, John slips back into the time of the Civil War and becomes Master Jack, confidant and defender of a charming white witch. It is the period and the home ground of Matthew Hopkins, Witchfinder General, and there is a convincing portrait of this revolting cheat. Not content with his hazardous visits to Cromwell's England, John brings Johanna back with him to modern Suffolk to become the 'yarb-mother' of the country folk. (Mr. Westall's Suffolk has deeper roots than the weekend cottage society which most of us see.)

It is a good idea, but Mr. Westall's novels are about people, not ideas. There is less conflict here than in, for example, ***The Wind Eye,*** but there is particular interest in the central figure. John is superficially very much a young man of his own time, a motor-cycling engineering undergraduate, rugger-playing and hard-swearing. His Achilles heel is a weakness for cats. By adopting the kitten he calls News, he not only guarantees himself access to the past but opens up the buried well of compassion in himself. As always with this most brilliant of writers, characters are clearly drawn in all their idiosyncratic oddity. There is a convincing local squire with his sexy modern wife, and the locals, contemporary peasants and importations alike—there is a lovely thumbnail sketch of a secondhand bookseller—are equally vivid.

The book makes demanding reading, not merely the acceptance of the improbable but the ability to follow the author's closely reasoned argument. But perhaps it is not absolutely necessary to understand it all. Surrender to a fascinating idea and to a tale supremely well told will bring its rewards.

M. Crouch, in a review of "The Devil on the Road," in The Junior Bookshelf, *Vol. 43, No. 2, April, 1979, p. 124.*

At a first reading I felt that the historical sources for ***The Devil on the Road*** were too obtrusive in the narrative, but a second reading made the careful structure of the book and the skilful correlations of past with present a good deal more apparent. . . . Since it would appear that young John Webster did in the end change the course of history, or at least of one small part of it, it is perhaps best not to examine too closely the logic of his interaction with the past but rather to surrender to the vivid details which ostensibly explain it—the atmosphere of the barn . . . , the cat who adopts him and seems to hold the secret of time-change, the Sealed Knot battle-spectacle which puts John into the necessary mood for communicating with Johanna, and above all the powerful image of the motor-bike and crash-helmet, seen as devilish engines by superstitious seventeenth-century folk. There is a moral in the book but it is implicit rather than dominant: those who accept the committed force and feeling of the story, its intermittent humour and strongly authentic idioms, will also accept the proclamation against violence and cruelty without feeling they are being bullied by the author. (pp. 3516-17)

Margery Fisher, in a review of "The Devil on the Road," in Growing Point, *Vol. 18, No. 1, May, 1979, pp. 3516-17.*

Topping even the British author's ***The Machine-Gunners*** and other splendid novels, Westall's latest is fast, utterly convincing and spiced by narrator John Webster's rakish delivery. . . . The suspense is artfully sustained as John tries to make sense out of the 17th and the 20th centuries as he slips almost on greased wheels from one to the other. This is a gripping, witty entertainment that readers will find themselves thinking about, long after they close the book.

A review of "Devil on the Road,"in Publishers Weekly, *Vol. 216, No. 10, September 3, 1979, p. 96.*

There are always problems with time travels which involve real histories, and ***The Devil on the Road*** does not escape them, though Westall handles the transitions with great subtlety and skill. But the writing is so charged and vigorous, the timing of the plot so carefully measured, that the customary difficulties are minimized.

John Webster seems very real indeed, and likable; and even better, there is a young cat, . . . who is surely one of the best and most charmingly drawn cats I've ever encountered in a book. Her presence in the story does for it what real cats can do for real life—she is all animal but still profoundly enigmatic, a creature of many wisdoms, a link between the known and the unknown. As such she epitomizes the story itself in all of its convolutions. The author is to be congratulated on a superb characterization here.

Without the cat and John Webster's hard-edged, vivid voice, ***The Devil on the Road*** would be just one more in terms of suspension of disbelief. And for this reader, at any rate, the book's final section, in which a group of characters from the past cross back into the present with John, allows disbelief to drop down again with a clunk. For me, the shape of the novel is damaged hereby, and the fragility of the premise fatally exposed.

But American teenagers ought to enjoy this story very much and identify easily with John in spite of his British idioms. He is blessedly three-dimensional and therefore more than welcome in a field where two-legged stools have been letting everybody down long enough. (p. 21)

Natalie Babbitt, "All Aboard the Broomstick!" in Book World—The Washington Post, *November 11, 1979, pp. 21-2.*

Set in both today's England and Civil War England, the book describes the experiences of John Webster in each time period. The author attempts to develop the main character and to set the basis for the novel before he allows Webster to traipse back and forth in time. The results are useless. . . .

[From the point when Webster] enters the barn, the story begins. Clues are laid to events that occur later. Illogicalities are logically unknotted. And the curious title's meaning is revealed. The denouement, however, depends on nearly nothing from the dull first section of the book.

What sustains the story is a fictionalized account of a witch hunt in Cromwell's England. Transported back to that era, Webster finds himself forced to decide whether to accept passively the obvious wrong of witch hunting like most inhabitants of that period or to resist. Factors like his ability to transcend time and knowledge of past events help him make his decision. In such instances, the reader is given a dose of suspense and morality.

Those two components rescue ***The Devil on the Road*** from the "So bad, it will never be stolen from the library" category. And even though the author treats hackneyed themes of time travel and witchcraft, he successfully deals with the themes by subordinating them to the chief personalities of the book rather than letting the themes dictate to the personalities their behavior. (Only occasionally do these primary personalities discuss anything that may serve as a catalyst to young reader's hormones, thus meriting the book a "B" rating.)

R. Greggs, in a review of "The Devil on the Road," in Best Sellers, *Vol. 39, No. 10, December 1979, p. 356.*

FATHOM FIVE (1979)

[The British edition of Fathom Five *features Jack Stokoe as the protagonist, while the American edition has Chas McGill as the main character.]*

Robert Westall's first book, ***The Machine-Gunners,*** attracted a lot of attention when it was published in 1975, and not only for literary and historical reasons. It won the Carnegie medal but still causes problems to many librarians and teachers. A Welsh librarian recently recalled that he had asked a group of teachers to read it for a seminar. Had they all enjoyed it? Yes. Did they think their pupils would enjoy it? Yes. Would they be using it in school? No, unanimously no.

The same controversies will surround the new book, ***Fathom Five.*** Westall has returned to the scenes of his own wartime youth: Newcastle lightly disguised as Garmouth. It is a few years later—the spring of 1943. Cem Jones is in the sixth form; Audrey Parton is working on the *News,* Chas McGill (Robin Hood and Superman rolled into one) has left the town, and Jack Stokoe is a very different hero. Sheila Smythson is the daughter of a bigwig. The four of them track down a spy.

There's a good deal of messing about in boats, and the book will undoubtedly be read by eleven and twelve-year-olds whose parents would prefer them to be reading Arthur Ransome. It is as far away from *Swallows and Amazons* as it is possible to be. Ransome knew about spying but he did not think that whores and drunks belonged in children's books. In fact, ***Fathom Five*** might claim some sort of record as the first book published in a children's list to mention syphilis.

It would be a pity, however, if timid teachers and librarians steered clear of this book. Certainly children won't be shocked by it. They may find it difficult; the plot is complex but convincing. Things like this really were going on, and it seems perfectly credible that these observant sixteen-year-olds should have got involved in them. The story is seen through Jack's eyes with a slangy, jerky, hectic style to match. Personally, I prefer Robert Westall exploring the relationship between truth, belief and legend (for instance in ***The Wind Eye***). In this book he goes entirely for realism. He touches on left-wing politics ("Hitlers come and Hitlers go but the *real* war, between workers and bosses, that never ends"), he shows a good understanding of human relationships (Jack and Cem; Jack and Sheila), but really the only thing that matters is the plot and the teeming life of the Low Street area of Garmouth in that wartime summer.

Ann Thwaite, "Alarms of War," in The Times Literary Supplement, *No. 4004, December 14, 1979, p. 125.*

Robert Westall is one of four or five notable British writers of fiction for children to have emerged in the seventies: a light crop, compared with that of the previous decade. His first book, ***The Machine-Gunners,*** deservedly won the Carnegie Medal for 1976. Since then he has published a book each year and has become firmly established. The next three books did not have quite the impact of the first, but all showed creative force and individuality and had a powerful emotional charge. . . .

[***Fathom Five*** is] a teenage novel: fairly gamey in parts, and concerned a good deal with adolescent matters (self-discovery, discovery of the other sex, discovery of what the world is about) which are not particularly interesting to pre-pubescent children.

The best parts of ***Fathom Five*** are not the teenage parts but those which it has in common with ***The Machine-Gunners.*** In the earlier story, a gang of children smuggle a machine-gun out of a crashed German bomber, perilously determined to make their contribution to the war effort, and almost causing disaster. Jack Stokoe, in ***Fathom Five,*** fishes out of the river a contraption which indicates that someone is transmitting vital information about Allied shipping to the Germans. The difference is that Jack's contribution is a real one; there *is* a spy, and Jack uncovers him.

The middle-of-a-war atmosphere, the life and speech of a Tyneside family, the picture of town and river are alive and vivid; the story of spy-detection is a strong one and (in the first few chapters) convincing. Yet the book goes off the rails. Partly the trouble is simply that the action becomes less credible. When Jack's two teenage girl friends dress up as whores in order to penetrate a disreputable part of town where policemen only go around in pairs, when Jack himself forms a beautiful friendship with the brothel-keeper, Nelly Stagg, who turns out to be a golden-hearted grandma-figure, suspension of disbelief becomes not so much unwilling as impossible.

Then, although Jack as the ordinary lad messing about on the Fish Quay Sands and scrapping with his pal Cem is fine, Jack as the incipient thinker and potential Oxford open scholar doesn't quite join up with that other Jack or carry real conviction. While Jack's relationships with his parents and his male friend have the ring of truth, his friendship with bourgeois Sheila is a thin, artificial construction. And the closing pages are imbued with a crude and surely unreasonable hatred for "the Bosses", who are implausibly shown as making a self-congratulatory party for themselves out of Jack's achievement while humiliating *him.*

One is reluctant to criticize a book for the elements which probably, in the author's eyes, made it worth writing. Yet I am sure that ***Fathom Five*** would have been more successful if it had attempted less. It would have worked better as a straight spycatching story with fewer social and psychological complications.

John Rowe Townsend, "Jack for All Seasons," in The Times Educational Supplement, *No. 3319, January 18, 1980, p. 41.*

The book is a compelling spy story for teenage readers in which the accidental discoveries and suspicions of a clever schoolboy convincingly succeed in exposing what officialdom has missed. But the true weight and strength of ***Fathom Five*** come from its compassionate depiction of war's unnoticed victims, and its harsh representation of the corruption, bigotry and social prejudice which set Garmouth at war with itself. Almost nothing and no one, its hero discovers, can be taken at face value. ***Fathom Five*** is a harsh, witty, passionate book: a better book than ***The Machine-Gunners,*** and that is praise indeed.

Peter Hollindale, in a review of "Fathom Five," in British Book News, *Children's Supplement, Spring, 1980, p. 18.*

The densely packed plot becomes at times confusing and lacking in cohesion. The pace is consistently fast, but the relentless action leaves little room for character development, which is unfortunate because many unusual and interesting characters are introduced. There is no reference to the children's previous experiences in ***The Machine Gunners;*** it is difficult to believe that these would have no impact. Yet once again, Chas comes to realize that war is not a game. The complex novel contains action, intrigue, and suspense but suffers from a lack of clarity and a monotonous tone as well as from the underdeveloped characterizations.

Christine McDonnell, in a review of "Fathom Five," in The Horn Book Magazine, *Vol. LVI, No. 5, October, 1980, p. 531.*

THE SCARECROWS (1981)

Robert Westall is an angry writer: angry with the present, with the past, with the female sex. His characters are choked with feelings they cannot express. His settings have a Hardyesque rankness and malevolence. Anger is the Westall fuel, but its power, like that of the medieval water mill in this new book, can prove to be the cause of its destruction.

The Scarecrows is saved from disappearing down its own emotional vortex by two things, both recognizable Westall characteristics: a terrifyingly acute understanding of teenage boys, and the presence of a menace from the past which sets into relief the terrors of the mind.

Continuing a progression up and around the English social scale, ***The Scarecrows*** is set in Sunday supplement land. Simon Brown, en route to Wellington, survives, just, his last term at a horrible (but recognizable) prep school. Unaware of what he is doing, he half kills the class bully after some flesh-creeping taunting in the dorm. The Head talks vaguely about growing up and glands, but Simon is conscious only of devils raging inside him—devils which vent their fury on his mother's new husband, a successful Scarfe-type cartoonist. Joe is everything Simon's own father was not—crass, corpulent, fleshly, bohemian, gentle, left-wing, and affectionate. But it is his mother's happiness that Simon resents even more than Joe, and his attempts at sabotaging it nearly succeed. Filled with loathing after spying on Joe and his mother's lovemaking, Simon sets up his dead father's army uniform to sit by the bed where they did *"all that"* (graphically described in this broadminded book).

Now the past intervenes. A presence emanates from the old watermill and takes shape in three frighteningly life-like scarecrows which gradually make their way from the mill across the turnip field to Joe's house. Simon identifies them as participants in a pre-war tragedy of passion that ended in murder and closed the mill for ever. The events of the past are going to be re-enacted unless Simon can break the power of the mill. . . .

The mill, at times silent and secretive in its bitter knowledge, at times pounding itself to pieces with pent-up fury, precisely expresses Simon's state of mind. Yet Westall is too good a writer to allow his imagery to intrude; or to overstate his parallels. How people talk and relate to each other, to their families and to themselves is what his work is really about. And despite its earnest intent, his story is exciting, agonizing, tender and terrifying by turns, and never fails to grip.

One gripe remains: when is Westall going to produce a likable female? His women are depicted as quasi-boys, thumb-sucking flirts or neurotic sex objects. Although narrated in the third person, ***The Scarecrows*** portrays an adolescent consciousness with consequent preoccupation with the physical and specifically sexual, and this is perhaps an excuse for the monstrous female threat. It does, nevertheless, make for a disturbing imbalance in this and other novels.

Sarah Hayes, "Threats from Within," in The Times Literary Supplement, *No. 4069, March 27, 1981, p. 339.*

Robert Westall is a writer with an obsession: violence. His books explore the destructive power of immature emotion, often using the supernatural as a mirror to reflect the mind's anguish. . . . [***The Scarecrows***] is a disturbing book; and, it seems to me, a disturbed one.

Westall is a talented writer, capable of achieving powerful effect, but in ***The Scarecrows*** he eschews the discipline which should harness passion. The book has no emotional shape, it simply blasts the reader with a scream of pain and insecurity. The pitch never varies. And in the end the resolution is not emotional but physical: the dramatic destruction of the mill.

What Robert Westall leaves out of account is anger's creative edge. There is no sense that anger is a valuable, necessary thing: it is simply a sort of bully inside the head, driving us to bestial atrocities. Not only does Simon's anger have no check, it has no balance. The contrast with other teenage books which deal uncompromisingly with adolescent anger—*A Game of Dark, The Owl Service, The Summer After the Funeral*—is stark, and not to Westall's advantage.

Westall is dealing in ***The Scarecrows*** with very tricky subject matter: and a certain crudity of apprehension, connected with this misconception of the nature and function of anger, lends an unwelcome voyeuristic feverishness to the more highly-charged scenes. The passages in which Simon eavesdrops on his mother and her new husband making love evoke a queasy shame in the reader which is artistically counter-productive. It is just this sense of complicity in Simon's psychotic jealousy which needs to be avoided if the book is to provoke a measured rather than an hysterical response.

The Scarecrows reads like a book written in a fury; a monument to misdirected energy. When so few writers for teenagers are prepared to face the central issues of life, it is sad that Robert Westall's gaze should be obscured by a film of blood.

Neil Philip, "Through a Film of Blood," in The Times Educational Supplement, *No. 3385, May 8, 1981, p. 27.*

The loss of innocence, and its accompanying outrage of emotions, is Robert Westall's questing ground. He crafts his plots from the dark centre of his characters, and draws his readers in by a touch on what they scarcely admit to themselves. Adults simply seem to see the brats behaving badly. Here is Simon adjusting to his mother's remarriage to an artist. The events are played out near an old mill, with scarecrows—the symbols between the present and the past. The hints are deeper, of course, and Freud is hovering. Robert Westall is a powerful writer, in every sense, but sometimes I wonder if he isn't also, intuitively, doing to his readers what Simon did to the scarecrows. (pp. 157-58)

Margaret Meek, in a review of "The Scarecrows," in The School Librarian, *Vol. 29, No. 2, June, 1981, pp. 157-58.*

To rid himself of hate, Simon must first come to terms with the darkness of the scarecrows—which he does, in a rousing and compelling climax. Although readers may encounter confusion at every turn of Simon's neurotic thought and act, the story is the author's most effective and tightly constructed piece of writing. Simon, Moreton, Simon's mother, even minor characters are clearly and believably developed, and Westall's empathy and understanding for these characters are unique. His storytelling, characterized by short, staccato sentences and some Briticisms, is, as usual, superior. Scarey, and Westall's best yet.

Jack Forman, in a review of "The Scarecrows," in School Library Journal, *Vol. 27, No. 10, August, 1981, p. 80.*

The psychological clearly dominates the supernatural element in this latest and most tightly integrated of Westall's highly charged and textured chillers. . . . (Hamlet in his mother's chamber might be Simon's model in cunning and Oedipal outrage.). . . . [The] final, heart-pounding destruction of the externalized terrors purges Simon's devils with the force their hold on him requires. Powerful currents, powerfully contained within the bounds of a hard-packed juvenile fantasy.

A review of "The Scarecrows," in Kirkus Reviews, *Vol. XLIX, No. 18, September 15, 1981, p. 1166.*

Heavy stuff, and the plot is unduly complicated. Moreover, Simon does seem uncommonly irascible in the face of his parents' efforts, especially those of his stepfather, to bring him into the family. Still, here are striking portraits of people whose needs often force them to hurt others. This is a bold and briskly written novel that takes a lot of chances. It should appeal to young readers who like their books vigorous, whatever the flaws.

Malcolm Bosse, in a review of "The Scarecrows," in The New York Times Book Review, *May 16, 1982, p. 29.*

BREAK OF DARK **(1982)**

None of the stories in ***Break of Dark*** has a young eye at the centre; none of them is on a theme that might be supposed to be of interest to young people in particular. This is not to say that young people won't enjoy them. . . .

They could be described as Robert Westall's Tales of the Unexpected. All have supernatural elements. The beautiful naked blonde who appears from nowhere in the first story, **"Hitchhiker,"** to inveigle the male narrator into fathering her golden triplets, is clearly not human—in spite of which the narrator's attitude may raise some hackles: "These creatures . . . could be running our world before I was an old man. And somehow I knew they would always be female; males they could pick up here—any male would do."

Fred, Alice and Aunty Lou, horrible relatives invented as a practical joke, turn out to have a life of their own; the rector of a city church finds himself booking a funeral for a healthy-looking gentleman aged 192; a seaside police sergeant is baffled by a stone horse-trough that swallows people's property. All these are well in the tradition of the eerie tale. They are technically accomplished, though not quite worth the space they occupy; the last of them, **"Sergeant Nice,"** sprawls over an inexcusable 51 pages.

The story that stands out is **"Blackham's Wimpey."** A German pilot, dying horribly in his blazing Junkers to the callous laughter of the crew that gunned him, returns to haunt not only this crew but their aircraft, driving men to death or madness. Oddly, the supernatural element here seems marginal to the real horror of air warfare, described with a conviction that makes the palms sweat. This story has the narrative power and emotional charge—and the violence—that make Westall at full strength a writer of disturbing brilliance.

John Rowe Townsend, "Power of Violence," in The Times Educational Supplement, *No. 3441, June 11, 1982, p. 40.*

In his first collection of stories, Robert Westall . . . shows himself a master of the art of creating eerie presences that can intrude into the sunlight of an ordinary day. His title ***Break of Dark*** is significant, for in each of the five stories something is heard, seen, or felt to have broken loose from its dark resting place. That is all the stories have in common, for their landscapes, characters and the nature of the breakout are all quite distinct. . . .

Robert Westall's robust style and settings have a solidity about them that makes the intrusion from the dark all the more uncomfortable. . . .

The façade of stolid reality and the familiar pettiness of ordinary people just occasionally cracks to afford a glimpse of the void. Mr Westall is quick to plaster over the crack, but the dark lingers on.

Sarah Hayes, "Glimpses of the Void," in The Times Literary Supplement, *No. 4138, July 23, 1982, p. 789.*

Robert Westall gets better and better. In fact these five stories make my point for me. I don't know in which order they were written, but the fantasy gets more subtle and more deeply integrated with the commonplaces of ordinary life from first to last. His theme throughout is the thin line which divides the placid homeliness of our everyday environment from the wonder and terror of the unknown. So we have a camper picking up a girl hitch-hiker who happens to be naked: she said her clothes had been stolen—a likely story! . . . Then a Wellington bomber becomes haunted by the ghost of a German pilot. A trifle overwritten, this one. For convincing nastiness, **"Fred, Alice and Aunty Lou"** takes some beating. . . . A shorter and on the whole more conventional tale about a haunted church gains credibility by its setting among the deserts of a Northern inner city. The last story—**"Sergeant Nice"**—has a gem of a central character, a gentle bobby in a seaside town grappling with problems of such vast improbabilities that only one whose enormous boots are firmly on the ground could comprehend them. A small masterpiece this, just the right length, with enough detail to win belief, not so much as to destroy the wonder and the terror.

Mr Westall is the lord of this no-man's-land on the edge of experience. He will surely win new admirers with this book, especially from those teenagers for whom reading is usually a repugnant chore. (pp. 155-56)

M. Crouch, in a review of "Break of Dark," in The Junior Bookshelf, *Vol. 46, No. 4, August, 1982, pp. 155-56.*

Five short stories recall Roald Dahl's bizarre tales for adults. Like his, these stories are rooted in the most ordinary English settings, but unlike his, they center on characters who are pleasant, reasonable, and attractive. Poor souls. Whether Westall writes about a young climber and his affair with a dazzling girl who turns out to be a shrewd extra-terrestrial, or a bomber crew in World War II whose radio blasts out the screams of a German pilot shot down some months earlier by the plane's former crew, the characters are driven to violent acts of heroism or retaliation in order to maintain their sanity or to protect their neighbors. . . . Well constructed and fast-paced, if without Dahl's slashing dazzle, each story touches on the supernatural. And each one, kept believable by the homely details of everyday life, is chillingly absorbing.

Ethel R. Twichell, in a review of "Break of Dark," in The Horn Book Magazine, *Vol. LVIII, No. 6, December, 1982, p. 663.*

THE HAUNTING OF CHAS McGILL AND OTHER STORIES **(1983)**

Eight British stories of ghosts, time-warps, and futurist fantasy—less consistent than the tales in ***Break of Dark*** (1982), with very little particular appeal to teenage readers. The most distinctive item is the most adult one: **"The Dracula Tour,"** in which a prim English housewife . . . finds herself being seduced by a certain count during a package tour to Transylvania. And **"The Vacancy"** is a strong, quick blend of *1984* futurism with a speck of sci-fi—as a bright, rebellious young man looks for a job in an England of epic unemployment. But, though **"The Night Out"** is an intriguing variation on the pressure-to-conform story (with a rough biker as the ambivalent hero), the other pieces are far less fresh: two excessively similar re-runs of *Twilight Zone*-style time travel; and several cats, ghosts, and creatures, including one that preys on "women alone; women in despair." Solid enough work, then, but—with British allusions and few youth concerns—no special treat. (pp. J209-J210)

A review of "The Haunting of Chas McGill and Other Stories," in Kirkus Reviews, *Juvenile Issue, Vol. LI, No. 21, November 1, 1983, pp. J209-J210.*

As might be expected in a collection of stories by the author of such superb novels as ***The Watch House*** (. . . 1978) and ***The Machine Gunners*** (. . . 1975), there is a great deal of quality writing here. Indeed, some of these selections shine like gems, especially those which deal with the mysterious powers of cats in a fashion reminiscent of H. P. Lovecraft. Another recurring theme which Westall deals with very skillfully is the bleakness of a future without meaningful and challenging work. The frustration of his young protagonists is palpable as they face a world which has no need of them and offers them no opportunity to develop either their skills or ideals. In spite of the author's keen insights and literary skills, however, there are two problems presented by this collection which almost guarantee that it will not find a wide audience. The first is his pervasive use of British expressions; the second and probably greater problem is the differing age levels for which the various stories seem written. Several seem written for fifth or sixth graders, while others are essentially adult. Hard core fans of Westall's previous work will find much to enjoy here, but most YAs may well find the aforementioned drawbacks too great to overcome, unfortunately.

Chuck Schacht, in a review of "The Haunting of Chas McGill and Other Stories," in School Library Journal, *Vol. 30, No. 5, January, 1984, p. 90.*

While none of the stories is actually frightening, they do provide pleasurable reading. This is mostly due to Westall's uncanny ability to mold dynamic and well-rounded characters. (Especially worthy of attention are the children he creates; they are reminiscent of those created by the late Frank O'Connor—most notably Jackie in "First Confession.")

Still, this is not a book for children. The language employed by the characters, while not sexually explicit, is nonetheless objectionable and often crude. And some of the themes arising out of the stories would be better appreciated by young and older adults. They will find ***The Haunting of Chas McGill and Other Stories*** pleasant bed-time fare.

Joseph M. P. R. Cocucci, S. J. in a review of "The Haunting of Chas McGill and Other Stories," in Best Sellers, *Vol. 43, No. 11, February, 1984, p. 432.*

This collection of short stories is at the same time horror, science fiction, and fantasy. Perhaps that is part of its trouble; it is uneven. There are some good stories, but most are not so good. With many, I was left with a feeling of incompleteness: the stories did not come to a satisfactory conclusion.

To me, a suggestion of horror is not horror. Many of these stories only hint at horror. Some attempt is made at supernatural happenings, but not much comes of it. **"Almost a Ghost Story"** is a good example. The title tells all. Another problem is the use of dialect which is hard for the reader to understand. **"Sea Coal"** is a good time travel story, marred by too much use of dialect.

Fred M. Gervat, in a review of "The Haunting of Chas McGill and Other Stories," in The Book Report, *Vol. 3, No. 1, May-June, 1984, p. 36.*

FUTURETRACK 5 (1983)

[Open-ended] but bleak and chilling, the conclusion of ***Futuretrack*** suggests a pessimistic view of man and his dependence on technology which is as necessary for young readers to contemplate as the predominantly active, hopeful views of [Geraldine Harris's *The Seventh Gate,* Susan Cooper's *Seaward,* Michael Ende's *The Never Ending Story,* Douglas Hill's *Exiles of ColSec,* and Monica Hughes's *Space Trap*]. Like Cormier, Westall takes as his theme the helplessness of private citizens against government, casting forward into the near future. Here England is controlled in social divisions where it seems that the Techs who provide the machinery of life, headed by the national computer affectionately known as Laura, easily dominate the stupidly arrogant Ests, upper-class survivors, and the Unnems, exiled beyond the Wire and offered mindless lives on Futuretracks inexorably binding them to the 'amusements' of video-games, motor-bikes and sex. There is, though, a more dangerous enemy, a secret committee conspiring to reduce the population by genetic control to a nation of pseudo-rustics bred in an artifical Fenland enclave. In the face of such appalling prospects the young hero, Henry Kitson, whose inexperience is balanced by a passionate curiosity, and his gallant ally, the motorbike champion Keri, have litle chance of survival, let alone victory over the planned future. Indeed, the victory they do achieve may point to an even greater subjection to the inconveniently enquiring mind of the computer Laura. The sardonic ending, with its suggestion that human nature has done little to improve in two thousand years, should not in fact induce pessimism so much as argument and resolve in the young people who see reflected in this turbulent, incisive tale a challenge to their intelligence and goodwill, a metaphor of the kind of world which apathy could in fact bring about. This is an extreme and a compelling example of the figurative use of science fiction.

Margery Fisher, in a review of "Futuretrack," in Growing Point, *Vol. 22, No. 5, January, 1984, p. 4194.*

Another tremendous narrative. . . .

Westall's urgent view of the near future is too convincing for comfort. There is not one aspect of this horrifyingly manipulated society which does not have its objective correlative in the society we inhabit today; everything extends logically from the present. Westall's extraordinary clearsightedness produces the true dystopia: a terrible warning about the day after tomorrow with an ending which in context can only be a gesture but taken out of its narrative context becomes a radical condemnation of the way we are allowing post-industrial Britain to be shaped. ***The machine-gunners*** is deservedly almost a standard text in secondary schools. ***Futuretrack 5*** ought to be as well. I'll go further: it *must* be.

Dennis Hamley, in a review of "Futuretrack 5," in The School Librarian, *Vol. 32, No. 2, June, 1984, p. 154.*

Westall's latest adventure is a science fiction story written along the lines of several recent Hollywood films which feature lots of violence, some sex and a view of a future world that will scare the pants off readers. . . . It is a clever story, both satirical and tongue-in-cheek, with obvious jibes at the British way of life, most especially its educational system. Not all American readers will appreciate the humor, and indeed the opening chapters can be rough going because it is hard to sort everything out, but in time the story becomes downright exciting. Even though there are some structural weaknesses and loose ends in the resolution, Westall's many fans and better readers of science fiction are in for a treat. (pp. 87-8)

Robert Unsworth, in a review of "Futuretrack 5," in School Library Journal, *Vol. 30, No. 10, August, 1984, pp. 87-8.*

[Robert Westall] combines spitting-fire prose of Swiftian zest with that gloomy dean's idealistic hatred of his fellows. ***Futuretrack 5*** has all the fierce indignation of *A Modest Proposal.* Continuous reading of Westall . . . produces in the reader a feeling of having been scoured for failing to be what mankind (yea, *man*kind, for women fare even worse) should become. . . .

The surface of Westall's narrative is as hard and fast as the technology he admires and despises. The pelting action is a subtle blend of text-times: the dialogue lasts as long as conversation would; the events are telescoped; emotions are one-word paragraphs ('Ridiculous'); settings are borrowed references ('I once saw a film about Berlin in 1945, all burnt out walls and rubble. Glasgow was like that. The worse wreckage was human'). Redemption lies in a kind of cosmic sympathy; but there is never a touch of tenderness.

Margaret Meek, "Fiction: 'Futuretrack 5'," in The Signal Review of Children's Books 2, *1984, p. 46.*

THE CATS OF SEROSTER (1984)

A murky, overlong blend of political intrigue, knightly mysticism, and psychical fantasy—all set in a vaguely medieval France. In the exciting opening pages, a provincial Duke, victim of a coup d'etat, is murdered during castle dinner with his twelve-year-old son. So the boy, with help from beloved royal cat Sehtek, kills his father's assassin, escapes—and takes refuge in a nearby mausoleum, where the elite of the Miw dwell: large, golden cats who communicate with each other by "sending" Tarzan-like dialogue back and forth. ("Why yellowcat go tell Horse? Why always yellowcat? Us good as yellowcat.") Meanwhile, as the Miw start plotting to restore the young Duke to his rightful throne, a wandering Englishman named Cam, something of a medieval hippie . . . , has a fateful encounter with a blacksmith—who gives Cam a magic knife and a letter addressed "To the Seroster." And Cam, amid a series of reluctant-knight adventures, will meet up with one of the Miw, a cat named Amon who leads him to the grand mausoleum. Eventually, then, Cam teams up with the Miw in the battle against the usurpers of the Dukedom: in accepting this mission, it seems, Cam himself thus *becomes* "the Seroster," a sort of warrior-saint and spiritual leader. . . . But, before the ultimate battle against the usurpers is won, Cam—who's ambivalent about sword-power—goes back and forth between his human self and his Seroster form; he gets unlikely support from "Father Death," a priest who has given up God for swordplay; and, at the last moment, Cam / Seroster manages to triumph . . . without unleashing a full-scale massacre. Presumably, then, there's a theme concerning warfare and violence somewhere within this dense pageant. Unfortunately, however, the fuzzy mystical notions here are further blurred by Westall's mannered narration. ("Then the gray-creature was fleeing, or was-not. Gray-creature disliked the Wetness; only came desperate in winter, when the Wetness was rockhardcold.") And the pace throughout is sluggish—as the focus keeps shifting from Cam to the various Miw to the largely extraneous doings of the usurpers. Despite some vividly imagined cat-world vignettes, then: a dense, demanding fable with only minor rewards. (pp. J108-J109)

A review of "The Cats of Seroster," in Kirkus Review, *Juvenile Issue, Vol. LII, Nos. 18-21, November 1, 1984, pp. J108-J109.*

The Cats of Seroster is a sword-and-sorcery fantasy featuring telepathic cats and a reincarnated warrior, set in a vaguely imagined and entirely unhistorical version of medieval France. It is an odd book from a writer as tough-minded as Robert Westall: its reworking of some of Tolkien's more stagey effects is as surprising as it is heavy-handed. Westall's powerful recent novel ***Futuretrack 5*** was a sort of children's *1984*, a lament for a generation deprived of hope. No one could guess from that angry, impassioned text that his next publication would be a conventional (and cliché-ridden) fantasy in which the villainy of the baddies consists in their rejection of the rule of an hereditary Duke. Whatever Westall's private convictions, the reactionary politics of fantasy have him securely bound.

What is most authentic in the book is the gut-wrenching violence. Just as there was much in ***Futuretrack 5*** and its predecessors that was disturbingly voyeuristic and brutal, so here Westall's inert narrative is quickened by images of tortured animals, of "a pregnant woman writhing at the stake in agony", of "a fat naked woman in bed with three black dogs and a monkey", of a man's face working "like a bowl of maggots".

Neil Philip, "Alien Intervention," in The Times Educational Supplement, *No. 3569, November 23, 1984, p. 38.*

Robert Westall's new novel is a historical fantasy. Part medieval derring-do, part allegory, part dream, it is aimed at only the most sophisticated teenager though most readers will find the second reading more rewarding than the first. There are too many narrative threads to follow and too many implications to absorb. Even the leitmotifs are circular: a path which leads onwards and always arrives in the same place; a knife that deals certain death yet confers immortality on its owner; a prophecy which is fulfilled in its overthrowing. Paradoxes prop up the structure of the novel like the impossible pillars of an Escher tower. . . .

This is a rich, violent, sombre novel, enlivened, like a medieval painting, by the occasional inappropriate grotesque. Robert Westall has never patronized his readers: here, with his darting unconnected sentences, constant shifting of scene, and teasing allusions he makes it positively difficult. Perhaps a generation reared on three-dimensional puzzles and micro games will find the effort less painful than their elders. Both should find the effort rewarding.

Sarah Hayes, "Prophecy and Paradox," in The Times Literary Supplement, *No. 4261, November 30, 1984, p. 1375.*

I sometimes think Robert Westall's policy is to write just one example of each dominant sub-species of contemporary literature to show he can do it better than anyone else and then go on to something new. ***The scarecrows*** was the best psychological thriller, ***Futuretrack 5*** the best dystopia—now, has he actually outgunned Richard Adams? Westall's cats are the heart of this absorbing, many-layered book. . . .

Just who and what the Seroster is turns out to be a real novelistic coup—the genuine surprise we should have known all along. Meanwhile, the elliptical, violent plot hurries us along with its gallery of vivid characters portrayed in pointed, funny, resonant prose. It culminates with about the most inventive, best-described battle I have ever read.

But the cats make the book. . . . In their actions is expressed empathically that very complex relationship between human and cat. In their imagined means of communication is a convincing understanding of the feline nature. The cats represent a major feat of the imagination which makes a good book outstanding. Robert Westall has done it again.

Dennis Hamley, in a review of "The Cats of Seroster," in The School Librarian, *Vol. 33, No. 1, March, 1985, p. 65.*

CHILDREN OF THE BLITZ: MEMORIES OF WARTIME CHILDHOOD (1985)

[***Children of the Blitz*** and John Costello's *Love, Sex and War: Changing Values 1939-1945* process] oral evidence to present an aspect of social experience during the Second World War; and the same problems of handling and referencing sources bedevil both. In the end, one is left with anecdotage rather than analysis; conflation of evidence and illustration of patterns are sacrificed, and the basic problems of oral evidence are tacitly left unconfronted. What, after all, do people tell the truth about? (p. 26)

[In Costello's book, the] intended function appears to be entertainment rather than analysis.

The same is true of Robert Westall's compilation of juvenile wartime reminiscences. Once again, sources are rarely attributed with precision; even the author's own contributions are coyly disguised as **"Boy, Tyneside"** (though made unmistakeable by a breathless style and a reliance on matey italicizing). Though weeding has taken place, the question of evaluating material is largely burked; an overall commitment to accuracy is not indicated by the mis-spelling of Mass Observation's Tom Harrisson throughout. The structure is anecdotal, chronological, unanalytical. There is some intrinsically interesting material, like a diary from the Orkneys, but some of the most vivid reminiscences, like Bernard Kops' memories of sleeping in the Underground, have already appeared in published memoirs. There is not much reliance on recent historical perspectives (this must be the first book since Eden's own memoirs to describe him as an anti-appeaser). There are, of course, some excellent stories, especially about unexploded bombs; and the whole thing is atmospheric in the way that, for instance, Elizabeth Bowen's *The Heat of the Day* is atmospheric. But the material dealt with is surely as skewed and disingenuous as that processed by any novelist. (p. 27)

Roy Foster, "Boy, Tyneside," in The Times Educational Supplement, *No. 3613, September 27, 1985, pp. 26-7.*

Readers of ***The Machine-Gunners*** and its sequel ***Fathom Five*** . . . will know of children's writer Robert Westall's ability to capture the drama and pathos of wartime as it impinges upon the lives of children. ***The Machine-Gunners*** . . . led many adults, who had been children during the Second World War, to send Westall accounts of their experiences. He has brought together a collection of these accounts in ***Children of the Blitz,*** along with several from previously published sources. Interspersed with vivid photographs, they form a lively and arresting profile of children's impressions and fears and prejudices during the period 1939 to 1945. . . . Of particular interest to readers of Westall himself are two accounts of children taking weapons and causing a stir of their own, the basis of his own fiction. Direct, blunt, funny, sad, heroic—this is a valuable gloss on Westall, a useful sourcebook for schools, and of interest to readers motivated by nostalgia.

C. S. Hannabuss, in a review of "Children of the Blitz: Memories of Wartime Childhood," in British Book News, *December, 1985, p. 760.*

[Westall] has organized these reminiscences, including many of his own, into chapters that range from spies (like gas, the source of much misplaced hysteria) to evacuation. The short anecdotes are profusely illustrated with archival photographs and cartoons, captioned by Westall in informative, often wry, detail. He does not exclude the horror ("one long nightmare, one long siren"), especially in the suffering of the poor, but the predominant tone is upbeat, as in the laconic story of a boy cycling with an unexploded bomb on his handlebars. A strong sense emerges of what it was like to be young at that time: blackouts, rationing, tedium, and also intense excitement and the satisfaction of being unequivocally on the right side.

Hazel Rochman, in a review of "Children of the Blitz: Memories of a Wartime Childhood," in Booklist, *Vol. 82, No. 12, February 15, 1986, p. 848.*

APPENDIX

The following is a listing of all sources used in Volume 13 of *Children's Literature Review*. Included in this list are all copyright and reprint rights and acknowledgments for those essays for which permission was obtained. Every effort has been made to trace copyright, but if omissions have been made, please let us know.

THE EXCERPTS IN CLR, VOLUME 13, WERE REPRINTED FROM THE FOLLOWING PERIODICALS:

The Advocates Newsletter, December, 1986. Reprinted by permission of the publisher.

The ALAN Review, v. 10, Winter, 1983. Reprinted by permission of the publisher.

American Jewish Historical Quarterly, v. LXVII, December, 1977. Copyright 1977, by the American Jewish Historical Society. Reprinted by permission of the publisher.

Appraisal: Children's Science Books, v. 1, Winter, 1967; v. 1, Spring, 1968; v. 1, Fall, 1968; v. 3, Spring, 1970; v. 3, Fall, 1970; v. 4, Spring, 1971; v. 5, Spring, 1972; v. 5, Fall, 1972; v. 5, Winter, 1972; v. 6, Fall, 1973; v. 7, Winter, 1974; v. 8, Winter, 1975; v. 8, Spring, 1975; v. 9, Winter, 1976; v. 9, Spring, 1976; v. 9, Fall, 1976; v. 10, Fall, 1977; v. 12, Spring, 1979; v. 13, Fall, 1980. Copyright © 1967, 1968, 1970, 1971, 1972, 1973, 1974, 1975, 1976, 1977, 1980 by the Children's Science Book Review Committee. All reprinted by permission of the publisher.

Appraisal: Science Books for Young People, v. 14, Winter, 1981; v. 14, Spring, 1981; v. 15, Winter, 1982; v. 15, Fall, 1982; v. 16, Winter, 1983; v. 17, Winter, 1984; v. 17, Spring-Summer, 1984; v. 18, Spring, 1985; v. 18, Summer, 1985; v. 19, Spring, 1986; v. 19, Summer, 1986; v. 19, Fall, 1986; v. 20, Winter, 1987. Copyright © 1981, 1982, 1983, 1984, 1985, 1986, 1987 by the Children's Science Book Review Committee. All reprinted by permission of the publisher.

Archaeology, v. 34, September/October, 1981. Copyright © 1981 by the Archaeological Institute of America. All rights reserved. Reprinted by the permission of the publisher.

The Babbling Bookworm, v. 7, June, 1979. Copyright 1979 The Babbling Bookworm Newsletter. Reprinted by permission of the publisher.

Best Sellers, v. 34, September 15, 1974; v. 34, January 1, 1975. Copyright 1974, 1975, by the University of Scranton. Both reprinted by permission of the publisher./ v. 36, August, 1976; v. 39, December, 1979; v. 39, February, 1980; v. 40, April, 1980; v. 41, September, 1981; v. 42, January, 1983; v. 43, February, 1984; v. 45, July, 1985; v. 45, January, 1986. Copyright © 1976, 1979, 1980, 1981, 1983, 1984, 1985, 1986 Helen Dwight Reid Educational Foundation. All reprinted by permission of the publisher.

Black Books Bulletin, v. 7, 1981. Copyright © 1981 by the Institute of Positive Education. All rights reserved. Both reprinted by permission of the publisher.

The Black Scholar, v. 8, December, 1976. Copyright 1976 by *The Black Scholar*. Reprinted by permission of the publisher.

The Book Report, v. 3, May-June, 1984. © copyright 1984 by Linworth Publishing Co. Reprinted by permission of the publisher.

Book Week—New York Herald Tribune, July 4, 1965; December 4, 1966. © 1965, 1966, *The Washington Post*. Both reprinted by permission of the publisher.

Book Window, v. 7, Summer, 1980. © 1980 S.C.B.A. and contributors. Reprinted by permission of the publisher.

Book World—The Washington Post, February 2, 1969. © 1969 Postrib Corp. Reprinted by permission of *The Washington Post*./ November 11, 1979; July 14, 1985; November 10, 1985. © 1979, 1985 *The Washington Post*. All reprinted by permission of the publisher.

Bookbird, v. VI (March 15, 1968); v. VIII (December 15, 1970); v. IX (September 15, 1971); v. XI (March 15, 1973); v. XII (March 15, 1974). All reprinted by permission of the publisher.

Booklist, v. 73, April 1, 1977; v. 74, October 15, 1977; v. 74, December 15, 1977; v. 75, September 1, 1978; v. 75, January 1, 1979; v. 76, December 15, 1979; v. 76, January 15, 1980; v. 76, February 1, 1980; v. 76, April 1, 1980; v. 76, June 1, 1980; v. 77, January 1, 1981; v. 77, February 15, 1981; v. 78, September 1, 1981; v. 78, March 15, 1982; v. 78, April 15, 1982; v. 79, September 1, 1982; v. 79, October 1, 1982; v. 79, November 1, 1982; v. 79, December 15, 1982; v. 79, January 1, 1983; v. 79, April 15, 1983; v. 80, September 1, 1983; v. 80, October 15, 1983; v. 80, April 15, 1984; v. 80, May 15, 1984; v. 81, September 15, 1984; v. 81, October 1, 1984; v. 81, October 15, 1984; v. 81, February 1, 1985; v. 81, March 15, 1985; v. 81, May 1, 1985; v. 81, June 15, 1985; v. 81, August, 1985; v. 82, September 1, 1985; v. 82, September 15, 1985; v. 82, October 1, 1985; v. 82, October 15, 1985; v. 82, December 1, 1985; v. 82, February 15, 1986; v. 82, March 1, 1986; v. 82, April 15, 1986; v. 82, May 1, 1986; v. 83, November 1, 1986. Copyright © 1977, 1978, 1979, 1980, 1981, 1982, 1983, 1984, 1985, 1986 by the American Library Association. All reprinted by permission of the publisher.

The Booklist, v. 37, May 1, 1941; v. 38, October 1, 1941./ v. 68, January 1, 1972; v. 69, May 15, 1973; v. 69, June 1, 1973; v. 70, December 15, 1973; v. 70, May 1, 1974; v. 70, November 15, 1974; v. 72, October 15, 1975; v. 72, November 1, 1975; v. 72, June 1, 1976. Copyright © 1972, 1973, 1974, 1975, 1976 by the American Library Association. All reprinted by permission of the publisher.

The Booklist and Subscription Books Bulletin, v. 58, September 1, 1961; v. 58, December 1, 1961; v. 62, December 1, 1965; v. 63, February 1, 1967; v. 64, May 1, 1968; v. 65, January 1, 1969. Copyright © 1961, 1965, 1967, 1968, 1969 by the American Library Association. All reprinted by permission of the publisher.

Books for Keeps, n. 23, November, 1983; n. 30, January, 1985. © School Bookshop Association 1983, 1985. Both reprinted by permission of the publisher.

Books for Your Children, v. 13, Spring, 1978; v. 15, Spring, 1980; v. 16, Summer, 1981; v. 17, Autumn-Winter, 1982; v. 20, Summer, 1985; v. 21, Autumn-Winter, 1986. © *Books for Your Children* 1978, 1980, 1981, 1982, 1985, 1986. All reprinted by permission of the publisher.

Books in Canada, v. 14, December, 1985 for "Identity Crisis" by Mary Ainslie Smith. Reprinted by permission of the author.

British Book News, December, 1985. © *British Book News*, 1985. Courtesy of *British Book News*.

British Book News, Children's Supplement, Spring, 1980. © *British Book News*, 1980. Courtesy of *British Book News*.

British Book News Children's Books, December, 1986. © The British Council, 1986. Reprinted by permission of the publisher.

Bulletin of the Center for Children's Books, v. XIII, September, 1959; v. XIII, November, 1959; v. XIV, January, 1961; v. XIV, May, 1961; v. XV, September, 1961; v. XIV, December, 1961; v. XV, May, 1962; v. XV, July-August, 1962; v. XVI, December, 1962; v. XVI, April, 1963; v. XVII, January, 1964; v. XVII, July-August, 1964; v. XVIII, July-August, 1965; v. 20, February, 1967; v. 20, March, 1967; v. 20, July-August, 1967; v. 24, November, 1970; v. 24, June, 1971; v. 25, January, 1972; v. 25, March, 1972; v. 26, November, 1972; v. 26, March, 1973; v. 26, April, 1973; v. 26, May, 1973; v. 27, September, 1973; v. 27, October, 1973; v. 27, November, 1973; v. 27, December, 1973; v. 27, March, 1974; v. 27, June, 1974; v. 27, July-August, 1974; v. 28, September, 1974; v. 28, January, 1975; v. 28, February, 1975; v. 28, March, 1975; v. 28, June, 1975; v. 29, April, 1976; v. 29, July-August, 1976; v. 30, September, 1976; v. 31, February, 1978; v. 32, September, 1978; v. 32, January, 1979; v. 32, March, 1979; v. 33, March, 1980; v. 33, May, 1980; v. 34, December, 1980; v. 34, January, 1981; v. 34, June, 1981; v. 35, October, 1981; v. 36, October, 1982; v. 36, November, 1982; v. 36, December, 1982; v. 36, January, 1983; v. 36, March, 1983; v. 36, May, 1983; v. 37, October, 1983; v. 37, February, 1984; v. 37, April, 1984; v. 37, June, 1984; v. 38, October, 1984; v. 38, December, 1984; v. 38, February, 1985; v. 38, April, 1985; v. 38, July-August, 1985; v. 39, September, 1985; v. 39, October, 1985; v. 39, December, 1985; v. 39, January, 1986; v. 39, February, 1986; v. 39, May, 1986; v. 40, October, 1986; v. 40, November, 1986; v. 40, December, 1986; v. 40, January, 1987. Copyright © 1959, 1961, 1962, 1963, 1964, 1965, 1967, 1970, 1971, 1972, 1973, 1974, 1975, 1976, 1978, 1979, 1980, 1981, 1982, 1983, 1984, 1985, 1986, 1987 by The University of Chicago. All reprinted by permission of The University of Chicago Press.

Bulletin of the Children's Book Center, v. VI, July, 1953; v. X, November, 1956; v. X, February, 1957./ v. XI, February, 1958; v. XI, April, 1958. Both reprinted by permission of the University of Chicago Press.

Canadian Children's Literature: A Journal of Criticism and Review, n. 4, 1976; n. 5 & 6, 1976; n. 15 & 16, 1980; n. 25, 1982; n. 31 & 32, 1983. Box 335, Guelph, Ontario, Canada N1H 6K5. All reprinted by permission of the publisher.

The Canadian Forum, v. 40, December, 1960. Reprinted by permission of the publisher.

Catholic Library World, v. 42, February, 1971; v. 42, July-August, 1971; v. 52, April, 1981; v. 54, December, 1982; v. 56, July-August, 1984. All reprinted by permission of the publisher.

Children's Book Review, v. IV, Winter, 1974-75. © 1975 Five Owls Press Ltd. All rights reserved. Reprinted by permission of the publisher.

Children's Book Review Service, v. 2, June, 1974; v. 6, Winter, 1978; v. 8, Spring, 1980; v. 10, March, 1982; v. 11, January, 1983; v. 11, Spring, 1983; v. 11, May, 1983; v. 11, June, 1983; v. 14, November, 1985; v. 14, January, 1986; v. 15, October, 1986; v. 15, November, 1986; v. 15, January, 1987. Copyright © 1974, 1978, 1980, 1982, 1983, 1985, 1986, 1987 Children's Book Review Service, Inc. All reprinted by permission of the publisher.

Children's Literature: Annual of the Modern Language Association Seminar on Children's Literature and The Children's Literature Association, v. 1, 1972; v. 4, 1975; v. 5, 1976. © 1972, 1975, 1976 by Francelia Butler. All rights reserved. All reprinted by permission of Francelia Butler.

Children's Literature Association Quarterly, v. 5, Summer, 1980; v. 7, Fall, 1982; v. 10, Spring, 1985. © 1980, 1982, 1985 Children's Literature Association. All reprinted by permission of the publisher.

Children's literature in education, v. 8 (Summer), 1977; v. 11 (Autumn), 1980; v. 16 (Spring), 1985. © 1977, 1980, 1985, Agathon Press, Inc. All reprinted by permission of the publisher.

Choice, v. 11, December, 1974. Copyright © 1974 by American Library Association. Reprinted by permission of the publisher.

The Christian Science Monitor, November 27, 1944./ October 23, 1978 for "Novels of Children Alone against the World" by Victor Kantor Burg; October 15, 1979 for "Urban Strife on Suburban Street" by Jerrie Norris; May 13, 1983 for "Cynthia Voight: Family Comes First" by Johanna Shaw-Eagle; December 2, 1983 for "Photos as Art and Education" by Darian J. Scott. © 1978, 1979, 1983 by the respective authors. All rights reserved. All reprinted by permission of the respective authors./ November 16, 1961; November 17, 1961; November 2, 1967; November 6, 1969; May 7, 1970; November 12, 1970; May 6, 1971; November 8, 1972; November 2, 1977; June 29, 1983; November 1, 1985. © 1961, 1967, 1969, 1970, 1971, 1972, 1977, 1983, 1985 The Christian Science Publishing Society. All rights reserved. All reprinted by permission from *The Christian Science Monitor.*/ December 10, 1946. Copyright 1946, renewed 1974, by The Christian Science Publishing Society. All rights reserved. Reprinted by permission from *The Christian Science Monitor.*/ December 9, 1954. Copyright 1954, renewed 1982, The Christian Science Publishing Society. All rights reserved. Reprinted by permission from *The Christian Science Monitor.*

Curriculum Review, v. 17, February, 1978; v. 18, February, 1979. © 1978, 1979 Curriculum Advisory Service. Both reprinted by permission of the Curriculum Advisory Service, Chicago, IL.

Early Years, v. 10, September, 1979; v. 14, January, 1984. © copyright 1979, 1984 by Early Years, Inc. Both reprinted with permission of the publisher, Westport, CT 06880.

English Journal, v. 66, September, 1977 for a review of "Never to Forget: The Jews of the Holocaust" by Alleen Pace Nilsen; v. 69, September, 1980 for "Looking Backward: Trying to Find the Classic Young Adult Novel" by Linda Bachelder and others. Copyright © 1977, 1980 by the National Council of Teachers of English. Both reprinted by permission of the publisher and the respective authors./ v. 74, November, 1985. Copyright © 1985 by the National Council of Teachers of English. Reprinted by permission of the publisher.

Freedomways, v. 16, second quarter, 1976; v. 19, first quarter, 1979. Copyright © 1976, 1979 by Freedomways Associates, Inc. Both reprinted by permission of the publisher.

Growing Point, v. 12, July, 1973; v. 13, January, 1975; v. 14, October, 1975; v. 18, May, 1979; v. 19, September, 1980; v. 19, January, 1981; v. 21, July, 1982; v. 22, May, 1983; v. 22, July, 1983; v. 22, November, 1983; v. 22, January, 1984; v. 23, July, 1984; v. 23, November, 1984; v. 25, July, 1986. All reprinted by permission of the publisher.

The Horn Book Magazine, v. LXI, March-April, 1985 for "Young Adult Books: I am a Storyteller" by Rosa Guy; v. LXII, July-August, 1986 for "Caldecott Medal Acceptance" by Chris Van Allsburg. Copyright © 1985, 1986 by the respective authors. All rights reserved. Both reprinted by permission of the respective authors./ v. XXVI, November-December, 1950. Copyright 1950 by The Horn Book, Inc., Boston. All rights reserved. Reprinted by permission of the publisher./ v. XXXV, August, 1959; v. XXXVI, December, 1960; v. XLIII, April, 1967; v. XLIII, August, 1967; v. XLIII, December, 1967; v. XLVII, August, 1971; v. XLVIII, August, 1972; v. XLVIII, October, 1972; v. XLVIII, December, 1972; v. L, April, 1974; v. L, August, 1974; v. L, December, 1974; v. LI, February, 1975; v. LI, April, 1975; v. LI, June, 1975; v. LII, April, 1976; v. LII, October, 1976; v. LIII, October, 1977; v. LIV, April, 1978; v. LV, October, 1978; v. LVI, June, 1980; v. LVI, August, 1980; v. LVI, October, 1980; v. LVI, December, 1980; v. LVII, June, 1981; v. LVII, August, 1981; v. LVIII, June, 1982; v. LVIII, October, 1982; v. LVIII, December, 1982; v. LIX, February, 1983; v. LIX, April, 1983; v. LIX, June, 1983; v. LIX, August, 1983; v. LX, August, 1984; v. LX, September-October, 1984; v. LX, November-December, 1984; v. LXI, January-February, 1985; v. LXI, March-April, 1985; v. LXI, May-June, 1985; v. LXI, September-October, 1985; v. LXII, January-February, 1986; v. LXII, March-April, 1986; v. LXII, May-June, 1986; v. LXII, September-October, 1986; v. LXII, November-December, 1986; v. LXIII, January-February, 1987; v. LXIII, March-April, 1987. Copyright © 1959, 1960, 1967, 1971, 1972, 1974, 1975, 1976, 1977, 1978, 1980,

1981, 1982, 1983, 1984, 1985, 1986, 1987 by The Horn Book, Inc., Boston. All rights reserved. All reprinted by permission of the publisher.

In Review: Canadian Books for Children, v. 3, Winter, 1969; v. 4, Spring, 1970; v. 8, Winter, 1974; v. 8, Spring, 1974; v. 12, Winter, 1978. All reprinted by permission of the publisher.

In Review: Canadian Books for Young People, v. 14, April, 1980; v. 15, April, 1981. Both reprinted by permission of the publisher.

Interracial Books for Children Bulletin, v. 7, 1976; v. 8, 1977; v. 9, 1978; v. 10, 1979; v. 12, 1981; v. 14, 1983; v. 16, 1985; v. 17, 1986. All reprinted by permission of the Council on Interracial Books for Children, 1841 Broadway, New York, NY 10023.

The Junior Bookshelf, v. 16, October, 1952./ v. 35, October, 1971; v. 37, August, 1973; v. 38, December, 1974; v. 41, April, 1977; v. 42, June, 1978; v. 42, August, 1978; v. 43, April, 1979; v. 43, June, 1979; v. 44, February, 1980; v. 44, December, 1980; v. 46, April, 1982; v. 46, June, 1982; v. 46, August, 1982; v. 47, February, 1983; v. 47, October, 1983; v. 48, February, 1984; v. 48, April, 1984; v. 48, June, 1984; v. 48, October, 1984; v. 50, June, 1986. All reprinted by permission of the publisher.

Junior Libraries, an appendix to *Library Journal,* v. 2, October, 1955; v. 4, September, 1957./ v. 6, November, 1959; v. 6, December, 1959. Copyright © 1959. Both reprinted from *Junior Libraries,* published by R. R. Bowker Co./ A Xerox Corporation, by permission.

Kirkus Reviews, v. XXXVII, January 1, 1969; v. XXXVII, January 15, 1969; v. XXXVII, May 15, 1969; v. XXXVII, October 1, 1969; v. XXXVII, November 15, 1969; v. XXXVIII, June 15, 1970; v. XXXVIII, July 1, 1970; v. XXXVIII, September 15, 1970; v. XXXVIII, October 1, 1970; v. XXXIX, February 15, 1971; v. XXXIX, October 15, 1971; v. XL, April 15, 1972; v. XL, June 15, 1972; v. XL, August 15, 1972; v. XL, October, 1, 1972; v. XL, October 15, 1972; v. XL, November 1, 1972, v. XL, November 15, 1972; v. XLI, February 1, 1973; v. XLII, January 15, 1974; v. XLII, February 1, 1974; v. XLII, June 15, 1974; v. XLII, July 15, 1974; v. XLII, December 1, 1974; v. XLII, December 15, 1974; v. XLIII, January 1, 1975; v. XLIII, October 15, 1975; v. XLIV, May 15, 1976; v. XLIV, June 15, 1976; v. XLIV, August 15, 1976; v. XLIV, September 1, 1976; v. XLIV, September 15, 1976; v. XLIV, October 1, 1976; v. XLV, May 15, 1977; v. XLV, September 1, 1977; v. XLV, October 15, 1977; v. XLVI, July 15, 1978; v. XLVII, January 1, 1979; v. XLVII, March 15, 1979; v. XLVII, October 1, 1979; v. XLVIII, June 1, 1980; v. XLVIII, October 15, 1980; v. XLVIII, November 1, 1980; v. XLIX, March 1, 1981; v. XLIX, August 1, 1981; v. XLIX, September 15, 1981; v. XLIX, October 1, 1981; v. XLIX, November 15, 1981; v. L, February 15, 1982; v. L, March 1, 1982; v. L, March 15, 1982; v. LI, March 15, 1983; v. LI, November 1, 1983; v. LIII, May 15, 1985; v. LIII, September 1, 1985; v. LIII, December 15, 1985; v. LIV, April 15, 1986; v. LIV, May 15, 1986; v. LIV, June 1, 1986; v. LV, January 15, 1987. Copyright © 1969, 1970, 1971, 1972, 1973, 1974, 1975, 1976, 1977, 1978, 1979, 1980, 1981, 1982, 1983, 1985, 1986. 1987 The Kirkus Service, Inc. All rights reserved. All reprinted by permission of the publisher.

Kirkus Reviews, Juvenile Issue, v. LI, September 1, 1983; v. LI, November 1, 1983; v. LII, May 1, 1984; v. LII, September 1, 1984; v. LII, November 1, 1984; v. LIII, March 1, 1985. Copyright © 1983, 1984, 1985 The Kirkus Service, Inc. All rights reserved. All reprinted by permission of the publisher.

Kirkus Service, v. XXXIV, December 15, 1966; v. XXXV, July 15, 1967; v. XXXV, October 1, 1967; v. XXXV, November 15, 1967; v. XXXVI, February 15, 1968. Copyright © 1966, 1967, 1968 The Kirkus Service, Inc. All reprinted by permission of the publisher.

Kliatt Young Adult Paperback Book Guide, v. XVI, January, 1982; v. XVII, September, 1983. Copyright © by Kliatt Paperback Book Guide. Both reprinted by permission of the publisher.

Language Arts, v. 54, November-December, 1977 for a review of "The Snopp on the Sidewalk and Other Poems" by Ruth M. Stein; v. 56, September, 1979 for a review of "The Queen of Eene" by Ruth M. Stein; v. 58, March, 1981 for a review of "All Times, All Peoples: A World History of Slavery" by Ruth M. Stein; v. 59, January, 1982 for a review of "Homecoming" by Ruth M. Stein; v. 59, March, 1982 for a review of "More than One" by Ruth M. Stein; v. 60, October, 1983 for a review of "Round & Round & Round" by Ronald A. Jobe; v. 60, October, 1983 for a review of "The Wreck of the Zephyr" by Ronald A. Jobe; v. 60, November-December, 1983 for a review of "Zoo Doings" by Marlene Ann Birkman; v. 60, November-December, 1983 for a review of "A Solitary Blue" by Ronald A. Jobe; v. 60, November-December, 1983 for "On the Writing of 'A Solitary Blue'" by Cynthia Voigt; v. 61, October, 1984 for a review of "I Walk and Read" by Ronald A. Jobe; v. 62, January, 1985 for "Critic's Choice" by Barbara Kiefer; v. 62, February, 1985 for a review of "The New Kid on the Block" by Ronald A. Jobe; v. 62, February, 1985 for "Reflection" by Joan Glazer; v. 62, November, 1985 for a review of "Dorothea Lange: Life through the Camera" by Janet Hickman; v. 62, December, 1985 for "Profile: Cynthia Voigt" by Dorothy Kauffman.

Library Association Record, v. 78, October, 1976; v. 79, January, 1977. © The Library Association 1976, 1977. All reprinted by permission of the publisher.

Library Journal, v. 65, October 15, 1940; v. 66, October 1, 1941; v. 69, November 1, 1944; v. 74, April 1, 1949; v. 74, September 15, 1949; v. 75, April 1, 1950; v. 77, October 15, 1952; v. 3, January 1957./ v. 7, November 15, 1960; v. 86, July, 1961; v. 86, December 15, 1961; v. 93, February 15, 1968; v. 96, May 15, 1971; v. 97, September 15, 1972; v. 104, December 15, 1979. Copyright © 1960, 1961, 1968, 1971, 1972, 1979, by Reed Publishing, USA, Division of Reed Holdings, Inc. All reprinted by R. R. Bowker Co., Division of Reed Publishing, USA, by permission of the publisher.

The Lion and the Unicorn, v. 3, Spring, 1979; v. 4, Summer, 1980; v. 4, Winter, 1980-81; v. 7-8, 1983-84. Copyright © 1979, 1980, 1981, 1984 *The Lion and the Unicorn.* All reprinted by permission of the publisher.

The Listener, v. 110, November 3, 1983 for "Ruined Fairy Tales" by Angela Huth. © British Broadcasting Corp. 1983. Reprinted by permission of the author.

The Nation, New York, v. 206, June 3, 1968. Copyright 1968 *The Nation* magazine, The Nation Company, Inc. Reprinted by permission of the publisher.

Negro Digest, v. 17, February, 1968. © 1968 Johnson Publishing Company, Inc. Reprinted by permission of *Negro Digest.*

The Negro History Bulletin, v. 30, October, 1967. Reprinted by permission of The Association for the Study of Afro-American Life and History, Inc.

New Directions for Women, v. 13, November-December, 1984; v. 14, May-June, 1985; v. 15, Spring, 1986. © copyright 1984, 1985, 1986 New Directions for Women, Inc., 108 West Palisade Ave., Englewood, NJ 07631. All reprinted by permission of the publisher.

New York Herald Tribune Book Review, November 13, 1949; November 12, 1950; March 11, 1951; May 17, 1953; November 14, 1954. Copyright 1941, 1949, 1950, 1951, 1953, 1954 I.H.T. Corporation. All reprinted by permission of the publisher./ November 13, 1955; December 11, 1955; November 4, 1956; November 18, 1956; May 12, 1957; May 11, 1958; September 11, 1960. © 1955, 1956, 1957, 1958, 1960 I.H.T. Corporation. All reprinted by permission of the publisher.

New York Herald Tribune Books, May 11, 1941. Copyright 1941 I.H.T. Corporation. Reprinted by permission of the publisher.

New York Herald Tribune Weekly Book Review, November 12, 1944. Copyright 1944 I.H.T. Corporation. Reprinted by permission of the publisher.

The New York Times, June 1, 1968; December 2, 1985. Copyright © 1968, 1985 by The New York Times Company. Both reprinted by permission of the publisher.

The New York Times Book Review, November 3, 1940; March 30, 1941; December 14, 1941; October 25, 1942; October 10, 1943; August 3, 1947; July 10, 1949; March 11, 1951; December 14, 1952; November 14, 1954. Copyright 1940, 1941, 1942, 1943, 1947, 1949, 1951, 1952, 1954 by The New York Times Company. All reprinted by permission of the publisher./ November 13, 1955; August 31, 1958; November 23, 1958; March 29, 1959; November 1, 1959; May 8, 1960; June 18, 1961; December 3, 1961; May 13, 1962; November 1, 1964; November 22, 1964; July 18, 1965; January 23, 1966; May 7, 1967; January 28, 1968; March 23, 1969; May 2, 1971; July 25, 1971; November 28, 1971; March 18, 1973; April 15, 1973; November 4, 1973; March 31, 1974; May 5, 1974; August 11, 1974; August 25, 1974; May 2, 1976; October 3, 1976; November 14, 1976; May 1, 1977; February 5, 1978; April 23, 1978; April 27, 1980; November 9, 1980; May 10, 1981; October 4, 1981; April 25, 1982; May 16, 1982; November 14, 1982; November 21, 1982; February 20, 1983; June 5, 1983; August 14, 1983; August 28, 1983; November 13, 1983; November 27, 1983; April 8, 1984; November 10, 1985; November 24, 1985; December 1, 1985; March 30, 1986; November 9, 1986. Copyright © 1955, 1958, 1959, 1960, 1961, 1962, 1964, 1965, 1966, 1967, 1968, 1969, 1971, 1973, 1974, 1976, 1977, 1978, 1980, 1981, 1982, 1983, 1984, 1985, 1986 by The New York Times Company. All reprinted by permission of the publisher.

Notes: The Quarterly Journal of The Music Library Association, v. 25, December, 1968 for a review of "Black Magic: A Pictorial History of the Negro in American Entertainment" by Gilbert Chase. Copyright 1968 by the Music Library Association, Inc. Reprinted by permission of the publisher and the author.

Publishers Weekly, v. 164, July 25, 1953./ v. 190, August 22, 1966. Copyright © 1966 by R. R. Bowker Company. Reprinted from *Publishers Weekly,* published by R. R. Bowker Company, by permission./ v. 197, March 2, 1970; v. 198, July 20, 1970; v. 199, May 3, 1971; v. 201, May 1, 1972; v. 203, January 15, 1973; v. 207, January 13, 1975; v. 209, April 19, 1976; v. 213, January 2, 1978; v. 215, February 26, 1979; v. 215, May 28, 1979; v. 216, September 3, 1979; v. 216, October 29, 1979; v. 216, November 12, 1979; v. 217, March 7, 1980; v. 218, October 31, 1980; v. 218, December 12, 1980; v. 219, April 10, 1981; v. 220, September 11, 1981; v. 220, December 4, 1981; v. 221, January 8, 1982; v. 221, February 5, 1982; v. 222, November 12, 1982; v. 223, March 11, 1983; v. 223, March 18, 1983; v. 223, April 8, 1983; v. 225, February 10, 1984; v. 225, April 13, 1984; v. 226, September 7, 1984; v. 226, November 2, 1984; v. 227, May 3, 1985; v. 227, May 31, 1985; v. 228, July 26, 1985; v. 228, August 2, 1985; v. 228, August 16, 1985. Copyright © 1970, 1971, 1972, 1973, 1975, 1976, 1978, 1979, 1980, 1981, 1982, 1983, 1984, 1985 by Xerox Corporation. All reprinted from *Publishers Weekly,* published by R. R. Bowker Company, a Xerox company, by permission./ v. 229, February 21, 1986; v. 229, April 25, 1986; v. 230, July 25, 1986; v. 230, September 26, 1986; v. 230, October 31, 1986; v. 230, November 28, 1986; v. 231, February 13, 1987. Copyright 1986, 1987 by Reed Publishing USA. All reprinted from *Publishers Weekly,* published by R. R. Bowker Company, a Reed Publishing company, by permission.

Quill and Quire, v. 46, November, 1980 for a review of "Petrouchka" by Jocelyn Allen; v. 51, October, 1985 for "Elizabeth Cleaver" by William Toye; v. 52, February, 1986 for "Enchanting New Views Help Re-Create Native Folk-Tales" by Eva Martin. All reprinted by permission of *Quill and Quire* and the respective authors.

Religious Studies Review, v. 10, April, 1984. Copyright © 1984 by the Council on the Study of Religion. Reprinted by permission of the publisher.

Saturday Review, v. 44, November 11, 1961; v. XLV, September 22, 1962; v. LI, November 9, 1968; v. LIII, November 14, 1970; v. LIII, December 19, 1970. © 1961, 1962, 1968, 1970 *Saturday Review* magazine. All reprinted by permission of the publisher.

The Saturday Review, New York, v. XXXVI, May 16, 1953; v. XXXVII, August 21, 1954; v. XL, December 21, 1957./ v. XL, May 11, 1957. © 1957 *Saturday Review* magazine. Reprinted by permission of the publisher.

The Saturday Review of Literature, v. 32, December 10, 1949; v. XXXIII, December 9, 1950. Copyright 1949, 1950 *Saturday Review* magazine. Both reprinted by permission of the publisher.

The School Librarian, v. 24, March, 1976; v. 29, June, 1981; v. 31, September, 1983; v. 31, December, 1983; v. 32, March, 1984; v. 32, June, 1984; v. 33, March, 1985; v. 33, September, 1985. All reprinted by permission of the publisher.

The School Librarian and School Library Review, v. 9, December, 1959. Reprinted by permission of the publisher.

School Library Journal, v. 21, January, 1975; v. 22, November, 1975; v. 23, November, 1976; v. 23, December, 1976; v. 23, April, 1977; v. 24, September, 1977; v. 24, April, 1978; v. 25, October, 1978; v. 26, October, 1979; v. 26, November, 1979; v. 26, February, 1980; v. 26, March, 1980; v. 26, April, 1980; v. 26, May, 1980; v. 27, October, 1980; v. 27, February, 1981; v. 27, March, 1981; v. 27, April, 1981; v. 27, May, 1981; v. 27, August, 1981; v. 28, September, 1981; v. 28, November, 1981; v. 28, January, 1982; v. 28, March, 1982; v. 28, April, 1982; v. 28, May, 1982; v. 29, November, 1982; v. 29, December, 1982; v. 29, January, 1983; v. 29, April, 1983; v. 29, May, 1983; v. 30, September, 1983; v. 30, October, 1983; v. 30, November, 1983; v. 30, December, 1983; v. 30, January, 1984; v. 30, May, 1984; v. 30, August, 1984; v. 31, September, 1984; v. 31, October, 1984; v. 31, November, 1984; v. 31, December, 1984; v. 31, April, 1985; v. 32, September, 1985; v. 32, October, 1985; November, 1985; v. 32, December, 1985; v. 32, January, 1986; v. 32, March, 1986; v. 32, April, 1986; v. 32, May, 1986; v. 32, August, 1986; v. 33, September, 1986; v. 33, October, 1986; v. 33, November, 1986; v. 33, December, 1986; v. 33, February, 1987; v. 33, April, 1987. Copyright © 1975, 1976, 1977, 1978, 1979, 1981, 1982, 1983, 1984, 1985, 1986, 1987. All reprinted from *School Library Journal,* Cahners/ R. R. Bowker Publication, by permission.

School Library Journal, an appendix to *Library Journal,* v. 11, September, 1964; v. 11, May, 1965; v. 12, December, 1965; v. 12, May, 1966; v. 13, October, 1966; v. 13, March, 1967; v. 14, February, 1968; v. 15, October, 1968; v. 15, January, 1969; v. 16, December, 1969; v. 16, February, 1970; v. 16, April, 1970; v. 17, October, 1970; v. 17, December, 1970; v. 18, September, 1971; v. 18, December, 1971; v. 18, April, 1972; v. 19, September, 1972; v. 19, October, 1972; v. 19, November, 1972; v. 19, December, 1972; v. 19, April, 1973; v. 21, October, 1974. Copyright © 1964, 1965, 1966, 1967, 1968, 1969, 1970, 1971, 1972, 1973, 1974. All reprinted from *School Library Journal,* Cahners/ R. R. Bowker Publication, by permission.

Science Books: A Quarterly Review, v. 3, December, 1967; v. 5, March, 1970; v. 6, September, 1970; v. 6, December, 1970; v. 6, March, 1971; v. 7, December, 1971; v. 7, March, 1972; v. IX, September, 1973; v. IX, December, 1973. Copyright 1967, 1970, 1971, 1972, 1973 by AAAS. All reprinted by permission of the publisher.

Science Books & Films, v. XII, May, 1976; v. XII, September, 1976; v. XII, December, 1976; v. 16, May-June, 1981; v. 18, November-December, 1982; v. 18, March-April, 1983; v. 19, January-February, 1984; v. 20, November-December, 1984; v. 20, May-June, 1985; v. 21, November-December, 1985; v. 21, March-April, 1986; v. 22, January-February, 1987. Copyright 1976, 1981, 1982, 1983, 1984, 1985, 1986, 1987 by AAAS. All reprinted by permission of the publisher.

Science Fiction Review, v. 14, November, 1985 for a review of "Kermit's Garden of Verses" by Neal Wilgus. Copyright © 1985 by Neal Wilgus. Reprinted by permission of the author.

Scientific American, v. 215, December, 1966; v. 229, December, 1973; v. 231, December, 1974; v. 245, December, 1981; v. 253, December, 1985. Copyright © 1966, 1973, 1974, 1981, 1985 by Scientific American, Inc. All rights reserved. All reprinted by permission of the publisher.

Signal, n. 28, January, 1979 for "How Real Do You Want Your Realism" by Robert Westall; n. 37, January, 1982 for "The American Connection" by Betsy Hearne. Copyright © 1979, 1982 The Thimble Press. Both reprinted by permission of the respective authors.

The Signal Review of Children's Books, 1, 1983; 2, 1984. Copyright © 1983, 1984 The Thimble Press. All reprinted by permission of The Thimble Press, Lockwood, Station Road, South Woodchester, Glos. GL5 5EQ, England.

The Signal Selection of Children's Books 1984. Copyright © 1985 The Thimble Press. All reprinted by permission of The Thimble Press, Lockwood, Station Road, South Woodchester, Glos. GL5 5EQ, England.

Social Education, v. 41, October, 1977. Copyright, 1977, by the National Council for the Social Studies. Reprinted from *Social Education* with permission of the National Council for the Social Studies.

The Social Studies, v. 59, November, 1968; v. 76, March-April, 1985. Copyright © 1968, 1985 Helen Dwight Reid Educational Foundation. Both reprinted with permission of the Helen Dwight Reid Educational Foundation, published by Heldref Publications, 4000 Albemarle Street, N.W., Washington, DC 20016.

The Times Educational Supplement, n. 3258, November 18, 1977; n. 3319, January 18, 1980; n. 3385, May 8, 1981; n. 3411, November 13, 1981; n. 3412, November 20, 1981, n. 3441, June 11, 1982; n. 3492, June 3, 1983; n. 3520, December 16, 1983; n. 3545, June 8, 1984; n. 3569, November 23, 1984; n. 3583, March 1, 1985; n. 3613, September 27, 1985; n. 3617, October 25, 1985; n. 3643, April 25, 1986. © Times Newspapers Ltd. (London) 1977, 1980, 1981, 1982, 1983, 1984, 1985, 1986. All reproduced from *The Times Educational Supplement* by permission of the publisher.

The Times Literary Supplement, n. 3312, August 19, 1965; n. 3484, December 5, 1968; n. 3501, April 3, 1969; n. 3719, June 15, 1973; n. 3785, September 20, 1974; n. 3826, July 11, 1975; n. 3836, September 19, 1975; n. 3900, December 10, 1976; n. 3949, December 2, 1977; n. 3966, April 7, 1978; n. 4004, December 14, 1979; n. 4034, July 18, 1980; n. 4051, November 21, 1980; n. 4069, March 27, 1981; n. 4121, March 26, 1982; n. 4138, July 23, 1982; n. 4190, July 22, 1983; n. 4200, September 30, 1983; n. 4261, November 30, 1984; n. 4324, February 14, 1986. © Times Newspapers Ltd. (London) 1965, 1968, 1969, 1973, 1974, 1975, 1976, 1977, 1978, 1979, 1980, 1981, 1982, 1983, 1984, 1986. All reproduced from *The Times Literary Supplement* by permission of the publisher.

Top of the News, v. 18, 1962. Copyright © 1962 by the American Library Association. Reprinted by permission of the publisher.

The Use of English, v. 31, Spring, 1980. © Granada Publishing Limited, 1980. Reprinted by permission of Grafton Books, a Division of the Collins Publishing Group.

Virginia Kirkus' Bookshop Service, v. XII, October 15, 1944; v. XIV, December 1, 1946; v. XVIII, February 15, 1950; v. XIX, June, 15, 1951; v. XIX, August 1, 1951; v. XX, September 15, 1952; v. XX, October 1, 1952; v. XXI, November 15, 1953; v. XXII, March 1, 1954; v. XXII, November 1, 1954.

Virginia Kirkus' Service, v. XXIII, November 15, 1955; v. XXIV, August, 15, 1956; v. XXIV, November 15, 1956; v. XXV, July 15, 1957; v. XXV, October 1, 1957; v. XXV, October 15, 1957; v. XXV, November 1, 1957./ v. XXVI, December 1, 1958; v. XXVII, February 1, 1959; v. XXVIII, August 1, 1960; v. XXIX, June 15, 1961; v. XXIX, November 1, 1961; v. XXX, July 15, 1962; v. XXXII, September 15, 1964; v. XXXIII, April 1, 1965; v. XXXIV, April 1, 1966. Copyright © 1958, 1959, 1960, 1961, 1962, 1964, 1965, 1966 Virginia Kirkus' Service, Inc. All reprinted by permission of the publisher.

Voice of Youth Advocates, v. 3, August, 1980; v. 4, December, 1981; v. 6, October, 1983; v. 7, April, 1984; v. 8, August, 1985; v. 8, December, 1985; v. 9, April, 1986; v. 9, August & October, 1986. Copyright 1980, 1981, 1983, 1984, 1985, 1986. All reprinted by permission of the publisher.

The Washington Post, December 17, 1985. © 1985, *The Washington Post Co.* Reprinted by permission of the publisher.

The Western Historical Quarterly, v. 6, October, 1975. Copyright 1975 by The Western Historical Quarterly. Reprinted by permission of the publisher.

Wilson Library Bulletin, v. 36, September, 1961; v. 57, November, 1982; v. 58, April, 1984; v. 60, March, 1986; v. 61, November, 1986; v. 62, January, 1987; v. 61, April, 1987. Copyright © 1961, 1982, 1984, 1986, 1987 by the H. W. Wilson Company. All reprinted by permission of the publisher.

The World of Children's Books, v. III, 1978; v. VI, 1981. © 1978, 1981 by Jon C. Stott. Both reprinted by permission of the publisher.

Young Adult Cooperative Book Review Group of Massachusetts, v. 13, October, 1976. Reprinted by permission of the publisher.

Young Readers Review, v. IV, November, 1967. Copyright © 1967 *Young Readers Review.* Reprinted by permission of the publisher.

THE EXCERPTS IN CLR, VOLUME 13, WERE REPRINTED FROM THE FOLLOWING BOOKS:

Arbuthnot, May Hill. From *Children and Books*. Scott, Foresman, 1947. Copyright, 1947, renewed 1974, by Scott, Foresman and Company. Reprinted by permission of the publisher.

Arbuthnot, May Hill. From *Children's Reading in the Home*. Scott, Foresman, 1969. Copyright © 1969 by Scott, Foresman and Company. All rights reserved. Reprinted by permission of the publisher.

Bader, Barbara. From *American Picture Books from Noah's Ark to the Beast Within*. Macmillan, 1976. Copyright © 1976 by Barbara Bader. All rights reserved. Reprinted with permission of Macmillan Publishing Company.

Bader, Barbara. From "The Caldecott Spectrum," in *Newbery and Caldecott Medal Books: 1976-1985*. Edited by Lee Kingman. Horn Book, 1986. Copyright © 1986 by The Horn Book, Inc. All rights reserved. Reprinted by permission of the publisher.

Baskin, Barbara H. and Karen H. Harris. From *More Notes from a Different Drummer: A Guide to Juvenile Fiction Portraying the Disabled*. Bowker, 1984. Copyright © 1984 by Barbara H. Baskin and Karen H. Harris. All rights reserved. Reprinted with permission of R. R. Bowker, Division of Reed Publishing, USA.

Books on American Indians and Eskimos: A Selection Guide for Children and Young Adults. Edited by Mary Jo Lass-Woodfin. American Library Association, 1978. Copyright © 1978 by the American Library Association. All rights reserved. Reprinted by permission of the publisher.

Cianciolo, Patricia. From *Illustrations in Children's Books*. Second edition. Brown, 1976. Copyright © 1970, 1976 by Wm. C. Brown Company Publishers. All rights reserved. Reprinted by permission of the author.

Cianciolo, Patricia Jean. From *Picture Books for Children*. Revised edition. American Library Association, 1981. Copyright © 1981 by the American Library Association. All rights reserved. Reprinted by permission of the publisher.

Cullinan, Bernice E. with Mary K. Karrer and Arlene M. Pillar. From *Literature and the Child*. Harcourt Brace Jovanovich, 1981. Copyright © 1981 by Harcourt Brace Jovanovich, Inc. Reprinted by permission of the publisher.

Dixon, Bob. From *Catching Them Young 1: Sex, Race and Class in Children's Fiction*. Pluto, 1977. Copyright © Pluto Press 1977. Reprinted by permission of the publisher.

Dole, Helen B. From an introduction to *Heidi: A Little Swiss Girl's City and Mountain Life*. By Johanna Spyri, translated by Helen B. Dole. Ginn and Company, 1927. Copyright, 1927, by Silver Burdett & Ginn Inc. Renewed 1955 by Margaret Dole McCall and Marguerite Davis. Used with permission of the publisher.

Eaton, Anne. From "Widening Horizons, 1840-1890: A Broader Field," in *A Critical History of Children's Literature*. By Cornelia Meigs and others, edited by Cornelia Meigs. Macmillan, 1953. Copyright, 1953, by Macmillan Publishing Company. Renewed 1981 by Charles H. Eaton. All rights reserved. Reprinted with permission of Macmillan Publishing Company.

Edwardes, Marian? From an introduction to *Heidi*. By Johanna Spyri. David McKay Company, 1922.

Egoff, Sheila. From *The Republic of Childhood: A Critical Guide to Canadian Children's Literature in English*. Second edition. Oxford University Press, Canadian Branch, 1975. © Oxford University Press, Canadian Branch, 1975. Reprinted by permission of the publisher.

Egoff, Sheila A. From *Thursday's Child: Trends and Patterns in Contemporary Children's Literature*. American Library Association, 1981. Copyright © 1981 by the American Library Association. All rights reserved. Reprinted by permission of the publisher.

Fisher, Margery. From *Who's Who in Children's Books: A Treasury of the Familiar Characters of Childhood*. Weidenfeld & Nicolson, 1975. Copyright © 1975 by Margery Fisher. All rights reserved. Reprinted by permission of the publisher.

Georgiou, Constantine. From *Children and Their Literature*. Prentice-Hall, 1969. © 1969 by Prentice-Hall, Inc. All rights reserved. Reprinted by permission of the author.

Guy, Rosa. From a promotional piece, Delacorte Press, 1983. Used by permission of Delacorte Press Books for Young Readers.

Haviland, Virginia. From "Rhymes: 'The Pack Rat's Day and Other Poems'," in *Children & Poetry: A Selective, Annotated Bibliography*. Edited by Virginia Haviland and William Jay Smith. Second edition. The Library of Congress, 1979. Reprinted by permission of the author.

Heins, Ethel L. From "A Decade of Children's Books: A Critic's Response," in *Newbery and Caldecott Medal Books: 1976-1985*. Edited by Lee Kingman. Horn Book, 1986. Copyright © 1986 by The Horn Book Inc. All rights reserved. Reprinted by permission of the publisher.

Huck, Charlotte S. From *Children's Literature in the Elementary School*. Third edition. Holt, Rinehart and Winston, 1979. Copyright © 1961, 1968 by Holt, Rinehart and Winston, Inc. Copyright © 1976, © 1979 by Charlotte S. Huck. All rights reserved. Reprinted by permission of Holt, Rinehart and Winston, Inc.

Hürlimann, Bettina. From *Three Centuries of Children's Books in Europe*. Edited and translated by Brian W. Alderson. Oxford University Press, Oxford, 1967. © Oxford University Press 1967. Reprinted by permission of the publisher.

Lacy, Lyn Ellen. From *Art and Design in Children's Picture Books*. American Library Association, 1986. Copyright © 1986 by the American Library Association. All rights reserved. Reprinted by permission of the publisher.

McSpadden, Joseph Walker. From "Johanna Spyri, the Author," in *Recollections of Johanna Spyri's Childhood*. By Anna Ulrich, translated by Helen B. Dole. Thomas Y. Crowell Co. Publishers, 1925.

Norton, Donna E. From *Through the Eyes of a Child: An Introduction to Children's Literature*. Second edition. Merrill, 1987. Copyright © 1987 by Merrill Publishing Company, Columbus, OH. Reprinted by permission of the publisher.

O'Neal, Zibby. From a promotional piece. The Viking Press, 1982. Reprinted by permission of Viking Penguin Inc.

Prelutsky, Jack. From "Through the Eyes of a Poet: Poetry Doesn't Have to Be Boring!" in *Through the Eyes of a Child: An Introduction to Children's Literature*. By Donna E. Norton. Second edition. Merrill, 1987. Copyright © 1987 by Merrill Publishing Company, Columbus, OH. Reprinted by permission of the publisher.

Rees, David. From *Painted Desert, Green Shade: Essays on Contemporary Writers of Fiction for Children and Young Adults*. The Horn Book Inc., 1984. Copyright © 1980, 1981, 1983, 1984 by David Rees. All rights reserved. Reprinted by permission of the publisher.

Sebesta, Sam Leaton and William J. Iverson. From *Literature for Thursday's Child*. Science Research Associates, 1975. © 1975, Science Research Associates, Inc. All rights reserved. Reprinted by permission of the authors.

Sendak, Maurice. From "Mother Goose's Garnishings," in *Children and Literature: Views and Reviews*. Edited by Virginia Haviland. Scott, Foresman, 1973. Copyright © 1973 Scott, Foresman and Company. All rights reserved. Reprinted by permission of the publisher.

Streatfeild, Noel. From "About This Book," in *Heidi*. By Johanna Spyri, translated by Joy Law. Watts, 1959. © copyright 1959 by Franklin Watts, Inc. Reprinted by permission of the Literary Estate of Noel Streatfeild.

Sutherland, Zena and May Hill Arbuthnot. From *Children and Books*. Seventh edition. Scott, Foresman, 1986. Copyright © 1986, 1981, 1977, 1972, 1964, 1957, 1947 Scott, Foresman and Company. All rights reserved. Reprinted by permission of the publisher.

Sutherland, Zena. From "Newbery Medal Books," in *Newbery and Caldecott Medal Books: 1976-1985*. Edited by Lee Kingman. Horn Book, 1986. Copyright © 1986 by The Horn Book, Inc. All rights reserved. Reprinted by permission of the publisher.

Thwaite, Mary F. From *From Primer to Pleasure in Reading*. Revised edition. The Horn Book, Inc., 1972. Copyright © 1963 by Mary F. Thwaite. All rights reserved. Reprinted by permission of the publisher.

Townsend, John Rowe. From *Written for Children: An Outline of English-Language Children's Literature*. Second revised edition. J. B. Lippincott, 1983, Penguin Books, 1983. Copyright © 1965, 1974, 1983 by John Rowe Townsend. All rights reserved. Reprinted by permission of Harper & Row, Publishers, Inc. In Canada by Penguin Books Ltd.

Usrey, Malcolm. From "Johanna Spyri's 'Heidi': The Conversion of a Byronic Hero," in *Touchstones: Reflections on the Best in Children's Literature, Vol. 1*. Edited by Perry Nodelman. Children's Literature Association, 1985. © 1985 ChLA Publishers. Reprinted by permission of the publisher.

Vincent, Gabrielle. From a promotional letter. Duculot Publishers, 1986. Reprinted by permission of Duculot Publishers. Translated for this publication, Gale Research Co. Translation copyright © 1986 Gale Research Co.

Zachert, Adeline B. From a preface to *Heidi*. By Johanna Spyri, edited by Adeline B. Zachert. Winston, 1924. Copyright, 1924, renewed 1951, by The John C. Winston Company.

CUMULATIVE INDEX TO AUTHORS

This index lists all author entries in *Children's Literature Review* and includes cross-references to them in other Gale sources. References in the index are identified as follows:

AITN:	*Authors in the News*, Volumes 1-2
CA:	*Contemporary Authors* (original series), Volumes 1-118
CANR:	*Contemporary Authors New Revision Series*, Volumes 1-19
CAP:	*Contemporary Authors Permanent Series*, Volumes 1-2
CA-R:	*Contemporary Authors* (revised editions), Volumes 1-44
CLC:	*Contemporary Literary Criticism*, Volumes 1-42
CLR:	*Children's Literature Review*, Volumes 1-13
DLB:	*Dictionary of Literary Biography*, Volumes 1-54
DLB-DS:	*Dictionary of Literary Biography Documentary Series*, Volumes 1-4
DLB-Y:	*Dictionary of Literary Biography Yearbook*, Volumes 1980-1985
NCLC:	*Nineteenth-Century Literature Criticism*, Volumes 1-14
SAAS:	*Something about the Author Autobiography Series*, Volume 1-3
SATA:	*Something about the Author*, Volumes 1-48
TCLC:	*Twentieth-Century Literary Criticism*, Volumes 1-23
YABC:	*Yesterday's Authors of Books for Children*, Volumes 1-2

CUMULATIVE INDEX TO NATIONALITIES

CUMULATIVE INDEX TO TITLES

Title Index

Title Index

Title Index